THE MUGHAL STATE 1526–1750

Oxford in India Readings

Themes in Indian History

Available in the Series

Kaushik Roy (ed.)	*War and Society in Colonial India* (OIP)
Ishita Banerjee-Dube (ed.)	*Caste in History* (OIP)
Aloka Parasher-Sen (ed.)	*Subordinate and Marginal Groups in Early India* (Second Edition, OIP)
S. Irfan Habib and Dhruv Raina (eds)	*Social History of Science in Colonial India*
Mushirul Hasan (ed.)	*India's Partition: Process, Strategy, and Mobilization* (OIP)
David Ludden (ed.)	*Agricultural Production and South Asian History* (OIP)
P.J. Marshall (ed.)	*The Eighteenth Century in Indian History: Evolution or Revolution?* (OIP)
Michael H. Fisher (ed.)	*The Politics of the British Annexation of India 1757–1857* (OIP)
Richard M. Eaton (ed.)	*India's Islamic Traditions, 711–1750* (OIP)
Jos J. L. Gommans and Dirk H. A. Kolff (eds)	*Warfare and Weaponry in South Asia 1000–1800* (OIP)
Ian J. Kerr (ed.)	*Railways in Modern India* (OIP)
Ranabir Chakravarti (ed.)	*Trade in Early India* (OIP)

THE MUGHAL STATE
1526–1750

edited by
MUZAFFAR ALAM
SANJAY SUBRAHMANYAM

OXFORD
UNIVERSITY PRESS

OXFORD
UNIVERSITY PRESS

Oxford University Press is a department of the University of Oxford. It furthers the University's objective of excellence in research, scholarship, and education by publishing worldwide. Oxford is a registered trademark of Oxford University Press in the UK and in certain other countries

Published in India by

Oxford University Press
22 Workspace, 2nd Floor, 1/22 Asaf Ali Road, New Delhi 110002, India

First Edition published in 1998
Oxford India Paperbacks 2000
Eighth impression 2015

ISBN-13: 978-0-19-565225-3
ISBN-10: 0-19-565225-8

Typeset in Times
by SJI Services, New Delhi 110 024

Printed in India by Repro India Limited

For our friends
in
Mughal and Ottoman Studies

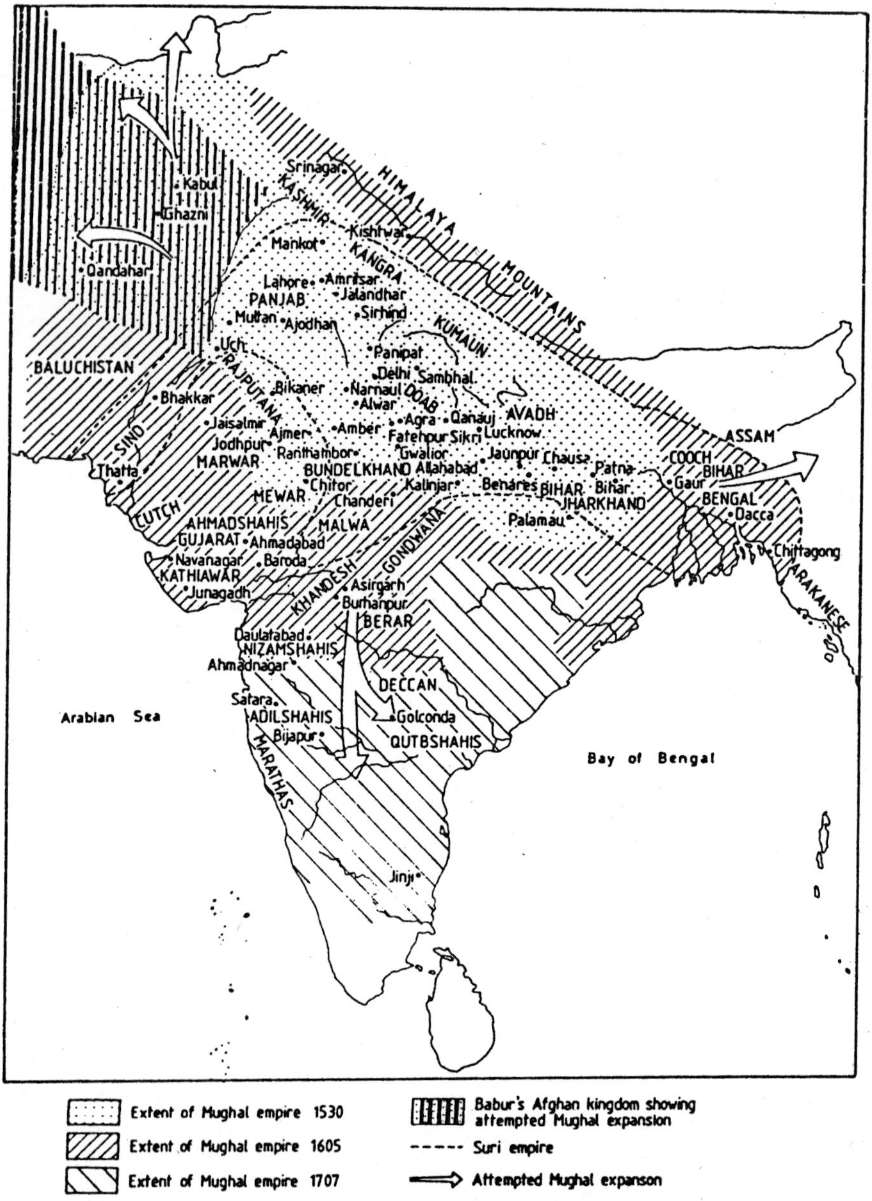
Srinagar
KASHMIR
HIMALAYA MOUNTAINS
Kabul
Ghazni
Qandahar
Kishtwar
Mankot
KANGRA
Lahore
Amritsar
Jalandhar
PANJAB
Sirhind
Multan
Ajodhan
KUMAUN
Uch
Panipat
BALUCHISTAN
RAJPUTANA
Delhi
Sambhal
Bikaner
Narnaul
DOAB
Alwar
Bhakkar
Jaisalmir
Agra
Qanauj
AVADH
Amber
Ajmer
Fatehpur Sikri
Lucknow
Jodhpur
ASSAM
SIND
Ranthambor
Gwalior
Jaunpur
Chausa
COOCH BIHAR
MARWAR
Thatta
BUNDELKHAND
Allahabad
Patna
Gaur
Chitor
Kalinjar
Benares
BIHAR
Bihar
MEWAR
Chanderi
JHARKHAND
BENGAL
CUTCH
Dacca
AHMADSHAHIS
MALWA
Palamau
GUJARAT
Ahmadabad
GONDWANA
Chittagong
Navanagar
Baroda
KATHIAWAR
KHANDESH
ARAKANESE
Asirgarh
Junagadh
Burhanpur
BERAR
Daulatabad
NIZAMSHAHIS
Ahmadnagar
DECCAN
Satara
Golconda
Arabian Sea
ADILSHAHIS
Bijapur
QUTBSHAHIS
Bay of Bengal
MARATHAS
Jinji
Extent of Mughal empire 1530
Extent of Mughal empire 1605
Extent of Mughal empire 1707
Babur's Afghan kingdom showing attempted Mughal expansion
Suri empire
Attempted Mughal expanson

Contents

Part 3:
Politics, Trade and Transformation

Part 4:
Regions and Realms of Resistance

Series Preface

This series focuses on important themes in Indian history, on those which have long been the subject of interest and debate, or which have acquired importance more recently.

Each volume in the series consists of, first, a detailed Introduction; second, a careful choice of the essays and book-extracts vital to a proper understanding of the theme; and, finally, an Annotated Bibliography.

Using this consistent format, each volume seeks as a whole to critically assess the state of the art on its theme, chart the historiographical shifts that have occurred since the theme emerged, rethink old problems, open up questions which were considered closed, locate the theme within wider historigraphical debates, and pose new issues of inquiry by which further work may be made possible.

Since its foundation in the sixteenth century the Mughal Empire in India has produced a rich historiography. Some contemporary works of the Mughal times, implicated in the very exercise of power, reveal the logic of this power. The writings of Mughal rulers, such as the *Babur Nama* in Turkish and the *Tuzak-i-Jahangiri* and Aurangzeb's letters in Persian, give us an insight into the minds of monarchs, and tell us of the different pressures they had to negotiate in building the imperial system. Clerics discussed the role Islam should play in the policies of rulers, and chroniclers recorded the working of the Imperial administration. European travellers reflected on the system through the eyes of the other. Francois Bernier's characterization of Mughal rule as Oriental Despotism, though partly disputed by his eighteenth century compatriot Anquetil du Perron, came to dominate western imagination.

The essays on the nature of Mughal power collected in this volume would give readers an idea of the questions that have troubled historians and the issues they have debated. Was the state an Oriental Despotism or a patrimonial bureaucracy? Was it a strong centralized power or a system based on regional power holders? Was the power built upon military might or through structures of patronage and networks of kinship? Did resistance lead to a crisis of authority or was it integral to its very constitution? The essays show how the focus has shifted over the years from the centre to the periphery, from the court to the locality, from the nitty-gritty of administration to the cultural rituals of kingship.

The introduction raises critical new issues in the study of Mughal history. The editors compare the Mughal dominion to other contemporary Asian empires, postulate the emergence of a new style of Imperial policy from the mid-seventeenth century, seek to revise the conventional wisdom about the fate of the Empire in the late seventeenth and eighteenth centuries and point to fresh directions of research.

Acknowledgements

The editors and publishers would like to thank the following for permission to include the present articles in this volume.

D.H.A. Kolff, 'A Warlord's Fresh Attempt at Empire', from *Naukar, Rajput and Sepoy,* Cambridge University Press, Cambridge, 1990, pp. 32–70.

Ram Prasad Tripathi, 'Turko–Mongol Theory of Kingship', from *Some Aspects of Muslim Administration*, 2nd edition, Allahabad, 1959, pp. 105–21.

J.F. Richards, 'The Formulation of Imperial Authority under Akbar and Jahangir', from J.F. Richards (ed.), *Kingship and Authority in South Asia*, Madison, South Asia Studies, 1978.

Norman P. Ziegler, 'Some Notes on Rājpūt Loyalties During the Mughal Period', from Richards (ed.), *Kingship and Authority*, 1978.

W.H. Moreland, 'Rank (*manṣab*) in the Mogul State Service', from *Journal of the Royal Asiatic Society of Great Britain and Ireland*, 1936, pp. 641–65.

Noman Ahmad Siddiqi, 'The *Fauidar* and *Faujdari* under the Mughals', from *Medieval India Quarterly*, Vol 4, 1961, pp. 22–35.

A. Jan Qaisar, 'Distribution of Revenue Resources of the Mughal Empire among the Nobility', from *Proceedings of the Indian History Congress*, 1965, pp. 237–42.

TAPAN RAYCHAUDHURI, 'The Agrarian System of Mughal India' *Enquiry*, New Series, Vol II, No 1, Spring, 1965, pp. 92–121.

S. NURUL HASAN, '*Zamindars* under the Mughals', from R.E. Frykenberg (ed.), *Land Control and Social Structure in Indian History*, Madison U.W.P., 1969, pp. 17–31.

JADUNATH SARKAR, 'The Condition of the People in Aurangzīb's Reign', *History of Aurangzeb, Vol 4*, Calcutta, 1924, pp. 436–72.

WILFRED CANTWELL SMITH, 'Lower-class Uprisings in the Mughal Empire', from *Islamic Culture*, Vol XX, 1946, pp. 21–40.

SATISH CHANDRA, 'Review of the Crisis of the Jagirdari System', from *Medieval India: Society, the Jagirdari Crisis and the Village*, Delhi, 1982, pp. 61–75.

ASHIN DAS GUPTA, 'Trade and Politics in Eigheenth Century India', from D.S. Richards (ed.), *Islam and the Trade of Asia*, Philadelphia, 1970, pp. 181–214.

KAREN LEONARD, 'The "Great Firm" Theory of the Decline of the Mughal Empire', from *Comparative Studies in Society and History*, Vol XXI, No. 2, 1979, pp. 151–67.

CHETAN SINGH, 'Conformity and Conflict: Tribes and the "Agrarian System" of Mughal India', *Indian Economic and Social History Review*, Vol XXIII, (3), 1988, pp. 319–40.

MUZAFFAR ALAM, 'Aspects of Agrarian Uprisings in North India in the Early Eighteenth Century', from S. Bhattacharya and Romila Thapar, (eds.), *Situating Indian History for Sarvepalli Gopal*, OUP, Delhi, 1986, pp. 146–70.

GAUTAM BHADRA, 'Two Frontier Uprisings in Mughal India', from Ranajit Guha, (ed.), *Subaltern Studies, Vol II*, Delhi, 1982, pp. 43–59.

J.F. RICHARDS AND V. NARAYANA RAO, 'Banditry in Mughal India: Historical and Folk Perceptions', from *The Indian Economic and Social History Review*, Vol XVII, 1, 1980, pp. 95–120.

This volume would have been richer if Professors M. Athar Ali, Irfan Habib and Iqtidar Alam Khan had granted permission to reproduce their essays.

Introduction*

Muzaffar Alam and Sanjay Subrahmanyam

Hindustan is a wide place, where there is an open field for all licentiousness, and no one interferes with another's business, so that every one can do just as he pleases.

—'Abd-ul-Qādir Badāyūnī, *Muntakhab-ut-Tawārīkh*.

The main pillar of government is to be well informed in the news of the kingdom. Negligence for a single moment becomes the cause of disgrace for long years.

—Muḥyī-ud-Dīn Aurangzeb ('Ālamgīr), *Aḥkām-i 'Ālamgīrī.*

This introduction sets itself three ambitious tasks. The *first* is to provide a synthetic, albeit somewhat subjective, overview of the state of Mughal studies as seen from the perspective of the mid-1990s. The *second* is to relate this overview to a selection of eighteen essays representing a variety of points of view and methodological positions, which derive moreover from different moments in the present century. The *third* task, perhaps the most difficult, is to use the selection of essays to indicate what seem to us to be some promising new avenues of research in the field. All three are daunting tasks, made more so by two self-imposed limitations. First, we have had to limit ourselves in our selection to writings in English. Further, we have chosen not to address or reproduce

**Acknowledgements:* We are grateful for remarks and suggestions to a number of colleagues who have seen various earlier drafts of this text. In particular, we thank the General Editors of this series, and above all C.A. Bayly and Romila Thapar, for their detailed comments.

selections from the vast corpus of primary materials (in Persian, as well as other Indian and European languages), leaving that task for another occasion.

But first, a series of rhetorical questions of characterization. What after all was 'the Mughal state'? Leviathan or paper tiger? Inexorable instrument of political and fiscal centralization, or mere carapace? Conquest-state or proto-national entity? The apparently anarchical open field sarcastically posited by Badāyūnī in the late sixteenth century (ostensibly in the narrow context of the heterodox savant, Sharīf Āmulī's welcome in Akbar's India, but in fact reflecting on wider traditions of Indian political culture), or the inquisitorial and absolutist information-gathering monarchy anxiously delineated by Aurangzeb a century later? The Mughal state even today, a century and a half after the exile of its last ruler Bahādur Shāh II to Rangoon, remains a hotbed of controversy around these two polar opposites. This volume, thus, addresses what is probably the single most active field of research in pre-colonial Indian history: the study of the Mughal state between the early years of its foundation in northern India by Bābur, and the close of the reign of Muḥammad Shāh. Faced with the vast historiography of this state in the twentieth century alone, the novice may have a sentiment of an embarrassment of riches of a sort that does not exist for the Sultanates of Delhi, Bijapur or Golconda, the kingdoms of Vijayanagara or Kerala in the early modern period. These riches are not only in terms of the body of modern writings, which in some respects do no more than reflect the vast collections of written materials, above all in Persian, but also in almost all the Indian vernaculars and even Sanskrit, on the royal scions of Chaghatay descent (*salāṭīn-i chaghtā*) in India. Vast and extensive chronicles, collections of documents in India and abroad, paintings and illustrations to manuscripts, as well as the architectural record of major and minor monuments, all reflect the enduring legacy of the Mughal state; they are also direct, and often deliberate, expressions of Mughal power, and are charged ideologically with the meanings that the Mughals themselves (and their state apparatus) tried to impose on their world. Since the English East India Company in the early part of its career as a landed political power (from, say, 1765 to 1793), saw itself quite explicitly as an heir to the Mughal dynasty, this prepossessing myth of the Mughals is also in part a creation of Company Bahādur.

But at the same time, the last years of the dynasty, and its immediate aftermath, also produced a nostalgic indigenous literature (above all in Urdu and Persian) that was contemporary to James Mill and Henry

Maine, wherein writers such as Ghālib or Muḥammad Zakā'ullāh (in his *Tārīkh-i Hindustān*) celebrated the erstwhile glories of the Mughals, and of high Mughal culture.[1] Tears were shed over Old Régime Lucknow and Delhi ('the last *mushā'ira* in Delhi'), with the medieval Persian genre of *shahr āshob*, that came in Mughal India in the early eighteenth century to signify 'decline' literature, now finding new twists and variants. This celebration of the Mughals coincided with the fresh attempt by the British (and other Europeans) to analyse Mughal institutions in the aftermath of 1857. The efforts of historians and philologists like H. Blochmann, whose understanding of the Mughals had advanced a considerable distance from the analyses of William Jones a century earlier, come to mind; in turn, the publication of a number of texts in Persian (notably in the *Bibliotheca Indica* series) from these years eventually enabled the positivistic history-writing of the early twentieth century.

Writings on the Mughals in the early years of this century are often bifurcated into the biased writings of the British and their 'communalist' acolytes (with the controversial legacy of H.M. Elliot clearly in the forefront), and the nationalistic reaction to these by Indian historians (with men like Jadunath Sarkar being obvious exceptions to this). But even a little reflection shows the dangers of adhering blindly to such a reading. In fact, the influence of British colonial writers such as W.H. Moreland on nationalist and even twentieth-century Marxist historians of the Mughals can be shown to be a profound one, while the positivist methodology inculcated by British historians of the inter-war years has retained a decisive influence on most practitioners in the field in India.[2] Labels can be somewhat misleading, since the Aligarh 'school' of ostensibly nationalist-Marxist writers often appears closer to these colonialist positions than the school of 'constitutional' nationalist historians who animated discussions at the Allahabad University in the 1940s and 1950s, and whose legacy has often been neglected. These historians attempted to rationalize the nature of institutions in the

[1]On Zakā'ullāh, see the classic work by C.F. Andrews, *Zakaullah of Delhi*, London, 1929; for an overview of the sort of literature referred to here, see Mujeeb Ashraf, *Muslim Attitudes Towards British Rule and Western Culture in India in the First Half of the Nineteenth Century*, Delhi, 1982.

[2]See, the works of W.C. Smith and Irfan Habib discussed below; also see K.M. Ashraf, 'Presidential Address to the Medieval India Section', *Proceedings of the Indian History Congress*, Pt I, 23rd Session, Aligarh, 1960, pp. 143–51.

medieval Indian past, at times modelling their efforts on the then prevalent studies of British 'constitutional history'.

The prosopographic and genealogical analysis of intellectual trends required to sort out these tangled threads and multiple heritages exceeds the scope of this introduction. But it is a task worth attempting, and requires far closer attention than has been paid hitherto to the institutions that have transmitted Mughal history, notably the Asiatic Society of Bengal, the Royal Asiatic Society, the Indian Historical Records Commission and the Indian History Congress. Suffice it to say for our purposes that modern Mughal historiography is crucially a product of a set of multiple lineages, some of which date back to Mughal times. This in turn surely sets the Mughals apart from a vast number of other South Asian medieval and early modern dynasties, whose histories had to be recovered and reinvented after a hiatus when a period of abject historiographic amnesia had been their lot.

South Asian state-building in the early modern period can be interpreted from more than one perspective, in any of these cases. There is among the possible candidates, first of all, a sort of internal or genealogical perspective, of the building of a state from the raw materials of earlier (and even partly contemporary, but soon to be defeated) regimes which normally leave a stamp on the state that 'succeeds' (in more senses than one). We can thus speak in a wider context of the influence of Byzantium or the Mamlūk Sultanate of Egypt on the Ottomans, or of the Mongols and the Tīmurid states of fifteenth-century Iran on the Ṣafavids, all the while aware that institutional continuity is not changelessness.[3] Here, the metaphorical content of the term 'state-building' is particularly useful, suggesting the making of an edifice not wholly *de novo*, but on an earlier site, using earlier structures or at least the rubble of earlier construction. But there is equally, a well-defined comparative or external perspective, which places a state within a larger geographical and synchronic reality; in the case of South Asia, this means posing developments regarded by most as peculiar and local in the Eurasian space which may seem naturally to lend itself to such an enveloping function. Thus, one might ask, how does one understand the historical trajectory of the Mughal state, in relation to its neighbours to the north and west, in particular the Ṣafavids and the Ottomans, to a lesser extent the Uzbeks in Central Asia?

[3]For a fine attempt to sort out the early history of the Ottoman state, and its relations to Byzantium, see Cemal Kafadar, *Between Two Worlds: The Construction of the Ottoman State*, Berkeley, 1995.

A Comparative Framework

It has long seemed to the present editors, from their respective points of view, almost self-evident that the Mughal state founded by Ẓahīr-ud-Dīn Muḥammad Bābur in north India in the 1520s could not have arisen *sui generis*, or be so unique as to defy comparison. It has, therefore, been somewhat puzzling why Mughal specialists have by and large refused, in the past few decades, to place the state they study in the larger context that includes Iran, Central Asia and the Ottoman empire, reinforcing at the same time existing barriers between the historiography on north and south India, and between pre-Mughal regimes and the Mughals.[4]

The rare exercises in pan-Asian comparison have been largely essentialist in character, seeking to identify and compare the 'key' institutions in all the cases, in the spirit of François Bernier, Karl Marx, or more recently Perry Anderson. What appears to unite these states, writes one historian in recent times, M. Athar Ali, are three structural constants: Islam, the lack of some 'European' institutions such as private property in land, and the failure to develop indigenous capitalism.[5] The *differentia specifica*, on the other hand, can be seen as variants in prebendal assignments, with the Mughal *jāgīr*, the Ṣafavid *tuyūl*, and the Ottoman *tīmār* being all related, but all somewhat distinct. We are led ineluctably, at the end of such an exercise, to a portrayal of the three states—which in the terms of contemporary Europeans of the sixteenth and seventeenth centuries were the Grand Mogor, the Grand Sufi (or more quaintly 'Sophy') and the Grand Turk—as 'a possible single category', which turns out to be nothing other than a

[4]For an Ottomanist's attempt at synthesis, see I. Metin Kunt, 'The Later Muslim Empires: Ottomans, Safavids, Mughals', in Marjorie Kelly, ed., *Islam: The Religious and Political Life of a World Community*, New York, 1984, pp. 112–36; Sanjay Subrahmanyam, 'State Formation and Transformation in Early Modern India and Southeast Asia', *Itinerario*, vol. XII (1), 1988, pp. 91–109. As we shall argue below, it is also important in this context to restitute Bābur, Humāyūn and Sher Shāh to their 'rightful' places, rather than focus excessively on the foundational character of Akbar's reign.

[5]M. Athar Ali, 'Political Structures of the Islamic Orient in the Sixteenth and Seventeenth Centuries', in Irfan Habib, ed., *Medieval India 1: Researches in the History of India, 1200–1750*, Delhi, 1992, pp. 129–40; also M. Athar Ali, 'The Passing of Empire: The Mughal Case', *Modern Asian Studies*, vol. IX (3), 1975, pp. 385–96.

revamped version of the familiar, not to say cliched, notion of the Asiatic Mode of Production!

Faced with such reductionist but widely current formulae, it is inevitable that researchers seeking new avenues will be dissatisfied. The point is that whereas historians have hitherto largely chosen to describe the *structure* of states it might be more fruitful to focus on the historical process of state-building. We suggest that researchers simultaneously trace evolution over time, and examine variation over space, in such an effort.[6] This is not to deny the need to open up more sophisticated studies of the institutional domain itself, to focus on other categories and subjects, such as Mughal legal institutions, their interest in customs and social practices, or their role in relation to the collection of information for administrative purposes (notably through such functionaries as the *waqā'i'-nigār* and the *sawāniḥ-nigār*). Again, the study of such offices as the *ṣadr*, the *muḥtasib*, or the *kotwāl* in Mughal India is still in its infancy, despite some efforts in the past.[7] But a word of caution is necessary too, for we should not assume that such institutions played the same part at various moments in Mughal history; while appearing to be solid structural elements that define an essential part of the state, they too evolved over both space and time, as Noman Ahmad Siddiqi's brief study of the office of *faujdār* (included in this volume) indicates.

Our focus in this volume is on the Mughals, yet it seems worthwhile to begin with at least a brief survey of the Ṣafavids and Ottomans, the two other states which figure largely in any comparative exercise. The differences are many, in terms of size and diversity of subject populations, extent of resources, geography, and so on, and to harp on these is to do no more than state the obvious. The purpose of comparison is, after all, not to argue for congruence. One may begin with a consideration of schematic views of the careers of these states: the Mughals from 1526 to 1857, the Ṣafavids from 1501 to about 1720, and the Ottomans from say 1300 to 1923. This bald statement of chronology already poses

[6]Sanjay Subrahmanyam, 'The Mughal State—Structure or Process? Reflections on Recent Western Historiography', *The Indian Economic and Social History Review*, vol. XXIX (3), 1992, pp. 291–321.

[7]See for example, Muhammad Zameeruddin Siddiqi, 'The Muhtasib Under Aurangzeb', *Medieval India Quarterly*, Vol. V, 1963, pp. 113–19; M.Z. Siddiqi, 'The Intelligence Services Under the Mughals, *Medieval India: A Miscellany*, vol. II, Bombay, 1972, pp. 53–60; and more recently still, M.P. Singh, *Town, Market, Mint and Port in the Mughal Empire, 1556–1707: An Administrative-Cum-Economic Study*, Delhi, 1985.

problems. The Ottoman state evidently had a career almost twice as long as the Mughals, and three times that of the Ṣafavids. It was not merely an early modern state, as the other two were in essence, but a relic of medieval times, as well as a survivor into the twentieth century.[8]

Within the context of the early modern period, the views of historians in respect of the Ṣafavids are largely extremely schematic. From the time of the charismatic figure of Shāh Ismā'īl, the dynasty's founder, the fundamental tension is portrayed as the need for the Iranian rulers to control the very elements who had brought them to power, namely their Turkmen tribal followers, the *qizilbāsh*. Ṣafavid rule is normally divided into three neat dynastic segments: 1501–88, 1588–1629, and 1629–1722.[9] The first phase is usually characterized by sociologically minded historians as a period of 'change and adjustment', during which, it is argued, an attempt was made to maintain a 'Turco-Persian condominium', which meant a compromise between the Turkmen *arbāb-i saif* ('lords of the sword'), and the Tajik *arbāb-i qalam* ('lords of the pen'). More recent historiography continues to note that, unlike Bābur, Shāh Ismā'īl was propelled by a powerful millenarian wave that saw him as semidivine, and defined his role as relating to establishing a universal order at the End of Time. In his own poetry in Turkish, written under the *takhalluṣ* of 'Khaṭā'ī' (the Sinner), Shāh Ismā'īl expressed an eschatological vision of his own role, portraying himself as a curious mix of 'Alī, Alexander and Jesus. Later rulers struggled to divest themselves of this too-heavy burden, gradually redefining Ṣafavid ideology and statecraft. In this context, attention is usually devoted to the second phase, identified with a single reign, that of Shāh 'Abbās (1588–1629), who is normally given overweening importance in Ṣafavid historiography, far surpassing even Akbar in the Mughal case or Süleymān in that of the Ottomans.

To 'Abbās is given the credit for four major changes. First, he is said to have fomented a sustained attack on *qizilbāsh* power by the creation of a 'third force', namely a set of Georgian, Circassian and

[8]The implications of this are partly developed in I. Metin Kunt, 'Development of the Ottoman State to 1600', in T. Aricanli, et al., *The Political Economy of the Ottoman, Ṣafavid and Mughal Empires* (forthcoming).

[9]Roger M. Savory, *Iran under the Safavids*, Cambridge, 1980; also Savory, 'The Safavid Administrative System', in Peter Jackson and Laurence Lockhart, eds., *The Cambridge History of Iran*, vol. VI (The Timurid and Ṣafavid Periods), Cambridge, 1986. Savory's work represents one of the orthodox poles in Ṣafavid studies.

Armenian fighting-men, at times proficient in the use of firearms. Second, 'Abbās' period is marked by a reorganization of the land-tax system, so that lands that had previously been assigned came to be under the direct control of the treasury (thus, the shift from *mamālik* to *khāṣṣa*).[10] Accompanying this was the third feature, namely the resettlement of populations, involving the relocation of Turkmen tribes and their displacement by Caucasian settlers, and the settlement of Armenian traders in urban Iran. Fourthly, these years are marked by a drastic reorganization and state centralization of trade, particularly in silk, so that 'Abbās becomes, in Vladimir Minorsky's oft-cited phrase, 'the largest capitalist' in the kingdom.[11] Finally, on a rather different note, it has been argued in recent times that the reign of 'Abbās witnessed a shift in the ideational basis of Ṣafavid rule: the definitive distancing of the Shah from his role as the *pīr-o murshīd* of the *qizilbāsh*, and a far closer relationship between the ruler and the '*ulamā*'.[12]

In contrast to these two phases, we have the last century of Ṣafavid rule, which is often seen as a working out in one fashion or the other of the accumulated contradictions of 'Abbās' reign. Usually neglected by historians, as is the case with all states once they have been diagnosed as in a state of 'decline', this period culminated, as is well-known, in the emergence of Ṭahmāsp Qulī Khān, or Nādir Shāh—which could be seen as further evidence of the eternal dialectic between pastoralists and sedentary settlers in Iran. Interestingly enough, contemporary travellers from Europe, such as Jean Chardin and Engelbert Kaempfer, suggest that one of the reasons for systemic tensions in the period was the overly centralized nature of the revenue economy, which tended to starve the outlying provinces not only of specie, but investible resources. This spatial dimension has, however, rarely been given much weight by historians of Ṣafavid Iran, who have preferred instead to stress that this state—unlike the Mughal and Ottoman domains—was

[10]Klaus Michael Röhrborn, *Provinzen und zentralgewalt Persiens im 16. und 17. Jahrhundert*, Berlin, 1966.

[11]Vladimir Minorsky, ed., *Tadhkirat al-Mulūk, a Manual of Safavid Administration*, London, 1943, p. 19.

[12]See Kathryn Babayan, 'The Waning of the Qizilbash: The Spiritual and the Temporal in Seventeenth-Century Iran', Ph.D. thesis, Princeton University, 1993, pp. 41–74.

relatively compact, and also did not expand a great deal over the two and a quarter centuries of Ṣafavid rule.[13]

To the extent that this is true, it tends to limit the applicability of a spatial approach to the Ṣafavid state. The relations between ruler and nobility (or *umarā'*), on the contrary, offer more fertile ground for comparison with the Mug͟hals. In general, the Ottoman historiography appears at present to be far richer than that on the Ṣafavids, at all levels. Chronologically, for the Ottomans, we have the conventional identification of a figure who consolidates the state, in Meḥmed II (r. 1451–81) assisted by his celebrated *wazīr* Karamani Meḥmed Pāshā, while the later reign of Süleymān (r. 1520–66) gives the lie to any standard model of rise, consolidation and decline by representing, as it were, a second wave of consolidation.[14] Still speaking chronologically, however, the Ottomans, whose career lasted far longer than that of the Ṣafavids or even the Mug͟hals, seem to move in 'slow motion' (to borrow a metaphor from Cemal Kafadar), relative to these other dynasties and states! The phase of consolidation endures over a century, and even 'Ottoman decline' in conventional historiography is an interminable process relative to the fairly quick *coup de grâce* delivered to the Ṣafavids, or the 150-year-long Mug͟hal 'twilight'.

On the other hand, a spatial or regional approach has clear potential in the Ottoman case, relative to that of the Ṣafavids. By the middle years of the sixteenth century, the Ottoman domains encompassed an astonishing *diversity* of territories, which went far beyond the initial heartland of Anatolia and Rumelia. In these territories, which extended from Basra to the Balkans, a variety of regional fiscal and power structures grew up, based on compromise as much as main force.[15] The

[13]For an important recent reconsideration, however, see Rudolph P. Matthee, 'Politics and Trade in Late Safavid Iran: Commercial Crisis and Government Reaction under Shāh Solaymān (1666–1694)', Ph.D. thesis, University of California at Los Angeles, 1991.

[14]Gilles Veinstein, 'L'empire dans sa grandeur (XVIe siècle)', in Robert Mantran, ed., *Histoire de l'Empire Ottoman*, Paris, 1989, pp. 159–226.

[15]A. Temimi, ed., *Les provinces arabes à lépoque ottomane*, Zagouhan, 1987, 3 vols; P.F. Sugar, *South-Eastern Europe under Ottoman Rule, 1354–1804*, Seattle/London, 1977; Stanford J. Shaw, *The Financial and Administrative Organization and Development of Ottoman Egypt, 1517–1798*, Princeton, 1958; Bruce McGowan, *Economic Life in Ottoman Europe: Taxation, Trade and the Struggle for Land, 1600–1800*, Paris/Cambridge, 1981; M.A. Bakhit, *The Ottoman Province of Damascus in the Sixteenth Century*, Beirut, 1982.

existence of this variety is implicitly recognized in one fashion or the other in much of the Ottoman historiography for the seventeenth century, which divides the domains into the heartland, the Arab provinces and the Balkans.[16] But this division appears also to be motivated by factors that are somewhat different from those which are significant in the Mughal case: namely the borders of twentieth-century nations and the nationalist historiographies of each of these regions that they have engendered thereby. While modern-day sectarian religious consciousness is mirrored in nationalist Indian and Pakistani approaches to Mughal history, the role played by regional and ethnic divisions is less marked in South Asia than with the Ottomans.

Contemporaries had a somewhat different way of looking at the question, and different criteria for the divisions they proposed. Thus, writing in 1653, during the reign in the Mughal domains of Shāhjahān, 'Alī Çavus describes the Ottoman domains in his *Risāle* as comprising thirty-four provinces, divided in his binary scheme into the oppositional categories of *khāṣṣ* and *sālyāne*, the latter including Egypt, Yemen, Habesh, Iraq, and North Africa. What set these provinces apart for him was the absence there of prebends (*ze'āmet ve tīmār*), and the fact that the Pādishāh drew revenues directly from them to pay off Janissary groups, with the surplus cash going directly to the central treasury. We thus see that the similar Perso-Arabic usage of *khāṣṣ* has rather different connotations in the three great 'Gunpowder Empires' (to use Marshall Hodgson's celebrated phrase) of the period.[17]

It is of course clear that the *sālyāne* provinces described above correspond largely to those parts of the Arab world which the Ottomans conquered in the first half of the sixteenth century. Equally, it is evident that many of these areas—Egypt, Yemen, Baghdad and Basra, for example—were far more closely linked to circuits of international trade, and also far more monetized than the Balkans, or even the Ottoman heartland. It appears logical therefore to adopt in these territories a fiscal system that differed from the 'classic' Ottoman one based on *ze'āmet* and *tīmār*, and as it happens this also permitted the accommodation, in some of these areas (such as Egypt), with pre-existent local elites. André Raymond has pointed out how Selīm I gave the

[16] See for example, Robert Mantran, ed., *Histoire de l'Empire Ottoman*, Paris, 1989, chs 9 and 10.

[17] Salih Özbaran, 'Some Notes on the Sālyāne System in the Ottoman Empire as Organised in Arabia in the Sixteenth Century', *Osmanli Arastirmalari, The Journal of Ottoman Studies*, vol. VI, 1986, p. 42.

charge of Egypt after the conquest to Kha'ir Bey, the former governor of Aleppo, with the Mamlūk title of *malik al-umarā'*, while at the same time naming Jānbardī al-Ghazālī (also a notable of the previous regime) as governor of Damascus. His reading of the evidence thus suggests to him that even after the Ottoman conquest 'the Mamlūks continued to dominate the administration of the Egyptian provinces', and he concludes moreover that, 'Far from being destroyed by the new regime, the old dominant aristocracy was called upon to share power, and it took little over a century before a representative of the Mamlūks, Rizwan Bey, again exercised a quasi-monarchical authority over Egypt (1631–1656)'. Again, in the case of the *vilāyet* of Tripoli, Raymond points to an Ottoman *kānūnnāme* of 1519–20, with the following revealing formulation:

> In the time of our *Pādishāh*, when justice reigns, it has not been permitted to make any innovation that does not belong to the ancient custom. The taxes fixed in the register, in a detailed and precise manner, which are the ancient taxes that have existed from time immemorial, are even now held to be due and have been written in the register.[18]

Thus here, conquest did not imply the erasure of older fiscal institutions or the older élite and their substitution on the basis of a unique imperial blueprint. Rather, the incorporation of new regions into the Sulṭān's 'well-protected territories' had complex consequences, at times even altering the essential structure of the state. Conquest thus was not teleological: first compromise and tribute, then abortive rebellion, and finally levelling and the imposition of uniform institutions. It was a halting process, with many possible outcomes.

It is interesting to compare, in a similar vein, the nature of the eighteenth- and nineteenth-century transitions in the Ottoman empire with the processes of 'regional centralization' that we will encounter in the Mughal case.[19] To sum up the state of the Ottoman historiography briefly, it was long held that the Ottoman state entered into decline from about the time of the Battle of Lepanto (1572), and then remained for nearly three centuries as the 'sick man of Europe', enviously eyeing its healthier neighbours to the west. Typical signs of this decline were

[18]André Raymond, 'Les provinces arabes (XVIe–XVIII siècles)', in Mantran, ed., *Histoire*, p. 356–7.

[19]See Ariel Salzmann, 'An Ancien Régime Revisited: "Privatization" and Political Economy in the Eighteenth-Century Ottoman Empire', *Politics and Economy*, vol. XXI (4), 1993, pp. 393–423.

taken to be 'peasant' rebellions (the so-called Celali revolts of the early seventeenth century), inflation and urban social unrest in the aftermath of the influx of American silver, the rise of revenue farming favouring new (and presumably unworthy) commercially oriented groups, and the rusting of the Ottoman war-machine in the absence of the earlier trend of incessant expansionary campaigning. In order to buttress this view, writers until the 1970s used not only Venetian consular reports (whose objectivity could of course be called into question), but a sort of indigenous 'decline literature' produced by the Ottoman élite itself, ranging from chroniclers to minor writers of memoirs. However, the newer historiography of the past two decades has tended to look sceptically at this elaborate edifice. The nature of revolts like the Celali rebellions now appears socially far more diverse than had been thought, and the effects of the silver inflow complex and diverse. What is clear is that social changes and readjustments were under way, and that certain social groups hitherto seen as low, unworthy and associated with 'shopkeeping' (what in Mughal terms would be called *dukāndārī*), were gaining new importance, amongst other things by using the practice of farming state revenues (*iltizām* to the Ottomans, *ijāra* in India). Older élites, with traditional skills, who felt left out of these processes took revenge by using their satirical pens to lampoon these 'new men', just as groups like Kayasthas and Khatris were made the butt of ridicule in eighteenth-century northern India. Thus, the comparison with the Ottoman transition, eventually leading to the creation of power centres dominated by regionally based *a'yān* (magnates), may prove rather fecund for the imaginative historian with a comparativist bent of mind.

The 'Systemic' Perspective

And so on to our primary object in this exercise: the Mughal state. Reviewing the literature of the last three decades on the Mughal state, one does not of course find a complete consensus, even among the scholars of what is known as the 'Aligarh school', the most influential of the streams in Mughal studies. Nevertheless, it is clear that the conventional wisdom uniformly stresses the systematic and also the *systemic* features of the Mughal state, focusing mainly on the state as a revenue sponge, or fiscal mechanism. Indeed, in the case of some historians, the 'achievements' of the Mughals in this regard are listed in a somewhat incongruous manner. Chief among these achievements is the efficiency, scale and might of the Mughal state in its period of glory; specific features often highlighted include the Mughal fiscal system, and the monetary system, based in the main on the silver *rupiya*, and supported by the gold *muhr* and the copper *dām* and *paisa.* A central role is equally given to the Mughal prebends, the ranking system (or *manṣabdārī*) and the revenue assignment (or *jāgīr*). In J.F. Richards' relatively recent formulation, the Mughals are even given credit for the burgeoning seaborne trade of the Indian subcontinent in the period from such ports as Surat, Thatta, Goa, Hughli, Balasore and Masulipatnam.[20] While the case for linking the prosperity of Surat and perhaps even Thatta with the Mughal empire can be made, neither Goa nor Masulipatnam lay within Mughal control during the years of their prosperity, so this appears to be a case of assigning the Mughal state too central a role in all economic processes of the area in the period.

Other more Marxist-influenced historians, like Tapan Raychaudhuri and Irfan Habib (the two leading contributors on Mughal matters to the *Cambridge Economic History of India*, volume I), are less celebratory of the empire perhaps, but equally insistent on its character as a tightly run system. To Raychaudhuri, (whose debt in the matter to Maurice Dobb's formulation of European feudalism is evident), 'the uncomplicated desire of a small ruling class for more and more material resources' explains most of the Mughal state's actions; in the case of the Mughals, he asserts, 'their economism was simple, straightforward and almost palpable ... there was no containing it until it collapsed under the weight of its own contradictions'.[21] The state must thus be seen primarily in fiscal–economic terms: it extracted resources unremittingly from the agrarian economy, 'in the form of land revenue assessed as a fixed share of the produce'. This claimed share, it is stated, varied 'from a third to a half or more of the output' in all of the empire.

The centrepiece of the structure, in the writings of Habib, Raychaudhuri and Richards, is the purported creation, during the period of Akbar (r. 1556–1605), of what is described as a vast, relatively uniform and centralized fiscal system, based on the collection of agrarian revenue. This structure is sometimes termed the Mughal 'agrarian system' (when what is really meant is only the 'fiscal system'), in what clearly reflects the decisive influence on Mughal specialists like Habib,

[20]J.F. Richards, 'The Seventeenth-Century Crisis in South Asia', *Modern Asian Studies*, vol. XXIV (4), 1990, pp. 625–38.

[21]Tapan Raychaudhuri, 'The State and the Economy: The Mughal Empire', in Tapan Raychaudhuri and Irfan Habib, eds., *The Cambridge Economic History of India*, vol. I, Cambridge, 1982, p. 172.

Raychaudhuri and Richards, of the British administrator-historian W.H. Moreland, whose volume *The Agrarian System of Moslem India* (1929) obviously provided the model (and even the title) for Habib's *The Agrarian System of Mughal India* (1963), an influential work whose argument may be found elegantly summarized in this volume in a review article by Tapan Raychaudhuri. Though replacing Moreland's apology for *Pax Britannica* with an ostensibly Marxist (and palpably nationalist) framework of analysis, as well as appreciably widening the set of Persian sources used, Habib in fact continued to share many of the analytical preoccupations and methodological preconceptions of his British predecessor, of which the single-minded pursuit of fiscality (and the administrator's anxiety about 'system') is a major symptom. What appeared to Moreland to be Oriental Despotism resurfaced in Habib as class-based exploitation, but the key questions and tools of analysis remained close, at times dismayingly so.[22] There is thus something of the British administrator's cadences in the Aligarh historian's eulogy of the so-called '*ẓabṭ* system', which Irfan Habib believes had assumed its 'final form' by about 1580. In Habib's own words:

> In 1574–75, Akbar took a series of important measures, which involved among other things, a new attempt to work out revenue rates. Information on yields, prices and the area cultivated was collected for each locality for a period of ten years, 1570–71 to 1579–80. On the basis of this detailed information, the revenue rates were now fixed directly in cash for each crop. The provinces of Lahore, Multan, Ajmer, Delhi, Agra, Malwa, Allahabad and Awadh were divided into revenue-circles, each with a separate schedule of cash revenue-rates (*dastūru'l 'amals*) for various crops ... [These] sanctioned cash rates were to be applied year after year, with such revision only as might be decreed by the administration in these rates from time to time.[23]

It is from examining the statistics generated by this *ẓabṭ* system, which evidently extended 'from the Indus to the Ghagra', that the inference that the Mughal state claimed, and even took, between a third and a half of agricultural produce—'the entire agricultural surplus', in

[22] In turn, Habib's analysis of Mughal decline as deriving from a class war, precipitated by the over-exploitation of the peasantry, is anticipated in many respects by Wilfred Cantwell Smith, 'Lower-Class Uprisings in the Mughal Empire', reproduced in this volume. Smith's paper was first published in 1946.

[23] Irfan Habib, 'Agrarian Relations and Land Revenue: North India', in Raychaudhuri and Habib, eds., *The Cambridge Economic History of India*, vol. I, p. 172.

Raychaudhuri's words—is drawn. The impression one gets is of a detailed cadastral survey, comparable say to those conducted by the generalissimo Toyotomi Hideyoshi in Japan in the 1590s (the so-called *taiko kenchi*).[24] Yet a reconsideration of the principal contemporary source on which such a statement rests leaves one somewhat uncertain. For rather than the routine administrative papers of a 'field-by-field' examination of agrarian production by the state, what we have is a summary compendium of revenue data in a far larger text, the *Ā'īn-i Akbarī*, of Shaikh Abu'l Faẓl ibn Mubārak (1551–1602), a contemporary and favoured courtier of Akbar. Heavily relied by the leading economic historians of the Mughal period, the *Ā'īn* is undoubtedly an unusual text by the standards of contemporary South Asia in terms of its scope and the sophistication of its author, a leading ideologue of Akbar's regime. But when read between the lines, it does not quite present a picture of unremitting centralization based on an elaborate and uniform bureaucracy which has 'penetrated' the countryside. Rather it suggests a picture of a quite different balance between *ẓabṭ* 'regulation' territories and the rest of the empire than one might gather from a section of the secondary literature. One way of ascertaining the extent of *ẓabṭ* is to see the extent of data available at the close of Akbar's reign on taxable land (*ārāẓī*). If data on this category is not available, it is obvious that no system based on an application of crop-specific revenue rates on measured land could have functioned in reality. Thus, provinces (*ṣūbas*) where we have no information on *ārāẓī* provide us a floor on (not an estimate of, we emphasize) 'non-regulation' territories. One may infer directly from the data that *at least* one third of revenue under the Mughals was collected in about 1600 by means other than the rather elaborate ones described by Habib.[25] Further, even those lands within the 'regulation' category are somewhat suspect. Aside from Allahabad, Awadh, Agra, Delhi, Lahore and Multan—provinces where the hold of the Delhi Sultanate and its late offshoots had been the strongest—much remains murky. In Bihar, only

[24]John W. Hall, Nagahara Keiji and Kozo Yamamura, eds., *Japan Before Tokugawa: Political Consolidation and Economic Growth, 1500 to 1650*, Princeton, 1981; Mary Elizabeth Berry, *Hideyoshi*, Cambridge (Mass.), 1982, pp. 111–26; also John W. Hall and James L. McClain, eds., *The Cambridge History of Japan*, vol. IV (Early Modern Japan), Cambridge, 1991.

[25]For a more detailed exposition of this point, see Muzaffar Alam and Sanjay Subrahmanyam, 'L'Etat moghol et sa fiscalité', *Annales HSS*, no. 1, 1994, pp. 189–217.

two-thirds of lands were unambiguously *ẓabṭī* in about 1600; and in Malwa too *ẓabṭ* is unlikely to have been extensively applied. In Gujarat, the *Ā'īn-i Akbarī* itself concedes that assessment is mostly based on *nasaq*, with measurement rarely practised, that is to say a fixing of revenues at a level for a long period based on some pre-existent principle; thus, here there is unlikely to have been *ẓabṭ* at all in 1600. As for Ajmer, a fair proportion of the land in this area was under chieftains, and measurement here too is unlikely to have been used to determine revenue assessment. Thus, the implicit notion that the central state was in a position to impose a uniform set of principles for taxation, and had the wherewithal and apparatus already in 1600 to implement its desires, appears suspect.

Besides what interest the *ẓabṭ* and measurement of *ārāẓī* questions may hold on their own, it should be noted that much of the statistical results in the Mughal historiography rest on the idea that summary revenue data can be squeezed to infer conclusions on anything from population, to urbanization, external trade, and even the 'gross national product' of Mughal India.[26] But if the relationship of revenue assessment to even agrarian production is tenuous in well over a third of the Mughal empire, these exercises must surely be treated with extreme caution. We must at the same time move from looking solely at numbers, and from fine-tuning the details within a largely unquestioned set of mutually reinforcing paradigms, to considering the paradigms themselves.[27]

Should we be content to reducing a complex political system to its agrarian fiscal aspects? Were there not other elements in the Mughal state (whether structural or processual) that might equally command our attention? When we begin to enter into such an exercise, of widening the bases of discussion, we are immediately faced with a series of major issues. The first specific problem concerns chronology, and the neglect of some periods in favour of others.

[26]Shireen Moosvi, 'The Gross National Product of the Mughal Empire, c. 1600', *The Indian Historical Review*, vol. XIII (1–2), 1986–7, pp. 75–87; also see S. Moosvi, *The Economy of the Mughal Empire, c. 1595: A Statistical Study*, Delhi, 1987.

[27]This critique is intended for not merely fiscal history, but Mughal economic history more generally; for a recent attempt, see Najaf Haider, 'Precious Metal Flows and Currency Circulation in the Mughal Empire', *Journal of the Economic and Social History of the Orient*, vol. XXXIX (3), 1996, pp. 298–364.

THE PLAY OF LIGHT AND SHADE

The Mughal dynasty was, like a number of others in Central Asia and Iran, a Tīmurid one, descended from the great figure of the 'Lord of the Conjunction' (*Ṣāḥib-i-Qirān),* Amīr Tīmūr Gūrgān, who had created a huge empire ranging over Central Asia, West Asia, and even a part of South Asia, from the fragments of the Chinggis Khanid dispensation. Between Tīmur's death in 1405, and the definitive installation of his direct descendant Ẓahīr-ud-Dīn Muḥammad Bābur, son of 'Umar Shaikh Mirzā, on the erstwhile throne of the Lodīs in northern India, well over a century elapsed.[28] This century and more did not efface the Tīmurid legacy, which in fact remained a crucial pole of orientation for the self-definition of the Mughal dynasty. As late as the reign of Shāhjahān (whose titulature significantly includes the claim to be the 'second *Ṣāḥib-i-Qirān* '), the Mughals continued to harbour territorial ambitions in Central Asia, motivated in part by the desire to effect a reintegration with the Tīmurid heartland.[29]

That the Indian Mughals were aware of and reflected on their Central Asian heritage, is a fact that is rarely given its due place in Indian historiography. Though dynasties in far earlier times, such as the Kushānas, had equally straddled the worlds of South and Central Asia, this spatial conception had largely been lost sight of during the Delhi Sultanate, whose rulers—while often of Central Asian origin—could not for a number of reasons (including political conditions in Central Asia) harbour territorial ambitions there. To understand this aspect of Mughal rule requires a temporal reorientation too. For, giving short shrift to the early history of the Mughal state in northern India, the great bulk of writings on the Mughal state focus on two periods, the first the reign of Akbar (1556–1605), the second the reign of his

[28]For a Central Asian perspective on Bābur, see Maria Eva Subtelny, 'Babur's Rival Relations: A Study of Kinship and Conflict in 15th–16th Century Central Asia', *Der Islam*, vol. LXVI (1), 1989, pp. 102–18.

[29]In this context, see the rather significant record of conversations in the 1620s between Jahāngīr, and Muṭribī of Samarqand, in Abdul Ghani Mirzoyef, ed., *Khāṭirāt-i-Muṭribī Samarqandī*, Karachi, 1977, pp. 19–20, 68–9 *passim.* The text is briefly summarized in Surinder Singh, 'The Indian Memoirs of Mutribi Samarqandi', *Proceedings of the Indian History Congress*, 55th Session, Aligarh, 1994, pp. 345–54.

great-grandson Aurangzeb or 'Ālamgīr (1658–1707).[30] In contrast, the pre-Akbar period, the half century after 1605, and the years after 1707 have been traditionally neglected in the historiography. There are some notable attempts at an earlier historiographic moment to render the first period its due, especially by S. Nurul Hasan, Simon Digby, Ahsan Raza Khan, Mohibbul Hasan and Iqtidar Husain Siddiqui.[31] These attempts at institutional analysis undoubtedly went deeper than the conventional political history of writers such as Rushbrook Williams. Some attempts at redress in respect of the last of these periods have also lately been witnessed, though many of these are based on somewhat tenuous evidence.[32] But, still on balance, the 'dark' phases we have identified still remain in the shade, and have so far been of little interest to persons other than, say, historians of architecture or music, whose position in the Mughal historiography is, unfortunately, a marginal one. This neglect is for a rather curious set of reasons. First, from the viewpoint of Indian historians writing with an eye to modern-day problems, and

[30] I.H. Qureshi, 'India under the Mughals', in P.M. Holt, Ann K.S. Lambton and Bernard Lewis, eds., *The Cambridge History of Islam*, vol. II, Cambridge, 1970, pp. 35–63; Irfan Habib, The *Agrarian System of Mughal India (1556–1707)*, Bombay, 1963; Jadunath Sarkar, *History of Aurangzeb*, 5 vols, reprint, Calcutta, 1973.

[31] For older, conventional, political narrative histories of Bābur and Humāyūn, see the Bibliography at the end of this volume. For attempts at institutional analysis, see S. Nurul Hasan, 'New Light on the Relations of the Early Mughal Rulers with their Nobility', *Proceedings of the Indian History Congress*, 7th Session, Madras, 1944, pp. 389–97; Iqtidar Alam Khan, *Mirza Kamran, a Biographical Study*, Bombay, 1964; Ahsan Raza Khan, 'Babur's Settlement of His Conquests in Hindustan', *Proceedings of the Indian History Congress*, 29th Session, Patiala, 1967, Pt I, pp. 207–20. Also the voluminous writings of Iqtidar Husain Siddiqui, for example, 'Wajh-i Ma'āsh Grants under the Afghan Kings (1451–1555)', *Medieval India—A Miscellany*, vol. II, Bombay, 1972, pp. 19–44. For a fine and imaginative piece on the period, see Simon Digby, 'Dreams and Reminiscences of Dattu Sarvani, a Sixteenth Century Indo-Afghan Soldier' (in 2 parts), *The Indian Economic and Social History Review*, vol. II (1), 1965, pp. 52–80; vol. II (2), 1965, pp. 178–94. We understand that this work is being revised and extended to be published as a monograph.

[32] C.A. Bayly, *Indian Society and the Making of the British Empire* (The New Cambridge History of India, vol. II. 2), Cambridge, 1988; David A. Washbrook, 'South Asia, the World System and World Capitalism', *The Journal of Asian Studies*, vol. XLIX (3), 1990, pp. 479–508.

a personality-oriented approach to history, Akbar and Aurangzeb are the hero and the villain respectively of the Mughal period. Jahāngīr and Shāhjahān, the Rosencrantz and Guildenstern amongst the *dramatis personae*, have yet to have their day. Second, from the perspective even of structure-oriented historians, it appears that the 'steel frame' of the Mughal empire (the metaphor is drawn, significantly once more, from the colonial ICS) was the *manṣabdārī* system, and hence the two crucial periods are obviously that in which this steel frame was put in place and that in which it was corroded: this brings us back to Akbar and Aurangzeb.

There have been minority voices raised from time to time, of course. Even from a purely fiscal perspective, the Afghan ruler of north India Shēr Shāh Sūr (1538–45), who forced the Mughal Humāyūn into exile in Iran, has sometimes been portrayed as the true creator of many key 'Mughal' institutions, be it the monetary system, or the notion of *ẓabṭ*. It is pointed out, for example, that the *rupiya* as a coin is first encountered in the Sūr ruler's reign, and that equally his system of *rai'* (or crop rates) anticipates many of the features of *ẓabṭ*.[33] This is not to deny of course that further evolution took place in Akbar's reign in both these spheres. The more plentiful availability of silver gave the *rupiya* greater prominence as the sixteenth century drew to a close, and equally the idea of *ẓabṭ* under Akbar and his advisor Todarmal did involve a fine-tuning of the Sūr crop-rate system, to take account of local variations. The interpretation that gives greater prominence to Sher Shāh rests largely, we should note, on the chronicle of 'Abbās Khān Sārwānī, *Tārikh-i Sher Shāhī*, written in Akbar's reign, and may reflect the chronicler's desire to portray his family's erstwhile patron as a sort of proto-Akbar. Even so, it is striking that the chief *ẓabṭī* territories in about 1600 were largely made up of the provinces already controlled by Sher Shāh; newly conquered provinces such as Gujarat, Bengal, Berar or Khandesh still tended to maintain their own distinct fiscal practices, as we have seen.

[33]Most recently, Iqtidar Alam Khan, 'The Mughal Assignment System during Akbar's Early Years, 1556–1575', in Habib, ed., *Medieval India I*, pp. 62–128, (especially pp. 79–80). For an early statement, W.H. Moreland, 'Sher Shah's Revenue System', *Journal of the Royal Asiatic Society of Great Britain and Ireland*, Pt I, 1926, pp. 447–59; S. Nurul Hasan, 'Revenue Administration of the Jagir of Sahsaram by Farid (Sher Shah)', *Proceedings of the Indian History Congress*, 26th Session, Ranchi, 1964, Pt II, pp. 102–7.

The other major development of Sher Shāh's period is well known, but perhaps not particularly well appreciated. Here the reference is to the building of a network of roads centred around a great arterial road, through the heartland of the Sūr domain, a road that later came to be termed the 'Grand Trunk Road'. As Sārwānī puts the matter in his chronicle:

> [Sher Shāh] built a road with *sarā'is* [rest-houses] which commenced from the fort that he had constructed in the Punjab and it ran up to the town of Sonargaon, which lay situated on the edge of the Bay of Bengal (*daryā-i shor*). He built another road that ran from the city of Agra to Burhanpur, on the borders of the Deccan. He made another road which ran from the city of Agra to Jodhpur and Chittor. He then built still another road with *sarā'is* which ran from the city of Lahore to Multan. In all he built 1700 *sarā'is* on the roads which lay in various regions and in every *sarā'i* he built apartments for both the Hindus and the Muslims.[34]

Obviously, one aspect of this road-building activity was its military utility. But at the same time, one cannot overlook the commercial significance of the process, for Sārwānī himself notes that 'in each *sarā'i* there was also a *bāzār* for buying and selling'. On the one hand, the attempt was clearly to improve the connections between the Sūr domains (especially the Ganga–Jamuna *doāb*) and the great trading routes extending into Central and West Asia via Kabul and Qandahar, something that Bābur had already contemplated in the late 1520s while conceiving a road to link Agra (which he had just conquered) to Kabul.[35] At the same time, we see in the period of Sher Shāh, the first stirrings of an attempt to bring the economy of Bengal into closer contact with that of northern India, after an interregnum lasting through much of the fifteenth and early sixteenth centuries, in which Bengal had become increasingly eastward oriented in its trade.[36] The expansion that was prosecuted during the reign of Akbar was thus in logical sequence to what had already occurred in this period, and some of the successful projects of conquest of the 1570s and 1580s—including that

[34] 'Abbās Khān Sārwānī, *Tārīkh-i-Sher Shāhī*, ed. S.M. Imamuddin, Dhaka, 1964 (English translation, B.P. Ambashthya, Patna, 1974), text, pp. 216–17.

[35] Mohibbul Hasan, *Babur: Founder of the Mughal Empire in India*, Delhi, 1985.

[36] John Deyell, 'The China Connection: Problems of Silver Supply in Medieval Bengal', reprinted in Sanjay Subrahmanyam, ed., *Money and the Market in India, 1100–1700*, Delhi, 1994.

of Gujarat—had already been conceived during the 1530s and 1540s, by Humāyūn and then Sher Shāh.

Recent work, most notably a monograph by Dirk Kolff (of which a chapter opens the present volume), has also added a valuable perspective on Sher Shāh's use of the 'military labour market' in sixteenth-century Hindustan. Kolff, whose work seems to build on the earlier insights of Simon Digby, shows how by the time of the first Mughal conquest of northern India in the 1520s, loosely allied groups, using such 'ethnic' designations as Afghan and Rajput, were tied together in complex systems of alliances, that were as important for Sher Shāh and Humāyūn, as they were for the contemporary politics of Malwa and Gujarat. The histories of these late 'regional Sultanates' have yet to receive the attention they deserve, but it is increasingly clear that horizontal ties, of both marriage and military give-and-take, structured the overarching lattice in which they operated; and that the ability to command the services of free-floating military groups was a key element in this precociously 'market-driven' polity. With the Mughals, things did change. The ability to open up a hierarchical chasm between themselves, and those whom they 'commanded' was part of the recipe of this newer style of kingship, analysed in another essay in this volume by Norman P. Ziegler, whose main focus is on how the Rajputs fitted into the Mughal political culture, with consequences for both themselves and the Mughals.

The transition from Afghan-style sovereignty (and its concomitant conception of political alliances) to that of the Mughals is of course one of the key questions of the sixteenth-century historiography. Besides the relative neglect of the Afghan role in laying the preconditions for successful Mughal expansion, it may be argued that the history of the Mughal dynasty itself has perhaps been posed in excessively teleological, linear, terms. The issue here centres in part on an ideological question: namely the basis of the Mughal claim to sovereign status, and the rights with which different members of the lineage were left as a consequence. Now, there is little doubt that in comparison to the early Tīmurids (and more generally with their Central Asian cousins), the Mughals managed to narrow down the peer group of the ruler; succession rivalries were always present, but the number of claimants was limited by direct descent. As several historians (represented in this volume by the important essay of J.F. Richards) have argued, the 'formulation of Mughal authority' was achieved by a two-pronged strategy: first, an illuminationist theory (of *farr-i īzadī*) with the fecund possibility of being variously interpreted by Islamic theologians, adherents of pre-Islamic Persian court ritual, and Rajputs; second, the creation of a sort of royal cult (*tauḥīd-i Ilāhī*) bearing an obvious resemblance to the early relationship between the Ṣafavid ruler and the *qizilbāsh*.[37] Both of these stressed the personal qualities of the ruler, and the notion of a single (rather than shared) sovereignty, as a riposte to what had been characterized by R.P. Tripathi, in a classic essay (whose conclusions were only partly qualified by Iqtidar Alam Khan in a subsequent discussion), as a 'Turko-Mongol theory of kingship'.[38] This in turn permitted a flexible interpretation of the *sharī'a*, as meaning primarily the preservation of social balance, in a situation wherein Muslims were demographically in a minority. Once more, the idea may have had intellectual roots in the reflection on kingship at the time when Muslim Persian *wazīrs* served *kāfir* Mongol rulers, but the formulation was put to a new and creative use in South Asia.[39]

Yet it should not be forgotten that these innovations emerged only after a period of considerable contestation, between the Mughals of the Ganga–Jamuna *doāb*, and others located in modern-day Afghanistan, with a far more Central Asian orientation. A key figure here, often neglected in Mughal historiography, is Humāyūn's son Mirzā Muḥammad Ḥakīm (1554–85), who was a more or less sovereign ruler of the Kabul region until his death.[40] Mirzā Ḥakīm maintained close relations with the rulers of Turan, and in particular 'Abdullāh Khān Uzbek; from the late 1560s, his court was a hotbed of Naqshbandī activity, with prominent members of that Sufi order even holding high state positions. The elimination of this kingdom was crucial from the Mughal viewpoint for several reasons. First, since the time of Bābur and Ḥumāyūn, Kabul had been an alternate centre of political power, drawing the Mughal centre of gravity away from Hindustan. Second, Mirzā Ḥakīm was able to portray himself, in contrast to his half-brother Akbar, as the pillar of an orthodox Sunnī state, building an alliance for example

[37]See J.F. Richards, 'The Formulation of Imperial Authority under Akbar and Jahangir', reproduced in this volume.

[38]See his introduction to Iqtidar Alam Khan, *The Political Biography of a Mughal Noble, Mun'im Khān Khān-i Khānān. 1497–1575*, Delhi, 1973.

[39]For an analysis, see Muzaffar Alam, 'Dīndārī and Jahāndārī: Sharī'a in Indo-Islamic Politics', in David Gilmartin, et al., *The Shaping of Indo-Muslim Identity in Pre-Colonial South Asia* (forthcoming).

[40]See Sanjay Subrahmanyam, 'A Note on the Kabul Kingdom under Muhammad Hakim Mirza (1554–1585)', in *La Transmission du savoir dans le monde musulman périphérique, Lettre d'information*, no. 14, 1994, pp. 89–101.

with the short-lived Sunnī ruler of Iran, Shāh Iṣmā'īl II (r. 1576–7). Third, Mirzā Ḥakīm had on at least two occasions (in the late 1560s and the early 1580s) posed an explicit threat to Mughal territories in the north-west, and also had significant support amongst the so-called Turani nobles of Akbar's court.

On his death, Mirzā Ḥakīm's memory was gradually absorbed into the Mughal historiography by a subtle process. Just as Mughal expansion into Central India permitted Akbar to take on the mantle of the Tomars and Baghelas, demanding as tribute not merely cash but key elements of symbolic authority (such as the musician Tansen, resident at the court of Rewa), the Mughals under Jahāngīr reinterpreted Mirzā Ḥakīm's role creatively. Thus, the *Akhlāq-i-Jahāngīrī* of Nūr-ud-Dīn Qāẓī al-Khāqānī, the first major book on *akhlāq* (ethics, including governance) produced under the Mughals in north India, in fact drew on the *Akhlāq-i-Ḥakīmī* by Ḥasan 'Alī bin Ashraf Munshī al-Khāqānī (Nūr-ud-Dīn Qāẓī's grandfather), a text written for and dedicated to Mirzā Ḥakīm and representing the orthodox view of rulership prevalent in his court. Qāẓī in fact reproduced verbatim large sections of the text by Munshī, while adding eight new chapters, more appropriate to the changed Mughal ideology of the early seventeenth century.[41] The point thus is that the Mughals were eclectic in their use of ideological formulations, and tried to reconcile the rather more austere vision of the Kabul court with their own circumstances in northern India, and with the ethical vision of, say, Naṣīr-ud-Dīn Tūsī.

This is not to belittle the extent or significance of the changes that took place in the last quarter of the sixteenth century, merely to put them in a rather more proper perspective. There was most obviously a matter of scale. By the early 1590s, when 'Abd-ul-Raḥīm, *Khān-i Khānān* under Akbar, conquered Sind and the Indus delta, the network of routes described by Sārwānī had extended considerably. Agra came to be linked not merely to Burhanpur but to Cambay, Surat and Ahmadabad. Lahore and Multan were for the Mughals not merely the gateway to Kabul, but to the ports of the mouth of the Indus. The tenuous link with Sonargaon under Shēr Shāh became a far more secure control over the ports of Bengal (with the exception of Chittagong, or Chatgam). Further, whereas Bābur, Humāyūn and Shēr Shāh were

[41]For a discussion, see Muzaffar Alam, 'Akhlaqui Norms in Mughal Governance' in M. Alam, et al. eds., *The Making of the Indo-Persian Culture: Indian and French Studies*, Delhi, 1999.

never seen either by themselves, or by their courtiers, as rulers at the same level as the Ṣafavids and Ottomans, such was not the case with Akbar.

The evolution of Mughal ideology under Akbar too is a surprisingly neglected subject. Whereas a great deal of attention has been devoted by historians to the sophisticated ideological articulations contained in the *Akbar Nāma* of Abu'l Faẓl (and in the *Ā'īn-i Akbarī*, which is a part thereof), not much has been written concerning the relationship between this text and the *Tārīkh-i Alfī*, an unfinished chronicle of Islam that Akbar had commissioned earlier in his reign, from about 1581. Inspired by a millenarian Islamic consciousness (in which Akbar's own contacts with Gujarat-based Mahdawīs may have played a role), the latter chronicle curiously enough does not begin with the *ḥijra* but instead—on the explicit instructions of Akbar—with Muḥammad's death, and already demonstrates the Mughal drive towards grandeur after the 1570s.[42] Again, even the Mughal–Ottoman diplomatic correspondence is testimony to the shift we have suggested took place.[43] In the mid-1550s, the Ottoman admiral Seyyidī 'Alī Reis, reports on a visit to the Mughal court that Humāyūn told him that 'the only man worthy to bear the title of Pādishāh is the ruler of Rūm, he alone and no one else in the world', an anecdote that is not devoid of significance even if it might have been apocryphal.[44] Such a thing could scarcely have happened by the middle years of Akbar's reign.

At the same time, however, many of the changes of the late sixteenth century were to be either consolidated or set aside later; for the circumstances and possibilities under Jahāngīr and Shāhjahān permitted innovations of a quite different order . We can see this quite clearly in respect of three major developments. First, on a politico-ideological plane, the gradual abandonment of the royal cult (*tauḥīd-i Ilāhī*) as a means of securing the notables to the ruler, which probably was visible

[42]S.A.A. Rizvi, *Religious and Intellectual History of the Muslims in Akbar's Reign, with Special Reference to Abu'l Fazl, 1556–1605*, Delhi, 1975, pp. 253–62; Subrahmanyam, 'The Mughal State—Structure or Process?', pp. 303–7.

[43]Naimur Rehman Farooqi, *Mughal–Ottoman Relations: A Study of Political and Diplomatic Relations between Mughal India and the Ottoman Empire, 1556–1748*, Delhi, 1989.

[44]Seyyidī 'Alī Reis, *The Travels and Adventures of the Turkish Admiral Sidi Ali Reis in India, Afghanistan, Central Asia and Persia*, ed. and trans. A. Vambéry, London, 1899 (reprint, Lahore, 1975).

already during the latter part of the reign of Jahāngīr. A further exploration of this would require a detailed analysis of the relationship between the Mughal dynasty and powerful Ṣufi orders, in particular the Naqshbandīs and Chishtīs, as also an exploration of the dialectical interaction of elements of 'pragmatism' and 'faith'. (*jahāndārī* and *dīndārī*) in the Mughal official ideology. In a certain sense, what we witness in Mughal India parallels trends in Iran in the same period, under Shāh Ṣafī and Shāh 'Abbās II. A second question, also of a cultural and ideological nature, is the opening up of the Mughal élite to certain European cultural and symbolic influences (visible both in art and architecture), though accompanied interestingly enough, with a hardening of attitudes towards the European trading and political presence (as witness the summary expulsion of the Portuguese from Hughli in 1632). It is in the seventeenth century, we may note in passing, that the key European texts on the Mughals (the basis of many later formulations) were produced: the war of succession between Shāhjahān's sons in the 1650s was watched with avid curiosity by intellectuals in Europe, fuelled by the writings of men such as François Bernier. This is not to argue that the European influence was the key to the dynamics of the Mughal state, far from it. Rather, it may well be time to rethink the simplistic, and rather nationalistic, formulation of Mughal autarky, that enjoyed so much success in South Asia in the decades after independence. There may be a good deal to learn here from the discussion in modern Japanese historiography concerning the 'European impact' of the years from 1580 to 1640, which far surpasses that in Mughal studies in its sophistication and subtlety.

Third, on a rather more conventional fiscal note, we may suggest that even the social basis of the fiscal system witnesses some evolution in these years. In particular, one notes the growing use in the seventeenth century of networks of bankers to transfer revenue to the centre from the provinces, and the consequent meshing of the fiscal system with commercial and financial networks; the counterpart of this was the growing direct participation by the Mughal nobility and the emperors themselves in trade. This question is a much debated one, and J.F. Richards for one has expressed scepticism about the importance of such transfers in comparison to transfers carried out by 'imperial messengers and armed escorts carrying coin and bullion'.[45] His

[45] J.F. Richards, 'Mughal State Finance and the Premodern World Economy', *Comparative Studies in Society and History*, vol. XXIII (2), 1981, pp. 285–308, especially p. 297.

response was in reaction to a provocative earlier essay by Karen Leonard (included in this volume), which had argued for a dependence of the Mughals on 'great firms' of bankers, and a subsequent shift of these bankers' loyalties away from the Mughals. Much detailed work is obviously necessary before any firm conclusion can be arrived at, but it would appear that far more evidence exists on the use of *huṇḍīs* for fiscal transfers than Richards suggests. Particularly, in the case of Gujarat, we can show that during the reigns of Jahāngīr and Shāhjahān, fiscal remittances to Delhi were closely tied to the *ṣarrāf* (or banker) network. This has been clearly demonstrated by H.W. van Santen, in his study of Dutch trade in Gujarat and north India in this period, which in part supports Leonard's hypothesis, but also modifies it in important respects. He argues that the transfers linking Gujarat to Agra had a significant 'centrifugal' as well as a 'centripetal' aspect: only the difference, or net balance, was transferred by cash. The rest was moved very largely through *huṇḍīs*, a process in which everyone from the *ṣūbadār* and *mutaṣaddī* to the Dutch Company participated. Single *huṇḍīs* between Surat or Ahmadabad and Agra, or vice-versa, could amount to as much as 50,000 or even 75,000 *rupiyas*, as his evidence from 1637–9 shows. Rates for the use of bills fluctuated seasonally, but the standard rate for a transfer from Agra to Surat was between 4 and 8 per cent, and that from Surat to Agra between 1.25 and 3 per cent.[46]

Just as the growing use of the *huṇḍī* to facilitate fiscal transfers between the outlying (and especially the maritime) provinces and the imperial centre was a feature that gained importance in the first half of the seventeenth century, so too royal and noble trade—while never accounting for more than a small portion of all commerce—grew more significant in the epoch, again adding a twist to ruling ideology. Shāhjahān's father-in-law, Āṣaf Khān, took an active part in the seaborne trade of ports such as Hughli and Surat, and even maintained an active correspondence with the Portuguese at Goa to this end.[47]

[46]Hans W. Van Santen, 'De Verenigde Oost-Indische Compagnie in Gujarat en Hindustan, 1620–1660', Ph.D. dissertation, Leiden University, 1982, pp. 117–32, 223–9; Sanjay Subrahmanyam, 'Introduction', in Subrahmanyam, ed., *Money and the Market in India*, Delhi, 1993.

[47]Sanjay Subrahmanyam, *The Portuguese Empire in Asia, 1500–1700: A Political and Economic History*, London, 1993, pp. 166–7; for documentation, see Sanjay Subrahmanyam, *Comércio e Conflito: A Presença Portuguesa no Golfo de Bengala, 1500–1700*, Lisbon, 1994, pp. 269–70.

Again, in the case of Sind, for example, several instances exist during the 1640s of advances of funds by the *shāhbandar* of Lahori Bandar and the *dīwān* of the *ṣūba* to merchants in the area from state funds, and the mint. In the 1640s, Mughal princes such as Murād Bakhsh, Aurangzeb and Dārā all used Thatta and Lahori Bandar as centres from which to prosecute commerce with Red Sea and Persian Gulf ports such as Kung and Mokha.[48] Surat too was a great centre for royal and noble trade in the 1640s and 1650s; for while Akbar and Jahāngīr had both owned shipping, the Mughal ruler most interested in maritime trade was clearly Shāhjahān.[49]

In fact, in the early 1650s, Shāhjahān on the advice of the Surat *mutaṣaddī* had half a dozen ships constructed in Gujarat, which he went on to deploy in the trade to Bandar 'Abbās and Mokha, more or less monopolizing the market in freight-carriage on these routes until 1663, when the ships were sold off to private merchants. Besides the rather obvious profits that such trade brought, and the need to keep maritime links open at a time when wars with the Ṣafavids had jeopardized trade on the overland route, it has been argued that Shāhjahān's trade was part of an implicit 'bullionist' orientation in Mughal state policy in the period. As the Dutch Company employee Gérard Pelgrom wrote in 1655:

> Were the King not to constrain his subjects to go through with the said passage with force, there would be few or perhaps even no traders to be found who would willingly risk their goods therewards, all merchants being made by His Majesty by a certain order to send a specified number of packs (of textiles) perforce to Mokha, even though the King very well knows that the owners will thereby gain but little interest, trying by these means to keep his view on increasing the textiles that are made in Gujarat and Hindustan (where most of his subjects live), and by the same means to bring a considerable sum of Spanish reals and ducats into his realm, as he otherwise has no gold or silver mines,

[48] Rashmi Seth, 'Some Aspects of the Economy of Sind in the Seventeenth Century', unpublished M. Phil. dissertation, Jawaharlal Nehru University, New Delhi, 1981; also Sanjay Subrahmanyam, 'The Portuguese, Thatta, and the External Trade of Sind, 1515–1635', *Revista de Cultura* (Macau), nos. 13/14, 1991, pp. 48–58.

[49] For Persian documentation on Mughal shipping at Surat at the time of Jahāngīr, see Shireen Moosvi, 'Mughal Shipping at Surat in the First Half of the Seventeenth Century', *Proceedings of the Indian History Congress*, 51st Session, Calcutta, 1990, pp. 308–20.

on account of which it is also deemed necessary that the Moors continue in this trade, for otherwise the artisans will be impoverished'.[50]

Penetrating the thickets of his syntax, it appears that Pelgrom's reading of Mughal 'state policy' was that it was part-bullionist, and part concerned to preserve artisan employment, in a period when Gujarat and north India had yet to recover wholly from the disastrous effects of the famine of the early 1630s. But one needs to go beyond this, as the policy in Shāhjahān's period where trade was concerned has a coherence that transcends regional imperatives. Just as Mughal princes came to participate in trade in Sind, the years from 1630 saw the Mughals make a concerted move to gain control of the maritime trade of Bengal as well. This meant that they had to reduce the role of the Portuguese traders settled in Hughli and Chittagong, something which they accomplished very successfully in the early 1630s in military campaigns against these areas. At the same time, Arakanese influence over trade in eastern Bengal had to be curtailed, which was also attempted—albeit less successfully.[51] But while in Surat and Sind, the royal family itself had taken the initiative, in Bengal it was noble trade, concentrated in the hands of a series of powerful *ṣūbadārs* and court-based grandees, that is conspicuous. This trend, begun in the period of Shāhjahān, continued into the reign of Aurangzeb, with the role of *ṣūbadārs* like Mīr Jumla and Shāyista Khān being well known in this respect.

It has been argued elsewhere that this shift in the attitude towards trade that one observes in the course of the seventeenth century can best be understood through an analysis of growing Iranian influence in the Mughal court in the first half of the seventeenth century.[52] This meant on the one hand that the sort of 'state mercantilism' espoused in Iran by Shāh 'Abbās was emulated in Mughal India, albeit with some changes; on the other hand, the long Iranian tradition of combining *imārat* and *tijārat*—statecraft and trade—found expression in Mughal domains, as it earlier had in the Deccan (and as it later was to do in

[50]Cited in Van Santen, 'De VOC in Gujarat', pp. 76–7.

[51]Syed Hasan Askari, 'The Mughal–Magh Relations down to the Time of Islam Khan Mashhadi', *Proceedings of the Indian History Congress*, 29th Session, Gauhati, 1959, pp. 201–13.

[52]Sanjay Subrahmanyam, 'Iranians Abroad: Intra-Asian Elite Migration and Early Modern State Formation', *The Journal of Asian Studies*, vol. LI (2), 1992, pp. 340–63.

Thailand). There is a certain obvious appeal to such an argument for the period of Jahāngīr, whose fascination with Shāh 'Abbās is well known. But moving away from a focus on the predilections of the ruler to the inertial momentum of the system is of essence here. By the seventeenth century, the Mughal court was conscious of itself as a rival and competitor of both Iran and the Ottomans; this inherently ambiguous relationship meant that mutual borrowings were more frequent than could safely be admitted by the chroniclers. We will hence submit that the classic formulation of the relationship between trade and politics in Mughal India, represented in this volume by the doyen of Indian 'maritime historians', Ashin Das Gupta, is in need of some rethinking. At the same time, the key problem posed by Das Gupta, of better integrating 'external relations' (whether political, commercial, diplomatic or cultural) with the rather insular mainstream of Mughal studies remains a *desideratum* even today.[53]

But the middle decades of the century, preceding the accession of Aurangzeb to the throne, are of interest for other changes as well. It is from these years, after all, that most of the surviving *dastūr ul-'amals,* the revenue manuals that are used by historians as testimony of the centralization of the Mughal state, date; equally, significant changes were made in precisely this epoch in a variety of other fiscal matters, including even the remuneration scales of the *manṣabdārs.* It is often forgotten that Shāhjahān's period also witnessed another important trend, one that remained unfulfilled however. This is the attempt to expand the extent of *khāliṣa,* relative to land held in *jāgīrs* or revenue-assignment. According to Irfan Habib, this expansion of *khāliṣa* extended into the early years of Aurangzeb's reign, and may be thought to be an act of 'deliberate policy', rather than a mere coincidence.[54] If this is indeed the case, we may see it as an abortive attempt at redefining the relative role and powers of the royal household in respect of the *amīrs* and *jāgīrdārs.* Equally, we should bear in mind that

[53] Although one may disagree with some of its theses, Ashin Das Gupta, *Indian Merchants and the Decline of Surat, c. 1700–1750*, Wiesbaden, 1979 (reprint, Delhi, 1995), remains a classic. For a more recent look at a number of its themes in a different regional setting, see Muzaffar Alam, 'Trade, State Policy and Regional Change: Aspects of Mughal–Uzbek Commercial Relations, c. 1550–1750', *Journal of the Economic and Social History of the Orient*, vol. XXXVII (2), 1994, pp. 202–27.

[54] Irfan Habib, *Agrarian System*, p. 272.

Shāhjahān's reign also sees the clearing of forested land, and the extension of cultivation acquiring the dimensions of a policy. According to the *Ḥaqīqat-i Ṣūba Bihār*, this was done as follows:

> From the time of Shāhjahān, it was customary that woodcutters and ploughmen (*tabrdārān wa tishādārān wa qalbahā*) used to accompany the troops, so that forests might be cleared and land cultivated. Ploughs used to be donated by the government. Short-term *pattas* (revenue-documents) were given fixed by the government at the rate of one *ānnā* per *bīgha* in the first year. *Chaudharīs* were appointed to keep the *ri'āyā* happy with their considerate behaviour and to populate the country.... There was a general order that whosoever cleared a forest and brought land under cultivation, such land would be his *zamīndārī*.[55]

Let us note then that many of the postures and attitudes of the Mughal state which are seen as inherent in the 'system' from its very inception (which usually means Akbar's reign), were in fact later improvisations and policies. The tendency has often been there to read back into the late sixteenth century institutional arrangements which evolved only later, apparently in order to sustain the idea that Mughal rule had already been perfected by Akbar's death. One of these institutions is the Mughal system of ranks for notables (*manṣab*), described by W.H. Moreland in a classic essay (included in this volume) as deriving from Mongol and Turkish practice, an interpretation subsequently refined and partly modified by Irfan Habib (although some of Habib's own premises on issues such as inflation are themselves questionable).[56]

Such a reading has a crucial bearing on our understanding of changes between 1650 and 1700 as well. If we are willing to consider that the middle decades of the seventeenth century witnessed a changed set of attitudes towards trade and traders, as well as a move towards 'centralization' (the extension of the *khāliṣa*), accompanying agrarian extension, the logic of change under Aurangzeb appears to have crucial

[55]Cited in Muzaffar Alam, 'Eastern India in the Early Eighteenth-Century "Crisis": Some Evidence from Bihar", *The Indian Economic and Social History Review*, vol. XXVIII (1), 1991, pp. 43–71.

[56]W.H. Moreland, 'Rank (Manṣab) in the Mughal State Service', reproduced in this volume; cf. also the article by Irfan Habib, 'The Manṣab System, 1595–1637', *Proceedings of the Indian History Congress*, 29th Session, Patiala, 1967, Part I, pp. 221–42. Permission to reproduce the latter paper here was unfortunately refused by the author.

elements of continuity with what had preceded it. The growing corpus of *dastūr ul-'amals* in Shāhjahān's period show the path to a gradual "canonization' (or perhaps one should say *qānūn*-ization) under his son. Aurangzeb's reign is when a sort of 'paper empire' emerges, with the growth of formalization, a greater insistence on measurement (at times through resurveys), and the systematization of information flows to the centre through *akhbārāt;* at the same time, and conversely, the ruler's epistles to particular officials are now reproduced as general statements of policy, and collections of royal letters and instructions come to abound.[57]

However, Aurangzeb went much further than Shāhjahān in the range of matters over which he chose to legislate. The most ambitious attempt in this direction is of course the voluminous and celebrated collection of reflections in Arabic by juriconsults, the *Fatāwā-i 'Ālamgīrī*, which appears, together with his famous *farmāns* to Muḥammad Hāshim and Rāsikdās, to be part of the first real attempt to impose a clearly defined legal system (influenced in particular by Hanafite jurisprudence) over the provinces under Mughal rule. It may be worth speculating whether this attempt at *qānūn*ization had anything to do with the rebellions that sprang up in his reign, which appear to have been as much related to an attempt to preserve and redefine local and regional autonomy, as part of a systemic, economically motivated 'crisis'.[58] Here, once more, we are reminded of the possibility of fruitful comparison with processes of what has been called 'centripetal decentralization' in the Ottoman state of the seventeenth and eighteenth centuries. Nevertheless, certain important, specific features of the Mughal religio-legal framework are also worth noting, since the contrast with the Ottomans helps bring these out rather more clearly. The office of the *qāẓī* obviously had an importance for the Mughals, and we may note their intervention in various forms of urban and even rural disputes, which were not necessarily

[57]Saiyid Ashraf Khān Ḥusainī, *Raqā'im-i-Karā'im, Epistles of Aurangzeb*, ed. S.M. Azizuddin Husain, Delhi, 1990; Shaikh Abu'l Fatḥ Qābil Khān, *Ādāb-i 'Ālamgīrī*, ed. 'Abdul Ghafur Chaudhari; 2 vols, Lahore, 1971; for a discussion, see Uriel Heyd, *Studies in Old Ottoman Criminal Law*, ed. V.L. Ménage. Oxford, 1973.

[58]Muzaffar Alam, *The Crisis of Empire in Mughal North India: Awadh and the Punjab, 1707–1748*, Delhi, 1986.

limited to purely religious questions.[59] While a definite *sharī'a* consciousness may be found in some part of the Mughal governing circles at all times (even though the totality of punishments dictated by the *ḥudūd* injunctions were rarely implemented), the meaning of the *sharī'a* itself was, as we have noted above, contested, and subject to interpretations in the light of politics. Once more, we should insist that placing the Mughals in a broader comparative sphere helps highlight certain major, unanswered questions. What, for example, was the place of arrangements such as *waqf* in the Mughal dominions and how did they evolve over time?[60] How can we explain the absence in Mughal India of the equivalent of the vast corpus of *sijill* documents (registers of cases from the courts of *qāẓīs*) that Ottoman historians have used to such telling effect for the writing of social and even micro-level economic history?[61]

[59]See Singh, *Town, Market, Mint and Port*, pp. 93–106, for some basic materials on the office of the *qāẓī* in Mughal towns; Van Santen, 'De VOC in Gujarat', for the intervention of the local *qāẓī* in disputes between the Dutch Company and indigo-growers of the Bayana region; and J.S. Grewal, 'The Qazi in the Pargana', in *Miscellaneous Articles*, Amritsar, 1974, pp. 38–73, for some materials from Punjab. The monograph by Alam, *Crisis of Empire*, pp. 111–16, 196, 211, contains a number of references to the changing role of the *qāẓī* in eighteenth-century northern India. For some interesting details, see Ghulām Ḥusain Siddiqī Firshorī Bilgramī, *Sharā'if-i-'Usmānī*, Department of History, Aligarh, Ms. 63; Qāẓī Aḥmadullāh, *Al-Musajjalāt fī Tārīkh-al-Quẓāt*, History Department, Aligarh, Ms. 87; further references may be found in documents of the UP State Archives, Allahabad, and in the *Akhbārāt Darbār-i Mu'allā* of the early eighteenth century.

[60]For an important study from Balkh, that is helpful to bring issues into focus, see R.D. McChesney, *Waqf in Central Asia: Four Hundred Years in the History of a Muslim Shrine, 1480–1889*, Princeton, 1991. For a study in the Indian context, see Rafat M. Bilgrami, *Religious and Quasi-Religious Departments of the Mughal Period, 1556–1707*, Delhi, 1984.

[61]For a very useful case study (with an extensive bibliography on both Anatolia and the Balkans), based on such documents, see Suraiya Faroqhi, *Men of Modest Substance: House Owners and House Property in Seventeenth-Century Ankara and Kayseri*, Cambridge, 1987. The regional archives for both the Maratha domains and Rajasthan in the eighteenth century remain to be exploited and may yield relevant legal material, albeit on a more modest scale than that of the Ottomans. Unfortunately, for Mughal India, we do not even have a collection of copies of *qāẓī*-court judgments comparable to the *Majmū'a-i Waṣā'iq* of sixteenth-century Samarkand (preserved in the Abu Rihan Al-Bīrunī Institute Library, Samarkand).

Rather than an exclusive focus on (often inappropriate) comparisons with Europe, a look to the Ottoman, Central Asian, and Iranian historical trajectories would certainly help in framing new issues, and in defining new institutional fields of inquiry.

Spatial Diversity : A View from the South

Our exposition so far has in fair measure centred on the issue of chronology, and the lack of logic that inheres in the neglect of certain extended periods of Mug͟hal history. The suggestion was, moreover, that the 'Mughal system' was certainly not born in 'adult' form; it grew and evolved both before and after Akbar's reign in quite significant ways. An alternative approach, that might serve to complement and shore up what has been discussed thus far, is to view the matter spatially. The Mug͟hal state's geographical extent was far different in 1700 from what it had been a century earlier, and Aurangzēb presided over a sprawling domain that extended well into southern India, besides stretching from the borders of Burma virtually to Central Asia. Within the notional 'boundaries' of this state were a diversity of territories and communities of varying statutes, as Chetan Singh's discussion of the problem of 'tribes' in relation to the notion of the 'agrarian system' of Mug͟hal India highlights; some have even spoken of defining a series of 'internal' frontiers, corresponding to this diversity of regimes that actually obtained. Nevertheless, it is safe to say that in the process of expansion in the seventeenth century, the Mug͟hals came to be seen in all of the subcontinent as the only true source of sovereignty, the only 'sovereign idea' as it were. Even the Marāthās, whose power de facto may have exceeded that of any Mug͟hal military force in the eighteenth century, continued to work largely behind a Mug͟hal facade, as indeed did the English East India Company in Bengal and Hindustan after 1765.[62]

It had not always been thus, of course. When Bābur established himself in north India in the 1520s, the rulers of Bengal, Orissa, and the Karnataka state (or Vijayanagara) certainly were seen—and saw themselves—as sovereign entities. The states of the Deccan had a more ambiguous status, as there is some evidence that they derived legitimacy from Iran—and as is apparent in the form of their diplomatic

[62]Alam, *The Crisis of Empire*; André Wink, *Land and Sovereignty in India: Agrarian Society and Politics under the Eighteenth-century Maratha Svarājya*, Cambridge, 1986.

correspondence with the Ṣafavids in the sixteenth and seventeenth centuries.[63] Of the already established states in 1530, there is no doubt that the one that cast the longest shadow was Vijayanagara, whose extent in that period was from Telengana and southern Maharashtra to the Madurai–Tirunelveli area in south India. The state was by no means a unitary and centralized one of course, although fiscal flows between distant regions and the imperial centre were sufficiently regular for us to view with scepticism the idea (propounded forcefully by the late Burton Stein) that the state was simply 'segmentary', with regions preserving autonomy and only recognizing the ritual superiority of the centre.[64] The power of this state was broken as a consequence of a long-drawn-out process, extending from the middle years of the sixteenth century to the 1650s. But it is not until the late seventeenth century that Vijayanagara as a 'sovereign idea' finally gave way in south India to the Mughals.

It is an interesting fact that while the Mughals themselves had very little directly to do with the decline of Vijayanagara, they are nevertheless indirectly implicated in it. At least one Telugu text, the *Rāmarājana Bakhair*, insists that the defeat of Vijayanagara forces by those of the Deccan Sultanates in 1565 was orchestrated by Akbar, who was himself present at the battlefield in this version![65] The *Bakhair*'s anonymous author was evidently struggling with the problem of how to locate the passing of the 'sovereign baton' at a concrete moment in space and time, and resorted to this device for the purpose. But much later, in the 1650s, the last ruler of Vijayanagara, Aravidu Sriranga, did maintain relations with Shāhjahān's court, in a last-ditch attempt to salvage some part of his domains, which had been overrun by Bijapur and Golconda forces from the late 1630s on. According to the letters of a spy in the Aravidu camp, Sriranga agreed to hand over a large treasure (including jewels and gold belonging to the major Vaishnava temple at Tirupati) to the Mughals, if only he were allowed

[63] See for instance, Nazir Ahmad, 'Letters of the Rulers of the Deccan to Shah Abbas of Iran', in *Medieval India: A Miscellany*, vol. I, Aligarh, 1969, pp. 280–300.

[64] Velcheru Narayana Rao, David Shulman and Sanjay Subrahmanyam, *Symbols of Substance: Court and State in Nayaka-period Tamilnadu*, Delhi, 1992, chs 2 and 3; contrast Burton Stein, *Vijayanagara* (The New Cambridge History of India, vol. 1.2), Cambridge, 1989.

[65] K.A.N. Sastri and N. Venkataramanayya, eds., *Further Sources of Vijayanagara History*, 3 vols, Madras, 1946, vol. III, pp. 224–5.

to retain a subordinate position under their dispensation, and keep the areas around Chandragiri and Velur (his twin court-towns) as his *waṭan jāgīr*. The Agra court seems to have been favourable to the idea, but the Golconda ruler acted quickly to nip it in the bud, by forcing Sriranga out of the region altogether.[66]

The eventual Mughal conquest of the region thus had to wait some three decades, and was actually accomplished by Aurangzeb only in the late 1680s, with some regions—such as Senji—continuing to harbour resistance even into the early eighteenth century. Some of this 'resistance' produced its own elaborate counter-narratives, as the celebrated case of Pap Rai or Sarvayi Papadu (to which we shall return briefly) demonstrates. Moreover, in the eastern Deccan and Karnatak Payanghat, the victory of the Mughals was rapidly followed by the re-formation of a set of regionally oriented sub-states, with the Āṣaf Jāhī state of Hyderabad and the Nawwābī state centred around Arcot in Tamilnadu being the two most conspicuous examples. However, prior to conquest proper, there had been a long period of incursions and an open and fluctuating frontier between the Mughal dominions and the Deccan Sultanates of Bijapur and Golconda. In the 1630s, these two Sultanates had formally declared themselves subservient to the Mughals, and over time the fiscal practice in Golconda tended to gravitate little by little towards a perceived Mughal style. Now in the early seventeenth century, fiscal administration in Golconda had been heavily mediated by revenue farmers on contracts of various lengths and with varying levels of permanence.[67] This was particularly true of the more productive coastal districts, while the less productive interior tended to be parcelled out in assignments, or held by autonomous chieftains called *nāyakas* (Persian *nāyakwariān-i 'iẓām*).[68]

As an arrangement, the Golconda practice in the first half of the seventeenth century was quite similar in crucial respects to what obtained further south, in the territories of the Chandragiri ruler, and the Nāyakas of Senji, Tanjavur and Madurai. Here too revenue-farming was common, and the ruling families were closely allied to an important semi-commercial, semi-warrior caste group, the Balija Naidus, whose ideology appears to have been closely reflected in the strategies adopted

[66]M.H. Rama Sharma, *The History of the Vijayanagara Empire*, ed. M.H. Gopal, 2 vols, Bangalore, 1978/1980, vol. II, pp. 288–94.

[67]H.K. Sherwani, *History of the Quṭb Shāhī Dynasty*, Delhi, 1974, pp. 439–41.

[68]J.F. Richards, *Mughal Administration in Golconda*, Oxford, 1975, pp. 18–19: Sherwani, *Quṭb Shāhī Dynasty*.

by these states. The major mode of assessing revenue in the more productive rice lands of the coast, both in Golconda and further south, was crop-sharing.[69] The application of crop rates for non-food crops (or for low value millets, etc.) was not unknown, but had not been systematized to a high degree. The states south of the Godavari in south-eastern India thus drew their resources from taxing rice production, trade, and the control of certain natural resources such as mines (we may recall here that Golconda was a major producer of diamonds in the epoch).

In the early seventeenth century, the interstate political system in the region has a classic 'domino' pattern. As the Mughals pressurized the Deccan Sultanates, they in turn pressed on Chandragiri, Senji and other states; the stabilization of state revenues became of essence in this situation. This situation tended to entrench revenue-farming even deeper, at least until the collapse of Senji and Chandragiri between 1649 and 1656–7. Thereafter, the Golconda Sultanate found itself in possession of extensive new resources in the so-called 'Karnatak', and gradually moved to redefine its fiscal methods in response to the new possibilities. This attempt occupied the late 1670s and early 1680s, and is often associated with Abu'l Ḥasan Quṭb Shāh's minister Mādannā Pandit, and his brother Akkannā. So far as we can gather, the attempt was largely one to redefine the *jama'-i kāmil* ('perfect assessment') more stringently, and lower the gap between assessment and collection. To this end, Mādannā deployed members of his own social group, Telugu Brahmans, as revenue officials; this attempt was stiffly resisted by Muslim notables, who saw the affair not merely as administrative reform but sectarian rivalry.[70] In this process, Abu'l Ḥasan Quṭb Shāh came to have the near-unique distinction of being reviled not only by the Mughal chroniclers, who accused him of making 'vagabond Hindus the managers and the administrators of the affairs of his State', but equally by contemporary Ṣafavid writers, such as Muḥammad Rābi', Persian ambassador to Thailand in the 1680s![71]

[69]Sanjay Subrahmanyam, *The Political Economy of Commerce: Southern India, 1500–1650*, Cambridge, 1990, pp. 327–36; Narayana Rao, et al., *Symbols of Substance*, pp. 103–5.

[70]Joseph J. Brennig, 'The Textile Trade of Seventeenth-Century Northern Coromandel: A Study of a Pre-Modern Asian Export Industry', Ph. D. thesis, University of Wisconsin, Madison, 1975.

[71]John O'Kane, ed. and trans., *The Ship of Sulaimān*, London, 1972, pp. 234–40.

But despite the 'bad press' that Mādannā and his associates have received, there seems to be some foundation to the idea that the fiscal reform they attempted formed the basis for the revenue-settlement of 'province *dār-ul-jihād* Hyderabad', formulated after the Mughal conquest by the *dīwān* Muḥammad Shafī in 1689–90. We note that this settlement was once again not based on land measurement (no *ārāẓī* statistics exist); rather it has figures for assessment (*jama*'), and established receipts *muqarrar ḥāṣil*), and the Mughal *dīwān* decided in the case of each region to increase the assessment by a greater or lesser extent depending on the gap between the two, and consultation with locally knowledgeable persons. It would be no exaggeration therefore to say that the Mughals on their conquest of Hyderabad gerry-built their fiscal system on what was already in place, namely the Mādannā settlement. While it is often assumed that revenue-farming was done away with, it is not clear that extensive evidence exists in support of such a contention. Certainly, the coastal districts were being farmed again within a half century of Mughal conquest, and the Dutch continued in the 1690s to retain the revenue farms (over villages like Konteru, Palakollu, Golepallem and so on) that they had held under Abu'l Ḥasan Quṭb Shāh. J.F. Richards would appear to be broadly accurate then when he asserts the following:

> The total impression that one gains is that the Mughal land-tax system in Hyderabad was, in fact, the decentralized system of Golconda with certain modifications. A new superstructure of Mughal revenue-officials functioned at the capital and other key administrative centres in the province.[72]

Naturally, these arrangements did not remain frozen over time, and evolved once into the second quarter of the eighteenth century.[73] From 1724, after his victory over a rival claimant Mubāriz Khān in the battle of Shakar Khera, a Turani noble originating from Bukhara titled Chīn Qilīch Khān (or Niẓām ul-mulk) set about consolidating his hold over six *ṣūbas* in the region, which were notionally subservient to the Mughals. Effectively, however, much of his activity concentrated in *ṣūba* Hyderabad itself, the erstwhile core region of the Golconda Sultanate.

[72]Richards, *Mughal Administration in Golconda*, p. 173.

[73]Muzaffar Alam, 'The Zamindars and Mughal Power in the Deccan, 1686–1712', *The Indian Economic and Social History Review*, vol. XI (1), 1974, pp. 74–91.

As documents published by Zahir Uddin Malik show, even within this region, a twofold policy was followed. The interior, or Telengana, was left to be dominated by powerful local chiefs and magnates, often descendants of the same clans who had controlled the locality under the Quṭb Shāhī rulers of Golconda. It was in the east, in a set of areas that encompassed Ibrahimpatnam, Devarkonda, and the coastal districts of Srikakulam, Masulipatnam, and Nizamapatnam, that Niẓām ul-mulk concentrated his efforts in the late 1720s and 1730s.[74] The three posts of *amīn*, *shiqdār* and *faujdār* were combined in a single person, who was given the duty of collecting the *jama*' but at the same time allowed to maintain substantial corps of troops from the revenue that he collected. In some instances, it is clearly stated that the collections from the coastal districts were to be remitted to Hyderabad by means of *huṇḍīs*. The trend seems to be towards consolidation and extension of revenue collection on the one hand, but on the other hand the new structure left the Āṣaf Jāhī state crucially dependent on the efficiency and goodwill of those who held these powerful joint posts. After 1740, the control of the coastal districts was effectively wrested from the Āṣaf Jāhs by a series of French and English interventions, and the experiment came to an end.[75]

Further south, it appears very likely that the fiscal administration adopted in Arcot by Sa'ādatullāh Khān and his successors after 1710 derived from the practice of Bijapur and Golconda administrators in the area: here too, one observes extensive recourse to revenue-farming, the deliberate attempt to seek links with ports such as São Tomé in the early eighteenth century, the close ties with coastal Muslim mercantile communities and so on.[76] Thus, the classic 'model' (indeed, ideal) of *ẓabṭ* derived from Sher Shāh could not be put in place here; the regional style of kingship, derived from the Nāyakas of the seventeenth century, and crucially dependent on the cult of consumption and enjoyment, operated as a ghost in the machine for the Arcot Nawwābs as much

[74]Zahir Uddin Malik, 'Documents Relating to Pargana Administration in the Deccan under Asaf Jah I', in *Medieval India: A Miscellany*, vol. III, Delhi, 1975, pp. 152–83.

[75]Karen Leonard, 'The Hyderabad Political System and its Participants', *The Journal of Asian Studies*, vol. XXX (3) 1971, pp. 569–82; Richards, *Mughal Administration in Golconda*, pp. 170–1; M.A. Nayeem, *Mughal Administration of Deccan under Nizamul Mulk Asaf Jah (1720–48 AD)*, Bombay, 1985.

[76]Susan Bayly, *Saints, Goddesses and Kings: Muslims and Christians in South Indian Society, 1700–1900*, Cambridge, 1989, pp. 151–5.

as for the Marathas who took over Tanjavur in the 1670s. But at the same time, by the late eighteenth century, a great degree of uniformity in administrative and fiscal terminology had come to exist between the Deccan and the Tamil country, as indeed between the area as a whole and other far-flung provinces and states which were under the nominal sovereignty of the Mughals. An examination of key legal and administrative terminology in Tamil reveals a very large number of Arabic and Persian-derivative words (ranging from *in'ām* and *mirāṣ*, to *wakīl* and *zamīn*), none of which can be encountered in common use in the area before about 1680. Thus, the seemingly Mughal institutions that the early British administrators of the Madras Presidency found there, and which are found reflected in their own references to *dahazāda*, *paimāish* and so on, were put in place not when the Mughal empire was at its 'glorious height' but in the eighteenth century!

It is clear that while this situation would arguably bear comparison with what was occurring in much the same period in Awadh (under Burhān ul-mulk and his successors), Punjab and Bihar, there are also significant points of difference that emerge.[77] Even if the evidence of substantial economic decline in none of these instances would stand up to close scrutiny, nevertheless the political configurations that come into place are rather varied. In Punjab, no strong regional state emerges until very late in the eighteenth century (with the consolidation under Ranjit Singh), and in Bihar too the attempts by a succession of governors to entrench themselves locally in the years 1700 to 1740 fail signally.[78] It is thus of significance that even within the northern Indian heartland of the Mughal empire, where *ẓabṭ* generally may have thought to have obtained, regional experiences differed widely. In short, the mere existence of *ẓabṭ* did not act as a 'levelling' mechanism, and other regional characteristics instead continued to play a crucial role in determining the trajectories of different areas in the early eighteenth century.

THE VIEW FROM THE EAST : BENGAL

There is thus some force to the idea of dismantling the master concept of the 'Mughal system' by using countervailing voices, that represent traditions at a higher level of disaggregation. In this section, we will continue to insist on the importance of the regional perspective by focusing on still another 'peripheral' region, Bengal. Unlike the south,

[77] Alam, *Crisis of Empire*.
[78] Alam, 'Eastern India in the Early Eighteenth-Century "Crisis"'.

which attracted Mughal attention relatively late, Bengal had already been a target of focus for Humāyūn in the 1530s. After a brief period under Sūr control, the region threw up a set of autonomous Afghan-ruled polities again in the 1550s and 1560s, and had to be re-annexed by Akbar's armies in the 1570s and 1580s, in a series of arduous campaigns.[79] Nevertheless, as late as the 1590s, a very large number of autonomous chieftains are recognized by the *Ā'īn-i Akbarī* in the area. To the north lay the important chiefdom of Kuch Bihar, founded by Bisva Singh, which expanded considerably in the course of the sixteenth century. By 1584, the military force commanded by Mal Gosāin, its chief, is reputed to have included 200,000 men on foot, 4000 horses, 100 elephants and a number of armed river vessels. To the south, another important chief of the period was 'Isā Khān, *zamīndār* of Bhati, who had a number of smaller *zamīndārs* subordinate to him. To the east (in modern day Bangladesh), Tajpur, Sylhet and Jessore were the places of residence of powerful *zamīndārs*, with the chief of Sylhet being an Afghan, Bāyazīd Karrānī. Similarly, the Orissa region too had located in it a number of powerful *zamīndārs*, in whose territories the Mughals had little say even after the 1580s.[80]

It is difficult to determine the extent of lands in Bengal which the Mughals could claim to 'directly administer', as distinct from those from which they collected *zamīndārī peshkash* (or tribute). The total revenues they claimed as *jama'* in the 1590s is reported by Abu'l Fazl in the *Ā'īn-i' Akbarī* to have been 598 million *dāms* from 787 *maḥāls*, which were in turn consolidated into 24 *sarkārs*, 19 in Bengal and the rest in Orissa. Roughly a sixth of the total (91.4 million *dāms*) is accounted for by the *sarkār* of Cuttack alone, with its 21 *maḥāls*. At the same time, however, the text of the *Ā'īn* makes it clear that the fiscal administration was based on the continuation of what had existed before Mughal conquest. Thus:

> The people are submissive and pay their rents duly. The demands of each year are paid by instalments in eight months, they themselves bring the *muhrs* and *rupiyas* to the appointed place for the receipt of revenue, as the division of grain between the government and the husbandsman is not here customary. The harvests are always abundant, measurement is not insisted upon, and the

[79] Tapan Raychaudhuri, *Bengal under Akbar and Jahangir: An Introductory Study in Social History*, 2nd edn, Delhi, 1966.

[80] Ahsan Raza Khan, *Chieftains in the Mughal Empire during the Reign of Akbar*, Shimla, 1977, pp. 177–200.

revenue demands are determined by the estimate of the crop. His Majesty in his goodness has confirmed this custom.[81]

Beyond suggesting that a form of *nasaq* (in the instance sometimes termed *muqṭà'ī* or fixed demand) was in use, and that crop-sharing (*batāī*) was not employed, the passage cited above is rather vague. What was the 'custom' that Akbar permitted to continue? It would appear that in part it preserved elements that had been determined in the Husain Shāhī period in Bengal (1494–1538), but was also overlaid with practices introduced by Sher Shāh, Sulaimān Khān Karrānī and so on, in the decades from 1530 to 1580. Now the Ḥusain Shāhī approach to fiscal collection and assessment can only be described as a patchy and uneven one. The administrative unit most commonly in use was the *arṣah*, which formed the basis for the later *sarkār*; the *arṣah* was further divided into *maḥāls*. That the control exercised over their domains by the Ḥusain Shāhīs was extremely uneven is testified to by several accounts, in particular the anonymous account of a Portuguese embassy to the Bengal court at Gaur. The Portuguese, who made the visit in 1521, followed a river-cum-land route from Chittagong, on the border with Arakan, all the way to Gaur in the north-west. En route, they dealt with a succession of local governors (*regedores*), who appear very often to have exercised a formidable autonomy—even if they were notionally 'appointed' by Gaur. These men, who held the post of *sar-i lashkar wa wazīr*, were appointed to key urban centres, and appear to have impinged relatively little on the countryside. That task was left to revenue-farmers, called *majmū'adārs* (or more rarely *ijāradārs*), who paid a fixed sum to the provincial treasury. Still another element in the state apparatus were men who held the post of *ghair maḥallī* (Portuguese *gromalle*), and were freewheeling agents of the Sulṭān's will, acting as his representatives in trade and mercantile ventures overseas, as well as to mediate between the province and the court.[82]

The evidence on early sixteenth-century Bengal, such as it is then, according to M.R. Tarafdar does 'not warrant the conclusion that there was a uniform system of provincial administration all over the

[81] Abu'l Faẓl, *Ā'īn-i Akbarī*, Persian text ed. H. Blochmann, 2 vols, Calcutta, 1867–77; English translation by H. Blochmann (vol. I), and H.S. Jarrett (vols. II and III) rev. D.C. Phillott and J.N. Sarkar, Calcutta, 1927–49, translation vol. II, p. 134.

[82] Geneviève Bouchon and Luís Filipe Thomaz, *Voyage dans les Deltas du Gange et de l'Irraouaddy: Relation Portugaise Anonyme (1521)*, Paris, 1988.

country'.[83] This emerges as much from contemporary literary evidence in Bengali, as from the Portuguese account we have cited above. When asked by one of the provincial *sar-i lashkar wa wazīrs* to hand over the gift the Portuguese had brought for the Sultan

'as there were many thieves in the land, and something might happen to us that might anger the King', the interpreter of the embassy replied 'that the present had to remain with us and we with it; and the land appeared most awful to us if such a great lord as the King was said to be, could be angered in what was his own [territory]; and that we had little hope of receiving any favour or mercy in such a land, for its lord was not even powerful enough to defend himself against his own subjects'.[84]

Now the most difficult of the subjects in question were of course the *zamīndārs*, amongst whom there were in turn (as we have seen) considerable differences in status and power. But this group was in itself not stable; several of the major *zamīndārīs* were founded in the course of the sixteenth century, and their 'customary' character was thus not beyond question. This is certainly true of a number of the Afghan *zamīndārīs* in Bengal, which were created after the fall of the Ḥusain Shāhīs in the 1530s. Again, in the time of Jahāngīr (r.1605–28), even the few big *zamīndārs* who had been displaced by Akbar are reported to have been restored to their old positions, with all their privileges. Numerous small *ta'alluqas* and petty *zamīndārīs* also seem to have been encouraged in between. It is evident that the Mughals only attacked these chieftains if they proved absolutely recalcitrant, and it is significant that while doing so they used not only Mughal armies but the forces of other *zamīndārs*. Mughal power in Bengal thus was established in a characteristic pattern, reminiscent in many ways of the first two centuries of the Delhi Sultanate: urban centres were the main focus of the Mughal presence, and the control of trade routes was crucial. The ports were also a priority, though conspicuously so only after the 1620s. Penetration into the countryside remained extremely limited until the late seventeenth century. The only manner in which this could be attempted was in the colonization of new lands. As the focus of population and settlement shifted eastward in Bengal over this period, new lands were brought under the plough, and what had been jungle now became paddy-fields. The Mughal state attempted to set itself up

[83]M.R. Tarafdar, *Husain Shahi Bengal, 1494–1538 AD: A Socio-Political Study*, Dhaka, 1965, p. 117.

[84]Bouchon and Thomaz, *Voyage dans les Deltas*, p. 223.

as arbiter of this expansion, by means of land grants on extremely favourable terms to specific groups. As a strategy however, this does not appear to have been wholly successful if indeed its intention was to curtail *zamīndār* power by the creation of an alternative gentry stratum (of *madad-i ma'āsh* and other *in'ām* holders). Nevertheless, it appears to have helped to an extent to promote the incipient Mughalization of the countryside in the eastern reaches of Bengal *ṣūba* in these centuries, paving the way for processes that we shall discuss below.[85]

The Mughal annexation of Bengal was hence not followed by any radical reorganization of the relationship between the central state and the local economy and society. The practice of *nasaq*, and the fact that revenue demand remained fixed, is suggestive moreover of a system not unlike fixed-rent revenue farming, where intermediaries rather than the central state bear the brunt of fluctuations (as well as reap the benefits of expansion). The *jama'* figures for Bengal thus remain relatively stable for almost three-quarters of a century after the Mughal takeover.[86] The increase that is visible from the 1650s was probably at least partly the result of territorial expansion, and the bringing of new eastern lands into the Bengal *ṣūba* during the *ṣūbadārīs* of Mīr Jumla and Shāyista Khān; it has also been argued by Richard Eaton that processes of ecological change and Islamization, both of which depended in a rather limited fashion on the Mughals, were responsible for such changes as did occur in the pattern of cultivation. Thus, the real impact of the Mughals on fiscal organization in Bengal had to await the eighteenth century—and even then was hemmed in by a number of constraints.

On the basis of size, strength, resources, geographical and strategic location, the important *zamīndārīs* in Bengal have been broadly classified in the existent literature into four types—the autonomous chiefs, the frontier *zamīndārs*, the big *zamīndārs* and the petty *zamīndārs*.[87] This analysis depends in large measure on a classic essay by S. Nurul Hasan (reproduced in this volume), which implicitly argues that the Mughal state was gerry-built in very large measure on its political relationship with the various levels of *zamīndārs*, a fact that the fixation with *manṣabdārī* and the 'agrarian system' in the Moreland–Habib analysis may have rather obscured. Following the lead of Nurul Hasan,

[85] Richard M. Eaton, *The Rise of Islam and the Bengal Frontier, 1204–1760*, Delhi, 1994, chs. 7 to 9.

[86] Cf. Habib, *Agrarian System*, pp. 400–1.

[87] Shirin Akhtar, *The Role of Zamindars in Bengal, 1707–1772*, Dhaka, 1982.

A.R. Khan, and others, we may suggest that in the case of Bengal, the Rajas of Kuch Bihar, Kuch Hajo, Assam and Tripura on the northern and north-eastern border fall in the category of autonomous chiefs. After the Mughal conquest, when Lakshmī Nārāyan and Parikshit Nārāyan, the Rajas of Kuch Bihar, pledged their allegiance and appeared personally at the court, they were recommended to be reinstated to their position by the *ṣūbadār* of Bengal and made allies of the Mughals. Similarly, the Rajas of Assam and Tippera were restored to their old possessions on the condition of regular payment of *peshkash.*[88] The Rajas of Bishnupur and Birbhum were among the most notable frontier *zamīndārs.* In the third category were the *zamīndārs* of Rajshahi, Rukunpur, Nadia, Dinajpur, Lashkarpur and Burdwan, who mostly controlled the inner contours of the province so that, even if they were not as high in terms of status and position as the autonomous and frontier Rajas, they formed the core of Mughal rule.

In the late seventeenth century, Bengal was rocked with a series of *zamīndārī* revolts. As the ordinary nobles in charge of the provincial government failed to rise to the occasion, Prince Muḥammad 'Aẓīm-ud-Dīn, better known as 'Aẓīm-ush-Shān, one of the ablest grandsons of Aurangzeb, was assigned the task of restoring law and order in the province. The Prince succeeded remarkably in his military mission; the rebels having been suppressed, revenues began to flow into the royal treasury as before.[89] Aurangzeb was however not satisfied. To deal with the problems he faced in the Deccan, he needed much more money from Bengal where the *zamīndārs* still paid low amounts in spite of the fact that lately there had been an enormous increase in production and thereby an improvement in the incomes of these *zamīndārīs.* While qualitative evidence points in such a direction, we do not unfortunately have much detailed quantitative data on the *zamīndārs'* exactions from peasants, and the internal administration of the *zamīndārīs.* However, the accounts of the Calcutta *zamīndārī* of the English East India Company

[88]Mirza Nathan, *Bahāristān-i-Ghaybī: A History of the Mughal Wars in Assam, Cooch Behar, Bengal, Bihar and Orissa during the Reigns of Jahāngīr and Shāhjahān,* English translation by M.I. Borah, Gauhati, 1936, vol. II, p. 521; J.N. Sarkar ed., *History of Bengal,* vol. II, Dhaka, 1948, p. 418; Raychaudhuri, *Bengal under Akbar and Jahangir.*

[89]Ghulām Ḥusain Salīm, *Riyāẓ-us-Salāṭīn,* ed. Maulavi 'Abdul Hak Abid, Calcutta, 1890 (English translation by Abdus Salam, reprint, Delhi, 1975), text, pp. 233–43; Munshi Salīmullāh, *Tārīkh-i-Bangāla,* ed. S.M. Imamuddin, Dhaka, 1979, pp. 12–32.

give us some idea of the rate of increase and the gap between the *zamīndār*'s collection, and his payments to the provincial treasury. The Company after acquiring *zamīndārī* rights over Calcutta (Kalkatta) village, Gobindpur, and Sutanuti in 1698 on the payment of Rs 1300 as its price, paid a total of Rs 1195 each year. This remained fixed for a long time, even at a later time when from the records collated by C.R. Wilson in his calendar, it appears that the Company obtained an income of Rs 27,265 per year.[90] It is naturally dangerous to generalize about *zamīndārī* income as a whole from this evidence. The increase in this case was exceptional because the English had established their commercial headquarters at Calcutta; by 1711, a number of bazaars had emerged around the town, and the rents from the houses in these bazaars formed a considerable part of the Company's income.[91] Still, even the increase in incomes from Gobindpur (which was at some distance from the town) has been estimated as having expanded sixfold in a decade, which is certainly a pointer to the considerable expansion even in areas which indirectly experienced the effects of the expanding overseas trade of the province.[92] It is also quite likely that the Company as a *zamīndār* enjoyed special privileges and concessions, and also may have managed to withhold more from the provincial treasury than other *zamīndārs.*

Still, even bearing all of these qualifications in mind, it would seem likely that the Calcutta *zamīndārī* accounts indicate the trend and direction of developments in *zamīndārīs* in Bengal in general in this period. The fact that the general set-up in late seventeenth-century Bengal was one where *jāgīr* assignments accounted for the bulk of *jama'* also helped the *zamīndārs* virtually to control the terms and nature of local revenue arrangements.[93] Those nobles who held *jāgīrs* in this province were usually persons posted elsewhere. Of course this was not unique to Bengal; but whereas in other provinces the *jāgīrdārs* agents were often their own associates who would apprise them more or less correctly of the true position, in Bengal these agents were usually local people—the *zamīndārs* themselves or their henchmen. Outsiders, it is

[90]C.R. Wilson, *The Early Annals of the English in Bengal*, reprint, Delhi, 1983, vols. I and II, vol. I, pp. 220, 225; vol. II.1, pp. 24–6, 29, 37–9, 53, 57, 66–9, 89–91; Saba Samiuddin, 'The Study of the Calcutta Zamindari of the East India Company in Bengal in its Early Phase', paper presented at the Indian History Congress, 42nd Session, Bodh-Gaya, 1981.

[91]Wilson, *Early Annals*, vol. II.1, pp. 170–1, 178–80.

[92]Samiuddin, 'The Study of the Calcutta Zamindari'.

[93]Salīmullāh, *Tārīkh-i-Bangāla*, p. 32; Habib, *Agrarian System*, pp. 271–3.

reported by the eighteenth-century chroniclers, avoided being posted in Bengal because of its humid and debilitating climate![94] The *jāgīrdārs* thus had to be content with what they received from the *zamīndārs*, the local intermediaries. Even if they realized that they were not getting their due, they had little hope of coping with *zamīndārī* strength. As the *jāgīrdārs* were a divided group with transient individual interests, they could never get together to discipline the *zamīndārs*; rather the *zamīndārs* could play them off against one another, colluding with one against another. Again, as a contemporary chronicle reports

> 'there was very little in the *khāliṣa* so that even the salaries of the soldiers put under the Prince's command and cash recipients (*naqdīs*) could not wholly be met out of the *mahāls* of the province. They had to be paid out of the other *ṣūbas*.'[95]

The reign of Aurangzeb had in general, we have noted above, been characterized by attempts to tighten administrative control, and in particular to improve the state's knowledge of the tax-base by means of more stringent measurement of *ārāẓī*.[96] It was in keeping with this spirit that a leading noble Mirzā Muḥammadī, entitled Kārṭalab Khān, but better known by his later title of Murshid Qulī Khān, who had earlier established his credentials as an ace financial manager, was sent as *dīwān* to Bengal in 1700 to reassess the revenue, and in order to take account of the recent expansion there. Ironically, it was the same Murshid Qulī Khān who founded a semi-autonomous state (*niẓāmat*) in Bengal, parallelling in some ways the developments we have surveyed in the eastern Deccan and Karnatak.

The Process of Regional Centralization

The set of processes that we shall discuss in this section brings us to the heart of a series of controversies concerning the nature of the eighteenth-century transition or 'crisis' in Mughal India, that have provoked heated and at times bitter debate in recent years. The general outlines of these debates shall receive more extended treatment below; let us begin with the specific, by looking at the nature of the transition in the case of Bengal, as a test case. Thus, we might ask, how, in fact, did Murshid Qulī Khān deal with the power of the *zamīndārs*, which

[94] Salīmullāh, *Tārīkh-i-Bangāla*, p. 32; Salim, *Riyāẓ-us-Salāṭīn* (text), p. 245.
[95] Salīm, *Riyāẓ-us-Salāṭīn* (text), pp. 245–6.
[96] Alam, 'Eastern India in the Early Eighteenth-Century "Crisis"'.

appears to have been so well entrenched? It has generally been suggested that the big *zamīndārs* were not simply the backbone of the early eighteenth-century *niẓāmat*, but they were allowed to be the real rulers if only they agreed to pay the stipulated revenue according to the old sixteenth-century Akbari–Todarmali arrangement. Murshid Qulī K͟hān, the first independent Mug͟hal *nāẓim* is held responsible for their supreme (and unprecedented) political and economic power.[97] As for the other *zamīndārs*, they, we are told, remained initially outside of the core of this *niẓāmat* and were thus of little significance in this transformation of Mug͟hal polity. The autonomous chiefs had always been sovereign, without ever being subjected to any well-defined Mug͟hal regulations and remained so under the Nawwābs. Munshī Salīmullāh and G͟hulām Ḥusain Salīm, two noted eighteenth-century chroniclers, give an account how these chiefs never bent their heads in submission and only on hearing the news of an imminent military attack by the Mug͟hal paid tributes.[98] In the frontier, Birbhum was brought under the Mug͟hals by Mīr Jumla in 1659. Later, Murshid Qulī K͟hān considered this *zamīndārī* to be very important since it guarded the western border against the Jharkhand chiefs. Bishnupur, surrounded by dense forests and the hilly terrains, remained almost free from Mug͟hal control.[99] These and many other *zamīndārīs* in the vast tracts of Jungle Mahal bordering Midnapore, Bishnupur, Birbhum and also some Rajput *zamīndārs* in Pachet, Chandrakona and Mynachora enjoyed a *peshkashī* status. In this category are also a number of petty frontier *zamīndārs* in the north and north-eastern region in Ghoraghat, Bengalbhum, Dakkinkol, Kamrup and Udehur.[100] The relations of these *zamīndārs* with the Mug͟hal government are portrayed as principally political and diplomatic. This then is the understanding in a good part of the current historiography.

[97]Philip B. Calkins, 'The Formation of a Regionally-Oriented Ruling Group in Bengal, 1700–1740', *The Journal of Asian Studies*, vol. XXIX (4), 1970. pp. 799–806; P.J. Marshall, *Bengal: The British Bridgehead* (The New Cambridge History of India, volume II.1), Cambridge, 1987; Munshi Mazibor Rahman, 'Nizamat in Bengal: A Study of its Rise, Growth and Decline, 1700–1757', unpublished M. Phil. dissertation, Jawaharlal Nehru University, Delhi, 1988.

[98]Salim, *Riyāẓ-us-Salāṭīn* (text); Salīmullāh, *Tārīk͟h-i- Bangāla*.

[99]Salīm, *Riyāẓ-us-Salāṭīn* (text), pp. 253–4; Hitesranjan Sanyal, 'Mallabhum', in Surajit Sinha, ed., *Tribal Politics and State Systems in Precolonial Eastern and Northeastern India*, Calcutta, 1987, pp. 74–142.

[100]Akhtar, *Zamindars*, p. 12.

It is our contention, however, that much of this analysis needs reconsideration. For the moment let us confine the discussion to the *zamīndārīs* of the inner tracts of the province only, while we review the *nawwābī* administration. The suggestion that Nawwāb Murshid Qulī Khān's policies encouraged the rise of a small but powerful group of *zamīndārs*, almost free to manage their internal affairs and that he converted a large and less stratified base of small landholders into a smaller but more stratified base of larger landholders cannot be accepted save with strong reservations.[101] On the contrary, the Nawwāb's principal concern on his arrival as the *dīwān* (the chief finance and revenue minister) in Bengal was to tighten his control over the countryside. Significantly, the new *dīwān* did not begin his reforms simply by appointing new assessors and collectors; according to the eighteenth-century Persian chronicles of Bengal, 'he made a proposal for transferring the *jāgīrs* of *manṣabdārs* of Bengal to Orissa, and this was approved'. Thereupon, the author of the *Riyāẓ us-Salāṭīn* adds,

> [He] transferred all the *sair ḥāṣil jāgīrs* except the *jāgīrs* of the *nāẓim* and *dīwān* from Bengal to Orissa, which had uncultivated, low revenue-yielding, rebellious and unsubdued *maḥāls*. Thus, he extricated the finances of Bengal from the grasp of the *zamīndārs* and *jāgīrdārs*, and brought about an increase in the income of the royal treasury, and by close scrutiny large economies were made, every year the *jama'* of the *ṣūba* increased.[102]

By extending the *khāliṣa*, Murshid Qulī Khān evidently intended to impose constraints in a more concentrated and organized manner on the *zamīndārs*. He achieved his goal partly by evolving a system that was in effect quite independent of Delhi, and more-or-less Bengal-based for the management of the *jāgīrs* of the *nāẓim*, *dīwān*, and some other imperial nobles and local officials. To the question of *jāgīr* administration, and how trends in it seem to signify a greater degree of what we may term 'local centralization' we shall return below. Let us first consider a passage of the *Riyāẓ us-Salāṭīn* to assess what Murshid Qulī Khān's revenue reforms meant for the *zamīndārs*.

[101]Calkins, 'The Formation of an Elite'; Raychaudhuri, 'The State and the Economy: The Mughal Empire', in Raychaudhuri and Habib, eds., *The Cambridge Economic History of India*, vol. I, p. 177. For the most recent version of this thesis, see John R. McLane, *Land and Local Kingship in Eighteenth-Century Bengal*, Cambridge, 1993.

[102]Salīm, *Riyāẓ-us-Salāṭīn* (text), p. 246.

He turned the *zamīndārs* of the province wholly into prisoners and bondsmen and appointed knowledgeable and honest revenue collectors over the *maḥāls* (*wa zamīndārān-i ṣūba rā bilkul muqaiyad-o-āsīr kardah wa 'ummāl-i wāqif kār wa diyānat shi'ār bar maḥālāt ta'aiyun namūdah*). He resumed the income from the *mufassal* and transferred the entire revenue payment (*mālguzārī*) to the headquarters (*ḥuẓūr*). He completely freed the income and expenditure (*dakhl-o kharch*) of the revenues from the clutches of the *zamīndārs* (*dast-i taṣarruf-i zamīndārān*) and confined their source of livelihood to *nānkār*.[103]

Far from conceding to the *zamīndārs* the highest position in the hierarchy of revenue administration, as has sometimes been asserted, Murshid Qulī therefore began his reform with an attempt to reduce them to total servility and subservience. We must not ignore the exaggerated Persian diction of the chronicler, of course, but the fact that Ghulām Ḥusain Salīm's statement is not wholly off the mark is borne out by an examination of a few administrative papers of the period from Bengal. For example, according to a list of officials from the early part of the reign of Bahādur Shāh (1707–1712), the responsibility for arranging the necessary *sīhbandī* and ensuring the realization of revenues of *khāliṣa* and *pāibāqī* (land earmarked for assignment in *jāgīrs*) in *ṣūba* Bengal was entrusted to 74 persons in charge of 92 *'uhdadārīs*; the documents also give specific details of the number and names of the *maḥāls*, whether they are *dar-o-bast* (full) or *qismat* (part/division), and the amounts. Among these *'uhdadārs*, only 30 can be identified as *zamīndārs*, including the four big *zamīndārs* of Burdwan, Rajshahi, Rukunpur and Ukhra, and the frontier Rajas of Birbhum, Bishnupur, and Pachet-Shergarh; 25 others are small *ta'alluqadārs*, *zamīndārs* and *chaudhurīs*. The remaining 44 are described as *karorīs*, *sazāwals*, *amīns*, *dāroghas*, *qānūngos* and *gumāshtas*, or are left unidentified.[104]

It is to be noted that in this list, the entire province had been divided into 13 *chaklās*, namely Karimabad (named after Prince Muḥammad Karīm, son of Prince Muḥammad 'Aẓīm-ush-Shān, and later renamed Murshidabad), Burdwan, Satgam, Baleshwar, Jahangirnagar, Sylhet, Akbarnagar, Jessore, Garhi Bari, Bhusna, Hijli, Ghoraghat, and Islamabad Chatgam, besides one *sarkār*—that of Kuch Bihar. This is significant because the general understanding in the literature, based largely on James Grant's analysis and the East India Company's *Fifth Report*, is that Murshid Qulī Khān regrouped the *maḥāls* into 13 *chaklās*

[103] Salīm, *Riyāẓ-us-Salāṭīn* (text), p. 252.
[104] Oriental and India Office Collections, London, Persian Mss. IO 4498.

only in 1722.[105] Indeed, many of the generalizations about the *zamīndārs'* position and the revenue administration of early eighteenth-century Bengal draw on these two early British accounts and are not supported by evidence in the early eighteenth-century records themselves. This is a question to be explored further, and which need not detain us here.

The *'uhdadārs*, whom we have mentioned in brief above, were evidently meant to act as a check on, as well as a support to, the routine revenue collectors (*amīns* and *muḥāṣṣils*). It must however be noted that only 486 *maḥāls* from these *chaklās* could be brought under this arrangement at this stage, covering about one-half (over 45 lakh rupees) of the total income from *khāliṣa* (which is stated to be one crore rupees in the chronicles). Again, it is worth noting that the *'uhdadārīs* were not uniformly distributed; 11 covered over one lakh rupees, another nine some fifty thousand rupees, and a smaller set of 13 some twenty thousand rupees. As for the rest, they were all small units, with one of them accounting for a mere Rs 67. But all the *'uhdadārs*, irrespective of size, were directly and independently accountable to the *ḥuẓūr* (headquarters of the *dīwān*).

The extension of the power of the *dīwān*, as it implied curbs on the local magnates, also tended to cause him to overshadow the *ṣūbadār* (governor), Prince Muḥammad 'Aẕīm-ush-Shān. The Prince thus not only resented Murshid Qulī's reforms, but even indulged in a series of intrigues and conflicts, allegedly going so far as to plan the assassination of the *dīwān*.[106] All this must have also restricted the full execution of Murshid Qulī's schemes. This also explains in part why not all *maḥāls* were covered under *'uhda* or any other such arrangement. In Bahādur Shāh's time, when 'Aẕīm-ush-Shān acquired a very high position at the Mughal court, Murshid Qulī was forced therefore to leave Bengal for some time. His successor as *dīwān*, Mīr Ẕia'ullāh, could not cope with the local situation, and was killed in Bengal in 1710; Prince 'Aẕīm, who had retained the governorship but chosen to stay at the court now had to recall and reappoint the experienced Murshid Qulī, who hence became both *dīwān* and *nā'ib ṣūbadār* (deputy governor) of the province. With additional powers in his hands, Murshid Qulī then extended his earlier work further, trying to bring the countryside

[105] Walter K. Firminger, ed., *Affairs of the East India Company, Being the Fifth Report from the Select Committee of the House of Commons*, vol. II, reprint, Delhi, 1984, pp. 188–90.

[106] Abdul Karim, *Murshid Quli and His Times*, Dhaka, 1963, pp. 19–23.

more and more under the control of the provincial headquarters. The measurement of land, direct contact with the peasants, extension of cultivation, and the preparation of elaborate accounts of each and every *maḥāl* seem to be prime endeavours in this phase. According to Salīm:

The revenue collectors on his orders sent *shiqdārs* and *amīns* to every village of each *pargana.* They measured the cultivated and waste land, approached each and every peasant individually, gave *taqāwī* loans to the indigent peasants, and [thus] undertook great efforts for the extension of cultivation. In every *maḥāl,* they obtained increases and enhancements [of revenue] preparing the *hast-o-būd* papers in accordance with the actual conditions and realising the *khām* income [tax levied on the actual cultivators] from harvest to harvest. As increases in the *māl* and *sāir* [followed] the increase in the yield of cultivation and economy of expenditure, the money receipts of the treasury doubled.[107]

Could we presume that by insisting on measuring the land, assessing the revenue on the *ri'āya,* and making the *zamīndārs* responsible for no more than its collection, in exchange for an allowance (*nānkār*), Murshid Qulī tried to extend to Bengal the *ẓabṭ* system of northern India? Our information does not permit us at present to arrive at any firm conclusion, but for the East India Company's *zamīndārī,* C.R. Wilson provides us some interesting and relevant data. In all the three divisions, Calcutta, Gobindpur and Sutanuti, the areas under jungle and wasteland were very large, leaving substantial scope for the extension of cultivation. The chief crop was paddy, almost equally distributed in the three units. But there was also some cultivation of tobacco and cotton, the two major cash crops. For Sutanuti and Gobindpur, we also have some details on the area under irrigation of different types. In Gobindpur, 10 *bīghās* and 3 *kāthās* were under wells, and 9 *kāthās* under tanks while in Sutanuti, 72 *bīghās* and 6 *kāthās* were under tanks and wells. Wilson also gives us some information about the caste groups in the region, particularly of the Brahmans as they claimed concessions and exemptions, and also of the other peasants in occupation of lands. Brahmans controlled 57 *bīghās* and 16 *kāthās* in Gobindpur, 109 *bīghās* and 16 *kāthās* in Calcutta, and 111 *bīghās* and 3 *kāthās* in Sutanuti.[108]

We also have some *madad-i ma'āsh* documents that throw some light on the period, and which show how closely Murshid Qulī Khān

[107]Salīm, *Riyāẓ-us-Salāṭīn* (text), p. 252.

[108]Wilson, *Early Annals,* vol. I, pp. 284–6; H.H. Wilson, *A Glossary of Judicial and Revenue Terms,* reprint, Delhi, 1968, pp. 85, 269.

insisted on ascertaining the area (*ārāẓī*) under cultivation. Some time in the reign of Farrukh Siyar (1712–19), Mihr Banu and 'Abd-ur-Razzāq *Durvesh* were granted 70 and 90 *bīghās* respectively from the cultivable wasteland of *parganas* Balinda and Anwarpur Raipur, in *sarkār* Satgam by an order from the central *wazīr*'s office in Delhi. But the grantees could not get possession of the lands, apparently because Murshid Qulī Khān did not permit the initiation of the procedural formalities for the takeover, which included measurement of lands and *chakbandī*, in order to settle scores with the *wazīr* Saiyid 'Abdullāh (with whom he had differences). The *parwāna* from the local office was issued only in 1721, when—following the death of Saiyid 'Abdullāh—Murshid Qulī received a fresh order (*ḥasb-ul-ḥukm*) from the new *wazīr*, Niẓām-ulmulk.[109] Throughout the *nawwābī* regime, *madad-i ma'āsh* grants continued to be specified in terms of their areas (*raqba-ārāẓī*), even if initially the grants were expressed in cash terms. Early in the reign of Muḥammad Shāh (1719–48), in 1727, 50,000 *dāms* from *pargana* Lashkarpur were granted, again by the office of the *wazīr* in Delhi, to one Maulavī Haibatullāh. But since villages were not specified in the original order, the local *dīwān* Sarfarāz Khān delayed its execution. Two years later, following repeated *parwānas* from the centre, the *nāẓim* Muḥammad Shujā'-ud-Dīn Khān directed the *dīwān* to specify the villages and measure the lands.[110] From another similar *madad-i ma'āsh* document of 1748, we can show the extent of the *nāẓim*'s control over and his interference in the 'internal' matters of even the big *zamīndārīs*. One Maulavi Muḥammad Naqī, in charge of a *madrasa*, had obtained from Ram Kant, *zamīndār* of Rajshahi, and Raghu Dev, *zamīndār* of Mahmudshahi respectively, 180 and 70 *bīghās* of land in *parganas* Qasimnagar and Mahabatpur, *sarkār* Bazuha. The *chaudharīs*, *qānūngos*, peasants (*ri'āyā*) and even the ordinary cultivators (*muzāri'ān*) refused to recognize the *zamīndārs*' act as valid until it was ratified by a *sanad* from Murshidabad under the seal of the *nāẓim*, 'Alīvardī Khān.[111] Such was the image of the *niẓāmat* even after it had received severe jolts from the Marathas in the 1740s.[112]

Thus, the semi-autonomous state created first by Murshid Qulī Khān, and then Shujā'-ud-Dīn and 'Alīvardī Khān, in the first half of

[109] West Bengal State Archives (Calcutta), Persian Sanad Registers (henceforth WBSA, PSR), vol. 10, ff. 1703a, 1708b.

[110] WBSA, PSR, vol. 13, f. 2147b.

[111] WBSA, PSR, vol. 1, f. 145a.

[112] K.K. Datta, *Alivardi and His Times*, Calcutta, 1939.

the eighteenth century, was thus not based simply on compromises, and a strengthening of the alliance with the local *zamīndārs*. Rather, arrangements such as *'uhda*, as well as later *pāyanām* and *ihtimāmbandī* were intended to create a sort of regional centralization, and to infringe on *zamīndārī* power. Thus, while the province was distancing itself from Delhi by breaking the tradition on *jāgīr* assignments et cetera, simultaneously some 'centralization' at a regional level was taking place. But this also meant that there was a struggle with Delhi, which tried to limit the Nawwāb's power in various ways.

No consideration of this process would be complete without mentioning the role therein of trade, both external and internal. Shipping statistics for the ports of Hughli and Calcutta show that Bengal's external trade was on the increase at the very period that Murshid Qulī and his successors were seeking to make the changes we have noted above.[113] But the importance of internal trade in foodgrains and other items should not be neglected either. Most of the *chaklā* headquarters were major centres of internal or external trade, suggesting that fiscal reorganization was linked with this question quite closely. In fact, the use in the struggle between Delhi and Murshid Qulī Khān of the 1717 *farmān* given by Farrukh Siyar to the English Company, permitting them freedom of internal trade using passes (*dastaks*), reinforces this notion.

This idea may appear similar to that put forward some years ago by Karen Leonard, in an essay that is included in this volume.[114] But whereas Leonard had stressed the role of great banking firms, we would prefer to suggest that many of the nobles themselves had an interest in trade. In the late seventeenth century, major nobles who had held the provincial governorship of Bengal, such as Shāyista Khān, also were interested in trade, not only in export goods but also possibly bulk agricultural products.[115] It is hardly necessary to emphasize the significance of

[113] Om Prakash, *The Dutch East India Company and the Economy of Bengal, 1630–1720*, Princeton, 1985; P.J. Marshall, *East Indian Fortunes: The British in Bengal in the Eighteenth Century*, Oxford, 1976, pp. 55–7.

[114] Karen Leonard, 'The "Great Firm" Theory of the Decline of the Mughal Empire', reprinted in this volume.

[115] Shāhnawāz Khān and 'Abd ul Ḥayy, *Ma'āṣir-ul-Umarā'*, ed., Maulavi Abd-ur-Rahim and Ashraf 'Ali, Calcutta, 1891, 3 vols.; English translation by H. Beveridge and Baini Prashad, Calcutta, 1952; text, vol. II, pp. 705–6; translation, pp. 835–6.

the well-known policy of *saudā-i khāṣṣ* followed by others, like Prince 'Aẓīm-ush-Shān. But it is certainly worth noting that a number of important local officials were themselves also traders before entering the official apparatus. Nūrullāh Khān, the *faujdār* of Jessore, Hughli, Burdwan and Mednipore, who died fighting against the rebel *zamīndār* Sobha Singh, is mentioned by both Salīm and Munshī Salīmullāh as a rich man and a merchant by profession (*mutamawwil-o-tijārat peshā*).[116] Early in the eighteenth century, Mirzā Luṭfullāh of Tabriz, who had settled in Bengal in connection with trade (*bar sabīl-i tijārat*), rose to be the governor of Orissa in the time of Nawāb Shujā'-ud-Dīn (1726–39), with the coveted title of Murshid Qulī Khān. The Nawāb even gave him a daughter in marriage. Later, in 'Alīvardī Khān's time (1739–56), he became the *nā'ib* (deputy governor) of Jahangirnagar Dhaka.[117] Mirzā Luṭfullāh and his associates Mīr Ḥabībullāh of Shiraz and Mīr Raẓī of Shustar (both of whom also held important provincial offices), are described by the eighteenth-century chronicles as *tājirzādas*, who maintained close contacts with Basra and Surat. Other Iranian and Central Asian traders in Bengal (*tujjār-i Mughaliya*) enjoyed their patronage and support.[118] At the same time, many of the major *zamīndārs* of Bengal in this period too seem to have had an interest in trade, and it would bear investigation as to whether their seats of power were also the major marketing centres of the region. There is thus an evident contrast between the situation here and in areas like Punjab, where Mughal nobles made alliances with local mercantile groups like the Khatris, who became more important as their subordinate allies in this period. In the case of Bengal, local mercantile groups seem to have been less important, and we have no obvious counterpart to the Multanis, while the ubiquitous Khatris have a rather different role to play here compared to northern India; as for the rising power of the Armenians in late seventeenth- and eighteenth-century Bengal, it too

[116]Salīm, *Riyāẓ-us-Salāṭīn* (text), p. 225; Salīmullāh, *Tārīkh-i-Bangāla*, p. 6.

[117]Mīr Ghulām 'Alī Āzād Bilgramī, *Ma'āṣir-ul-Kirām*, Hyderabad, 1913, 2 vols., vol. II, p. 222.

[118]Bilgramī, *Ma'āsir-ul-Kirām*, vol. II, p. 224; Salīm, *Riyāẓ-us-Salāṭīn* (text), pp. 299, 344; Ghulam Husain Ṭabaṭabai, *Siyār-ul-Muta'akhkhirīn*, vol. II, Lucknow (n.d.), p. 498.

offers an instructive case in contrast.[119] But nevertheless, the interest of Shāyista Khān, Buzurg Ummed Khān, 'Aẓīm-ush-Shān and other high Mughal officials in trade is evident from the 1660s onwards. In the disputes between European and Asian traders in the centres of Bengal, it appears that the *ṣūbadārs,* and later the Nawwābs often intervened in favour of the latter. The shift in overland trade routes through the Gangetic valley to Central Asia in the late seventeenth and early eighteenth century may have further increased their interest in maritime trade.

The case of Bengal seems to confirm the need to study the region in order to understand the nature of the early eighteenth century transition. Relations between the Nawwāb and the *zamīndārī* structure here do not seem to have followed the same pattern as in some other regions. Also, the importance of trade in the Bengal case is clearly greater than in some of the other regions. The Nawwābs of Bengal were attempting to redefine their relationship with both the agrarian economy and society, and commerce in the first half of the eighteenth century. But the logic of change could not proceed to its conclusion after the 1750s, once Bengal became a part of the larger political structure put into place in the subcontinent by the English East India Company.

THE ISSUE OF MUGHAL 'DECLINE'

If the Mughal historiography in general has been marked by a curious lack of debate, and a rather artificial 'consensus' resultant from this fact, one issue that has given off both heat and light is the vexed question of Mughal 'decline' and the transition to colonial rule. Now, it should be emphasized in this context that, despite the 'consensus' noted above, at least two distinct approaches have held sway in the study of the dynamics of the Mughal state during the present century. *One* is seemingly the older-fashioned, and focuses on the personalities of rulers, their achievements, their originality or lack thereof.[120] Historical agency is seen in this approach to reside principally with the élite, who

[119] Alam, *Crisis of Empire*, pp. 169–75. The Khatris in Bengal did found some major *zamīndārīs*, notably that of Burdwan (for which see McLane, *Land and Local Kingship)*. However, the point is that the nature of their social insertion was somewhat different from that which they had in Punjab. It may be noted in passing that, by the eighteenth century, there were a sufficient number of Khatris in eastern India for a branch to be termed the 'Purbiya Khatris'.

[120] Sarkar, *History of Aurangzib*; Qureshi, 'India under the Mughals'.

shape the empire when talented, and who cause its decline when dissolute or incompetent. It is a view that evidently shares a great deal with the perspective of Mughal chroniclers' themselves, to whom individuals from the élite naturally seemed somewhat larger than life, or at least larger than their contemporaries. Such an approach is represented in this volume by a chapter from Sir Jadunath Sarkar's *magnum opus* on Aurangzeb, a work that is at once Whiggish in its judgements and personality-centred in its approach even to the largest historical questions.

The *second* approach, in the Mughal case to a large extent shaped by the influence of a sort of Marxist-flavoured history, is one that has ostensibly dominated the debate in South Asia since at least the 1950s.[121] Here, on the face of it, institutions rather than individuals are the primary focus of attention, social groups are identified with particular material interests, and the logic of rise, peak, and decline is associated with tensions stemming from systemic rather than psychological contradictions. In the past three decades, the writings that lie within this framework have further subdivided: the one sub-stream stresses the tensions between an imperially appointed, and numerically calibrated élite—the *manṣabdārs*—and the amorphous mass of the peasantry; the other, associated with the work of Nurul Hasan and those who followed him, lays (as we have noted above) far more emphasis on the tensions between state and rural-based 'gentry' (or *zamīndārs*), as determinants of the dynamics of the Mughal state, especially in its phase of decline—which is to say after about 1700.[122]

Cross-fertilization between even the two polar approaches noted above has not been unknown in the past few decades, especially from the pens of Western historians (above all, those trained in American universities in the 1960s or early 1970s). The most favoured synthesis, at times given a Weberian flavour by its proponents, is that it was the nature of institutions (or processes of state formation) that gave such enormous and arbitrary power to a few individuals, who became the fulcra of the system. To put the matter slightly differently, it is argued in this synthesizing approach that the balance of institutional forces tugging in different directions left a large vacuum, which was filled by a few individuals with the emperor being the central shaft of the

[121] Habib, *Agrarian System;* M. Athar Ali, *The Mughal Nobility under Aurangzeb*, 1966; new revised edition, Delhi, 1997.

[122] S. Nurul Hasan, 'Zamindars under the Mughals', reprinted in this volume; Khan, *Chieftains in the Mughal Empire*.

umbrella of empire, in one picturesque formulation.[123] Thus, it was the peculiar nature of the Mughal *system* itself to be arbitrary and delicately balanced on the whims or predilections of a few. Such an approach, we may note in passing, also has adherents in the recent historiography of South-east Asia, where we encounter the further ingenious construction that if the 'idea of power' in the political culture was based upon such a notion of arbitrariness, then power itself would as a consequence become arbitrary.[124] The approach is, besides, not merely ingenious but convenient; if stated as a preamble, it permits the return to the central theses of the older personality-oriented generation.

In relation to these two well-established and familiar approaches, it would be presumptuous to suggest that this introduction has done more than raise some questions, and seek to provoke readers to rethink the bases of the usual generalizations on the Mughal state. It is conceivable, moreover, that such a rethinking might help in taking fresh stock of the histories of the Ottoman and Ṣafavid states in the same period, as stated at the outset. Our reading of the literature leads us to believe that some conclusions of a comparative nature concerning the three states, focusing on issues of chronology and regional diversity, are certainly feasible.

Our focus here has been on how the Mughal state came to be fashioned and refashioned in the period from 1530 to 1750. The argument has largely stressed two hitherto neglected points: first, that the Mughal state evolved throughout this period, and had not been 'perfected' by 1600 as is often assumed, and second, that the incorporation of new regions into the Mughal domain necessitated adjustments to local conditions, so that the state eventually resembled a 'patchwork quilt' rather than a 'wall-to-wall carpet'. After about 1700, however, we witness a second phase of transformation. In sum, it may be asserted that the shift from the political configuration of the seventeenth century to that of the eighteenth century in India is marked above

[123]Stephen P. Blake, 'The Patrimonial-Bureaucratic Empire of the Mughals', *The Journal of Asian Studies*, vol. XXIX (1) 1979, pp. 77–94; M.N. Pearson, Political Participation in Mughal India', *The Indian Economic and Social History Review*, vol. IX (2), 1972, pp. 113–31, as also M.N. Pearson, 'Shivaji and the Decline of the Mughal Empire', *The Journal of Asian Studies*, vol. XXXV (2), 1976, pp. 221–35.

[124]Benedict Anderson, 'The Idea of Power in Javanese Culture', in Claire Holt, Benedict Anderson and James T. Siegel, eds., *Culture and Politics in Indonesia*, Ithaca (NY), 1972, pp. 1–69.

all by the rise of regional states and kingdoms in place of the Mughal state. Such a transition is of obvious interest for any study of the Islamic world in the epoch, since the only other state comparable to the Mughal one in dimensions—the Ottoman empire—also seems to undergo a similar shift in roughly the same period.

Why did these transformations occur? Personality-oriented historians of an earlier generation have spoken in terms of a degeneration in the character of the Mughal rulers and the principal nobles as reason enough for the transformation, which they were certain was to be seen as 'decline'. The relatively misogynist amongst them have seen the influence of the harem, in the 'feminine' weakness shown by the later Mughals. A somewhat more sophisticated argument, to be associated with Jadunath Sarkar and his disciples, posed the main reason for the political fragmentation of the period as the religious policy of Mughal rulers such as Aurangzeb, whose orthodox Sunnism was presented as the main reason for the alienation of Hindu regional élites; Aurangzeb, writes Sarkar, 'was the worst ruler imaginable of an empire composed of many creeds and races, of diverse interests and ways of life and thought'.[125] In turn, Marxist-oriented historians (here represented by a thoughtful essay by Satish Chandra on the '*jāgīrdārī* crisis') sought their own explanations in materialist terms, linking the transformations of the period with *jāgīrdārī*, and the so-called 'agrarian crisis', that is a crisis in the distribution of revenue assignments (*jāgīrs*) to claimants, and problems in the collection of revenue as well as production itself, on account of the effects of inflation, rapid expansion in the number of claimants, excessive Mughal coercion, etc.[126] Irfan Habib, in particular, followed—as we have brought out—the lead of the influential work of W.H. Moreland in exaggerating the despotic and exploitative character of Mughal rule as the main reason for Mughal decline.[127] Habib's close associate, Athar Ali has linked the decline to an

[125]Jadunath Sarkar, *Anecdotes of Aurangzeb*, reprint, Calcutta, 1988, p. 20.

[126]Habib, *Agrarian System;* Satish Chandra, *Medieval India: Society, the Jagirdari Crisis and the Village*, Delhi, 1982 (see especially sections reproduced in this volume); J.F. Richards, 'The Imperial Crisis in the Deccan', *The Journal of Asian Studies*, vol. XXXV (2), 1976, pp. 237–56.

[127]W.H. Moreland, *From Akbar to Aurangzeb: A Study in Indian Economic History*, London, 1923; Irfan Habib, 'Potentialities of Capitalistic Development in the Economy of Mughal India', *The Journal of Economic History*, vol. XXIX (1), 1969, pp. 32–78; also Habib, *Agrarian System*, Conclusion; finally Noman Ahmad Siddiqi, *Land Revenue Administration under the Mughals, 1700–1750*, Bombay, 1970, pp. 1–3, 92–101.

imbalance between claimants to positions in the *manṣabdārī* hierarchy and available resources in terms of *pāibāqī*, or land to be assigned.[128] Later studies have however begun to diverge from this formulation. Some have spoken of a tripartite relationship between *jāgīrdārs*, *zamīndārs* and peasants as determining the nature of the 'crisis'.[129] In a recent work on Awadh and the Punjab by one of the authors of this introduction, a fourth dimension was brought in, in the form of the *madad-i ma'āsh* holders, who seem to have played an important role in determining the nature of the struggle for control of resources in this period.[130]

Rather than insist too greatly on the existence of a single logic that informs 'Mughal decline', it might be worthwhile to focus here, even if only briefly, on the vast variety of regional experiences. The 'successor' states that arose in the erstwhile Mughal domains during the years from roughly 1720 to 1850 varied greatly after all in terms of resources, longevity and principal character. Some of them—like Awadh in the north or Hyderabad in the south—were located in areas that had harboured regional states in the immediate pre-Mughal period, and thus could hark back to an older local or regional tradition of state formation. But others were states that had a more original character and derived from very specific processes that had taken place in the course of the late sixteenth and seventeenth centuries. In particular, many of the post-Mughal states were based on ethnic or sectarian groupings—the Marathas, the Jats and the Sikhs for instance—which had no real precedent in medieval Indian history. Rather than focus on personality or class alone, it is clear that notions of 'community' too are important for our analysis; further, moving away from the purely materialist logic of many of the formulations surveyed above would help us focus on cultural dimensions of the Mughal state, as a way of explaining both its longevity and its demise. In this context, one question that surely merits more detailed exploration is the linguistic one: the support lent by the Mughals to Persian as a sort of 'imperial language', and the resulting tensions between Persian and the vernaculars in the course of the career of the Mughal state.[131] Resistance

[128] Athar Ali, *Mughal Nobility*.

[129] Chandra, *Medieval India*.

[130] Alam, *Crisis of Empire*, pp. 110–22, *passim*.

[131] For a more detailed exposition of this point, see Muzaffar Alam, 'The Pursuit of Persian: Language in Mughal Politics', *Modern Asian Studies*, vol. XXXII, no. 2, 1998, pp. 317–49.

to Mughal claims may thus often be found not in the Persian-language materials (be they chronicles, correspondence, or revenue documents) that have hitherto formed the staple of Mughal historians, but in other texts, whether written or oral. Indeed, as Gautam Bhadra, in the context of eastern India, and J.F. Richards and Velcheru Narayana Rao in the context of the Deccan, have shown, a more nuanced and decentred history of the Mughals would ideally combine the Persian and vernacular, the written and the oral. We have deliberately included these essays towards the end of the present volume, to point to innovative trends in the historiography of the past two decades, that should in our opinion be further developed and consolidated. In particular, Narayana Rao and Richards made a significant contribution to a more nuanced use of unconventional semi-literary materials for history writing, by using the powerful myth of the 'anti-hero' from the Gamalla caste, Sarvayi Papadu, who appears portrayed in the darkest hues in early eighteenth-century Mughal chronicles. From their reading of these materials, we see the deep interpenetration of the logic of 'imperial' and 'communitarian' perspectives on the past and history, which serves as a check on romantic views of pristine, communitarian consciousness, existing wholly independently of the intrusive potential of state structures. More careful and sophisticated research on Mughal questions may thus not only contribute to, but significantly modify, regnant assumptions on, the nature of 'subaltern' history in South Asia.[132]

The context of what might be called 'resistance' to the Mughals was undeniably rather complex. We may take the relatively well-known case of Mughal–Maratha relations. Theoretically, by the early eighteenth century, the Mughals claimed rights over a far larger area than had ever been the case under Akbar, Jahāngīr or Shāhjahān. This area included large parts of southern India, over which central rule was never actually consolidated. Taking advantage of their somewhat ambiguous relations with the Mughals, and claiming to be the agents of Delhi, various Maratha clan-chiefs (*sardārs*) often made partial claims on the revenues of these areas, as *chauth* and *sardeshmukhī*. This was the case, for example, in Mysore in the 1720s and 1730s; Mysore had notionally come under the sovereign umbrella of the Mughals in the

[132]For an interesting perspective from 'below', based on a seventeenth-century Persian text, see the discussion of the *Tazkira-i Pīr Ḥassū Tailī* by Surat Singh, summarized briefly in M. Athar Ali, 'Sidelights into Ideological and Religious Attitudes in the Punjab during the 17th century', in *Medieval India: A Miscellany*, vol. II, Bombay, 1972, pp. 187–94.

late 1690s, as the result of an embassy sent to Aurangzeb by Chikka-devarāya Wodeyār, then ruler of Mysore. In effect, this meant that Mysore was to pay a periodic tribute (or *peshkash*) to Mughal representatives in the south, but there was a problem in doing so. Since Mughal authority in the Deccan and south was itself divided, several possible channels of tribute existed. Mysore thus sought to make use of this ambiguity, playing off the celebrated Nizām-ul-mulk, who himself in these years founded a dynasty at Hyderabad, against the Mughal representative at Arcot, thereby putting off the tribute payment. A further factor in the fiscal politics of Mysore were the Marathas, and some clans among them made it a regular practice to raid the Mysore capital of Srirangapatnam.[133] In this way, overlapping and at times conflicting claims were all justified with reference to a Mughal centre that was distant, and lacked a sustained interest for the most part in these affairs.

As such then, few if any of the so-called 'successor states' to the Mughals that emerged in the early eighteenth century made a direct attack on Mughal legitimacy, or sought to challenge Mughal claims head on. To the extent that such a frontal challenge (as distinct from a rebellion conducted within a shared understanding of the framework of authority) can be located in the period, it comes from the far north-west of the Mughal domain. Eventually, however, this challenge was to have repercussions that were felt by the Marathas and other groups. In this context, we may note that the north-west frontier between the Mughals and Ṣafavids had always harboured elements which possessed the potential to destabilize the balance between these states. The area, which falls largely in present-day Afghanistan, also had a tradition of religio-political movements, often intended to provide a direct challenge to the Mughals or Ṣafavids. An important instance is of the Raushaniyya movement of Bāyazīd Anṣārī and his successors, which was crushed by the Mughals in the late sixteenth and early seventeenth centuries.[134] Again, in the reign of Aurangzeb, a frontal attack on the legitimacy of his rule was made by the Pashtun leader, Khushḥal Khān Khatak, though in this instance from the standpoint of orthodox Islam. Significantly, in Khushḥāl Khān's poetic and other literary works, there was also an

[133]Sanjay Subrahmanyam, 'Warfare and State Finance in Wodeyar Mysore, 1724–25: A Missionary Perspective', *The Indian Economic and Social History Review*, vol. XXVI (2), 1989, pp. 203–33.

[134]For a discussion, see Joseph T. Arlinghaus, 'The Transformation of Afghan Tribal Society: Tribal Expansion, Mughal Imperialism, and the Roshaniyya Insurrection, 1450–1600', Ph.D. thesis, Duke University, 1988.

explicit and nostalgic yearning for the time of Shēr Shāh Sūr, the Afghan who had expelled the Mughal ruler Humāyūn from Hindustan.[135] The spirit of these writings was translated into action in the early eighteenth century, when Mīr Wais Khān Hotak, a leader of the Hotak clan of Ghilza'is, succeeded in carving out a Pashtūn state based at Qandahar, under the nose of the Ṣafavid governor of the area. Between 1709 and 1715, Mīr Wais ruled Qandahar unofficially, but his successors were not so modest. His son, Mīr Maḥmūd, first attacked Kirman in Iran, and then—in 1722—took Isfahan itself and proclaimed himself its ruler. However, the Ghilza'i success was not to last long, as they were challenged both by their fellow Pashtūns—the Abdālīs— and by the plans of Nādir Qulī Afshār, a Ṣafavid subordinate who harboured substantial ambitions of his own.[136]

Between Mīr Maḥmūd's death in 1725, and 1731, Nādir Shāh rapidly consolidated his hold over eastern Iran, and placed a severe check on the rise of Pashtūn power. Subsequently, he marched into Afghanistan and later the Mughal territories, sacking Delhi in 1739. His success in welding together a disparate set of territories, while operating outside the system of Mughal sovereignty, provided a model for the Pashtūns, after his death in 1747. Many from the Abdālīs and Ghilza'is had been employed by Nādir Shāh, and they had had an opportunity to learn at close quarters. Among those who had been subordinate in this way to the Afshār conqueror was Aḥmad Khān, a member of the relatively small Sadozai lineage of Abdālīs. It fell to Aḥmad Khān to assume leadership of the Pashtūns in 1747, in the wake of Nādir Shāh's assassination, after his election by a congregation of Pashtūn Khāns at a shrine near Qandahar. His trajectory took him into conflict with the Mughals, then the Marathas, and finally acted as a crucial catalyst in the formation of the Sikh state in north India. Nādir Shāh's ephemeral, but significant, success, which contemporaries saw in terms of the effeminate weakness of the court of Muḥammad Shāh, can equally be understood institutionally, as reflecting a redistribution of resources between a resource-hungry, and militarily well-supplied 'marginal area', and an imperial centre that was all too susceptible to such 'tribal breakouts'.

[135] Ashraf Ghani, *Production and Domination: Afghanistan, 1747–1901*, New York, forthcoming. We are grateful to the author for allowing us access to the manuscript.

[136] For an overview of these processes, see Jos J.L. Gommans, *The Rise of the Indo-Afghan Empire, c. 1710–1780*, Leiden, 1995.

The causes for the weakening of the Mug͟hal centre are thus best sought in a series of local and regional dynamics, such as those relating Delhi to Punjab, Awadh and the Deccan, which permitted Nādir Shāh to launch his famous raid on Delhi and north India in 1739–40, an expedition that proved highly damaging to Mug͟hal prestige. Again, there is no doubt that the single most important power that emerged in the long twilight of the Mug͟hal dynasty was again one that should primarily be understood in the context of a region, namely the Marathas. Initially deriving from the western Deccan, the Marathas were of course a very loose, open-status, peasant-warrior grouping (akin to others analysed by Kolff in another, earlier, context), that rose to prominence during the rule, in that region, of the Sulṭāns of Bijapur and Ahmad-nagar. The most important Maratha clan, the Bhonsles, while very probably of pastoralist origin, had held extensive prebendal rights under the 'Ādil Shāhī rulers, and these were consolidated in the course of the 1630s and 1640s, as Bijapur expanded to the south and south-west. Shāhji Bhonsle, the first prominent member of the clan, drew substantial revenues from the Karnatak region, in territories that had once been controlled by the rulers of Mysore and other chiefs who derived from the collapsing Vijayanagara kingdom. One of his children, Shivaji, emerged as the most powerful figure in the clan to the west, while his half-brother Vyamkoji was able in the 1670s to gain control over the Kaveri delta, and the kingdom of Tanjavur.[137]

The successes of Shivaji were not given to his son and successor Sambhaji, who as is well known was captured and executed by the Mug͟hals in the late 1680s. His younger brother, Rājarām, who succeeded him, faced with a Mug͟hal army that was now on the ascendant, moved his base into the Tamil country, where Shivaji too had earlier kept an interest. He remained in the powerful fortress of Senji (earlier the seat of a Nāyaka dynasty subordinate to Vijayanagara) for eight years in the 1690s, under siege by a Mug͟hal force, and for a time it may have appeared that Maratha power was on the decline. But a recovery was effected in the early eighteenth century, in somewhat changed circumstances. A particularly important phase in this respect is the reign of Shāhū, who succeeded with some acrimony in 1708. Lasting some four decades, to 1749, Shāhū's reign is marked by the ascendancy of a lineage of Chitpāvan Brahmin ministers, who virtually

[137]For a summing up of conventional wisdom, see Stewart Gordon, *The Marathas, 1600–1818* (The New Cambridge History of India vol. 11.4), Cambridge, 1993, pp. 59–90.

came to control central authority in the Maratha state, with the Bhonsles reduced to figureheads. Holding the title of Peshwa, the first truly prominent figure of this line is Bālāji Vishwanāth, who had aided Shāhū in his rise to power. Vishwanāth and his successor Bāji Rāo I (Peshwa between 1720 and 1740) managed to bureaucratize the Maratha state to a far greater extent than had been the case under the early Bhonsles. On the one hand they systematized the practice of tribute-gathering from Mughal territories, under the heads of *sardeshmukhī* and *chauth*. But equally, they seem to have consolidated methods of assessment and collection of land revenue and other taxes which were in fact derived from the Mughals.[138] Much of the revenue terminology used in the documents of the Peshwa and his subordinates derives from Persian, and this suggests a far greater continuity between Mughal and Maratha revenue practice than might have been imagined.

By the close of Shāhū's reign, a complex role had been established for the Marathas. On the one hand, in the territories that they controlled closely, particularly in the Deccan, these years saw the development of sophisticated networks of trade, banking and finance, the rise of substantial banker-houses based at Pune and with branches extending into Gujarat, the Ganges valley and the south, and an expansion of the agricultural frontier. At the same time, maritime affairs were not totally neglected either, and Bālāji Vishwanāth took some care to cultivate the Angria clan, which controlled a fleet of vessels based in Kolaba and other centres of the west coast. These ships posed a threat not only to the new English settlement of Bombay, but to the Portuguese at Goa, Bassein and Daman. On the other hand, there also emerged a far larger domain of activity away from the original heartland of the Marathas, which was either subjected to raiding or given over to subordinate chiefs. Of these chiefs, the most important were the Gaikwāḍs, the Sindhias and the Holkars. Also there were branches of the Bhonsle family itself, which established themselves at Kolhapur and Nagpur, while the main line remained in the Deccan heartland, at Satara. All of this should be understood not only through the logic of class conflict (peasants and 'gentry' versus 'prebendal aristocracy'), but in the context of region-based community identities. A complex mix of local patriotism, religious rhetoric, and invented genealogies, provided the

[138] Stewart Gordon, 'The Slow Conquest: The Administrative Integration of Malwa into the Maratha Empire, 1720–1760', *Modern Asian Studies*, vol. XI (1), 1977, pp. 1–40, reproduced in Gordon, *Marathas, Marauders and State Formation in Eighteenth-Century India*, Delhi, 1994, pp. 23–63.

raw material to define the markers around which these dynasties improvised an identity that both depended on, and sought to define a distance from, the Mughals.

Similar complexity and paradox confront the researcher who looks into still another of the variety of regional and 'communitarian' experiences of the period, namely the case of the Sikhs, a group whose identity crystallized only gradually and in an uncertain fashion from the sixteenth century. By the time of the death of the last Sikh Gurū, Gobind Singh, in 1708, the Sikhs had emerged, like the Marathas, as a regional threat to Mughal dominance. Oddly enough, this was partly the result of the assumption of leadership in the Punjab by one Banda Bahādur, a Maratha who had come under the Gurū's influence during the latter's last days at Nanded in Maharashtra. Between 1709 and late 1710, the Sikhs under Banda Bahādur enjoyed dramatic successes in the *sarkārs* of Sarhind, Hissar and Saharanpur, all of them ominously close to Delhi. Banda set up a capital at Mukhlispur, issued coins in the names of the Gurūs (a particular signal of *lèse-majesté*), and began to use a seal on his orders even as the Mughals did. In late 1710 and 1711, the Mughal forces counter-attacked, and Banda and his forces retreated. Expelled from Sarhind, he then moved his operations west, into the vicinity of Lahore. But here too he was unsuccessful, and eventually he and his forces were forced to retreat to the fort of Gurdas Nangal. There, they surrendered to Mughal forces after a prolonged siege, and Banda was executed in Delhi in 1716.[139]

This phase of activity is particularly important for two reasons. First, as distinct from the sporadic militancy shown under the Gurūs Hargobind and then Gobind Singh, it is now that a full-scale rebellion against Mughal authority by the Sikhs breaks out for the first time. Second, Banda Bahādur's role in the matter itself, which is somewhat enigmatic, lends the affair a curious flavour. Some of Banda's letters speak of orthodox Islam as an enemy to be rallied against, thus suggesting that the Sikhs at this time were moving somewhat away from their initial orientation as mediators between popular Hinduism and Islam. Further, this early Maratha–Sikh alliance prefigures later coalitions that were to emerge in the context of the Abdālī attacks on Punjab.

The quelling by Mughal forces of the Sikhs under Banda Bahādur did not mean an end to Sikh resistance to Mughal claims. In the 1720s and 1730s, Ramdaspur, or Amritsar, emerged as a centre of Sikh activity, partly because of its pre-eminence as a pilgrimage centre. Kapūr

[139]For an earlier discussion, see Alam, *Crisis of Empire*, pp. 134–55.

Singh, the most important of the Sikh leaders of the time, operated from its vicinity, and gradually set about consolidating a revenue-cum-military system, based in part on compromises with the Mughal governors of the province. Other Sikhs were however less willing than Kapūr Singh to deal with the Mughal authorities and took the paths of social banditry and raiding.[140] These activities acted as a damper on the attempts by the Mughal governors of Lahore *ṣūba* to set up an independent power-base for themselves in the region. First 'Abd-uṣ-Ṣamad Khān and then his son Zakariyā Khān attempted the twin tracks of conciliation and coercion, but all to little avail. After the latter's demise in 1745, the balance shifted still further in favour of the Sikh warrior-leaders, some of whom like Jassā Singh Ahluwālia, later the founder of the kingdom of Kapūrthala, emerge into prominence in the 1740s. The mushrooming of pockets under the authority of Sikh leaders was thus a feature of the two decades preceding Aḥmad Shāh Abdālī's invasion of the Punjab, and took place not merely in eastern Punjab but in the Bari *doāb*, not far from Lahore itself.

Now, the Sikh chiefdoms too continued many of the courtly, authoritative and administrative practices initiated by the Mughals. The main subordinates of the chiefs were given *jāgīr* assignments, and the Persianized culture of the Mughal bureaucracy continued to hold sway.[141] Unlike the Gurūs themselves, who, as is well known, were exclusively drawn from Khatri stock, the bulk of the Sikh chieftains tended to be of Jat origin, drawing disparaging remarks from at least some contemporary writers who spoke of them as *shūdras*. Particularly disparaging also was the French mercenary, Colonel Antoine Polier, who wrote of them in the 1770s:

'As for the Seeks, that formidable aristocratical republick, I may safely say it is only a defenseless state such as this. It is in fact a Hydra. Each Zemindar from the River Attock to the city of Hansy-Hissar and to the Gates of Delhy, who lets his beard grow, cries Wah Gurroo, eats pork, wears an iron bracelet, drinks bang, abominates the smoking of tobacco and can command ten horse-

[140]For a summing up of recent scholarship, see J.S. Grewal, *The Sikhs of the Punjab* (The New Cambridge History of India, Vol II.3), Cambridge, 1990. Also see Satish Chandra, *The Eighteenth Century in India: Its Economy and the Role of the Marathas, the Jats, the Sikhs and the Afghans*, Delhi, 1986.

[141]See Indu Banga, *Agrarian System of the Sikhs*, Delhi, 1978; and Banga, 'The Jagirdari System of Maharaja Ranjit Singh in the Light of His Orders', in Satish Chandra, ed., *Essays in Medieval Indian Economic History*, Delhi, 1987, pp. 110–116.

men, sets up immediately for a Sikh Chief, and as far as in his power aggrandizes himself at the expence of his weaker neighbours; if Hindoo or Musalman so much the better, if not, even amongst his own fraternity will he seek to extend his influence and power; only with this difference in their intestine divisions from what is seen every where else, that the husbandsman and labourer in their own districts are perfectly safe and unmolested, let what will happen around them.[142]

It was one such chief, Ranjīt Singh, grandson of Charhat Singh Sukarchakia, who eventually welded these principalities for a brief time into a larger entity, from 1799 to 1839. But this was realized in a context already dominated by the growing power of the English East India Company. Within ten years of his death, the British had annexed Punjab, and so this period can be seen as the last gasp of the old regime polities in India. His rise to power was based on superior military force, partly serviced by European mercenaries, and by the strategic location of the territories that he had inherited from his father, Mahān Singh. Ranjīt Singh's kingdom combined disparate elements. On the one hand, it represented the culmination of Sikh rebellions against Mughal rule, that had gone on for almost a century. On the other hand, it was based on the intelligent application of principles of statecraft learnt from the Mughals and Afghans.[143]

Such relatively ephemeral but dramatic successes at state-building as that of Ranjīt Singh are rare but not unique. One can find other instances in the context of the eighteenth century, where consolidation was rapidly followed by reversals. Such instances can be divided into two categories, those where the consolidation of a particular state proved a threat to British power and was hence undermined (the case of Mysore under Haidar and Tipu), and others where the logic of consolidation and decline appears to be autonomous of the British. In the latter category, we can place the case of Jaipur (earlier Amber) in eastern Rajasthan, a Rajput principality controlled by the Kacchwāha clan. From the sixteenth century, the Kacchwāhas had been subordinate to the Mughals, and had as a consequence gradually managed to consolidate their hold over the region around Amber in the course of the seventeenth century. The crucial role played in high Mughal politics by members of the clan like Rāja Mān Singh thus paid dividends, and the chiefs were permitted to maintain a large cavalry and infantry force.

[142]Antoine Louis Henri Polier, *Shah Alam II and His Court*, ed., Pratul C. Gupta, reprint, Calcutta, 1989, p. 100.

[143]The authoritative study is by J.S. Grewal, *The Reign of Maharaja Ranjit Singh: Structure of Power, Economy and Society*, Delhi, 1981.

In the early eighteenth century, the ruler Sawāi Jai Singh took steps to increase his power manifold. This was done by arranging to have his *jāgīr* assignment in the vicinity of his home territories, and taking on land in revenue farm, which was gradually made permanent. By the time of his death in 1743, Jai Singh (after whom Jaipur came to be named) had emerged as the single most important ruler in the eastern Rajasthan region.[144]

The eighteenth century thus appears not only as the century of the regional state, but that of the 'ethnic state'. Rohillas, Jats, Sikhs and Marathas, were among a series of groups who sought to create semi-independent dispensations under the carapace of Mughal sovereignty. There is a danger for the historian here, of seeing these identities in primordial terms, and in viewing Mughal decline as no more than the re-emergence of old, regionally rooted, ethnic identities. Nothing could be farther from the truth. Though the regional idiom was used consistently, and with success by these groups, and though they dug deep into the mythic resources of regions, the regional identities that were formed in the eighteenth century were themselves the product of a complex interaction between region and empire. Both came to be redefined in this process.

Some Concluding Remarks

At first glance, the above discussion suggests that the first half of the eighteenth century was a period of considerable political turmoil in India, one in which regional states were formed with some rapidity, and there was a great deal of fluidity in the system. Did this political turmoil have a clear counterpart in terms of generalized social and economic dislocation? This does not seem to have been unambiguously the case. It is of course true that raids by military forces would have caused dislocation, and the practice of destroying standing crops was followed by armies during most of the century. On the other hand, economic warfare and the attempts to destroy the productive base of a rival state were relatively uncommon in the first half of the eighteenth century. But after 1750, recourse was taken increasingly to the harshest

[144]See for example, S.P. Gupta, *Agrarian System of Eastern Rajasthan*, Delhi, 1987, and Dilbagh Singh, *The State, Landlords and Peasants: Rajasthan in the 18th Century*, Delhi, 1990, both of whom suggest that whatever the situation in the latter half of the eighteenth century, there was no 'crisis' in material terms prior to 1740 in eastern Rajasthan.

of measures. The destruction of irrigation tanks, the forcible expropriation of cattle wealth, and even the forced march of masses of people, were not unknown in the wars of the 1770s and thereafter. All these must have had a deleterious effect on economic stability and curtailed the impulse towards growth.

But such negative effects can also be exaggerated. When viewed from Delhi, the eighteenth century (and especially the period after 1740) is certainly a gloomy period. The attacks of Nādir Shāh, then of Aḥmad Shāh Abdālī, and finally Rohilla attempts to hold the Mughals to ransom, left the inhabitants of the city with a sense of being under permanent siege.[145] But this perspective can hardly have been shared by the inhabitants of other centres in India, be it Thiruvananthapuram, Pune, Patna or Jaipur. There is a process of economic reorientation that accompanies the political decentralization of the era, and it is on account of this that the experience of Delhi and Agra cannot be generalized. However, even the trajectory of the regions was mixed. In some, the first half of the eighteenth century witnesses continued expansion—the cases of Bengal, Jaipur, and Hyderabad, for example—while others are late bloomers, like Mysore or the Punjab. No single chronology of prosperity and decline is likely therefore to fit all the regions of India in the epoch.

It would also appear that the mid-eighteenth century marks a significant point of inflection in key processes. This is for a variety of reasons, some obvious and others less so. For example, the engrossing by the English Company of the revenues of Bengal *ṣūba* (or province) had the effect of eventually reversing the direction of flows of precious metals into the area. Whereas Bengal had earlier attracted considerable quantities of gold and silver in exchange for its exports, this pattern no longer held to the same extent. Similarly, on the external trade front, the latter half of the eighteenth century saw the growth, under the aegis of the Company, of semi-coerced forms of crop production, the case of opium being a prominent one. But another reason why the latter half of the eighteenth century differs from the period before about 1750 is in terms of the economic costs and consequences of war. In the post-1750 period, warfare became more disruptive of civil life and economic reproduction than before, and at the same time the new technologies in use made it a far more expensive proposition. The use of firearms

[145]Thus, see for example Zahir Uddin Malik, *The Reign of Muhammad Shah, 1719–48*, Bombay, 1977. Also, Ralph Russell and Khurshidul Islam, *Three Mughal poets: Mir, Sauda, Mir Hasan*, Cambridge (Mass.), 1968.

on a large scale, of mercenaries, the maintenance of standing armies, all of these are likely to have changed the character of war. But it does appear too strong to term the processes of the post-1750 period as a total inversion of what went before.

It would thus appear to us that the eighteenth century 'crisis', as it is so often termed in the literature, worked at different levels. High court politics was no doubt one of the important factors in the period of Farrukh Siyar and Muḥammad Shāh, but the role of powerful individuals in the regions who mediated with the *zamīndārs* cannot be ignored either. Finally, the nature of changes and of expansion in the local economies of the different regions also seems to have had an impact on the formation of regional states.[146] Thus, the study of the eighteenth-century material transition in Mughal India would require, on the one hand, a return to a focus on the region and detailed data available on conditions there, and on the other hand a close re-examination of the conventional materials on which Mughal history has been based, namely the court chronicles, both from centre and province. This is what we have attempted to illustrate above with reference to southern India, the Deccan or Bengal, and the literature of the past decades enables us to reconstitute a disaggregated picture rather than one based on a single, central, motor.

We are aware that the approach tentatively proposed here, may seem heretical to those who see the fragmentation of the Mughal empire as a disaster for Indian society. Indeed, in the context of discussions among Indian historians, it is often claimed that a denial of the thesis of eighteenth-century anarchy and decline is tantamount to an apology for the British Empire. Our contention is precisely the reverse. The fixed cycle of rise, consolidation and decline, with eighteenth-century anarchy as its endpoint, even though not an invention of the English East India Company officials but of indigenous south Asian intellectuals and literati of the eighteenth century, was nevertheless extremely convenient to justify the idea of *Pax Britannica*. Once again, the notion of the Mughal state as an all-powerful Leviathan, with a bureaucratic 'steel frame', and uniform institutional structure that smoothly replaced the dynamic of region and locality, owes much to an idealized vision of the British Empire in India, projected backwards into the late sixteenth century.

[146] Chetan Singh, *Region and Empire: Panjab in the Seventeenth Century*, Delhi, 1991; Bayly, *Indian Society and the Making of Empire*.

A survey of the literature produced on the Mughal state in the course of this century thus is salutary, showing both encouraging signs of considerable evolution in certain spheres, and the gloomy landscape of relative stasis in others. In the privileged sphere of fiscal and economic questions, the urgent need remains to go beyond the paradigm set out by W.H. Moreland in the 1920s, a task to which the greater part of the historians of the 'Aligarh school' have signally failed to address themselves. But there is also the need to put fiscality in its place by focusing on other questions, whether of a materialist nature or not. The Mughals produced a series of powerful popular myths that live on not only in tales of Bāz Bahādur, or Chhatrasāl, or Tānsen and Baijū Bāwra, or Akbar and Bīrbal (in the last of which elements of tales surrounding Rāja Bhoja, and Krishnadeva Rāya both find echoes), but in a variety of local and regional histories, as much in the oral as in the written traditions.[147] They also produced a form of 'global theatre' that ensured that the word 'Mogul' would be enshrined in the English language as a synonym for riches and power, and in this writers like the Portuguese chronicler Diogo do Couto the French physician François Bernier and the Venetian jack-of-all-trades Nicolò Manuzzi (or Manucci) had a major part to play.[148] The task before us is thus not only the positivistic one of separating 'myth' from 'reality', but of understanding the complex dialectic between the two. The challenge and prospect that lies before the historian of Mughal India is thus a daunting one; it remains to be seen whether the methodological renewal that is in the process of transforming so many other fields in Indian history will eventually blow much-needed winds of change into this domain as well.

[147]For a recent collection that addresses and partly historicizes some of this vast variety of oral materials, see Cathcrine Champion, ed., *Traditions orales dans le monde indien* (Collection Puruṣārtha), Paris, 1996. In a related vein, but with a more textual orientation, see B.L. Bhadani, 'The Profile of Akbar in Contemporary Rajasthani Literature', and Shirin Mehta, 'Akbar as Reflected in the Contemporary Jain Literature in Gujarat', both in *Social Scientist*, vol. XX (9–10), 1992, pp. 46–53, 54–60. For some materials that remain between the oral and written traditions, see for example Winand Callewaert, ed., *The Hindi Biography of Dadu Dayal*, Delhi, 1988, which recounts an apocryphal meeting between Dadu and Akbar.

[148]For a first approach to this question, based largely on English-language materials, see Kate Teltscher, *India Inscribed: European and British Writing on India, 1600–1800*, Delhi, 1995. These issues will be explored in greater depth in a monograph in preparation by Sanjay Subrahmanyam, *Mughals and Franks: Ethnography and Realpolitik in Indo-European Relations, 1500–1750* (provisional title).

PART 1

The Formulation and Consolidation of Authority

1

A Warlord's Fresh Attempt at Empire*

D.H.A. Kolff

Long after they migrated to India in search of land and a soldier's career, the Afghans of Hindustan remained organized as war-bands, ready to migrate with their women, children, tents, and flocks to whatever camp their chiefs would determine upon.[1] In politics they likewise tended to stick to old ways and, when one of their leaders became king of Delhi in 1451, their attitude towards him and his successors remained ambivalent for several generations. The problems of legitimacy were not really solved. Indeed, the Afghan aristocracy of the Lodi period (1451–1526) never quite learnt to live with an indivisible kingship. The experiment of a dual monarchy was tried on more than one occasion; in 1517 it was abolished for the last time only after a good deal of campaigning and intrigues amongst the *amirs* of the realm.[2] The repeated division of the sultanate of the Lodi family was characteristic of a segmented Afghan society which used the enmities in the royal kin to fight its own and did what it could to fan them. It was a two-way process. The sultans were partners in the feuds of their great nobles and the heads of the aristocratic families were drawn inescapably into conflicts within the ruler's family. The kings were reminded again and again that they had to keep up appearances

*Chapter Two of D.H.A. Kolff, *Naukar, Rajput and Sepoy* (first published Cambridge: Cambridge University Press, 1990).

[1]Simon Digby, 'Dreams and Reminiscences of Dattu Sarvani, a Sixteenth Century Indo-Afghan Soldier', *Indian Economic and Social History Review*, 2, 1965, 58.

[2]Hameeduddin, 'The Lodis', in R.C. Majumdar (ed.), *The Delhi Sultanate (The History and Culture of the Indian People, VI)*, Bombay, 1960, 148.

and share part of the gains of kingship with the high aristocracy. Yet, a trend towards stronger kingship is discernible. The Afghan nobles had no doubt felt at ease with the gregarious ways of Bahlul Lodi (1451–89), who had no throne erected for himself but shared the carpet with his peers.[3] His son Sikandar (1489–1517) had slowly asserted royal authority in the pastoral confederation of tribal lords over which he presided, but he had done so without outraging aristocratic sentiment. Ibrahim, the last sultan of the dynasty (1517–26), however, appears to have followed a policy of outright suppression of his *amīrs*' independent manners. He required them to observe proper court ceremonial and set out to 'purge their minds of any thoughts of equality based on clannish affinity with the king.[4]

By thus trying to impose new attitudes upon his *amīrs*, Ibrahim threatened the equilibrium and cohesion of the kingdom. He was out to prevent them from periodically reasserting their position through conflicts that involved not only the nobility of the kingdom but also the royal family and thereby kingship itself. But he could never hope to succeed in restraining the chiefs without a corresponding change in the segmentary institutions of Afghan rule in Hindustan. This he failed to do. Nobles who found that the new rules of the game did not allow them to contend for status and profit the way they felt was their birthright, left the arena of the Lodi sultanate, either by declaring themselves independent or by seeking help from outsiders like the Mughal Babur in Kabul.[5] The king could not destroy such great aristocratic rebels against his rule without destroying the legitimacy of Lodi rule itself: too much custom and right were on their side. Understandably, his kingdom had already begun to fall apart before his final defeat at Panipat in 1526.

This, however, would not prove the end of Afghan rule in Hindustan. Within a decade after Panipat, it reasserted itself, this time on a different footing. This essay addresses itself to the question of whether the power base of Sher Khan Sur, who would be king of Delhi from 1540 to 1545, differed institutionally from that of the Lodis. It will be my contention that, at least initially, his reign presents a new departure in north Indian history. He significantly changed the segmented aristocratic military polity as it had existed in Lodi times. First and foremost this is clear from the way he entered the military labour market and from the alliances his army encompassed.

[3]Ibid., 142.
[4]Ibid., 149.
[5]Ibid.

Abbas Khan's Message

Abbas Khan Sarwani who, about 1580, wrote a history of the great Afghan Sher Shah,[6] began his work by tracing the origin of Afghan immigration into northern India. The movement of poor tribesmen from Afghanistan to the rich plains of India, he contended, had provided the manpower for the armies of the Lodi and Sur dynasties that, with an interruption of only fourteen years, had ruled in Hindustan from 1451 to 1555. Abbas relates how Sultan Bahlul Lodi was at first just one of many petty kings of northern India who was left at peace so long as he remained stuck within the walls of Delhi, but whose city was besieged by the sultan of Jaunpur as soon as he had left it on an expedition to subdue Multan. Bahlul, however, knew his rivals' weak spot. He told his nobles that none of these kings had a 'national [*qaumdār*] following of their own', whereas, far in the north-west, he had a large number of kinsmen who were valorous and poor and who, if brought to India, would firmly establish his hold over the country. A message was sent to the chiefs of Afghanistan in which Bahlul told them that the preservation of the honour of their kinswomen in Delhi was their affair as well as his. He would share all his possessions with them, he said, as with brothers, keeping only the sovereignty of India for himself. And so they descended to the plains 'like ants and locusts', as the usual cliché has it, to serve Bahlul. The Jaunpur king could not withstand these spirited tribesmen. It is true that he had 'elephants like mountains' and 'innumerable zamindars', but he lacked, Abbas implies, the human resources that Bahlul now commanded: 'dear and near ones ... imbued with the spirit of honour and prestige'. Jaunpur was defeated. The Afghans were richly rewarded with *iqtā's* (fiefs) and more of them began to stream into Hindustan every day.[7]

Here, one feels, Abbas Khan is mainly at pains to preach unity to the Afghans of his own time in which Afghan power had yielded to that of the Mughals. He pleads for a revival of national pride amongst his immigrant countrymen. But as far as historical truth is concerned, one cannot but have one's doubts about Abbas' contention that Bahlul's success was exclusively due to his appeal to ties of kinship and

[6]The names Farid (proper name), Sher Khan (title conferred about 1526) and Sher Shah (title as sultan of Hindustan from 1540 onwards) are all used in this essay to denote the same person.

[7]Abbās Khan Sarwani, *Tārīkh-i-Śēr Sāhi*, trans. B.P. Ambashthya, Patna, 1974, 5–9; *The Tārīkh-i-Shēr Shāhī* (Persian text and English Translation) ed. S.M. Imamuddin, Dhaka, 1964, 1, 4.

nationhood amongst the Pathans.[8] Certainly, there were ethnic and geographic factors working in his favour. As a Lodi Afghan in control of Delhi and most of the Punjab, he had easy access to the finest recruiting grounds that could be imagined. Perhaps there were also demographic forces pushing men from the hills to the plains of Hindustan. Yet only his success in war enabled him to turn all this to advantage. Most of his new men must have been simply soldier-adventurers, many of them no doubt experienced fighters, who were drawn by Bahlul's growing fame as a leader rather than by feelings of tribal obligation. Good 'marginal' soldiers were a rare commodity and would remain so for centuries.

But Bahlul's plentiful fortune as a military commander procured for him the wealth the lavish distribution of which allowed him, firstly, to be selective as to whom he permitted to serve in his camp and, secondly, to maintain a certain discipline. This, I suggest, must have been the grain of truth in Abbas' assurance to his readers that, in those early days, there was no factionalism or rivalry amongst the Afghans. On the contrary, 'they looked to the well-being of their nation and never felt jealous of the prosperity of others'. Among Bahlul's *amīrs* the same self-denying spirit prevailed: 'If they knew that their Afghan brethren had better prospects elsewhere, they immediately allowed them to go there with their recommendations, so that they might not be taken to be the ill-wishers to their nation and tribe.'[9] Perhaps this is not just an idyllic myth. In Bahlul's time, the influx of Pathan soldiers into Hindustan very likely grew so intense at one point, that even *amīrs* could pick their men. As long as the supply of men exceeded demand, they were in a position to prevent intertribal and interfactional quarrels from impairing the fighting quality of their hosts. But all this lasted only as long as their coffers and those of their king were full of booty and tribute, that is to say as long as military fortune smiled on them.

Abbas, the Afghan historiographer on whom we shall continue to rely to a great extent in the following pages, was clearly in need of a Golden Age and found it in the reigns of Bahlul and Sikandar Lodi (1451–1517). His demography may contain some truth, as we saw, though, already for at least 200 years before Bahlul, thousands of Afghans had been serving in the Punjab and Hindustan. Abbas, however,

[8]Here and elsewhere in this study the words Afghan and Pathan are used interchangeably. See on Abbās also, Harbans Mukhia, *Historians and Historiography During the Reign of Akbar*, Delhi, 1976, pp. 160–5.

[9]Abbās, *Tārīkh*, 12.

was out to make another point, to wit, that the glorious Afghan empire in Hindustan was lost in the 1520s not by the sword, but, as he has Sher Shah say, 'through the feuds that the Afghans had developed among themselves'.[10] In the final paragraph of his work Abbas admitted that these feuds were part of 'the very temper' of the Afghans as a people. But they were not ineradicable. Sher Shah, he said, had completely wiped out 'the contentions, disputes, fights, and feuds which were ingrained in the very temper of the Afghans ... whether they be in Hind or Roh'.[11] What Sher Shah achieved in the 1530s and 1540s was, according to Abbas, not only a restoration of, but also an improvement of Afghan rule as it had been under Bahlul. It was his greatness to have overcome, for once, the ingrained weakness of the Afghan race.

What then was so particular about this sultan? What exactly did he change? More than any other historian, Abbas answers this question. He points not to the kind of man Sher Shah was, though like Bahlul he must have been a leader of exceptional ability, but to the basis of the relationship between him as an employer and the men on whom he built his kingdom. In this respect Sher Shah apparently could afford to act on new principles to a degree that clearly set him apart from the Lodis.

An important departure from ancient Afghan custom was Sher Shah's rule that the laws of inheritance did not obtain in public affairs. To the Afghan community, the matter must have been fraught with emotion. The tension between the royal prerogative and tribal equality had hardly been problematic during the time of Bahlul Lodi, the founder of the dynasty who, when inviting his kith and kin, had promised to share with them as brothers whatever territories and kingdoms would come into his possession. His son Sikandar, however, decided that, whenever one of his nobles died, his treasures and chattels were to be divided according to the Afghan law of inheritance, whereas his *parganas* and soldiers would be conferred on the son whom the king considered most able. This principle was revived by Sher Shah who also refused his own relatives a share in the *parganas* conferred on him by the Lodi king, telling them: 'This land is not the country of Roh that I should make divisions equally among brothers. The country of Hind is completely under the laws of its king and here nobody has any share

[10]Ibid., 104, 117, 452.

[11]Ibid., 787. Hind is India and Roh is the home country of the Afghans in Afghanistan.

in it. There is no question of seniority, juniority or fraternity here.'[12] In Hindustan, the sultan's law prevailed over tribal distributive custom and inheritance. Elsewhere, Abbās told an anecdote to remind his audience how proper it was that loyalty to one's family and tribe yield to service to a leader like Sher Shah, because 'the safety of that one man who is powerful and capable leads to the well-being of the seven climates'.[13] Throughout his history, Abbas stresses the importance of Sher Shah's empire as the embodiment of Afghan unity,[14] firmly founded on the principles of subordination, discipline, and royal control over the tribal immigrants, however egalitarian the outlook of these freebooters originally may have been. Sher Shah's empire was not a tribal state. On the contrary, tribal custom and closeness of kinship ties is dismissed as belonging to the sphere of personal affairs and is not allowed to impinge on the 'public' interest.

Abbas particularly wanted to stress the discontinuity he saw between the Lodi period and the rule of Sher Shah. After 1526, the old solutions had lost their validity; Bahlul's recipe was no longer applicable. The Lodi dynasty had been based in large measure on a principle opposed to that of discipline; their monarchy had been floating on a loose confederation of aristocratic clan segments. At crucial moments internal feuds proved their undoing, however brave the Pathans might have been individually.[15] The Lodi nobility had lost their kingdom to the Mughals and, in the opinion of Abbas, this failure of theirs disqualified them from future leadership over the Afghans. The point of the insufficiency of genealogy to justify any claim to a share in empire is duly stressed in his history. The aristocratic descendants of the Lodis were judged unfit to serve as advisers under Sher Shah's new dispensation. They had the seal of failure on their foreheads. Providence now favoured another type of leadership.[16] Therefore, Sher Shah was right when he did not join Sultan Mahmud a son of the last Lodi king who rose against Mughal rule in 1537.[17] The dethronement of the dynasty had exposed

[12]Ibid., 99. See also the *Tārīkh-i-Daulat-i-Shēr Shāhī* which quotes Sher Khan as saying: 'In the matter of conquest and the business of administration, the ties of kinship are not to be observed', in Nirodbhusan Roy, 'New Light on Sher Shah's Early Career', *Journal of the Asiatic Society, Letters*, 18, 1952, 57; see also page 60.

[13]Abbās, *Tārīkh*, 271, 272.

[14]Ibid., e.g. 255, 265, 269, 375, 383.

[15]Ibid., e.g. 382.

[16]Ibid., 375, 443, 450.

[17]Ibid., 209.

the politics of the faction-ridden Afghan élite as hopelessly inadequate in the changed circumstances.

Sher Khan entered the race with a handicap. As late as 1537 aristocratic opinion was that the leadership of a Lodi was necessary to rouse, hold together, and legitimize an attempt at restoration of Afghan authority. The rebellion of Mahmud was an expression of the shared aspirations and the common system of values of the autonomous chiefs of the great Afghan clans. Sher Khan was an outsider to this kind of politics. Abbas himself admits that, if the only hope was for a refurbished confederation of the old type, his hero 'did not command sufficient respectability amongst the Afghans' to compete with the aristocrats.[18] He was a member of the Sur clan, a minor Afghan group, and his pedigree was singularly unimpressive. In the diplomatic game of tribal politics he was at a natural disadvantage. Yet precisely for this reason, if Sher Khan was to respond at all to the crisis of Afghan unity, he would have to come up with something new. Like Ibrahim Lodi, he would as king make changes in the old etiquette concerning the respect shown by the *amīrs* to their sultan and vice versa. But whereas Ibrahim had the advantage of a certain dynastic legitimacy, Sher Khan first had to build a basis of power for himself that was imposing enough to make his nobles obey him. Though it took him 40 years before he was successful, this is what he did achieve.

In a revealing sentence Abbas explained why Sultan Mahmud, the Lodi pretender of 1537, though his respectability for a while won him a large following of allied noblemen, was bound to fail. 'Since Sultan Mahmud', he wrote, 'did not possess the real hold over the country and the treasures, he could not maintain a force of his own.'[19] The prince had no access to the agrarian resources and the hoards of Hindustan and, therefore, could not afford to maintain a sizeable number of soldiers in his pay. Clearly, Abbas is at pains, from the first chapter of his book to his concluding sentence—in which he said that Sher Khan gave peace and tranquillity to peasants and soldiers—to explain how through a long career his hero was successful exactly on the issues where prince Mahmud failed.[20] In Sher Khan's view, he suggests, the crucial ingredients of politics were not the famous lineages of the Afghan nation, but soldiers, treasure, peasants, and the revenue they paid.

[18]Ibid., 207.
[19]Ibid., 212.
[20]Ibid., 788.

Long before he became sultan and probably as early as the second decade of the sixteenth century, Sher Khan, then still only named Farid, began building a base for himself around Sasaram in what are now the Rohtas and Bhojpur districts of western Bihar. Called to the area in about 1511 by his father to administer two *parganas*, he found himself at first without troops of any description. The story goes that he had 200 saddles made and then borrowed horses from the village headmen, which means that these people were capable of war, because in India a horse was a war-horse. Perhaps what Sher Khan tried here was the forced disarming of the local peasantry. Anyway, with these horses he equipped the young Pathans of the district, telling them: 'I will provide you with subsistence, allowance and clothings and whatever booty in the shape of cash or kind falls into your hands will be yours. I will never covet them.' The valorous amongst them he would provide with maintenance fiefs.[21] It is clear from these and similar remarks that he did not collect a loose gang of retainers around him: his soldiers received their equipment from their leader and received a basic payment from him, or, to use the Indian idiom, they ate his salt. The *parganas* he administered and from which he took agrarian taxes, were also his recruiting ground. In fact, the management of land, as practised by Sher Khan, was linked to the recruitment of peasant-soldiers. According to another sixteenth-century chronicle, he put an early stop to the ancient system of forced labour in his *iqtā*' and remitted various kinds of imposts levied by his predecessors, with the result that 1000 husbandmen, amongst them even Rajputs from Marwar, migrated and came to live under his protection.[22] Later on, we find that Sher Khan, then the virtual ruler of Bihar, returned to his home counties for some months to manage his lands and collect an army.[23] The Sasaram area became Sher Khan's most securely held district virtually by his own efforts. Not surprisingly, once he had become king of Hindustan, of the Punjab, and of Bengal, he had his tomb built in these otherwise obscure southern marches of his realm.

Though we shall have to say something on the subject later, Abbas clearly suggests that Sher Khan's troops were exclusively Afghans.[24] And indeed, he seems to have gone to great lengths to enlist as many men from that nation as he could, first from the Sasaram area and later from elsewhere as well. In the 1530s when probably already over 50

[21] Ibid., 26, 27.
[22] Roy, 'New Light', 53, 54.
[23] Abbās, *Tārīkh*, 208; see also 757 and Roy, 'New Light', 58.
[24] Abbās, *Tārīkh*, 384, 454 and *passim*.

years old, he at last emerged as the one and only Afghan warlord of north India. He doubtlessly realized that aggressive recruitment methods minimized the possibility of a competing rallying point of Afghan solidarity emerging elsewhere in Hindustan. In building up his strength, he resorted to harsh expedients. 'Those Afghans', Abbas says, 'who had taken to the life of mendicants and indolence on account of their misfortune, were made to give up this life and were enlisted again as soldiers. Those who refused to take to soldiery and continued the life of mendicancy were killed.'[25] Recruiting officers or, if one prefers a less modern expression, press-gangs, were sent to the communities of Pathans which, particularly after their defeat at the hands of the Mughals in 1526 and 1527, had spread far and wide, but in the first place to Bihar.[26] One of Sher Khan's men was even reported to have led all the Afghans of Gujarat and Mandu to his army in the north.[27]

Once in camp, military life turned out to involve hard physical labour, most spectacularly the erecting of the earthen entrenchments with which Sher Khan seems invariably to have surrounded his encampments. To a certain degree such hardships were apparently also imposed on Pathan noblemen. For one of these aristocrats, who felt unequal to the exertions required by Sher Shah, this was a reason to try and escape from camp.[28] Others swallowed their pride and became accustomed to this kind of life; perhaps they derived some consolation from the sight of a party of respectable Mughals who, as two fellow-historians of Abbas tell us, were working in camp as common labourers at the circumvallation constructed each day.[29]

In yet another aspect this army astonished Sher Khan's contemporaries. Its soldiers were not only disciplined and used to an idea of

[25] Ibid., 249.

[26] Ibid., 121; Digby, 'Dreams'. 55, 64.

[27] Abbās, *Tārīkh*, 447. Some contingents of Afghans, however, remained beyond his control, Digby, 'Dreams', 58.

[28] Abbās, *Tārīkh*, 542, 543, 586n, 588n.

[29] H.M. Elliot and J. Dowson (eds), *The History of India as told by its own Historians: The Muhammadan Period*, London, 1867–77, iv, 394n, quoting the *Waqī'āt-i-Mushtāqī* and the *Tārīkh-i-Daudī*. See on the Timurids buildings such ditches and on their *Wagenburg* in fifteenth-century Iran and Turkey, John E. Woods, *The Aqquyunlu: Clan, Confederation, Empire: A Study in 15th/9th Century Turko-Iranian Politics*, Minneapolis and Chicago, 1976, 112, 175. Also Halil Inalcik, 'The Khan and the Tribal Aristocracy: The Crimean Khanate under Sahib Giray I', *Harvard Ukrainian Studies* 3/4 (1979-80), pt. I, 460.

soldiering that involved more than just fighting battles, they were also subjected by Sher himself to a certain kind of drill. In 1542, he was in a position to surprise the ex-king of Malwa with a military spectacle that may have been quite new in India at the time. 'When the royal umbrella came in sight', runs a report, 'the cavalry drew their sabres, galloped forwards towards the umbrella, dismounted from their horses, and saluted the king in due form, as was their habit on the day of battle. Each division did this in succession.'[30] Soldiers and king thus solemnly acted out the devotion that bound them to each other in a manner that pronounced the role of the nobility as largely irrelevant. But this demonstration of loyalty also conveys the orderly impression of an exercised manoeuvre. Indeed, Sher Khan is quoted by Abbas as reminding his men on the morning of the battle at Kanauj in 1540 that he had imparted training to all of them. This may certainly be regarded as a striking innovation which, as far as we know, sets apart the army of Sher Khan from that of his predecessors as well as from many of the later Indian armies.[31]

Sher Khan's novel methods of recruitment, labour and drill must have made life in his camp hard as compared to conditions under the Lodis. Yet, there were plenty of Afghans who voluntarily joined his standards when they heard that he was, as Abbas says, 'greatly eager to organize them'.[32] After Sultan Bahadur Shah of Gujarat lost control of Malwa in 1535, for instance, the Afghans who had been in his service joined Sher Khan. As with Bahlul Lodi in the fifteenth century, Sher Khan's success in politics and in battle must have made service with him seem attractive. Even the aristocrats gave up their scorn of him when they saw him prosper.[33] But the common soldiers in particular favoured him and they enjoyed his favour. He could not have held his nobles in check if he had not kept his promises to the ranks.

But by what method did Sher Khan achieve this? How did he find the means to keep his promise? Abbas points out that the men in the army were fully equipped, received whatever money they demanded

[30] Ibid., 393n, quoting the same sources.

[31] Abbās, *Tārīkh*, 451. However, according to Ahmad Yadgar, in the late 1530s Humayun had men come from Badakhshan to train his troops in up-to-date methods of warfare, Abbās, *Tārīkh*, 302. For a story about Sher testing a man's skill as an archer, see N.B. Roy, 'Anecdotes of Sher Shah (from the manuscript of Tārīkh-i-Dāudī)', *Islamic Culture* 32, 1958, 260–1.

[32] Ibid., 249.

[33] Ibid.

and grew so affluent that their number increased daily.[34] This, of course, was the basis of any warlord's success. Abbas himself, as we shall see, gives Bibi Fateh Malika as an example of a rich *amīr,* whose inherited wealth enabled her to set herself up as a formidable military power.[35] But the information we have is not detailed. What we should like to know is to what extent fixed and regularly paid salaries were a feature of these armies and, most crucially, whether soldiers were paid directly out of Sher Khan's treasury or through the intermediary of *muqta's* (fief-holders) and jobber-commanders. The first question is impossible to answer categorically though Abbas mentions monthly salaries several times in his history, which would lead us to assume that they were the rule at least for a portion of the army.[36] As to the second question, the answer must be that possibly a number of soldiers received pay directly from the treasury, but that the majority, especially those serving away from the capital or the royal camp, was paid by the army officers out of their *iqtā's.* The problem was to make sure that this last category of soldiers received regular pay.

As the inspection, however strict, of his officers' accounts was not a sufficient means to control their spending, Sher Shah introduced the systematic branding of horses, a practice which, according to Abbas, was quite new, though the device seems to have been tried before by Alauddin Khilji in the early fourteenth century.[37] Sher Shah was well aware how, during the reign of Ibrahim Lodi (1517–26), the nobles used to dismiss most of their men as soon as *iqtā's* came into their possession, and how afterwards, having enriched themselves from their unduly large income as *muqta's,* they used to forsake their sultan and join another master.[38] His system was designed to avoid a repetition of this. He preferred to have the horses of his men branded in his own presence and, after he had inspected the rolls of soldiers and horses presented to him, he used 'with his own tongue' to announce their monthly pay, while he also personally fixed the monthly emoluments of newly enlisted soldiers. This was done, amongst other reasons, in order 'that there should be no discrimination *(farq)* between the rights

[34]Ibid., 121, 757.

[35]Ibid., p. 252

[36]Ibid., pp. 129, 754, 755, 774.

[37]Ibid., pp. 753, 754; Abu-l-Faẓl, *The Akbarnāma of Abu-l-Fazl (Bibliotheca Indica)* trans. H. Beveridge, Calcutta, 1897–1921 (reprint, Delhi, 1972), vol. 1, 399.

[38]Abbās, *Tārīkh*, pp. 753, 795n.

of the nobles and the soldiers [and] that the nobles may not be able to deprive the soldiers of their dues ...'[39]. There is no doubt that the sultan in this way made a considerable impact. The Mughals would revive the system.

It is true that Abbas elsewhere draws the attention of his readers to the case of an *amīr* who, when appointed to the charge of the faraway province of Sind, was exempted from branding.[40] But this was clearly an exception. More importantly, Sher Khan's soldiers soon learnt what they were entitled to. They knew they could count on the protection of their master if any noble threatened to deprive them of it. Once the governor of Malwa in conjunction with his aristocratic entourage reserved for himself some of the income meant for distribution to the soldiers. Upon this, 'two thousand noted horsemen' decided they would submit the case to the king who, Abbas commented, they knew showed no favour to a man simply because he held a large army or because he was one of the *amīrs* belonging to his own nation. Understanding that Sher Shah would never forgive them if they left their post on the frontier of the realm to resort to his court *en masse,* they sent a *vakīl* and set up a separate camp at a distance from that of the governor. Sher Shah's reporters told him about the affair before the horsemen's *vakīl* or spokesman appeared before him. The sultan promptly had a letter written to the Malwa governor reminding him that he had introduced the branding of horses with the intention that the nobles should not encroach on the rights of the soldiers. 'Have you no shame', he asked, 'before the people and fear of God above that you have acted contrary to my laws?' On receipt of this letter, the governor abused his nobles for their bad advice, got on his horse, rode to the camp of the 2000, offered them his excuses and brought them back to the main camp, 'bestowing on them rewards and favours'. When the *vakīl* of the soldiers returned he was given a horse and a robe of honour while amongst the poor the governor distributed a large sum of money, thus restoring his relationship with God as well as with the common man.[41] For, Abbas seems to imply, the sultanate of Sher Shah was built on those two relationships, and any nobleman had better acknowledge the fact.

Compared to Lodi times, therefore, the distribution of the financial means of the realm was organized on new principles. To sum up, Sher

[39]Ibid., p. 754.
[40]Ibid., 533.
[41]Ibid., 772–8.

Khan's attempts emphasized subordination and employment by the centre, not horizontal alliances with aristocratic leaders, pastoral tribes and warlords. Sher Khan penetrated the military labour market along a vertical axis with, amongst others, agrarian-based troopers or, as we might perhaps call them, an emerging gentry in his home counties in Bihar and in the *qasbas* situated on the east–west river and land routes that formed the main frame of his realm. This did not, of course, mean he tried to monopolize recruitment—that, in India, is impossible, as can be shown—but it did mean centralization to the extent that it was feasible. Now what was feasible? Sher Khan's approach presupposes the command of independent means. We need to know, first, what these were and how they were used. Secondly, it is necessary to inquire whether Indian conditions allowed a programme of centralized recruitment and distribution to become a permanent feature of politics and state formation.

TREASURE

It is difficult to understand Sher Shah's reign unless we can find an answer to the question of the origin of the resources with which he financed the personal fidelity of his soldiers who alone could keep the Afghan aristocracy in check. For the period after 1540, when he controlled the great plains of northern India, the answer is clear. At that time, a careful management of the fiscal resources of the country was feasible enough; regular pay to the army and, therefore, army discipline could be guaranteed. After the battle of Kanauj, Sher Shah devoted himself wholeheartedly to this difficult task. He may have been helped by a continuation of the period of agricultural expansion that had probably characterized the Lodi period. Anyway, though some tribute from the outer regions of the realm still came in, much depended now on his ability in a systematic way to tap into the agricultural resources of Hindustan. On this score, Sher Shah's achievement was reputedly great. Historians, including Abbas, have, probably not without reason, drawn attention to the innovations he introduced in the administration of the land revenue adding that these served as the inspiration for the later agrarian settlements of Todar Mal during Akbar's reign.[42] Thus, after Sher Khan's famous victories at Chausa (1539) and Kanauj (1540) had put the agrarian resources of Hindustan at his disposal, land revenue became the all-important element of his income.

[42]Ibid., 755–32, Percival Spear, *A History of India*, vol. 2, Harmondsworth, 1962, 27, 28.

The early years before 1529 do not present much of a problem either. Until that year he was simply a successful commander who divided his time between the ruthless but efficient administration of his father's *parganas* in south Bihar[43] and service with a variety of chiefs mainly in Oudh as well as with Ibrahim Lodi and the Mughal king Babur. Abbas, the historian, did not deny that a good deal of loot fell into the hands of his hero and that, while serving in the camp of the Lodis, he was able to make savings.[44] Yet, however great his success as a revenue assignee and as a soldier of fortune, being a member of the Sur clan and unconnected with any of the powerful clans of the Ghilzai tribe that dominated Afghan politics in Hindustan, there was not much of a future for him either in the Mughal camp or amongst the remnant of the Lodi confederation: politics were on too big a scale there for an as yet comparatively insignificant professional soldier to be much in demand. In 1529, he left the camp of the Mughals and joined the service of the newly established Nuhani (or Lohani) sultanate of south Bihar, a more modest enterprise.

For Sher Khan this field of action had the advantage of being close to his home base, his recruiting grounds in the Sasaram–Benares area, and of allowing full scope for his personal initiative as a military commander. For the Nuhani sultan, the fact that he was not supported by tribal sentiment and family relationships of any significance meant that he promised to be a stable element of the otherwise baffling scene of Nuhani factionalism. Perhaps that is the reason he was selected for a position of trust: that of guardian *(atālīq)* of the minor prince Jalal Khan. When the sultan died shortly afterwards and his widow ruled for a while on behalf of her son, Sher Khan, the outsider, maintained himself in his position at court. And, when the sultana also died, 'the entire management of the kingdom of Bihar now devolved upon him'.[45] In this way he appears to have won a measure of independence for himself that was far removed from his earlier inferior position as a dispensable

[43] Abbās, *Tārīkh*, pp. 27–32. See on the controversy about whether Sher settled for the revenue with the village chiefs or with the peasant cultivators, S. Nurul Hasan, 'Revenue Administration of the Jagir of Saḥsaram by Farid (Sher Shah)', *Proceedings of the Indian History Congress*, Sec. II, (Medieval India), 26 (1964), 102-7, and Hussain Khan, *Sher Shah Sur, Ustad-i-Badshahan alias Sher Shah Suri*, Lahore–Rawalpindi–Karachi, 1987, 55–8. I tend to side with Nurul Hasan who thinks Sher dealt with the chiefs.

[44] Ibid., 27, 47.

[45] Ibid., 107, 108

mercenary in Lodi or Mughal service. Yet he was still essentially a servant of the Nuhani clan and in times of crisis had to fall back on his military skill and on the income from his own modest home counties around his town of Sasaram. It is doubtful whether he would have been able, faced as he was with the claims of the jealous Nuhani lineage chiefs, to lay his hands on a large part of the sultanate's revenues. We are, therefore, still left with the question as to the origin of the resources on which Sher Khan built his power during the crucial ten years between 1529 and 1539.

Abbas' answer to this is abundantly clear: treasure. Immediately after his account of Sher Khan's emergence as the guardian of the young Jalal Khan, he mentions the subject for the first time. And throughout his account of the decade preceding Sher Khan's overthrow of Humayun, the issue of how his hero came into the possession of wealth accumulated by others remains perhaps the single most important theme of his narrative. Then, as the story reaches the end of the decade, the subject is dropped as abruptly as it was taken up. Abbas is silent about the enormous spoils which must have fallen into the hands of the Afghans immediately after the two decisive battles of 1539 and 1540. Whereas this is perhaps explained by the delicacy of the subject of these Mughal defeats for an author writing during Akbar's reign, he also makes no mention of the acquisition of treasure by Sher Shah during the five years of his kingship. The reason is, no doubt, that the loot of those years was no longer a vital explanatory element in the story he had to tell. During the preceding decade, it had been a different matter. Indeed, there was a wide gulf separating, on the one hand, Sher Khan's modest circumstances before 1529, when he made a living in the pay of several provincial governors, rulers and warlords, and, on the other hand, the state of his affairs in the 1540s when he had seated himself on the throne of Hindustan and could dispose of its entire land revenue. It was treasure, talent and luck alone that enabled him to cover the distance between the two.

The hoarded wealth that fell into Sher Khan's hands between 1529 and 1539 came from the strong-rooms of both *amīrs* and sultans. The exact dates of these acquisitions are difficult to establish. Assuming a rough chronology to be Abbas' intention, we follow the order in which he has placed them. The list starts with Sher Khan's alliance with a certain Makhdum Alam, an *amīr* in the service of the king of Bengal, who was in charge of Hajipur in north Bihar across the Ganges from Patna. When the Bengal sultan sent an army to assert his authority in north Bihar and perhaps wring south Bihar from the hands of the

Nuhanis, Sher Khan succeeded in defeating this expedition. 'The huge amount of spoils', Abbas comments, 'in the form of treasures, horses and elephants, etc. which fell into the hands of Sher Khan made him master of the resources.'[46] Now the king of Bengal sent another force to subdue Makhdum Alam who so far had taken no part in the fighting. Sher Khan sent a contingent of troops to his aid receiving as a trust Makhdum Alam's earthly possessions. When the latter was killed in battle, this wealth fell to him as his ally.[47] Thus, to begin with, war booty and wealth confided to him by an ally added to Sher Khan's property.

As a result of his central position in the Nuhani court, Sher Khan appears to have had access, perhaps not to the revenues, but to the treasure of the kingdom of south Bihar. Part of it he seems to have sent as *peshkash* to the Mughals to serve his own diplomatic ends.[48] His growing power and independence and his method of handling the spoils that the Nuhanis regarded as theirs caused a crisis in the little sultanate. He lost the confidence of one Nuhani faction which now left Bihar in search of help, carrying away to Bengal the young sultan Jalal Khan. In the battle that inevitably followed, Sher Khan was again victorious over the Bengalis. 'All the treasures, elephants, equipages, and train of artillery fell into the hands of Sher Khan who thus escaped the disgrace of subjection to others and he now became the master of the kingdom of Bihar.'[49] Jalal Khan fled back east. It is not certain whether on this occasion Sher Khan acquired the royal treasure of the Nuhani kingdom of Bihar or whether it was taken to Bengal by Jalal Khan. But we have already noticed that his good use of this treasure had played a role in his rise as a regional political leader in Bihar.

Next in Abbas' account are the resources that three widows yielded to Sher Khan. In medieval India it was not unusual for aristocratic women to assume conspicuous roles. In an élite society torn by rivalry and war at frequent intervals, a woman's brothers and husband often died violent deaths leaving her at the head of family affairs. Also, as girls were married young, there was always a good chance of their surviving their husbands. Thus, noblewomen wielding impressive financial and military power were a common feature of the political scene. As allies they were more eagerly sought after than men, as a measure

[46]Ibid., 109.
[47]Ibid., 110.
[48]Ibid., 119.
[49]Ibid., 129. Cf. Roy, 'New Light', 61.

of control over their resources was a natural corollary of any kind of partnership.

In 1526, the Lodis had been driven from Delhi and Agra by the Mughals and from their Agra treasury Babur had distributed huge gifts to his family, to the tribes of his army, as well as to several recipients in Central Asia.[50] But there was more in the way of Lodi wealth in Hindustan. In the 1530s, a provincial treasure of the defeated dynasty was still kept in the fort of Chunar, not far to the west of Sher Khan's home *parganas.* The fort was held by Lad Malika, the widow of a professional Sarangkhani soldier to whom the Lodis had entrusted it. She was assisted by three Turkoman brothers who were at loggerheads with her stepsons. These partisans of hers, in an effort to strengthen their position, arranged for their mistress' marriage to Sher Khan.[51] On that occasion she presented to Sher Khan '150 precious jewels, 7 maunds of pearls, 150 maunds of gold' as *peshkash.* After this her new husband brought 'all the parganas in the environs of the fort' under his control. Subsequently, he married Guhar Gosain, the—perhaps converted, Hindu—widow of Nasir Khan Nuhani and took into his possession sixty *mans* of gold from her. 'His power', Abbas adds, 'came to be fully established.'[52]

Even more important than these marriage alliances was his connection with Bibi Fateh Malika, a lady of unrivalled respectability. She was a Farmuli *shaikhzāda,* i.e. a member of the second most powerful clan of the Lodi sultanate;[53] her father had been a sister's son of Sultan Bahlul Lodi and her husband had been the descendant of a famous *shaikh*, a religious man of great prestige. She belonged, in short, to the high aristocracy of Hindustan. And she was rich. Her father had possessed some inherited wealth. Being 'a man of prudence', he had, during the prosperous and peaceful years of Lodi rule, taken only few

[50]Bābur, *Bābur-Nāma of Zahiru'd-dīn Muhammad Bābur Pādshāh Ghāzī*, trans. A.S. Beveridge, 1922 (reprint, Delhi, 1970), 522, 523.

[51]Abbās, *Tārīkh*, pp. 201–6, 221n. Abu-l Fazl, *The Akbarnāma of Abu-l-Fazl (Bibliotheca Indica)* trans. H. Beveridge, Calcutta, 1897–1921, (reprint, Delhi, 1972), I, 288. See below for the place of the Sarangkhanis in fifteenth-century north India.

[52]Abbās, *Tārīkh*, 206. This *man*, or maund, perhaps weighed something like 13 kg. See also Elliot and Dowson, *History*, IV, 343–6 (Abbas Khan).

[53]Nizamuddīn Ahmad, *The Tabaqāt-i-Akbari of Khwajah Niẓāmuddin Aḥmad (Bibliotheca Indica)*, Persian text, ed. Brajendranath De, Calcutta, 1913–35, trans. Brajendranath De, Calcutta 1927–39, I, 356.

soldiers in his service and had, as a result, made great savings. The whole *sarkār* of Awadh and other *parganas* had been given to him by Bahlul and during more than a generation these *iqtā's* were never changed. It was said that he never purchased anything but gold and jewels. He had no issue except Bibi Fateh Malika who thus became heiress to the family treasure.[54] Her husband seems to have been more of a fighter than his father-in-law and must have spent some of his riches on soldiers. However he soon died. Bibi Fateh Malika now told her husband's younger brother Bayazid to employ more soldiers 'and that she would give money for it'.[55] This chief subsequently quite successfully opposed the Mughals Babur and Humayun, but his early death and the consolidation of Mughal power in Awadh left the lady to her own devices. She could have taken refuge with the Baghela Rajput raja of Bhata—later known as Rewa—as so many wealthy Afghans did during these critical years. But another possibility now was Sher Khan, a man no doubt of spurious descent, but at least an Afghan and an adroit leader on whom fortune seemed to smile.

Indeed, Sher Khan plotted to bring her 'under his control by adopting a variety of artifices and cunning devices'. To let go such treasure would have been 'a matter of grief to his heart till eternity'. If we are to believe Abbas, he tried to convince her that all the *amīrs* of the Lodi sultans and their sons had exalted him, Sher Khan, by taking shelter with him. Whatever may have been said during the negotiations, she must have known that this was not true. All the same, in the end she did not join the Bhata raja but came to Sher Khan's camp. For the latter it was a political breakthrough and financially the advantages were enormous. The wealth of this noblewoman enabled him to take the initiative against Bengal. About 1535 he took 300 *mans* of gold from her leaving her only a small amount of gold and the fief he had conferred upon her so that she might not become dependent on others. Having equipped his army with this money, he set out on his conquering expedition to Bengal. However, in this case a marriage alliance as with Lad Malika and Guhar Gosain was out of the question. The embarrassed Farmulis might have felt compelled to become the Sur leader's allies, but they had not lost their pride and when Sher Khan's son asked Bibi Fateh Malika to marry her daughter to him, she refused and Sher Khan did not judge it politic to press her on the matter.[56]

[54] Abbās, *Tārīkh*, 250.
[55] Ibid., 252.
[56] Ibid., 250–5.

The next catch was probably the greatest of all. This time it was straightforward loot again. Sher Khan's rise to power in Bihar had been worrying the Afghan nobles in Humayun's service for some time, but the emperor himself had not taken much notice of him. Moreover, Sher Khan had befriended the Mughal governor of Jaunpur by sending him *peshkash,* which in this case amounted to a kind of honourable bribe consisting, according to one source, of some *mans* of gold.[57] He had thus been able for some years to conduct an aggressive war towards the east. In 1537 he again sent an expedition to the east laying siege to the Bengali capital city of Gaur. This at last compelled Humayun to move in his direction. Humayun's Mughal comrades proposed to take Chunar first, Sher Khan's strongest fort, but the Afghan aristocrats in his entourage were now eager to get at their low-born rival with as little delay as possible. There was an added reason for their hurry. 'The counsel of the old', their leader pleaded, 'is that as there is a huge treasure lying in the fort of Gaur, the fort of Gaur should be taken first'; after that, the capture of Chunar would become an easy task. Humayun did not listen to this advice, whereupon the old Afghan could only comment gloomily that as Sher Khan would soon acquire the treasures of Gaur, there was no doubt that he was in the ascendant.[58] So it happened: Gaur fell to the Bihari Afghans in 1538 and, though Sher Khan could only with difficulty find enough porters and beasts of burden to transport its huge riches, most of this wealth arrived safely in Rohtas in his home country by a route through the Jharkhand hills.[59]

Other sources support the picture as give by Abbas, particularly as regards the Gaur spoils. The chronicler Muhammad Kabir says that the ransom agreed upon for lifting the first siege of Gaur in 1536–7 was nine lakhs of rupees.[60] He also reports that when Humayun occupied Gaur in 1538, after Sher Khan had left, a huge treasure that the latter had not been able to find, was discovered under a *cabūtra* and sent towards Agra on 500 mules along with a large force to escort it. This whole precious consignment, however, was seized by the Afghans and sent to Sher Khan at Sasaram.[61] The *Tārīkh-i-Dāudī* says that Sher Khan, on his return from Gaur, got hold of the huge treasures of

[57]Quoted by Ambashthya from the *Waqī'āt-i-Mushtāqī* and probably also from the *Tārīkh-i-Daudī*, ibid., 305n.

[58]Ibid., 257, 258.

[59]Ibid., 262, 274, 275. Elliot and Dowson, *History*, v, 112 (Niamatullah).

[60]Quoted by Ambashthya from Kabir's *Afsana*, Abbās, *Tārīkh*, 295n.

[61]Quoted by Ambashthya from the same source, ibid., 367n, 368n.

Maharath Chero, a tribal raja of south Bihar.[62] Abul Fazl, who clearly found the subject of Sher Khan, this 'seditious impostor', exceedingly unsavoury, also mentioned the role of finance in his rise to power. According to him Sultan Bahadur of Gujarat (1526–37) sent a subsidy to Sher Khan through merchants and summoned him to his side. But Farid, he wrote, who in a short space of time 'by craft and unrighteousness surpassed the rebels of the age', did not join Bahadur, but 'made the money into capital for sedition'. Another tale, apparently written down in the seventeenth century and explaining Sher's victory over Humayun by his seizure of the latter's treasure, nicely, though erroneously, summed up ten years of Sur successes.[63] Even more striking is that stories of the kind we have been quoting from sixteenth- and early seventeenth-century historians, were apparently current for centuries in the heartland of Sher Shah's empire. There, people about 1820 still knew that the *rauzas* (gardens) of Sasaram and Chainpur were paid for from the hoarded riches which a commander of Sher Shah had seized from the Chainpur fort and which Sher had not wanted to appropriate for his own use.[64] As long as his memory lasted, his name conjured up images of unheard-of accumulations of treasure and of lavish spending.

Portuguese sources are as emphatic as Abbas Khan in pointing out Sher Khan's special interest in finance and his success in obtaining treasure. In the early 1530s, they report, he quarrelled with the treasurer of the army of King Nusrat Shah of Bengal (1518–33), who then largely controlled Bihar. This resulted in an affray in which the commander of the camp was killed. Later, he was again present when the Bengal army in Bihar rebelled against the new king of Bengal, Mahmud Shah (1533–8). In the battle that followed, Mahmud was victorious, but Sher Khan got away with the treasure of the defeated army.[65] In 1536–7, as we saw, he invaded Bengal himself and got as far as Gaur, Mahmud Shah's capital. His army, on this occasion, consisted of 40,000 horsemen, 1500 war elephants, 200,000 foot and 300 boats each of which had two rowers and three archers. Mahmud paid him thirteen lakhs of

[62]Quoted by Ambashthya, ibid., 363n.

[63]Abu-l Fazl, *Akbarnāma*, I, 328, 401. S.A.A. Rizvi, *Religious and Intellectual History of the Muslims in Akbar's Reign*, Delhi, 1975, 504.

[64]F. Buchanan, *Journal of Francis Buchanan, Kept During the Survey of the District of Shahabad in 1812–13*, ed. C.E.A.W. Oldham, Patna, 1926, 120.

[65]Fernão Lopes de Castanheda, *História do descobrimento e conquista da Índia pelos Portugueses*, Coimbra, 1924–33, Book VIII, ch. cix, 379, 380.

gold, valued at 525,000 *pardaus,* to get rid of him, the deal being that Sher Khan would recognize Mahmud as his lord and publicly pay him his respects. The captain of the Portuguese, who was present with the Bengalis during the negotiations, counselled against this bargain as Sher Khan, he said, would no doubt use this money to continue his war of aggression.[66] He was right, because in 1537–8 the Afghan returned, this time accompanied by 100,000 horse and 300,000 foot—inflated numbers no doubt, but interesting if compared with the lower numbers cited for the preceding expedition—demanding the same sum again from the king, telling him this was going to be an annual contribution. This time the king refused, whereupon Sher Khan plundered the city. The Portuguese could not be very exact as to the value of the jewels, pearls, *aljôfares* ('seed-pearls') and of the gold and silver that was taken from the city's palaces, but over a period of seventeen days they saw 300 'calaluzes', i.e. rather large rowing boats, carrying these treasures to the other side of the Ganges, whence they were brought to Sher Khan's stronghold Rohtas in Bihar. It was rumoured that all this was worth 60 million (pieces?) of gold.[67]

Though quantification of the accumulated wealth of diverse origin flowing towards Sher Shah in south Bihar in the 1530s is clearly impossible, the evidence of its enormity is convincing. Perhaps the best indication of its vastness and of its importance for his rise to power in Hindustan, is the fact that in Abbas' account these data become crucial explanatory ingredients. In large parts of his exposition of Sher Khan's career between 1529 and 1539, he allows these acquisitions of treasure to dominate his narrative. They must have been a conspicuous element in the reports of Sher Shah's relatives and contemporaries. Abbas knew quite a number of such men intimately and he was in an easier position to interview them as he himself was related to Sher Shah's family.[68] Chronology may have faded from their minds but the stories of how their chief acquired his gold and silver during a period when he was only reluctantly taken notice of by his fellow-Afghans, had made a

[66]Ibid., Book VIII, ch. cxxviii. 410. João de Barros and Diogo do Couto, *Da Ásia,* Lisbon, 1777–80, Déc. IV, Book ix, ch. vii, 500, 501. I assume what is meant here is the *pardao de tanga* or *tanqat*, worth about one and a half future Mughal rupees.

[67]Castanheda, *História*, bk. VIII, ch. clxxvii, 486, 487. Barros, *Da Ásia,* Déc. IV, bk. ix, ch. viii, 503–6.

[68]Abbās, *Tārīkh*, 110. A sister of Sher Khan had been married to a Sarwani relative of Abbas Khan.

lasting impression on them. To Abbas—and this is saying something about his quality as a historian—these frequent references were no bizarre tales of oriental riches. On the contrary, he emphasizes the theme to tell us something essential about the polity Sher was building at the time, the so-called second Afghan empire that differed so much from the first, Lodi, sultanate.

Some of the massive resources that fell to Sher Khan were no doubt spent on *peshkash* and presents to those lords of Hindustan with whom he could as yet not cope on the battlefield. But the emphasis was on the distribution of income to his own men. We have mentioned the theme earlier. From 1529, Sher Khan was using his position amongst the Nuhanis of south Bihar almost exclusively to increase the number and discipline of his retainers. This was exactly the cause of the rupture between him and the proud Nuhani faction around the young sultan Jalal Khan.[69] 'Whatever new territories, treasures and wealth came into his hands, he spent them over appointing fresh retainers and granted to the new entrants the jagirs to their hearts' content, while he gave nothing to the Nuhanis out of his new jagir.' In the end he even told Jalal Khan quite frankly, that, as he saw it, this was in the best interests of both the king and the kingdom.[70] He thus attacked the tribal basis of the realm and replaced it by a new distributive principle that may be regarded as one of Sher Khan's main political innovations. Fixed payment and discipline replaced clannish loyalty. He is quoted as telling anyone who entered his service: 'Whatever monthly pay and stipends I will fix for you ... I will not reduce it even by one grain of rice. But you will not have to commit oppression and crime and quarrel with anyone.'[71] Besides their salary his soldiers also received their share of the spoils of battle. After an encounter with the Mughals in Bihar they all got at least four horses and many boxes containing valuables.[72] Thus, by the end of the 1530s, Sher Khan's name was associated with victory,

[69]Ibid., 119. Abbas does not mention Sher Khan's marriage to Dudu, the widowed queen of the Nuhanis, see Roy, 'New Light', 60.

[70]Abbās, *Tārīkh*, 111, 112, *Jāgīr* is the Mughal term for what in Sher Shah's time would have been called an *iqtā'*.

[71]Ibid., 129.

[72]Niamatullah, *History of the Afghans*, trans. Bernard Dorn, 1829–36, reprint, London–Santiago de Compostela, 1965, 115. Ambashthya, as so often, gives a slightly different translation, see Abbās, *Tārīkh*, 354n. See also Elliot and Dowson, *History*, v, 112 (Niamatullah).

treasure, good pay for soldiers and minor, well-disciplined commanders and, consequently, good service from the rank and file.

Such distributive practice attracted large numbers of horse and foot.[73] A worried Mughal commander is said to have reported that when, early in 1535, Humayun had embarked on his Gujarat campaign, Sher Khan had only 6000 horsemen under his command, but that only a few years later he had 70,000 of them at his disposal and spent twelve crores on their pay.[74] Though, again, one can have one's doubts about the reliability of these figures, the message of the historians is clear: they draw attention to the extraordinary qualities of Sher Khan as a recruiter, disciplinarian and paymaster, in short, to his methods as an employer of men. Abbas, in his concluding chapter, is perhaps more explicit. 'All through the day', he explains, 'he distributed gold like the sun and remained busy with the scattering of pearls like [a] cloud and that was why the Afghans rallied round him and the country of Hindustan came under him.'[75]

We can accept this judgement without reserve. After 1539 Sher Khan, now entitled Sher Shah, remained keen to restrict the élite's independence and to maintain personal control of his power base, his army. But he set about perfecting his system in two respects. The aim was to preserve, under the changed circumstances, the distributive polity that had taken shape in the 1530s and of which the army was the central institution. Firstly, as the supply of the hoarded treasures of Hindustan into his coffers largely ceased with the re-establishment under his leadership of regular government, he became increasingly dependent for his income on the agrarian resources of the country, supplemented perhaps by tributary payments from the fringes of his empire. A regularly assessed land revenue, for which he became rightly famous, became the major source of his income. Secondly, after 1539, a set of fixed rules that ensured the payment of salaries to soldiers became feasible. An essential element of the system chosen was the branding of horses to which we have already alluded.

Sher Shah, therefore, after his seizure of the sultanate, responded to the changed circumstances by effecting both a new fiscal policy and new procedures of spending. Both reforms were crucial if the kind of army built by Sher Shah was to survive in less troubled times. Indeed,

[73] E.g. Abbās, *Tārīkh*, 206.

[74] Translated by Ambashthya from the *Waqī'āt-i-Mushtāqī*, ibid., 307n; see also 235n.

[75] Ibid., 769.

the political economy that Sher Shah endeavoured to establish in Hindustan between his accession to the throne in 1539–40 and his death in 1545 was largely conditioned by the need to preserve intact the main instrument of his power: a well-recruited, well-paid, trained, and disciplined professional army of horse and foot. Abbas significantly ended his work by concluding that, as a sultan, Sher Shah gave peace and tranquillity to peasants and soldiers alike,[76] that is to say, that his new income policy worked as well as his policy of expenditure. If there is truth in this, it should be worthwhile taking a closer look at the recipients of his distributive system. Were all of them drawn from an exclusive ethnic category, the Afghans, or did some of them originate from the peasant strata that the king took so much pains to satisfy and turn into a prop of the state he built?

Afghans and Non-Afghans

In other words, who were Sher Khan's soldiers? On this score our faithful historian, Abbas, fails us entirely. He describes himself as 'the author of the annals of the kingdom of the Afghans'[77] and we, therefore, cannot blame him if his bias throughout his history is clearly Afghan, though his emphasis on the role of the Sarwanis, the clan to which he himself belonged, is less excusable. Inevitably, there were things which he could or would not take notice of. But was Sher Khan's career really such an exclusively Afghan affair?

It probably was not. To begin at the beginning, Farid's—to use his proper name, for Sher was a complimentary one later acquired—father and grandfather did not enter the service of any Afghans at all except for a period immediately after their arrival from Afghanistan when they served a Sur kinsman of theirs in the Punjab. At some point during the 1480s they, along with other Surs, joined Jamal Khan Sarangkhani, the governor of Hissar in present-day Haryana. Later, they moved as retainers of the Sarangkhanis to Jaunpur when the family was put in charge of that area. This connection with members of the Sarangkhani family would last for decades. The Sarangkhanis were Turkbachchas, i.e. they descended from the Turkoman or Mamluk slaves, who had served the Tughluq dynasty of Delhi in the fourteenth century—just as Indian slave-soldiers had served to the west of the Indus—and who, in north India, continued as an important element in military society afterwards.

[76]Ibid., 788.
[77]Ibid., 3, 4.

No doubt, these men had not lost the reputation for loyalty that characterized all slave soldiers. Their gangs must have been much in demand in the unstable and segmented warrior polity of fifteenth-century north India. In their forts they often kept great riches and military stores. When, in 1527, Ilyas Khan Turkbachcha was captured by Babur, one of the latter's followers got hold of two lakh *man* of grain, 2000 *man* of oil and also a few thousand *man* of pearls and jewels. The Lodis used their troops in certain key posts to counterbalance the power of the unruly Afghan clans.[78]

Thus, when Sikandar Lodi in or about 1498 tightened his grip on Jaunpur, which had been an independent kingdom not long before, he sent Jamal Khan Sarangkhani there with 12,000 horsemen. The strong fort of Chunar was given to another Turkoman, a relative of Jamal Khan. So the Lodi sultan created a non-Afghan base right in the centre of Hindustan to serve as a check on the surrounding *iqtā's* and provinces held by the Sarwani, Farmuli and Nuhani noblemen. As we saw, however, Jamal Khan Sarangkhani had a number of non-aristocratic Sur Afghans amongst his retainers. These he took with him and gave them as fiefs a number of *parganas* in the present Mirzapur, Bhojpur and Rohtas districts south of the Ganges.[79] This narrow area formed the strategic link between Awadh and Jaunpur on the west and Bihar on the east. It had never been brought fully under the control of any of the sultans of Hindustan. The Surs, therefore, now had to safeguard the passage of troops across the Ganges ferry at Chausa as well as on the stretch of the Delhi to Bengal road that ran across their area. As one of them, Farid's father was put in charge of two *parganas*, sufficient

[78]The identification of the Sarangkhanis as Turkbachchas is taken from Kalikaranjan Qanungo, *Sher Shah and his times: An Old Story Retold*, Bombay, 1965, 67n. See also Iqtidar Husain Siddiqui, *Mughal Relations with the Ruling Indian Elite*, Delhi, 1983, 20, and Niamatullah, *Niamatullah's History of the Afghans, pt I (Lodi Period)*, trans. Nirodbhusan Roy, Santiniketan, 1958, 30. See for the Turkbachchas also A. Halim, 'The Foundation of the Saiyad Dynasty', *Journal of Indian History 31* (1953), 201–9; *32* (1954), 157–69; 33 (1955), 32, 38; Al-Badāoni, *Muntakhab-ut Tawarikh*, trans. G.S.A. Ranking, Calcutta, 1898, I 360, 362, 365; Abū'l Faẓ'l, *Ā'īn*, II 176, 195, 297. In my opinion, other 'Turk' or 'Turkoman' commanders may as well have represented the Mamluk tradition, see, e.g., Siddiqi, *History of Sher Shah Sur*, Aligarh, 1971, 53, 69, 107, 136.

[79]Abbās, *Tārīkh*, 12, 14, 15; Siddiqui, *Mughal Relations*, 18–20, 22, 26, 43, 46–7, 52, 179, 183. The erstwhile Shahabad district has now been partioned into Bhojpur and Rohtas.

for the maintenance of 500 men. One of the *parganas* was Sasaram, which would become the central *qasba* of Sher Khan's home counties.

So, about 1498, Farid and his father, Hasan, left the Punjab for Hindustan with the Sarangkhanis and spent twenty years in the largely Turkbachcha enclave in the east of the Lodi sultanate. During this period we may assume that, from about 1501 to 1511, Farid was a freelance soldier-administrator in the Jaunpur neighbourhood and, between 1511 and 1518, managed the family *parganas* at Sasaram. He then probably served another Sarangkhani at Agra only to return to the family base on the death of his father in 1524.[80] But even after he joined the Nuhani Afghans of south Bihar in about 1525, his association with non-Afghans remained a vital factor in his rise to power, as is shown by his service as a client of the Mughals between 1527 and 1529[81] and, most importantly, by his marriages with Guhar Gosain, who can hardly have been an Afghan, and with the Sarangkhani, i.e. Turkoman or Turkbachcha, widow Lad Malika, as well as by his alliance with Bibi Fateh Malika, a Farmuli, and therefore a member of a group of families that were *shaikhzādas*, not Afghans, though related to Afghans by marriage.[82] Inevitably, the composition of his army in the 1530s must to some extent have reflected these non-Afghan connections. It is clear, for instance, that after his alliance with the three Turkbachcha or Turkoman brothers and his marriage with their chief, Lad Malika, the Chunar contingent, which must entirely or largely have consisted of Turkbachcha professional soldiers, was henceforward part of his army.

But this does not exhaust the issue of the Sur relationship with non-Afghans. Even more striking than the Turkbachcha link are the connections that allied Hasan and Farid with Rajputs. A bardic poem from Rajasthan, the 'Qaimkhan Raso', caused one of Sher Shah's biographers to surmise that Hasan's first wife, Farid's mother, was 'a daughter of

[80]See Qanungo, *Sher Shah*, 66–75. The chronology is based on B.P. Ambashthya, 'The Accounts of the Ujjainiyas in Bihar,' *Journal of the Bihar Research Society*, 47(1961).

[81]Bābur, *Bābur-Nāma*, 652, 659. Qanungo, *Sher Shah*, 76–88. Abbās, *Tārīkh*, 103–7. The Portuguese were also told that Sher Khan had served Babur and Humayun, Barros, *Da Ásia*, Déc. IV, Book VI, ch. iii, 23, and Dec. IV, Book ix, ch. vi, 488.

[82]On the identity of the Farmulis, see I.H. Siddiqui, 'Rise of the Afghan Nobility under the Lodi Sultans (1451–1526 AD)', *Medieval India Quarterly* 4, 1961, p. 122.

the ruling Qaimkhani Rajput family of Fatehpur–Jhunjhun (Shekhawat)' near Narnaul in Haryana where Hasan's father in the late fifteenth century held an *iqtā'* for the maintenance of 40 horsemen.[83] At about that time Hasan Sur was himself in the service of another Rajput in the Shekhawat area, a certain Raimal.[84] Though the Persian chronicles of the period rarely refer to these things, in medieval times there was nothing extraordinary about non-Afghan women being received in Afghan households,[85] nor about Afghan soldiers serving Rajput masters. As examples of the latter phenomenon we may cite Rana Sanga of Mewar and the Baghela raja of Bhata, both of whom received Pathans in their armies in the period after the battle of Panipat in 1526.[86] Perhaps we may go one step beyond this and suggest that Afghans and Rajputs were not really exclusive or even distinct ethnic groups at all. Fuchs found that among Indian tribes the title of Pathan, i.e. Afghan, is assumed 'by any member of the Hindu military caste who is converted to Islam', adding that 'such men find admittance into the Pathan ranks and are adopted by a clan or tribe in the same manner as some wealthy aboriginals are admitted into the Rajput caste'.[87] Similarly, if

[83]Qanungo, *Sher Shah*, xi. See Jan Kavi, *Kayam-Khan-Raso*, Jaipur, 1953. The name of Qaimkhani makes one wonder whether these Rajputs were perhaps of Turkbachcha origin. In the *Waqī'āt-i-Mushtāqī* an anecdote is told about a Shaikh Farid, who in Roy's opinion apparently is the future Sher Shah, in which it is said that 'Shaikh Farid Turk was a Sur', Niamatullah, *History*, 171. See also Abu-l Fazl *Ā'īn*, II, 205, 282, where the annotator says they are Chauhans converted to Islam. Cf. the Qaim Khan, *zamīndār* of Jhunjhunu, mentioned in Harish Chandra Tikkiwal, *Jaipur and the Later Mughals 1707–1803 AD: A Study in Political Relations*, Jaipur, 1974, 4–6. See also Sunita Budhwar, 'The Qayamkhani Shaikhzada Family of Fatehpur–Jhunjunu', *Proceedings 39th Indian History Congress*, Hyderabad, 1978, I, 412–25.

[84]Abu-l Fazl, *Akbarnāma*, I, 327.

[85]See, for instances from Lodi family history, Hameeduddin, 'Lodis', 151n, 153n. Raja Bihar Mal Kachhwaha, the first Rajput later to enter Mughal service had a previous alliance with Hajji Khan, the Sur governor of Mewat and Ajmer to whom he offered his daughter, see Douglas E. Streusand, 'The Formation of the Mughal Empire, 1556-1582', unpublished Ph.D. thesis, University of Chicago, 1987, 120.

[86]Bābur, *Bābur-Nāma*, 562. Digby, 'Dreams', 64. Niamatullah, *History*, 164n.

[87]Stephen Fuchs, *Aboriginal Tribes of India*, Delhi, 1973, 85. This practice was not restricted to tribes, see the passage from the 1911 Census Report quoted in William L. Rowe, 'The New Cauhāns: A Caste Mobility Movement in North India', in James Silverberg, ed., *Social Mobility in the Caste System in India* (CSSH Suppl. 3), The Hague–Paris, 1968, 66.

Farid's grandfather was a Rajput, this does not mean he was not an Afghan, because his being a Muslim—temporarily or for good—entitled him to the name of Afghan if he should adopt that identity and live up to it, for instance by serving an Afghan lord.

This may seem quite a heretical thing to say, but I suggest that, according to the ways of the north Indian military labour market, in the pre-Mughal period, 'Afghan' as well as 'Rajput' were soldiers' identities rather than ethnic or genealogical denotations. It was merely to register membership of the war-band they had decided to join that, until quite later on, Indian soldiers were known by such names. It is perhaps appropriate here to quote a British recruiting officer, Garrett, who wrote on his experience during the years 1917 and 1918 in the Punjab that 'there were a large number of families of the Hindu Ẓamīndār class of which those members who had enlisted in the army had, as a matter of course, become Sikhs'. Those staying at home remained 'Hindus' until, as a result of the intensive recruitment during the later stages of the war, they were induced also to join up, in which case they also became Sikhs. 'It was', Garrett continued, 'an almost daily occurrence for—say—Ram Chand to enter our office and leave it as Ram Singh—Sikh recruit.' Finally, he observed acutely that 'conversion on other than military grounds just before the war was not common'.[88] This, in other words, was by no means 'religious conversion' as we understand the term; just as the cases of the weaver whose success made him a Shaikh and of the Muzaffarnagar farmers who became the famous Sayyids of Barha, it represented an inflection of social status or professional identity[89]. What at first sight might seem to be a change of religion, is often a device to register either recruitment or professional success whether military or otherwise. Very often the Rajput to Afghan change—and, one may add, the peasant to Rajput change—was a similar kind of affair, indicating the pervading impact of soldiering traditions on north Indian social history. The military labour market, in other words, was a major generator of socio-religious identities.

Therefore, for Sher Khan and men like him who were aiming at building up political power and entered the military labour market of north India with the treasure and the credit commensurate to their ambition, ascriptive status and ethnic identity were no barrier to recruitment. On the contrary, identities were easily adapted to and even shaped

[88]*Census Punjab 1921*, xv, pt 1, 179.
[89]See Kolff, *Naukar, Rajput and Sepoy*, 18–19.

by any new alliances concluded. In this way the Turkbachchas of north India were probably entirely absorbed into the Afghan 'nation', just as was the case with many Shaikhzadas and Rajputs.

For most Rajputs, however, the switch to an Afghan identity, even under Afghan sultans, was often unnecessary, because Rajputs carried on a military tradition in their own right and they were frequently much in demand as such. Thus when Farid's father, in about 1498, moved to the Sasaram neighbourhood of south Bihar, an understanding with the local families of Rajputs became as indispensable for him, if he was to maintain himself in his *parganas*, as it had been earlier in the Shekhawat area of Rajasthan. Fortunately, thanks to a bardic source of information dating from 1663, we know a good deal about the most important of the clans in this territory, the Rajputs of Bhojpur. A short account of their history will inevitably lead us face to face with the imposing personality of the future Sher Shah. They were a group of fighters, who had, during the course of the fourteenth century, found their identity as Ujjainiya Panwar Rajputs. They felt—or, at the latest in the seventeenth century, came to feel—that they were related to the famous Panwar royal family of Ujjain in Malwa and, indeed, they may well have migrated from that region to Hindustan as adventuring soldiers. In 1324—their tradition has preserved the year—the clan was strong enough to successfully challenge its tribal master in south Bihar, one of the regionally dominant Chero chiefs. They now founded their own estate of Bhojput in the present-day Bhojpur district and ceased marrying their daughters to the Cheros, a decision tantamount to a declaration of political emancipation.[90] But they had to face the rulers to the north of the river Ganges, especially those of Jaunpur who coveted control of the ferry at Chausa. Manoeuvring for a position that would enable them to check traffic on the strategic Benares–Patna road just as the Cheros had done before them, they alternately met profit and disaster.

The seventeenth-century *khyāt* that is the source for the history of the Ujjainiyas of this period, records that, in 1394, the Sharqi ruler of Jaunpur crossed the ferry at Chausa with his army and halted at Baksar about 20 kilometres to the east of the ferry. Baksar was then probably, as it was 400 years later when Buchanan visited it, a holy place celebrated in Brahman legend, where assemblies of pilgrims were held

[90] Ambashthya, 'Accounts', 426.

several times a year in order to visit the temples and bathe in the Ganges.[91] According to the *khyāt*, some of the Sharqi ruler's 'Yavanas', i.e. foreigners, seeing a few Brahmans performing their *sandhyā* prayers on the bank of the Ganges, interfered with them. The Ujjainiya Rajputs thereupon took up the cause of the Brahmans of Baksar and chased the Yavanas from that place. The Sharqi ruler, however, soon defeated the Ujjainiyas and plundered Bhojpur, demolishing, the *khyāt* adds, its temples. The episode, duly emphasized in the Ujjainiya literary tradition, provided an early historical base for the social relationship which grew up between the Bhojpur Rajputs and the pilgrimage centre of Baksar.

After their defeat, the Rajputs fled to the hills and forests, began a life of pillage and plunder, and generally continued harassing the Sharqi foreigners. In 1400, as their enemy, the Jaunpur man, had died, they felt safe enough to leave the jungle and to resettle the area they considered their own. But, as with all *zamīndārs*, their negotiating position depended on their prowess as soldiers. From 1417 to 1449 and between 1455 and 1457 they again spent long years in the wilderness.[92] After these unruly years, they appear to have adjusted to paying a more or less regular tribute to the Sharqi sultans until that kingdom was merged in the Lodi empire. When Jamal Khan Sarangkhani was sent to Jaunpur as the governor of the Lodis, he soon established a hold of some kind or other over the Ujjainiya country. Once more their chief, a man by the name of Durlabh Deva, retired into the forest. This time, however, his exile did not last long. Farid's father Hasan, sent in about 1498, as we saw, by Jamal Khan to administer a stretch of half-subjugated country that was meant to yield him enough for the maintenance of 500 soldiers, knew by experience that it was best to try to come to an understanding with these Rajputs. 'Hasan Khan' the *khyāt* records, 'far from fighting with the Ujjainiyas, befriended them. Durlabh Deva accepted the suzerainty of Hasan Khan and began to rule over Bhojpur'.[93]

[91]Buchanan, *Shahabad*, 65, 71. Bābur visited the place in 1528 and noticed 'between 40 and 50 landing-steps' on the river bank that were, however, washed away during the next monsoon, Bābur, *Bābur-Nāma*, 660. See also Alexander Cunningham, *Report for the Year, 1871–72 (Archaeological Survey of India, III)*, Calcutta, 1873, 64–6; C.R.P. Sinha, 'Buxar in Archaeological Perspective', *Journal of the Bihar Research Society* 49, 1963, 107–10.

[92]Ambashthya, 'Accounts', 427–30.

[93]Ibid., 431

From this point onwards, the tone of the *khyāt* I have been quoting changes. Chronicle turns into romance. The only theme henceforward is the relationship between the Ujjainiyas and Hasan's son Farid, the future Sher Khan. I will confine myself to giving the bare facts. Badal, Durlabh Deva's eldest son, neglected by his father, who in 1500 chose the son of a younger wife as his heir-apparent, left his home accompanied by his followers and 'braved the unbearable pains of jungle-life'. Though the bard informs us that he spent his days hunting, one may assume that he kept himself going by gang warfare and pursued his feud as so many Rajputs in his situation did.

This is clearly related to the theme of the Rajput son, who, ostensibly as his father's rival but also as the champion of his clan, takes to the jungle and performs his *bhūmiyāvat,* his raid in search of a territory of his own. It is a role no Rajput family, it often seems, could do without for long. One day, when he was resting with his men by the side of a water-tank, Badal saw 'a young Yavan', a foreigner, on horseback coming towards him. It turned out to be Farid, who, disgusted with the hold his step mother had gained over Hasan Khan, had left Sasaram and was now on his way to Jaunpur to try his fortune in the world. As he was all alone, Badal asked him how he would manage. Farid replied (and there is here perhaps an allusion to his later name of Sher, i.e. tiger or lion): 'Nobody teaches the art of hunting to the cub of the lion and the latter never waits for his associates in hunting,' There was plenty to eat in the forest, he said. 'Like you, I also can hunt the animals when I feel hungry and take rest by the side of the streams.' The Rajput was duly impressed. Badal and Farid had a meal sitting side by side and found their respective life stories strikingly similar. In the end, the two young men 'having swords in their hands, took vows to remain friendly to each other all through their lives and to help each other in times of misfortune. They then embraced each other and separrated.[94]

One cannot, however, help wondering whether this was all there was to it. The *khyāt* uses the incident to explain why Farid, as soon as he was called back to Sasaram in 1511 to administer his father's *parganas,* sent Badal a horse and a robe of honour and forced Durlabh Deva to allow to his eldest son his share in the management of the Ujjainiya clan estate.[95] But we know that, in 1542, Farid, then Sultan Sher Shah, told the story of how as a young man, during the same decade which Badal spent in the jungle, he had led a life that must

[94] Ibid., 432, 433.
[95] Ibid., 433, 434.

have been in many respects similar to that of his outlawed friend. He recalled how he 'fell in with a party of thieves and highway-men, with whom he associated for some time, plundering the country all round; till one day, when seated in a boat with his new comrades, he was pursued "by his enemies", who, after a conflict, were completely victorious. Upon this, placing his bow and arrows on his head, he plunged into the water, and after swimming for three *kos* escaped with his life'.[96] It is tempting to conjecture that the bard's account of Badal and Farid's joint meal and their oath at the water-tank telescopically sums up an association that may have been less ephemeral.

Yet it would be rash to accept Abu-l Fazl's view of Farid as a mere robber and to reject the report that during that same first decade of the sixteenth century, Farid must have received an administrative and even a literary training of sorts in the Jaunpur area.[97] Both some experience as an outlaw and a certain grounding in Persian documents were valuable assets for a political entrepreneur in the medieval context. The combination goes some way to explaining Farid's success after 1511 when he became the manager of the family *parganas*. Also, the information as to Farid's liking for books is too precise to be put aside lightly and is perhaps confirmed by his being chosen about 1529 as the guardian *(atālīq)* of the Nuhani sultan's young son. On the other hand his management of his father's *parganas* shows features that remind us of Mughal practices against the Rajputs of western Hindustan during Jahangir's reign. 'The powerful *zamīndārs*', writes a biographer of Sher, 'were not spared, in spite of their requests. They were surrounded in their villages; the dense forests which were used by them as hide-outs were cut down; and then they were killed to the last man. It is said that not a trace was left of the old population, for the children and women who survived their men were captured and sold into slavery. And, new peasants were brought there to carry on cultivation.'[98] The evidence, therefore, seems to be that Farid, like so many of his contemporaries, owed his early achievements to a combination of soldiering and ruthless administration and that, as had been the case with his father, a friendly understanding with one or more of the local Rajput families was of great help to him.

During the 1511–18 period, as Farid lived at Sasaram, he and Badal remained allies. It was a brotherhood beyond all genealogical or

[96] Elliot and Dowson, *History*, IV, 393n. See also Abbās, *Tārīkh*, 585n, where the *Waqī'āt-i-Mushtāqī* and the *Tārīkh-i-Dāudī* are used.

[97] Abu-l Fazl, *Akbarnāma*, I, 327, 328. Abbās, *Tārīkh*, 14.

[98] Ibid., 96, 107, 108. Siddiqui, *Sher Shah Sur*, 18, see also 72.

ideological allegiance. Thanks to it, both prospered. Badal was in a position to collect 'thousands of Ujjainiyas' around him. The term Ujjainiya soon came in general use to denote soldiers recruited and led by members of the Ujjainiya clan. Only a few of them, however, can have belonged to the kin of the Bhojpur Rajputs; the remainder must have been mustered from the numerous men who could easily be engaged by anybody whom luck appeared to favour, especially in the so-called Purab area of eastern Hindustan, which was, or anyway would become, a famous recruiting area and in whose centre Bhojpur and Sasaram were situated. 'Ujjainiya', in other words, rather than a genealogical concept or a clan name, now became a soldiers' identity, the name of an open category of fighting men whose mere recruitment under Ujjainiya leadership caused them to be labelled as Rajputs. Some of them, of course, may even earlier have considered themselves as Rajputs, but Bhumihars, Brahmans and many categories of peasants may also have been amongst them.

Badal soon had a sizeable number of auxiliaries in his pay and he must have appreciably added to Farid's strength. But when, in 1518, Farid left for Agra to try his luck there and when Durlabh Deva died soon after, a struggle for the Bhojpur *gaddī* inevitably followed. Badal was killed by one of his half-brothers. His wife with her two sons, Gajpat and Bairishal, fled and passed the traditional number—often met in ballads and folk-songs for periods of adventure and hardship spent away from home—of twelve years 'amidst the jungle people in the deep ravines of the mountains'. Not until 1532, when Gajpat was eighteen years old, did his mother send the boys to serve her husband's old ally Sher Khan, who was now building up his strength in south Bihar and who received them well. Gajpat and Bairishal now collected 'two thousand Ujjainiyas' and killed their rival uncle with Sher Khan's help whereupon Gajpat was seated on the *gaddī*.[99] The Bhojpur Rajputs, under Gajpat's leadership, amply repaid Sher Khan during the following years, rendering invaluable military assistance. During the battle of Surajgarh in which Sher Khan defeated the Bengal army, he put 3000 picked Pathans and 2000 Ujjainiyas in his first line.[100] The battle was won and, according to the *khyāt*, the Bengali general was killed at the hands of Gajpat. Sher Khan was much pleased. 'All the spoils of war, comprising elephants, horses and other equipments, which had fallen into the hands of Maharaja (Gajpat) were allowed to be retained by

[99] Ambashthya, 'Accounts', 434, 435.
[100] *Ibid.*, 437.

him. At the time of departure of the Maharaja (Gajpat) he (Sher Khan) tied with his own hand the bejewelled sword to hang round his (Maharaja Gajpati's) waist, bound his arm with a jewelled armlet, gave a string of pearls round his neck, fixed a bejewelled Kalangi in his Sirpech (headdress), gave a horse, head-to-foot dress and a sword for prince Bairishal, and gave Buxar as jagir to him (Maharaja Gajpat).' Again, the relationship between the Ujjainiyas and the pilgrimage centre is stressed. Soon after this, the chronicle said, Gajpat brought his new fief of Baksar under his control and went to live there along with his Ujjainiyas.[101]

Though the published part of the *khyāt* unfortunately stops here, there is every reason to believe that the relationship between Sher Khan and Gajpat was a lasting one. It is reported that Sher Khan, presumably after he had become sultan, conferred the title of raja and the districts of Rohtạs and Shahabad on Gajpat.[102] The relationship was indeed a necessary one from the point of view of both, firstly because they were close neighbours, their headquarters lying only some 70 kilometres apart, and secondly, because each of them compensated the weakness of the other. Since the struggle for the succession to the Bhojpur *gaddī* of 1519–20, the rivalry in the Ujjainiya family had never stopped and Gajpat, though, as we saw, with Sher Khan's help successful against his uncle in about 1533, soon found himself faced with another rival, a cousin of his by the name of Dalpat. Just like Gajpat, Dalpat had been driven out of the Bhojpur country as a young boy with his widowed mother. He had found refuge with his mother's brother at Arail in the present-day Allahabad district and stayed there until, in 1538, his uncle produced him before Humayun and got a Mughal *farmān* for the conferment of Bhojpur issued in his favour. For a while, he became the master of the family estate and Gajpat retired to Sher Khan, his protector. Thus, Sher Khan and Humayun each had their own clientele among the Ujjainiyas; the dividing line between the great protagonists of Hindustan split even a relatively obscure Rajput family on the frontiers of the sultanate. Though Gajpat, no doubt with Sher Khan's help, recovered the *gaddī* and could maintain himself there until his death in 1577, the rivalry between the branches of the family would survive him.[103]

[101] *Ibid.*, 438.

[102] *Imperial Gazetteer*, XI, 378.

[103] Ambashthya, 'Accounts', 439, 440, and genealogical table opposite p. 424.

His lineage's factionalism rendered Gajpat dependent on continuing help from his powerful neighbour at Sasaram. But on the other hand the alliance with the Ujjainiyas proved an equally invaluable asset for Sher Shah. As Rajput chiefs and as the protectors by heritage of the Brahmans of the pilgrimage centre of Baksar, they had access to the recruiting grounds of Eastern Hindustan to an extent that complemented Sher Khan's personal style of recruitment. Though Sher Khan's entrepreneurship as a warlord allowed him to rise above the segmentary bickerings of the Afghan aristocrats, he could neither demilitarize northern India nor dissolve the old ties and the security that bound locality, lineage and old identities to hundreds of leaders all over his realm. He needed these *zamīndārs* as allies as much as they needed his treasure and loot. Achievement and ascription had to strike a balance of some sort.

It is certain that Sher Khan tried hard to do just this. He had more *zamīndārī* contingents like that of the Ujjainiyas in his army. It is only because the Ujjainiya clan was to survive as an important family locally, recognized as Panwars by the Rajputs of Rajasthan, and allowed a place in a Rajasthani bardic *khyāt*, that we know so much about their association with Sher. In any case there appears to be some reason to assume that, though he emphasized the direct recruitment of individual soldiers to be disciplined and paid under his personal supervision, and though he could afford to avoid loose alliances with aristocratic Afghan warlords, Sher Khan must have made frequent use of more or less powerful non-Afghan middlemen, whether Turkbachcha, Rajput or 'tribal'. Often these men commanded resources Sher had no access to. In addition to their kinship ties and the historical identities they represented, they had patrimonial estates and forts of their own. They may also to a certain extent have engaged in trade and the asking of protection money from caravans. They may have been horse dealers as both Bahlul Lodi himself and Sher Khan's grandfather Ibrahim had once been.[104] But above all, such men were dealers in manpower. And because much of the military labour force of Hindustan was bound to remain beyond Sher's immediate control, he could not do without these men in his attempt to rearrange the best bits of it and then direct these units to empire building.

[104]Niamatullah, *History*, 27, 28; Abu-l Faẓl, *Akbarnāma*, 1, 326. Roy, however, denies that Bahlul was ever a trader, though his father and grandfather were.

To sum up, such were the conditions of the segmented military society of sixteenth-century India, that Sher Khan was to some extent debarred from directly tapping the human resources of the Turkbachchas, the Farmulis, the Rajputs, the Bhumihars and the Brahmans of Hindustan. He needed men like the three 'Turkoman' brothers in the fort of Chunar and the Ujjainiya subcontractors. In the lower Doab, the Gautam Rajput family of Argal, to cite another example, fought several battles for Sher Khan against Humayun.[105] On the other hand, there seems to have been only a single Afghan nobleman of old respectability put in charge of a *sarkār* and given a high *suwār* (cavalry) rank in Sher Shah's empire. Other members of the old aristocracy were only given small maintenance fiefs.[106] If, therefore, Sher's army was by no means entirely recruited by Sher himself directly from the peasantry, he was clearly in undisputed command and could choose his own companions in leadership.

As commanders then, Sher chose quite a few Afghans, though practically all of them descended from 'obscure families the members of which never appear to have occupied any important position in ... the Lodi period'. Amongst them were the manumitted slaves Haji Khan Sultani and Habib Khan Sultani. The Abyssinian slave or ex-slave known as Habsh Khan whom Sher employed to superintend the building of a citadel in the fort of Rohtas, is another example.[107] Then there are the three sons of one of his slaves, who cannot have been an Afghan by birth as only free men could claim that identity. Two of these sons at different times bore the title of Khawas Khan, the second of whom became Sher's most trusted and prominent commander.[108] It is possible that the soldiers of this family of slaves successfully arrogated to themselves the name of Afghans; the second Khawas Khan anyway seems to have done so. Another of Sher Shah's outstanding military leaders was Barmazid Gaur, or Kaur. Qanungo contends that this man was a Gaur Rajput called Brahmajit. Siddiqui, a later biographer, points out that this man's name was Kaur, i.e. 'one-eyed'. If this is so, then the lack of a community name may, as in the case of Khawas Khan, indicate low social origins. Anyway, we must assume that many thousands

[105]F.S. Growse, 'Notes on the Fatehpur District', *Journal of the Asiatic Society of Bengal* 54, 1985, pt I, 155, 161.

[106]Siddiqui, *Sher Shah Sur*, 44.

[107]Ibid., 34; Buchanan, *Journal*, 51.

[108]Abbās, *Tārīkh*, 100, 261 and *passim*; Abu-l Fazl, *Akbarnāma*, 1, 615. Badaoni, *Muntakhab*, 1, 537; Siddiqui, *Sher Shah Sur*, 66–87

of this commander's soldiers also were 'Hindus'.[109] Even in the Lodi period, for that matter, it was a common occurrence for an Afghan *amīr* to have non-Afghan personal retainers and, as one instance shows, for hundreds of Meo tribals—from Rajasthan—to serve as guards in the contingents of an Afghan commander. One can only guess at the composition of the army of Shujaat Khan Sur, who was another of Sher Shah's great commanders, and who led the household troops of the sultan.[110] The Surs, though not as aristocratic as the Farmulis, might, like the latter, be described as spurious Afghans, in the same sense as in the nineteenth century some Rajputs were spoken of as spurious, i.e. as not answering to the then generally accepted genealogical or ethnic criteria of historical identities. I no longer accept these rigid criteria and suspect that in the ranks of these armies social identities could be achieved in a manner that was diffuse and dynamic. Indeed, if aristocratic notions about lineage had as little place in Sher's dispensation as I think they had and if so many of Sher Khan's commanders were slaves in the process of emancipation or adventurers and peasants in the process of achieving an Afghan or Rajput identity, we are far removed from the world of caste and 'ascribed' status that for so long was regarded as central to the social history of India.

Abbas Khan could be silent about his pluriformity and could present a picture of Afghan harmony, because clearly ethnic conflict was not a prominent feature in Sher Shah's camp. As we saw, Sher Shah had built his army not just as a loose confederation composed of Afghan factions and other ethnic groups but as a distributive structure of comparatively well-paid and disciplined soldiers. Badaoni rightly remarks on the preciousness to Sher Shah of the individual trooper.[111] During the 1530s, luck as well as shrewd politics had made him the master of huge treasures. After 1540 an energetic fiscal policy remained a feature of his reign. And inasmuch as he succeeded in securing for his men a fair distribution of the resources of the realm, he pushed ethnic and factionalist rivalry into the background. The most important institution of Sher Shah's reign was no longer the clan or a particular tribe, nor the court, but the army camp. The physical expression of this was the earthen entrenchment with which Sher, to the surprise of his contemporaries, invariably surrounded his camp. Within this clearly defined

[109]Qanungo, *Sher Shah*, 419–21; Abbās, *Tārikh*, 514–18; Siddiqui, *Sher Shah Sur*, 88–95. See for Khawas Khan's 'Hindu' noblemen and retainers, ibid. 79, 80.

[110]Ibid., 125–9, 252; Niamatullah, *History*, 120, 176.

[111]Badaoni, *Muntakhab*, I, 477.

little world, Sher Shah's word was law. The citizen of the camp was the common soldier rather than the noble confederate. Abbas Khan's history seems irrefutably to testify to Sher Shah's success in integrating widely differing groups in a polity characterized by a new distributive intensity. For these men, one might say, the opportunities of an aggressive and enterprising kingship carried more weight than any pedigree or bond of ethnicity. The challenges of ethnic loyalties, if any, and of the Lodi heritage of segmentary, aristocratic politics, were largely overcome by direct recruitment based on merit, a leadership that owed very little to ascribed status, alliances with minor commanders, and the lavish distributions of, first, the windfall of loot, and, later, once the empire was established, of the revenues of a regular agrarian administration.

But did this really work in the end? If aristocratic solidarity and the politics of alliance that had been the props of the Lodi segmentary state were rejected in order to build a more stable—perhaps one should say 'early modern'—state, what sources of legitimacy and integrative solidarity did it depend upon? Was Sher Shah, to use the idiom of political science, as successful a creator of solidarity as he was an administrator?

Admittedly, in Indian political science—I am referring to Kautiliya's *Arthaśāstra*—treasure *(koṣ)* is one of the essential elements of kingship and, as a source of legitimacy, seems to have occupied at least as high a place as the *khutba* (the official Friday prayer in the name of the sultan) and the *sikka* (right to coinage) derived from Islamic tradition. There is indeed a political quality about Indian hoarded wealth and treasure trove as is testified by Indian folklore. Riches in Indian stories are often miraculously unearthed, almost as Sher Shah found his, and states immediately spring into existence. A hidden treasure is a hidden kingdom and its rediscovery was enough for the rays of royalty to shine again in the world. Such was the power of the treasure brought to light by Prithiraja at Nagaur in the twelfth century, 'amounting to seven millions of gold, the deposit of ancient days'. And as late as the eighteenth century, a Bihari poem proudly and at some length explained the emergence of the Darbhanga kingdom as based on the plunder of an enemy's camp.[112] To bury a hoard with one's comrades-in-arms

[112]James Tod, *Annals and Antiquities of Rajasthan, or the Central and Western Rajput States of India, 1829–32*, ed. W. Crooke, London, 1920, I, 300; Narayan Singh and G.A. Grierson, 'The Battle of Kanārpī Ghāt', *Journal of the Asiatic Society of Bengal* 54, 1885, pt I, 16, 35.

was, inversely, the establishment of a bond that would one day find its consummation in royalty. A hidden treasure was the centre of a kingdom to come and of a political solidarity that did not require the actual distribution of its riches to be real. The results of one of Sher Khan's battles with the armies of Bengal in about 1534 was that, as an eyewitness remembered later, 'countless booty' had fallen into his hands and into those of his companions; it consisted of 400,000 gold coins *(mohurs)*. Sher proposed not to send this money to Humayun, their nominal overlord, but to bury it for the time being and to covenant with an oath on the Quran to maintain secrecy about the place of the burial. The decision amounted to the establishment of Sher's hidden kingdom, which would take many years to become manifest. One of the friends (a non-Muslim?) asked to be exempted from the oath, saying his word would be enough. And it was, because, though the allies never had an opportunity to return to the place, their four lakh covenant was not broken as long as their gold remained where it was, serving as the pledge of their faith to each other and contributing to the status of its chief even from its secret vault.[113]

Meanwhile, Sher Shah did portion out most of his hoarded and fiscal wealth. The widening circle of people sharing in the largesse of the pretender was the reality of his expanding kingdom. His gift economy seemed tantamount to a new political nation that cut across ethnic and communal boundaries. To Jaisi, the great mystic, who wrote his tale of love, the *Padmāvatī*, during Sher Shah's reign, this was the essence of his legitimacy as a king. None of the great rulers of former ages, he sang, equalled Sher Shah. His treasures, like the Ocean and Mount Meru, were inexhaustible. 'The kettle-drum of his generosity soundeth at his court, and the fame thereof has gone even across the ocean. The world touched this Sun, and became of gold compact, so that poverty fled and went beyond the borders of his kingdom. He who but once approacheth him and asketh, for all his life is free from hunger and from nakedness. Even that [King of old] who performed ten horse-sacrifices—even he gave not holy gifts like him. So generous hath Sultan Sher Shah been born upon the world, that none hath e'er been like him, or will be, nor doth anyone give such gifts.'[114]

Yet, though Sher made most of his wealth politically, there were problems. In order to draw attention to the risk of distributive politics irrespective of 'primordial' identity or ethnic claims, it is pertinent to

[113]Roy, 'New Light', 60, 61.
[114]A.G. Shirreff, *Padmāvatī, of Malik Muhammad Jaisi Calcutta*, 1944, 14.

mention once more Sher's general Khawas Khan. Abu-l Fazl said of him that he extorted money from people with one hand and distributed it with the other in order to gain popularity. There were always several hundred *faqīrs* attached to his household: '*malang* (a kind of Muslim ascetic), *Langotaband* (Hindu ascetics who put on only loincloth), *Yaran-i-Pyara* (also Muslim ascetics), *jogis* and *munis* (Brahmans, exclusively devoted to religion) and *gibrs* (fire worshippers)', who received daily allowances of money, grain and cooked food. Often there were lavish meals with separate menus for Hindus and Muslims. Sufis assembled in his house every Thursday night when there was music. Because of this, there were differences of opinion with the orthodox amongst the Muslim learned 'and disagreement arose with regard to the upholding of the rights of the soldiery'.[115] This case may indicate that indiscriminate distributive practice, ideologically based on heterodox eclecticism, could be found unpalatable by the orthodox '*ulamā* of Islam.

The answer could be to try and avoid an alliance with orthodox Islam, just as Sher Shah tried to avoid all alliances with powerful identities. But an understanding with *zamīndārs* and with Afghan troopers was still essential for him and to ignore the '*ulamā* later in his reign would not be easy for him. There are several questions suggested by Khawas Khan's predicament. What exactly was the price which one paid (and which Sher Shah tried hard to avoid paying) for an alliance in Indian medieval politics? If India's multiplicity of identities represented as many integrative concepts, as many communities of memory and expectation, what chance did Sher Shah stand of transcending this pluriformity? And if he could not altogether avoid all alliances, what channels of communication could he establish, what balance could be struck between allies whose claims clashed with each other? These questions are relevant to Sher Shah's relationship with the learned Islamic community, but they should equally be asked with reference to his attitude towards the Rajputs of Central India with whom he would clash in a dramatic way.[116]

[115]Siddiqui, *Sher Shah Sur*, 76–9. See also N.B. Roy, 'Some Interesting Anecdotes of Sher Shah from the Rare Persian ms. of Tazkirat-ul-Mulk', *Journal of the Asiatic Society, Letters* 20, 1954, 226.

[116]These themes are explored in later chapters of Kolff, *Naukar, Rajput and Sepoy*, in particular Sher Shah's relationship to Silhadi, the commander in Central India.

2

The Turko-Mongol Theory of Kingship*

Ram Prasad Tripathi

The Chaghtai conqueror Bābar came to India with ideas that were not quite similar to those of either the early Turkish rulers of Delhi or the Afghans. Claiming the blood of Changīz Khan and Timūr in his veins Bābar could also claim a system of ideas which reflected the Mughal, the Turkish and the Islamic cultures. By geographical situation, family alliances and political relations the house of Bābar could not but imbibe consciously or unconsciously the traditions and beliefs of all those peoples.

The Turks, the Iranians and the Mongols all considered the position of a sovereign as something higher than simply a leader. The story of the birth of the ancestor of Changīz Khan clearly indicates the element of supernatural origin of his personality. He was, according to the legend, the Son of Light. Such a belief was quite in keeping with the star worship that had continued to prevail among the Mughals down to the fourteenth century if not later. The semi-divine origin of the family of Changīz coupled with the enormous prestige of his success and career had made his house an object of inspiration and awe, and had preserved sovereignty in his family up to the sixteenth century. Sovereignty was regarded as their birthright not on the strength of some vague traditions as was the case with Balban's house, but on actual facts of centuries of history. Such was the spell of the house of Changīz Khan that even Timūr could not venture to break it, and thought it

*Chapter 9 of Part I of R.P. Tripathi, *Some Aspects of Muslim Administration* (first published, Allahabad, 1936).

advisable to exercise full power in the name of a descendant of Changīz and feel contented with the humble title of Amīr or Beg.

The Mughal Khan—the Great Khan—was different from the Khalīfa of Islamic theory. The Great Khan was purely a political and military and not a religious leader. It was no part of his duty to enforce a well-defined and immutable code of divine or quasi-divine system of law as was the case with the Khalīfa. While the Islamic conception of the sovereign hedged the Khalīfa round by the Shari'at Law the Mughal sovereign had no such limitations. He was a political sovereign pure and simple.

It is true that there was a sort of election even among the Mughals in determining the Great Khan but the choice was very narrow and had nothing to do with any spiritual or religious connotations.

Another important feature of the Mughal polity was that of dividing the empire among the princes not on a territorial but tribal basis. The tribes were assigned to them and they were established in the territory inhabited by them. These princes exercised almost full powers of government within their jurisdiction and were practically independent. Theoretically, however, they recognized the suzerainty of the Great Khan who ruled in Mughūlistān—the homeland of the Mughals. The theory had gained reality from the traditions and conventions prevailing among the Mughals.

These were some of the leading ideas that were mixed up with the Islamic theories and practices in the course of time. Although the authenticity and antiquity of the *Malfuzāt-i Timūrī* is not beyond question, they might reasonably be taken to embody the ideas which were believed to be prevailing in the time of Timūr. They unmistakably show the fusion of the Mughal and Islamic ideas that must have taken place by the time of Timūr.

The central point in Timūr's conception of sovereignty was his belief that the various offices in an earthly empire are symbols of those in the Empire of God.[1] This idea was imparted to him by, or at least had the sanction of, Qutb ul-Aqtāb Zainuddin Abu Bakr, his spiritual guide. Timūr believed that 'since God is one and hath no partner, therefore, the viceregent (King) over the land of the Lord must be one'.[2]

[1]Malfuzāt, *Institutes, Political and Military, written originally in the Mogul Language by the Great Timour, improperly called Tamerlane, first translated into Persian by Abu Tauleb al-Hussaini and thence into English with marginal notes by Major Davy,* Oxford, Clarendon Press, 1773. For similar ideas see Hāfiz Ābrū, Oriental and India Office Collections, London, Mss, Or. 2774, f. 3v.

[2]Ibid., 86–8, 228.

Accordingly he lays down that the King must make the people feel that he is not under the influence of anybody.[3] It does not, however, mean that he inculcated the unrestrained use of power. He himself showed considerable regard for his nobles and officials and has emphasized the importance of consulting the wise just as Balban and others had done. But the final decision lay with the sovereign who might or might not follow such counsels.[4]

Timūr was not satisfied with being a purely military and political leader. He was brought up in Islamic traditions, hence he had a religious view of kingly office. With supressed exultation but obvious satisfaction he gives a full copy of the letter (*maktūb*) of the great scholar Mīr Sayyid Sharīf conferring on him the title of the promoter and renovator (*Murawwaj wa mujaddid*) of the religion of Muhammad. He was the eighth of the line of such promoters. In each century there was one. The previous seven in the order of time were Umar 'Abdul 'Aziz, Māmun, Muqtadir Billah, Azaduddaula, Sultan Sanjar, G͟hāzān Khan and Aljaitu Khan.[5] It is significant that the last two Mughal sovereigns and Timūr have been linked in the same chain at one end of which appear the names of the Umayyad and Abbasid Khalīfas. It is also said that both Timūr and Shāhrukh Mirza read the Khutba in their own names in the mosque like some previous Khalīfas.[6]

Under the Timurids the old Mongol custom of dividing tribes among the princes was transformed into a territorial division of the empire. Timūr himself divided his empire among his sons and his practice later on was followed by his successors. Nevertheless the occupant of the throne of Samarkand had some glamour which others lacked but there does not appear to be any reality in it.

In one respect the grandfather of Bābar, Abu Sa'īd Mirza, introduced a great change in the policy of Timūr. Although in practice the Timurids enjoyed full powers and were sovereign in their own jurisdiction, yet in theory they had left the fiction of the ultimate sovereignty of the Great Mughal Khan undisturbed. Abu S'aīd, however, gave a

[3]Ibid., 220–1.

[4]Ibid., 9, 11, 15

[5]Ibid., 178–96

[6]'Abd-ul-Qadir Badauni, *Muntakhab-ut-Tawārīkh*, ed. Ahmad Ali, Kabir-ud-Din Ahmad and W.N. Lees in 3 vols, Calcutta 1864–9. English tr. G.S.A. Ranking (vol. 1), W.H. Lowe (vol. 2) and T. Wolseley Haig (vol. 3) reprint, Delhi, 1973, 268, Niẓām-ud-Dīn Ahmad, *Ṭabaqāt-i Akbarī*, ed. Barun De, 3 vols (vol. 3 revised by M. Hidayat Hosain) Calcutta, 1913, 1927, 1931 and 1935; English tr. by B. De, Calcutta, 1936–7.

rude shock when he said to the Mughal sovereign Yunis Khan: 'The old order of things has been changed, you must now lay aside all your pretensions, that is to say, the mandates will be issued in the name of the dynasty[7] (of Timūr) because, I am Pādshāh in my own right.'[8] This step was resented by the Mughals and aggravated the hostility that they bore to the Timurids. It might be for that reason that Abu S'aīd did not inscribe on the coin any new and high title.[9] In fact he remained contented with the titles of Sultān and Mirza.

As to the women, they exercised enormous powers in the state and there are cases when during a period of interregnum or of the minority or absence of the sovereign they exercised the powers of regency. In this respect they offer a strong contrast with the women of the time of the early Turkish rulers of Delhi. Among the latter normally, the harem exercised little influence, and paradoxical as it might appear they had to their credit Raziyyah who was sovereign in fact and theory. The Mughals while permitting great influence normally to women did not recognize her title to hold sovereignty. This point has been clearly brought out in the letter that Shāh Begum of Badakhshān wrote to Bābar. She said, 'Though I, being a woman, cannot myself attain the sovereignty, yet my grandson Mirza Khān can hold it.'[10] This claim was recognized by Bābar fully.

Like the Ṣafavis, the Timurids did not consider minority a disqualification for attaining sovereignty. Bābar was himself a minor, though the eldest son of his father, when he got the throne. The Mughals of Farghana supported even the claim of Jahāngīr Mirza who was younger than Bābar. They did not show any reluctance to recognize a minor as their sovereign like the early Turks and the Afghans in India.

In the time of Bābar the nobility was very powerful. The nobility and the religious classes both exercised great power in Central Asia. As the early days of Bābar were full of troubles and anxiety it was natural that he should show respect for them. Indeed, at times he had to humiliate himself before them and follow their advice to their satisfaction.

By 1507, Bābar felt it advisable to assume formally the title of *Pādshāh.* He had established himself securely in Kabul, had got an

[7]Mirza Haidar Dughlat, *Tārīkh-i Rashīdī,* English tr. E. Denison Ross, London, 1895–98, 172.

[8]Ibid., 83–4.

[9]S. Lane Poole, *Coins of the British Museum,* London, 1892, vol. x.

[10]*Rashīdī,* 203.

upper hand of the Arghūns[11] and was the best of the surviving descendants of Abu Sa'īd Mirza. The political link between him and the Mongol Khān was cut off and the latter had been thrown into the shade by Shaibāni Khān. By the death of Sultān Husain Baiqara he was left the best representative of the house of Timūr.[12] Besides all these things the necessity for asserting himself had also arisen. The growth of the Ottoman pretensions in the east, the rise of the Safavis in Persia and of the Shaibānids in Mawaraunnahr (Central Asia) were calculated to throw into oblivion the descendants of Timūr who once exercised sway over all of them. The Ottoman Sultan held the title of Qaiṣar, the Ṣafavi of Shāh and the Shaibānids of Sultān. Taking a hint, probably, from the intentions of Abu Sa'īd Mirza, Bābar also assumed the high and distinctive title of Pādshāh.

Bābar's own outlook was more practical and political than religious. Although he had unbounded faith in the will of God and had versified the Islamic law for the guidance of his second son, his memoirs do not show any superstitious and morbid regard either for the schoolmen or the details of the law. The ease with which he could adjust his actions to the wishes of Shāh Isma'īl Safavi is a good example of his general outlook.

As one proud of his ancestry and believing in the inherent right of the Timurids to rule, Bābar was a believer in the hereditary right to sovereignty. In his letter to Sultān Sa'īd regarding the succession to the authority in Badakhshān he laid emphasis on the 'hereditary rights' of the heir.[13] He could not understand and expressed surprise at the custom of Bengal where any person who could kill the ruler, and usurp the throne received the homage of the officials and the people. He was astonished at the theory of the Bengalis: 'We are faithful to the throne; we loyally obey whoever occupies it.'[14]

Unlike some of the great Turkish Sultans of Delhi, Bābar was social and mixed rather freely with his officials. He would even accept social invitations from his officials and would participate in dining, drinking and drugging. He relied on his personal charm and influence rather than on a highly artificial social etiquette. Sometimes he gave audience

[11]L.F. Rushbrook Williams, *An Empire Builder of the Sixteenth Century*, Delhi, 1962, 95.

[12]English tr. A.S. Beveridge, Zahir-ud-Din Muhammad Babur, *Babur-Nama*, London, 1992, i. 344 r.

[13]Ibid., i. 274; *Tarīkh-i Rashīdī* 389; Abu'l Fazl, *Akbar Nāma*, i. 115–16.

[14]Ibid., 482–3.

to foreign envoys in a most informal manner, and he himself says how on one occasion he shouted from the house-top where he was drinking with his private friends, asking an envoy to come up![15]

In his letter to Humāyūn written in 1529, almost at the end of his career, he summed up his final opinions regarding sovereignty: 'No bondage equals that of sovereignty; retirement matches not with rule.'[16] He advised him to 'take counsel and settle every word and act in agreement with well-wishers.' Bābar himself acted accordingly. These ideas were not very different from those of his predecessors in India, but in that letter there was one statement that had a strong flavour of Central Asia. Referring to the probable dispute between Humāyūn and Kāmrān he says that 'the rule had always been adhered to that when thou hadst six parts Kāmrān had five'.[17] Personally, however, so far as the sovereign power (*pādshāhi*) was concerned, Bābar did not like the idea of the division of authority. On one occasion during the Kabul period he had remarked that 'partnership in rule is a thing unheard of'.[18] In spite of his political experience Bābar seems to have failed to see that territorial divisions between princes and the maintenance of sovereign authority over the whole do not match well and kept the state in perpetual tension. The early Turkish rulers and the Afghan rulers of Delhi, excepting Bahlūl, fully realized the dangers inherent in the policy. It did not always work well even in Central Asia and there were no better chances for it in India.

The Timurids were free from any belief in the legal superiority of the Khalīfa, dead or living. The position of the first four Khalīfas was however different. They had come to enjoy an extraordinary place in Muslim thought. They had acquired a semi-religious and sanctified position never attained by any Khalīfa of any dynasty. Their name on the coins indicated nothing more than a respect to their memory and an act of piety. Moreover, by the time Bābar conquered India even the nominal Khalīfa of Egypt had disappeared. That the Timurids could ever aceept any position of inferiority to the Ottoman Sultan was entirely out of the question. Indeed, they considered themselves superior to the Ottomans.

The succession of Humāyūn had in its background an interesting episode. Nizāmuddin Khalīfa, the Vazīr of Bābar, was suspected of

[15]Ibid., 402. The envoy was Darvish Muhammad.
[16]Ibid., 625–7.
[17]Ibid.
[18]Ibid., 293.

some grievance against Humāyūn and therefore is said to have intrigued to raise to the throne Mahdi Khwāja, a brother-in-law of Bābar. Mahdi Khwāja was reported to have uttered in a monologue words signifying his intention to kill Khalīfa on coming to the throne. On hearing his remarks Khalīfa changed his mind, ordered Mahdi to be interned, and calling Humāyūn from Sambhal raised him to the throne. Bābar called in the high officials and made them offer their homage to Humāyun.[19] If Humāyūn had been really superseded a very dangerous precedent would have been created quite in the infancy of the Mughal empire and would have proved a source of endless troubles. The recognition of Humāyun, the eldest son of Bābar, was a happy begining and might have led to healthy traditions if the course of events that followed had not weakened its force.

The Mughal principle of the division of the empire was put to a test soon after the death of Bābar. There was no great difficulty felt at the beginning regarding the theoretical position of the sovereign. Humāyun was unanimously recognized by the Mughals as the successor of Bābar to the sovereignty of Delhi; and the *khutba* was read and coins were struck in his name. The practical question, however, was the way in which the empire was to be divided between the brothers. Should the same proportion of six to five hinted at by Bābar be maintained?

For the first time the experiment of division was seriously tried in India. It must at once be recognized that the conditions under which the experiment was made were very unfavourable. The Mughal empire had not yet gained a firm and strong footing in India and its enemies were yet very powerful and threatened to destroy it. But the tradition of the Mughals and even the wishes of Bābar were there. There was practically no escape out of it. The division was made. Askari and Hindāl Mirza were comparatively moderate in their ambitions but Kāmrān insisted on the lion's share and got it. No other Sultan of Delhi would have tolerated such an arrangement, and the perplexity exhibited by Humāyun indicates that he too was nervous.

In the early stages nothing untoward happened. Apparently things appeared to be getting on well. The *khutba* was read in the name of Humāyun in Delhi, Kabul and Ghazni. The plan was not very likely to succeed. If it had succeeded, then a possible solution might have been found out of the evil that took a violent form in the later days of Shāhjahān

[19]Abul Fazl, *Akbar-Nāma*, ed. H. Blochmann, 3 vols, Calcutta, 1873–87, English tr. H. Beveridge, reprint, Delhi, 1977, I, 117.

and after the death of Aurangzeb. The wars of succession would not have been then so bitter as to paralyse the Mughal empire.

As the difficulties of Humāyūn increased in volume the hollowness of the arrangement became more and more visible. After his final defeat at the hands of Sher Shāh, Humāyūn thought of falling back upon Badakhshān. But Kāmrān refused to permit him to pass through Kabul on the grounds that it had been given by Bābar to his (Kāmrān's) mother. Humāyūn was thunderstruck at this reply and urged that Bābar had specifically declared his intention not to give Kabul to anybody for all his sons were born there.[20] It was then that Humāyūn must have realized that the division of the empire meant something more than simply an administrative arrangement. The final blow was given when Hindāl was also obliged by Kāmrān after a siege of four months to drop the name of Humāyūn and insert his name in the *khutba* at Qandahar also,[21] in spite of the attempts of Bābar's respected sister. Thus the first and the last experiment of the Mughals to introduce the principle of division of authority broke down in India.

Humāyūn had a mystic bent of mind, and as such probably believed that the phenomenal world was only a shadow of the reality that the human eye cannot ordinarily see. He had also faith in astrology like many a Timurid. As a Muslim he also believed that the king was the shadow of God on earth and therefore was expected to do within his sphere what God did in relation to his creation.

The cumulative effect of all those ideas resulted in a theory that was reflected in the institutions evolved out by him. He believed that just as the sun was the centre of the material world, similarly the King whose destiny was closely associated with that great luminary,[22] was the centre of the human world. Accordingly, he constituted the servants of the state in 12 orders, of which he himself was the centre.[23] A tent with 12 divisions corresponding to the signs of the zodiac was constructed to symbolize the lattices through which the light of Empire shone.[24] In all this he might have drawn inspiration from the institutions of the Mughals and Timūr, or even from the ideas of the Shi'as.

[20]Gulbadan Begum, *Humāyūn Nāma*, ed. and tr. A.H. Beveridge, London, 1902, 147.

[21]Ibid., 161–2

[22]Khwand Mir, *Humāyūn Nāma*, British Museum, Mss. Nos. Or 5850 and 1762, ed. and published as *Qānūn-i Humāyūnī* by M.H. Hosain, Calcutta, English tr. B. Prasad.

[23]Khwand Mīr, *Humāyūn Nāma*.

The most glaring manifestation of his ideas was during his stay at Gaur where he introduced a new form of Court etiquette. In Bengal he used to cast a veil over his crown, and when he removed it the people used to say, 'Light has shone forth!' He also washed his sword in the river and said, 'Upon whom shall I gird the sword'.[25]

This manifestation led some people to believe that Humāyun claimed divinity, and when he was in Persia he was taunted for his pretensions.[26]

The early Turks believed in the theory that the King was the shadow of God on earth. But no one seems to have given so much emphasis to it as Humāyun. His first official historian, Khwand Mir, calls him a personification of the spiritual and temporal sovereignty (*Jām'ai Sultanati Haqīqī va Majāzī*)[27] and, his Majesty the King, the shadow of God (*Hazrati Pādshāh Zill-i-Ilāhī*).[28] He was believed to receive institutions and inspiration from God (*Ilhāmāti Rubbāni va Vāridāti Subhānī*).[29] His rival Sher Shāh also appears to have believed that his mind received special suggestions and directions from God.[30] The latter had better justification to think so than the former! With all this there is little wonder that Abul Fazl in his exuberance uses the word *insān-i kāmil*, or the perfect man, for him.[31]

In the whole range of the Muslim history of India, there is hardly anything more amusing and significant than the transfer of sovereign power for a few hours[32] to the water-carrier who saved the life of Humāyūn. Gulbadan who was then old enough to understand things,

[24] *Akbar Nāma*, Beveridge, 361.

[25] Badaoni, Ranking, 573.

[26] Badaoni, loc. cit., *Afzal-ul-Tawārikh* gives a letter of Shah Tahmāsp where a reference to such pretensions is found. Br. M., 4678 f., 193 v.

[27] Kh. Mir, *Humāyūn Nāma*, Or., 1762 f., 126 r.

[28] Kh. Mir, *Hamāyūn Nāma*, f. 133 r.

[29] Kh. Mir, *Humāyūn Nāma*, f. 133v. Also see *Akbar Nāma*, I, 120.

[30] This can be clearly inferred from the anecdotes given in Abdullah's *Tārīkh-i-Dāudī*, British Museum, Ms. Nos. Or. 1701 and 197, ed. I.H. Siddiqi, Aligarh, 1969.

[31] *Akbar Nāma*.

[32] Gulbadan, 140, says two days. Jauhar Aftabchi, *Tazkirat-ul-Waqiat*, British Museum Ms. 16711, English tr. Charles Stewart, reprint, Delhi, 1970, f. 25v. Stewart 19, says two hours (*Sā't*). Whatever be the duration the fact of transfer is there. The sovereign according to Muslim theory cannot transfer his sovereign right to any man or assembly, B.D. Macdonald, *Development of Muslim Theology, Jurisprudence and Constitutional Theory*, London, 1903.

and was present at Agra says that Humāyūn made the water-carrier actually sit on the throne and 'ordered all the Amirs to make obeisance to him. The servant gave everyone what he wished and made appointments (*manṣab*)'. This strange expression of gratitude involved a principle that had no justification in the Islamic law or precedent among the Timurids or rulers of Delhi. It implied that sovereignty was a personal property of the *pādshāh* who could bestow it upon anybody or do with it as he pleased. It was not approved by Kāmrān, and Hindāl did not attend the Court of the water-carrier, the former being ill and the latter having gone to Alwar. What 'Askari did we do not know. Probably he attended it like other Timurid nobles. The event itself though of no practical importance is significant enough of the attitude of Humāyūn towards the sovereign power. Indirectly it brought to light the nature of the interpretation that Humāyūn put upon the idea of hereditary right.

In spite of the grand notions of Humāyūn regarding the position of the *pādshāh* and his expectations of receiving absolute obedience from the nobles, the latter on more than one occasion forced their will on him. The first occasion was in Bengal when Humāyūn found himself stranded there owing to the activities of Sher Shah in his rear. Supported by 'Askari the officers obliged Humāyūn to augment their regiments, increase their stipend, and advance a large sum of money in hard cash.[33] Even when Humāyun's days of adversity were over and Kāmrān was a prisoner in his custody the nobles offered him a bold front. As Humāyun seemed to be unwilling to inflict drastic punishment on Kāmrān, they told him plainly that they had suffered long enough for him and were no more prepared to see their wives and children in captivity or under torture.[34] 'The matter had passed beyond bounds, it could no longer be coped with.'[35] In spite of Humāyūn's evasions the officers remained 'firm in their request'. Humāyūn then asked them to put down their demands in writing. They asked for the execution of Kāmrān, and supported their demand with legal opinions. Humāyūn did not go to that extent but had at least to order Kāmrān to be blinded.

After Humāyūn had disposed of his brothers he commended to his men the ideal which the followers of Shāh Isma'īl Safavi had placed

[33]Jauhar, 14–15.

[34]Gulbadan, 201. See also *Tabaq. Akb.*, 165 r. Jauhar, though not so explict refers to the matter, Br. M. Ms., f. 121 v., Stewart (104).

[35]*Akbar Nāma*, Beveridge, I, 603.

before them. They were so loyal that they 'flung themselves from a skyhigh mountain to seize his (Shāh's) handkerchief'.[36] Humāyūn did not realize that Shāh Isma'īl had enjoyed a religious status and a national position that no Timurid could claim from his subjects. Not long after he was made to realize the difference when his officers objected to go with him to Kashmir on military and political grounds. When they found Humāyūn determined they deserted him so completely that he was compelled to abandon his intention and return to Kabul.[37]

Like his father and the Surs, Humāyūn was not willing to recognize any power politically superior to him. He however, did not assume the title of Khalīfa. Although in Mecca and Medina the Khutba was read in the name of the Ottoman Sultan, he, like his father, did not attach any importance to it. Humāyūn had not forgotten the humility to which Bāyazīd Ildiram was reduced by Timūr. In fact he had cited the incident in one of his bombastic letters to Bahādur Shah of Gujarat. In his last days when the Turkish Admiral Sidi 'Ali Rais praised before him the power and dignity of the Ottoman Sultan, Humāyūn expressed his utter indifference and complete surprise.[38] Though he did not object to Sidi Rais praying for his sovereign in a Friday prayer, the incident was so insignificant that no one except the loyal Admiral took notice of it!

[36]*Akbar Nāma*, Beveridge, I, 557.

[37]A.N. I, 330, *Tabaq. Akb.*, p. 165 r. Jauhar, Charles Stewart, *Private Memorirs of the Moghul Emperor Humayun by Jouhar* (English tr.) London 1832, reprint, Delhi 1970, 107.

[38]Sidi Ali Reis, *Travels and Adventures of a Turkish Admiral (1553–1556)* English tr. A. Vambéry, London, 1899, 51–3. Sidi 'Ali makes Humāyun say (what he hardly would have said) 'that the ruler of Turkey was the only man worthy to bear the title of Pādshā ... he alone and no one else in the world'.

3
The Formulation of Imperial Authority under Akbar and Jahangir*

J.F. Richards

Introduction

After AD 1720 the Mughal empire was no longer a tightly centralized political entity. Muhammad Shah (AD 1719–48) and his successors could no longer freely command the flow of money, goods, information and personnel to and from the capital nor direct the inter- and intra-provincial movement of these entities, Nevertheless, in spite of its sudden political collapse, the legacy of the imperial system remained. The imperial model for concentration and power retained its compelling appeal for Marathas, Jats, Rajputs, Sikhs, and ultimately the British. The expansion, and consolidation, of the empire had irrevocably reordered human relationships throughout the subcontinent in virtually every aspect of society.

As late as the first years of the nineteenth century, the Mughal agrarian order decayed, but still recognizable, offered a rationale and techniques for recognition and assimilation of aristocracies rooted in local control of land and peasants. The imperial land tax structure still set limits, levels and acceptable modes of assessment and collection for the state's share of agrarian production. Under the East India Company and the princely states the Mughal currency system flourished in its essential metrology, bi-metallic composition, coin types, and minting system. Mughal courtly rituals, etiquette, terminology, honorific symbols, etc. retained their appeal in virtually every region. Imperial aes-

*From J.F. Richards, ed., *Kingship and Authority in South Asia* (Madison: University of Wisconsin South Asian Studies, 1978).

thetic standards in painting, calligraphy, literature, architecture, still provided a cultural reference point. Imperial techniques for the management, recruitment and control of military élites continued to have great influence. Debased and distorted Mughal numerical ranks, and the ubiquitous *jāgīr* or lands assigned for salaries and troop maintenance were utilized by Rajput and French rulers alike.

Most dramatic of these survivals was the continuing near-monopoly of the later Mughal emperors over the dispensation of legitimate authority in the form of Mughal offices, ranks and honours. The downward movement of these rights, in the absence of a centralized political order (as Stewart Gordon has shown), is one of the continuing aspects of high politics in the eighteenth century. As is well known, the East India Company found it useful to perpetuate the fiction of Mughal supremacy as late as 1857. The tenacity with which the imperial myth of authority retained its fascination, and utility for the tough, calculating politicians, military leaders and kings of eighteenth- and early nineteenth-century India is somewhat baffling. Nonetheless, such longevity does suggest that for a very long period of time, as much as a century or more, imperial authority, embodied in the Emperor, systematically destroyed and/or assimilated to it all competing sources of legitimate rule. Only in exceptional circumstances did the rebel Bhonsle Maratha dynasty (prior to 1689) and the Sikh Khalsa rise independently. On the one hand, this is perhaps only stating the obvious: that an imperial structure existed before 1720. On the other hand, it raises the central issue behind the truly impressive achievements of the 'Great Mughals'. Why and how were the Mughal Emperors able to create a system of symbols, and rituals necessary for a pervasive network of authoritative, hierarchical relationships? Why and how did this authority system develop so firmly that it allowed the Emperors to mobilize the active energies of the imperial political elect, i.e. the nobility and their military followers, the burgeoning civil service, and other official groups such as the '*ulama* in state employment? Preceding Indo-Muslim dynasties in north India failed in precisely this area. The Afghan Lodi rulers were never able to overcome satisfactorily fissiparous tendencies among their nobles and fellow tribesmen.

Akbar, after surviving at least one attempted coup and two concerted rebellions (in 1567 and 1579–80), fashioned new relationships between himself and his military/administrative élite. In part, Akbar succeeded by a careful balancing of old and new ethnic groups as he rapidly expanded his cadre of army commanders and administrators to keep pace with the speed of territorial conquest.[1] But Akbar's political achievement was far more difficult than the simple balancing of ethnic and factional interests within the élite.[2] He and his advisers successfully shaped a new individual and group identity: that of the imperial *mansabdār* or *amīr*, i.e. a military commander and imperial administrator. The wealth, powers, status and lifestyle of the *amīr* or noble became and remained a pervasive model of secular attainment for ambitious, able, men whether rajas, lineage chiefs, aristocratic Muslim migrants to India or even peripatetic European adventurers.

Akbar carefully fostered the inherited advantages of his own personality. A complex mixture of acute intelligence, great sensitivity and warmth, and an easy, yet never abandoned dignity marked his overwhelming appeal as a political leader. His open style was remarkable for an Indo-Muslim autocrat. As Father Monserrate observed:[3]

> It is hard to exaggerate how accessible he [Akbar] makes himself to all who wish audience of him. For he creates an opportunity almost every day for any of he common people or of the nobles to see him and to converse with him; and he endeavours to show himself pleasant-spoken and affable rather than severe toward all who come to speak with him. It is very remarkable how great an effect this courtesy and affability has in attaching him to the minds of his subjects.

By a series of symbolic acts, Akbar built upon his personal appeal to establish an image or metaphor of the Emperor's person as an embodiment of the Empire. To challenge or destroy the Emperor's person was

[1] cf. Iqtidar Alam Khan, 'The Nobility Under Akbar and the Development of His Religious Policy, 1560–1580', *Journal of the Royal Asiatic Society* (1968), pp. 29–36.

[2] S.A.A. Rizvi in his recent *Religious and Intellectual History of the Muslims in Akbar's Reign* (New Delhi, 1975), has been the first scholar to notice and to discuss the intellectual connections between the ideology of illumined descent set forth in the *Akbar-Nama* and the doctrines of the most important Iranian philosophical schools. However, the great significance of Professor Rizvi's finding has not yet been fully understood or recognized. Partly this is due to less than full development of the argument and partly to difficulties with the organization of the volume as a set of topical essays.

[3] António Monserrate, *Commentary*, tr. and ed. J.S. Hoyland and S.N. Banerji (London, 1922), p. 197. Monserrate also noted that Akbar 'is especially remarkable for his love of keeping great crowds of people around him and in his sight and thus it comes about that his court is always thronged with multitudes of men of every type, though especially with the nobles …'. Ibid., p. 198.

to challenge or destroy the imperial system, for they were identical. In furthering this metaphor, Akbar (or his advisers) established a degree of paramount spiritual authority for the Emperor unprecedented in previous Indo-Muslim experience. This assertion merged with the recognized familial charisma residing in direct descent from the Timurid line which, for Muslims at least, connoted legitimate monarchy. All of these elements were eventually expressed by Abul Fazl in a dynastic ideology which explicitly set out Akbar's infallible, unchallengeable authority.

Glorification of the Emperor's person in this manner provided a basis for more intense, emotive ties with the imperial nobility. The latter increasingly felt a sense of direct, personal obligation to the Emperor. The ruler and his élite shared a complex Indo-Persian etiquette and ritual which delimited and patterned transactions of authority and subordination. Over time, *amīrs* and even lesser commanders and administrators displayed similar, predictable, responses to the rituals and symbols of imperial authority. By the time Jahangir, who followed his father's policies, completed his 22-year reign, in 1627, the system was firmly set. Younger generations, sons of nobles anticipating imperial service from childhood, were readily assimilated into the imperial élite.

From an external perspective, the bureaucratic structure of the empire with its specialized offices, systematic procedures, and hierarchies of technically proficient officials, was the most impressive aspect of the empire. However, the core of the imperial system embedded within the outer structure was formed by the complex matrix of ties of loyalty and interest between the *amīrs* and the Emperor.

However, the system could only have succeeded by transforming the values of high-status warrior-aristocrats of diverse origins. The sense of honour for each *amīr* had to shift from personal, lineage, or sectarian pride—that of the 'free' warrior chief—to a more impersonal, imperial pride—that of the 'slave' warrior—administrator. In this transformation the search for the display of martial honour necessarily changed from bardic or epic glory immortalizing feats of victory (or defeat) in battle, to chronicled fame testifying to service of the Empire and its Master. Honour in the latter case also became advancement, i.e. the greater honour of promotion or movement nearer to the person of the Emperor. Honour found in unconditional service and obedience was a salient characteristic of the new role for an imperial commander. The sense of discretionary personal honour of the warrior-aristocrat, leader of a lineage group or war band, obviously did not disappear altogether, but its subordination to a less parochial concern within the imperial context was generally assured.

The Public Image

In common with all gifted political leaders, Akbar, from his earliest days of independent rule (i.e. from about 1560), virtually intuitively, presented to various social groups and tested for responses facets of his public personality. Akbar's personal behaviour and traits evolved coterminously with his strategic and administrative policies. The sixteenth-century version of political reporters and analysts: courtiers, nobles at court, agents of nobles and *mansabdārs* sent to the imperial audiences, agents of tributary rajas or of mercantile houses; spies of as yet unconquered regional kingdoms, all carefully watched every perceived and reported action or speech of the Emperor. Close, unremitting public scrutiny (aided by Akbar's inclination towards open accessibility) gave the young Emperor an opportunity to create an image of certain, absolute (but not capricious) power. Gradually, by a series of symbolic actions undertaken during the first two decades of his mature reign, he underscored the fact that no minister, no noble, nor any group could challenge or limit that authority. After 1580, with the entrance of Abul Fazl to the select group of the Emperor's closest advisers, the Emperor's approach shifted towards a more didactic, verbally expressed ideology.

One of Akbar's earliest public expressions of his intended autonomy emerged from his decision not to make Delhi the imperial capital. Instead he embarked upon an extensive programme of urban construction and fortification. For two and a half centuries Delhi had been the unassailable redoubt, the refuge for Indian Muslims and the seat of the Sultans of Hindustan. By moving first from Delhi to Agra, and later to his own capital at Fatehpur Sikri (as shown below) Akbar reduced existing associations of legitimate rulership with Delhi. Neither Akbar nor a possible rebel henceforth could easily claim the imperial throne by virtue of possession of the citadels, the palaces, or the active support of the volatile populace of the old imperial city.

For more than 15 years, Akbar diverted much of his resources towards the building of three massive palace-fortresses: Agra, defending the gateway to central Hindustan; Allahabad (formerly Prayag), commanding the eastern Gangetic valley; and Lahore, capital of the Panjab and a Muslim military base since Ghaznavid times. The Emperor and his builders and architects designed walls and battlements of dressed stone construction running thousands of yards to encircle each city and its palace and citadel (e.g. at Agra the 'enclosure wall ... consists of a solid sandstone rampart just under seventy feet in height and nearly one and a half miles in circuit').[4] The elaborate array of palace and official buildings placed within each fortress allowed the Emperor to move freely and comfortably with his household and central administration from one to the other city as political or military considerations demanded direct supervision or command. To complete the new imperial strategic pattern, Akbar designed a smaller, but strongly defended, fort at Ajmer, the northern gateway to Rajasthan. Ajmer fort became the headquarters for the Mughal governor of the directly controlled districts in Rajasthan, and defender of the plain against possible future Rajput revolts. Finally, older fortifications at the extremities of the northern plains were strengthened. Attock and Rohtas forts (built by Sher Shah Sur) on the Indus and Jhelum rivers guarded the northwest trunk route to Lahore, while the identically named Rohtas fort, served as a major stronghold in the eastern Gangetic valley.

Akbar firmly broke with the Delhi-centred political tradition in 1571, when he selected a site for a new imperial capital at Sikri, a village located some 20 miles from Agra. Renamed Fatehpur Sikri, the new capital, despite its characteristic red sandstone battlements, was primarily a courtly city—essentially dependent upon the proximity of Agra for economic and military support. Akbar's meticulous concern (continuing for well over a decade) for site selection, for the spatial arrangement of buildings and streets, for the distinctive shared style of building architecture in red sandstone has long been seen as an aesthetic effort of great appeal and near-genius.[5] However, the city was also a firm political statement and symbol of the new order. The uniform architecture, and configuration of streets and public buildings designed only for the needs of centralized rule and administration, proclaimed the Emperor's personal and dynastic supremacy. Enclosed within the walls, adjacent to and dependent upon the palace rose the great public mosque of the city, an integral part of the urban plan. So also did the tomb of Shaikh Salim Chishti, a Sufi mystic and recluse who, before his death, had often met and discussed spiritual questions with the Emperor (as noted below). Thus, the new capital contained both a great congregational mosque and the tomb (*dargāh*) of a widely revered, still-

[4]See Percy Brown, *Indian Architecture* (Islamic Period) (Bombay, 1968 5th edn.), pp. 92–6 for a description of these structures. Unlike Lahore, Agra, or Allahabad, Fatehpur Sikri 'was never intended to be of any strategic value being purely a ceremonial capital', (p. 94).

[5]cf. S.A.A. Rizvi, 'Mughal Town Planning Fathpur Sikri: A Case Study', *Abr-Nahrain*, XV, pp. 98–112.

worshipped Sufi saint—the binary institutions of legal and mystic Indian Islam.

Within the city, the single most dramatic symbol of Akbar's autocratic rule extant is the interior design of the arcaded audience chamber (the *Dīwān-i Khāss*) intended for more restricted court audiences (as opposed to the *Dīwān-i 'Amm*, the Hall of Public Audience). At the precise centre of the two-storey open hall stands a massive pillar and platform carved of red sandstone.[6] Towards the top of the great column a vertical series of three carved circular brackets (or corbelling) begin radiating outward. The uppermost (and largest) bracket supports the heavy square platform. From this square platform diagonal passageways, guarded by carved railings, reach to the four corners of the hall. Whether, in actuality, Akbar used the so-called 'throne' platform as a throne support or not, or whether, as local legend has it, he sat on his throne beneath the great pillar, is unimportant. The pillar dominates the physical space of the grand audience hall just as Akbar dominated the new political and social space of the empire in the sixteenth century.

Choosing Sikri as a site also underscored the young Emperor's widely noted mystical affinities—a tendency which would later buttress his assertion of spiritual authority. The village of Sikri was the residence of Shaikh Salim, whom Akbar frequently visited, for, as Abul Fazl puts it, there existed 'a bond of union between them'.[7] Such marked attraction between these two powerful figures must have attracted considerable popular attention. Obviously, Akbar, a young, vigorous and victorious Emperor created a sense of drama in virtually all his actions. Shaikh Salim was renowned as 'one of the greatest Shaikhs of Hind, and a high master of the different stages of the advancement in the knowledge of God'.[8]

[6]E.W. Smith, *The Mogul Architecture of Fathpur Sikri*, Archaeological Survey of India, *Annual Reports*, XVII and XVIII (4 vols) (1895–96), I., p. 22 and plates. This work contains a description, scaled drawings and plans, and plates for each of the remaining edifices of the city. The frontispiece to vol. I is a much reproduced plan of the city's remains. A more readily accessible colour plate of the throne pillar may be found in Bamber Gascoigne, *The Great Moghuls* (London, 1971), p. 102. A small accompanying inset photograph shows the arrange-ment of the four diagonal passageways intersecting at the top of the pillar.

[7]'Abd-ul-Qadir Badauni, *Muntakhab-ut-Tawārīkh*, ed. Ahmad Ali et al., 3 vols Calcutta, 1864–69; trans. T.W. Haig et al., reprint, Delhi, 1973–83 I., p. 112 (translation).

[8]Ibid., I., p. 140.

Recognition by the Shaikh implied, at least, the validity of Akbar's mystical concerns. The latter is also inherent in the seeming intensity of Akbar's religious struggle. Two publicly reported mystic episodes took the external appearance of trance-like seizures associated with the hunt. The earliest, in early adulthood, apparently arose from Akbar's unanticipated solitude in the desert. The second, in mid-life occurred in 1578, when the court was engaged in the mass slaughter of all quarry within a ring fence (a *gamargha* hunt prepared by beaters days in advance of the event). Suddenly, the Emperor experienced 'the sublime joy' of the 'attraction (*jazaba*) of the cognition of God', in Abul Fazl's terms or 'a strange state and strong frenzy' in the words of a hostile critic.[9] Upon recovery, Akbar immediately forbade the killing of those animals surviving. Later he proclaimed that on certain days the slaughter of animals was to be prohibited. He also cut his hair in the style of an ascetic.[10]

In the long-prevailing Sufi tradition of pastoral concern, Shaikh Salim also counselled Akbar in regard to the aspiring dynast's most vexing problem: his inability to produce a live male heir from among his wives. Finally, when Shaikh Salim foretold the birth of the long-awaited first prince of the line, the grateful Emperor named his son Salim (later the Emperor Jahangir). After Shaikh Salim died in 1571, Akbar selected Sikri for his new capital, renaming it Fatehpur Sikri, or 'Place of Victory'. To preserve his mentor's memory, the Emperor directed construction of a carved white marble tomb within the courtyard of the great public mosque at Fatehpur. The tomb, located at what had become a busy imperial metropolis, rapidly became a major pilgrimage site (*dargāh*) for worship of Shaikh Salim as a saint.[11]

By thus emplacing Shaikh Salim's tomb within the walls of the Fatehpur Sikri mosque, Akbar was able to draw upon that perceptible sanctity adhering to it, and to assimilate this to his own authority. Moreover, he did not permit Shaikh Salim's sons to succeed him, nor even to retain control over and management of the newly established *dargāh* and its enormous potential for secular profit and spiritual status. Instead, in another measure of incorporation, Akbar strongly encouraged

[9] Abul Fazl, *Akbar-Nama*, tr. H. Beveridge, 3 vols. reprint (Delhi, 1977) II, pp. 348–56. Badauni, II, p. 261. The earlier incident occurred when Akbar was hunting wild asses in the desert (see Abul Fazl, *Akbar-Nama*, II, p. 522.)

[10] Abul Fazl, *Akbar-Nama*, II, p. 356.

[11] Badauni, I, p. 140. The tomb is one of the finest extant examples of Mughal building.

the sons and grandsons to enlist in his service as *mansabdārs.* Several of these men, attaining high ranks, provided exceptional service for the empire, while continuing to retain an aura of spiritual distinction as descendants of Shaikh Salim.[12] Perhaps the most distinguished member of this group was the general and governor Islam Khan Chishti, architect of the early seventeenth-century Mughal conquests in Bengal, under Jahangir. As governor and conqueror in distant Bengal, Islam Khan began challenging Jahangir's imperial authority by adopting various royal perquisites (e.g. the 'viewing', or *jharoka*, of the governor on a balcony at set times of day by the general populace). In part, Islam Khan felt he could challenge the spiritual aspect of the Emperor's inherited, illumined authority by citing his own descent from Shaikh Salim.[13] The latter point implies, at least, that Akbar's own connection with the incorporation of a leading family of the Chishtiyya was of some importance to him, in that he could assimilate and share the mystical qualities of that family.

The Emperor extended his ties with the Chishtiyya to other sections of the order. Since 1562, he had regularly visited the sacred tomb of the founder of the Chishtiyya order, Khwaja Muinuddin Chishti at Ajmer.[14] In 1570, fulfilling the terms of a vow made prior to the birth of his son, Akbar walked the 228-mile distance from Agra to Ajmer to worship at the tomb and to give thanks for his gift. However, when bitter, open quarrels broke out among the supposed descendants of the Khwaja over division of the Emperor's gifts to the shrine, Akbar reacted much as he did with the corrupt official *'ulama* of his administration: he ordered an investigation. The legitimacy of these descendants proving to be dubious, he expelled them, seized control of the shrine and appointed an imperial *mansabdār* as superintendent. This officer was to utilize the gifts and income of the tomb for proper charitable purposes such as the repair and maintenance of mosques, or other such enterprises.[15] That Akbar's interest in the Chishtiyya originated in genuine religious concerns, his frequent pilgrimages leave little doubt; that he was able to make use of control over two major Chishtiyya

[12] Rizvi, *Religious and Intellectual History*, pp. 182–3.

[13] See Jadunath Sarkar (ed.), *History of Bengal, Muslim Period, 1200–1750* (Patna, 1973 reprint edn), p. 282.

[14] For one of Akbar's first visits to Ajmer in 1562, see Abul Fazl, *Akbar-Nama*, II, p. 243.

[15] Abul Fazl, *Akbar-Nama*, II, pp. 510–11.

shrines and his growing influence over members of the order in an ongoing ideological struggle with the orthodox *'ulama* is also likely.

Certainly, association with the Chishtiyya, one of the most well-regarded Sufi orders of north India, must have added to Akbar's political appeal and his own popular reputation as a mystic. Thus, by 1590, when Abul Fazl began a systematic affirmation of Akbar's claim to universal authority in the *Akbar-Nama*, he included an anecdote which indirectly stated Akbar's superiority over even the most famed Chistiyya saint. In the narrative for the year 1568, Abul Fazl noted that Akbar had made a vow (similar to that made after Salim's birth) that if he could capture the massive Rajput fortress at Chitor, he would walk the full distance from Chitor to Ajmer in order to worship at the tomb of Khwaja Muinuddin. However, soon after the king and his entourage had started out, along the route came a message from the attendants of the shrine (still at that point the purported descendants of Khwaja Muinuddin), saying:[16]

> ... his holiness the Khwaja had appeared in a vision and announced that the spiritual and temporal king [i.e. Akbar] had ... formed the intention of visiting the shrine of his humble self on foot, and had directed them [his living disciples] to restrain the caravan conductor of truths way from his design by every means in their power. If he knew the amount of ḥis own spirituality he would not bestow a glance on me the sitter-in-the-dust of the path of studentship.

By the 1580s Fatehpur Sikri rapidly added the economic functions of a true city. Court income and expenditures, the flow of taxes and tribute, as well as the type of demand usually associated with a major imperial capital, diverted local regional and inter-regional trade from Agra to the new site. Merchants and contractors dependent upon court-generated trade necessarily responded to the new shift by migrating to Fatehpur. Constant building by the grandees of the empire, as well as lesser officials and merchants began to create the appearance of a more spontaneous, less planned urban space. Residential suburbs appeared outside the enclosure walls. Suddenly, however, the Emperor moved his entire court and administration to the palace-fortress at Lahore, presumably to better supervise operations against the Yusufzai, a rebellious Pathan tribe in the Hindu Kush. Not to be reoccupied thereafter, Fatehpur Sikri was gradually deserted leaving its shell in a Pompeii-like effect virtually intact.

[16]Ibid., pp. 476–7.

Whether the threat from the Afghans merited this sudden response on Akbar's part, or whether he moved for a mixture of motives is difficult to determine. It may be that what was becoming a most rigid, set daily court ceremonial, (clearly necessary for the continuing socialization and disciplining of the new nobility being formed), carried out in essentially an artificial urban setting, bore the danger of isolating and eventually incapacitating the Emperor. The Indo-Persian court rituals from which Mughal practices were largely derived, were primarily an elaborate metaphor for overwhelming authority and political stability. But, as such, these reassuring images of unchanging order could confine, circumscribe and, in extreme cases, destroy the ruler.

Any contradictions between a more passive, immobile ceremonial role for the Emperor, and a more aggressive, active role undoubtedly intensified with the enhanced wealth and size of steady territorial growth. Akbar's characteristically innovative solution to this tension was to revert to the ambulatory court camp capital of his Turko-Mongol ancestry. Although every Chaghtai, Timurid ruler and noble was at ease living and moving with tents, the true precedent or model for the Mughal imperial camp must be traced back to the practices of Timur and even earlier to the army encampments of the Mongols.[17] Akbar revived and expanded upon this tradition by devising a mobile capital containing all the necessary parts of the central administration: his household, his official audience and consultation halls, the imperial archives, and chancery; the treasury and mint; the horse stud and elephant stables; field and siege artillery; armouries and powder magazines; court attendants, and bodyguards; kitchens and bazaars; and the larger portion of the central army. Each of the accompanying noble encampments replicated these arrangements on a smaller scale. The gigantic size and precise organization of the imperial camp capital was a source of amazement and a staple description for those foreign travellers or visitors reporting back to their European or Middle Eastern homelands.

Akbar's camp, after his departure from Fatehpur Sikri in 1585, became a mobile version of that capital. Instead of dressed stone, the camp contained structures of canvas tenting, timber, supports, rope, thousands of yards of cloth passageways, and rich carpeting and hangings. Moreover, each tent and structural component was duplicated so that a second camp could be sent on ahead for assembly and erection

[17]Ruy González de Clavijo, *Narrative of the Embassy to the Court of Timour*, trans. and ed. C.R. Markham, Hakluyt Society, no. 26 (London, 1856), pp. 140–63, *passim*.

in preparation for occupancy at the end of the day's march. Clearly, this giant organism was far different in its conception and use than the fast-moving military column which Father Monserrate accompanied on Akbar's march toward Kabul in 1579.[18] In the slower-moving court-camp the Emperor placed his residence pavilion, unvaryingly at the centre of the east end of a rectangle running along an east–west axis some 1500 yards in length. Akbar occupied a two-storeyed red-dyed canvas structure, the highest in the camp. The residence area was surrounded by a cloth-walled, screened enclosure, 150 yards square. Inside this royal space the Emperor had reception facilities for private consultations with his seniormost officers, ambassadors or other dignitaries. All of the Emperor's tents were dyed scarlet, the Timurid and, previously, the Sasanian royal colours.[19] The next westward segment of the formal encampment was alloted to enclosed and closely guarded harem tents. The third section towards the west provided space for a gigantic audience tent and its elevated throne. When closed, the audience tent was the *Dīwān-ī Khāss* or 'select' audience hall, when opened, it extended to an uncovered roped area to accommodate the largest public audiences (i.e. the *Dīwān-ī 'Amm*).[20] Finally, at the western border of the enclosure, the various official administrative tents housing the treasury, etc. were placed.

Tents for the princes and most distinguished nobles were pitched at alloted distances within the royal enclosure respectively on the right and left sides of the Emperor's quarters. Other nobles erected their residence structures and cover for their entourages in sites determined by their rank, and current favour at court, surrounding and facing the

[18]On the march to Kabul, the Mughal grand army was scarcely encumbered by the paraphernalia of the courtly camp. As Father Monserrate commented: 'He [Akbar] carried those black standards, the sign of war to the death, which Timur the Lame—ancestor of the Mongol kings—had been wont to employ in his wars.' Monserrate, *Commentary*, p. 73.

[19]Clavijo, *Narrative*, p. 145. cf. G. Widengren, 'The Sacral Kingship of Iran', International Congress for the History of Religions, *La Regalita Sacra* (Leiden, 1959), p. 254. 'The king's proper dress was red, thus associating him with the class of warriors, for red was the colour of this class in Indo-European society ...'.

[20]See Abul Fazl, *Ain-i Akbari*, Blochmann trans., I, p. 47 ff. for a description and drawings of the layout of the encampment. M.A. Ansari, in *Social Life of the Mughal Emperors (1526–1707)*, has compiled from the *Ain-i Akbari* and other sources a more detailed and comprehensive plan and description, Ansari, pp. 201–2.

royal enclosed rectangle. On the outer perimeter of the court-camp were various bodies of troops, bodyguards, as well as the artillery park. A neatly ordered bazaar and residence area for merchants, etc. met the supply needs of the camp.

In function, but in appearance as well, the imperial encampment bore a striking resemblance to Fatehpur Sikri. Noticeable similarities exist between the unchanging plan of the mobile capital and the urban space of the stationary capital. If Abul Fazl's drawings are to be trusted, even the external design of the tents of the camp and the surviving buildings of Fatehpur Sikri contain similar features. For example, in cross-section the south facade of the imperial palace at Fatahpur (the *Mahal-i Khāss*) looks very much like the east wall of the canvas two-storeyed structure used for the Emperor's private quarters (the *Gulāl-bār*). Similar comparisons can be made, structure by structure. The design of the arcades of the tents virtually duplicates the earlier design of the buildings.[21]

Numismatic evidence also suggests identification of the imperial camp with the capital of the empire. After Akbar's departure from Fatehpur Sikri, the encampment seems to have become the true seat of legitimate imperial authority—regardless of its location or whether the Emperor was actually journeying. According to P.L. Gupta's arguments, the camp-mint became the leading centre of coinage for the empire. Rather than being struck with the name of a town or city, gold and silver coins bore legends such as 'struck at the camping ground of good fortune' (*Zorb Mu'askari-i Iqbāl*). By the year 1000 AH (the Muslim millennium from the Hijra Muhammad, i.e. 1591–92) gold and silver issues from Akbar's camp carried the legend *Dār-ul Khilāfat* or the 'seat of the caliphate', in other words the capital of the Caliph of the Age, Akbar. More humble copper issues from the camp-mint carried only the name of the often-obscure town adjacent to the camp when the coins were struck. These names, however, can be correlated with the known movements of Akbar during the latter years of his reign.[22]

[21]Cf. the illustration in the Blochmann edn of the *Ain-i Akbari*, plate IV, p. 50 with Smith, *Mogul Architecture*, I, plate II.

[22]P.L. Gupta, 'The Mint-Towns of Akbar', in H.R. Gupta, *Essays Presented to Sir Jadunath Sarkar*, 2 vols (Hoshiarpur, 1958), I, pp. 154–69. See also L.N. Kurkuranov, 'The "Urdu" Issues of Emperor Akbar', *Museum Notes*, American Numismatic Society, XV (1969), pp. 137–40. Gupta's analysis draws upon the observations of S.H. Hodivala, 'Abul Fazl's Inventory of Akbar's Mints', *Journal of the Asiatic Society of Bengal*, new series, XVI (1922), pp. 165–90.

To summarize, first Akbar designed and built Fatehpur Sikri as a completely new capital devoid of any of the political associations of Delhi, Lahore or any of the other long-occupied Muslim cities. His own creation, Fatehpur Sikri, was thus completely identified with Akbar's policies and personal authority. Later, concerns for defence and perhaps as we have suggested, rejection of possible ceremonial immobilization, led to the abandonment of Fatehpur. Thereafter, the imperial camp rather than a specific city, became Akbar's capital, titled the seat of the *Khilāfa.* For the Indo-Muslim rulers of Hindustan prior to Akbar, including his father and grandfather, possession and political domination of Delhi was of supreme importance. Similarly in the earlier Central Asian tradition of the Timurids, possession of Samarkand, coronation, and political support from the populace was a matter of continuing concern. Akbar reversed this fixed concern, fusing, instead, all authority within himself and ultimately within the dynasty which succeeded him.

Dynastic Ideology

Towards the end of Akbar's third regnal decade, the Emperor had identified and attracted to him a significant addition to that small coterie of his closest advisers. Abul Fazl and his brother, the poet Faizi, were as capable, versatile, and imaginative as earlier entrants to this select cluster of Akbar's 'companions'. However, unlike men such as Todar Mal, primarily a superb administrator, Abul Fazl's breadth of vision, powers of political analysis, and trained understanding of philosophy, mysticism, and the other disciplines of Islam, made him an outstanding ideologue and propagandist for Akbar. That Abul Fazl and Akbar were attracted to each other despite the difference in status and years is manifest.

From the time of his appearance at court, Abul Fazl began erecting an intellectual scaffolding upon which to build a Timurid dynastic ideology—an edifice firmly establishing a new legitimacy for Akbar and his descendants. If done well, such an ideology would pre-empt the challenges certain to re-emerge from the fissiparous claims of the Mirzas (Akbar's collateral Timurid princes) or from new coalitions of disgruntled orthodox *'ulama* and imperial grandees. Abul Fazl achieved this end by asserting the divinely illumined right of the Emperor to rule mortals with lesser qualities. The actual development of the new imperial doctrine was the result, however, of a brilliant partnership, in which Akbar's own intuitive sense of political need, his desire for broad political support (the most useful context in which the adjective 'tolerant' can be applied to the Emperor) and what seems to have been a mystical sense of his own mission, found a direct response in the mind of Abul Fazl. The latter, with a few collaboraters, began to express the dynastic formula in a number of modes: discussions at court, eulogistic poetry, and a continuing and wide-ranging official and private correspondence.[23] Abul Fazl's most systematic exposition of the new ideology is set out in the best-known Mughal history, the voluminous *Akbar-Nama*, an annual recounting of the events for 47 regnal years along with its equally bulky appendix: the three volumes of the *Ain-i Akbari*, an imperial manual and gazetteer. After years of effort, Abul Fazl presented the magnificently bound and calligraphed first volume of the finished manuscript to Akbar at a court audience in 1595. To further aid the intended effect of the work, several hundred miniature paintings, found on virtually every page, illustrate the most dramatic events described in the work.[24]

Outwardly, the *Akbar-Nama* is merely another example in an extensive genre of Indo-Islamic court eulogies, perhaps more ambitious than most, but little more. A more careful reading reveals that the *Akbar-Nama* is also unquestionably a product of serious, historical scholarship. Abul Fazl based his detailed narrative upon official records, no longer extant, and upon interviews with eyewitnesses and participants in events. At the core of the work, however, permeating nearly every passage, is an ideology of authority and legitimacy. The aim of Abul Fazl's panegyric is to demonstrate either openly or subtly with every possible rhetorical device, his master's superiority to ordinary men. That is, Akbar's claim to rule over all men rested on an ultimate legitimacy far surpassing the accidents of conquest, coup or secession. Even the solemn recognition of authority in the recurring

[23]cf. Rizvi, *Religious and Intellectual History*, pp. 300–22 for discussion of Abul Fazl's extant letter books.

[24]The *Akbar-Nama* paintings from this earliest manuscript are in the collection of the Victoria and Albert Museum, London. Other manuscript versions of the history, apparently widely circulated in the royal and noble circles of Mughal India, were also similarly illustrated by imperial artists. Gavin Hambly, in *Cities of Mughal India: Delhi, Agra and Fatehpur Sikri* (New York, 1968), p. 24 has included a large colour reproduction of a painting by Govardhan, 1602–5, depicting Abul Fazl presenting the second volume of the *Akbar-Nama* to Akbar in a court scene. The latter is part of an *Akbar-Nama* manuscript in the possession of the Chester Beatty Library, Dublin.

prayers of the Indo-Muslim community (i.e. the *Khutba*) was weakened by the intercession of fallible human agency.

In direct contrast to the fallible nature of the ordinary Indo-Muslim Sultan, Akbar was a superior being, existing ontologically closer to God, to true reality. This assertion was confirmed by the hidden light passed to its final recipient through a chain of ancestors (see below). Moreover, the ineffable radiance emanating from the brow of Akbar was perceptible only to superior men—men whose spiritual capacities were highly developed, and who could recognize the signs of true authority. For adepts, or for those men willing to be properly instructed, the veil guarding the outpouring of light from Akbar was removed, and his true nature revealed. He had esoteric knowledge and authority greater than the recognized interpreters of the Sharia, (i.e. the *Mujtahid* of the age), than the most saintly of Sufi masters (*Pīr*) or the most renowned of the charismatic saviours (*mahdi*).[25]

Such an assertion was not a rhetorical device in the accepted conventional description of the Indo-Muslim Sultan as the 'Shadow of God'. Faizi, in one of his eulogistic quatrains (*rubā'iyat*) says:[26]

> He [Akbar] is a king whom on account of his wisdom, we call *zūf unūn* [possessor of the sciences] and our guide on the path of religion. Although kings are the shadow of God on earth, he is the emanation of God's light. How then can we call him a shadow?

[25]Akbar's assertion of the right of final judgement between the various interpretations and interpretations of the sacred law resulted from his long struggle with the conservative '*ulama* holding state positions in the 1560s. The final resolution of this appeared in the much discussed 'testimony' (*mahzar*) of 1579. This document, signed under duress by the chief Qazi and the Sadr of the Empire, stated 'that the rank of a just Sultan is higher in the eyes of God than of a mujtahid'. The most comprehensive discussion of this conflict is that of Rizvi in *Religious and Intellectual History*, pp. 141–75. For Akbar's incorporation of the most prominent Chishti family and shrine under his authority see below. For the attitude of Akbar toward Bayazid Ansari (d. 1572) who claimed to be a *hadi* or 'guide' possessing a divine call to lead his followers in the path of the Prophet Muhammad, see also S.A.A. Rizvi, 'Rawshanīyya Movement', *Abr-Nahrain*, VI (1965) pp. 62–91; VII (1967–8), pp. 62–98. Instead of using the name Rawshaniyya or 'Followers of Light' for this predominantly Afghan movement, Abul Fazl employed the term *Tarīkian* or 'Followers of Darkness'. A Mughal armed contingent eventually hunted down and killed Bayazid in the Hindu Kush.

[26]Abul Fazl, *Ain-i Akbari*, I, p. 631.

Thus, Akbar possessed refulgent power which was the gift of 'the world-adorning Creator'.[27] He obtained this power and its accompanying piercing quality of vision in a process both miraculous and intricate.

The masterfully composed miniature paintings found within the pages of the Victoria and Albert manuscript (one of the first *Akbar-Nama* manuscripts if not the original), in addition to their aesthetic appeal, served to enhance the central theme of the narrative. The great artists directing each painting carefully planned the compositions to depict each of the major incidents and affairs of the history, usually on facing pages of the manuscript. In a seldom appreciated aspect of their genius, the Emperor's artists, image after image, conveyed Abul Fazl's view of Akbar: 'absolute light which would carry ... conviction as an image of absolute power'.[28] More than 50 paintings survive, directly portraying the Emperor. In these, the artists contrast the divine order, self-control and harmony of the Emperor as illumined person, with the turgid, struggling disorder of those unwieldy masses of men and mankind seen in the remainder of the painting.

To achieve this ideological end (transmuted to an aesthetic focus for the series), the Emperor's master painters avoided obvious techniques such as differential scaling for the Emperor's figure, elaborate identifying dress, symbols of authority or even, in many instances, rendition of Akbar's figure as the central compositional focus of the painting. Frequently, on first viewing, he appears as a still, nearly unnoticed figure, who, after a few moments of study, becomes truly dominant. Although dressed very simply in colours contrasting with the apparel of those near him, Akbar always bears characteristic, recognizable features. Other men may be identifiable by careful portraiture in one painting, but in another remain anonymous. The Emperor consistently is iconically supreme. In each composition, intersecting curves, rhythms, stresses and lines lead the viewer's eye to a figure which is the source

[27] Abul Fazl, *Akbar-Nama*, II, p. 501.

[28] Debra Brown Levine, 'The Victoria and Albert Museum *Akbar-Nama*; A Study in History, Myth and Image', 2 vols, Ph.D. dissertation (University of Michigan, 1974), I, p. 47. The artists of the Mughal atelier had progressed in the course of nearly 30 years from the single plane conventions of the perfected Persian miniature style to the use of new European techniques of 'deep space'. The latter combined receding horizon lines, visual curves, and diminished figure size. Experimentation with these new devices clearly enabled the painters to avoid more obvious visual clichés such as actually attempting to show divine light coming from the Emperor's brow.

of intense potential energy—a calmly controlled energy which engenders harmony in the confusing mass of human action. By means of such subtle techniques the court painters presented to the cognizant reader of the *Akbar-Nama* the radiant, infallible, powers of their master and patron. The Emperor's synergistic capacity calmed and directed the energies of his servants, his subjects, and ultimately of all mankind.

Abul Fazl explicitly states the core of his ideology in the introductory *Akbar-Nama* passages describing Akbar's ancestry and descent.[29] Beginning with Adam, the ancestor of all men, Abul Fazl in 52 human generations traces the passage of the hidden Divine refulgence until it reaches and illumines the spirit and intelligence of Akbar, its intended recipient. Akbar's 'heaven descended forefathers' from the seven planets all came to earth as 'kings, kings of kings, kingdom bestowers and king makers [who] governed the world by God-given wisdom and true insight'. Adam, born 7000 years ago, was the first ancestor (as, of course, he is for all men).[30] Thereafter, Abul Fazl briefly lists five biblical prophets before reaching Ikhnush[31] or Enoch, who, among his other accomplishments 'guided men to the reference of the Great Light [the sun]'.[32] The continuing line of male descent leads through Joseph to his son Turk, ruler of Turkestan, thus shifting from biblical prophets (common to Islam and Christianity) to the first Turko-Mongal figure.[33]

Mughal Khan, the son of a Turk, is the first eponymous ruler in an unidentified series of nine Mughal (or Mongol) kings. The last, or ninth generation of the dynasty, is defeated, massacred and dispersed by an enemy. The survivors retire in confusion to a mountain valley, Mughalistan, hidden far to the east.[34] After 2000 years in seclusion, a most important natal event occurs. Alanquwa (Alan-qo-a) a Mughal

[29]To substantiate these points Levine analyses a number of well-known paintings. See, for example an incident at the siege of Chitor, the great Rajput fortress in the painting. 'Akbar Uses Sangram to Shoot Jaimal at the Siege of Chitor', Levine, I, pp., 63–4.

[30]Abul Fazl, *Akbar-Nama*, I, p. 143.

[31]At this juncture, Abul Fazl engages in a lengthy digression in which he explains the Hindu and Jain views on the age of the universe. These essentially cyclical cosmologies suggest that countless Adams may well have begun each of innumerable ages of man. Ibid., p. 154.

[32]Ikhnush is also Hermes, a key figure in the philosophy of Suhrawardi Maqtul (see below).

[33]Ibid., p. 168.

[34]According to Blochmann, this withdrawal to Mughalistan derives directly from the Mongol traditions. Ibid., p. 175n.

princess, married to Zubun Biyan, king of Mughalistan, becomes a childless widow when her royal husband dies prematurely. But Alanquwa is a woman of the utmost purity from whose forehead shone the 'lights of theosophy' (*anwar Khudā shināsī*) and the 'divine secrets' (*asrār' ilāhī*). As the princess lay sleeping in her tent one night, a ray of light miraculously entered her body and impregnated her.[35]

The progeny born from this conception were triplets, three brothers, who collectively were called 'nairun' or 'light-produced'. Abul Fazl describes the introduction of the divine illumination into the body of Alanquwa, and its transmission to her sons as the 'first manifestation' (*aghāz zahūr*) of the divine origin of Akbar. From the eldest of the three brothers, who possessed the illumination of his mother to the greatest degree, the hidden light passed through generation after generation until the *Shāhinshāh* of mankind, Akbar, was born in 1542.[36]

Following short notices of nine Turko-Mongol rulers, members of the chain of descent, Abul Fazl arrives at Chingiz Khan (Temuchin), who, somewhat surprisingly, he does not glorify. In an apologetic passage he concedes the prevailing Islamic view of Chingiz Khan as a destructive monster. But the myopia of most men means that 'everything which comes into existence in the world of evil [its] real nature the superficial cannot percieve'.[37] That is, one of Chingiz Khan's well-hidden virtues is that he bore the veiled light for his descendant who would benefit men as much as his distant ancestor had harmed them.

Rapidly descending the generations from the early thirteenth and the late fourteenth centuries, Abul Fazl begins his most extended discussion to that point. Amir Timur Gurgan of Samarkand the 'Lord of Conjunctions of the Planets' (*Sāhib Qirān*) was, of course, the conqueror of those Central Asian lands in Balkh, Badakhshan and Ferghana inherited by his politically fragmented fifteenth-century descendants. Moreover, Timur's exploits, his control of Samarkand, his methods of rule afforded a source of legitimacy for all subsequent Timurid princes as well as a model of conquest and rule on the greatest possible scale. Timur was 'a hero fit for and capable of a great sovereignty'(*wālā'ig*

[35]Ibid., p. 179; Abul Fazl, *Akbar-Nama*, 3 vols (Lucknow edn.), I, pp. 51–2. I have used this edition of the *Akbar-Nama* text to verify key passages and phrases from the translation because the Bibliotheca Indica edition was not accessible at the time of writing.

[36]*Akbar-Nama*, (trans.), I, p. 180; (text) I, p. 52.

[37]Ibid. trans., I, p. 196.

Saltanat).[38] Always, 'the lights of celestial victories illumined that world conqueror', whose feats of both destruction and reconstruction in Central Asia forecast those of his sixteenth-century descendant in Hindustan and the vast, heavily populated regions of the subcontinent.[39]

Thus, formal legitimacy for the Timurids began when, in April 1370 Amir Timur, firmly seated on a throne in Samarkand, placed on his own head the 'crown of world conquest'.[40] More than three decades later, at considerable expense and effort, he ensured complete recognition as a true Muslim king: 'In the pulpits of Mecca, Medina and other holy places, the *khutba* was read in his name.'[41] Babur, in a practice followed by his son, grandson, and all subsequent Timurid rulers, began his dynastic genealogy with Amir Timur (or *Sāhib Qirān*, the posthumous title). The magnificently calligraphed, etched iron seals and ceremonial gold coins of the dynasty invariably bear this official statement of dynastic authority.[42] Surviving manuscripts of histories of Timur, profusely illustrated, also demonstrate that these were not merely formulaic expressions, but represented a deep and continuing interest in Timur (and one suspects in measurement against his achievements) on the part of emperors such as Shah Jahan (1627–58), reigning at the apogee of the empire.[43]

[38]Ibid., (trans.), I, p. 204; (text), I, p. 61.

[39]Ibid., (trans.), I, p. 210, (text), I, p. 62. '*wa anwār fatūhāt āsmānī bar ruzgār ān jahāngīr 'ālam-peraya'*.

[40]Ibid., (trans.) I, p. 208; (text), I, p. 61. '*ikhlīl-ī kishwār-kishā'ī*'.

[41]Ibid., (trans.) I, p. 212; (text), I, p. 62. The term used for monarchy is *farmānrawāī*.

[42]For a seal of Babur see Momin Mohiuddin, *The Chancellery and Persian Epistolography Under the Mughals* (Calcutta, 1971), p. 77. For a more elaborately decorated seal of Akbar, bearing the *tughra*, see the picture, text and translation in B.N. Goswamy and J.S. Grewal, *The Mughals and the Jogis of Jakhbar* (Simla, 1967), pp. 57–61. (The *tughra* was a square, etched, vermilion rendition of the Emperor's titles placed beside the official seal at the head of all formal rescripts.)

[43]See Khan Sahib Abdul Muqtadir, 'Note on a Unique History of Timur and his Descendants in Iran and India ...', *Journal of the Bihar and Orissa Research Society* III, 175–263. The handsomely calligraphed and illustrated 'Tārīkh-i-khāndān-i-Timuriyah' was compiled by an unidentified author in Akbar's reign. It bears an autograph note of Shah Jahan describing its contents as 'the history containing an account of the circumstances of Hazrat Sahib Qiran, the "world seizer" and his descendants' (p. 268).

Concluding his account of Timur, Abul Fazl pursues the lineage from Miranshah, son of Timur, to Sultan Muhammad Mirza (of the second generation), to his son Sultan Abu Said Mirza (1427–64), ruler of Samarkand and most of Transoxania (of the third), to 'Umar Shaikh Mirza (1456–94), one of 11 sons of Abu Said Mirza (of the fourth generation). Until his accidental death, 'Umar Shaikh Mirza ruled the valley of Ferghana from the city of Andijan, revived and repopulated under Timurid rule. By this time, the Turko-Mongol appanage system ensured that the Timurid ancestral territories were free of centralized control. Three of 'Umar Shaikh Mirza's siblings also ruled as kings: one at Kabul, one at Samarkand, and one at Kunduz. This generation of Timur's descendants was continuously engaged in a swirling struggle for dominance and for survival against the challenges of other siblings of the Chaghtai line anxious to rule. The forceful intrusion of the Uzbeks from the steppe, added another confusing dimension to the political milieu.

However, when Babur assumed the deceased 'Umar Shaikh Mirza's responsibilities at Andijan (supported by various adult advisers), the divine illumination flared out again for the first time since the exploits of Amir Timur. Abul Fazl compares Babur's seizure of Delhi and retention of the city against desperate Rajput and Afghan resistance with the feats of Sultan Mahmud of Ghazni, Sultan Muhammad of Ghur, and Amir Timur, all of whom commanded gigantic armies. That Babur could emulate their example by taking and holding the heart of Hindustan with only 13,000 followers was proof of 'divine aid'. Therefore, Babur was the 'carrier of the world-illuminating light' (*hāmil nūr jahān āfrūz*), which would reach its full glory in only two generations.[44]

As one might expect after the long narrative of descent, Abul Fazl, in his account of the life and reign of Humayūn, minimizes the latter's apparent incompetence and defeats, to stress the imminent appearance of Humayun's son, Akbar. Prior to his flight and wandering exile, Humayun's 'shining forehead' lit the world with the power of the divine light which, originating 'in the time of the ocean pearl-shell Alānqūā', had traversed the centuries and generations hidden 'under the veils of women in travail'.[45] At the foreordained nativity of Akbar, the divine illumination would shine forth in its full glory (but only for those capable of proper perception). Humayun's political failures were simply calamities assigned by God to 'quicken the attention of the

[44]Abul Fazl, *Akbar-Nama*, I (trans) I, pp. 243–5; (text) I, p. 76.
[45]Ibid. (trans.) I, p. 287.

"noble-minded", or to alert them that showing forth of the final cause of that light to wit, the holy incarnation of his majesty, the king of kings was at hand'.[46]

Humayun, defeated and despairing in 1540, found reassurance in a majestic night vision. God sent him an illumined message that 'an illustrious successor whose greatness shone from his forelock' would be bestowed upon the exiled ruler—a successor whose greatness would more than rectify his father's losses.[47] The nativity of Akbar was further presaged by a mysterious light which entered the bosom of Akbar's putative nurse.[48] God's all-powerful, omniscient will had determined that the moment was at hand for bringing forth the receptacle for that hidden light so long in its passage through the ages.[49]

Hyperbolic and excessive as the above treatment of Akbar's ancestry may seem, it was not entirely a concoction of Abul Fazl's inventive mind. If the doctrine were to have any widespread recognition and response it necessarily needed to possess and retain an easily recognizable affiliation with already existing religio-political traditions. Thus, Abul Fazl fused two well-known doctrines: the ancient origin myth of the Mongols and the illuminationist theosophy of Suhrawardi Maqtul, the Persian mystic and philosopher.

The probable source for Abul Fazl for the traditional Mongol genealogical motif is one of the Mongol histories widely available in the sixteenth century. Mirza Haidar, who compiled a history of his Mongol ancestors 40 years before the writing of the *Akbar-Nāma*, in the mid-sixteenth century, states: 'All histories [i.e. of the Mongols] trace the genealogy of ... Alankua Kurkluk, back to Japhet, son of Noah (upon them be peace) and detailed accounts of all her ancestors are given in these histories.'[50] All the Mongol chronicles available to Mirza Haidar included variants on the story of the conception by means of a divine light of Alankua Kurkluk (which means an immaculate woman) and the subsequent birth of her son Burunjar Khan. However, Mirza Haidar minimizes this clearly pagan, pre-Muslim motif, and begins his full narrative only after the acceptance of Islam by the Mongols in Transoxania. He comments that 'the object of this book [the *Tārīkh-i*

[46]Ibid., p. 353.

[47]Ibid., p. 42.

[48]Ibid., p. 44–5.

[49]Mirza Muhammad Haidar Dughlat, *Tārīkh-i Rashīdī*, trans. N. Elias and E.D. Ross, *A History of the Moghuls of Central Asia* (London, 1895), p. 5.

[50]Ibid.

Rashīdī] is not to tell tales such as these, but simply to point out that Burunjar Khan was born of his mother without a father'.[51] That Mirza Haidar thought it necessary to include any mention of the myth suggests its earlier importance and possible appeal to Mongol pride even in the sixteenth century. Collective oral (and written) memories of vast conquests over a humbled Muslim world three centuries before could not have faded so easily.[52]

Abul Fazl leaves not doubt as to the source of the illuminationist theme systematically interwoven with the Mongol myth of descent. In the course of his description of the five biblical prophets down to Ikhnush or Hermes, Abul Fazl states that he has been following the commentary of 'the very learned Shahrazūrī'.[53] The 'Tārīkh-i-Hukama' by Shamsuddin Muhammad Shahrazuri (d. 1243 AD) is a collective Arabic biography of pre-Muslim and Muslim philosophers and sages. Included among these is the life of Shihabuddin Suhrawardi Maqtul (d. 1191 AD) the spiritual and intellectual master of Shahrazuri, and founder of the 'Eastern' or 'Ishraki school of Persian philosopy. For his adaptation of the Mongol genealogy, and portrayal of Akbar's antecedents Abul Fazl freely utilized many aspects of Suhrawardi's complex system.

The central vision of the 'Ishraki school (that is, Suhrawardi and those who followed his teachings) 'regards Beings and Knowledge as irradiations of the Pure Light which rises in the East'. In other words, Suhrawardī's 'East' is not merely the eastern philosophy of Neoplatonism, but the east of the origin of light and the metaphorical 'East of Thought'. 'Ishrak (the east), as a symbol of light, 'is not

[51] Ibid.

[52] Abul Fazl, *Akbar-Nama*, I, p. 157. In 1101 AH (1602–3) Prince Salim, later the Emperor Jahangir, commissioned the paraphrased translation from Arabic into Persian of Shahrazuri's work (titled in Arabic *Raudatu'l Afsah wa Nuzhatu'l Arwah*). This was completed in 1610 during Jahangir's reign by Maq ud'Ali Tabrizi. See Muhammad Ashraf, *A Concise Descriptive Catalogue of the Persian Manuscripts in the Salar Jang Museum and Library*, 3 vols (Hyderabad, 1965–6), II, p. 238, Catalogue no. 595. Hermann Ethé, in the *Catalogue of the Persian Manuscripts in the India Office Library*, lists another copy of the same manuscript, but ascribes the original to Shamsuddin Muhammad *Suhrawardi* instead of Shahrazuri, no. 614, p. 249. For the transmission of 'Ishraki ideas to India in the fifteenth and sixteenth centuries see Rizvi, *Religious and Intellectual History*, pp. 40–2, and for direct influence of 'Ishraki thought upon Abul Fazl see ibid., pp. 339–73.

[53] R. Arnaldez, '"Ishrākī" and "Ishrākīyyūn"' *The Encyclopaedia of Islam*, 2nd edn.

reduced to the general notion of illumination which confers upon the spirit a truth inaccessible to the abstract concepts of reason; it is more fundamentally, a delight in the source of all light, whence proceed all beings and all authentic knowledge.'[54] All life, all 'reality' in the world, according to Suhrawardi, is light given existence by the constant blinding illumination of the Light of Lights (*nūr-al anwār*), or God. The degree of luminosity each being or object possesses is a measure of its ontological reality and also an expression of its self-awareness.

God's light reaches earth and mankind through the intervention of a hierarchic chain of dazzling angels. In this descending vertical or longitudinal order of angels, the supreme archangel. receives the 'divine irradiation' of God, veils its intensity and transmits the remainder of the light to the next subordinate angel until the chain is ended at the fixed stars in the heavens. This, the feminine order of angels, is a vertical chain of love and acceptance by means of which light and life reach earth. The horizontal, latitudinal order of angels, existing beside one another, is the 'masculine' order of domination. These platonic archetypes preside over a still lower order of angels who govern the human soul. The dominant force within this lower order of 'lordly lights' is the guardian angel for mankind, the Angel Gabriel (identified with the spirit of the Prophet Muhammad), the revealer to man of true knowledge of God.

Each individual human soul possesses a core of light imprisoned within the body. This luminous core or 'divine spark' is divided or separated from an angelic light still remaining in the heavens (the soul's guardian angel) in order to enter the body. Thus man's soul longs to be reunited with its angelic counterpart. Of three groups of men, the lowest have lives shaded by ignorance and wickedness; the second have attained some measure of goodness, or enlightenment; and the third consisting of the saints have already become aware of their own illumination and that of God. They are the true theosophists and masters of the age. Masters like Plato or Suhrawardi himself understood both illumination and the limits of rational discursive thought. For Suhrawardi, the origins of this wisdom of the east, i.e. of the firmament of the stars in his geographical symbolism, was first revealed to man by the prophet Hermes. The latter's teachings followed two chains of transmission,

[54]The following synopsis is drawn from Seyyid Hossein Nasr, *Three Muslim Sages* (Cambridge, Mass., 1964), pp. 52–82.

one through Persia and the second through Greece. Suhrawardi felt that he recombined the two modes of thought.[55]

Although the above is only a summary of Suhrawardi's 'Ishraki philosophy, we can readily discern its influence upon Abul Fazl. His emphasis upon Hermes in describing the earliest of the bibilical prophets is apparent. So also is his adaptation of the concept of a chain of transmitters possessing a divine luminosity so intense that it must be veiled to prevent harm. The direct generation of human life by a star, a feminine angelic form, and the subsequent transmittal of this inner light to Akbar clearly gave him the enhanced awareness of Suhrawardi's 'Master of the Age'. Simultaneously, however, conception induced in the Mongol princess by light from a star enabled Abul Fazl to utilize the basic male–female opposition in Suhrawardi's angelology.

The vertical 'longitudinal' chain of generative, loving, stars and the horizontal, 'latitudinal' array of protecting, commanding guardian angels has its counterpart or parallel in the extended *Akbar-Nama* portrayal of Akbar's character. With alternating love and sternness, he extends his esoteric knowledge (the 'light from his brow') to all his subjects. In the well-known doctrine of *sulh-i kul* 'peace for all', appearing later in the *Akbar-Nama* we find a shorthand expression of Akbar's nurturing and punishing roles. Rather than simply 'toleration' of the Hindu or non-Muslim subjects of the empire, Abul Fazl was subtly clearing the way for a broader ideology of imperial concern which would abate the grim tensions between rulers and ruled seen in earlier Indo-Muslim regimes.[56]

Imperial Discipleship

The ideological formula of the *Akbar-Nama* (as distinct from the narrative text) drew together, and made more coherent, Akbar's eclectic, publicly displayed religious practices—the apparent resolution of an incessant, at times tortured spiritual quest. In so doing Abul Fazl

[55]Nasr provides a summary of the two parallel chains of transmission (p. 62). 'The Master of *Ishrāq* therefore considered himself as the focal point at which the two traditions of wisdom that had at one time issued forth from the same source were once again unified. He thereby sought to synthesize the wisdom of Zoroaster and Plato.'

[56]For a discussion of the earlier conception of proper relationships between rulers and ruled, see C.E. Bosworth's description of the Islamic 'power-state' in *The Ghaznavids* (Edinburgh, 1963).

succeeded in integrating into a comprehensive symbolic framework the illumined dynastic legitimation of the Timurids with Akbar's predilection for worship of the sun. This made a broad appeal to the imperial official élite, to the landed regional aristocracies (i.e. the *zamīndārs*) and to varied groups of other local notables in the empire.[57] If viewed in this way, the hoary scholarly controversy over the nature and purpose of Akbar's so-called 'Divine Faith' has been misdirected. Since the early nineteenth century, generations of historians in sorting out the various rituals and beliefs of Akbar, have tried to determine influences and filiation—whether Zoroastrian, Sufi, Nath Yogia, or Brahminical practices and beliefs. A general tendency has been to treat the 'Divine Faith' as a bizarre concoction of Akbar's fertile intellect.[58]

By 1583, Akbar had apparently rejected public prayer and other formal aspects of orthodox ritual Islam in what seems to have been a steady process of religious questioning. In place of Muslim prayer, Akbar began to worship the sun publicly four times a day with prostrations, facing east before a sacrificial fire and accompanying rituals of his own invention. The latter, according to Badauni, included, among others, recitations of 1001 synonymous Sanskrit names for the sun at the noontime ceremony.[59] His continuing interviews with famed holy men of all sects and the religious debates carried on at Fatehpur Sikri were obviously part of this effort. In addition, various forms of abstinence (exceptional for an Indo-Muslim ruler) marked his behaviour. Akbar avoided excessive meat eating, sexual intercourse, and alcoholic consumption.[60] Possibly persuaded by the Hindu doctrines of metempsychosis, Abkar had the crown of his head (the tenth opening of his body) tonsured to allow his soul to escape freely at the moment of death.[61]

[57]To what extent Abul Fazl's origin myth for the Timurid dynasty retained any appeal for Akbar's successors is uncertain. A privately compiled, unofficial history of the early eighteenth century does reproduce a summary of the myth for its account of Akbar's reign. Khafi Khan, in the first volume of his *Muntakhab-ul Lubāb* provides the essentials of the birth of the three light-conceived Mongol princes and the passage of the interior light to Akbar. Khafi Khan, *Muntakhab-ul Lubāb*, Bibliotheca Indica, 3 vols (Calcutta, 1869).

[58]Cf. the comments of S. Roy, in his contribution to R.C. Majumdar (ed.) *The Mughal Empire, the History and Culture of the Indian People* (Bombay, 1974), VI, pp. 138–40.

[59]Rizvi, *Religious and Intellectual History*, p. 338.

[60]Ibid., p. 390.

[61]Ibid.

One of the most controversial and puzzling aspects of the 'Divine Faith' is the Emperor's ability to attract a number of his courtiers and highest official élite to his beliefs. Blochmann, the late nineteenth-century translator of the bulk of the *Akbar-Nama*, compiled a listing of 18 nobles who could be identified as adherents or disciples or Akbar and subscribers to the new 'Divine Faith'. Based on this enumeration, the generally accepted interpretation has been that the disciples were part of a tiny group equivalent to an élite 'order' in the British knightly, honorific sense. However, S.A.A. Rizvi in a recent analysis of the body of references pertaining to this issue, has concluded that the term 'Divine Faith' was misapplied by Blochmann. The enlistment of disciples by Akbar simply cannot be dismissed as the egomania of the Emperor aided by the sycophancy of his courtiers. Instead, imperial discipleship, possessing a serious political purpose, found its ideological grounding in the *Akbar-Nama* and Akbar's symbolic association with the sun and light. In Rizvi's view, discipleship represented a major effort to create an exceptionally loyal and reliable cadre of nobles, carefully screened and recruited to form a body of life-guards. Far more than 18, unspecified as to total number, but clearly substantial bodies of men, were inducted every week in groups of twelve into this more intense relationship with the person of the Emperor.[62]

At noon on Sunday, the Emperor himself presiding, the newly selected disciples underwent an initiation ceremony. Each Muslim initiate signed a declaration repudiating the orthodox bonds of conventional (*taqlīdī*) Islam and agreeing to reverence Allah directly. He also swore to accept four degrees of devotion: the unhesitating willingness to sacrifice one's life (*jān*), property (*māl*), religion (*dīn*) and honour (*namūs*) in the service of the Master (Akbar). During the ceremony, the new disciple placed his head on the feet of the Emperor in the fashion of the Sufi disciple's prostration (*sijdah*) to his master or *Pīr*. Upon conclusion of the ceremony, the Emperor raised up the supplicant, and, placing a new turban upon his head, gave him a symbolic representation of the sun, and a tiny portrait of Akbar to wear upon his turban.[63] Thus, the four degrees of devotion were a means 'to unify the new Mughal élite around the ... throne'.[64] Instead of the ties of common ancestry, ethnicity, and familial hereditary service which bound Babur's tiny élite to him, Abkar's Persian, Rajput, and Khatri,

[62]Ibid., pp. 391–2. For the Persian terms see Badauni (text), II, p. 304.
[63]Rizvi, p. 401.
[64]Ibid., p. 398.

and Indian Muslim disciples were widely disparate in their beliefs and ethnicity. Exacting such a solemn commitment to an Emperor who had reached the highest degree of purity, knowledge and ontological status possible for a mortal, was one solution to the recurrent problem of challengeable legitimate rule, and an alternative to the potentially divisive balancing of factions within the élite.

Popular understanding of the Emperor's assertions of divinely sanctioned ancestry, illumined wisdom and spirituality, clearly permeated among the populace of the court/camp and other major urban centres of the empire. Ultimately this understanding became so pervasive that a continuing memory of Akbar's powers was even absorbed into the folk culture of rural society within the various regions of the empire.[65]

Discipleship, however (although evidently its existence was not secret), was never publicized by Abul Fazl or the Emperor in the same fashion. Certainly, the nobility, and more informed observers from the secondary and tertiary ranks of the imperial political élite, must have fully comprehended the true significance of discipleship. But, unfortunately, extant written references to its operation in the last decade or so of Akbar's reign are muted.

Jahangir, who seems to have been caught in the dilemma of imitation versus rebellion against his father, common to the sons of men of extraordinary stature, did perpetuate the imperial order of disciples. He demanded worship from his disciples in the mode established by his father. Unlike Akbar, however, he viewed many of the renowned saintly figures of his time as competitors, rather than spiritual masters.[66] Interesting direct testimony to this effect comes from the letters and journals of Sir Thomas Roe, ambassador from James of England to the Mughal Emperor. A university graduate, a minor aristocrat with a family mercantile background, a courtier and diplomat of long experience, and

[65]E.g. in his description of the Kunbis, the most numerous peasant caste in Maharashtra, R.V. Russell detailed the birth customs of the caste from ethnographic material collected in the first years of the twentieth century. If the labour of a Kunbi woman were unduly prolonged, among the folk remedies recounted 'she is given water to drink in which a Sulaimāni onyx or a rupee of Akbar's time has been washed;...the virtue of the rupee probably consists in its being a silver coin and having the image or device of a powerful king like Akbar'. 'Kunbi', in R.V. Russell, *Tribes and Castes of the Central Provinces of India*, 4 vols (London, 1916), II, p. 29.

[66]E.g. Jahangir's response to the Sikh Guru Arjun's untimely, accidental meeting with Prince Khurram during the latter's rebellion against his father.

possessor of a high level of analytic intelligence, Roe's observations are worth considering. Moreover, in the course of nearly three years (January 1615 to September 1618) in attendance at the court camp of Jahangir, Roe was able to establish an affable relationship (partly based on drink) with the Emperor who seems to have enjoyed the company and the supplies of the ambassador. In a lengthy letter to the Archbishop of Canterbury written at the end of October 1616, Roe reported on the general perception of Akbar's religious position:[67]

> Ecbar-shae [Akbar] himself continued a Mahometan, yet he began to make a breach into the law; Considering that Mahomett was but a man, a King as he was, and therefore reuerenced, he thought hee might prove as good a Prophett himself.

Roe noted, however, that Jahangir:[68]

> Falling upon his father's conceipt, hath dared to enter farther in, and to professe himselfe for the Mayne of his religion to be a greater Prophett than Mahomett; and hath formed to himself a New Law, mingled of all ...

Imperfect though his understanding of the subtleties of Akbar and Jahangir's doctrinal position may have been, Roe correctly grasped from his informants at court the unusual nature of such religious beliefs. His assessment of Jahangir undoubtedly reflects the commonly held view in the court and capital that the Emperor was pressing assertion of his religious authority more openly than Akbar had found necessary.

Considerable evidence also exists that Jahangir imitated his father's practice of selecting and initiating disciples from among his most favoured nobles. In a short passage from his memoir, Jahangir mentions Shaikh Ahmad Lahauri, newly promoted to the office of *Mīr 'Adl*, who had been initiated as a disciple by Akbar before Jahangir's accession. One of Shaikh Ahmad's duties in his new office was to advise 'who is worthy of receiving *shast wa shabah*', i.e. the seal (or ring) and the imperial likeness which were the symbols of discipleship. Then Jahangir describes the details of the enrolment ceremony. His account is in

[67] William Foster (ed.), *The Embassy of Sir Thomas Roe to the Court of the Great Mogul, 1615–1619*, 2 vols (London, 1894, Hakluyt Society, new series), II, pp. 313–14.

[68] Ibid., p. 314.

essential agreement with Abul Fazl's description.[69] Roe himself, although again he was not fully aware of the entire significance of the event, became a disciple at Jahangir. In August 1616, more than a year and a half after his arrival at court, Jahangir favoured the ambassador by enacting, without warning, the ceremony of initiation. Roe describes this in some detail:[70]

August 17—I went to visit the King, who, as soone as I came in, called to his woemen and reached out a picture of himselfe sett in gould hanging at a wire gould Chaine, with one pendant foule pearle, which he delivered to Asaph Chan [Asaf Khan, the *wazīr*] warning him not to demand any reuerence of mee other than such as I would willingly giue, it beeing the Custome, when soever hee bestowes any thing, the receiuer kneeles downe and putts his head to the ground. ... So Asaph Chan came to mee, and I offered to take it in my hand; but hee made signe to putt of my hatt, and then putt it about my neck, leading mee right before the king. I understood not his purpose, but doubted hee would require the Custome of the Country called *Size-da* [i.e. the full prostration of *Sijdah* of discipleship]; but I was resolved rather to deliure up my present. Hee made sign to mee to giue the king thancks, which I did after my owne Custome. Whereatt some officers called me to *Size-da*, but the King answered no, no, in Persian. So with many gratious woordes sent mee, I returned to my place. You may now Iudg the kings liberallitye. This guift was not woorth in all 30 *li.*, yet it was five tymes as good as any hee giues in that kynd, *and held for an especiall fauour, for that all the great men that weare the kings Image (which none may doe but to whom it is given) receiue noe other than a meddall of gould as bigg as sixpence, with a little chayne of 4 inches to fasten it on their heads,* which at their owne Chardg some sett with stones or garnishe with pendant Pearles.

A more significant indication of the growing significance of the master–disciple tie in Jahangir's reign, lies in the response of nobles and *mansabdārs*—especially the younger men, members of a new generation coming to maturity since Akbar's death. In this context, we are fortunate that the autobiographical memoir, of 'Alauddin Isfahani, a Persian noble known as Mirza Nathan, has survived. This extraordinary document contains a full account of Mirza Nathan's career and service

[69]Rizvi, *Religious and Intellectual History*, p. 400 quotes the full passage. In checking the original text, Professor Rizvi has found that a mistranslation of a critical sentence in the English edition makes it appear that Jahangir is referring to his father's practice of initiation, not his own.

[70]Foster, I, pp. 244–5. A portion of this passage is also quoted in Rizvi, *Religious and Intellectual History*, p. 404.

on the marches of Muslim expansion in north-eastern Bengal an Assam during the second and third decades of the seventeenth century. The *Bahāristān-i-Ghaybī*, written in the third person in Persian, was completed by Mirza Nathan in 1632.[71] His account is one of the most important sources for the operations of the imperial armies in the riverine terrain of that region against the unsubdued Bengali rajas. Later, the Mughal commanders were forced to meet the aggressive attacks of the Ahom mass armies pressing down the Brahmaputra valley. However, the *Bahāristān* is also noteworthy for its recounting of the details of the personal life, emotions and reactions of the author, who as he attained experience and maturity rose in rank and status to become an *amīr* or noble.

In 1607, Mirza Nathan as an adolescent youth, accompanied Ihtimam Khan, his father, to the eastern frontier. Ihtimam Khan was posted to serve as commander (*Mīr Bahr*) of the imperial war fleet of armed river boats in use in Bengal. Shortly after his arrival in Bengal, Mirza Nathan became seriously ill and lapsed into a fever. His condition deteriorated until, on the seventh night of sickness, the young officer had an awesome vision. In his sleep 'the king of the spiritual and temporal domain', (that is Jahangir) appeared and addressed him: 'O Nathan! Is this the time for a tiger to lie down? Arise, we have granted you security from pain and trouble by our prayers to the Almighty and Omnipresent Lord. Be quick, and placing the foot of manliness and sincerity in your devoted work be a comrade to your great father and be his support.' In the morning, Nathan awoke, fully cured and convinced of his mission. Through his father and the governor of Bengal, Islam Khan Chishti, Nathan sent a petition to the Emperor entreating the favour of enlistment as one of his disciples—reciting the detail of his mystical vision. Somewhat later, an imperial messenger returned

[71]Mirza Nathan, *Bahāristān-i Ghaybī*, ed. and trans. M.I Borah, 2 vols (Gauhati, 1936). The only extant manuscript of this text is that possessed by the Bibliothèque Nationale (Paris). As with a number of other exceedingly important sources for Mughal India, this was discovered by Jadunath Sarkar by a careful reading of the Bibliothèque Nationale's catalogue. Sudhindra Nath Bhattacharya has made extensive use of the *Bahāristān* manuscript in his chapters on the early seventeenth-century Mughal advances to the east in Bengal and Assam in Jadunath Sarkar (ed.) *The History of Bengal Muslim Period 1200–1757* (Patna, 1973, reprint edn), pp. 234–315. Bhattacharya, (and Sarkar earlier) has shown that the details of Nathan's work are generally accurate while the Assamese chronicles refer to him by his title, in the context of an able enemy commander.

bearing a tiny portrait (*shabah*) of Jahangir 'adorned with a genealogical tree' of the Timurid dynasty. Although he was not brought back to court for a personal ceremony, by placing this image in his turban, Mirza Nathan openly displayed devotion to his master and membership in the imperial elect.[72]

In referring to Jahangir, Nathan frequently used the terms *pīr*, *murshīd*, or even *qibla* as a synonym, i.e. equating the Emperor with that portion of a mosque towards which worshippers directed their prayers. That Nathan equated his service to Jahangir with a form of worship seems a reasonable inference. At one point in the narrative, the young disciple, speaking under great stress, states that for six years on the Bengal frontier he had always considered his imperial service 'to be greater than the worship of God'.[73] It is to the nature of Mirza Nathan's service as a disciple, and the authoritative relationship between the elect body of disciples and the Emperor to which we now turn.

New Imperial Identities

By the early years of the seventeenth century the diverse Mughal élite had become a corporate body of paid officers, with status and posting ultimately determined by the wish of the Emperor. Most members of this motley élite depended almost entirely on their imperial careers for a livelihood and worldly success. A minority—Rajputs, some Afghans and Indian Muslims—retained hereditary ties to landed patrimonial domains to which they could return if necessary.[74] By various devices (such as the numerical ranking system and titles) Akbar successfully subordinated dozens of particularistic group identities and jealously guarded personal dignity to the demands of authority. Touchy, bellicose

[72]Nathan, *Bahāristān*, I, pp. 17, 74. The recurring genealogy in this, as in other contexts, is apparently a reference to the illumined descent of Akbar and Jahangir. It is also analogous to the genealogy of masters and disciples given Sufi initiates by their Shaikhs.

[73]Ibid., I, p. 295. In a later portion of the memoir the Mirza uses all three terms of refer to Jahangir. Ibid., II, p. 743.

[74]M. Athar Ali has reproduced a dramatic mid-seventeenth-century description by a Mughal bureaucrat of the 'various classes and groups of persons from every race and people [who] have sought asylum in the Imperial court' both foreigners and Indians and 'men of the pen and men of the sword'. M. Athar Ali, *The Mughal Nobility Under Aurangzeb* (Aligarh, 1966), p. 15. For a discussion of partrimonial holdings or *watan-jāgīrs*, see ibid., pp. 79–80.

views of the honour of the individual warrior-soldier were transmuted into an acceptance of group and individual honour enhanced in service to the Emperor. Somewhat paradoxically, as the bureaucratic systems of the empire evolved, the Persian, Indo-Muslim, Brahmin, Khatri, and Kayastha technicians who extended, consolidated and maintained the administrative system, also acquired martial, warrior values to accompany their inclusion. They too were assimilated into the general, military- oriented honour-bound system of ranks, rewards, and assignments emanating from the Emperor.

For this new military–administrative service élite, a basic model and idiom seems to have derived from the centuries-old tradition of Islamic corporate military slavery. Always closely associated with the Turks, this institution was a time-honoured means of incorporating ethnic groups for reliable service to dynasties of Sultans, often insecure and themselves of slave origin. To have immediately at hand bodies of troops and cadres of slave commanders, at least partially deracinated, beholden to the King for their lives and employment, was an invaluable tool for the parvenu Muslim ruler. Legally free though they were, the Mughal nobles and lesser *mansabdārs*, especially those on the Muslim side, did adopt some of the attitudes of military slaves.

The term *bandah* or slave was actually employed by the Mughal nobility in reported speech. For example during a heated altercation between Islam Khan Chishti (a grandson of Akbar's preceptor), the overbearing governor of Bengal, and his war fleet commander, Mirza Nathan's father, Ihtimam Khan, the latter stood and protested to the governor: 'You forget yourself' (meaning the governor had gone too far). Islam Khan also rose and shouted: 'I am that very Islam Khan whom your master [i.e. Jahangir] has asked you to serve and attend.' Replying in the same tone Ihtimam Khan said, 'I also am not inferior to you. Every one of us is the slave of the master.'[75] Such usage reflected that of Jahangir, who frequently referred to or addressed his officers as 'slaves'.[76] Usage of such terminology in both spoken and written language suggests that normative connotations developed over centuries of corporate military slavery in the Muslim world, helped to shape the expectations, style and intensity of the relationship between the imperial master and his servants as well as the collegial and hierarchical relationships among that body.

[75]Nathan, *Bahāristān*, I, p. 27.

[76]Jahangir, *Memoirs of Jahangir*, 2 vols, trans. A. Rogers, ed. H. Beveridge (London, 1909–14), *passim*.

The practice of escheat carried out by both Akbar and Jahangir in regard to the treasuries, mansions, armouries, stables, and other property of their deceased servants, certainly supports this interpretation. Contrary to the precepts of canonical law for the inheritance of free Muslims, but permissible of course for slaves, the practice remained unchallenged and unremarked upon save by foreign observers. When Mirza Nathan's father, Ihtimam Khan died suddenly of illness, the governor of Bengal quickly instituted the regulation procedure. On the fifth day of mourning, at a formal ceremony, the governor, Islam Khan, bestowed robes of honour upon Mirza Nathan and the other bereaved relatives. Afterwards, the Mirza surrendered his father's and his own elephants, and the guns, munitions and accounts of their joint armoury. He also confined the armoury treasurers and cashiers to ensure an accurate audit. At a legal proceeding held in the provincial *diwān*'s office (the *kachari*) the Qazi and the Superintendent of the court witnessed formal transfer of the dead officer's treasury, and other valuable property (save for a few personal items) to the agents of the governor. The Bengal governor then sent the sealed, secured money and valuables directly to the capital, along with the head accountant of Ihtimam Khan. The latter, Tula Ram, was expected to produce for verification his dead master's complete accounts of income and expenditure.[77] After concluding this procedure, the governor promoted Mirza Nathan from 100 *zāt*, 50 *suwār* to 500 *zāt*, 250 *suwār*, gave him two female elephants from his father's herd, and transferred seven *parganas* (subdistricts) from the *jāgīr* holdings of his father (necessary to defray the Mirza's increased salary and allowances).[78]

Emerging from this master–slave connection between the Emperor and his service élite were two more intensely felt bonds. The first, that of discipleship, for an elect chosen by the Emperor, we have already discussed. The second, that growing out of familial hereditary service, by the early 1600s was becoming of equal or even greater importance. *Khānazāds*, both Hindu and Muslim, had proven their devotion, reliability and capabilities over as many as three or even four generations.

[77]Nathan, *Bahāristān*, I, pp. 205–10. This procedure conforms to that described by Athar Ali, *The Mughal Nobility*, pp. 63–4. Aurangzeb seems to have confined his expropriations to those debts left outstanding to the imperial treasury. The earlier Emperors seized all properties and gave what they chose to the heirs.

[78]Nathan, I, pp. 206–9. The governor also advanced the Mirza money to pay for the funeral ceremonies of his father ibid. I, p. 203.

In Jahangir's time, the term *khānazād* (literally, 'son of the house') seems to have connoted actual residence in or connections with the imperial court palace or camp. To the extent that even the childhood and maturation of the *mansabdār* was known to the imperial family—as in the case of Mirza Nathan himself—the term may have referred to a type of informal page system for the harem and palace. Later, as the century progressed, *khānazād* came to have the wider meaning of pride in hereditary imperial service alone, without the necessary impetus of an initial personal relationship with the Emperor. Moreover, the conception permeated downward from the apex of the élite, the *amīrs* and nobles of 1000 *zāt* or more, to middling and lower *mansabdārs* and private officers in the service of imperial grandees. Obviously, if properly nurtured, *khānazādī* was a powerful conception which could intersect with the dynastic ideology put forward by Abul Fazl.

Mirza Nathan's night vision of the Emperor and his eagerness to act upon this occurrence, presumably derived from his birth and upbringing as a *khānazād*. When Prince Khurram, later Shah Jahan, rebelled and arrived in Bengal, he referred to the Mirza as 'one of the special servants of our Court, ... who was brought up from childhood under our feet'.[79] Undoubtedly rhetorical, Shah Jahan's phrasing nonetheless does convey a sense of personal familiarity with Nathan in boyhood and adolescence. Possibly, as the new generation of a Persian émigré family in imperial service, Nathan did grow up in the Emperor's giant household. Under such circumstances, if Nathan (as he seems to have) demonstrated qualities of military leadership and administrative skills, he received preferment and early command responsibilities in common with other able young *khānazāds* of similar background. As we have seen, further zealousness could bring the reward of discipleship and concomitant membership in an especially devoted élite cadre of *mansabdārs*.

Sustaining the bonds of hereditary familial service, and discipleship, was relatively easy for the Emperor at the imperial capital. Private, less formal audiences and interviews at fixed hours in the Emperor's consultation rooms or tents (the so-called *ghusul khāna* or 'bath-room') obviously provided opportunities for exhortation, private orders, and other matters with trusted *mansabdārs*. During the great daily 'public' assemblies in the audience hall of the palace or camp, the Emperor and his officers enacted formal rituals of authority and subordination. Imperial officers called before the throne offered at a minimum several

[79] Ibid., II, p. 702.

gold coins (*muhurs*) to the Emperor. After the sovereign uttered formal verbal confirmation of promotions, new titles, postings, etc., he favoured the officer with a full or partial robe of honour, a horse or an elephant, jewelled weapons, money or other artefacts. Most of the gifts for personal use thus bestowed could be construed to have some symbolic reference to the body and person of the King: e.g. the robe of honour, if not actually worn by Jahangir, was brushed momentarily across his shoulder.[80]

In the case of military campaigns, however, the Emperor rarely supervised or commanded in person. Thus, during the five years from 1608 to 1613 when Islam Khan energetically directed the conquest and administrative organization of Mughal Bengal, Jahangir remained at the imperial capital (either Agra, Lahore, or Kashmir in the hot season). Similarly, during later campaigns against the Arakanese or the Ahoms, Jahangir never visited Bengal in person. Moreover, the complete absence of any reference to a visit to court in Mirza Nathan's narrative suggests that he, and perhaps other mid-ranked field commanders, remained on the eastern frontier without recall for years on end (possibly even the 16 years from 1608 to 1624 covered by the memoir).

How, in view of such prolonged separation from the imperial centre, could even a pretence of personalized authority and loyalty between Emperor and disciple of *khānazād*, endure? One tangible, continuing contact with the Emperor was the confirmation of promotion in rank and a concomitant rise in pay, status and responsibility (or punitive demotion) following recommendation in the reports of the Bengal governor. From his first promotion to 500 *zāt*, 250 *suwār* at the death

[80]Cf. Thomas Roe, who received from Jahangir 'a cloth of gould Cloake of his owne, once or Twice worne, which hee caused to bee put on my back, and I made reverence ..., it is here reputed the highest of fauor to give a garment warne by the prince, or being New, once layed on his shoulder'. Roe, *Embassy*, II, p. 334. cf. the early analysis of F.W. Buckler in which he points out that kings in the Middle East, both ancient and Muslim, all employed the robe of honour. When the 'Eastern King' gave these dresses to his servants, 'he was incorporating into his own body, by means of certain symbolical acts, the persons of those who share his rule' (p. 239). In Arabic, *khil'at* and in Persian *saropā*, the robe of honour, as it is customarily translated, conveys 'some idea of continuity or succession' and 'that continuity rests on a physical basis, depending on contact with the body of the recipient with the body of the donor through the medium of clothing' (p. 241). F.W. Buckler 'The Oriental Despot', *Anglican Theological Review*, X, 1927–28, pp. 238–49.

of his father in 1612, Mirza Nathan progressed upward until, in 1621, after his part in the suppression of a Muslim *zamīndār's* rebellion, he became a noble or *amīr*, at 1000 *zāt*, 500 *suwār*. The imperial rescript sent to the Mirza, signed jointly by Jahangir and his wife Nur Jahan, also gave him a new honorific identity, the title Shitab Khan and a robe of honour.[81] To complete the transaction Mirza Nathan (now Shitab Khan) sent 42,000 rupees to the Empress Nur Jahan to acknowledge the superior value of the great favour bestowed upon him.

Other, personal gift exchanges with the distant master presumably helped to prolong this illusion. On various occasions, Nathan received via a special imperial messenger, a set of soft shawls (probably from Kashmir); a shield directly from the hand of the Emperor; and two sets of pendant pearl earrings (form among a set of 36 pairs sent to the Bengal commanders).[82] Whenever possible, Nathan organized a wild elephant hunt (a *kheda*) and sent his best captives to court as reciprocal personal offerings to the Emperor.[83]

Officers in Bengal, in common with their colleagues in other parts of the empire, also received written orders (*farmāns*) sealed with the great seal and *tughra* of the Emperor. Such special rescripts were brought rapidly from the court by either one or a pair of mace bearers, or by gentlemen cavalry troopers (*ahadīs*). Reception of such an order demanded that the recipient act as if the Emperor himself were arriving in person: riding with his retainers several miles to meet the messengers (if they sent advance notice); performing the court obeisance; and placing the object on his head and eyes and even kissing it before opening the container. The Emperor employed a more pointed form of personal substitution as well, in which his messenger, usually a man of considerable but not noble status and rank, at an appropriate moment recited verbatim injunctions, orders and reprimands to amplify the written orders.

In an attempt to reduce the notorious factiousness and inefficiency of Qasim Khan, governor of Bengal after Islam Khan, Jahangir sent a revenue officer, Ibrahim Kalal, with orders of censure for the governor,

[81]Nathan, II, p. 666. The interval between 500/250 was accomplished in two steps, the first to 625/250 for Nathan's part in the conquest of Kuch (ibid., II, p. 503); the second 700/350 to reward him for his assignment to pacify the Dakhinkul country and finally to the status of a noble at 1000/500 (ibid., II, p. 632.).

[82]Ibid., I, pp. 299–300.

[83]Ibid., II, pp. 667–87.

the provincial *dīwān*, the *bakhshī*, and the Bengal newswriter. When the envoy arrived at Dacca, the provincial capital, the governor met him, performed the proper obeisances to the imperial order, and installed the messenger in quarters near the governor's palace. The next morning, when the Governor, his three chief officers and all his army commanders (*khāns*) were assembled in the audience hall, Ibrahim Khan solemnly delivered from memory the Emperor's verbal rebuke to each of the four chief officers in turn. Without soliciting a reply he left rudely and abruptly to return to court.[84]

Such devices as these may have been effective in reasserting and strengthening the converging modes of personal authority and personal service: Emperor and disciple; Emperor and hereditary servant (*khānazād*); and Emperor and military slave—gradually fusing into what was to prove to be for the Indo-Muslim political tradition, a remarkably durable structure of imperial control. Clearly, the ability to perceive the person of the Emperor behind the material symbols of protestation, or his voice in the speech of a surrogate had become an imperial ritual—just as necessary for all nobles as acceptance and usage of the niceties of Indo-Persian courtly etiquette. Nevertheless, the bedrock of imperial authority lay in its appeal to a value for more pervasive. Jahangir, in rebuking the faulty leadership of Qasim Khan, stressed the governor's gravest excess:[85]

> Although through our kindness to slaves we address with our pearl-scattering tongue Qāsim Khān as our son, it is incumbent upon him to protect the honour of the imperial officers, high and low. It is also obligatory on the part of our slaves, for the sake of protecting their honour, to prefer death to the adoption of any dishonourable conduct.

The Emperor's admonishment was double-edged, for he was censuring the governor for plundering the house, and violating the honour of the provincial *dīwān* (fiscal officer), while at the same time he was also censuring the *dīwān* for not defending and asserting his honour as a warrior and imperial servant.

Whether 'men of the pen' or 'men of the sword', *khānazāds* or foreign-born aristocrats, rural Indian Muslims or urbane Persians, or Turks or Rajputs, the paradoxical appeal to enhancement of honour by submission to the Emperor's personal and dynastic authority cut across

[84]Ibid., II, pp. 307–10.
[85]Ibid., I, p. 309.

previously impassable social boundaries. Slaves could only possess honour, especially dignity of the warrior, in the reflection of a master of numinous powers and consummate honour. At the same time, however, it was the responsibility of the noble or *mansabdār* to preserve his individual honour and that of his family, status, group, or lineage. He must firmly demonstrate his readiness to defend his sexual honour, if the modesty or chastity of his women be threatened; his patrimonial honour, if the security and sanctity of his residence and property (including slaves and servants) be endangered; his familial honour, if his blood relatives be assaulted; and his religious or sectarian honour, if the sacred symbols of his religion be blasphemed. If the warrior-noble, or warrior-*mansabdār* could not thus uphold his reputation or name as an adherent of the code of the warrior, his utility as an imperial servant, as a commander or administrator of men was severely curtailed. At any time a threat to the warrior-commander's honour could come from other *mansabdārs* engaged in the ceaseless struggle for individual or group precedence (i.e. honour) from the Emperor. Or, alternatively, defeat in battle could cause the same threats from a different source. Under the most desperate circumstances in battle, the warrior-commander must be prepared for an epic sacrifice (or martyrdom in Muslim idiom) to retain his personal honour, his lineage honour and the honour of the Emperor, his master.

Violent, self-sacrificial death on the battlefield certainly found an important place in the Indo-Muslim martial tradition, in the ideal of the *ghāzī*. However, the norms of that tradition also placed more pragmatic restraints upon the self-destructive urge of the warrior, which in the emotional stress of perceived defeat or reverse could be expressed in battle as a desire for release for death, with personal honour intact. But for the servant of an imperial master or in the case of Mirza Nathan, a select and ardent disciple, such a response was self-indulgent since it did nothing to further either the reputation or the possessions of the Emperor.

These elements are sharply etched in Mirza Nathan's memoir. After more than a decade of service in Bengal, he suffered one of his few disastrous defeats in a battle with the Ahoms. Themselves an aggressive power, the Ahoms were expanding down the Brahmaputra valley when they first clashed with the Mughal armies.[86] Possibly grown somewhat

[86]For a detailed discussion of the Ahom–Mughal wars, inadequately analysed in general treatments of the Mughal empire, see Sarkar, *History of Bengal*, pp. 295–7.

careless, Mirza Nathan had moved his troops forward to the extremity of Mughal territory at Ranihat. Here he built a stockade fort and out-lying watchtowers, brought up his women and entire household, and supply establishment (*mahal*), while waiting for fresh troops to build up his battle-depleted forces.[87]

In one of the more dramatic episodes of the lengthy narrative the Ahom armies discovered the presence of the Mughal outpost. Acting under the personal orders of the Ahom king, they attacked quickly and in force. The first night after making contact, the Ahom generals utilized one of their most successful tactics: rapid construction of an immense wooden, palisaded stockade wall at a distance of one cannon shot opposite the outer wall of the Mughal fortification. The next day the Ahom general outmanoeuvered Mirza Nathan by generating a false report that the Mughal supply and communications line to the rear was blocked. This drew off part of the depleted Mughal force, whom Mirza Nathan sent to restore communications. Moreover, Shaikh Kamal, a Mughal noble who had clashed earlier with Mirza Nathan in a dispute over possession of *jāgīr* lands, held up the sending of reinforcements and supplies. The first full-scale Ahom assault resulted in occupation of the outlying Mughal stockade and total encirclement of Mirza Nathan's weakened forces. During the following night, the Ahoms, constructing a wooden and earthen wall fronted by a ditch, totally invested the imperial stockade walls. During the next day they regrouped and rested in preparation for the final assault. The Ahom commanders sent a demand to Mirza Nathan to surrender, offering to spare the lives of the imperial garrison.

At this point, a small group of 13 imperial *mansabdārs* evaded the Ahom guards and entered the fort. The 13 horsemen constituted a small lineage group of Usmani Afghans, serving as field cavalry at low ranks (possibly 20 to 80 or 100 *zāt*) who had campaigned with Mirza Nathan on earlier occasions. Disobeying the orders of Shaikh Kamal they had travelled to the Mirza's assistance. That night, distraught, Mirza Nathan was preparing to die fighting: he dismissed his servants and camp followers, ordering them to flee in the hope that the Ahoms would not bother with them. Next, in consultation with his officers and troops, Mirza Nathan found full agreement with the argument that they should reject the Ahom demand to surrender. He and his Muslim officers and troops each wrapped his shroud (*kafan*) around his head.

[87] See ibid., II, pp. 588–606 for the extended narrative of this episode.

They sent a reply to the Ahoms: 'As we have taken the salt of Jahāngīr, we consider martyrdom to be our blessings [*sic*] for both the worlds. You will see what [feats] we perform before you till our death.' Nathan, bringing out his gold plate and utensils from his household, ordered the paymasters to meet the salary arrears of all his soldiers. He then demanded of all Muslims that they take an oath on the Koran, and all Hindus that they swear 'according to Hindu custom' that they would remain together and 'would accept martyrdom following one another's footsteps'.

Remaining somewhat detached from these proceedings, the small groups of Usmani Afghans approached Nathan and argued that he should act rather than simply wait to be killed in the trap which the fort had become. They appealed to his obligation to avenge both his betrayal by Shaikh Kamal and his defeat and dishonour by the Ahoms for he had 'neither a son nor a brother ... who would be able to take vengeance on [his] internal and external foes'. Nor would his defeat and slaughter help the prestige of the empire. Implicit in the latter argument was the perception that a glorious death in defeat, while satisfying the individual honour of the self-sacrificing commander, was, in essence, selfish, and not commensurate with the more important interests of the Emperor and the empire. Dead, Mirza Nathan also could not satisfy the imperative of vengeance for betrayal (by Shaikh Kamal) and defeat by the Ahoms.

Persuaded by these arguments, Nathan loaded his field artillery on his elephants, and organized his soldiers into an assault column. The one remaining elephant served to carry Mirza Nathan's wife, sister and a companion. He put the women in charge of Nik Muhammad Bek (whose family had served Nathan's family for four generations) with orders to kill the women if Nathan died in battle. Thereafter Nik Muhammad Bek was to 'display whatever manliness you can and attain happiness'. Surprisingly, Nathan then ordered the 50-odd women remaining in the fort to perform immolation by fire, in the Hindu rite of *jauhar*. Several Mughal soldiers who were afraid of losing their honour if captured, joined the women in this rite of collective suicide. These preparations completed, the Mughal commander led his column from the fort. A running, desperate engagement followed, but as the Afghans had predicted, Nathan and at least some of his dispirited army managed to cross the Brahmaputra river to safety. The following day Nathan removed his turban (presumably with the Emperor's image attached) wrapped a ragged black shroud around his head, and made an oath not to remove it until he had avenged his defeat. A fresh army soon recruited, after several months of campaigning he won a substantial victory over the Ahoms. His officers were thus able to persuade him to remove his self-inflicted symbol of disgrace and put on his turban of honour once again.

4
Some Notes on Rājpūt Loyalties During the Mughal Period*

Norman P. Ziegler

Loyalty can be defined as a feeling of attachment to something outside the self, such as a group, an institution, a cause, or an ideal. The sentiment carries with it a willingness to support and act in behalf of the objects of one's loyalty and to persist in that support over an extended period of time and under conditions which exact a degree of moral, emotional, and material sacrifice from the individual.

Loyalties emerge out of the social matrix, and the processes of loyalty formation, growth, and change are closely akin to those involved in the process of identification.[1]

The question of Rājpūt loyalties during the Mughal period is a complex and paradoxical one. As dealt with in much of the literature on Rājpūts and Rājasthān, it partakes of the wider controversy among contemporary Indian historians about the nature of Muslim rule in India and local reactions to that rule. For some, Muslim and more particularly Mughal rule represents an era of religious tolerance and national unification, in which Rājpūts participated under the banners of their clan leaders, to whom they directed primary allegiances, as soldiers and administrators because of the prestige and benefits they gained through association with the Mughal throne.[2] For others, Rājpūt struggles for

*From J.F. Richards, ed. *Kingship and Authority in South Asia* (Madison: University of Wisconsin South Asian Studies, 1978.)

[1] J.H. Schaar, 'Loyalty', in D.L. Sills (ed.), *International Encyclopedia of the Social Sciences* (New York, 1968), vol. 9, p. 484.

[2] For example, see M. Athar Ali, *The Mughal Nobility Under Aurangzeb* (New York, 1970, reprint); Irfan Habib, *The Agrarian System of Mughal India* (New York, 1963); S. Nurul Hasan, 'Zamindars under the Mughals', in R.E. Frykenberg (ed.), *Land Control and Social Structure in Indian History* (Madison 1969), pp. 17–32 reproduced in this volume.

independence and their resistance to the Mughals have become symbolic of general Hindu resistance to Muslim domination. They explain Rājpūt co-operation with the Mughals with reference to conquest, cooption and collaboration out of political or economic necessity.[3]

Upon closer examination, the question of loyalties becomes much more diffused than the above views suggest. It is the purpose of this essay to examine the nature of these loyalties and the reasons behind Rājpūt fidelity to the Mughal throne in some detail. Such an examination is of importance for a number of reasons. Firstly, the Rājpūt alliance with the Mughals represents one of the more prominent Mughal 'successes', in contrast, for example, to the proverbial failure of Mughal relations in the Deccan. This alliance evolved into one of the primary supports of the empire and its partial dismemberment under Aurangzeb during the Rājpūt wars of the 1680s, historians of India often cite as one of the contributing causes of decline. Secondly, Mughal penetration into Rājasthān in the late sixteenth and seventeenth centuries involved the incorporation of a separate cultural group with its own distinct history, myths and customs within the larger orbit of north Indian politics, and the gaining of its active participation in the policies and goals of the empire. The Rājpūts occupied a relatively isolated frontier region of marginal agricultural importance, which is an extension of the great geographical and cultural shatter belt extending across Central India from Kāthiāvāṛ to Orissa, an area marked by great internal subdivision. This area was also a strategic transitional zone situated between larger cultural centres in Gujarāt and on the north Indian plain, criss-crossed by trade routes running between these larger centres.[4] Thirdly, our understanding of Rājpūt loyalties pertains to broader concerns with the functioning of imperial systems as a whole, and their problems with integration and control, authority and legitimacy.

[3]For example, see A.C. Banerjee, *Lectures on Rajput History* (Calcutta, 1962); V.S. Bhargava, *Marwar and the Mughal Emperors* (Delhi, 1966); J. Tod, *Annals and Antiquities of Rajasthan or the Central and Western Rajpoot States*, ed. by W. Crooke (London), 3 vols.

[4]For a discussion of the geographical significance of Rājasthān, and of regions in general, see O.H.K. Spate, *India and Pakistan: A General and Regional Geography* (London and New York, 1957), pp. 11, 44–57, 565–6; B.S. Cohn, 'Regions Subjective and Objective: Their Relation to the Study of Modern Indian History and Society', in R.I. Crane (ed.), *Regions and Regionalism in South Asian Studies: An Exploratory Study* (Durham, North Carolina, 1967), pp. 5–38.

The specific examination of Rājpūt loyalties is complicated by the variation in Rājpūt response, both with respect to particular individuals and through time. The differing reactions of Rāṭhoṛ Rāo Candrasen Māldeot of Jodhpur, Mārvāṛ, and his paternal nephew, Rājā Surajsiṃgh Udaisiṃghot, to Mughal rule are symbolic of this variation. Rāo Candrasen succeeded to the rulership of Jodhpur in 1562, shortly after Akbar's succession to the Mughal throne in 1556, and spent most of his life until his death in 1581, fighting Mughal armies which had invaded Mārvāṛ under the initial phases of Mughal expansion into Rājasthān.[5] In contrast, Rājā Surajsiṃgh spent the whole of his life, both before his succession to the rulership of Jodhpur in 1595, and after in active participation in imperial affairs in the Deccan and elsewhere in north India. His involvement in external affairs was so great that the Mārvāṛī chronicle of his reign records his having said, when Jahāngīr ordered him home to settle some local problem: 'What will I do if I go home? I don't know anything about affairs at home. I have left sole responsibility for their management in the hands of [my Pradhāṇ, Jeso Bhāṭī] Goyaṃdās [Mānāvat].[6]

The differing reactions of these two individuals we can explain to some degree with reference, on the one hand, to the Mughal attack upon Rāo Candrasen's position and land, and on the other, to Rājā Surajsiṃgh's long period of tutelage and socialization under the Mughals both as a boy and after Akbar personally confirmed his succession, and to specific obligations and personal attachments he had developed through this contact. But this does not offer a complete explanation, for Rāo Candrasen's brother, Udaisiṃgh, the father of Rājā Surajsiṃgh, whose lands the Mughals also took away, joined the Mughal standard even while his brother fought in exile from Mārvāṛ. Other Rāṭhoṛs, who were clan brothers of Candrasen also did the same. Why? How do we explain their actions? Socialization and the formation of personal obligations are important considerations in a few instances. But for the majoity of Rājpūts, contact with the Mughals was both indirect and intermittent, and Rājpūts, dealt with them and reacted to them more on the basis of locally derived sentiments.

[5] 'Aitihāsik Bātāṃ', *Parampara*, ed. N.S. Bhāṭī (Copāsnī, Rājasthānī Śodh Saṃsthān), pt 11, 1961, pp. 78–87.

[6] Naiṇsī, *Mārvāṛ rā Parganām rī Vigat*, ed. N.S. Bhāṭī (Jodhpur Rājasthān Prācyavidhyā Pratiṣṭhān), vol. 1 (1968), p. 97. This translation from the Mārvāṛi chronicle and others to follow are mine.

For an understanding of Rājpūt loyalties during this period, we must, therefore, turn to local political culture, that is to the system of empirical beliefs and the constellation of normative orientations which defined situations in which political actions took place and which provided a subjective orientation of the action.[7] In turning to aspects of political culture in an attempt to explain, in a broad sense, Rājpūt cultural response to Mughal domination, I am making a series of assumptions about the nature of loyalties and the functioning of pre-modern political systems in general. These are:

1. Loyalty—'the willingness to support and act in behalf of the objects of one's loyalty'—depends not only upon identification, which defines who one is with relation to others and one's place among them, and obligation, which bespeaks of duty and obedience, but also upon notions of what is 'right' and 'wrong' as defined in cultural terms. These aspects speak to questions of integration, of concepts of place and membership, and of shared values and institutions.[8]

2. Loyalty also depends upon a community of interest between the personal aims and aspirations of individuals and the objects of their loyalty, be they individuals or institutions. Loyalty thus is a product both of an individual's personal identification and his private satisfaction.[9]

3. In a broader context, loyalty depends upon conceptualizations of order, upon myth and bodies of 'significant symbols' which define that order, and which speak to ultimate goals, to what is as well as to what ought to be.[10] Such myths and symbols act both to rationalize present situations and to shape them.

[7]S. Verba, 'Comparative Political Culture', in L.W. Pye and S. Verba (eds), *Political Culture and Political Development* (Princeton, 1965), p. 513; Schaar, 'Loyalty', p. 484.

[8]E. Shils, 'Deference', in J.A. Jackson (ed.), *Social Stratification* (Cambridge, 1968), pp. 107, 120. See also by Shils, 'Charisma, Order and Status', *American Sociological Review*, 30 (April 1965), no. 2, pp. 199–213; L. A. Fallers, 'The Predicament of the Modern African Chief: An Instance from Uganda', *Inequality: Social Stratification Reconsidered*, (Chicago and London, 1973), pp. 42–55.

[9]Schaar, 'Loyalty', p. 485.

[10]C. Geertz, 'The Impact of the Concept of Culture on the Concept of Man', in Y.A. Cohen (ed.), *Man in Adaptation: The Cultural Present*, (Chicago, 1968), p. 24; and, 'Religion as a Cultural System', in M. Banton (ed.), *Anthropological* Approaches to the Study of Religion (New York and Washington, 1966), pp. 7–9; D. Schneider, *American Kinship: A Cultural Account* (Englewood Cliffs, NJ, 1968), p. 1.

4. In pre-modern societies, because of the nature of the economy, technology and the system of communications, which preclude high degrees of integration and contribute to the distribution of power and authority among various individuals and groups at different levels within the society,[11] loyalties are channelled both through a variety of primary and secondary groups, and subject to the influence of competing norms and standards, making for their multiplicity and the possibility of conflict. The latter is particularly the case in periods of stress and change.

Case Histories

This examination begins, perhaps somewhat arbitrarily, with the presentation of three case histories of individual Rājpūts who lived during the Mughal period. These cases are meant to provide an initial perspective on the lives and actions of Rājpūts and will serve as a backdrop to the following discussion. In addition, they serve the purpose of shifting our focus away from a preoccupation with local Rājpūt rulers and their actions and policies, which has dominated most studies of Rājasthān.

The case histories and much of the following discussion I have drawn from the genealogies (*pīḍhiyāṃ/vaṃsāvaliyāṃ*), clan histories (*khyāt-bāt*) and administrative chronicles (*vigat*) of the Rāṭhoṛ Rajpūts of Mārvāṛ, western Rājasthān. The documents themselves date from the mid-seventeenth century. They are comprised largely of local oral traditions, supplemented with information from written documents of genealogists and various Rājpūt courts, which Mahārājā Jasvaṃt Siṃgh of Jodhpur (1638–78) had his Dīvāṇ, Muṃhata Naiṇsī Jaimalot, compile and submit to writing. They represent part of an extremely important body of Rājpūt literature, which arose in response to Mughal contact and subsequent Rājpūt efforts both to reinterpret local values and ideologies, and to defend local positions of rank and authority.[12]

[11] B.S. Cohn, 'Political Systems in Eighteenth Century India: The Benares Region', *Journal of the American Oriental Society*, Vol. 82, no. 3, (July–Sept. 1962), pp. 312–13.

[12] I have discussed these sources and their importance elsewhere in detail. See N.P. Ziegler, 'The Seventeenth Century Chronicles of Mārvār: A Study in the Evolution and Use of Oral Tradition in Western India', *History in Africa: A Journal of Method*, Vol. III (1976); and 'Mārvārī Historical Chronicles: Sources for the Social and Cultural History of Rājasthān', *Indian Economic and Social History Review*, vol. XIII, no. 2, Apr–June 1976, pp. 219–50.

Case I: Rāṭhoṛ Māṃḍaṇ Kuṃpāvat[13]

Māṃḍaṇ was a Rājpūt of the Kūṃpāvat *khāṃp* (twig) of Mārvāṛ Rāṭhoṛs, and the son of Kūṃpojī Mahirājot, from whom this branch of Rāṭhoṛs stems. His ancestry goes back in direct line of descent to Rāo Riṇmaljī Cūṃḍāvat (*c.* 1428–38), his great-great-grandfather, who first consolidated Rāṭhoṛ rule in central Mārvāṛ at Maṃḍor and whose son, Rāo Jodhojī Riṇmalot (*c.* 1453–89), founded Jodhpur city. Māṃḍaṇ's great-grandfather was Akhairāj Riṇmalot, eldest son of Rāo Riṇmaljī. Akhairāj received an area around the village of Bagṛī (10 miles east of Sojhat town in eastern Mārvāṛ) as his patrimonial inheritance shortly after Rāo Jodhojī established his new seat of rulership at Jodhpur, and he proceeded to consolidate his authority there by capturing the area from some other Rāṭhoṛs of the Sīṃdhaḷ *khāṃp*.

Akhairāj's son, Mahirāj, and his son, Kūṃpo, continued to occupy villages in the area of eastern Sojhat until the time of Rāo Gāṃgo Vāghāvat (ruler of Jodhpur, *c.* 1515–32). At this time, Kūṃpojī, who had been a retainer (*cākar*) of Rāo Vīramde Vāghāvat, the younger brother of Rāo Gāṃgo and Ṭhākur of Sojhat, joined Rāo Gāṃgo. Rāo Vīramde had been engaged in considerable hostilities with Rāo Gāṃgo over control of lands in Mārvāṛ until his death around 1530. According to the Mārvāṛī *khyāts*, Kūṃpojī changed sides because of offers from Rāo Gāṃgo and his son, Kuṃvar Mālde, of villages which exceeded those he held in Sojhat in value. Kuṃvar Mālde, who succeeded Gāṃgo to the rulership of Jodhpur in 1532, particularly valued Kūṃpo's prowess as a warrior, and Kūṃpojī rose under Mālde to become one of his foremost Pradhāṇs (military commander).

Mālde granted Kūṃpoji authority over several large tracts of land in Mārvāṛ and elsewhere, which Mālde's armies had conquered during the years of expansion in the early part of his reign. One of these areas included the village of Āsop (50 miles north-east of Jodhpur city) and others nearby, which eventually became the *ṭhikāṇa* (seat of rule) of the Kūṃpāvats descended from Māṃḍan Rāṭhoṛ.

Māṃḍaṇ himself was probably born during the latter years of Rāo Gāṃgojī's rule at Jodhpur, and he served along with his three elder brothers under his father in the armies of Rāo Mālde, while growing up in Āsop. Then in 1544, his father and at least two of his elder

[13]For references to Māṃḍaṇ Rāṭhoṛ and his family, see Paṃdit Rāmkaraṇ Āsop, *Āsop kā Itihās* (Jodhpur, n.d.), pp. 16–56; *Naiṇsī rī Khyāt*, ed. P.V. Muni, III (Jodhpur 1964), pp. 80–6 124–33, 274; 'Aitihāsik Bātāṃ', pp. 40–5, 51, 58–9, 74–5, 91; Naiṇsī, *Vigat*, I, pp. 38, 43–5, 56, 63, 77.

brothers were killed in the battle of Samel against Sher Shāh Sūr, whose victory here effectively ended Rāo Mālde's expansion in western Rājasthān and much reduced his authority throughout Mārvāṛ.

Āsop was included among the areas over which Mālde lost control to Sher Shāh, and although Māṃḍaṇ continued to serve under Rāo Mālde for a number of years after his father's death, he finally left Mārvāṛ with his family and personal retainers sometime around 1555–6. The reasons behind Māṃḍaṇ's migration from Jodhpur are unclear, but at least one local source indicates that they were directly related to Mālde's much reduced control within Mārvāṛ and his inability to provide his retainers with lands.

When Māṃḍaṇ left Jodhpur, he proceeded to Delhī, arriving there at the time of Akbar's succession to the Mughal throne in 1556. He appears to have joined Akbar's service soon thereafter, for the *khyāts* record that in 1557, he received Āsop and 13 other villages in Mārvāṛ in *jāgīr* from Akbar. He also held the area of Jhūṃjhaṇūṃ in central Rājasthān in *jāgīr* for a short time.

It is unclear how long Māṃḍaṇ initially remained in Akbar's service, for he is next mentioned as having joined Rāo Candrasen, who succeeded Rāo Mālde to the rulership of Jodhpur in 1562. This period was an extremely unsettled one in Mārvāṛ, which came under Mughal attack in the mid-1560s. In the early 1570s we find Māṃḍaṇ again leaving Mārvāṛ shortly before Akbar's troops forced Rāo Candrasen himself into exile in the Arāvallī hills in 1574. This time, Māṃḍaṇ proceeded to Mevāṛ, where he became a retainer of Sīsodiyo Rāṇo Udaisiṃgh Sāṃgāvat (*c*. 1537–72), and his son and successor, Rāṇo Pratāp Udaisiṃghot (*c*. 1572–95).

The *khyāts* make much of the fact that while Māṃḍaṇ stayed in Mevāṛ he also took revenge for the murder of one of his brothers who occupied a village near Sojhat in Mārvāṛ, and who had been killed by a Sīṃdhaḷ Rāṭhoṛ named Sīho over a dispute about the possession of some horses. Upon learning of his brother's death, Māṃḍaṇ raided into Mārvāṛ and killed Sīho in a battle near the village of Jaitāran (some 60 miles due east of Jodhpur city). This battle and the death of Sīho led to further hostilities with the Sīṃdhaḷs who sought to avenge Sīho, and ended only when Rāo Candrasen sent a small force of troops to assist Māṃḍaṇ.

Māṃḍaṇ then rejoined Rāo Candrasen during the latter's period of exile in the Arāvallīs and southern Rājasthān, returning to Mevāṛ to continue serving under Rāṇo Pratāp in 1581, upon the death of Rāo Candrasen. Rāṇo Pratāp was himself involved in a struggle with the

Mughals at this time, and we find Māṃḍaṇ leaving Mēvaṛ sometime between 1582 and 1583, to join Rāo Candrasen's brother, Udaisiṃgh Māldeot. Udaisiṃgh was then an imperial *mansabdār* of Akbar, living at Samāvalī (near Gwālior), to which Akbar had sent him to quell some disturbances of local Gujars and which Akbar later granted him in *jāgīr*.

In 1583, Akbar appointed Udaisiṃgh Māldeot (better known as the Moṭā Rājā) ruler of Jodhpur and granted him the title of 'Rājā' and a *mansab* of 1000 *zāt*. Māṃḍaṇ then returned to Jodhpur along with the Moṭā Rājā and served under him and his successor, Rājā Surajsiṃgh, until he was killed in 1603, while leading operations against Rāṭhoṛs in far western Mārvāṛ who refused to submit to the authority of the Jodhpur ruler. During this latter period, Māṃḍaṇ also held a *mansab* under Akbar, for the *khyāts* record that Akbar directly granted him Āsop and other villages as a separate *jāgīr* upon his return to Mārvāṛ.

I have little information about Māṃḍaṇ's wives or daughters and their places of marriage. He did have seven sons, three of whom succeeded him to the ṭhakurship of Ṭhikāṇa Āsop and played roles of varying importance in the history of Mārvāṛ. There is also some information about his personal retainers.[14] Several of them were Bhāṭī Rajpūts of the Jeso *khāṃp* (see Case II concerning the Jesā Bhāṭīs), and at least one was a Sonagara Cahuvāṇ of the Sāṃcor branch. All of them were individuals who followed Māṃḍaṇ on his wanderings through Rājasthān and north India, and at one time or another held villages under him. The Jeso Bhāṭī connection with Māṃḍaṇ is of particular interest because it extends back to the time of Māṃḍaṇ's grandfather, Mahirāj Akhairājot. Mahirāj had married the daughter of Jeso Bhāṭī Bhairavdās Jesāvat, and she became the mother of Māṃḍaṇ's father, Kūṃpojī. Two of Bhairavdās Jesāvat's brothers' sons afterwards became retainers of Kūṃpojī and died with him at the battle of Samel in 1544. The sons and grandsons of one of these Bhāṭīs continued on in the service of Māṃḍaṇ, along with other close relations who joined them in his service. The *khyāts* contain no further information on marriages between Māṃḍaṇ or his family and the Jesā Bhāṭīs, but it is highly probable that some of these Bhāṭīs also married their daughters to either Kūṃpo or Māṃḍaṇ.

[14]For information on Māṃḍaṇ's retainers, see *Naiṇsī rī Khyāt*, I (1960), p. 243; II (1962), pp. 172, 178, 181, 184, 187, 192.

Case II: Bhāṭī Surtāṇ Mānāvat[15]

Surtāṇ was a Bhāṭī Rajpūt of the Jeso *khāṃp*, the second son of Māno Nīṃbāvat and fifth generation in descent from Jeso Kalikaraṇot, from whom this *khāṃp* stems. His ancestor, Jeso, was the eldest son of a younger son of Rāvaḷ Kehar Devrājot, the ruler of Jaisaḷmer (*c.* 1361–94). He had migrated from Jaisalmer to Nagaur in late fifteenth century. Here he apparently entered the service of the Khānazāda Muslim ruler of the area,[16] from whom he received the village of Bhāuṃḍo which he held on patrimonial tenure and which remained in his family intermittently thereafter until the time of Surtāṇ Mānāvat. Later on, he left Nāgaur and went to Mevāṛ, where he held the villgae of Thāṇo and others from the Sīsodiyo Rāṇo, under whom he served as a retainer.

His descendants did not remain in Mevāṛ long. We find several of his sons in Mārvāṛ at the time of Rāo Sūjo Jodhāvat, ruler of Jodhpur (*c.* 1492–1515). Sūjo had married Jeso's half-sister while still a Kuṃvar, and it appears to have been this tie which brought the Jesā Bhāṭīs to Mārvāṛ and out of which the rather enduring relations between them and the rulers of Jodhpur developed.

Surtāṇ represented a younger son of the elder branch of the Jeso *khāṃp*. He was descended from Jeso's eldest son, Āṇaṃd, about whom the Bhāṭī genealogy gives no information. Āṇaṃd appeared to have returned either to Jaisaḷmer or to have gone to Nāgaur and Bhāuṃḍo village from Mevāṛ. Āṇaṃd's eldest son, Nīṃbo, later migrated into Mārvāṛ at the time of Rāo Mālde (*c.* 1532–62), under whom he took service. Mālde granted him the village of Lavero (some 35 miles north of Jodhpur city). Nīṃbo held Lavero until his death in 1544, in the

[15]For references to the Jesā Bhātīs, Surtāṇ Mānāvat and his family, see *Naiṇsī rī Khyāt*, II, pp. 75–7, 152–3, 157–8, 160; III, pp. 7, 103–5; Naiṇsī, *Vigat*, I, pp. 96, 99; 'Aitihāsik Bātāṃ', p. 90; *Tavārīkh-Jaisaḷmer*, comp. and ed. Muṃhata Nathmalji and Sevak Lakhmicand (Ajmer, 1891), pp. 42–5, 101; *Baṃkīdās rī Khyāt*, ed. P. J. Muni (Jaipur, 1956), p. 119; *Rāṭhoṛom kī Khyāt Purāṇī Kavirājjī Murārdānjī ke Yahāṃ se Likhī Gaī*, MS no. 15672, no. 2 (Rājasthān Prācyavidhya Prātiṣṭhān, Jodhpur, Rājasthān), p. 418; V.N. Reu, *Mārvāṛ kā Itihās* (Jodhpur, 1938), I, p. 192, fn. 2; G.H. Ojhā, *Rājpūtāne kā Itihās*, IV Ajmer, (1938), pt 1, pp. 374–5.

[16]The Khānazāda Muslims were a minor branch of the Muslim kings of Gujarāt, and ruled Nāgaur between 1400 and 1535, when Rāo Mālde of Jodhpur captured the area. See Naiṇsī, *Vigat*, II (1969), p. 421; M.A. Chaghtai, 'Nagaur, A Forgotten Kingdom,' *Bulletin of the Deccan College Post-Graduate and Research Institute*, no. 1 (Poona, 1939), pp. 175–6.

great battle against Sher Shāh Sūr. His eldest son, Māno, in turn served under Mālde and then Moṭā Rājā Udaisiṃgh, both before Udaisiṃgh succeeded to the rulership of Jodhpur in 1583, and for a short time thereafter until his death.

Surtāṇ was probably born in the late 1560s or early 1570s, while his father served under Udaisiṃgh at Phaḷodhī, the area of northern Mārvāṛ which Udaisiṃgh had received as his inheritance upon Rāo Mālde's death. With Surtāṇ at Phaḷodhī were also his elder brother, Goyaṃdās, who later rose to the position of Pradhāṇ of Jodhpur under the Moṭā Rājā and his successor, Rājā Sūrajsiṃgh Udaisiṃghot (*c.* 1595–1619), and a younger brother, Sādūl, who died of gunpowder burns at the battle of Rājpipla in Gujarāt in 1583. Sādūl had accompanied the Moṭā Rājā there to suppress the rebellion of Pātsāh Muzaffar Khān.

When the Moṭā Rājā succeeded to the rulership of Jodhpur in 1583, he granted all three brothers joint possession of Lavero and other surrounding villages. These villages appear to have been divided equally among the brothers (the texts are not specific here), for the Bhāṭī genealogy records Surtāṇ as holding the villages of Kelāvo (some 10 to 12 miles south of Lavero), Vikūṃkohar (30 miles west of Lavero) and 20 others in addition to Lavero, which seems only a general designation. The genealogy also notes that Surtāṇ held Kelāvo specifically until 1605. Possession of all of these villages continued after the death of the Moṭā Rājā in 1595, under his successor, Rājā Sūrajsiṃgh.

There is little information about Surtāṇ's activities while he served as a retainer under the Moṭā Rājā. In the early years of Rājā Sūrajsiṃgh's rule, he took part in local operations in Mārvāṛ connected with bringing the *pargana* of Sojhat under Sūrajsiṃgh's control. This *pargana* Akbar had taken from Rājā Sūrajsiṃgh's brother, Sakatsiṃgh, and granted to the Rājā in 1600, and there were problems associated with the transfer of authority relating to Sakatsiṃgh's unwillingness to relinquish the land until the arrival of an imperial *farmān* from Delhī.

Then in 1605, Surtāṇ accompanied his brother, Goyaṃdās, and the Rājā of Jodhpur with an army to Gujarāt, where he took part in the battle of Māṃḍav against the Kolīs. He seems to have performed well in battle, for Sūrajsiṃgh afterwards rewarded him with the grant of the important village of Bhādrājūṇ and 25 others, which he then occupied instead of those around Lavero. For some unexplained reason, these villages were taken away in 1607, and he again received his previously held villages around Lavero.

In 1611, Surtāṇ accompanied Rājā Surajsiṃgh to the Deccan. While away from Mārvāṛ, Rājā Surajsiṃgh had given Surtāṇ's brother, Goyaṃdās, and his own son Kuṃvar Gajsiṃgh Sūrajsiṃghot, authority over Jodhpur. Goyaṃdas, who was *pradhāṇ* of Jodhpur, employed the services of one of Surtāṇ's *ṭhikāṇa* administrators, a man by the name of Muṃhata Keso, during Surtāṇ absence. Muṃhata Keso's actions embittered Surtāṇ, for when he learned about his Muṃhata's 'defection', he left his post in the Deccan, returned to Mārvāṛ and killed Keso. In response to this murder, Surtāṇ's brother, Goyaṃdās, drove him out of Mārvāṛ.

Surtāṇ then fled to Nāgaur, where he became a retainer of Kachvāha Mādhosiṃgh Bhagvaṃtdāsot, the brother of Rājā Mānsiṃgh of Aṃber. Mādhosiṃgh, an imperial *mansabdār* with a rank of 3000/2000, held this area in *jāgīr* from Jahāngīr between 1606 and 1616.[17] Surtāṇ also received his ancestral village of Bhāuṃḍo from Mādhosiṃgh at this time, where he settled.

Surtāṇ's receipt of this village immediately brought him into conflict with Rāṭhoṛ Narsiṃghdās Kalyāṇdāsot, who occupied the village prior to Surtāṇ's arrival. Rāṭhoṛ Narsiṃghdās was the son of Kalyāṇdās Rāymalot (see Case III below), and a great-grandson of Rāo Mālde Gāṃgāvat of Jodhpur. According to the Mārvāṛī sources, there were several outbreaks of hostilities between Narsiṃghdās and Surtāṇ, both at the time Surtāṇ took possession of Bhāuṃḍo village and shortly thereafter, when Narsiṃghdās brought a small contingent of retainers including his two brothers, Īsardās and Mādhodās, several Meṛtiyā Rāṭhoṛs and other Rajpūts, against Surtāṇ. During the latter attack, which took place in May 1613, both Surtāṇ and Narsiṃghdās were killed.

[17]The Mārvaṛī sources all note that Surtāṇ settled in the land of Sīsodiyo Bāno Sāgar Udaisiṃghot, but this assertion seems incorrect. Sāgar held Nāgaur in *jāgīr* for only one year between 1601 and 1606. He was one of the younger sons of Rāṇo Udaisiṃgh Sāṃgāvat of Mevāṛ. Jahāngīr had given him the title of 'Rāṇo' and the *jāgīr* of Citoṛ and Nāgaur at the time he sent Prince Parviz into Mevāṛ against Rāṇo Pratāp. Sāgar held the title and the *jāgīr* of Citoṛ until 1619, when Jahāngīr took away the title and replaced it with that of 'Rāvat' and granted him a *jāgīr* outside of Mevāṛ. See Naiṇsī, *Vigat,* II, p. 422; *Naiṇsī ṛī Khyāt,* I, p. 391; Ojhā, *Rājpūtāne kā Itihās,* II (1932), pp. 796, 815; *Kavirāj Murārdānjī kī Khyāt kā Tarjuma,* MS no. 25658, no. 1, (Rājasthān Prācyavidhyā Pratiṣṭhān, Jodhpur, Rājasthān), p. 608; Abu'l-Fazl, *The A'īn-ī-Akbarī,* trans. H. Blochmann, ed. S.L. Gloomer (Delhi, 1971), pp. 460–1.

Surtāṇ's brother, Goyaṃdās, and Kuṃvar Gajsiṃgh of Jodhpur immediately took revenge for the death of Surtāṇ by killing one Rāthoṛ Rajpūt who had taken part in the attack on Surtāṇ. The hostilities did not end here. They can be traced in the Mārvāṛī genealogies two more generations and led at least to two other deaths. In order to escape further retribution from Surtāṇ's brother, Rāthoṛ Narsiṃghdās's brothers, Īsardās and Māhodās, apparently left Mārvāṛ sometime around 1616, for Burhānpur in the Deccan. There they met Rājā Surajsiṃgh and entreated him to end the hostilities, for which they claimed no fault. At the same time, they declared the Rājājī to be their father and further entreated him to retain them. Surajsiṃgh in turn prevailed upon Mohabat Khān to accept them as retainers, which he did. Īsardās was later killed in the Deccan fighting under the command of Mohabat Khān's son, while Mohabat Khān himself killed Mādhodās in Kābul, over an insult relating to the imperial family.

While Īsardās and Mādhodās escaped the revenge of the Bhāṭīs, Īsardās's son, Narhardās, did not. The last trace of hostilities I have come across relates to his death at the hands of Bhāṭī Goyaṃdās Mānāvat's son, who killed him while he was on his way from the Deccan to Mārvāṛ, when they happened to cross paths along the way.

I have no information on Surtāṇ's wives or daughters. He had six sons, five of whom remained in Mārvāṛ and served under the Jodhpur rulers. There are also references to two Rājpūts who were his personal retainers. One of these men was Bhāṭī Mādho Riṇmalot, the son of Surtāṇ's father's brother, Riṇmal Nīṃbāvat. The other was a Jodho Rāṭhoṛ named Jasvaṃt Hamīrot. It is significant with regard to Rāṭhoṛ Jasvaṃt, that his brother, Bhopat Hamīrot, had married one of Surtāṇ's sisters, whom Surtāṇ's brother, Goyaṃdas, had given to him in marriage after the death of their father.[18]

Case III: Rāṭhoṛ Kalyāṇdās Rāmalot[19]

Kalyāndās was a Rajpūt of the Jodho *khāṃp* of Mārvāṛ Rāṭhoṛs stemming from Rāo Jodhojī Riṇmalot, the founder of Jodhpur city. He was

[18]For information on Surtāṇ's personal retainers, and on the Rajpūts involved in hostilities with him and his family, see *Naiṇsī rī Khyāt*, II, p. 161; *Rāṭhoroṃ kī Khyāt*, pp. 417–18, 531–2; *Kavirāj Murārdānjī kī Khyāt*, pp. 606–10.

[19]For references to Kalyāṇdās and his family, see *Kavirāj Murardānjī ki Khyāt*, p. 605; *Rāṭhoroṃ kī Khyāt*, pp. 188–90; Naiṇsī, *Vigat*, II, p. 77; Ojhā, *Rājpūtāne kā Itihās*, IV, pt 1, p. 360.

the son of Rāymal Māldeot and the grandson of Rāo Mālde Gāṃgāvat, the ruler of Jodhpur. According to the Rāṭhoṛ genealogy, Kalyāṇdās's father, Rāymal, became a retainer of Akbar shortly after Akbar's succession ot the Mughal throne in 1556. Why Rāymal left his father, Rāo Mālde, and joined Mughal service is unclear, but his migration from Mārvāṛ occurred during the period of Mālde's much restricted rule in Mārvāṛ after the battle with Sher Shāh Sūr in 1544. Rāymal was also a younger son of Rāo Mālde, born of a minor queen, Rāṇī Hīrāde Jhālī, the daughter of Jhālo Mānsiṃgh of Halod,[20] which may have influenced his decision to leave. I have no information about the village or villages he held from Mālde in Mārvāṛ, nor the extent of his patrimony.

Rāymal appears to have been only a low-ranking *mansabdār* in Akbar's service, but Akbar did grant him the fort of Sīvāṇo (60 miles south-west of Jodhpur city) and surrounding villages in *jāgīr*. He held these until his death around the time that Moṭā Rājā Udaisiṃgh succeeded to the rulership of Jodhpur in 1583.

From all indications, Rāymal's son, Kalyāṇdās, continued in Akbar's service after his father's death and also received Sīvāṇo in *jāgīr*. It is also likely that he had been born at Sīvāṇo during the early part of his father's tenure there, but the Mārvāṛi texts supply no details. They mention only that Kalyāṇdās was an imperial servant at Lāhor, and that he was killed around 1589, by his paternal uncle, Moṭā Rājā Udaisiṃgh.

Two different versions of events leading up to his death exist. According to one, Kalyāṇdās became angry one day while engaged in imperial duties (presumably at Lāhor), and killed a Sayyid, who was a *mansabdār* of Akbar. When Akbar learned of the murder, he ordered the Moṭā Rājā to kill Kalyāṇdās, who had meanwhile fled to Sīvāṇo and taken refuge in the fort there. According to the other version, Kalyāṇdās took offence at the Moṭā Rājā's marriage of his daughter, Jodh Bāī, to Prince Salīm, shortly after the Moṭā Rājā succeeded to the Jodhpur throne.[21] The Rāṭhoṛ genealogy records that Kalyāṇdās threatened to kill both Moṭā Rājā Udaisiṃgh and Prince Salīm on account of this marriage to the 'Turks'. When news of Kalyāṇdās's threats reached Akbar, he ordered the Moṭā Rājā to kill him. In agreement with the first account, this version also states that Kalyāṇdās fled to

[20] *Naiṇsī rī Khyāt*, II, p. 256; *Rāṭhoṛoṃ kī Khyāt*, p. 142.

[21] For details regarding this marriage, see Bhargava, *Marwar and the Mughal Emperors*, pp. 58–9.

Sīvāṇo. Both accounts indicate that the fort fell to Moṭā Rājā Udaisiṃgh in 1589, and that Kalyāṇdās died here in battle along with his several wives, who performed *jauhar* from the fort walls.

I have no information on Kalyāṇdās's wives or daughters. He had several sons, mentioned in connection with Bhāṭī Surtāṇ Mānāvat (see Case II, above). I also find one reference to a personal retainer of his, a Jeso Bhāṭī named Khetsī Ūdāvat. Khetsī took part in the battle of Sīvāṇo fort and was wounded there. Afterwards, Kānha Kisnāvat, the son of one of Ketsī's father's brothers, who was a servant of the Moṭā Rājā, picked him up from the field and cared for him. Khetsī then also joined the service of the Moṭā Rājā, under whom he held the village of Jāṭivās near Jodhpur city.[22]

Primary Loyalties and the State

During the Mughal period, there were two primary units of reference and identification for a Rājpūt. These were his brotherhood (*bhāībaṃdh*) and his relations by marriage (*sagā*). In the widest sense, the brotherhood was a patrilineal unit of descent represented by the clan (*vaṃs/kuḷ*), which included all those related by ties of male blood to a common ancestor (*vaḍero*). However, the clan was generally widely dispersed over different territories within Rājasthān and was not itself a corporate group in the sense that it enjoyed joint control over a specific territory. The functionally corporate units were smaller brotherhoods, namely, internal segments of the wider clan (*khāṃp* or *nak*),[23] consisting of from three to five or six generations and including all

[22]For references to Kalyāṇdās's retainer and Jeso Bhāṭī Kānha Kisnāvat, see *Naiṇsī rī Khyāt*, II, pp. 164–5, 173.

[23]Rajpūt clans are internally segmented first into branches (*sākh/sakhām*), and then into lesser divisions of *khāṃp* (twig), and *nak* (bud). Each unit is designated by a particular name which may be either that of an ancestor, from whom the line descends, or that of a local territory, where the line first became established. *Gotra* affiliations are generally found at the level of *khāṃp*. But in Rājasthān, a clan or several branches of a clan often have the same *gotra* designation. The *gotra* name determines the boundaries of exogamy.

members related by close ties of male blood, their wives,[24] sons and unmarried daughters.[25]

Territory which the brotherhood controlled often carried the name of the brotherhood itself, with the suffix *vaṭ* or *vaṭi* (share/portion) attached to the name and indicating lands obtained through the division of shares among brothers (*bhai vaṃṭ*). This territory the brotherhood also referred to as its birthplace or homeland (*vatan/janm-bhom*). It was both the centre of the brotherhood's origin and expansion, and the land from which it was felt to derive its sustenance and strength. The two entities, brotherhood and land, were felt to be inseparably linked and mutually supportive. The symbol of this linkage was the *piṃḍa*, a ball of food or clay made either from the sustenance of the land or the land itself, which the brotherhood offered up to its ancestors, who had conquered and enjoyed mastery over the land before them. One finds references to mortally wounded Rājpūts mixing their blood with the land to form *piṃḍas* and offering these up before death.[26] Such acts represented the return of strength to the land and its nourishment of the brotherhood, which preserved the 'body' and enabled it to continue to rule.

While these corporate brotherhood acknowledged ties to the wider clan and paid varying degrees of deference to 'senior' or 'ruling' line by descent within the clan,[27] in general they looked upon themselves

[24]Wives are included as members of the brotherhood, because it is felt that upon marriage a woman becomes transformed into a person related by male blood to her husband and his brothers. See *Naiṇsī rī Khyāt*, II pp. 327–8; III, p. 163; *Brandreth's Treatise on the Law of Adoption in Rajpootana* (with notes by Col. J.C. Brooke), (Calcutta, 1871), pp. 5, 22; 'Law and Practice in Cases of Adoption and Succession to Sovereignties in Rajputana', Rajputana Agency Office Historical Record 27, 75/General, vol. I (1846, 1853, 1859) (National Archives of India, New Delhi), p. 11.

[25]*Naiṇsī rī Khyāt*, I, pp. 64, 119; 'Vāt Tiḍai Chāḍāvat rī', *Vātāṃ ro Jhumakho*, ed. M. Sarma (Bisau, n.d.), pt 3, p. 40.

[26]Aitihāsik Bātāṃ', p. 43. *Piṃḍa* can mean both 'ball (of food or clay)' and 'body'.

[27]This expression of deference applied primarily to brotherhoods not too far removed genealogically from the senior or ruling line. Those which had branched off many generations back generally granted no deference at all and considered themselves totally independent of the authority of the senior line. This hierarchical differentiation of territorial units and settlements based on descent is similar to that Kashi Nath Singh discusses with reference to Rājpūt settlements in eastern Uttar Pradesh. See Kashi Nath Singh, 'The Territorial Basis of Medieval Town and Village Settlement in eastern Uttar Pradesh', *Annals of the Association of American Geographers*, LVIII (1968), pp. 203–20.

as separate and distinct units. Each claimed equal prerogatives and rights to precedence over land by descent. Other brotherhoods of the same clan comprised more distantly related 'brothers', occupying territories separate from their own, and were no different from the brotherhoods of other Rājpūt clans located nearby.

The other primary unit of reference and identification for the Rājpūt was his *sagā*, those to whom he gave daughters and/or from whom he received wives in marriage. This relationship was of particular importance, for at the same time that the act of marriage was seen to unite a woman with her husband's brotherhood, it was also seen to create an alliance. The term in Mārvāṛī (western Rājasthānī) for both betrothal and alliance is *sagāī*, a derivative of *sagā*. After marriage, the husband's father usually gave his son's wife a new name, which symbolized her 'birth' into the brotherhood. But the members of her father's brotherhood still continued to call her 'sister' (*bāī*), and strong relations of support and affection between a mother's brother (*māmā*) and his sister's son (*bhāṇej*) figure prominently in the Rājpūt literature.[28] In addition, individual Rajpūts themselves were identified not only by the name of their father and his brotherhood, but also by the name of their mother's father or brother and his brotherhood. Genealogical entries in particular display this feature, listing individuals as daughter's son (*dohitro*) or sister's son of a certain Rājpūt clan, one of its subdivisions, or a particular individual.

The importance of *bhāībaṃdh* and *sagā* as primary or primordial units of reference and identification persisted during the Mughal period because of their centrality in defining who a Rājpūt was. There were also units of natural affinity which called forth immediate sentiments of reciprocity, support and assistance, and in this sense organized the basic loyalties of most Rājpūts.[29] They did not necessarily command all his allegiances, however, for the complex of loyalties within territories which particular brotherhoods dominated display complexities generated by structural features of these groups themselves. We can

[28]For example, see *Naiṇsī ri Khyāt*, III, pp. 63–4, 68–9.

[29]C. Geertz, 'The Integration Revolution: Primordial Sentiments and Civil Politics in the New States', in C. Geertz (ed.), *Old Societies and New States: The Quest for Modernity in Asia and Africa* (New York, 1963), pp. 108–29; Shils, 'Deference', pp. 107–15. Shils defines centres as those positions which 'exercise earthly powers and which mediate man's relationship to the order of existence' (p. 107).

distinguish several different institutions or organizational principles which governed these groups and influenced the direction of loyalty.

Among some brotherhoods, which remained relatively undifferentiated during this period, kinship remained the dominant institution. This characteristic is particularly true, for example of semi-independent Rāṭhoṛ brotherhoods in far western Mārvāṛ, in the desert tracts of Maheva and Bāhaṛmer (modern Millānī), which remained largely outside the influence and control of more powerful groups in central Mārvāṛ and had limited contact with the Mughals, either directly or indirectly. Within them, unilineal descent and the principle of equality among brothers with regard to right of access to land prevailed.[30] Internal differentiation among brothers concerning positions of rank and authority also remained minimal, there being only a nominal leader or chief (*dhaṇī*) and respected and influential members (*pāñc lok*) besides the brothers, their wives and children. In addition, though positions of leadership within the group passed to candidates, which the brothers as a whole selected from among identified 'senior' blood lines, these candidates were only first among equals (*primus inter pares*), and their positions depended totally upon both their generosity and the will and acquiescence of their brothers.[31]

Elsewhere, however, brotherhoods were more highly stratified and their membership internally differentiated on the basis of wealth and access to positions of power and authority. The organization of these brotherhoods was also greatly influenced by two additional institutions, namely rulership and clientship. These institutions were closely interrelated and in contrast to the relatively undifferentiated, corporate brotherhood, were not defined in terms of kinship and associated territory, but in terms of hierarchical ties and common allegiance among residential groups and individuals to a superior—the local ruler (*ṭhākur*). It was these ties and allegiances which both defined a local kingdom (*rāj*) of a Rajpūt ruler and determined the extent of his territory. They also formed the primary basis of solidarity within that kingdom.

Local rulers of these kingdoms were often representatives of senior lines by descent within particular clans. But one also finds examples of junior lines, such as the Jodhā Rāṭhoṛs of Mārvāṛ, which had superceded senior lines through conquest of strategic territories and risen to greater prominence, maintaining for themselves the right to provide

[30] *Naiṇsī rī Khyāt*, III, p. 161.
[31] Ibid., II, pp. 43, 329–30.

successors to the position of local rulership. Kinship and descent as principles of organization were operative primarily within the families of these rulers, in the determination of succession and rights to positions of authority, and in matters of inheritance. Generally, a ruler designated his heir (*pāṭvī*) from among his immediate sons, and in turn transmitted to him greater authority and status than accorded other sons. This heir was not necessarily the eldest son, but more often the son of either a favourite wife or the chief queen (*paṭrāṇī*), who held customary right to provide the successor. This son always received the major share of land in his inheritance, while other sons received only minor shares for their maintenance.[32]

Outside the immediate family of the ruler, clientship was the prime determinant of both access to land and to positions of authority.[33] Clients as a body included not only Rājpūts of the same clan and brotherhood as that of the ruler, but also other Rājpūts from different clans and brotherhoods. The texts generally refer to them as *cākar*, which carries the general meaning of servant, but in Mārvāṛi usage, designates a 'military retainer,' one who held rights over villages on the condition of provision of arms to a superior, or who was included as a member of his patron's personal household. The latter was referred to as residing in the *vās* (residence, ward) of the patron. Examples of the movement of individual Rājpūts from area to area within Rājasthān and outside appear frequently in the Rajpūt literature, as the history of Māṃḍaṇ Rāṭhoṛ attests (see Case I), and point to an important and enduring feature of this society.

The relationship between a local ruler and a client consisted of a set of obligations incumbent upon each party. The client generally owed both allegiance and service to his patron, which he acknowledged with a vow, sworn before a *devata* in a local temple.[34] Service entailed both the provision of arms or military service, and other forms of attendance upon the person of the patron himself.[35] This obligation a client additionally acknowledged because he had eaten the salt (*lūṇ*) or the grain (*mūṃg/dhāṇ*) of his patron, which symbolized both his dependence upon and indebtedness to the patron, who maintained him. In return for this allegiance and support, the patron was obliged both to protect his client and to favour him with land and other forms of remuneration.[36]

[32] Naiṇsī, *Vigat*, I, p. 95.
[33] Ibid., II, pp. 61, 63.
[34] Ibid., II, p. 61.
[35] *Naiṇsī rī Khyāt*, II, p. 273.

Within a kingdom, only clients who maintained direct ties with a ruler were designated *ṭhākurs*, the term which also defined a local ruler.[37] But hierarchical ties of patronage and clientship extended throughout all levels of Rājpūt society, a feature which all three case histories presented above display. Clientship was an important institution in Rājasthān because it superseded kinship as a basis of organization. In addition, it not only regulated access to land and to positions of authority, but also made available to a local ruler, upon whom clients depended for favours and rewards, a coercive force which he could in turn employ to support and to strengthen the local hierarchy itself.[38]

While the institutions of rulership and clientship existed in Rājasthān prior to the Mughal period, they developed greatly during the sixteenth and seventeenth centuries at the expense of kinship as a basis of organization. Their development was a direct function of Mughal policy of indirect rule, which both assumed the right to appoint successors to positions of rulership in Rājasthān, and in turn supported them with arms and resources in the form of *jāgīrs* of ancestral lands (*vatan jāgīrs*) inside Rājasthān and other lands outside.[39] These added resources and support allowed local rulers to consolidate their own spheres of authority and to greatly centralize their own administrations. It is in this period, by the early seventeenth century, that we see the first true Rājpūt 'states' so much discussed in the literature on Rājasthān, in the sense that there was a defined and institutionalized locus of power (the local ruler), from whom regulations emanated with appropriate sanction

[36]'Aitihāsik Bātāṃ', p. 52.

[37]Ibid., p. 57–8.

[38]Scholars are just beginning to give the institution of clientship in Rājpūt kingdoms of Rājasthān and its importance for political development the attention it deserves. African studies of this institution are much more complete and offer good models for similar detailed studies in Rājasthān. For example, see L. Mair, *Primitive Government* (Baltimore, 1964), pp. 166–89; and also 'Clientship in East Africa', *Cahiers d'études Africaines*, II, no. 6 (1961), pp. 315–25; J. Goody, 'Feudalism in Africa?', *Journal of African History*, IV, no. 1, (1963), pp. 1–18; L.A. Fallers, *Bantu Bureaucracy* (Chicago, 1965).

[39]*Jāgīrs* outside Rājasthān were particularly desired because of their greater value than the desert lands of Rājasthān. For an example of the comparative value of these lands, see the list of *jāgīrs* that Rāṭhoṛ Mahārājā Jasvaṃtsiṃgh Gajsiṃghot of Jodhpur held between 1638 and 1678: *Srī Mahārājā Srī Jasvaṃtsiṃghjī kī Khyāt*, MS no. 15661 (Rājasthān Prācyavidhyā Pratiṣṭhān, Jodhpur, Rājasthān pp. 3–13.

and enforcement.[40] Through the late sixteenth and seventeenth centuries, the Mughal Emperors also granted local rulers more extensive authority over local areas, thus effecting through time a shift in the centres of authority. This shift in turn allowed local rulers increasing control over the primary source of honours and rewards in the local hierarchical system—access to land.

An example from Mārvāṛ is instructive here. When Moṭā Rājā Udaisiṃgh succeeded to the rulership of Jodhpur in 1583, Akbar granted him only four and one-half *parganas* of Mārvāṛ in *jāgīr*: Jodhpur, Sojhat, Pokaraṇ (over which he had no authority due to Bhāṭī possession), Sīvāṇo (in 1589), and one-half of Jaitāraṇ.[41] Other areas of Mārvāṛ he granted on separate tenures to Rāṭhoṛs and other Rājpūts alike. However, by the time of Rājā Gajsiṃgh Surajsiṃghot (1619–38), the Moṭā Rājā's grandson, the Mughal Emperor had granted the Jodhpur ruler control over nine *parganas* of Mārvāṛ, including Jodhpur, Sojhat, all of Jaitāraṇ, Pokaraṇ (over which there was still no authority), Phalodhi, Meṛto, Sīvāṇo, Jāloṛ (between 1620 and 1626) and Sāṃcor (between 1622 and 1636).[42]

As local rulers gained wider control over lands which representatives of their own clans had traditionally dominated, they sought to transform relationships on these lands from those based on kinship and customary access by birthright, to inter-relationships based on service and exchange. The resistance they met with from clan brothers in their attempts, the *khyāts* attest to at great length. This resistance generally took the form of challenging the basis upon which a ruler claimed dominance over an area or his right to precedence at all, and often ended in armed conflicts. Tell us, who has the authority to give or to take [this land].? He who has granted you Jodhpur has also given [this land] to us[43] is the classic response of clan brothers, meant to evoke sentiments of the brotherhood and values of equality and rights to inheritance of and dominance over land by birth. These sentiments and values form an undercurrent during the Mughal period which resurfaced periodically, and it is important to note that differing interpretations of rights to particular lands play a role not only locally, but also in connection with Rājpūt adherence to the Mughal throne.

[40]See E.R. Service, *Origins of the State and Civilization: The Processes of Cultural Evolution*, (New York, 1975), pp. 14–15, 71–102.

[41]Naiṇsī, *Vigat*, I, pp. 73,76–7.

[42]Ibid., I, p. 95 105–9, 124.

[43]*Naiṇsī rī Khyāt*, III, pp. 117–18.

The process of transforming relationships on the land also included the increasing bureaucratization of these relationships as administrative procedures became more sophisticated in these local kingdoms. An indication of this bureaucratization with regard to Mārvāṛ, for example, is the beginning issuance of written titles or deeds (*paṭo/paṭa*) to villages. Already by the early Mughal period, the possession of such deeds had acquired a legitimacy which superseded prior claims to land based on descent or based on verbal grant.

The *paṭo* in contrast was modelled upon Mughal prototypes for the granting of *jāgīrs* and purported to be a movable grant based on prebendal tenure. It gained wide usage in Mārvāṛ during the late sixteenth and seventeenth centuries and included not only the writ legitimizing access to a village or villages, but also a valuation (*rekh*) of these villages for the determination of the number of troopers and animals ṭhākurs were to supply to the ruler for military service. In addition, local rulers also initiated a fee of investiture (*nazrāna*), which they charged upon all *ṭhākurs* at the time of succession, based upon a percentage of the total *rekh* valuation of their villages.

These innovations began during the rule of Moṭā Rājā Udaisiṃgh, the first Rāṭhoṛ ruler of Jodhpur to come into close and enduring contact with the Mughals, and his son, Rājā Sūrajsiṃgh.[44] Under Moṭā Rājā Udaisiṃgh, *paṭās* appear to have been issued for the most part only to heads of families and to have designated particular villages which were handed down in these families. But by the time of Mahārājā Jasvaṃtsiṃgh (1638–78), deeds were issued not only to heads of families, but also to junior members, and individual Rājpūts were regularly transferred from one village to another in a similar fashion to Mughal *mansabdārs* holding *jāgīrs*. From genealogical evidence, it also appears that while in the early years, local rulers confined grants to particular local areas where individual brotherhoods were concentrated, later on they moved their *cākars* about over increasingly wider areas, effecting by this mechanism the breakup of local lineage territories.[45] In addition, the Mārvāṛi texts indicate that *cākars*, whether clan brothers of the local ruler or not, all performed service as

[44]Bhargava, *Marwar and the Mughal Emperors*, p. 78. Munsi Hardayāla, *Majmuī Hālāt va Iṃtizām Rāj Mārvāṛ, 1883–1884*, (Jodhpur 1885), I, pp. 353, 440.

[45]For some examples from one such genealogy, see *Nainṣī rī Khyāt*, II, pp. 155–60.

candidates for the receipt of *paṭas* (*umedvārī rī cākrī*) before they actually gained access to lands.[46]

We frankly do not know enough about the effect of such bureaucratization upon the allegiances of individual Rajpūts.[47] I have alluded to instances of Rajpūt discontent and disregard for the authority of local rulers above. Information from the reign of Mahārājā Jasvaṃtsiṃgh of Jodhpur adds further corroboration. A Mārvāṛī text notes, for example, with reference to the *pargana* of Pokaraṇ in north-western Mārvāṛ:

> In the *pargana* of Pokaraṇ, the descendants (*pāḷā*) of Rāṭhoṛ Jagmāl Mālāvat are local land holders (*bhomiyas*). In the *mauza* of Cāṃpo ... they have taken over and enjoy the rule of much land. They do not perform much service (*cākrī*).... Together they total about 100 horsemen (*asvār*) and 400 footmen (*pāḷā*).[48]

Despite the above indication of problems of control and of the fulfilment of obligations, one of the direct results of these administrative changes was the increase in the availability of positions of rank and prestige, both on a local and supra-local level. On the whole, these changes contributed to the institutionalization and strengthening of dyadic, personalized bonds between a ruler and clients, at the same time that they furthered the breakup of territorial brotherhoods. They also acted to channel loyalties and allegiances more through local hierarchies of authority, and thus to counteract the prior diffusion of primary loyalties to individual brotherhoods. These structural changes have additional cultural implications of importance for understanding

[46]For a reference to this custom, see *Muṃḍiyāṛ rī Rāṭhoṛāṃ rī Khyāt*, Ms. no. 15635, no. 2 (Rājasthān Prācyavidhyā Pratiṣṭhan, Jodhpur, Rājasthān), p. 143.

[47]There are also indications from actual figures given in the administrative texts that local administrations consistently overvalued many villages. This problem, which is one among many involved in the process of bureaucratization, and the effects in general of structural and administrative changes in the Rājpūt polities require detailed attention scholars have not yet given them. A number of these problems are the subject of present research of this writer, based on the analysis of several rather detailed genealogies of different Rājpūt brotherhoods contained in the seventeenth-century chronicles. An example of such a genealogy is the 'Jeso Bhāṭīrī Pīḍhī,' *Naiṇsī rī Khyāt*, II, pp. 152–95. This genealogy covers nine generations of Bhāṭīs present in Mārvāṛ during the sixteenth and seventeenth centuries and provides a wealth of information on villages held and local activities.

[48]Naiṇsī, *Vigat*, II, p. 234.

Rājpūt loyalties, which I will discuss in detail in the final section of this essay.

The interplay of these varying principles of organization and the complex of overlapping loyalties and affiliations built up around them is illustrated in the pattern of territorial relationships within the *ṭhikāṇa* of Bhādrājūṇ, *pargana* Jodhpur, Mārvāṛ, in the seventeenth century.[49] The internal organization of this *ṭhikāṇa* is representative on a smaller scale, of the organization of larger territorial states under local Rājpūt rulers during the Mughal period.

In the seventeenth century, the *ṭhākurs* of Bhādrājūṇ, who belonged to the Ratansiṃghot Jodhā *khāṃp* of Mārvāṛ Rāṭhoṛs, held their lands from the rulers of Jodhpur, also Jodho Rāṭhoṛs. Although members of the senior line of Ratansiṃghots had held these lands since the time of Rāo Mālde, the *ṭhākurs* date the beginning of their real possession from 1596, when Rājā Sūrajsiṃgh of Jodhpur issued the first *paṭo* of Bhādrājūṇ to Rāṭhoṛ Mukaṃdās Sādūlot.[50] The lands of Bhādrājūṇ consisted of the head village of Bhādrājūṇ itself, plus a number of other surrounding villages, which the *ṭhākurs* referred to as their *caurāsī* (literally, 'eighty-four villages'), and as the *janm-bhom* (birthplace) of the Ratansiṃghot Jodhās. Along the outer margins of the *ṭhikāṇa* were designated villages, which the *ṭhākurs* of Bhādrājūṇ granted to Rājpūts of clans different from the Rāṭhoṛ. These Rājpūts were all personal *cākars* of Bhādrājūṇ, who held lands on informal 'patrimonial' tenure and owed loyalty and service directly to the *ṭhakurs.* Some of these Rājpūts were also the *sagā* of the *ṭhākurs,* having given their daughters to them in marriage. This outer ring of villages under non-Rāṭhoṛ Rājpūts the *ṭhākurs* of Bhādrājūṇ considered the first line of defence of the *ṭhikāṇa*, based significantly upon *cākars* who held no local claims to land and were solely dependent upon the *ṭhākurs* of Bhādrājūṇ.

[49]I obtained most of my information about this *ṭhikāṇa* from the present Kuṃvar of Bhādrājūṇ, Srī Gopāḷsiṃghjī, and from a family history of the *ṭhikaṇa.*

[50]The first Jodho Rāṭhoṛ Ṭhākur of Bhādrājūṇ was Ratansiṃgh Māldeot, a younger son of Rāo Mālde of Jodhpur, to whom Mālde gave this land after its conquest from the Siṃdhaḷ Rāṭhoṛs in the 1530s. Ratansiṃgh held the area for a time, then left and entered Mughal service under Akbar, from whom he received a *jāgīr* in the *pargana* of Ajmer. The lands of Bhādrājūṇ later returned to his family, when his son, Sādūl, received them in *paṭo* from Rājā Sūrajsiṃgh Udaisiṃghot, *Kavirāj Murārḍānji kī Khyāt*, pp. 613–16; *Rāṭhoṛām rī Khyāt evam Bhādrājūn rī Khyāt* (private MS of the Ṭhākurs of *ṭhikāṇa* Bhādrājūṇ, Mārvāṛ), pp. 31–57.

Internally, the best and most defensible lands and villages the Bhādrājūṇ *ṭhākurs* held themselves. Other villages internal to the area passed to cadet lines of the *ṭhikāṇa* which received shares by right of birth, but whose members also held their lands on the basis of service and loyalty to the 'senior' line. These areas they in turn divided among the members of their immediate families, larger shares as well as greater rank being conferred on those chosen to succeed to the headships of families. Often, individual members of these cadet families received separate lands directly from the Bhādrājūṇ Ṭhākurs in return for special services they had performed. In addition, some Ratansiṃghot Jodhās from these cadet lines held certain villages within the boundaries of the *ṭhikāṇa* in *paṭo* directly from the ruler of Jodhpur, which he had awarded them for direct services to the throne. There is also evidence that in *ṭhikāṇas* like this one, some members of the brotherhood held additional *jāgīrs* directly from the Mughal emperors.[51] Finally, many of the descendants of the Bhādrājūṇ *ṭhākurs*, principally sons who either decided to seek their fortunes elsewhere, or who did not succeed to positions of authority, left the area and became *cākars* of other Rājpūts or of the Mughals.[52]

Over and above these ties of loyalty and service structured around descent and patron–client relationships, the senior ṭhākurs of Bhādrājūṇ also had ties of alliance through marriage which extended beyond the *ṭhikāṇa*. Their *sagā* included several different *khāṃps* of Rājpūts such as those of the Bhāṭīs of Jaisaḷmer, the Solaṃkī Cāhuvāṇs of Sāṃdor and others.[53] Many of their brothers from cadet lines also appear to have taken wives and given daughters to the same brotherhoods that they did.[54]

The inter-relationship one sees among Rājpūts between marriage and clientship, noted not only here in connection with *ṭhikāṇa* Bhādrājūṇ, but also in the case histories of Rāṭhoṛ Māṃdaṇ Kūṃpāvat

[51] *Rāṭhoroṃ kī Khyāt*, pp. 465–8.

[52] *Bhādrājūṇ rī Khyāt*, p. 49.

[53]. Ibid., pp. 48, 55, 76.

[54] I have not personally been able to trace these marriage ties and am indebted both to Kuṃvar Arjunsiṃghji of village Oṃkalī, a member of one of the cadet lines of the Bhādrājūn Ṭhākurs, and to Henri Stern of the CNRS, Paris, for collaborative information. Stern in particular has traced marital networks among Meṛtiyā Rāṭhoṛs of the Goḍhvāṛ, Mārvāṛ, and notes that senior *ṭhākurs* by descent both regulate the marriages of members of junior branches and arrange them with lines with which there are already established alliances.

(Case I) and Bhāṭī Surtāṇ Mānāvat (Case II), points to another important feature of marriage and relations among *sagā* which must be mentioned here. The rite of marriage not only acted to form an alliance between two families and brotherhoods, which entailed mutual support and assistance; it also created a fundamental spatial or territorial relationship among *sagā*. This relationship appears to have developed out of the custom known in Rājasthān as *sāḷā kaṭārī*, according to which a sister's husband (*bahanoī*) presented special gifts of clothing and/or land (*kaṭārī*—literally 'dagger') to his wife's brothers (*sāḷā*) in a separate ceremony at the end of the wedding itself. A sister's husband's presentation of gifts fulfilled his obligation to return a gift to his wife's brothers who had given him a woman in marriage.

The clearest reference I have to this custom is a note in one of the Mārvāṛi texts about two sons of Rāo Jodhojī Riṇmalot (c. 1453–89), the founder of Jodhpur city, Mārvāṛ, who married their uterine sister to the Muslim Khān of Nāgaur in order to acquire some land:

> Karamsī and Rāypāl Jodhāvat were uterine brothers [*sagā bhāī*], sons of Rāṇī Bhāṭiyāṇī Pūra and daughter's sons of Bhāṭī Rāo Vairsal Cācāvat.[55] Rāo Jodho had given them the village of Nāhaḍhsar.[56] Later on, they went to Nāgaur and married their uterine sister, Bhāgāṃ, to [Khānazāda] Salhai Khān. Salhai then gave them Āsop and Khīṃvsar in *sāḷā kaṭārī* and since that time, these lands have been incorporated within the territory of Jodhpur.[57]

It is unclear from either Mārvāṛi chronicles or genealogical references, whether in this case, lands received in *sāḷā kaṭārī* were combined with clientship. Most frequently, however, it is clear that individual Rājpūts used marriage ties to gain access to land from their sister's husband or other family memebrs. On having become the client of some *ṭhākur*, they customarily married a sister or a daughter to him in exchange for land already granted.[58] The important point here is that marriage

[55]A Kelhaṇ Bhāṭī, ruler of Pūgaḷ and the founder of Vairsalpur, some 100 miles east of Jaisaḷmer city, Rājasthān, in the early sixteenth century, *Naiṇsī rī Khyāt*, II, p. 117.

[56]Nāhaḍhsar is located near Bīlāṛo, some 40 to 45 miles east of Jodhpur city, Mārvāṛ.

[57]Naiṇsī, *Vigat*, I, p. 40.

[58]Several of the sons of Jodho Rāṭhoṛ Sādūḷ Ratansiṃghot, for example, who did not succeed him to the ṭhākurship of Bhādrājūṇ, are recorded in the Rāṭhoṛ genealogy as having lived at the 'home of the Solaṃkīs', their *sagā*. *Rāṭhoṛoṃ kī Khyāt*, pp. 615–16. See also, fn 51 above.

alliances provided another institutionalized means of gaining access to land, rank and prestige, and seems to have created more effective and durable bonds than vows of allegiance on the part of a client to his patron.

The specific sentiment regarding territory and territoriality which derived from this relationship and its potential importance for understanding Rājpūt loyalties, is expressed in a passage from a seventeenth-century Mārvāṛi text relating to the time of Mahārājā Jasvaṃtsiṃgh of Jodhpur. Jasvaṃtsiṃgh had received the *pargana* of Pokaraṇ (north-western Mārvāṛ) in *jāgīr* from Pātsāh Shāh Jahān upon his succession to rulership in Mārvāṛ in 1638. His father, grandfather and great-grandfather had also all held Pokaraṇ in *jāgīr* from Mughal emperors. But for a period of more than 50 years, they had possessed no authority over this area and derived no revenue from it because it was under the control of the Bhāṭīs of Jaisaḷmer.[59] However, in 1649, Bhāṭī Rāvaḷ Manohardās Kalyāṇdāsot[60] died childless and Rāmcaṃd Siṃghot, a Bhāṭī from a distant collateral line of the ruling family, succeeded him. When Jaswaṃtsiṃgh learned of Rāvaḷ Manohardās's death and Rāmcaṃd's succession, he immediately petitioned Shāh Jahān both directly and through his paternal aunt, Bāī Śrī Manbhāvatījī,[61] who was resident in Shāh Jahān's harem, to allow the conquest of Pokaraṇ from the Bhāṭīs. He gave the following reasons:

> The *pargana* of Pokaraṇ is part of my Imperial *jāgīr*, but I have no authority over the area. For many years, Rāvaḷ Manohardās, who was my *sagā*, held it, and for this reason, I made no complaints. Now, however, Bhāṭī Rāmcaṃd Siṃghot has succeeded to the throne of Jaisaḷmer. He is someone whom I have no reason to leave in control of Pokaraṇ. If you will allow me, I will attack Pokaraṇ and assert my authority over it.[62]

[59]Bhāṭī rule over Pokaraṇ dates from 1575–1576, when Rāo Candrasen mortgaged it to them while in exile from Mārvāṛ. See Naiṇsī, *Vigat*, I, p. 70; II, p. 297; 'Aitihāsik Bātāṃ', p. 78; Reu, *Mārvāṛ kā Itihās*, I, p. 157; Ojha, *Rājpūtāne kā Itihās*, IV, pt 1, p. 347.

[60]Ruler of Jaisaḷmer, *c.*1633–49. *Tavārīkh-Jaisaḷmer*, pp. 56–8.

[61]Manbhāvatījī was the daughter of Rājā Sūrajsiṃgh Udaisiṃghot of Jodhpur, and was married to Prince Parviz, brother of Shāh Jahān, in 1623, in return for Parviz's grant of Meṛto *pargana* in Mārvāṛ to Rājā Gajsiṃgh Surajsiṃghot of Jodhpur, whose uterine sister she was. She remained a resident of Shāh Jahān's harem after the death of Parviz in 1626. Naiṇsī, *Vigat*, I, p. 108; *Rāṭhoṛom kī Khyāt*, p. 207.

[62]Naiṇsī, *Vigat*, II, p. 298.

Marriage relations between the Rāthoṛ rulers of Jodhpur and the Bhāṭī rulers of Jaisalmer go back over many generations. Those most pertinent here are Jasvaṃtsiṃgh's father, Gajsiṃgh's, marriage both to a daughter of Bhāṭī Rāvaḷ Kalyāṇdās Harrājot (1623–33), and to one of his son, Rāvaḷ Manohardās Kalyāṇdāsot (1633–49), and Jasvaṃtsiṃgh's own marriage to a daughter of Rāvaḷ Manohardās.[63] These alliances acted to create a sentiment of corporate territoriality which cross-cut that of the brotherhood, but was in many respects strikingly similar to it.[64] Inherent in both were expected rights of access to and use of land.

To sum up, we must conceive of Rājpūt loyalties and identifications on a local level in terms of both descent, operative within the brotherhood among those related by ties of male blood, and sets of hierarchical, dyadic relationships based on service and exchange, operative within a kingdom between a ruler and his servants. Each of these institutions or sets of relationships also possessed a territorial aspect, based on the extent of kin recognition which defined the *vatan* of a brotherhood, and based on structural ties between a ruler and his retainers, which defined the territory of the kingdom. Cross-cutting all levels and included within the concept of 'territory' were also affiliations through ties of alliance and marriage with *sagā*.

Many of these local institutions and the sentiments surrounding them the Rājpūts were able to transfer directly to their relations with the Mughals, with whom they formed not only patron–client ties, but also marriage alliances. This transference does much to explain Rājpūt loyalty to the Mughals. However, it must be noted that although the different principles of organization among Rājpūts were often mutually supportive, they were also often in direct conflict with each other. This conflict is particularly evidenced between corporate egalitarianism and hierarchy, and centred most directly upon questions of access to and control over land and the direction of allegiances. Such conflict arose especially when local groups manipulated these alternative and inconsistent principles, one local and the other gained through contact with

[63]For a complete list of Jodhpur rulers' marriages with the Bhāṭīs of Jaisalmer from the time of Rāo Mālde, see *Tavārīkh-Jaisaḷmer*, pp. 50–3, 56, *Rāṭhoroṃ kī Khyāt*, pp. 138, 142, 164–5, 193, 198, 212; *Naiṇsī rī Khyāt*, II, p. 98; *Muṃḍīyār rī Khyāt*, pp. 100, 138.

[64]The sentiment of corporate territoriality within the brotherhood is expressed in one Mārvāṛi tradition in the words of a Rajpūt: 'If [the land] is under my paternal uncle, it is also my land.' *Naiṇsī rī Khyāt*, II, p. 141.

more sophisticated, outside authorities and reinterpreted in terms of local ideology, for their own ends during periods when powerful rulers of their own clans dominated or attempted to subordinate them.[65]

The overlapping nature of jurisdiction and loyalties and the inconsistent and often incongruent nature of norms of conduct and rights are typical of this frontier region in a process of transition. The conflict over the direction of loyalty is logically reflected within Rājpūts themselves. This type of internal conflict explains much about the seemingly quixotic movements of Rāṭhoṛ Māṃḍaṇ Kūṃpāvāt (Case I) back and forth between the Mughals, non-Rāṭhoṛ Rājpūt rulers and Rāṭhoṛ rulers of Jodhpur. The lives of many other minor Rājpūts of this period display the same disconnected quality in their search to reconcile the demands of brotherhood with those of a servant, and at the same time fulfil personal desires for achievement. This conflict is also reflected in the cyclical nature of Rājpūt political organization over time, and its fluctuation between more and less centralization. Stability gained during the Mughal period rested primarily upon Mughal support of local rulers, who in turn were able to enforce their authority and to command the allegiance of subordinates.

Society Moving Towards an Image of Itself

The conflict over principles of organization among Rājpūts also reflects itself significantly in a corresponding conflict over norms of conduct and values, and the appropriateness of certain kinds of behaviour in contexts which called for different standards. This conflict shaped both local interactions among Rājpūts themselves and individual Rājpūt responses to the Mughals. In spite of these conflicts, however, what is interesting about Rājpūt relations with the Mughals is the

[65]For example, see Naiṇsī, *Vigat*, II, pp. 48–51. This phenomenon is not particular to Rājasthān. A number of scholars studying marginal, frontier regions have commented about similar conflicts and their bases at length. See M. Fried, 'On the Evolution of Social Stratification and the State', in S. Diamond (ed.), *Culture in History: Essays in Honor of Paul Radin* (New York, 1960), pp. 723–4; E.R. Leach, *Political Systems of Highland Burma* (Boston, 1970), pp. 8–16; F. Barth, *Principles of Social Organization in Southern Kurdistan* (Oslo, 1953), pp. 9–10. Barth notes with respect to the shatter zone of southern Kurdistan that 'such a situation produces familiarity with various competing normative systems, principles of organization and power hierarchies. This familiarity on the part of the villager leads to attempts at manipulating these various systems and principles'.

relative constancy of their loyalties. The reasons behinds this constancy appear to lie in the complex of Rājpūt cultural beliefs about rank and in their own myth of order and authority. This last section will deal more specifically with this conflict over norms of conduct and with the sets of cultural beliefs which lay behind Rājpūt political actions.

The traditional Rājpūt literature of the seventeenth century conceptualized the norms of conduct appropriate for Rājpūts in terms of general rules which symbolized Rājpūt *dharma*. This *dharma* was felt to be an inborn, moral code for conduct, which each individual inherited by birth along with an innate potential to fulfil it.[66] Fulfilment enabled in turn both the maintenance and the increase of rank within the order of castes, and the achievement of salvation.[67]

The general rules of this code the texts set forth in terms of three basic axioms: avenging the death of one's father (*bāp rai vair leṇau*), fulfilling one's morally appointed task or duty of fighting and dying in the service of one's master (*sām/dhaṇī rai kām āṇau*),[68] and refraining from *gotrakaḍaṃb* (literally, 'destruction of the *gotra*'), that is killing of other members of the same *gotra* or clan, a sin to which great demerit (*avguṇ*) was attached.[69]

None of these rules is exclusive of the others. All are in some sense mutually supportive and the texts view them as defining a 'general' Rājpūt *dharma*, which encompassed behaviour appropriate to the different networks of relationships of which Rājpūts of this period were a part. However, it is important for analytical reasons to separate out these rules, for they pertain to specific sets of relationships and there are major areas of incompatibility among them. We see in the cultural system as in the actual social system, inconsistencies and conflict expected of a society in transition. This incompatibility marks the Rājpūt as being divided in a very direct sense within as well as often against himself.

The two rules regarding avenging the murder of kinsmen and refraining from *gotrakaḍaṃb* logically apply to the brotherhood. They both emphasize aspects of solidarity, corporate equivalence and the expectation that individuals whose social existence is defined with reference to this group, will render support, particularly against outsiders.

[66] *Naiṇsī rī Khyāt*, I, p. 75.

[67] See M. Marriott and R. Inden, 'CasteSystems', '*Encyclopaedia Britannica* (1974), for their discussion of South Asian conceptions of caste and ranking.

[68] *Naiṇsī rī Khyāt*, II, pp. 270–1.

[69] Ibid., II, p. 266; 'Aitihāsik Bātāṃ', pp. 57–8.

They also emphasize the importance of the preservation of the body, the unit of shared male blood or substance, collectively possessed of inherent powers *(baḷ)* which enabled it as an entity both to control and to maintain rule over land. This cultural notion of the brotherhood as a collective body possessing inherent powers is important for our understanding of the emphasis placed upon both the enjoining of murder with the unit and upon the exacting of blood vengeance.

The avenging of the murder of close kinsmen was incumbent upon brothers because a death at the hands of an outsider represented defeat, humiliation and subordination through loss of power. Acts of vengeance thus took the form of acts of equalization, involving either the murder of a member of the offending party or of the offender himself. This 'trading of bodies' reasserted the relative balance of power and preserved the rank and the honour (as precedence)[70] of the Rājpūts. When different clans and *gotra* were involved, they usually confirmed the settlement of such hostilities through gifts of daughters in marriage and the formation of alliances (*sagāī*),[71] thus asserting a new pattern of relationships among themselves.

Rājpūt honour, both collective and individual, and the concern with its preservation form an integral part of the overall concern with the maintenance of the power and rank of the brotherhood. Both the preservation and assertion of honour are also intimately associated with concepts of the body[72] and display general features of Rājpūt regard for prestige and for outright domination. Honour demanded that a Rājpūt abjure cowardice,[73] that he contest any insult to his person or his family,[74] and that he be generous.[75] It also demanded that he protect those dependent upon him, particularly his women, from violation,[76] for

[70]J. Pitt-Rivers, 'Honor', in D.L. Sills, (ed.), *International Encyclopedia of the Social Sciences*, vol. 6, p. 505. Pitt-Rivers notes that: 'claim to honor depends always, in the last resort, upon the ability of the claimant to impose himself. Might is the basis of right to precedence, which goes to the man who is bold enough to enforce his claim, regardless of what may be thought of his merits.'

[71]*Naiṇsī rī Khyāt*, II, p. 336.

[72]Pitt-Rivers, 'Honour', p. 505.

[73]One often reads in the Rājpūt literature of Rājpūts taking vows never to flee in battle. For an example, see *Naiṇsī rī Khyāt*, III, pp. 158–60.

[74]*Naiṇsī rī Khyāt*, III, pp. 62–78.

[75]Ibid., II, p. 313.

dishonour inhered not only in the violation of one's women, but also in the necessity of bowing before and giving a daughter in marriage to a superior. Both implied symbolic castration or mutilation of the body, and hence subordination.[77] This concern with honour perhaps best explains Rāṭhoṛ Kalyāṇdās Rāymalot's (Case III) detestation of Moṭā Rājā Udaisiṃgh's marriage of his daughter to Prince Salīm, and his subsequent break from the Mughals.[78]

In addition, honour demanded that a Rājpūt continually assert his own position of superiority and authority in relation to those in equal or subordinate positions around him. This assertion took various forms, most notably that of exhibitions of prowess and of conquest, such as bravery in battle, the capture of land, animals and also women. It is important to note that in addition to the above situation involving Rāṭhoṛ Kalyāṇdās (Case III), and marriage or personal insult as a point of honour, the texts mention many instances in which individual Rājpūt relations with Mughal equals or superiors were disrupted because of an incident connected with a Muslim's harem. One of the more celebrated of the incidents involved Rāṭhoṛ Rāo Amarsiṃgh Gajsiṃghot, the elder brother of Mahārājā Jasvaṃtsiṃgh of Jodhpur. Amarsiṃgh was a *mansabdār* of Shāh Jahān, who presented Nāgaur, in Mārvāṛ, to him in *jāgīr* at the time of his father's death and the succession of Jasvaṃtsiṃgh to the rulership of Jodhpur in 1638.

[76]Ibid., III, p. 261: see also Pitt-Rivers, 'Honor and Social Status', in J.G. Peristiany (ed.), *Honour and Shame: The Values of Mediterranean Society*, (Chicago, 1974, reprint), pp. 45–6. Pitt-Rivers notes that honour is accorded to men and women differently. For men, it resides in manliness, courage and his ability to protect. For women, it resides in sexual purity and restraint. A man's honour is therefore closely involved with that of his women, whose sexual purity it is his duty to protect. Adultery or violation of a woman represents failure of duty, and hence brings dishonour and the defilement of manliness.

[77]G. Morris Carstairs, *The Twice-Born: A Study of a Community of High-Caste Hindus* (Bloomington and London, 1967), pp. 159–60. Carstairs notes with reference to Rājpūts that all those who occupy positions of subservience are forced to enact a symbolic self-castration. In the Rājpūt traditions, subordination of a person often takes the form of mutilation of him personally or of his possessions, such as his animals. See, for an example, *Nainsī rī Khyāt*, III, pp. 71–3.

[78]The usual interpretation given to such a reaction—Hindu Rājpūt dislike of marriages to Muslim superiors, which implies a strong communal sentiment—seems invalid here.

According to the Mārvāṛi chronicles, Amarsiṃgh developed a relationship with the wife of Ṣalābat Khān shortly thereafter, and he used to visit her often in the absence of Salābat himself. This union later led to Amarsiṃgh's murder of Salābat in a knife fight, when the latter tried to end Amarsiṃgh's visits to his wife, and finally to Amarsiṃgh's own death during a fight which broke out in the imperial *darbār* in Delhi, at the hands of a Gauṛ Rājpūt and others, whom Shāh Jahān had deputed to kill him.[79]

Alongside the normative rules of conduct and of honour which pertained to the brotherhood and the clan was the injunction commanding the service of one's master. This rule of *dharma* was, of course, appropriate for those hierarchical relations between a master and servant or a patron and his client, and represents an undoubted accretion to the body of Rājpūt cultural tradition during the fifteenth through seventeenth centuries, when these social relationships became both more common and more significant among Rājpūts.

Sām or *sāmī* and *dhaṇi* are Mārvāṛi words meaning 'God, master, ruler or sovereign and husband.' They are often used interchangeably in the Rājpūt literature with the term *ṭhākur,* which carries a similar set of meanings. *Kāmāṇau* means simply 'to fulfil a duty or appointed task', but is generally limited in usage to the following context: *vaḍo Rājpūt kām āyo*—'the great warrior died fighting in battle', implying therein the appointed duty to which Rājpūts themselves were born. The expressive rule of *dharma*—to fulfil one's appointed task of fighting and dying in battle in the service of one's master—therefore embodied within itself a complex symbolism relating to cultural conceptions of the kingdom, sovereignty, authority, power and rank.

The kingdom itself was conceived of as the product of marriage between a ruler, who was both God and master (*ṭhākur*) and husband (*dhaṇī*), and the land (*dhartī*—from Sanskrit *dharitrī*—'a female bearer'), which was his wife. The land the *ṭhākur* had himself conquered and was in turn bound to protect and to nourish in order that it continue to bear fruit (*phal*). This he did in his role as *vaḍo dātār* or great giver, for he was both the giver of grain and nourishment (*annadāta*), and paradoxically, the giver of his life in the protection of his kingdom and the moral order of castes within it (*jhūṃjhār*). He was also the parent

[79]*Muṃḍiyāṛ rī Khyāt,* pp. 124–9; see also 'Aitihāsik Bātāṃ', pp. 82–3, for another example of such an incident.

(*maīt*—literally 'mother and father')[80] of all the people (*lok*) of the kingdom, who were in his care, and he exercised his control and supervision through his sons (*beṭā*),[81] who were his servants or clients (*cākar*) as well as his wards (*vās*).

It was felt that a *ṭhākur* obtained the necessary power to conquer and to rule a kingdom through devotion to and service in behalf of his god or goddess (*ṭhākur, kuḷ devata/devī*), who granted him the boon (*var*) of sovereignty (*ṭhākurāī*) and power (*baḷ*) as a favour (*parsād*) for his devotion.[82] The *ṭhākur* (ruler) in turn became a worldly deputy of the *ṭhākur* (God), ruling his earthly kingdom in his stead. Beneath him were other *ṭhākurs*, who were his servants to whom he had transmitted the substance of his power and authority, which enabled them to rule smaller kingdoms within his own.

Service (*cākrī/sevā*) therefore signified, on one level, service for the *ṭhākur* as God in his various froms of *kuḷ devata* and *kuḷ devi*. On another level, it meant service for the *ṭhākur*, who was ruler, or for the *ṭhākur*, who held a *ṭhikāṇa* and was himself a servant (*cākar*) of the ruler. Service was seen as a form of worship, expressed through acts of devotion and self-sacrifice, which involved both a willingness to support a superior and to offer one's life in battle in his behalf. The most devoted servant was one who kept nothing to himself, but gave all including himself to his master.[83] Through such service, a Rājpūt fulfilled his morally appointed task of fighting to protect and sustain

[80] *Maīt* also means 'ancestor' or 'progenitor'. *Naiṇsī rī Khyāt*, I, p. 62; Naiṇsī, *Vigat*, II, p. 57; *Kavirāj Murārdānji kī Khyāt*, p. 608.

[81] In the Rājpūt literature, Rājpūts are often referrred to simply as son (*beṭo*), of a *ṭhākur*, or as either his *saput* (worthy son) or *kaput* (unworthy son), depending upon proper fulfilment of obligations. *Naiṇsī rī Khyāt*, III, p. 87; Naiṇsī, *Vigat*, II, p. 52.

[82] *Naiṇsī rī Khyāt*, I, pp. 3, 11–12; II, pp. 267–72.

[83] Ibid., III, pp. 149–50. It is significant in this context that one finds a relatively large number of instances in the Rājpūt chronicles in which Rājpūt's are involved in acts of self-mutilation and also suicide. The latter is the ultimate act of self-sacrifice, the offering of one's body to the *devata*. Though some of these acts seem to be genuine, others clearly involve attempted extortion of favours from the deity, and point to an important aspect of manipulation which is part of all hierarchical relationships. See *Āsop kā Itihās*, pp. 70–80; *Naiṇsī rī Khyāt*, II, p. 162; 'Aitihāsik Bātāṃ', pp. 87–8.

his kingdom and its people, and he received in exchange either salvation through death, or rewards for his devotion.[84]

This embedding of dyadic, patron–client ties in a myth of salvation and the obtainment of power and rulership extended to internal ranking among Rājpūts themselves, based on the subjective evaluation of outward differences in degrees of sovereignty and power among Rājpūts. Those who were felt to have been least devoted to the service of their master are categorized in the traditions as *chuṭe* or *pādrā* Rājpūts (minor or petty Rājpūts). They were *caurāsī dhaṇis* (masters of 84 villages) and *bhāībaṃdh bhomiyās*.[85] *Bhomiyo* means both 'one knowledgeable about a local area, a local' and 'one of the soil (*bhom*)'. It designated members of brotherhoods, who jointly controlled small areas of land, which was considered cultivated soil rather than land which was ruled (*dhartī*). Within the brotherhood, sovereignty was also seen to be diffused and to be dispersed among all members, each of whom possessed an equal share.

This diffusion of sovereignty marked the reason *bhomiyās* were both subordinate to and inferior in rank to the *ṭhākurs*, who were felt to have performed greater service in behalf of their masters. The *ṭhākurs* were the *rājvī* (those of royal blood)[86] and the *vaḍā ghar rā choru* (the sons of great houses).[87] They possessed greater power and sovereignty than the *bhomiyās*, because these attributes were felt to be concentrated in their bodies, giving them proportionately greater ability to rule, to protect and to grant favours and rewards. Some, who were seen to have performed exceedingly great service were rulers of kingdoms (*rāj*), while others ruled lesser kingdoms (*ṭhikāṇa*) subordinate to them. The sovereignty concentrated within the body of a *ṭhākur* himself was also seen to be transmitted to his offspring in the form of his seed (*bīj*), and to his servants through his favours (*parsād*—literally, 'transvalued substance') which acted in turn to embody power within them.[88] The hierarchy of rank among Rājpūts thus directly reflected the hierarchy of power and authority.

[84] *Naiṇsī rī Khyāt*, II, pp. 272–3.

[85] Ibid., III, p. 8; *Rāṭhoṛoṃ kī Khyāt*, p. 88.

[86] *Rāṭhoṛoṃ kī Khyāt*, pp. 72–3.

[87] Naiṇsī, *Vigat*, I, p. 10.

[88] This transfer of power and authority was taken in a very literal sense, and seen to involve the actual transfer of physical substances embodying inherent qualities, which acted to transform the nature of the servant who 'ingested' them. *Naiṇsī rī Khyāt*, III, p. 292.

In understanding medieval Rājpūt cultural conceptions of rank, power and sovereignty, it is important to note that the Muslim was also included within this hierarchical scheme as a Rājpūt. The traditions generally represent the Rājpūt *jāti* (caste) as being divided into two categories: Muslim (or Turk) and Hindu.[89] This category of 'Muslim' within the Rājpūt *jāti* did not include all Muslims, but only those who were warriors and who possessed sovereignty and power equal to or greater than the Hindu Rājpūt. The Muslim emperor in particular, held a position of high rank and esteem, and the traditions often equate him with Rām, the pre-eminent Kṣatriya cultural hero of the Hindu Rājpūt.[90] What basically distinguished the emperor from local Rājpūt rulers was simply his possession of greater sovereignty and power and his greater ability to grant favours and rewards. Within Hindu Rājpūt cultural conceptions, Hindu Rājpūt service for the Muslim emperor or one of his subordinates was thus no different from service for a local ruler or *ṭhākur.*

I have emphasized throughout this essay the internal inconsistencies with respect to affiliations and obligations with which Rājpūts of this period lived. The rules of *dharma* display similar inconsistencies, for carried to logical extensions, the rules of service to one's master came into direct conflict with other tenets of Rājpūt dharma emphasizing support for the brotherhood and the demerit attached to killing members of the same *gotra* or clan. A typical example of this conflict comes from a tradition about the time of Rāṭhoṛ Rāo Mālde of Jodhpur and his expansion within Mārvāṛ:

> During the time of Rāo Mālde, there were powerful Rājpūts from branches of many different clans in his service. It was a time of great and valorous deeds of bravery and heroism. All of his Ṭhākurs were renowned for their feats in battle.
>
> Jaito Paṃcaīṇot Rāṭhoṛ was one of his great Ṭhākurs a man who never failed to live up to his vows. He would not allow anyone to act improperly before Rāo Mālde. Rāo Mālde attacked with zeal, and then began to contemplate the capture of nearby Bīkāner, Meṛto, Sīvāṇo and Sojhat.[91] He spoke of his plan to Jaito, but Jaito replied: 'I will not commit *gotrakaḍaṃb*.' When he heard these words the Rāojī became depressed. Then Jaito said: 'Don't be so downhearted. I will do whatever you order me to do...'[92]

[89] *Naiṇsī rī Khyāt*, III, p. 70; 'Aitihāsik Bātāṃ', p. 61.
[90] *Naiṇsī rī Khyāt*, I, p. 220.
[91] All of these areas were under Rāṭhoṛ Rajpūts.
[92] 'Aitihāsik Bātāṃ', pp. 57–8.

The contradictions apparent here between the differing aspects of Rājpūt *dharma*—support for the brotherhood and service for one's master—are underlying themes in the Mughal period as a whole. Their interplay provides additional insight into the actions of Rāṭhoṛ Māṃḍaṇ Kuṃpāvat (Case I) and the instability of his attachments to the Mughals and non-Rāṭhoṛ rulers.

The reason the Rajpūt traditions stress the demerit of *gotrakaḍaṃb* to the extent they do, however, undoubtedly relates to the fact of its progressively greater occurrence during the Mughal period. Moṭā Rājā Udaisiṃgh's killing of his own paternal nephew, Rāṭhoṛ Kalyāṇdās Rāymalot, at the orders of Akbar (Case III), and Rāṭhoṛ Kuṃvar Gajsiṃgh's participation along with Bhāṭī Goyaṃdās Māṇāvat in the avengement of Bhāṭī Surtāṇ's death against other Rāṭhoṛs (Case II) both attest to this phenomenon. They represent on a broader level an aspect of the process involving the shift in the ideology of honour from concerns with the brotherhood and norms of conduct appropriate to it, to concerns with powerful, individual rulers, local and imperial, from whom honour increasingly derived as they came more to control entitlements to rank and land.[93]

This shift in ideology was facilitated, I think, by the myth of the Rājpūt which acted as a powerful psychological force in medieval Rājasthān. This myth became greatly developed during the Mughal period in the hands of the Cāraṇ bards of the Rājpūts, and provided not only a model of relationships as they were found in reality, but also a model for relationships as they should be.[94] I have already detailed elements of this myth relating to the structure of a kingdom, the manner of transmission of power and authority and the order of rank. But there are other aspects of importance for understanding Rājpūt actions, which concern the traditions relating to the origin of the Rājpūt *jāti*.

According to myth, Rājpūts (from Sanskrit *rājaputra*—'son of a king') were not true Kṣatriya rulers themselves, but only their sons and descendants. Preceding their rise in different areas of Rājasthān, their Kṣatriya ancestors had lost their sovereign rule and this loss had been

[93]This process is a familiar one to students of European history. For example see Baroja's discussion with respect to medieval Spain: J.C. Baroja, 'Honour and Shame: An Historical Account of Several Conflicts', in J.G. Peristiany (ed.), *Honour and Shame: The Values of Mediterranean Society*, (Chicago, 1974, reprint) pp. 81–137.

[94]Geertz, 'Religion as a Cultural System', pp. 3–9.

followed by a period of *vikhau* (distress and penance), during which confusion prevailed, castes became mixed and the proper moral order and hierarchy of society collapsed. The Rājpūts themselves were felt to be products of this confusion and mixing, and thus to be both lower ranked and less powerful than their Kṣatriya ancestors. It was only through great service and devotion to their various deities that some Rājpūts had succeeded in regaining small kingdoms and reasserting the proper order of relations within them. History itself, during this period of reassertion, the traditions conceptualize as a fluctuating movement in time back and forth between the order of a kingdom (*rāj*) and the confusion (*vikhau*) caused by its disruption.[95]

This process of consolidation and reassertion of order the Mughals greatly facilitated in Rājasthān during the sixteenth and seventeenth centuries, and from the Rājpūt point of view, this was a period when society moved towards an image of itself, towards an image of what it ought to be. This process only faltered when outside attacks threatened the stability and endurance of kingdoms. And it is during times of *vikhau* that we see a few spectacular examples of local Rājpūt rulers, who perhaps most lived the myth, such as Rāṭhoṛ Rāo Candrasen Māldeot, spending years of their lives surrounded by a small, fluctuating band of followers, fighting Mughal armies from the hills, while other members of their clan and brotherhood served under the Mughals and sought individual recognition for themselves and an opportunity to build their own kingdoms. I should emphasize that concerns with hierarchy, order and confusion occurred among Rājpūts at all levels of Rājpūt society, whenever land and its counterpart, rulership, were in doubt. Famines, which caused hardship and forced migration, attack or usurpation of land by others all were symbolic of confusion and disorder, and the casting of rank in doubt.[96]

[95]We can also trace the emergence of the Rājpūt *jāti* in Rājasthān in the inscriptions of some of the clans, which generally refer to themselves only as Rājpūt after the fifteenth century, when an important sociological change in the subjective perception and attribution of rank occurred. Prior to this time, they refer to themselves as Kṣatriya. For a discussion of this interesting problem and a more complete analysis of the myth, see Ziegler, 'The Seventeenth Century Chronicles of Mārvāṛ', and Ziegler, 'Action, Power and Service in Rājasthānī Culture: A Social History of the Rājpūts of Middle Period Rājasthān', unpublished Ph.D. dissertation (University of Chicago, 1973).

[96]For an interesting case history, see 'Aitihāsik Bātāṃ', pp. 68–73.

I shall close this final section of the essay with a brief examination of the history of relations between the Meṛtiyā Rāṭhoṛs of *pargana* Meṛto, Mārvāṛ, the rulers of Jodhpur and the Mughals, which reflect the important role this myth played in Rājpūt society. This examination will also serve to re-emphasize the interplay between the various principles of organization and associated values, and the various networks of relationships in which Rājpūts were involved, which affected the direction of their loyalties in this period. These relations passed through a series of stages during the sixteenth and seventeenth centuries, the first of which was characterized by internal conflict among Rāṭhoṛs over rights to land and to precedence, and the seeking of outside aid and support for local pretensions to rulership and positions of rank.

The land of Meṛto had originally come under Rāṭhoṛ control in the late fifteenth century, when Dūdo Jodhāvat and his elder uterine brother, Varsiṃgh, who were among the younger sons of Rāo Jodhojī Riṇmalot of Jodhpur, received it as their share of patrimonial inheritance from their father and proceeded to carve out their own rule over the area. The lands of Meṛto thus became the *vatan* of the sons and descendants of these two men, from whom the Meṛtiyo *khāṃp* stems. Dūdo, the younger brother, eventually superseded the sons of Varsiṃgh, to whom the headship of the Meṛtiyās had passed, and it was to his son, Vīraṃde Dūdāvat, that the headship passed in the early sixteenth century.

Under Vīraṃde, the Meṛtiyās, who before had been only *bhomiyās,* began to emerge as a powerful brotherhood on the borders of eastern Mārvāṛ, while Vīraṃde himself sought to establish a small kingdom within the lands of Meṛto and to the east, incorporating Ajmer. But beginning with the period of Rāo Mālde's rule in Jodhpur (1532–62), the Meṛtiyās and Vīraṃde came under increasing pressure from the Jodhpur rulers to acknowledge the precedence and authority of the Jodhās and to perform service under them. Rāo Mālde was greatly involved in establishing and consolidating a large kingdom of his own in Mārvāṛ, and was able to conquer the land of the Meṛtiyās and to subordinate them by force for a time early in his reign. His rule over Meṛto effectively ended, however, in 1544, when Sher Shāh Sūr defeated him at the battle of Samel with the help of Vīraṃde Dūdāvat, his brothers and other followers.

After losing his land to Rāo Mālde, Vīraṃde and his followers had proceeded to Delhi to plead their case and to seek the aid of Sher Shāh in regaining Meṛto and reasserting their 'rightful' position of rulership over it. And after the defeat of Mālde at Samel, Sher Shāh granted the rulership of Meṛto to Vīraṃde, and then to his son, Jaimal Vīramdevot, when Vīraṃde died shortly thereafter.[97]

Sher Shāh, upon whose support Jaimal depended for the retention of his position, died in 1545, and Rāo Mālde then again was able to conquer Meṛto and to drive Jaimal out of Mārvāṛ. Mālde proceeded to convert half of the lands of Meṛto into his own crown land, but he granted the other half to Meṛtiyo Jagmāl Vīraṃdevot, a brother of Jaimal, who had become a *cākar* of his after failing to succeed Vīraṃde to the headship of Meṛto.[98] This split in the direction of loyalties among brothers is a common phenomenon in the Rājpūt literature and reflects once again the cross-cutting of allegiances and the importance of gaining positions of local rank and precedence. Jaimal himself meanwhile migrated with his followers to Citoṛ during this period of distress, and settled in the land of Sisodīyo Rāṇo Udaisiṃgh Sāṃgāvat, his *sagā*[99] to whom he offered his services in return for villages. After a short period here, he, like his father before him, also proceeded north, this time to the *darbār* of Akbar Pātsāh, to plead his case against Rāo Mālde. Akbar proved sympathetic and confirmed him in his position of local rulership with a grant of Meṛto in *jāgīr* after he had declared his allegiance and submission to the Mughal throne. He also sent an army with Jaimal to help him recover Meṛto, which opened Akbar's initial phase of penetration into Mārvāṛ.[100]

Akbar's troops quickly defeated Rāo Mālde's forces at Meṛto, and Jaimal again assumed the ṭhakurship of this land. Akbar, however, soon thereafter revoked his *jāgīr* because of his protection of the local Muslim commander of Nāgaur, who had incurred imperial disfavour and fled from Nāgaur to Meṛto and then on the Gujarāt. This Muslim had originally helped Jaimal retake Meṛto and Jaimal appears to have developed a close personal relationship with him. While Jaimal owed allegiance to Akbar, his sense of identification and obligation seems here to have rested with the commander of Nāgaur, to whom he felt a more primary sense of loyalty. With the loss of his *jāgīr*, Jaimal again left for Citoṛ with his followers, where he was killed in battle in 1568, along with his brother, Īsardās, fighting against Akbar.[101]

[97]Naiṇsī, *Vigat*, II, pp. 56–8.

[98]Ibid., II, pp. 62–3; *Rāṭhoṛoṃ kī Khyāt*, pp. 520–1.

[99]At least one of Jaimal's sons and a number of his grandsons appear to have married into the Sīsodiyo ruling house. *Rāṭhoṛoṃ kī Khyāt*, pp. 465–8.

[100]Ibid., p. 461.

[101]Ibid., p. 462; Naiṇsī, *Vigat*, II, p. 68.

With the death of Jaimal, Akbar granted half of Meṛto in *jāgīr* to Jaimal's brother, Jagmāl, who had become a *mansabdār* of his upon the death of Rāo Mālde in 1562, and married one of his daughters to Akbar in exchange for the *jāgīr*.[102] The other portion of Meṛto Akbar reserved as imperial *khālsa* and placed under his own administrators.

Jagmāl held Merto in *jāgīr* for about four years. Upon his death in 1572, Akbar granted half shares of the *pargana* to two of Jaimal's sons, Surtāṇ and Kesodās. Both of these Rājpūts had remained with the Rāṇo of Mevāṛ for some time after their father was killed at Citoṛ. But they eventually also proceeded to Delhi to meet Akbar and attempted to regain their lands and their positions. The *khyāts* record that their paternal cousin, Narhardās Īsardāsot, the son of Īsardās Vīramdevot, facilitated Akbar's acceptance of their entreaty. Narhardās had joined Akbar's service after his father's death at Citoṛ alongside Jaimal, and had given one of his daughters in marriage to the Emperor.[103]

Both of Jaimal's sons, Surtāṇ and Kesodās, who remained in Mughal service after Akbar's grant of Meṛto in *jāgīr* to them, were eventually killed while performing imperial duties outside of Mārvāṛ. Meṛto then passed to their sons, until Akbar included all of the *pargana* within the *jāgīr* of Jodhpur Rājā Sūrajsiṃgh in 1604.[104] This grant marks the beginning of the second stage in these relations. This stage began in protest, when the Meṛtiyō Ṭhākurs and their brothers and followers went in a body of 2000 before Akbar to complain against Jodhpur authority over their lands. Akbar, however, denied their petition,[105] and Meṛtiyā fears about Jodhpur domination also soon faded when Rājā Sūrajsiṃgh confirmed most Meṛtiyās in control of individual villages within the *pargana*. Most Meṛtiyā allegiances also appear to have shifed to Rājā Surajsiṃgh at this time, under whom they began performing service, although some Meṛtiyās continued to hold *jāgīrs* in Mārvāṛ and elsewhere directly from the Mughals.[106]

The whole of Meṛto *pargana* remained in the *jāgīr* of Rājā Sūrajsiṃgh from 1604, until his death in 1619. In that year, Jahāngīr sequestered it and presented it to his son, Prince Khurram, the *Ṣubahdār* of Ajmer. Khurram appears to have divided up the area among his

[102] *Rāṭhoṛoṃ kī Khyāt*, pp. 520–1.
[103] Ibid., pp. 462–4, 471–2, 512–13; Naiṇsī, *Vigat*, II, pp. 69–72.
[104] *Rāṭhoṛoṃ kī Khyāt*, pp. 464–6, 472.
[105] Naiṇsī, *Vigat*, II, p. 73.
[106] *Rāṭhoṛoṃ kī Khyāt*, pp. 466–73.

Rājpūt servants, granting the town of Meṛto itself and a large number of villages to Sīsodiyo Rājā Bhīm Amrāvat.[107]

This transfer of authority to an outsider caused no apparent local disturbances, and Meṛtiyā alliances through marriage with the Sīsodiyās appear to be the reason, though I have not been able to trace the exact relationships involved here.

In 1622, however, when Prince Khurram (Shāh Jahān) revolted against his father, Jahāngīr appointed Prince Parviz Ṣubahdār of Ajmer with authority over Meṛto. Parviz at first allowed local Rājpūts to remain in control of their villages.[108] But in 1623, he granted Meṛto in *jāgīr* to the Sayyids. When news of this development and the threat of outside occupation of Rāṭhoṛ lands reached Mārvāṛ, there was great local consternation. Rājā Gajsiṃgh, eldest son and successor of Rājā Sūrajsiṃgh, immediately sent representations to Prince Parviz through Navāb Mohābat Khān, with whom he had developed a close personal relationship through serving under his command in several campaigns, saying:

> For many days now, I have enjoyed the fruits of Rājā Surajsiṃgh'ssuccesses. I have been able to retain the command and loyalty of all of his [Meṛtiyā] followers, who were in hopes that I would quickly receive Meṛto [in *jāgīr*] These Rājpūts have stayed with me for so long only with the expectation of my regaining [this land]. Now my Rājpūts in the *darbār* have heard that the Prince has given Meṛto to someone else, and these [Meṛtiyā] Rājpūts of mine are leaving.[109]

When the Navāb received this petition, he considered it prudent to have Meṛto granted to Rājā Gajsiṃgh in order not to cause disaffection among the Rājpūts. He then prevailed upon Parviz, who gave the *jāgīr* of Meṛto to Gajsiṃgh. Gajsiṃgh in turn married his uterine sister, Manbhāvatījī, to Parviz in exchange.[110]

Both this reaction of the Meṛtiyās as well as their earlier one are similar to that of Rājā Sūrajsiṃgh, the father of Gajsiṃgh, when he learned that Jahāngīr was revoking his *jāgīr* of Phaḷodhī and presenting it to Rāo Sūrajsiṃgh of Bīkāner. Rājā Sūrajsiṃgh of Jodhpur had himself been born at Phaḷodhī and he refused to give up his control there,

[107] Naiṇsī, *Vigat*, I, pp. 106, 112; II, p. 73.
[108] Ibid. II, p. 74.
[109] Ibid. II, p. 75.
[110] Ibid., I. p. 108; *Rāṭhoṛoṃ kī Khyāt*, p. 207. .

writing to his men posted at the fort: Phaḷodhī is my *janm-bhom.* I will not give it up. I will ask the Pātsāh not to transfer the authority.[111]

Upon representation at the Mughal court, Jahāngīr was prevailed upon to reverse his decision and to grant Phaḷodhī once again to Rājā Sūrajsiṃgh. Phaḷodhī remained under the Jodhpur rulers, except for a period of four years when it was under a brother of the ruler, until the death of Mahārājā Jasvaṃtsiṃgh in 1678.[112] We see in both examples a joining of concerns relating to the land as the sustenance of the brotherhood and control over land as the symbol of a *ṭhākur* and his rule of a kingdom.

From this point on, Meṛtiyā relations with both the ruling house of Jodhpur and the Mughals stabilized. Throughout the reigns of both Rājās Gajsiṃgh and Jasvaṃtsiṃgh, Meṛtiyā loyalties remained channeled primarily through the local ruler of Mārvāṛ to the Mughals. And although their *vatan* became increasingly broken-up as these rulers asserted greater centralized rule within Mārvāṛ, Meṛtiyās who remained in Mārvāṛ and offered their services to them also retained and gained access to individual ṭhākurships through this relationship, whether in Meṛto itself or in other local areas. This pattern was broken only after the death of Jasvaṃtsiṃgh in 1678, when Aurangzeb initiated the Rājpūt 'wars' of the 1680s. The cycle discussed above then began to repeat itself as local lands came under attack and Rājpūts began to lose control over their kingdoms.

Conclusions

During the Mughal period, Rājpūts from the frontier zone of Rājasthān were involved in a complex process of change and transition, which affected their society as this area became increasingly incorporated within the larger political and cultural system of north India. This process influenced the development not only of local social and political structures around which Rājpūts organized their lives, but also their system of local values and ideals, by which Rājpūts judged themselves and their actions. This period of transition and the resultant pressures which it brought to bear, confronted Rājpūts as individuals and as members of larger groups with a series of choices about the nature of their identification, their obligations and the direction of their loyalties. It

[111] Naiṇsī, *Vigat,* II, p. 7.
[112] Ibid., I. pp. 94–5, 106, 124.

also generated considerable conflict, both internal and external, over questions of support, rights to land, precedence and honour.

This conflict was itself symptomatic of a society undergoing a process of change and of the ambivalence of individuals in such a society, who seek to fulfil expectations deriving from overlapping and often contradictory sets of relationships and associated values of which they had become a part. These conflicts remained endemic during the Mughal period, both in isolated individual situations as well as in larger contexts, and speak to the problems of control in an area lacking an integrated system of shared values and norms.

Despite the endemic nature of this conflict, which for the most part was limited to small-scale actions and incidents, Rājpūt support for and adherence to the Mughal throne became an enduring feature of this period. This support and loyalty rested primarily upon a basic 'fit' between Rājpūt ideals and aspirations, expressed in local myth and symbol, and Mughal actions in this area, which did not challenge fundamental Rājpūt tenets regarding order and precedence. Mughal policy of support for local rulers, of alliance through marriage, and of granting lands in return for service and allegiance all found a base of support in local ideology and allowed Rājpūts in turn to find fulfilment of their own ideals through subordination and loyalty to the Mughal throne. Only in periods when the Mughals directly contradicted these tenets concerning order and precedence did Rājpūts withdraw their support and shift the direction of their loyalties. In sum, the Rājpūt alliance with the Mughals can be seen as a product of identification and obligation generated through the establishment of personal bonds and affiliations, sanctioned in local custom, and the fulfilment of cultural aspirations and ideals, defined in local myth and symbol.

PART 2
Fiscal Organization and Social Structure

5 Rank (*manṣab*) in the Mogul State Service*

W.H. Moreland

In this essay I propose to examine the position held by the executive officers of the Mogul Empire in the light of some new documentary evidence, and from a standpoint different from that occupied by earlier writers on the subject. It is well known that there was no differentiation between civil and military employment: all officers, from the princes of the blood down to what would now be called sergeants and corporals, formed a single state service, in which each individual had a definite rank or position (*manṣab*); and ordinarily each of them had to maintain out of his emoluments a contingent of cavalry available for the Emperor's work. Some officers might receive their emoluments in cash, but as a rule payment was made by an assignment of the land revenue of a specified area (*jāgīr*), which the recipient made his own arrangements to collect. The questions at issue relate mainly to the remuneration of officers and the size and constitution of their contingents.

To begin with, it is necessary to examine the terminology. In the literature of Akbar's reign an officer's rank is, with very few exceptions, described by a single word, a numeral with the suffix *-ī*, the nearest English equivalent for which is the colloquial *-er*: *hazārī*, for instance, may be rendered '1000-er'. I shall speak of this form of description as 'single rank'.

In the literature of Jahāngīr and Shāh Jahān the regular method of description is what I shall call double rank. The 'single rank' term is followed by the word *ẓāt* ('person'), and by a numeral with the word *suwār* ('troopers'), but *ẓāt* is sometimes omitted. *Hazārī ẓāt haft ṣad suwār* is an example, which may be rendered '1000-er personal 700 troopers'.

*First published in the *Journal of the Royal Asiatic Society* (1936).

In the same period we find, in a comparatively small number of cases, what I shall call triple rank; the double rank description is followed by a number of troopers *sih-aspa dū-aspa*, that is to say, troopers possessing two or three horses, and an officer might be described as *hazārī ẓāt haft ṣad suwār, sih ṣad suwār sih-aspa dū-aspa*, or 1000-er personal 700 troopers 300 troopers with two or three horses. To shorten the last expression I shall write '2–3h.'.

Promotion in the service might take one of three forms, in personal rank, in trooper rank, or in 2–3h. rank; and the subject may be illustrated by a sketch[1] of the career of Raja Jai Singh of Amber, whom we shall meet again. Jai Singh succeeded as Raja in 1621, but he was then too young for service, and was appointed to the comparatively modest rank of 2000 personal 1000 troopers, or as I shall write for brevity, 2000/1000. Two years later he was ready to serve, and started on his active career as 3000/1400. Soon after Shāh Jahān's accession he was promoted to 4000/3000, then 4000/4000, then 5000/4000, and then, in the tenth regnal year, 5000/5000. This was the highest rank to which an officer could ordinarily rise: Akbar had made a rule[2] that ranks above this should be reserved for princes of the blood, and, while exceptions were subsequently made, they were rare. Accordingly, Jai Singh's further promotions were by way of 'triple rank'; in the eleventh regnal year he was made 350 2–3h., and rose by successive steps till in the 24th regnal year he became 5000/5000/4000. His subsequent career lies outside the present inquiry.

In the literature the transition from single to double rank occurs in the first year of Jahāngīr,[3] so suddenly that a reader might be tempted to infer that double rank was introduced in that year. As a matter of fact it existed under Akbar,[4] and, as I shall show, it was introduced by him in his eleventh year; the change in the literature must mean merely that at this time double rank began to be entered regularly in the court journals, on which both the *Tūzuk* and the *Bādshāhnāma* were clearly based. The first mention I have found of triple rank is in Jahāngīr's tenth year,[5] but it would not be safe to infer that it was then a new

[1]*Tūzuk, The Memoirs of Jahāngīr*, trans. A. Rogers, ed. H. Beveridge (Oriental Translation Fund), London, 1909–1914, ii, 219, 257; *Bādshāhnāma*, I, i, 120, 296; I, ii, 86, 248, 294; *II*, 272, 3 683, 719; and some documents cited below.

[2]*The Ain-i Akbari*, Persian text in *Bibliotheca Indica*, i, p. 179.

[3]*Tūzuk*, i, between pp. 60 and 71.

[4]*Akbarnāma*, iii, 1031, 1069, 1077; *Ain* i, 179.

[5]*Tūzuk*, i, p. 299.

creation; I have failed to find any evidence to show the date or circumstances of its introduction.

It is unnecessary to refer in detail to the earlier writers who attempted to explain this cumbrous nomenclature and bring it into relation with facts. Blochmann[6] was obviously groping; von Noer[7] contributed nothing material; and Horn[8] erected, if I understand him rightly, an unsubstantial structure on some of Blochmann's guesses, accepted as facts. The account which holds the field in England is that which was offered in 1903 in Irvine's *Army of the Indian Moghuls,* and is contained in two sentences which I will quote. The discussion of personal rank is followed by the words:

> As an additional distinction, it was the custom to tack on to a *manṣab* a number of extra horsemen. To distinguish between the two kinds of rank, the original *manṣab*, which governed the personal allowances, was known as the *ẕāt* rank, and the additional men were designated by the word *suwār.*[9]

The description of *suwār* rank begins as follows:

> The grant of *suwār* rank in addition to *ẕāt* rank was an honour.... The table of pay in Blochmann, i. 248 and that given above [not reproduced here] are exclusively for the *ẕāt* rank, from which money the officer had to maintain his transport, his household, and some horsemen. For the *suwār* rank there was a separate table, pay for these horsemen being disbursed under the name of *tābīnān.*[10]

The effect of these passages is that an officer holding double rank had to maintain two contingents: (*a*) 'some horsemen' paid out of his personal salary; and (*b*) some 'extra' or 'additional' horsemen paid from the allowance provided for this purpose. This idea of two contingents prevails in the subsequent literature, but it will suffice to quote one illustration from Vincent Smith: 'Another complication was introduced by the grant of *suwār* rank in addition to the personal (*ẕāt*) class

[6]H. Blochmann, translation of vol. I of the *Ain-i-Akbari* in *Bibliotheca Indica* (Calcutta, 1871), i, p. 239 ff.

[7]von Noer, *The Emperor Akbar*, trans. A.S. Beveridge (Calcutta, 1890), i, p. 267.

[8]Paul Horn, *Das Heer und Kriegswesen des Gross-Moghuls* (Leiden, 1867–1877), pp. 11–21.

[9]William Irvine, *Army of the Indian Moghuls,* p. 5.

[10]Ibid., p. 9.

rank, that is to say, an officer was allowed to add and draw extra pay for a supplementary body of *suwārs* or horsemen.'[11]

Irvine quoted no authority for his statement that 'some horsemen' were paid from an officer's personal salary, and I cannot make the omission good, for I have found no passage to support it. The truth appears to be that, following previous writers, he started with the very natural assumption that personal rank must involve the maintenance of a contingent; and if that assumption is correct, the idea of two contingents for 'double rank' follows logically. The question of the strength of these contingents was not examined by Irvine in detail; he rightly rejected[12] Horn's view that under Akbar personal rank denoted the actual strength, but thought that 'the figures had possibly some connection with the number of men', a connection which, he suggested, had ceased to exist in the reign of Shāh Jahān.

An alternative account has, I understand, been current in India for some time, but the first place where I have found it in print is an article by Mr Abdul Aziz in the *Journal of Indian History*.[13] According to this account, the official descriptions mean just what they say: personal rank was purely personal, and by itself involved the maintenance of no troopers, the number of which was denoted, or indicated, by the trooper rank; and an officer with 'double rank' had to maintain only one contingent, not two. I do not propose to review the arguments advanced by Mr Abdul Aziz; taking them as a whole, they seem to me to come very near to actual proof, or at the least, make this view definitely more probable than that offered by Irvine. In a later number[14] of the same journal Mr C.S.K. Rao Saheb arrived independently at the same conclusion regarding trooper rank, and proceeded to argue that personal rank denoted the strength of a contingent of infantry which every officer had to maintain out of his salary. I hope to discuss the latter contention in the journal where it appeared, and here I will say only that in my judgement the case for infantry contingents is not established.

I now turn to examine the general question in the light of some documents of a kind which have not hitherto been available to students—a series of assignment orders issued by the revenue ministry in the reign of Shāh Jahān. The story of these documents is as follows. Some years ago, when I was collecting material for a study of the

[11] Vincent Smith, *Akbar the Great Mogul*, p. 364.
[12] Irvine, *Army of the Indian Moghuls*, p. 58.
[13] Abdul Aziz, *Journal of Indian History* (August 1930), pp. 138–63.
[14] C.S.K. Rao Saheb, *Journal of Indian History* (August 1935), pp. 205 ff.

Mogul agrarian system, I made such search as was possible for records of the kind, but I failed to find a single document earlier than the middle of the eighteenth century, and I was driven to the conclusion that the quest was hopeless. Recently, however, I learned that some documents of the sort I wanted had come to light among the old records of the Jaipur State, and His Highness the Maharaja very kindly allowed me to obtain photostats of them. I owe a special debt of gratitude to Mr C.U. Wills, C.I.E., who brought the existence of these documents to my notice, obtained the requisite sanction, and made all the arrangements for the supply of photostats.

Among the documents are three assignment orders issued to Raja Jai Singh, the first in AH 1018, when he was promoted to the rank of 5000/5000/350, the second in Rajab, AH 1090, when he was 5000/5000/3000; and the third in Ramazān of the same year on his promotion to 5000/5000/4000. All three are obviously 'common form', and they may reasonably be accepted as samples of the ordinary procedure of the period: their form agrees generally with that given by Irvine[15] for the period of the later Moguls. The text of the orders is short, and (omitting compliments) merely recites that the Raja holds a certain rank and that his assignment has been fixed 'as below'; then follows a lengthy schedule, which gives (1) the Raja's claim to salary and allowances, (2) a comparison with his former claim, (3) any necessary adjustments, and (4) a list of areas assigned in satisfaction of the claim so calculated. For the present purpose the relevant portion is that in which the claim is set out; the originals are, of course, arranged in the manner of the period, with totals at the top, and details stretching down the page in irregular columns, not ruled off; in the following reproduction of the statement of claim formulated in Ramazān, 1060, which is given as a sample, I have rearranged the items for convenient printing:

5000 TROOPERS, viz. 4000 2–3 h., 1000 *barāwardī*.			
SANCTIONED CLAIM:			
Individual: (? amount of) salary of 5000-er		100	laks of dāms
Contingent: 5000 troopers, sanctioned		720	laks of dāms
	Total	820	laks of dāms
DETAIL OF CONTINGENT:			
4000 2–3 h., sanctioned		640	laks of dāms
1000 *barāwardī*		80	laks of dāms.
	Total	720	laks of dāms

[15] Irvine, *Army of the Indian Moghuls*, p. 17.

The terminology in the original is as follows. The troopers (*suwār*) are distinguished in two classes, *sih-aspa dū-aspa*, and *barāwardī*; the latter is a technical term, and for the present I do not attempt to translate it. 'Sanctioned' throughout represents *muqarrara*, which clearly points to the 'sanctioned scale', as we should now say. 'Claim' represents *talab*. 'Individual' represents *khāsa;* the correlation of this word with *ẕāt* (personal) is obvious. 'Salary' represents *sālāna*, 'yearly pay'; the word just before it is badly written, and I cannot say with confidence whether it is *miqdār* (amount) or something else. 'Contingent' represents *tābīnān*, the regular word for an officer's troopers regarded as a body.

On the face of it this statement of claim is in accordance with the view that an officer holding 'double' or 'triple' rank had to provide only one contingent. There is an individual salary determined by the personal rank, and there is provision for the contingent indicated by the other items of the rank: there is nothing more. Irvine's view becomes highly improbable, or almost impossible, when the actual figures are scrutinized. It is true that the salary (Rs 250,000) looks very large when the value of money is taken into account; but necessary expenses were correspondingly heavy. The cost of maintaining the transport obligatory for a 5000-er was reckoned by Blochmann[16] to be over Rs 10,000 a month, more than one-third of the salary sanctioned by Akbar, and just half of that which was allowed to Raja Jai Singh. The cost of managing and policing the assignment must have been substantial, especially when the land lay at some distance from the officer's station; and any loss resulting from bad seasons necessarily fell on him, for the high pitch of the revenue made it certain that the peasants could not bear the burden. Out of the balance the Raja had to maintain his position as one of the great nobles of the empire at a time when extravagance had reached its highest point, and to offer periodical costly presents to the Emperor: if, as the claim shows, 18 lakhs of rupees were allowed for a nominal contingent of 5000 (representing at this period from 1200 to 1600 effectives), the number of troopers that could be provided from the balance of personal salary would be at the most trifling.

These documents then seem to me to tell strongly against Irvine's view; I proceed to examine the whole question of officer's rank from a standpoint different from that of previous writers. The tendency has been to regard the state service as a static organization, so that the

[16]Blochmann, *Ain*, i, p. 241.

facts of Shāh Jahān's reign could be explained directly by those of Akbar's, and vice versa. I prefer to start by allowing for the possibility that the organization changed with changing times, and to review the recorded facts against the known background of administrative, military, and financial history. So treated, the story of rank presents five successive phases.

In the first phase, numerical rank appears as a military fact; the 1000-er was a man who commanded 1000 troopers, and nothing else. In the second phase, effective strength fell below nominal, and the titular 1000-er might command only a few hundred troopers. In the third phase, this divergence was recognized, and it was regulated by the introduction of double rank: the 1000-er who commanded 100 was not degraded from his titular rank, but became 1000-er personal 100 troopers; and the trooper rank was a military fact. The fourth phase was a repetition of the second; effective strength again fell below the nominal, and trooper rank ceased to be a military fact. The fifth phase was the reorganization effected by Shāh Jahān.

The first phase carries us back to Chingīz and Tīmūr. To quote a recent biographer[17] of the former, 'In accordance with an immemorial usage, he divided it [his army] into thousands, hundreds, and tens. Experienced leaders, personally known to the Khān, were appointed to be commanders of the thousands and hundreds.' This was in the day of comparatively small things; a little later the organization was carried higher, and the thousands 'were united into groups of two, three or five thousands, and into larger units—army corps—myriads', the historic *tūmān* of 10,000 troopers. Tīmūr's organization, as it can be seen in his *Memoirs*,[18] was essentially similar, and under these men—conquerors rather than rulers—there was no need, and no room, for anything in the way of honorary or personal rank as distinguished from command.

The second phase carries us from Tīmūr to the early years of Akbar. The fifteenth century was a time when effective strength might be expected to fall: instead of one great conqueror, there were several kingdoms, some of them quite petty, and nothing is more striking in the early pages of Bābur's *Memoirs* than the smallness of the numbers which might suffice to win a throne. But it is most unlikely that the

[17]B.Y. Valdimirtsov, *The Life of Chingis-Khan*, trans. D.S. Mirsky (London, 1930), pp. 58, 69.

[18]H. Elliot and J. Dowson, *The History of India as Told by its Own Historians* (London, 1867–77), iii, pp. 394 ff.

Tīmūrids, with their pride in their glorious past, should discard the historic titles of the higher commands; it is much more probable that the titles should survive, while the strength of the commands fell.

Bābur brought the Tīmūrid system to northern India,[19] and continuity is established by such facts as the survival of the foreign title *Yūzbāshī* for the 100-er, that of *Amīr-ul Umarā* for the highest rank, or the conferment of the *tūmān-togh*, the historic standard of the *tūmān*, as a military distinction. In his *Memoirs* Bābur did not give the numerical rank of his officers, but frequent incidental references show that they were members of a regular service with formal appointments and promotions, and a line drawn between 'great Begs' and 'Begs', corresponding perhaps to the later distinction between Amīrs and Mansabdārs. Two passages in his *Memoirs* establish the fact, which is antecedently probable, that in his time the titular commands had become nominal. On p. 170 we find: 'A few days later the Khāns joined to me Ayūb with his *tūmān* and Jān Hasan with the *Bārīn tūmān*—1000 to 2000 men in all.'[20] Under Tīmūr, two *tūmāns* would have been 20,000 men, but in Bābur's time effective strength was one-tenth or less of nominal. Again on p. 277: 'It is an evil noticeable to-day that effort must be made before the man, dubbed Beg because he has five or six of the bald and blind at the back, can be got into the Gate [i.e. on guard] at all.'[21] The sarcastic exaggeration of that sentence shows that Bābur was worried by the conditions which were to worry Akbar—the wide divergence between nominal and effective strength; and the reality of this second phase is proved by the best possible witness.

I can find nothing to show that Humāyūn made any attempt at reform, and the third phase began in Akbar's eleventh year, when he superimposed trooper rank on the existing system. The fact is recorded briefly in the *Akbarnāma*[22] in a passage which Beveridge[23] rendered as follows: 'As the branding department has not then emerged into being, at this time the number of attendants[24] for all the officers and

[19]Vincent Smith in *Akbar the Great Mogul* asserted that the system of numerical rank was 'borrowed directly from Persia'. But there is no evidence of this loan, and the truth is that, while the system prevailed over a large part of Asia, it was brought to northern India by the Tīmūrids.

[20]*Bāburnāma*, trans. A.S. Beveridge (London, 1921), p. 170.

[21]Ibid., p. 277.

[22]*Akbarnāma*, Persian text in *Bibliotheca Indica*, ii, p. 270.

[23]H. Beveridge, translation of the *Akbarnāma* in *Bibliotheca Indica*, ii, p. 403.

[24]Text, *Naukarān*. This word is used occasionally as a synonym for *suwār*, e.g. by Nizamuddīn Ahmad, p. 383.

servants of the threshold was fixed, so that everyone should keep some persons in readiness for service.' The technical terms are not used in this passage, but its meaning is obvious, and it may be illustrated by a passage from Badāonī quoted by Blochmann:[25]

> It was settled that every Amīr should commence as a commander of twenty ... and when, according to the rule, he had brought the horses of his twenty troopers to be branded, he was then to be made a *Ṣadī*, or commander of 100, or more. ... When they had brought to the musters their new contingent complete, they were to be promoted according to their merits and circumstances to the post of *Hazārī* [or higher].

The title of Amīr was reserved for officers of the higher ranks; the position of the dividing-line is obscure,[26] but in Akbar's days it seems that all above 500 might be so styled, though under Shāh Jahān it was confined to those of 1000 (personal) or more. Stress must not be laid on Badāonī's numbers, because he was apt to exaggerate for effect, but his language is in accordance with that of the *Akbarnāma*, and it shows that each high officer received a second rank, which might be quite small, but was intended to be a hard fact; the essential thing was that 'some persons' should be ready for service, and the second, or trooper, rank denoted the number which each officer should keep ready. His old high rank was not abolished, but on the introduction of trooper rank it ceased to signify command, and became merely personal.

This change of system affecting the entire state service ought to have been recorded in the *Ain*, but in fact it does not appear. The silence of the official record is not, however, a matter of much importance: I have shown elsewhere[27] that the *Ain* must be supplemented by the *Akbarnāma* in order to give a full account of Akbar's administrative activities in the revenue department, and we now find that the same thing is true in the military department also. As a matter of fact, however, the text of the *Ain*[28] implies the existence of the regulations which are not formally set out, and shows that the reform effected was gradual. At first Akbar relied on the preparation of descriptive rolls, but dishonest practices were not thereby eliminated, and sham troopers rode to the muster on borrowed horses; then, after seven years, came the branding regulations, which are set out at length in the *Ain*,[29] and which

[25] Blochmann, *Ain*, i, p. 242.
[26] The authorities are set out by Abdul Aziz, pp. 157 ff.
[27] *The Agrarian System of Moslem India*, p. 108.
[28] *Ain*, i, pp. 175–6.
[29] Ibid, pp. 190 ff.

were certainly well adapted to secure the military and financial benefits which the official record claims. This explains the introductory words in the passage quoted from the *Akbarnāma*; when Abul Fazl wrote, the branding system had been in operation for many years, but he had now to describe action taken before its introduction. It is reasonable to infer that from this time on the contingents were kept at or near their nominal strength, so long as these rules were enforced, or in other words, so long as Akbar was there to insist on their enforcement. Thus in this third phase trooper rank must be regarded as a reality, though a certain amount of dishonesty may have survived.

Before passing to the next phase a few words are called for regarding the form of the basic passage in the *Akbarnāma*. In his translation Beveridge noted a lack of connection with the earlier portion of the paragraph, and his note is correct in regard to form, though not to substance. The preceding sentences tell us that at this time Akbar took measures to ensure that the assignments given to his officers should be worth their face value, and the paragraph thus shows that in this year he took up the question of service reorganization as a whole. Contingents and assignments alike were shams; the practice was to offer payment on paper for paper troopers; and the reforms were directed to giving real payment for real men. But the passage regarding rank is brought in clumsily, with a casual 'and'; it breaks the even style which Abul Fazl usually maintained; and, in our eyes, it is a very summary treatment of a matter of great importance. The probable explanation of these features is that it was an afterthought. The silence of the *Ain* indicates that this particular regulation was not among Abul Fazl's materials, and it was made long before he came to Akbar's court; probably some critic, quite possibly Akbar himself, hearing the draft read over, pointed out the omission, and this hurried insertion was the result.

The fourth phase, in which the contingents denoted by trooper rank fell below nominal strength, comes with the reign of Jahāngīr, and, differing in this respect from those which have now been reviewed, there is no direct evidence of its reality. Our knowledge of the reign, however, is such as to make it practically certain, or at least to throw the burden of proof on anyone who should assert that one of Akbar's institutions survived in its integrity when the rest were crumbling. We know that Jahāngīr's reign was characterized by progressive administrative inefficiency, lack of financial control, lavish promotion, and instability of tenure; we know that the officers of the service were engaged largely in a struggle to get as much money as possible for themselves. To economize on their contingents was their most obvious course, since the great bulk of their assignments was earmarked for this purpose; Raja Jai Singh, as we have seen, drew a crore of *dāms* for himself and more than seven crores for his contingent and the proportion was probably not very different in the earlier period; it seems to me to be reasonable to say that, in these circumstances, only an exceptionally keen soldier, or an exceptionally honest man, would have kept his contingent up to strength, when the Emperor had ceased to trouble himself about such matters. The tradition of making money in this way had been strong in the days of Akbar. We may allow that his fight against it was successful for the time, but we cannot suppose that he had eradicated the tendency, which would again become effective as soon as his restraining influence was removed. A critical and independent chronicler of Jahāngīr's reign would perhaps have told us what actually happened, but we possess no such chronicle, and the *Tūzuk*, our primary source for the period, is the last place in the world where such facts would have found a place. The reality of this phase thus rests, not on contemporary evidence, but on inference from established facts.

The fifth, and last, phase is what I have called Shāh Jahān's reorganization. We know from the statements of various writers, and notably from the *Maasīr-ul Umarā*,[30] that Shāh Jahān reorganized the finances of the empire, which at his accession were in a most unsatisfactory condition, and this action must have involved changes in the position of the state service, which was by far the largest head of expenditure; even after the reorganization it received in assignments more than 85 per cent of the entire land revenue.[31] The contemporary chronicles do not tell us what was done, but the date of action is fixed by English records, and its nature is apparent in the documents preserved at Jaipur and other sources of the period.

The position which Shāh Jahān had to face was this. As the result of his father's lavish promotions, he had on paper an army larger than he could pay for, and also larger than he needed; but its effective strength was small, because the contingents maintained by officers had fallen far below the nominal figures. To have insisted on the contingents being brought up to full strength would have meant bankruptcy, and also widespread disaffection in the service. The alternative of letting things stay as they were would equally have meant bankruptcy, and

[30] *Maasīr-ul Umarā*, Persian text in *Bibliotheca Indica*, ii, pp. 813 ff.
[31] *Bādshāhnāma*, Persian text in *Bibliotheca Indica*, ii, p. 710.

also military weakness, which would have been fatal to his projects of conquest. The facts on record indicate that he effected a compromise, on the one hand scaling down the contingents, and on the other reducing the emoluments of his officers, so that on balance they were better off than under Akbar, though their clandestine profits may have been less than under Jahāngīr.

First, as to the date of this reorganization. In February 1628 the English merchants at Agra wrote that Shāh Jahān had taken his seat on the throne on the 4th of that month, and on 17 March they reported as follows: 'The present occurrences at Court is a gennerall lessening of former livings and mayntenance of all degrees of the late King's amraws and servants.'[32] The subsequent reports from Agra have not survived, but their tenor can be inferred from the letter sent home in April 1630, by the Council at Surat, which reported that Shāh Jahān's empire was at peace, he 'having pollitickly wrought his owne securitie by ... impovrishing his amrawes or nobles by taking from them all their treasure and livings, allowing noe more then wil maintaine them barely in an ordinary state'.[33] These last words are perhaps too strong, for the new scale of remuneration was still exceedingly liberal when judged by modern standards, but on these records it is safe to say that Shāh Jahān began his reorganization as soon as he was seated firmly on the throne, and that it had become effective by the early months of 1630.

Next, as to the measures adopted. The scaling down of the contingents appears from a passage in the *Bādshāhnāma*,[34] which tells us that as a general rule Shāh Jahān's officers were required to muster either one-third or one-fourth of the troopers indicated by their trooper rank; the higher proportion applied when they were serving in the province where their assignments were situated, and the lower when they were serving elsewhere. The statement is introduced by the words: 'Among the regulations of this exalted reign (*daulat-i wālā*) is this.' Blochmann[35] took these words to mean that the regulation had been made by Shāh Jahān, and that is a natural reading in such a context; but the word *daulat* may mean realm as well as 'reign', and the scholars whom I have consulted agree with me in thinking that the phrase, standing by itself, cannot safely be taken as furnishing conclusive proof that the regulation was made by Shāh Jahān. The probability that it was his

[32]*The English Factories in India (1624–29)*, pp. 240, 271.
[33]Ibid., 1630–33, p. 33.
[34]*Bādshāhnāma*, ii, p. 506.
[35]Blochmann, *Ain*, i, p. 244.

work remains, for it is very hard to conceive of Jahāngīr making such a rule, but it would be a reasonable and natural step for the son to take in order to get the father's army into some sort of order, that he should say to his officers: 'I won't require you to maintain all the men you are supposed to pay, but I will insist on a fixed minimum being always at my service.' Akbar had done the same thing, though in a different way. It is not then formally proved that Shāh Jahān made the regulation in question, but the probability that he did so is very great.

As to the reduction of emoluments, Irvine[36] and Abdul Aziz[37] have shown from later records that the salaries of officers under Aurangzeb and his successors were on a much lower scale than those recorded in the *Ain*[38] as having been fixed by Akbar. The reductions in the grades from 7000 to 500 average 37 per cent all over; between 7000 and 1500 they range from 26 to 42 per cent, and in the lower grades from 32 to 60 per cent; while their quantitative importance can be judged from the fact that the yearly salary bill for these grades in Shāh Jahān's twentieth year works out at 2¾ crores of rupees on the new scale as against nearly 4½ crores on the old. The two scales are further differentiated by the fact that while Akbar fixed monthly salaries in rupees, in later times they were stated in *dāms* per annum. Now among the Jaipur documents is a *farmān* issued by Shāh Jahān in 1630, which shows that in that year salaries were allowed substantially on the new and lower scale, which can safely be regarded as the result of his 'lessening of former livings'.

This document is of interest as containing the earliest schedule of emoluments and assignments which has yet come to light. Its main purpose was to inform Raja Jai Singh of the appointments conferred on 21 of his adherents who had offered their services to the Emperor; and the schedule on the reverse, which is nearly eight feet in length, gives the rank and emoluments of each of these officers. It differs from the documents already cited in giving only the totals of emoluments, but these can be distributed precisely between personal salary and allowance for contingent, because by a fortunate accident it contains several pairs of what algebraists call simultaneous equations, the solutions of which furnish rigorous proof, and not merely probabilities. A single example of these equations may be given. One officer received the rank of 80/30, and was allowed 386,100 *dāms*. Another received

[36] Irvine, *Army of the Indian Moghuls*, p. 8.
[37] Abdul Aziz in *JIH*, p. 150.
[38] *Ain*, i, p. 180 ff.

the rank of 80/20, and was allowed 208,100 *dāms*. Both were in Class III of the grade, because trooper rank was less than half of personal,[39] and therefore they drew the same salary, but the first had 10 troopers more than the second; it requires no elaborate display of formulae to show that the difference of 88,000 *dāms* in total emoluments represents the allowance for ten troopers, and it follows by the ordinary algebraic procedure that the salary of the grade and class was 122,100 *dāms*.

These equations give us the salary allowed to each of the 21 officers. Eliminating duplicates, we have 13 cases, which are compared in the following table with Akbar's scale, and with that for the later period.

OFFICERS' SALARIES
(in thousands of *dāms* yearly)

Grade and Class	Akbar's scale	1630 scale	Later scale
600 II	1320	862.5	900
400 II	840	478.5	480
400 III	720	462	460
300 II	600	379.5	380
300 III	576	363	360
200 II	456	313.5	280
200 III	432	280.5	260
150 III	384	254.1	210
100 II	288	198	180
80 III	168	122.1	120
50 III	110.4	75	75

Obviously the salaries of these ranks were substantially on the later scale, and in all cases far below what Akbar had paid. The minor differences between the last two columns may be explained on the hypothesis that the reduced scale was subsequently modified in detail, but it is also possible that some or all of them may be due to individual allowances or deductions, taken into account in the schedule, but not shown separately; the change in level is, however, beyond question.

These figures relate to the lower ranks of the service. For the higher ranks we have the fact, established by the Jaipur assignment orders, that from Shāh Jahān's eleventh year onwards Raja Jai Singh drew a crore of *dāms* yearly, or Rs 250,000; this was the salary he would have drawn under Aurangzeb, while on Akbar's scale he would have been

[39]Ibid., p. 179.

entitled to Rs 360,000. The English reports already cited justify the inference that this reduction also dated from the first or second year of the reign.

The other and larger item in an officer's emoluments, the allowance for his contingent, brings us into an obscure region, which has to be explored step by step. To begin with, it must be understood that the rates of troopers' pay given in official records do not mean that each trooper was paid at the rate stated. They were essentially contract rates: an officer was allowed so much money to maintain so many men; what he actually paid to each man was his own affair. In the next place, it must be remembered that the ordinary trooper owned his horse (or horses) and his arms and other equipment; the pay was more than a personal wage, for it covered a complete fighting unit. In the third place, it is obvious that, in order to secure the mobility which is of the essence of cavalry, some sort of remount service was indispensable, and this took the form of a requirement for men with more than one horse of their own; a *dū-aspa*, or trooper owning two horses, was from the military standpoint worth more than a *yak-aspa* or trooper with a single horse, and a *sih-aspa*, or trooper with two remounts, was worth still more. Akbar's rule[40] was that officers' contingents should be composed of these three classes in the proportion of three, four, and three, giving on the average 20 horses for 10 troopers (Blochmann's figure of 18 horses is a miscalculation.) Under Shāh Jahān the rule was, as we shall see, more complicated.

The data for pay of troopers given in the *Ain*[41] point to an average allowance of about Rs 25 monthly, or 12,000 *dāms* yearly, per head, but they were superseded by a later order,[42] which introduced a new scale, giving for ordinary troopers an average of Rs 20, or 9600 *dāms* yearly, calculated on the proportion of horses to troopers which has just been stated; and this rate is mentioned occasionally as prevailing during Jahāngīr's reign, as for instance, by William Hawkins.[43] The *farmān* of 1630 shows that in Shāh Jahān's third year the rate allowed for ordinary troopers was 8800 *dāms*, a reduction of one-twelfth, but the later documents prove that from the eleventh year onwards it was 8000 *dāms*, a figure which still prevailed in Aurangzeb's time. An entry in the assignment order of Shāh Jahān's eleventh year suggests that

[40]Ibid., p. 188.
[41]Ibid., p. 175–87.
[42]*Akbarnāma*, iii, p. 672.
[43]William Hawkins, *Early Travels in India*, ed. W. Foster, p. 114.

this second 'cut' was made towards the end of the tenth year, but the point is not free from doubt, and it is enough to say that Shāh Jahān began by a reduction of one-twelfth on Akbar's rate, and that before his eleventh year he had established a reduction of one-sixth in all. In addition to this substantial reduction we have to take into account the operation of what I shall call the Rule of Months, a rule which emerges for the first time in Shāh Jahān's reign.

We do not possess this rule in so many words, and its operation is known to us mainly from the passage in the *Bādshāhnāma* which has already been quoted to establish the fact that contingents had been scaled down. In that passage the standing regulation that officers should bring to muster a third or a quarter of their trooper rank was quoted in order to explain the special concession made to the expeditionary force sent to conquer Balkh. We are told that in view of the distance to be traversed by that force, Shāh Jahān reduced the proportion to one-fifth, so that an officer holding double rank as 5000/5000 was required to muster only 1000 troopers; and the kinds of these 1000 troopers are then detailed according to the number of months in a year for which the officer received his allowance. Following previous writers, I will set out this passage in tabular form:

No. of months	Kind of Troopers			No. of horses (calculated)
	3-horse	2-horse	1-horse	
12	300	600	100	2200
11	250	500	250	2000
10	–	800	200	1800
9	–	600	400	1600
8	–	450	550	1450
7	–	250	750	1250
6	–	100	900	1100
5	–	–	1000	1000

There was thus a definite correlation between the amount of the allowance and the proportion of remounts. In order to realize his full claim, an officer had to maintain a reasonably mobile contingent: 22 horses for every 10 troopers; if he had only 16 horses for 10, he lost 25 per cent of the allowance, and so on.

As the text stands, these figures were fixed specially for the Balkh expedition and we must not generalize from the details, but we hear of the Rule of Months incidentally elsewhere, and it must be accepted as a general regulation, the figures of which were perhaps modified for this special occasion; it would have been quite impossible to improvise the rule at this time, for to do so would have involved a complete revision of assignments at the moment when the officers concerned were starting for a distant objective. Its effect was necessarily to reduce the average allowance per trooper below the figure which I have given, unless (what is perhaps improbable) every officer succeeded in qualifying for the full twelve months' allowance.

To resume this portion of the argument, we find that the following changes had occurred between Akbar's later years and Shāh Jahān:

(1) Effective strength of contingents scaled down to one-third or one-quarter of nominal;

(2) Officers' salaries reduced substantially—on the average by more than one-third;

(3) Allowances for contingents reduced by at least one-sixth with further reductions in case of lack of mobility.

These changes seem to me to hang together and form part of a scheme. It is scarcely possible to conceive an all-round reduction in emoluments being made by itself, whether all at once or by stages: reduction appears reasonable and natural as part of a compromise, in which officers' contingents were reduced simultaneously. They received smaller assignments, but had to spend less on their contingents; on balance, their net income was substantially larger than in Akbar's time, while there was a very definite inducement to maintain their contingents in a reasonably mobile condition. Here we have the main features of Shāh Jahān's reorganization.

Some idea of its financial effect can be obtained by calculating the cost to the empire of a real as opposed to a nominal trooper. Under Akbar this was, as we have seen, eventually Rs 20 monthly. Under Shāh Jahān, when effective strength was either one-third or a quarter of nominal, the figure was either Rs 50 or Rs 67, or on the average practically three times what Akbar paid. I have shown elsewhere[44] that no general rise had occurred in silver prices between the two reigns, but it is possible that, with the growth of luxury, serviceable horses had come to cost substantially more, and part of the increase in cost per effective head may perhaps be attributed to this cause.

I have described this reorganization as the last phase in the story, and the description is justified by the fact that the position during and after Aurangzeb's reign, as described by Irvine and Abdul Aziz, was

[44]W.H. Moreland, *From Akbar to Aurangzeb*, London, 1923 pp. 170 ff.

substantially identical with that which existed in the reign of Shāh Jahān: the general procedure, the scale of salaries, the classes[45] and allowances for troopers, all agree. There was, however, an epilogue, which reproduced the second and fourth phases, in that the effective strength of the contingents once again fell. I have not attempted to collect evidence for a change which was inevitable in the circumstances of the time, but I may reproduce Irvine's quotation[46] telling how in Muhammad Shāh's reign a 7000-er 'never entertained even seven asses, much less horses or riders on horses'. That great noble of the decaying empire may fairly stand beside Babur's Beg with 'five or six of the bald and blind at his back'.

Such is my reading of the story of rank in the Mogul Empire. The first three phases are established by contemporary evidence; the fourth rests at present on inferences from recorded facts; the fifth rests partly on direct evidence and partly on inference. The validity of these inferences could probably be determined by the discovery of a series of documents for the reigns of Akbar and Jahāngīr, similar to those which I have used for Shāh Jahān.[47] In order to complete the account I have offered, it is necessary to examine the nature of a distinction between two classes of troopers which appears in the Jaipur documents and in the later records.

In the specimen statement of Raja Jai Singh's claim given on an earlier page troopers are classed as either *sih-aspa dū-aspa* or *barāwardī*, the former allowed for at 16,000 *dāms*, and the latter at 8000; and the distinction recurs in later documents to the close of the period. The latter class was the commonest, and all that I have written regarding the allowances for ordinary troopers in Shāh Jahān's reign

[45]Irvine's *Tābīnān-i barādarī* (p.10) must, I think, be a misreading for *barāwardī*. There is nothing like it on f. 144*b* of *Add.* 6599, the authority he quotes, but on f. 146 (which is part of the same section) the word *barāwardī*, which is discussed below, appears as a sub-heading under *tābīnān*—just as it does in all the Jaipur documents.

[46]Irvine, *Army of the Indian Moguls*, p. 59.

[47]At the request of Sir Reginald Glancy, His Highness the Maharaja of Bikaner has most generously sent me photographs of two *farmāns* which his predecessor Rai Rai Singh received from Akbar, but unfortunately these documents have at some time or other been backed, presumably for preservation, and the schedules written on the reverse are concealed by the backing. I have heard of no other relevant documents of Akbar's reign and so far there is no trace of any issued by Jahāngīr.

refers to it: troopers of the former class were allowed only to officers who held 'triple rank', and the relative importance of the two classes can be seen from the fact that in Shāh Jahān's twentieth year the nominal contingents of all officers from the 7000 to the 500 grade inclusive comprised in round numbers 373,000 *barāwardīs* out of a total nominal strength of 423,000.[48] The names of both these classes are technical terms, which cannot be interpreted directly from a dictionary. The first ought to mean that in this class every trooper had at least one remount, but, as we shall see, it might denote a contingent without a single remount among 2000 troopers. The second may mean either 'enlisted' or 'assisted'; but by this time it must have acquired the sense of 'entered on a particular list', or else 'assisted in a particular way'.

The nature of the first class is indicated clearly by the conclusion of the passage in the *Bādshāhnāma* relating to the Balkh expedition. We have seen that this passage details the composition of the contingent to be furnished by an officer ranking as 5000/5000; it then passes to the case of 'triple rank', and states that an officer of that rank should bring to brand twice (*ẓi'f*) as many *barāwardī* troopers as the number of *sih-aspa dū-aspa* troopers of his rank. According to the dictionaries the word *ẓi'f* may mean 'equal' as well as 'double', but the sense in this passage is fixed by the example which follows: 'for instance an officer of 5000/5000/5000, whose assignment is for twelve months, should bring to brand 6000 three-horse, 1200 two-horse, and 200 one-horse troopers, and so in proportion.' A glance at the table given above will show that the composition of his contingent was precisely the same as that of an officer of 5000/5000, but the number was twice as large, 2000 instead of 1000; and it follows that, if an officer's assignment was for five months, his 2000 troopers might not have a single remount between them.

Thus from the military standpoint there were not two classes of troopers but only one, and the distinction was merely a matter of accountancy; for if there had been a real difference in quality, an officer ordered to Balkh would have had to discard his trained 2–3 h. troopers, and hastily recruit twice as many *barāwardīs* in their place, which would be a wholly impossible way of mobilizing an expeditionary force. It follows that the pecuniary advantage of 'triple rank' lay in the difference between the flat rate per head which an officer received, and the average rate at which he was able to secure his troopers. In the

[48]These figures are calculated from the list of officers in *Bādshāhnāma*, ii, pp. 717 ff, excluding those who were dead when it was compiled.

case of the Balkh expedition when one-fifth of the nominal contingent had to be mustered by officers of 'double rank' and two-fifths by officers of 'triple rank', the Emperor paid in effect a flat rate of Rs 1000 per effective trooper; if the market rate was Rs 1000 per head, the two officers would be financially in the same position; but if the market rate was Rs 800, an officer with 'double rank', furnishing a contingent of 1000 troopes, would save Rs 200,000, while one with 'triple rank', furnishing 2000 troopers, would save Rs 400,000. 'Triple rank' might therefore be a profitable as well as an honourable distinction; and since it is impossible to believe that troopers cost as much as Rs 1000 per head, the pecuniary advantage may have been important.

The position in Shāh Jahān's reign is thus clear, but it is difficult to reconcile his nomenclature with that of Akbar's time as disclosed in the *Ain.*[49] The ordinary trooper was then one whose horse (or horses) had been branded in accordance with the rules in force; the *barāwardī* was by definition a poor but suitable man, who received 'the requisites for troopership'. The last words are not explained in the text, and it is uncertain whether they cover the supply of a horse, or merely arms and equipment, but in any case it is clear that in Akbar's days the *barāwardī* was a man who, unlike the ordinary trooper, required, and received, some sort of finançial help.

The label *sih-aspa dū-aspa* has not been found in the literature of Akbar's reign, and one small piece of evidence suggests that it is an abbreviation which came into official use under Shāh Jahān. I have said above that Jai Singh's assignment orders are obviously 'common form', but there is one difference of detail: in the later orders the heading *sih-aspa dū-aspa* is used, just as it appears in the *Bādshāhnāma* and in subsequent records, but in the first order, that of AH 1048, it appears in three places as *sih-aspa dū-aspa yak-aspa,* and in one of them the words *ba ẓabiṭa*, or 'according to the regulation of' are prefixed. In Akbar's time contingents had, as we have seen, to be composed in a specified proportion of troopers owning one, two, and three horses, and that class might well be described by such a heading; but it is too cumbrous for use in tabular matter and the abbreviation *sih-aspa dū-aspa* would suffice. There may then be substantial continuity of terminology between the two periods, but this would not explain why the special class of Akbar's time had become the ordinary class under Shāh Jahān, while Akbar's ordinary class has become special. It is an admissible guess that, in the demoralization of Jahāngīr's reign,

[49] *Ain*, i, pp. 115 ff.

the help (whatever it was) which Akbar offered to poor but competent troopers came to be given lavishly and without discrimination, until most troopers were *barāwardī*; this would explain the change in nomenclature between the two periods, but in the absence of evidence it is useless to travel further in the realm of conjecture.

6
The *Faujdar* and *Faujdari* Under the Mughals*

Noman Ahmad Siddiqi

EVOLUTION OF THE INSTITUTION

The term *faujdar* appears to be of pre-Mughal origin.[1] Under the Surs the word seems to have been used merely in the sense of a military commander. However, *faujdari* as an organized executive institution with a well-defined jurisdiction was developed under the Mughals. It appears that the jurisdiction of the *faujdar* extended over the entire area under his charge which included his own *jagir* as well as the assignments of those who might have been serving elsewhere in the province or in the other parts of the Empire. Thus the new institution gave stability to the local administration, strengthened the central authority and facilitated the deployment of *mansabdars* in different parts of the Empire, without disturbing the existing arrangement of the revenue assignments in lieu of the salary.

Although chronicles such as the *Akbar Nama* and the *Tabaqat-i-Akbari,* rarely use the term *faujdar* to denote the executive head of an administrative charge, a critical examination of the relevant evidence contained in the *Ain-i-Akbari* reveals that the institution had been fully developed by the fortieth year of Akbar's reign.

*First published in *Medieval India Quarterly*, vol. IV (1961).

[1]Abul Fazl, *Akbar Nama*, 3 vols, Bib. Ind., Calcutta, 1873–87, vol. II, p. 37; cf. P. Saran, *The Provincial Government of the Mughals, (1526–1658)*, Allahabad, 1941, p. 210.

The available evidence of the chronicles suggests that the conquest of a province having been completed, Akbar entrusted the overall administration to a noble of high rank, who later on came to be known as Subahdar. A number of nobles, holding comparatively smaller ranks, were attached to the Subahdar as his lieutenants who served as the executive heads of the administrative charges in which the newly conquered province was divided. These subordinate nobles, in the chronicles, are collectively described as *umara* and individually referred to as Hakims of the charges assigned to them. They were entrusted the *ayalat, hukumat* or *imarat* of the charges. It appears that they were also assigned *jagirs* (the entire area or a part of their charges) in lieu of their salaries and as such they were sometimes referred to as *jagirdars* also known as *iqtadars* or *tiyuldars*.[2] On the other hand, the relevant evidence contained in the *Ain-i-Akbari* indicates that the administration of a few parganas was entrusted to a noble of proven prowess and integrity and that such an officer was known as *faujdar*.[3] The functions and duties ascribed to him in the *Ain* indicate that he combined in himself the office of an executive officer and that of a military commander.[4] Thus it may be seen that the executive head of an administrative charge in the chronicles is described as the Hakim whereas the *Ain* gives him the official appellation of the *faujdar*. The territorial jurisdiction of the Hakim might comprise a few parganas, a *sarkar* or more than a *sarkar*. The *faujdar*'s territorial jurisdiction, as set down in the *Ain*, extended over a group of parganas. The inference is that by the fortieth year of the reign the institution had been organized on

[2] *Akbar Nama*, II, pp. 143, 169, 331; *Akbar Namah* III, p. 33; Khwaja Nizam ud-Din Ahmad, *Tabaqat-i-Akbari*, ed. B. De, 3 vols, Bib. Ind., Calcutta, 1913–35, vol. II, pp. 222, 253, 378; Abdul-Hamid Lahori, *Badshah Nama*, 2 vols, Bib. Ind. Calcutta, 1866–72, vol. II, pp. 332; Mohammed Salih Kanboh Lahori, *'Amal-i-Salih*, ed. G. Yazdani, 4 vols (vol. IV Index), Bib. Ind., Calcutta, 1912–46, vol. II, p. 371, 'Ali Muhammad Khan, *Mir'at-i Ahmadi*, 2 vols and Supplement, ed. Nawab Ali, Baroda, 1927–28 and 1930, vol. I, pp. 210, 212, 223, 226, 235.

[3] Abul Fazl, *A'in-i Akbari*, ed. Blochmann, Bib. Ind., Calcutta, 1887, vol. I, p. 196: the text reads as *A'in-i Faujdari: Dar juz-i chand parganat badidbani-ye yaki az dilawaran kam az andaza-shanas durust paiman baz guzarad, wa an ra badan nam khwanad.*

[4] *A'in-i Akbari*, I, p. 197. The relevant evidence in the *Tabaqat-i-Akbari* and later sources shows that for policing the charge a network of *thanas* or outposts was established within each charge.

a more systematic basis and the Hakim in the administrative jargon came to be known as the *faujdar*.[5]

Jurisdiction of the Faujdar

The territorial jurisdiction of the *faujdar* has been a subject of some controversy among the students of Mughal administrative institutions. The proposition that the territorial jurisdiction of the *faujdar* extended over an administrative charge which was quite independent of the fiscal units of the *sarkar* and pargana has been questioned and it has been maintained that the territorial jurisdiction under a *faujdar* coincided with the fiscal division of a *sarkar*.[6] A careful examination of the relevant evidence, contained in the chronicles and administrative documents, however, reveals that the *faujdari* constituted an independent administrative unit and its territorial limits varied from place to place and from time to time.

Under Akbar

The available evidence for the reign of Akbar suggests that generally a charge was as large as a *sarkar* and the noble administering such a charge was known as Hakim. Thus the *Tabaqat-i-Akbari* refers to Shihab-Uddin Khan as the Hakim of Sarkar Saraunj and Shah Budagh Khan as the Hakim of Sarkar Sarangpur (975 AH/1567–8).[7] The parallel passage in the *Akbar Nama* describes Shihab-Uddin Khan as the *faujdar*

[5] It appears that either the term *faujdar* did not fit in with the style of Abul Fazl and Nizamuddin or it did not convey till the closing years of thirties, the administrative power and position of the executive head of an administrative charge. However, when the *Ain* was compiled the executive head of an administrative charge was given the official appellation of the *faujdar* and his functions and duties were set down in the *Ain-i-Akbari*. In the chronicles compiled in the seventeenth century, the *faujdar* is almost invariably used to denote the executive head of an administrative charge which came to be known as *faujdari* although occasionally he might be referred to as Hakim.

[6] Dr Saran in his work *The Provincial Administration of the Mughals* (pp. 88–109) rejects the proposition put forth by Moreland that within a Suba there were two separate divisions entirely distinct from each other, one *sarkar* for fiscal purposes and the other a purely administrative division under the *faujdar*. On the other hand he maintains that a *sarkar* invariably constituted a fiscal as well as an administrative division. His inference is based on evidence contained in the Qazwini's *Badshah Nama*.

[7] *Tabaqat-i-Akbari*, II, p. 222.

of Saraunj and Shah Budagh is reported to have been holding the charge *(hukumat)* of Sarangpur[8] (975 AH/1567–8). Abul Fazl also states that Sarkar Patan was entrusted to Khan-i-Kalan and Sarkar Broach and the adjoining areas to Qutab-Uddin Khan[9] (980 AH/1572–3). In 971 AH/1563–4 Qasim Khan was administering the charge of Nornol (a *sarkar* in the province of Agra.[10] Thus it may be reasonably presumed that under Akbar the administrative charges were fairly large and generally an administrative charge comprised a *sarkar* and in some cases even an area larger than a *sarkar.* But no uniformity can be claimed nor can it be asserted that the jurisdiction of a *faujdar* invariably extended over an entire *sarkar.* On the other hand there is some evidence to show that even as early as 980 AH/1572–3, a charge smaller than that of a *sarkar* did exist. In 980 AH/1572–3 AD the administration of Dhaulqah and Danduqah was entrusted to Sayyid Hamid Bokhari.[11] A reference to the statistical account of the twelve provinces, given in the *Ain-i-Akbari* will show that Dhaulqah and Danduqah were two *mahals* in the *sarkar* of Ahmadabad.[12] According to the author of the *Mirat-i-Sikandari,* Pargana Baroda was assigned to Aurang Khan.[13] It appears that by the fortieth year of the reign some organizational changes were introduced and an attempt was made to organize the institution on a more systematic basis. The functions and duties of the *faujdar* were enumerated and his territorial jurisdiction was defined. The evidence contained in the *Ain*, viz. that the territorial jurisdiction of a *faujdar* extended over a few *parganas,*[14] suggests that it was not necessary that each *sarkar* should be placed under a single *faujdar*

UNDER JAHANGIR

During the reign of Jahangir the administrative charge under a *faujdar* came to be known as *faujdari.* According to the *Tuzuk-i-Jahangiri,*

[8] *Akbar Nama,* II, p. 331.

[9] Ibid., I, p. 33, cf. *Tabaqat-i-Akbari,* II, p. 373.

[10] Ibid., III, p. 198.

[11] Ibid.., III, p. 33 The parganas of Dhaulqah and Simi and Tappa Janpur were held by Sayyid Hamid and Sayyid Mahmud Bokhari under Sultan Muzaffar Shah. They remained in their possession as their *jagirs* under Akbar. *Mirat-i-Sikandari,* p. 370.

[12] *Ain-i Akbari,* II, English tr. H.S. Jarrett, ed. and corrected by J.N. Sarkar, Calcutta, 1949, pp. 252–3.

[13] Sikandar bin Manjhu, *Mirat-i Sikandari,* eds S.C. Misra and M.L. Rahman, Baroda, 1961, p. 55.

[14] *Ain-i-Akbari,* Text pp. 197–8.

Mubarak Khan was entrusted with the *faujdari* of Hisar[15] and Mir Mughal was given the *faujdari* of Sarkar Sambhal.[16] Similarly, there are references to the *faujdaris* of the *sarkars* of Sarangpur, Mewar and Alwar.[17] The evidence described above reveals that the administrative charge was known as *faujdari.*[18] This evidence seems to contradict the inference based on the statement in the *Ain* that the territorial jurisdiction of the *faujdari* might have extended over an area which was smaller than that of a *sarkar.* However, it may be pointed out that the cases recorded in the *Tuzuk-i-Jahangiri* were those of the more prominent nobles and related to *faujdaris* which might be among those which later came to be known as *faujdari-i-umdah,*[19] comprising a *sarkar* or a region even larger than a *sarkar.* Presumably, smaller units existed, though their existence is not specifically recorded.

Under Shahjahan

The available evidence for the reign of Shahjahan indicates that the size of *faujdaris* varied from place to place. In 1045 AH/1635–6, Najabat Khan was serving as the *faujdar* of the Valley of Kangra and Lashkar Khan as the *faujdar* of Lakhi Jungle.[20] Appointment of *faujdars* is on record for the *sarkar* of Gorakhpur, the suburb of Akbarabad, the *sarkar* of Lucknow and Baiswarah and for the pargana of Baroda.[21] A critical examination of the evidence adduced above shows that the jurisdiction

[15]Nur ud-Din Muhammad Jahangir, *Tuzuk-i Jahangiri,* ed. Saiyid Ahmad Khan, Aligarh, 1864, p. 55.

[16]Ibid., p. 161.

[17]Ibid., pp. 85, 157, 203.

[18]Jahangir's *farman* dated 22 May, 1607 AD, Maghribi Collection, Central Records Office, Hyderabad. It records the appointment of Jan Beg to the office of the *faujdari-i-Baroda.* Relevant evidence contained in the Supplement of the *Mirat-i-Ahmadi* shows that the Sarkar Baroda comprised four *parganas,* namely Baroda, Bahadurpur, Dabohi and Senore. While Baroda and Dabohi constituted separate *faujdaris,* those of Bahadurpur and Senore were attached to the *faujdari* of Baroda (Supplement, pp. 204, 205). The inference is that at some stage the *faujdari* of *sarkar* Baroda was split up into two smaller administrative charges. However, in actual practice the two *faujdaris* could be assigned to a single officer (*Mirat-i-Ahmadi,* pp. 289, 290). It may be pointed out that occasionally the charge was still referred to as *hukumat.* See *Tuzuk-i-Jahangiri,* p. 161.

[19]*Mirat-i-Ahmadi,* II, p. 4.

[20]*Badshah Nama* I, pt II, p. 1.

[21]Ibid. I, pt II, pp. 14, 242, 243, 545.

of a *faujdari* extended sometimes over a region which was larger than a *sarkar*, sometimes over a *sarkar*, and at other times it was limited even to a single *pargana*.[22] A passage in the *Khulasat-us-Siyaq* indicates that Saad Ullah Khan, the Wazir, introduced some changes in the local administration. He created the administrative unit of the *chakla* which comprised a few *parganas*, and each *chakla* was placed under a *faujdar*.[23] Whether the new administrative unit of *chakla* was created throughout the Empire is a matter of conjecture. The available evidence suggests that in certain provinces the administrative division of *chakla* was created whereas in other provinces the old administrative units of *faujdari* continued. We know that in the province of Delhi Chakla-i-Hisar was administered by a *faujdar*.[24] An appointment order contained in the *Siyaq Nama* shows that Chakla Faizabad in Kashmir was placed under a *faujdar*.[25] Thus we can infer that in some provinces the new administrative division was introduced. However, the detailed account of the *sarkars*, *parganas* and *faujdaris*, given in the Supplement of the *Mirat-i-Ahmadi*, contains no reference to *chakla*. Neither does the *chakla* find any place in the text of the *Mirat-i-Ahmadi*. The inference is that in Gujarat the new administrative division was not introduced and the old units of *faujdari* continued. Similarly, the *Waqai-i-Ajmer* contains no reference to *chakla*, but there is some evidence to show that the *faujdars* were administering a *pargana* or a *sarkar*.[26] It can be, therefore, suggested that in Ajmer the old system continued.

Under Aurangzeb

For the reign of Aurangzeb the relevant evidence is available in the sources such as the *Mirat-i-Ahmadi*, the *Siyaq Nama*, the *Alamgir Nama*, the *Insha-i-Roshan Kalam* the *Nigar Nama-i-Munshi* and the *Waqai-i-Subah Ajmer*. However, the nature of the administrative unit of the *faujdari* can be best studied in a passage recording the appointment of a number of *faujdars*, contained in the *Mirat-i-Ahmadi*, together with

[22] *Selected Documents of Aurangzeb's Reign, 1659–1706*, ed. Yusuf Husain Khan, Hyderabad, 1958, p. 98.

[23] *Khulasat-us-Siyaq*, Aligarh Muslim University Manuscript, ff 25b, 26a–b.

[24] *Gwaliar Nama*, B.M. Rieu II. Add. 16859 ff. 52 b, 65b.

[25] *Siyaq Nama*, Litho, Nawal Kishore Press, Lucknow, p. 67.

[26] *Waqai Ajmer-o-Ranthambor, AD 1678–80* Asafiya Library, Hyderabad, Fann-i-Tarikh, 2242, transcript from Daftar-i-Diwani, Hyderabad, available in the Research Library, Department of History, Aligarh Muslim University, pp. 400, 402, 403.

the detailed description of the *parganas* and the *faujdaris* in each *sarkar,* contained in the *Supplement* of the same work. The appointments were made in Gujarat in the year 1083 AH/1672–3. Five of these appointments along with the charges assigned to the respective *faujdars* are given below in a tabular form:[27]

Name of the *faujdar*	Charge or charges	*Sarkar* in which *faujdari* was assigned
1. Kamal Jalori	Palanpur (pargana)	Patan
2. Muhammad Jafar	(a) Jargal (a *thana* in pargana Sarnal)	Ahmadabad
	(b) Khorwarah (a *thana* in pargana Naryad)	Ahmadabad
3. Sayyid Mahmud Khan	(a) Baroda (pargana)	Baroda
	(b) Dabhoi (pargana)	Baroda
	(c) Nadot (pargana)	Nadot
	(d) Bilparah (pargana)	Ahmadabad
	(e) Kajnah (a *thana* in pargana Khambayat)	Ahmadabad
4. Shah Wirdi Beg	(a) Islamabad (a *thana* in pargana Thamna)	-do-
	(b) Azamabad (pargana)	-do-
	(c) Mamurabad (pargana)	-do-
5. Muhammad Muzaffar	Kari (pargana)	-do-

An analysis of the appointment list reveals that the territorial jurisdiction under the five *faujdars* differed widely and that the administrative units under these *faujdars* can be classified into the following categories:

1. The territorial jurisdiction of a *faujdar* extended over or coincided with a single *pargana* as in the cases of Kamal Jalori, the *faujdar* of Pargana Palanpur and Muhammad Muzaffar, the *faujdar* of Pargana Kari.

2. The territorial jurisdiction of a *faujdar* might extend over more than one *thana,* lying in two different *parganas* as in the case of

[27] *Mirat-i-Ahmadi,* I, pp. 289, 290.

Muhammad Jafar, the *faujdar* of the *thanas* of Jargal and Khorwarah, lying in the *parganas* of Sarna and Naryad respectively.

3. The territorial jurisdiction of a *faujdar* extended over four parganas and a *thana* in the fifth pargana, in two different *sarkars*, as in the case of Sayyid Mahmud Khan.

4. The territorial jurisdiction of the *faujdar* extended over two parganas and a *thana* as in the case of Shah Wirdi Beg.

The evidence contained in the list of appointments is more or less corroborated by the detailed account of the *sarkars*, *parganas* and *faujdaris*, contained in the Supplement of the *Mirat-i-Ahmadi*.[28] In the account under reference, Palanpur and Kari are given as independent *faujdaris* each under a *faujdar*. Similarly, Islamabad, Azamabad and Mamurabad, assigned to Shah Wirdi Beg, constituted a single *faujdari*. The territorial jurisdiction comprising the *faujdari* under Sayyid Mahmud Khan is also confirmed in its essential by the evidence contained in the *Supplement*. We read that the *faujdari* of Baroda comprised the *parganas* of Baroda, Bahadurpur and Senore, in Sarkar Baroda, and Pargana Nadot in Sarkar Nadot. A comparison of these details with the details given in the appointment list will reveal that Pargana Baroda and Pargana Nadot are common to the charge assigned to Sayyid Mahmud Khan and the detailed account of *faujdari* of Baroda given in the *Supplement*. However, the parganas of Dabohi and Bilparah and Thana Kajnah in Pargana Khambayat are not included in the *faujdari* of Baroda. We can read between the lines that these places were specified in the appointment order and two *parganas*, namely Bahadurpur and Senore which formed a part of the Baroda *faujdari* were excluded from the *mahal-i-faujdari* of the appointment on account of some immediate administrative necessity.[29]

An examination of the evidence contained in the *Mirat-i-Ahmadi* and its Supplement indicates that the *faujdari* constituted a separate and distinct administrative unit which was quite independent of the fiscal divisions of *sarkar* and *parganas*. Such an administrative unit might comprise a few *thanas*, a *pargana* or a number of *parganas*.

Thus we see that the *faujdari* constituted an administrative unit. The inference drawn on the basis of evidence contained in the *Mirat-i-Ahmadi* is amply borne out by the relevant evidence contained in other

[28]*Mirat-i-Ahmadi*, Supplement, pp. 196, 200.

[29]Bhupat Rai, *Insha-i-Roshan Kalam* Mir Abdus Salam Coll., 109/339, Aligarh, f. 8 a–b. An examination of the evidence in the *Insha-i-Roshan Kalam* reveals that such minor adjustments were a routine administrative practice.

sources. The *Nigar Nama-i-Munshi* contains an appointment order of the *faujdar* of a pargana.[30] We learn elsewhere that Sher Andaz Khan was appointed the *faujdar* of a few *mahals*, the home land of Bais clan. However, it appears that the *parganas* of Lucknow, Bijnore and Sandilah, assigned as *jagir* to a prince, and the *mahals* assigned to Aziz Khan and other *mansabdars* were excluded from the administrative unit of his *faujdari* and therefore he could not take any action against the rebels and robbers who had settled in these *mahals*.[31] The *Insha-i-Roshan Kalam* contains some more references about the *mahal-i-faujdari* and the *faujdari* of *Mahal* Baiswarah.[32] The evidence under examination establishes it very clearly that the *faujdari* constituted an administrative unit which was known as *mahal-i-faujdari*. It also indicates that the Baiswarah was a regular unit of *faujdari* but on account of administrative expediency certain *mahals* specified in the appointment order for the office of *faujdari (sanad-i-faujdari)* were excluded from the jurisdiction of the *Faujdar* of Baiswarah. To sum up, the territorial limits of the administrative charge of the *faujdari* varied from place to place and from time to time and whereas the smaller units might comprise only a few *thanas* or one *pargana* the larger units comprised many *parganas* or even a *sarkar*. Between them were the average size *faujdaris* comprising three or four *parganas*. It appears that the *faujdaris* were classified into more than one category and the important and first grade *faujdaris* were comparatively fewer, which came to be known as *faujdari-i-umdah*.[33] It may be suggested that it was the appointment was to these *faujdaris* which finds a place in the chronicles while appointment to smaller *faujdaris* can be traced in the *Waqais* or in the provincial histories such as the *Mirat-i-Ahmadi*.

A general review of the evidence mentioned above suggests that while under Akbar and Jahangir a *sarkar* frequently formed a unit of *faujdari*, later smaller units became more common. This development signified that the *faujdar* tended to be more of an executive officer rather than a military commander and that the state was able to take greater interest in the maintenance of law and order. In other words, the civil aspect of the office was being emphasized. Moreover, the

[30]*Nigar Nama-i-Munshi*, Litho, Nawal Kishore Press, Lucknow, p. 84; cf. *Mirat-i-Ahmadi*, I, pp. 97, 256, 290; *Waqai-Suba Ajmer*, pp. 400, 402, 403.

[31]*Insha-i-Roshan Kalam*, 3, a–b.

[32]Ibid., f. 4, b, 5, a–b. .

[33]*Mirat-i-Ahmadi*, II, p. 4.

development was closely related with the problem of providing *mansabs* and offices to the ever-increasing number of *mansabdars.*

Thana

The administrative charge known as *faujdari* comprised a number of *thanas* or military outposts. At each of these number of *sawars* were stationed under a Thanadar. It appears that Akbar took energetic steps for the organization of a network of *thanas.* In 975 AH/1566–7 he reached Mauhi[34] in *Sarkar* Bijagarh in Malwa, and engaged himself in establishing *thanas* in the province. Qazi Khan Badakhshi, Sharif Khan Atka, Mujahid Khan and Subhan Quli, along with 3000 *sawars* were stationed in Mauhi, and Abdur Rahman Beg, at the head of 500 *sawars,* was posted in the hills of Madariyah.[35] We are further told that the work of establishing the *thanas* was soon completed.[36]

Later works such as the *Mirat-i-Ahmadi* and the *Insha-i-Roshan Kalam* throw some light on the internal organization of a *faujdari.* A careful examination of the account given in the *Supplement* of the *Mirat-i-Ahmadi* reveals that within a *faujdari* there were a number of *thanas,* described as *zamima* or *painam* of the *faujdari,* i.e. the *thanas* attached to the office. The *sawar* rank attached with the office of each *faujdari* is specified but the number of *sawars* to be stationed at each *thana* not given. The inference is that the office of the *faujdari,* carried with it a fixed number of *sawars* and it was left to the *faujdar* to station soldiers in various *thanas* under him.[37] In addition to these *thanas,* in some *faujdaris* there were a number of *thanas* described as *huzuri* or *huzuri mashruti.* The ranks attached with these *thanas* are separately specified.[38] There is some evidence to show that in these *thanas* the appointments of the Thanadars were made by the central government, by virtue of royal orders, directly or at the recommendations of the Nazim or the Diwan of the province.[39] It appears that these Thanadars were to a considerable degree independent officers who could receive

[34]In the English rendering of the *Ain-i-Akbari,* the place is given as Mahoi. See *Ain-i-Akbari,* Jarrett II, p. 206.

[35]*Tabaqat-i-Akbari,* II, pp. 322–9.

[36]Ibid., II, p. 390.

[37]Cf. *Insha-i-Roshan Kalam,* f. 5b. *Selected Documents of Aurangzeb's Reign,* p. 41.

[38]*Mirat-i-Ahmadi, Supplement,* pp. 194, 196, 199, 200.

[39]Ibid., p. 6, 189.

orders directly from the central government.[40] Nevertheless, they were probably placed under the overall supervision of the *faujdar* and were expected to co-operate with him in maintaining law and order. These *thanas*, it may be suggested, were created to ensure the efficient working of the local administration and also to provide a check against an overambitious *faujdar*, who in the absence of energetic and powerful *mansabdars*, acting as independent officers in the vicinity, might have nourished the idea of paying scant respect to the imperial regulations or indulged in oppression of the people.

Thus the unit of *faujdari* appears to have been a *thana*. While some of the *faujdaris* comprised the *thanas* described as *huzuri* as well as those known as *painam* or *zamima* others comprised only the latter. This appears to have been the general pattern but variations in actual practice cannot be ruled out. In the case of certain *faujdaris* no *thanas* are given under the *zamima* which seems to suggest that the charge was directly administered from the *faujdari* headquarters. Another possibility is that within the *faujdari* in the areas assigned to the *jagirdars* there might have been no regular *thanas* but the responsibility of maintaining law and order in a general way vested in the *jagirdars*. In either case in an emergency the *faujdar* of a charge could be called upon to enforce imperial regulations and restore law and order.[41]

[40]We read in the *Selected Waqai of the Deccan* (ed Yusuf Husain Khan, Hyderabad, 1953) that Shah Muhammad Khan the *thanadar* of Kalam wrote to Iraj Khan, the *faujdar* of Elichpur that in compliance with his orders the former was making preparations to proceed to Aurangabad. In the meantime the order of the Bakshi-ul-Mulk was received that Shah Muhammad should send his son along with the contingent to Aurangabad and himself should stay in the *thanadari* (*Selected Waqai of the Deccan*, p. 87, dated 11 May 1692 AD). Incidentally, the evidence reveals that the *faujdar* had some authority over the *thanadar* who could directly receive orders from the court. Some of the *thanadars* enjoyed considerably high ranks and were given the charge of *thanas* which were of great strategic importance. Maharaj Jaswant Singh held the *thanadari* of Jamrud in the fourteenth year of Aurangzeb's reign. His rank is given as 7000/7000, Samsam ud-Daulah Shahnawaz Khan, *Maasir ul-Umara*, 3 vols, ed. Abd ur-Rahim and Ashraf Ali, Bib. Ind., Calcutta, 1888–95 III, p. 603). Similarly, Fateh Ullah Khan Alamgir Shahi, the *thanadar* of Lohgarh in Kabul held a rank of 3000/1200. (*Maasir-ul-Umara*, III, p. 47).

[41]*Insha-i-Roshan Kalam*, ff, 1. a–b, 2a.

Appointment and Transfer

The appointment of a *faujdar* was made by virtue of a royal order and the appointment order bore the seal of Bakhshi-ul-Mulki.[42] An examination of the *arzdasht* contained in the *Insha-i-Roshan Kalam* reveals that the *faujdar* received orders directly from the Emperor and submitted his petition directly to the court.[43] The tenure of the office of the *faujdari* does not seem to have been fixed. It varied from place to place and time to time. But the transfer of the *faujdar* was a well-established administrative practice. A connected account of the office of the *faujdari* in a few *sarkars* will give some idea about the tenure of the office.

Faujdari of Sorath

In 1045 AH Mirza Isa Tar Khan, who held the rank of 5000/4000, was appointed the *faujdar* and *tiyuldar* of Sarkar Sorath. He served as *faujdar* till 1052 AH, when he took over the charge of the *subahdari*. Inayatullah Khan, the son of Mirza Isa Tar Khan, who held a *mansab* of 2000/500, served as *faujdar* from 1052 AH. Mirza Isa Tar Khan again resumed the charge in 1054 AH and remained in office till 1061 AH when Muhammed Saleh, son of Mirza Isa Tar Khan, was appointed the *faujdar* of Sorath. He was replaced by Qutb ud-din Khan Kheshgi in 1063 AH who served till 1072 AH. In 1072 AH. Sardar Khan was appointed the *faujdar* of Sorath and continued to serve till 1078 AH when Diler Khan was appointed the *faujdar* of Sorath. In 1080 AH Diler Khan proceeded to the court and the *faujdari* was given back to Sardar Khan. The latter served as *faujdar* till 1094 AH when he was appointed the Subadar of Thata.[44]

Faujdari of Patan

Mir Shamsh was appointed the *faujdar* and *tiyuldar* of Patan in 1062 AH. He was replaced by Mujahid Jalori in 1066 AH. In 1066 AH Qutb-ud-Din was appointed the *faujdar* and *tiyuldar* of Patan. Dildar Beg replaced Qutb-ud-Din as *faujdar* in 1068 AH.[45]

[42] *Siyaq Nama*, p. 67.

[43] *Insha-i-Roshan Kalam*, ff. 2b. 3ab, cf. *Mirat-i-Ahmadi*, I, pp. 257–8.

[44] *Mirat-i-Ahmadi*, I, pp. 210, 212, 213, 216, 228, 240, 253, 257, 274, 276, 305, 306.

[45] *Ibid.*, p. 226, 232, 240.

Faujdari of Baroda

Dildar Khan the *faujdar* of Baroda died in 1040 AH. In the same year Aqa Afzal, known as Fazil Khan, was appointed the *faujdar* of Baroda. He proceeded to the court in 1046 AH. We do not know who served as *faujdar* of Baroda between 1046 AH and 1056 AH. But in 1055 AH Sultan Yar and Asfand Yar jointly held the office of the *faujdari* of Baroda. In 1062 AH Sultan Yar was appointed the *faujdar* of Baroda.[46]

Faujdari of Idar

Sher Singh was serving as the *faujdar* of Idar in 1071 AH. He was replaced by Sardar Khan in 1071 AH but in 1072 AH Sardar Khan was appointed the *faujdar* of Sorath and Sher Singh resumed the charge of the *faujdari* of Idar. In 1079 AH, Sardar Khan was transferred from Sorath and was appointed the *faujdar* and *tiyuldar* of Idar. In 1080 AH Sardar Khan was again appointed the *faujdar* of Sorath. We do not know who served as *faujdar* of Idar between 1080 AH and 1098 AH. but in that year the charge was given to Muhammad Bahlol Sherwani.[47]

Functions

An examination of the available evidence reveals that the range of the *faujdar*'s functions was very wide, and his authority extended over military, police, judicial and revenue affairs. His prime function, it appears, was to maintain law and order within his jurisdiction, and to take necessary military action against those who dared to defy the authority of the state.[48] At the same time he was associated with the local judiciary and land revenue administration.

Military and Police Duties

In the *Ain*, the *faujdar* appears to have been a military commander who assisted the civil authorities in enforcing the imperial regulations. When a peasant, an *amalguzar* of *khalsa*, or a *jagirdar* proved rebellious, the *faujdar* induced him to submit by fair words. In case persuasion failed, the *faujdar*, on the authority of a written request of the principal officers, proceeded to chastise the disobedient. He was required to pitch his camp in the neighbourhood of the rebels and continually inflict loss upon their persons and property, but not to risk an immediate general

[46]Ibid., pp. 208, 211, 222, 227.

[47]Ibid., pp. 253, 257, 294, 295.

[48]*Jahangir's Farman*, dated 22 May 1607 AD; Maghribi Collection, Central Records Office, Hyderabad, Deccan.

engagement. The *Ain* also contains instructions tor capturing a fort, and for the disposal of the booty. It was the duty of the *faujdar* to see that his soldiers were well equipped, and to make necessary arrangements in case a soldier lost his horse for one reason or another.[49]

Similarl functions have been assigned to the *faujdar* in some works compiled in the reign of Aurangzeb. He was required to keep the rebels and the unruly within the proper limits, to demolish their forts, and to protect the *ryots* and *malguzars* (i.e. *zamindars* who paid land revenue). He saw to it that the blacksmiths did not manufacture guns.[50] He appointed Thanadars in the *thanas* who took necessary measures to prevent drinking and other activities prohibited by the Holy Law.[51] It was the *faujdar*'s duty to check the acts of theft and robbery, within his jurisdiction. He was required to recover the stolen and looted property, and to apprehend the thieves and robbers. The recovered property was to be restored to the owner and the culprits were to be punished. In case he failed to recover the stolen or looted property, he was accountable for it.[52]

According to an appointment order contained in the *Nigar Nama-i-Munshi*, the *faujdar* was required to maintain law and order, prevent robbery and ensure the safety of the roads and highways.[53] A number of letters contained in the *Insha-i-Roshan Kalam*, throw interesting light on the functions actually performed by the *faujdar*, and corroborate the evidence contained in the administrative manuals which enumerate the functions and duties of the *faujdar*. In an *arzdasht* contained in the *Insha-i-Roshan Kalam*, Sher Andaz Khan, a faujdar stationed in the province of Awadh, recounts his exploits against a rebel *zamindar*. It appears that he reached the charge assigned to him in the month of Ramzan[54] (the year is not given) and gave necessary assistance to the officers entrusted with the administration of the *khalsa*, and to the *jagirdars*. He led an attack against Lal Sahi, the *zamindar* of Manuhar Karah,

[49]*Ain-i-Akbari*, I, p. 197.

[50]*Siyaq-Nama*, p. 67, *Selected Documents of Aurangzeb's Reign*, p. 41.

[51]It appears that some *thanas* were described as *huzuri* and Thanadars in these *thanas* were appointed directly by the Emperor (See *Mirat-i-Ahmadi*, Supplement pp. 193, 194, 198, 208).

[52]*Selected Waqai of the Deccan*, p. 97; *Siyaq Nama*, p. 67; *Selected Documents of Aurangzeb's Reign*, p. 41.

[53]*Nigar Nama-i-Munshi*, p. 78; also see, pp. 79, 84; cf. *Selected Documents of Aurangzeb's Reign*, p. 41.

[54]Ninth month of the Islamic Calendar.

who had rebelled, had not paid the land revenue, and caused distress and trouble to the inhabitants and travellers in the vicinity. Sher Andaz Khan took note of the report submitted by the agent of the *jagirdar* and of the complaint made by the men of noble birth and good status of the area and led an expedition against the *zamindar.* After some fighting, the *zamindar* and a large number of his followers were killed.[55] In another *arzdasht,* contained in the same work, we learn that Khudadad Afghan, the *gumashta* of Aziz Khan, the *jagirdar* of *pargana* Hadhadah and Unam, plundered the village Husain Nagar, killed 600 Muslim men and women, captured 700 bankers and artisans and carried away cash and kind valued at 10 lakh of rupees. A complaint was made to the Emperor who issued orders to the *faujdar* to take necessary action. The *faujdar* in compliance with the royal order, sent his men, who brought Khudadad with them and presented him before the Qazi. Khudadad confessed his acts of transgression and agreed that he would restore, within the next eight days, the cash and goods looted by him to their rightful owners. Later on an order was received that Khudadad should be sent to the court, and it was complied with by the *faujdar.*[56]

Judicial Functions

The *faujdar* appears to have been associated with the work of dispensing justice. The court was attended by the *faujdar,* the Qazi and the Diwan, and while the *faujdar* presided over the proceedings the cases were decided in consultation with each other.[57] We read in the *Nigar Nama-i-Munshi* that the *faujdar* was required to decide cases in accordance with the Holy Law and in consultation with the officers entrusted with the administration of justice. Morecover, he was asked to see to it that no one indulged in activities which were prohibited by the Holy Law.[58]

Some light on the nature of the *faujdar*'s judicial functions is thrown by a *farman* contained in the *Mirat-i-Ahmadi,* and a document preserved in the UP State Records Office, Allahabad. It appears that in 1073

[55] *Insha-i-Roshan Kalam,* f. 1 b.

[56] Ibid., f. 4 b.

[57] *Selected Waqai of the Deccan,* p. 79. We read that on 22 May 1662 AD Khwaja Beg, the *faujdar,* Qazi Fazl, and Lal Chand Diwan came to the court. Khwaja Beg the *faujdar* laid down that the court should be held thrice a week, on Sunday, Monday and Wednesday, so that the imperial servants should assemble and execute the business of the state in consultation with each other.

[58] *Nigar Nama-i-Munshi,* pp. 78, 79; cf. *Mirat-i-Ahmadi,* I, pp. 257–8.

AH/1662–3 a large number of inhabitants from Sarkar Sorath went to the court and complained against the *faujdar.* A *farman* (in 1074 Hp 1663–4) was issued to Sardar Khan, the *faujdar* of Sarkar Sorath. In the *farman,* the *faujdar* was asked to exert his utmost to dispense justice to the complainants of the cities, towns and villages of Sarkar Sorath and to see to it that the strong did not oppress the weak. In cases and claims pertaining to the Holy Law he was to decide the cases in consultation with the Qazi, Mufti and Mir Adl. In cases which came under the purview of the revenue ministry and other imperial regulations, he was to decide them in conformity with the prescribed laws and regulations and in accordance with the established practice.[59]

An examination of the evidence described above reveals that the *faujdar* participated in deciding cases pertaining to the Holy Law but in such cases he consulted the judicial officers such as Mufti, Qazi and Mir Adl. In cases which fell under the purview of revenue and other imperial regulations of general nature no consultation with officials of the judiciary has been stipulated. The evidence might be construed to indicate that in such cases the *faujdar* was the sole authority to dispense justice to the complainant. The division of judicial power between the *faujdar* and the Qazi can be inferred from a document dated Muharram 1080 AH/1669, preserved in UP State Records Office, Allahabad. It records the proceedings of a case decided in the court of the Qazi of Gorakhpur. It appears from the document that a complaint was lodged with *faujdar* Fidai Khan Jiv on behalf of Shaikh Yusuf, the son of Shaikh Zakariyya, to the effect that Shaikh Sibghat Ullah, the father of Shaikh Na'im Ullah, had taken unlawful possession of the *farman* granting 200 bighas of land to Shaikh Zakariyya, and by producing the said *farman* had also obtained the possession of the plot of land specified in the said *farman.* In spite of many efforts to obtain the said *farman,* it was not given back to Shaikh Yusuf, son of the deceased Shaikh Zakariyya, and therefore, it was prayed to the *faujdar* that the rightful claim to the *farman* should be investigated by him in consultation with the Qazi. Fidai Khan Jiv summoned Shaikh Na'im Ullah, the son of Sibghat Ullah, and the parties were directed to appear before the court of Abdul Wahab, the Qazi of the city of Gorakhpur. The Qazi investigated the point of law. The defendant admitted the claim of the plaintiff, disclaimed all his rights in the land specified in the *farman,* and handed over the *farman* to the *wakil* of the plaintiff to be delivered to

[59] *Mirat-i-Ahmadi,* I, pp. 257, 258.

the latter. The agent proceeded to deliver the *farman* to the plaintiff so that he might take possession of the land specified in the *farman*.[60]

Revenue Administration and the Faujdar

The *faujdar* was also associated with the land revenue administration. He was directly responsible for the collection of land revenue from the *zamindars* who normally evaded payment of land revenue and paid only under threat of force to be employed against them, and were described as *zortalab*. The *faujdar* could entrust the collection of land revenue from such *zamindars* to the Karori or nominate an intermediary and authorise the Karori to collect the assessed land revenue from the former. In case he entrusted the work of collection to the Karori and the land revenue could not be collected, the *faujdar* would be accountable for it. If the Karori did not collect the land revenue, he was required to deposit it with the *faujdar* and not to keep it with him on account of adjustment of his claim for commission on the collections. He was told that he should proceed to the office of the *faujdar* and prepare the account showing the amount collected from *ryoti* and *zortalab* areas. Later on, the commission on collections from the *zortalab* area could be adjusted.[61]

The *faujdar* was also indirectly associated with the land revenue administration as he was required to render necessary assistance in collection of land revenue to the Amil in *khalsa* or *jagir* lands, on a written request from the latter.[62] However, it was explicitly laid down that the *faujdar* should not plunder a village unless a written request to the effect was forthcoming from the Amil. On receipt of a written request for assistance, the *faujdar* was required to take hold of a few muqaddams of the unruly village and persuade them to abstain from acts of disobedience and unruly conduct. If they responded favourably to the words of persuasion, the *faujdar* was required to obtain written consent from the Amil. However, if the Muqaddams, goaded by their inborn obstinacy, refused to submit, the *faujdar* should pillage the village and chastise the rebels. Nevertheless, no harm was to be done to

[60]*Allahabad Documents* no. 204. Uttar Pradesh State Archives, Allahabad, Mughal revenue records in Persian.

[61]*Siyaq Nama*, p. 68.

[62]*Ain-i-Akbari*, p. 197; *Siyaq Nama*, p. 67; *Insha-i-Roshan Kalam*, f. 3a.

the *ryots.* The booty acquired from the village was to be handed over to the Amil who should give a receipt to the *faujdar.*[63]

The present study of the institution of the *faujdar* is rather brief and tentative. However, it reveals that the *faujdar* occupied a key position in the local administration under the Muhgals. He combined in himself the office of a military commander and, that of the executive head of the administration charge known as *faujdari.* At the same time he was closely associated with the judiciary and land revenue administration. Such an officer must have possessed sufficient military and administrative talents, in order to discharge, even to some extent, the manifold functions attached to his office. A study of the administrative achievements of the innumerable *faujdars* who served for centuries under the Mughals can give a much better insight into the administrative conditions in which the people lived and worked. The *faujdars* under the Mughals were required to ensure the continuity of administrative practices and inspire confidence in the aims and objectives of the Mughal administration. An assessment of the measure of their success and failure, based on comprehensive data, can be a fruitful subject for further investigation.

[63] *Siyaq Nama*, p. 67; pp. *Ain-i-Akbari*, I, p. 169; *Insha-i-Roshan Kalam*, f. 2a; *Nigar Nama-i-Munshi*, pp. 78, 79.

7

Distribution of the Revenue Resources of the Mughal Empire among the Nobility*

A. Jan Qaisar

General statements have often been made with regard to the income and economic position of the nobility of the Mughal Empire. However, until now, to the knowledge of the present writer, no attempt has been made to work out a reconstruction in anything approaching statistical terms, of the pattern of distribution of the revenue income of the Mughal Empire among the various strata of the Mughal ruling class.

The present attempt at statistical presentation of such distribution is based on one or two assumptions regarding the Mughal administrative procedures, which are borne out by such documentary evidences as we possess. The principal assumption is that when a salary was sanctioned for an officer, and he was assigned a *jagir*, his pay claim (*talab*) as determined by the pay schedules, was exactly the same as the *jama* or *jamadami* entered in the imperial register against the territorial units comprising his *jagirs*. This *jama* represented the revenue income of the territory as estimated or fixed by the Mughal administration, and did not by any means correspond to the actual income (*hasil*). The difference between the two figures, namely, *jama* and *hasil*, led to the introduction of the so-called months-scale.[1]

Now if in these circumstances, we could know on the one hand the total amount of salary bill claimed by the various ranks of the Mughal *mansabdars*, and on the other, the total *jama* of the empire for the same year, we can work out the share of each rank in the total estimated

*First published in the *Proceedings of the Indian History Congress*, 1965.

[1]For details, see Irfan Habib, *The Agrarian System of Mughal India* (Aligarh, 1963), pp. 264–6 and *n*. Also cf. M. Athar Ali, *The Mughal Nobility Under Aurangzeb* (Bombay, 1966), pp. 46–53.

revenue resources of the empire. We would not thereby know the actual cash income of officers of various ranks, but their relative share in the total actual income may be assumed to correspond largely with the share in the estimated income.[2]

It happens that for the twentieth year of Shah Jahan, we are in possession of practically all the data required for the kind of statistical enquiry suggested above.

In the first place, the official pay schedules are available: there is a pay schedule sanctioned in the fourteenth year of Shah Jahan,[3] and another sanctioned under the signature of Saadullah Khan, the *diwan* of Shah Jahan.[4] The two schedules are identical, and therefore we can with confidence establish what were the actual pay scales in the twentieth year.

In the official history of Shah Jahan's reign, the *Badshahnama* of Abdul Hamid Lahori, we have a list of the *mansabdars* (including the four princes) holding the ranks of 500 *zat* and above, with specifications of the *zat* and *sawar* rank for each.[5] Applying the pay schedules, we can work out the salary sanctioned for each of these *mansabdars*, and obtain the total amount of the salary claimed by the various categories of the *mansabdars*. Finally, we have in the same work a province-wise statement of the *jamadami* of the entire empire for the same year (the twentieth).[6] We can therefore set our figures for the salary claims against the *jama* of the whole empire.

In making calculations on this basis, our statistical presentation is not affected by the fact that some of the *mansabdars* were not given *jagirs* but obtained their salary in cash. Just as the ordinary *jagirdars* did not get the estimated income from their *jagirs*, so also the *mansabdars* who happened to be paid in cash from the imperial treasury were generally put on a particular months-scale, and so only paid a part of

[2]Since we would be concerned with the *jama* and not with the *hasil*, our calculations will not involve any consideration of the implications of the months-scale.

[3]cf. *Selected Documents of Shah Jahan's Reign*, Daftar-i-Diwani, Hyderabad, (1950), pp. 79–84. It was issued under the signature of Islam Khan.

[4]*Dastur-ul Amal-i-Alamgiri*, Add. 6598, ff. 121a–123a. cf. Irfan Habib, *Agrarian System*, p. 258; Athar Ali, *Mughal Nobility*, pp. 47–8.

[5]*Badshahnama*, II, *Bibliotheca Indica*, 1868, pp. 717–52. Lahori has also given another list of the *mansabdars* from 500 *zat* upwards for the tenth year of Shah Jahan's reign (ibid, I, pp. 292–328), but this list cannot be used for our present enquiry because Lahori does not give the *jama* of the same year.

[6]Ibid, II, pp. 710–11.

their nominal pay claim. It may be denoted further that their cash salaries came out of the revenues of the *khalisa* which in the twentieth year of Shah Jahan's reign had a *jama*[7] amounting to about one-seventh th of the total *jama*.[8] We have simply assumed that each pay claim of the *mansabdars* was met either directly by a *jagir* carrying an equal amount of *jama* or indirectly by accounting for a share in the *jama* of the *khalisa* equal to their pay claims.

A few notes are called for with regard to the calculation of the salary bill of each *mansabdar*. The pay of *zat* and *sawar* ranks was fixed separately. The pay for each *zat* rank was stated in the schedules; there being three rates for each *zat* rank according to whether the *sawar* rank of the *mansabdar* was equal, half or more than half, or less than half.[9] Since Lahori sets out both *zat* and *sawar* ranks of each *mansabdar*, the salary for each *zat* rank could be determined according to the rates for the three grades in the schedules.[10] As far as the pay of the *sawar* rank, this is to be calculated by multiplying the number of the *sawar* rank by 8000 *dams In the case of the do-aspa-sih-aspa sawar* ranks, the factor will be 16,000 *dams* and not 8000 *dams*.[11]

The results of the calculations are set out in two detailed tables appended to this essay. The first table (Table A) gives the total salary bill (including claims against *zat* and *sawar* ranks) of the holder of each *zat* rank and the ratio of the salary bill to the total *jama* in the case of each rank. The second one (Table B) gives the total amount of salary bill, itemized as *zat* salary and *sawar* salary, for the holders of each *zat* rank. The percentages of the *zat* and *sawar* salaries separately have been set out with reference to the total salary bill for each *zat* rank.

[7]*Badshahnama*, II, p. 713 (*khalisa* had 120 crore *dams*). cf. Irfan Habib, *Agrarian System*, pp. 69, 272.

[8]*Badshahnama*, II, p. 710. The total *jama* was 880 crore *dams*.

[9]See *Ain-i-Akbari*, Nawal Kishore, I, pp. 123–4. It should be denoted that the difference in salary claims for the three grades or classes in each *zat* rank was not only slight when compared to the total salary claim of these grades, but it followed a particular pattern. For example the difference between the I, II and III grades' salary claims from 1500 *zat* to 5000 *zat* was uniformly 3 lakh *dams;* again from 900 zat to 500 zat the difference was uniformly 50,000 *dams*.

[10]However, the *zat* ranks from 6000 upwards were not covered by this regulation (cf. *Selected Documents of Shah Jahan's Reign*, pp. 79–80).

[11]W.H. Moreland, 'Rank (*mansab*) in the Mogul State Service', in this volume (first published in *Journal of the Royal Asiatic Society*, 1936, pp. 641–65).

Lahori's list of the *mansabdars* and princes of the twentieth year gives the name of 578 *mansabdars*, out of which 133 were dead by 1647–8. We have naturally excluded the salary of the dead from our calculation and thus we get 445 *mansabdars* (including the princes). The total number of *mansabdars* serving under Shah Jahan at this time is said to have been 8000.[12] Thus Lahori's list of the *mansabdars* contains the names of only 5.6 per cent of the total number of the *mansabdars.*

The total estimated revenue of the empire for the twentieth year of Shah Jahan's reign was 880 crores of *dams.*[13] The total salary claims, for both *zat* and *sawar* ranks, calculated according to the schedules discussed above, of the 445 princes and nobles, amount to 541.9 million *dams* out of which the total *zat* salary of the same number of rank-holders amounts to 1228.7 million *dams.*

A detailed examination of Appendix Table A would show that 445 *mansabdars* (including the four princes) or a bare 5.6 per cent of the total *mansabdars*, numbering 8000, held 61 per cent of the entire estimated revenue of the empire. The high incidence of the concentration of the control of the fiscal resources is highlighted by the following examples:[14]

Number of *mansabdars* (including the princes)	*Zat* rank	Percentage of the total *mansabdars* (8000)	Percentage of the total *jama*
445	from 500 upwards	5.6	61.5
115	" 2000 "	1.4	44.0
73	" 2500 "	0.9	37.6
35	" 4000 "	0.4	28.2
25	" 5000 "	0.3	24.3
10	" 6000 "	0.1	13.8
4 princes	" 12000 "	0.05	8.2

Thus, at the top of the hierarchical bureaucracy of the Mughal empire, a mere 73 princes and nobles, who constituted only 0.9 per cent of the total number of the *mansabdars,* controlled 37.6 per cent of the total *jama*, or in other words, more than one-third of the total estimated

[12]*Badshahnama*, II, p. 715.
[13]Ibid., p. 709.
[14]See Table A.

revenue. On the other hand, 7555 *mansabdars* who constituted 94.4 per cent of the total number of *mansabdars*, claimed in the form of salaries 25 per cent or at the most 30 per cent of the total estimated revenue of the empire, allowing a margin for the *khalisa* expenditure other than that of paying cash salaries to the *mansabdars* (*naqdis*).

However, a fairly large portion of the salary bill of each *mansabdar* appears to have been earmarked for expenditure on maintaining a contingent equivalent to his *sawar* rank. This pattern emerges after an analysis of the separate figures of the *zat* and *sawar* salary claims of each *mansabdar* as well as of the various ranks.[15]

The total salary claim for the *sawar* ranks of the 445 *mansabdars* and princes amounted to 4182.2 million *dams*. This amount accounts for 77.2 per cent of the total salary claim, both *zat* and *sawar*, of the 445 rank-holders. This enormous amount spent on the maintenance of troopers becomes more significant by the fact that 445 individuals (up to 500 *zat* rank) drew 47.5 per cent of the total *jama* of the empire as their *sawar* salary. A scrutiny of Table B appended to this essay reveals that the claim allowed for the maintenance of the troopers in each rank was not less than 70 per cent of the total salary claim of 445 *mansabdars*.[16] This would indicate a huge diversion of the resources of the Mughal state to military organization. But, perhaps, there is an element of overstatement here, since it is quite possible that the *mansabdars* did not actually spend on their troops the whole amount they claimed against their *sawar* ranks.

A further possible aspect of our enquiry could be the working out of the shares of each grouping of the nobles such as the Iranis, Turanis, or *zamindars*, *khanazads*, etc. For the purpose of such an extension of our enquiry, however, one will have to work out the social origin of each of the *mansabdars* mentioned in Lahori's list. It is conceivable that an extended study on these lines might yield interesting results.

In the end I may say that though while presenting these tables, I am struck by the pattern of distribution they reveal, I am also conscious of the various limitations of presenting such a statistical account. It may have tended to present an over simplified view of what was indeed a complex system. However, my purpose would be served if this helps to focus attention on this very important subject and provokes deeper study of the problem.

[15]See Table B.

[16]Except in the rank of 900 zat where it is 67.6 per cent.

Appendix Table A

Rank	Total number	Total salary bill for both *zat* and *sawar* ranks (millions of *dams*)	Percentage of assessed revenue income (*jama*)
Princes (above 7000 *zat*)	4	724.0	8.2
7000 *zat*	4	400.0	4.5
6000 "	2	88.0	1.0
5000 "	15	929.7	10.5
4000 "	10	336.8	3.8
3000 "	33	743.4	8.4
2500 "	5	87.2	0.9
2000 "	41	562.4	6.3
1500 "	35	353.3	4.0
1000 "	70	451.1	5.1
900 "	18	78.9	0.9
800 "	30	146.2	1.6
700 "	52	179.1	2.0
600 "	25	86.0	0.9
500 "	101	244.8	2.7
Total	445	5410.9	61.5

Appendix Table B

Rank	Total salary bill (million *dams*)	Pay against *zat* rank (million *dams*)	Percentage of total salary bill	Pay against *sawar* rank (million *dams*)	Percentage of total salary bill
Princes	724.0	124.0	17.1	600.0	82.9
7000 *zat*	400.0	56.0	14.0	344.0	86.0
6000 "	88.0	24.0	27.3	64.0	72.7
5000 "	929.7	149.7	16.1	780.0	83.9
4000 "	336.8	77.6	23.0	259.2	77.0
3000 "	743.4	189.0	25.4	554.4	74.6
2500 "	87.2	23.2	26.6	64.0	73.4
2000 "	562.4	152.0	27.0	410.4	73.0
1500 "	353.3	92.1	26.0	261.2	74.0
1000 "	451.1	131.5	29.2	319.6	70.8
900 "	78.9	25.6	32.4	53.4	67.6
800 "	146.2	35.8	34.5	110.4	75.7
700 "	179.1	53.0	30.0	186.1	70.0
600 "	86.0	22.3	25.9	63.8	74.1
500 "	244.8	73.0	29.8	171.0	70.2

8

The Agrarian System of Mughal India: A Review Essay*

Tapan Raychaudhuri

Once in a very long while something happens to stir the shallow, turbid and yet extensive waters of Indian historiography. The publication of Irfan Habib's *The Agrarian System of Mughal India*[1] is generally recognized—even in the most unlikely quarters—as one of these rare occasions. The detailed knowledge on which the volume is based would satisfy the most rigorous demands of India's traditional scholarship: the not-so-whispered accusation of glib generalization, based on ill-understood and inadequate data, often levelled against the Indian protagonists of the analytical approach to history, would be quite pointless in this particular case. What is much more important, a large mass of data has been brought together here within a framework of clear and sober analysis to reconstruct a crucially significant area of India's past. Besides, the volume is something more than the product of an individual's effort. In recent years at Aligarh a small group of young scholars have succeeded in building up something like a historical 'school' in the true sense of the term. Habib's *Agrarian System* is the first major product of this new Aligarh 'school' and thus marks a fresh point of departure in Indian historiography.

Our knowledge and understanding of Indian agrarian society in the pre-colonial era, as derived from Moreland, Baden-Powell, Maine, etc. on the one hand and Marx and the Marxists on the other, are essentially simplistic, which fact perhaps explains the striking and unexpected similarity of views as between the British officials and the radical

*First Published in *Enquiry* (n.s.), 1965.

[1]Irfan Habib, *The Agrarian System of Mughal India* (Bombay, 1963).

thinkers mentioned above. The image generally projected is of an undifferentiated mass of small peasants, held together in fraternal village communities exercising by virtue of immemorial custom the communal right of hereditary occupation over arable land and pasture, subject only to revenue exploitation by the superior political-military authorities who expropriated the surplus directly or through power delegated to intermediate levels of authority. In this pre-class society, private ownership of land had not emerged: the concept was, in fact, irrelevant. For the situation, in Moreland's words, was 'antecedent to the process of disentangling the concept of private right from political allegiance'. In Marxist terms, the basic *fact* of communal property—which was really no property in the bourgeois sense—was masked by oriental despotism with 'the despotic government suspended over the small communities'. To repeat, property in land was irrelevant in these circumstances wherein cultivation was not a right but an enforceable duty. The 'self-sustaining unity of manufacture and agriculture' containing 'all the conditions for reproduction and surplus production' within the village community explains the economic viability and self-perpetuating character of this elementary form of social organization which could resist disintegration as much as evolution. Within this essentially changeless system, superficial mutations occurred through the aggregation of small states into empires, entailing changes in assessment and collection and in the composition of the exploiting class. These did not however affect either the organization or the relations of production. The sharers in the expropriated surplus might be of diverse origin, but they were identical in their economic functions and foundations. In so far as the only mentionable changes in agrarian society concerned this class, unconnected with production, the basic thesis of changelessness is not affected. At most, the variation in the degree and manner of revenue extraction permitted a limited range of fluctuations in output and the producers' share of it. But *strictly* limited; because most of the time in most places the expropriation of the surplus was as near total as was practicable.[2]

[2]The above account is a very brief summary of analysis and description elaborated, and endlessly repeated, in a vast body of literature. The best known among these are the works of Moreland. Baden-Powell's *The Indian Village Community*, Sir Henry Maine's *Village Communities: East and West* and Marx's *Letters on India* (the ideas contained in it were further developed in R.P. Dutt's *India Today)*. These works may differ in approach, emphasis and terminology, but the above summary is a fairly accurate representation of their common conclusions. For a brief, authoritative exposition of these views one may refer to W.H. Moreland, *India at the Death of Akbar*, pp. 96–8 and Karl Marx, *Pre-Capitalist*

This simple abstract model has been repeatedly put forward as the standard pattern of agrarian organization in Asia, and not by Marxists alone. Of course, one knew there were local differences; but these differences were considered to be either deviations from the norm or subsumed by the fundamental uniformity of socio-economic organization throughout this vast continent. In other words, the view that the local and regional variations were not significant enough was established pretty firmly. This image of the Oriental Society, with capital letters in appropriate places, is reborn, Phoenix-like, from time to time, of course with a seasonal change of feathers. Wittfogel's *Oriental Despotism* is perhaps the latest—but not the last, one apprehends—formidable *avatara* of this immortal bird.

Fortunately, over the last three decades or so, at a safe distance from the grand theory, specialists on different regions of Asia have produced a number of monographs which, when compared, bring out the striking individuality of socio-economic organizations in different parts of Asia, often within the same country. The abstract model of pre-class ante-property village communities, based on self-sufficiency, with the state in the role of an incubus, hardly fits any of these regional patterns. Even as a tool of analysis it has lost much of its value, unless one treats it as a starting hypothesis to be abandoned for the most part by the time one has finished investigation. The works of Van Leur, Schrieke and Meilink-Roelofsz on the Indonesian archipelago, of Doreen Warriner on the Middle East, of Lambton on Persia have all done their bit to demolish the image of a universal Oriental Society.[3] To this growing library of studies on Asian societies, Habib's work is a very important addition. This detailed empirical study, though not free from the natural limitations of a general survey covering the whole of Mughal India and a wide time span, brings into focus the distinctive

---

Economic Formations, p. 35 (Hobsbawn's Introduction). The formulations in *Pre-Capitalist Economic Formations* are rather different from those in Marx's *Letters on India*, the identification of oriental society as a pre-class society being the most significantly different formulation developed in the former work. The implications of this analysis in the context of Mughal agrarian society is discussed later in this essay.

[3]J.C. Van Leur, *Indonesian Trade and Society;* Schrieke, *Indonesian Sociological Studies;* Doreen Warriner, *Land and Poverty in the Middle East* (London, 1948); A.K.S. Lambton, *Landlord and Peasant in Persia* (OUP, 1953); Meilink-Roelofsz, *Asian Trade and European Influence* (The Hague, 1962).

traits of India's agrarian economy during a significant phase of the pre-colonial era.

The new light thrown on the nature of land rights perhaps marks the most significant point of departure from the traditional views sketched above. The self-contradictory yet simultaneously held theses that land ownership was an unknown category and that the king was the owner of all lands have both been proved to be equally incorrect. Private ownership of urban land and royal purchases of such lands from the subjects are evidence enough to disprove such theses. More significant however is the clear recognition in contemporary sources of the right of ownership (*milkiyat*) in agricultural land as something different from mere usufructuary right. The *milkiyat*, implying in practice the right of hereditary occupation including the right to rent out, is shown to have been generally vested in the *raiyat* or primary *zamindars*—terms which were more or less identical in connotation. An indirect evidence of the fact is that the individual peasant family, and not the village or the *zamindar*, is invariably the assessee for revenue purposes.[4]

Milkiyat in agricultural land under the Mughals was not, according to Habib, the same as 'ownership' as understood today. The *raiyat* had no right to alienate his land freely. Cultivation as a right was vested hereditarily in the peasant, but it was also an obligation from which no peasant was exempt. He was thus not a free agent: if the land belonged to him, he also belonged to the land and hence was not very different in his rights and obligations from the European serfs. Besides, his right of hereditary occupation was at times interfered with in practice, if the land was lucrative enough to attract new peasants whenever the old occupants were forced out. The most striking proof of the peasants' subject status was the large-scale abandonment of cultivation by *raiyats* who had no other means of escaping an intolerable revenue burden.[5]

The above picture of peasants' rights differs from the traditional view mainly on one point, viz. the identification of the peasant as *malik*. Very recently, however, other researchers have suggested further modifications of the older views on the subject. Both Nurul Hasan and B.R. Grover have referred to numerous cases of sale of land by the *raiyats*, though Grover concedes that such transactions, relatively

[4]Habib, *Agrarian System*, pp. 113f, 174, 230.
[5]Ibid., pp. 115, 118.

speaking, were extremely rare.[6] Where they differ from Habib is in their rejection of the view that the peasants did not have the right to sell their land without any constraints. In Grover's opinion, Elphinstone's statement regarding the territories conquered from the Peshwa, 'that a large portion of the Ryots (Mearassees) are proprietors of their estates, subject to the payment of fixed land-tax to the government;... their property is hereditary and saleable, and they are never disposed while they pay their tax', applies to Mughal India as well. He, however, makes some important distinctions: in Mughal India, fallow and forest 'belonged' to the state, only the cultivated land being under peasant proprietorship, a significant modification of the popular views on communal ownership of land. Secondly, while Habib has written only of income differences among the agricultural classes, Grover identifies an irregular hierarchy of land rights: the peasant proprietors (*riaya*) who cultivated their own land (*khudkashta*) or had the right to rent out their land, tenants (*muzarian*) holding lands from the *riaya*, *pahikashtkars* who owned land in a village where he did not live and *muqarari riaya* with hereditary rights of transfer, mortgage and sale of land, who, after reserving a holding for personal cultivation, farmed or rented out the residual land.[7] Ravinder Kumar's recent thesis on 'State and Society in Maharashtra in the 19th Century'[8] discloses a picture of rural society in the early nineteenth century essentially similar to Grover's account. This fact suggests a continuity of socio-economic organization which authorizes certain hypotheses about the agrarian system of Mughal India. Habib has hazarded a guess correlating the different levels of money income with the different strata of rural society (*zamindars*, rich peasants and poor peasants).[9] He has not enquired into the possible composition of the different strata. In Maharashtra in the early nineteenth century, there was very little correlation between the level of land rights on the one hand and the size of the landholding, and the agriculturists' income on the other, though social and political power in the village was concentrated in the hands of the hereditary peasant proprietors, both rich and poor.[10] One wonders

[6]N. Hasan, 'The Position of the Zamindars in the Mughal Empire', *Indian Economic and Social History Review*, vol. I, no. 4, 1963–4; B.R. Grover, 'Nature of Land-Rights in Mughal India', ibid., vol. I, no. 1.

[7]B.R. Grover, ibid., 3–5

[8]Ravinder Kumar, 'State and Society in Maharashtra in the 19th Century', Australian National University (Canberra, 1964).

[9]Ibid., pp. 119–20.

[10]Ibid., ch. I.

if the unstable conditions of the late seventeenth century generated a similar asymmetry so that there were *muzarian* or *pahikashtkars* richer than the local *zamindar, khudkashtkars* and the rentier peasant proprietors. A further point worth investigating is the consequence of such likely shifts in economic power in terms of social and administrative authority.

Our knowledge regarding the lowest strata of agrarian society—the people without any proprietory or tenancy rights in land—is still very inadequate. Habib has added some useful details to Moreland's statements[11] on agricultural labourers and 'village serfs' in India. He mentions cultivators who tilled other people's land, *chamars* who 'worked for wages in the fields of cultivators and Zamindars', *dhanuks* who husked rice and other groups who worked as guides and porters. The assumption that the 'landless' were not numerous is not consistent with another possibility, viz. that the bulk of the untouchables, a significant proportion of Hindu society, were excluded from occupancy rights. The phenomenon, somewhat puzzling in the context of a very favourable land–man ratio, is explained in terms of the rigid caste system, the rigidity in its turn being ascribed to hereditary divison of labour necessitated by rural isolation and self-sufficiency.[12] But isolation and self-sufficiency of villages have not generated such immobility in other societies, to wit, in those of medieval Europe. Inadequacy of capital supply—Habib mentions how large sections of the peasantry depended 'wholly upon credit for their ability (to cultivate)'—partly explain the origin of this class.[13] One may however, have to fall back on social anthropology for a more satisfactory explanation.

Where in all this does one come across the proverbial village community, owning the land communally and redistributing it periodically among the coparceners? According to Habib, there is not 'the slightest suggestion anywhere in our sources' that the occupancy or proprietory right was ever held in common or land distributed periodically; the village community developed only in 'some spheres outside that of production.'[14] This does not, however, finally lay a familiar ghost. True, the *Smriti* literature from very early times speaks exclusively of private property in arable land, laying down elaborate rules for inheritance, division and disposal. Yet, on the other hand, nineteenth-century

[11]W.H. Moreland, *India at the Death of Akbar*, pp. 112–14.
[12]Habib, *Agrarian System*, pp. 120–2.
[13]Ibid., p. 120.
[14]Ibid., pp. 119, 123.

British officials do describe communal ownership and periodic redistribution.[15] The discrepancy may be explained in one of several alternative ways. A more exhaustive study of the sources may disclose the existence of communal ownership in the seventeenth century. The phenomenon of periodic distribution may have developed in the days of political and administrative anarchy. (It is unlikely that the British administrators made a mistake about such a distinctive practice.) At another level, except with regard to this important issue of redistribution, there is no essential contradiction between Habib's position and the mid-nineteenth-century evidence. To the nineteenth-century British administrators, ownership implied something more than the right of occupancy and alienation: its other essential characteristics included 'the right of regulating occupancy and appropriating rent'.[16] We know from Grover's study[17] that the renting of arable land was a familiar practice in the seventeenth century. In the North Western Provinces in the nineteenth century the tenant did not pay any rent in cash or kind to any individual peasant proprietor. He was only obliged to contribute a relatively larger share of his produce (as compared to the contribution of the coparceners) to the common pool which covered the 'expenses of the village'—the *Kharj-i-deh* of the seventeenth-century documents—as well as the revenue demand. The tenant was thus the tenant of the village community, not of any individual proprietor. As yet there is little to indicate that the position in the *raiyati* villages in the seventeenth century was different from the one described above.[18] Development of private ownership from communal property, with vestiges of the earlier organization still clearly discernible, has been a characteristic feature of several Arab countries until very recently. The Arabs recognized private property in livestock, but only communal property in land whence developed the *mushaa* system in Palestine, Transjordan and Syria—a form of semi-collective ownership with regular reallotments—until considerations of efficiency led to the establishment of individual titles only in the days of the mandate.[19] Habib has ascribed

[15]See S.C. Gupta, *Agrarian Relations and Early British Rule*, p. 52f and the authorities cited by him.

[16]Ibid.

[17]Ibid.

[18]Grover's casual reference in 'Nature of Land Rights' to renting out of land by individual peasants does not vitally affect this hypothesis.

[19]Warriner, *Land and Property*, pp. 18–21.

thegradual dissolution of the village community such as it was to the growth of commodity production.[20] One wonders whether a probable transformation of communal rights in land was at least partly the product of the same forces. Since, however, the evidence of the *Smriti* texts traces private property in land back to a much earlier period, such an explanation is not very satisfactory. As in the Arab countries, so here, powerful landlords and assignees, often living in the cities, may have contributed to a weakening of the communal tradition.[21] Besides, one must not exaggerate the alienation of the village community from productive enterprise. Communal effort and control were far from unimportant when the cost of repayment of loans, purchase of seeds (in some cases) and the maintenance of canals was met from the communal pool to which every villager contributed.[22]

Not so much outside the scope of production as outside the control of land, the village community was a reality in a number of ways, particularly in connection with the management of the financial life of the village, including the collection and payment of revenue. Two interesting facts emerge in this connection: first, that there were villages without headmen who were represented by any villager selected for the purpose in the community's dealings with officialdom; secondly, village headship (*muqaddami*) became in many cases a hereditary property which could be and often was bought and sold. Inequalities of landholding often derived from the *muqaddam*'s extra holding of 2½ per cent of the village lands equivalent to his perquisite of 2½ per cent of the revenue.[23] But as has been indicated above, the size of one's holding and one's status in the rural hierarchy were not evenly correlated. There must have been other sources of inequality besides the perquisite of village officials. A minority of well-to-do peasants has been a characteristic feature of many agrarian societies in the pre-capitalist era. We have inter alia the notable example of the Russian serfs who were allowed to trade and became millionaires.[24] Growth of the market for agricultural products may have favoured the enterprising and the fortunate and colonizing efforts further aggravated the inequalities. And during the unsettled years the progress from wealth to ownership and hence the suppression of communal rights were perhaps

[20]Ibid., p. 128.

[21]Ibid., p. 6.

[22]Habib, *Agrarian System*, pp. 126–7.

[23]Ibid., pp. 126–7, 128–30.

[24]J. Blum, *The European Peasantry from the Fifteenth to the Nineteenth Century* (Washington, 1960), p. 22.

a natural process. Yet these are but surmises and we are still nowhere near the history of the Indian village communities and do not even know where, when or in what forms the institution actually existed. Habib's statement regarding the members of the *bhaiyachara* community belonging to one caste probably refers to the coparceners only and indirectly supports the thesis of dominant castes, if we read history backwards. Even on this point doubts are raised by Grover's description of multiple caste *zamindari* as well as *raiyati* villages.[25]

In trying to understand the nature, organization and economic basis of agrarian society, it is not enough to concentrate on the character of the peasantry, its position *vis-à-vis* the state and vice versa. In fact very often the label 'feudal' is fixed to a society on the basis of the role played in it by intermediary groups standing between the authority of the state and the masses subject to it—a role assessed in terms of political–administrative–military power and control over land.[26] The fascinating but not very fruitful exercise seeking to ascertain the degree of feudalism in terms of the classic West European model—complete with military obligation, commendation, subinfeudation, manors and serfs—or the even more exciting one which seeks to pin down the crucial feature of feudalism is not terribly relevant to our purpose. An analysis of the character and role of the intermediary groups is nevertheless important for they significantly affected the distribution of the produce and helped define the conditions of agricultural production as also the producer's social and economic status, itself an important factor in stimulating or retarding production. Fortunately, much of the recent research on the Mughal agrarian system has concentrated on this question so that enough is known to authorize more or less precise conclusions.

An regards the *mansabdar-jagirdars*, once wrongly considered the major intermediary group, much of the familiar details are confirmed anew the fact of the *jagirdar*'s claim being on revenue, not on land, the transferability of the *jagirs* except in the case of *altamgha* and *watan jagirs* and the central authority's efforts to enforce the standard revenue regulations in the assigned lands as well, in order to check the

[25] Habib, *Agrarian System*, p. 123; Grover, 'Nature of *Dehat-i-Taaluqa* etc.', *Indian Economic and Social History Review* (*IESHR*), vol. 2, nos 2 and 3.

[26] For a recent instance of the identification of the Indian economy in the ancient period as 'feudal' on the basis of land grants to non-producing groups, see R.S. Sharma, 'Land-grants to Vassals and Officials in N. India (*c.* AD 1000–1200)', *Journal of Economic and Social History of the Orient*, vol. IV, pt I (1961) and 'The Origins of Feudalism in India c. AD 400–650)', ibid., vol. I, pt 3 (1958).

possibilities of oppression, have now been discussed with a wealth of documentary evidence.[27] The impression left by this restatement of known facts is that the system of revenue assignment in lieu of cash salary was simply a convenient arrangement for maintaining the bureaucracy: it rid the central government of a fair measure of irksome responsibility with regard to collection and disbursement without any corresponding reduction in authority or increase in the revenue burden. Other facts, mentioned but not sufficiently emphasized, suggest a very different situation. Without any long-term interest in the territory assigned to him for a short period, the *jagirdar* unhesitatingly fleeced the peasant. Complaints to the higher authorities, permitted in theory, were nearly impossible in practice and were at best ineffective. The system of farming out *jagirs*, discouraged by the government, apparently to little purpose, further aggravated the situation. The financial crisis of the Mughal empire, in the later years of Aurangzeb and afterwards, with too many *mansabdars* and not enough *jagirs* to go around led to a steady deterioration all round:[28] a government unable to provide adequate revenue assignments could hardly have told its revenue assignees how to behave towards *ryots* and the impoverished *jagirdar* now had an additional incentive to squeeze the producer. The significance of these facts becomes clear if one remembers that the *khalisa*, directly under the revenue administration of the central government, never accounted for more than 1/5th of the total assessment except for a brief period under Akbar.[29] Thus in the greater part of the imperial territories, there does not appear to have been any check on the unlimited exploitation of the rural population. The real measure of the subjection of the peasantry is to be assessed in terms of what went on in the assigned territories, and not in the *khalisa* where practical considerations, if nothing else, partly restrained the oppressors. Abandonment of cultivation on a large scale and the mass migration of peasants—phenomena likely to occur only when the agriculturist's income is reduced to a point below the already meagre subsistence level—make sense only in the context discussed above. A government, dependent for its existence on the income from agriculture, which it was eager to maintain and extend, could not have gone on killing the geese that laid the golden egg's year after year. The assignee, briefly enjoying an inadequate and precarious income from his *jagir*, could not on the other

[27]Habib, *Agrarian System*, pp. 260, 273, 296–7, 318, 320–3.

[28]Ibid., p. 270; Noman Ahmad Siddiqi, 'Revenue Administration of the Mughal Empire in the First Half of the 18th Century', unpublished Ph.D. thesis (Aligarh Muslim University).

[29]Habib, *Agrarian System*, pp. 271–2.

hand care less as to what happened to the ryot. Seizing the entire harvest or taking the population in slavery could be for him, but not for the state, a rational source of profit. N.A. Siddiqi in his thesis[30] has described the gradual impoverishment and exit of the big *jagirdar*, replaced by a class of men who bought from the *jagirdar* or otherwise secured the right to collect revenue over parts of the erstwhile big *jagirs*, a right which eventually became hereditary in many instances. An increasingly strong school of thought would have us believe that the virtual dissolution of the Mughal empire in the eighteenth century was accompanied by a gradual extension of peace and prosperity in many of the virtually independent provincial kingdoms. One wonders whether the mutations in the *jagirdari* system had something to do with this improvement.

It is with regard to the nature and role of *zamindari* rights that recent research has dug up the most significantly new information. A careful scrutiny of the well-known manuscripts of the *Ain* has revealed that the *zamindars* were not simply a princely class that managed to survive here and there mainly outside the heartland of the empire; the *Ain* actually mentions the castes of the *zamindars* for practically every *sarkar* in the imperial territory, a fact which was overlooked earlier owing to editorial errors in the printed editions of the compendium.[31] The *zamindars* were in fact to be found everywhere, in *jagir* as well as *khalisa* territory.

[30] Siddiqi, 'Revenue Administration of the Mughal Empire'.

[31] Habib, *Agrarian System*, pp. p. 136f. Habib has, however, not been quite fair to Moreland in ascribing to him without adequate qualifications the view 'that the *zamindars* in Mughal times really meant a vassal chief and could not exist in the directly administered territories of the empire' (p. 136). Moreland in his *India at the Death of Akbar* (pp. 3–4) clearly states: ' In various parts of the Empire we find that the local administration was in the hands of men who are spoken of consistently as 'zamindars'... *it would be a mistake to regard these zamindars as necessarily equivalent to Princes or Chiefs;* the word covers everybody, other than a grantee or an official, who stood between the peasants and the Emperor, and it may mean a land-holder in the modern sense, a chief, or a rebel ... *we hear of them in the Gangetic plain, where Akbar's supremacy was definitely established;* we hear of them in the borderlands ... and we find them in Rajputana, *and in the mountainous country south of Allahabad and Benares* ... and if we possessed detailed knowledge of the position of individuals, we should probably find a wide variety of superior tenures, ranging from what would now be termed landholders to rulers in subordinate alliance with the Emperor. ... '(emphasis mine) Far from contradicting Moreland's conclusions, recent research has actually proved his surmises to be correct.

They were however not a homogeneous class. In fact even the term 'intermediary' would not apply to large sections covered by that multi-purpose nomenclature. The different types of *zamindars* had, however, one thing, besides their name, in common: in contradistinction to other elements in the rural society, they represented a higher level of rights and privileges. Any analysis of the class divisions in rural society must primarily concentrate on these superior rights of the *zamindars*; the stratification of rights at the level of the actual cultivators (including what Nurul Hasan has described as the primary *zamindars*)[32] was itself determined by these superior rights. There is a continual shift in the character and composition of the various types of *zamindars*. The levers of change and the element of dynamism in the rural society were closely interlinked with this particular process: any vital change in the role of the *zamindars* implied a change in the class structure of agrarian society.

Historically, the *zamindari* rights appear to have been derived from two sources which were at times intermingled. The *zamindaran-i-umda* or the chieftains as well as Nurul Hasan's 'intermediary *zamindars*' enjoying the rights to collect revenue and some administrative power over relatively small territories were repositories of independent or semi-independent political and military authority some time or other. The 'primary *zamindars*', indistinguishable from the *riyaya*, who had the right of regulating occupancy and appropriating 'rent', were the original colonizers and settlers of the soil or their descendants: such at least was the theoretical basis of their rights and a certain degree of political authority appears to have been originally implicit in it, particularly when the cultivating *zamindar* was simply the scion of a proliferating family which once also collected revenue and exercised administrative power.[33] These was, however, nothing static about the position of these groups. The erstwhile political authority undertook to pay *peshkash* (tribute), or became a *mansabdar* of the empire holding his territory as *watan jagir*, not necessarily coterminous with his ancestral lands. The *zamindari* status of the 'intermediary *zamindar*', however hoary its antiquity, was derived, under the Mughals, from imperial *sanads* formally conferring the 'office'. Under the *sanad*, the *zamindar* became a *malguzar*, an official responsible for the collection of revenue from the land under his control, almost invariably more extensive than

[32]'Hasan, 'The Position of zamindars'.
[33]B.R. Grover, 'Nature of *Dehat-i-Taaluqa*'.

his ancestral holding.[34] From this point there are movements in two different directions. The *zamindar* might become a *sadr zamindar* with jurisdiction over numerous *parganas* or (outside Bengal) a *taaluqdar* with superior rights over smaller *zamindars* who paid their revenue through him. Still a cog, however big, in the wheel of the revenue administration, the *taaluqdar* before long consolidated his rights in the nature of perquisites and eventually laid claim to proprietorship over the territories under his control. Secondly, the *zamindari* rights might suffer a dilution or diminution as well generating in the process other forms of control over land. The Bengal *taaluqdars*—both independent (i.e. *huzuri*, paying revenue directly to the state) and dependent (i.e. *muskuri*, paying revenue through some *zamindar*)[35]— secured rights essentially similar to that of the *zamindars* through colonization, purchase or gift and thus emerged as a distinct level of intermediaries. The frequent sales and partitions of the *zamindari* and *taaluqdari* lands often reduced the individual holding to a size which forced the individual *zamindars* to become, once more, a *khudkashta* ryot, paying revenue through the real or putative head of the family, now a chief *zamindar*. But even such *khudkashta* ryots, as discussed above, shared in the right to determine occupancy. This pattern of stratification was complicated by criss-cross relationships created by the combination of different levels of rights in the hands of the same individuals.[36] The bewildering complexity of land rights which characterize the British period of Indian history, particularly the minute stratification found in certain parts of Bengal, assumed their final proportions in comparatively recent times, but the origins are surely traceable to the Mughal period.

The *zamindars*, other than the *khudkashta* ryots, were not the owners (*malik*) of the soil. What rights the chieftains actually exercised *vis-à-vis* the tillers and the land under them, is not yet very clear. Bernier's statement affirming that the peasants were better off under the autonomous chieftains seems reasonable in view of the chieftains' vested interest—not shared by the *jagirdars*—in long-term agricultural prosperity. Nurul Hasan has, however, questioned its veracity. The 'intermediary *zamindars*'—who often enjoyed certain perquisites in their capacity of village headmen (*chaudhuri*)—were entitled to a share of the revenue as their *zamindari* perquisite, which assumed different

[34]Hasan, 'The Position of the Zamindars'.

[35]B.R. Grover, 'Nature of *Dehat-i-Taaluqa*'.

[36]Ibid.

forms and names in different parts of the country, but was never very lucrative. The right to these perquisites and to collect revenue was owned by the *zamindar* and was in fact freely sold. Besides, the *zamindar* collected additional cesses (*abwabs*) and had his personal lands over which he enjoyed full proprietory rights. What the *zamindars* did with their personal land remains something of a mystery. Grover says that they generally got it 'cultivated by others'. Does this imply some sort of demesne farming with forced or wage labour or simply that the land was rented out? The same author adduces evidence to prove that rent, as distinct from revenue, was paid to the proprietors usually as a specified proportion of the produce. The primary *zamindars* also received rent, probably on a communal basis, from the *pahikashtkars* and *muzarian*.

The position in Bengal was somewhat different from elsewhere: here the *zamindar* paid a fixed amount to the state apparently not based on any calculation of the produce, an arrangement somewhat similar to that under the Permanent Settlement. Presumably, the *zamindari* perquisite in such a case was not a fixed proportion of the revenue demand.

The *zamindari* rights had a caste basis—increasingly heterogeneous through sale and transfer of rights, yet never completely destroyed. Another basis of the *zamindar's* power was the armed retainers, either peasants impressed into military service or mercenaries paid in cash or rent-free lands. The caste basis evidently was relevant for all types of *zamindars;* the armed retainers were maintained by the chiefs and intermediate *zamindars* only.[37]

One more group stood between the revenue-payer and the state: the grantees who held their land by virtue of their religious merit—the Muslim 'army of prayer' whose services were by no means inessential to the state, and the Hindu Brahmins, Vaishnavs, etc. Holding their lands from the state as well as *zamindars* and *jagirdars*, such grantees actually enjoyed only a claim to revenue and not to any proprietory rights in the land. At least this appears to have been the position of the Muslim *aimadars;* it is likely, but not certain, that the Hindu grantees were in a similar position. Individually, these revenue assignees were not important, as the lands under their individual control were seldom very extensive. As a group, they accounted for as much as 5.4 per cent

[37]The above discussion is based on the articles by N. Hasan and B.R. Grover already referred to and Habib, *Agrarian System*, ch. v.

of the revenue in some areas.[38] The grants, resumable in theory and at times in practice, appear to have been generally treated as hereditary.[39] In their impact on agrarian life, the grantees were comparable to small *jagirdars* except that they had a long-term interest in their assignment. To describe them as parasitical is misleading, since in the eyes of their contemporaries they surely rendered a service of great importance.

Can we, in the light of all this new information, tackle a basic question, namely the precise character of the peasantry and its determinants? Attempts to answer it in terms of the familiar categories—degree of independence or subjection and extent of proprietory rights—can not elicit any clear formulation. One reason for this lack of clarity is that we have no definite notion as yet of the relative proportions of the different categories of peasants. Obviously our question can have very different answers depending on whether the peasant proprietors or tenants or landless labourers constituted the majority or at least very significant proportions of the total. Possible regional variations which are casually referred to but nowhere investigated by any of the scholars mentioned above raise further difficulties. It would be a matter for surprise if in a country of continental proportions the same basic pattern was to be found everywhere. In conditions hardly more dynamic than those of seventeenth century India, Western European feudalism flourished in a relatively limited area while Scandinavia and regions east of the Elbe developed socio-economic systems of a very different character.[40] Nearer home, in Syria, Lebanon, Iraq and Transjordan, Doreen Warriner has identified regional variations in agrarian organization caused by topographical and historical factors.[41] The possible impact on agrarian society of differences in fertility, water supply, altitude, proximity to the urban market, levels of culture, etc. needs to be enquired into. Conceivably, data on most of these points are very inadequate, but such a statement is not authorized until at least the questions have been posed. What we have at the moment is an introductory general statement which fits together scattered evidence relating to dif-

[38]Habib, *Agrarian System*, p. 314. This figure does not include the grants made to Hindus, or by agencies other than the imperial government.

[39]Sheikh Abdur Rashid, 'Siyurghal Lands Under the Mughals', *Sir Jadunath Sarkar Commemoration Volume* (1958), '*Madad-i-Maash* Grants Under the Mughals', *Journal of the Pakistan History Congress* (1959).

[40]cf. Marc Bloch, *Feudal Society*, Introduction and ch. I.

[41]Warriner, *Land and Property*, pp. 3f, 18f. Similar regional variations in modern India have been discussed in Chen Han-Seng, *Agrarian Regions of India*. See Alice and Daniel Thorner, *Land and Labour in India*, ch. IV.

ferent regions and points of time and material collected from the administrative records of a central authority which necessarily sought to impose at least a certain measure of uniformity. Notwithstanding the great value of such a statement as a starting point, it may induce a misleading assumption of unchanging uniformity. If such uniformity was in fact there, one could be sure of it only after comparing different regions over a period of time.[42]

Within the limits of our inadequate knowledge, one may hazard certain very tentative formulations: we have here a class society with clearly articulated proprietory rights of various categories as also complex and divergent patterns of stratification. Some sections of the peasantry were the owners of the bulk of the agricultural land, while others had occupancy rights as tenants or were landless. Ownership included the right of alienation, rarely exercised in practice. The state and other extractors of revenue might expropriate the entire surplus, but seldom evicted the peasant from his land. But if cultivation was a right, it was also a duty enforced by the state. This probably meant that while the individual peasant might sell his land, the state tried to ensure that the land should not remain fallow. 'Normally', the peasant cultivated the land and the state or the intermediaries collected revenue; conflict between the right and the duty to cultivate did not arise; the peasant was not free only in the sense that custom or law did not restrict the revenue burden. Conflict arose when the revenue demand became intolerable. It is indeed doubtful how far the 'normal' situation described above was the one usually encountered. Peasants unwilling to pay revenue, *raiyat-i-zor talab*, were by no means exceptional. When their resistance failed, they tried to give up cultivation and run away. In law, they were not allowed to abandon cultivation; in fact, they frequently did so. It was at this point that the state sought to enforce the obligation to cultivate and the subjection of the peasant became something more than theoretical. In the later years of Aurangzeb's reign such conflicts and the mass migration of peasants became more and more frequent. We have here no doubt a form of subjection involving in extreme circumstances even the possibility of physical destruction:

[42]For a discussion of possible approaches to local and regional variations within the general framework of a country's agrarian history, see Professor Postan's review of Kosminsky's *The English Village in the 13th Century* (Leningrad, 1935) in *Economic History Review* (1936). In this field, Marc Bloch's *Les caractères originaux de l'histoire rurale française* is perhaps the best-known example of generalizations based on a comparative study of local and regional history.

but compared to the serfs in medieval Europe or Assam peasants obliged to render labour service to the Ahom kings or Malabar *kanamkars* tied to the soil working for the *janmi* landowners,[43] the peasant in Mughal India in the *khalisa* lands was closer to freedom than dependence in terms of socio-economic organization. One may ask if even this measure of dependence was not the result of the gradual removal of customary checks on the revenue burden, particularly under the Mughals. There are examples of a free peasantry gradually reduced to subjection in other parts of the world, e.g. Iran under the later Abbasids[44] and the Byzantine empire during the high Middle Ages. In the latter case, scarcity of labour is known to have prompted the efforts at subjection.[45] This may have been an important influence in the Indian case as well; the fact that sections of the population had no right to occupy land further restricted the available labour force.

The data discussed in this article probably authorize an important distinction between two categories of the peasantry. The juridical independence and proprietory rights of the peasantry evidently meant something in the *khalisa* lands, because of the state's long-term interest in agricultural prosperity. But the position in the *jagir* lands appears to have been very different. The *jagirdar*, ephemerally connected with particular revenue assignments, is not really integrated with the structure of agrarian society: he might be said to represent, in Marxist terms, 'the despotic government suspended over the small communities'. He was very different from the *iqtadar* or *jagirdar* of the Turko-Afghan days, who often developed hereditary connections with the land assigned to him and thus came to constitute a stratum in rural society. With the courts and camps as his focal points of interest, the *jagirdar-mansabdar* was a non-rural phenomenon, disposing of the bulk of the agricultural surplus (since he accounted for the bulk of the imperial revenue), but not concerned with the control of production or its means. Under his practically despotic irresponsible authority, the condition of the peasantry was probably the hardest and the incentives to production correspondingly the lowest and this despite the feeble state effort to protect the peasantry. It seems reasonable to conclude then that there

[43]See S.K. Bhuiyan, *Anglo-Assamese Relations*, ch. 1 and Logan's *Malabar* for discussions of the position of the dependent peasantry in these parts of India. It has been suggested later in this article that the ryots in the *jagirs* were probably far more dependent than their counterparts in the *khalisa*.

[44]Ann K.S. Lambton, *Landlord and Peasant in Persia*, (OUP, 1953) pp. 4, 5ff.

[45]*Cambridge Economic History of Europe*, I, pp. 192, 221.

were two categories of ryots: the one, in the *khalisa*, enjoyed a considerable degree of independence limited only by a heavy revenue demand and an obligation to cultivate which was at the same time a right and another, in the *jagir* lands, semi-servile in practice, frequently constrained to abandon their meagre and precarious livelihood. At times, owing to financial pressures on the administration, this line of distinction is wiped off. The key to the actual position of the agriculturist is hence to be sought not in social or economic organization but the manner in which administrative and political power was distributed and deployed.

Cutting across the distinction between the *riaya* in the *khalisa* and those in the *jagirs* is a second criterion of classification—the distinction between the *zamindari* and the *raiyati* villages. Whether the *zamindars* in their own interest acted as a shield for the masses of cultivators is a point worth investigating: the *a priori* arguments can cut both ways. What is certain is that the chiefs, intermediary *zamindars* and *taaluqdars* were a rural class disposing of a portion of the agricultural surplus and as such created a pattern of stratification different from the one to be found in the *raiyati* villages, where the proprietory rights and the class structure were differently articulated. If there was no significant development of a land market, there was surely a very considerable volume of dealings in *zamindari* rights—the rights to dispose of a stated proportion of the surplus. By the end of the Mughal period, a mutation had taken place: the *taaluqdar*'s proprietory right had been gradually extended from a share in the produce to a control over the means of production; he was staking his claim to the *milkiyat* of the village lands, crucially including the authority to determine occupancy. Then there are the assignments based on religious merit, but these did not really introduce a distinct stratum in the hierarchy of land rights, for they merely represented the transfer of a fraction of revenue income from the state, the *jagirdar* or the *zamindar* to men of religious merit. In fine, the changes in the structure of land rights took place at two levels. At the level of the *khudkashtkars*, *pahikashtkars* and the *muzarian* the control of the actual means of production was the question at issue; evidently, there was vertical mobility, mainly upwards in terms of rights, but both ways so far as income and the size of holding were concerned. The limits of such mobility are worth investigating in a precise time space context. For one thing, a *pahikashtkar* could evidently become a *malik* only in lands he himself and colonized, a constraint which could have considerable potentiality as an incentive to extension of cultivation. At another level, the rights which undergo mutation were concerned with shares in the produce and control over men rather than on land. Towards the end of our period, the two processes tend to merge.

Mutations in agrarian relationships may be causally related to economic pressures or incentives or both. Certain facts taken in isolation would suggest that incentives were practically absent from the Mughal agrarian system. If 50 per cent of the gross produce was actually extorted from the producer[46]—that is, if this was the reality and not simply an administrative 'ideal'—then the peasant could hardly have been left with a subsistence income in any accepted sense of the term. Such a paradoxical situation may nevertheless be economically viable for a period of time, because the 'below subsistence income', implying very low caloric content of food, may result in reduced longevity rather than abandonment of cultivation, where the peasant has no alternative means of survival. Habib's reading of the contemporary evidence that everything that could be taken from the peasant was in fact taken—whether this amounted to 50 per cent of the gross produce or not—is perhaps very near the mark, subject to one important qualification. Through all the harrowing contemporary accounts of the poverty of the masses, one fact does emerge: the living standards of the poor were not the same everywhere. To take a single instance, Bowrey found it difficult to get small coins worth a *rupia* in the Orissa villages where there was also an acute scarcity of foodstuff; by contrast, he found Bengal a land abundant in all the necessities of life. Since the peasant's income—the residue left after the payment of revenue in cash—depended not only on the magnitude of revenue demand, but on the price he could get for his produce, conditions of the market acquire an importance in this context, and these were not uniform throughout the country. One must also take into account the possible lack of uniformity in the vigour of revenue administration, particularly in the *zamindari* villages. In short, peasants with an income somewhat above the subsistence level were probably not altogether an unknown phenomenon. If this is correct, then the existence of incentives to production cannot be ruled out.

A comparison between the levels of agricultural productivity and income in the Mughal period with those in the twentieth century was first made by Moreland.[47] The relative insignificance of this exercise has been obscured by polemical issues and the fact that such com-

[46]Habib, *Agrarian System*, pp. 190f, 195.

[47]Moreland, *India at the Death of Akbar*, 115f.

parison should concentrate on the structure of the economy rather than on the levels of output has been lost sight of. Habib has reopened the question; but his preoccupation remains the same as Moreland's. Moreland's hypothesis that the average agriculturist's income had, if anything, improved in the British period was based, inter alia, on a major fallacy, 'that in any particular region the numbers of the rural population have varied approximately with the area under cultivation',[48] because labour productivity, in the absence of technological change, had remained constant. The argument ignores the phenomenal growth of disguised unemployment in agriculture and the consequent possibility of a reduction in per capita income and output in this sector. Habib postulates a possible decline in income and productivity per acre on the familiar ground that with expansion of population inferior land was brought under cultivation. In addition to the very effective arguments put forward by Moreland against this line of reasoning, one may point out that colonization and extension of cultivation were regulated by a set of factors, including mere contingency, of which relative fertility of the soil was only one. The assumption that extension of cultivation necessarily meant the bringing of less fertile soil under the plough needs to be empirically validated before one can accept it. There is, however, an argument in favour of relatively higher labour productivity in the Mughal period. According to the evidence of our census data, significant growth in population in India is a post-World War I phenomenon primarily caused by the control of epidemic diseases.[49] If one may read history backwards from this evidence, Mughal India with its history of continuous wars, famines and epidemics, must have had, at most, a very slowly increasing population. Habib has, however, adduced enough evidence to prove the fact of substantial expansion of the area under cultivation during this period, a thesis supported with regard to Bengal by Abdul Karim's monograph on Murshid Quli Khan. An expanding agriculture with the population remaining more or less constant means an increase in labour productivity. Even in conditions of unchanging techniques this may have happened, if the pressures and incentives then at work forced, as seems likely, the idle or under-employed labour, e.g. in the joint families, to bring new land under cultivation.

How the pressures of revenue demand frequently cut into the meagre subsistence income of the peasant has been discussed by all

[48]Ibid., p. 111.

[49]K. Davies, *Population of India and Pakistan*, pt II.

writers on the subject. Habib and Siddiqi have indicated an increase in this pressure during the declining days of the empire. The former ascribes a number of risings in northern India and the Maratha upheaval to this increasing pressure on the agriculturist and identifies this 'agrarian crisis' as a major factor in the decline of the empire. Whether he has overemphasized the role of the agrarian crisis or not is a question that can be answered only when we have a critical assessment of all other elements in the situation. That the contemporary sources, mostly written by officials involved in administrative problems, 'put the greatest store by the economic and administrative causes of the upheaval'[50] is, however, no proof that these were in fact the most crucial issues. Attempts to assess the relative weights of different factors in a process as complex as the decline of an empire is always rather baffling. The nature and causation of the peasants' risings may be a more rewarding subject of investigation. An interesting fact to be remembered in this connection is that in other parts of the world agrarian risings are known to have occurred when conditions were improving as well as in situations of growing fiscal burden.[51] The role of religious movements in securing a cohesion, often across mutually conflicting class interests, which makes resistance possible is also worth investigating.[52]

Besides the undoubtedly heavy pressure on the peasant, a system of incentives was also in operation. The revenue concessions, particularly those granted when land lying fallow was reclaimed or wells were repaired, were among the more obvious instances of such incentives.[53] At the level of the revenue-collecting *zamindar*, there was obvious advantage in encouraging colonization of new territory which was appreciated and acted upon at least in Murshid Quli's Bengal. At the level of the actual cultivator, one wonders whether the power, prestige, as also the marginal economic advantages associated with the status of the *malik* and *zamindar* in rural society did not encourage the tenant-cultivators to colonize unclaimed territory where alone they

[50]Habib, *Agrarian System*, p. 339.

[51]See for instance F.W.N. Hugenholtz, *Drie Boerenopstanden uit de Viertiende Eeuw* (Haarlem, 1949). The author discusses how the French jacquerie of 1358 was the result of fiscal burdens while the English and Flemish risings of 1381 and 1323–8 respectively took place when conditions were improving.

[52]Habib has actually referred to the cohesive influence of Sikhism, though not of the Bhakti movement in Maharashtra, but not analysed its implications as a factor in agrarian unrest.

[53]Habib, *Agrarian System*, pp. 252–3.

could hope to acquire it. Both the settled peasant and the colonist could count upon some form of external assistance in their productive efforts. Interestingly enough, this external assistance did not assume the form of state-controlled irrigation which was insignificant in Mughal India: so far as this period is concerned, the grand thesis of hydraulic society has no legs to stand on.[54] The peasant was in fact helped in a way which has a very important bearing on our understanding of the contemporary economy: *taqavi* loans were granted, apparently on an extensive scale, by the state and the *zamindars* and these were supplemented by loans from the village moneylenders.[55] This fact suggests a penetration of capital into primary production to a degree never suspected before and traces the control of the moneylender on the peasant to a point of time much further back than the late nineteenth century. It further indicates that the primary producer was not concerned with exchange merely as a form of economic activity required to secure the wherewithal for the payment of revenue; the process of production itself had become partly dependent on exchange operations. In order to continue his agricultural production, the peasant mortgaged or 'pre-sold' the whole or a part of his produce and the cash he got in return was used to replenish his stock, buy seed-grain or maintain himself and family until the harvest season. Market forces penetrated into the peasant's world of subsistence-based isolation in other ways as well. We now have fairly convincing evidence of a steady upward trend in agricultural prices —probably in the urban retail market.[56] It has been suggested that the benefits of this price rise went exclusively to the middlemen. There are reasons for doubting this hypothesis. The demand for agricultural products in the urban centres was very great and all sources of supply were in positions of equal disadvantage with regard to access to the market. In such situations, while the middlemen are likely to profit most, peasants too may experience an upward trend in their income.[57] A more solid piece of evidence supports my contention: that

[54] Ibid., p. 256.

[55] Ibid., pp. 120, 131–2, 254–5, 239–42; also see Grover's articles referred to above.

[56] Ibid., pp. 81, 89, 91, 249. Habib has not made it clear as to which price he is discussing. Thought his sources also are somewhat vague on this point, it does appear that both the *Ain* and the *Factory Records* mention retail prices only, mainly in the urban markets.

[57] Compare for instance the situation in Tudor England when the growth of the London food market powerfully affected areas which had access to it. While the rentiers profited most from the situation, the peasants also enjoyed a rising standard of living. See Ramsey, *Tudor Economic Policy*, pp. 44f.

the peasants were responsive to new demand is proved by the striking expansion of tobacco cultivation in course of our period. If the producer had nothing to gain from the cultivation of a new cash crop, he was hardly likely to have undertaken it from a sheer propensity to innovation.

The above facts lead to a basic query regarding the nature of the Indian economy under the Mughals. The term 'monetization' and 'money economy' have been bandied about frequently enough in the literature on economic history, usually to the undoing of those who have indulged in this evidently tempting pastime. The temptation to apply these precious terms to Mughal India are indeed strong: the revenue demand, accounting for a third to one half of the total agricultural produce, was now on a cash basis; a vast and complicated mechanism of exchange attended to the distribution of this surplus over a land area of continental proportions; credit institutions of a fairly sophisticated variety helped in the functioning of administration, commerce and even agriculture;[58] and there was a steadily expanding export trade. There is however, one serious snag in the argument. Even forgetting that we do not know what part of the revenue was actually collected in cash, the available evidence is fairly conclusive on one point: the village sold, but hardly ever purchased anything from the outside world. So far as the consumption needs of the villagers, the bulk of the population, were concerned, the pattern of self-sufficiency was not affected. Grover has provided evidence to show that there was some exchange between small groups of neighbouring villages who stood in relations of mutual economic complementarity to one another.[59] We do not know, however, the extent of this pattern of economic organization. Besides, this too is a form of self-sufficiency with a group of villages rather than a single village as the basic unit. The relationship of mutual exchange between town and country which developed in Europe in the later Middle Ages and its consequences in terms of specialization and division of labour are absent from the Indian scene.[60]

[58]Irfan Habib, 'Banking in Mughal India', *Contributions to Indian Economic History*, I, 'Usury in Mughal India', *Comparative Studies in History and Society*, (1964).

[59]Grover, '*Raqba-Bandi* Documents of Akbar's Reign', *Proceedings of Indian Historical Records Commission* (1961).

[60]There is some evidence of localization of manufactures, but this phenomenon was rather limited in extent and appears to have developed mainly in connection with the export trade leaving the bulk of the economy unaffected. See my *Jan Company in Coromandel* (The Hague, 1962), Introduction and last chapter; and 'Some Patterns of Economic Activity and Organisation in 17th Century India', *Proceedings of the Second International Economic History Conference*.

A large monetized sector did develop. The agricultural surplus extracted in the form of revenue was to be distributed among a numerous body of nobles, soldiers, bureaucrats, servants and retainers. Traders, middlemen, usurers and dealers in money provided the machinery for distribution. This very large segment of the population—the urban population accounted for a very high proportion of the total[61]—did not produce anything for their own consumption. They 'sold' their services, in one form or another, for a money income which they used to purchase their necessities of day-to-day existence or for hoarding. But the share of the produce taken away from the peasants was so high that the surplus, if any, left in their hands was evidently not enough to create a rural market for consumer goods. Hence, for all practical purposes, the process of monetization stopped at the border of village India. The villager sold his produce so as to pay the revenue, now demanded in cash, and may be partly to repay the moneylender unless he preferred payment in kind. For the rest, his life was geared to a tradition-based distribution of the rural produce among agriculturists, craftsmen and village servants. Habib mentions that compared to present times area for area, with a much smaller population, Mughal India had a much larger number of villages.[62] This is what one might have expected, for the imperfections of the market prevented the growth of large centres of specialized production and when technique is inefficient, a self-sufficient unit cannot be very large. Grover's groups of mutually complementary villages probably added up in area to single medium-sized villages of later times.

Recent literature indicates a certain dynamism in the agrarian society of Mughal India, whatever its limitations in terms of increasing efficiency of the economy. Do we have evidence of a change as compared to earlier times? Such evidence is implicitly there, though its full articulation would depend on further research. The transition from a decentralized revenue administration with practically hereditary *jagirdars*, collection in kind and relatively unobtrusive central administrations to the Mughal system of revenue demand in cash, transferable *jagirs* and the increasing financial needs of a powerful, expanding and centralized empire is crucial in this context. It seems that in pre-Mughal India, despite some urban development, the distinction between town and country was far less marked; with rare exceptions, the ruling class extracted their share of the surplus in kind and used it directly for their own consumption and that of their retainers, sometimes making over

[61] Habib, *Agrarian System*, p. 76.
[62] Ibid., p. 12.

their claims on revenue in particular areas to their men for the latter's maintenance; an elaborate machinery of exchange for the distribution of the surplus was not necessary under these circumstances. This is pretty close to the Marxian model of a subsistence-based agrarian society supporting an autocratic power. Only it was not classless. There is nothing to indicate that the class divisions in agrarian society as well as property rights in land originated with Babur's victory at Panipat. Yet, as the 'intermediate *zamindar*' ceases to derive his claims on revenue from political-military jurisdiction and becomes a *malguzar*, ostensibly a revenue official living in the village, he becomes more closely integrated with the structure of rural society. He is now a villager with specified claims on the produce. No doubt these claims have the flavour of superior rights, but they are not based on the fiats of any local petty autocrat. The changes implicit in the structure of economic life discussed in this article are, however, much more far reaching than this. If our thumbnail sketch of the pre-Mughal society is correct, then under the Mughals the Indian economy had passed from a level of loosely integrated units of self-sufficiency to one where there is a vast monetized sector, involving the extensive development of internal commerce. The increased needs of the administration and the system of transferable *jagirs* almost certainly meant a screwing up of the revenue pressure compared to earlier times. Whether this happened through a process of substitution or superposition of claims on the producer is not terribly important. All available evidence seems to indicate that the magnitude of revenue demand deprived the producer of nearly the entire surplus and thus undermined the possibilities inherent in the growth of a relatively complex economic system, itself made possible and partly caused by the emergence of a strong centralized state integrating politically and administratively—and in some ways, economically as well—a land area of continental proportions.

9
Zamindars under the Mughals*

S. Nurul Hasan

The *zamindar* class played a vital role in the political, economic, and cultural life of medieval India. During the Mughal period its importance increased, and its position in society became more complex.[1] The surplus of agricultural production, appropriated from the peasants, was shared among the emperor, his nobles, and the zamindars, and the power exercised by the *zamindars* over the economic life of the country—agricultural production, handicrafts, and trade—was tremendous. In spite of the constant struggle between the imperial government and the *zamindars* for a greater share of the produce, the two became partners in the process of economic exploitation.

Politically, there was a clash of interests between the Mughal government and the *zamindars*. Most of the administrative difficulties which the Mughal emperor had to face were the result of the *zamindars*' activities. At the same time, the administration had to lean heavily on their support. In the cultural sphere, the close links of the *zamindars* with the imperial court contributed in no small measure to the process of cultural synthesis between the distinctive traditions of the various communities and different regions, and between the urban and rural cultures. At the same time, the separatist, localist, and parochial trends received powerful patronage from the *zamindar* class. The Mughal empire

*From R.E. Frykenberg (ed.), *Land Control and Social Structure in India History* (Madison: University of Wisconsin Press, 1969).

[1]The following discussion of the *zamindars* is aimed at focusing the attention of historians on the urgent need for a detailed study of the working of the *zamindari* system during the Mughal period. The opinions expressed are tentative and are based on only a small fraction of the evidence available.

achieved its great power largely because it could secure the collaboration of this class; but the inherent contradictions between a centralized empire and the *zamindars* were too deep to be resolved. These contradictions within the Mughal empire contributed to its downfall even before the Western powers were established in the country.

The word '*zamindar*' gained currency during the Mughal period. It was used to denote the various holders of hereditary interests, ranging from powerful, independent, and autonomous chieftains to petty intermediaries at the village level. Before the Mughals, the chieftains were designated as *rajas, rais, thakurs,* and so on, while the small intermediaries would be termed *chaudhuris, khots, muqaddams,* etc. The Mughal practice of using the same generic term for the holders of widely varying types of landed interests is a reflection of the Mughal desire to reduce the chieftains to the status of intermediaries while compensating them in other ways.

The existence of the various types of landed interests was the result of a long process of evolution spread over several centuries. By the close of the twelfth century, a pyramidal structure had already been established in agrarian relations. Even though there were important regional differences, the nature of land rights in most parts of the country was basically similar. During the sultanate period (1206–1526), significant changes in land rights occurred, but the essential features remained more or less the same. However, the process of change accelerated during the Mughal period.

Zamindars in the Mughal empire may be classified in three broad categories: *(a)* the autonomous chieftains; *(b)* the intermediary *zamindars;* and *(c)* the primary *zamindars.* These categories were by no means exclusive. Within the territory held by the autonomous chieftains were to be found not only vassal semi-autonomous chiefs, but also intermediary as well as primary *zamindars.* While the intermediary *zamindars* exercised jurisdiction over groups of primary *zamindars,* most of the intermediary *zamindars* were also primary *zamindars* in their own right. A chieftain might exercise primary rights over some lands and intermediary rights over others, while simultaneously enjoying 'sovereign' or 'state' powers over his dominions.

It may be noted that the territories held by the *zamindars* were not separate from the *khalisa* or *jagir* lands. The distinction between the *jagir* and the *khalisa* lay only in the distribution of the state's share of the revenue. If the revenue from a particular area were deposited in the imperial treasury, it would be deemed to be *khalisa*; if it were to be assigned to an officer in lieu of salary, it could be considered a *jagir*. Thus, the *khalisa* as well as the *jagir* comprised various types of *zamindaris*. A careful study of the various types reveals that there was hardly a *pargana* in the Mughal empire in which there were no *zamindars*.[2]

The Chieftains

The chieftains were the hereditary autonomous rulers of their territories and enjoyed practically sovereign powers. Since the establishment of the sultanate the Sultans had tried to obtain from these chieftains the recognition of their overlordship and imposed on them the obligation to pay regular tribute and to render military assistance to the sultanate whenever called upon. But there were many cases of resistance or rebellions; and the nature of control exercised by the imperial government depended upon the extent of military pressure which it could bring against the chieftains. On a number of occasions, during the course of struggles against the sultan's authority, the ruling houses of the chieftains were altogether overthrown or their territories substantially reduced. Conversely, taking advantage of the weakness of the imperial authority, the chieftains would on occasion assume independence, or extend their territories. In either case, the rights of the vassals of the chieftains and of the intermediary or primary *zamindars* were not substantially affected. By the time Akbar (1556–1605) came to the throne, such autonomous chieftains held sway over the major portion of the Mughal empire; many who had accepted the overlordship of the Surs had by now become independent.

Akbar and his successors not only continued the policy of the sultans of demanding from the chieftains a recognition of their overlordship, the payment of tribute, and the rendering of military assistance, but also introduced the following new elements in their treatment of the chieftains:

1. Akbar was the first emperor who realized the importance of forging powerful links between the empire and the chieftains by absorbing many of them in the imperial hierarchy and the administrative machinery. This policy was continued by his successors; and it is estimated that during the latter half of Aurangzeb's reign (1658–1707), 81 persons belonging to the ruling houses of the chieftains held *mansabs* of 1000 horsemen and above, representing almost 15 per cent of the

[2]See Irfan Habib, 'The Zamindars in the *Ain*', *Proceedings of the Indian History Congress* (Allahabad, 1958).

total number of *mansabdars* of a 1000 or more horsemen.[3] When a chieftain received a high *mansab* (a military rank regulated by the supposed number of horsemen the holder of the title could bring into the field), he also received a substantial *jagir* for the support of his troops. The revenue from this *jagir* would far exceed that of the chieftain's hereditary dominion; for example, the *jagir* granted to a *mansabdar* of 5000 *zat*, 5000 *sawar*, was expected to yield a yearly revenue of 8.3 lakhs of rupees which was several times the income of many of the principal Rajput rulers.[4] This policy resolved to an appreciable degree the basic contradiction between the chieftains and the imperial power and made it more fruitful for them to seek promotion in the imperial service than to cast off the imperial yoke and attempt to expand their territory in defiance of imperial authority. The imperial service also provided to the retainers and clansmen of the chieftains lucrative employment as well as a share in the plunder while conducting campaigns on behalf of the empire. Apart from bringing monetary advantages, imperial service was a source of power to the chieftains and enabled them to strengthen their position by recruiting and maintaining large armies.

2. The Mughals asserted the principle which later came to be known as that of 'paramountcy'. This meant that a chieftain depended for his position on the goodwill of the emperor rather than on his inherent rights. Only such of the chieftains were designated 'rajas' as were given the title by the emperor. While generally conforming to the law of primogeniture and hereditary succession, the Mughals asserted the right of 'recognizing' a younger son or even a distant relative of a deceased *raja* as his successor. The emperor Jahangir (1605–27) specifically claimed this right when he rejected the nomination of a younger son by Rai Rai Singh of Bikaner and nominated the elder one instead. Similarly, on the death of Raja Man Singh of Amber, the claims of Maha Singh, the son of Man Singh's eldest son, were overruled, and Bhao Singh, a younger son of Man Singh, 'was given the principality of Amber with the lofty title of Mirza Raja'.[5] When Raja Sangram, the chieftain of Kharakpur in Bihar, incurred the displeasure of the emperor

[3]M. Athar Ali, *The Mughal Nobility under Aurangzeb* (Bombay and New York, 1966), p. 13.

[4]This figure was calculated on the basis of the eight-month scale. The *zat* rank was the personal rank of the officer, while the number of his horsemen was indicated by the *sawar* rank.

[5]*Tuzuk-i-Jahangiri* (Aligarh, 1864), p. 130. Also see pp. 106 and 145.

and action was taken against him, he was killed and his territories were taken over in *khalisa*; but after some time they were restored to his son, Raja Rozafzun. During Shahjahan's reign (1627–58), the claim of Jaswant Singh of Marwar was upheld in preference to that of his elder brother on the grounds that he was the son of the favourite wife of the late *raja*, a decision the reverse of that made by Jahangir with regard to Bikaner. The assertion of this right of the emperor to decide who would be the ruler of a principality not only strengthened the control of the central government over the chieftains, but also gave the latter a sense of personal obligation to the emperor. The well-known policy of matrimonial alliances with the houses of the leading chieftains further strengthened the sense of attachment of the chiefs to the emperor. The Mughal insistence that the chiefs should remain in attendance at the court of the emperor or a governor, or should be represented there by one of their close relatives if they themselves held posts elsewhere, helped to consolidate the imperial hold over the chiefs.

3. Although all the sultans had claimed the right to call upon their vassal chiefs to render military assistance to the sultanate whenever required to do so, the Mughals were successful in utilizing systematically the military services of even such chieftains as did not hold *mansabs*. In practically all the major campaigns conducted by the Mughals the contingents of the vassal chiefs played a prominent part. For example, during the reign of Akbar a number of the leading chiefs of south Bihar served under Raja Man Singh in the Orissa campaign of 1592. At about the same time in Gujarat, many vassal chiefs were required to provide contingents of *sawars* or horsemen, at the call of the governor. The troops supplied by the chieftains contributed appreciably to the military might of the Mughal empire. How greatly valued was this military obligation of the chiefs may be judged from Jahangir's statement describing the importance of Bengal in terms of the obligations of its chiefs to supply 50,000 troops rather than in terms of the enormous revenue it provided.[6]

4. The Mughal emperors appear to have pursued the policy of entering into direct relationship with the vassals of some of the more important chieftains, thus reducing the power of these chieftains and creating a new class of allies. The most obvious example of this policy may be seen in the case of Garha Katanga where Akbar established direct relations with the vassals of the Garha chief. Sometimes the vassals of

[6]Ibid., p. 7.

the ruling chiefs were directly offered imperial *mansabs* as in the case of Marwar after Jaswant Singh's death.

5. Of great importance was the Mughal attempt to treat the hereditary dominions of the autonomous chiefs as *watan jagirs*. This meant that theoretically the chiefs were supposed to have the status of *jagirdars*, and thus were subject to the imperial revenue regulations, but exercised *jagirdari* rights in hereditary succession over their territories, which were consequently immune from transfer. Even though this theory could be applied mainly to the chiefs who were enrolled as *mansabdars*, the imperial government made attempts to change the character of the tribute payable by the chiefs into land revenue assessed on the basis of the actual production. It is difficult to estimate the extent to which the Mughals succeeded in this effort as we find that a very large number of chiefs continued to pay tribute on an irregular basis, which was known as *peshkash*.[7] However, even in fixing the amount of the *peshkash*, the Mughal administrators tried to obtain data regarding the area under cultivation, the crop pattern, and the revenue realized by the chiefs from their vassals or subordinate *zamindars*. The information in the *Ain-i-Akbari* regarding the states of the chieftains and the account of the revenue settlement of Gujarat conducted by Todar Mal in the sixteenth century provide the most obvious evidence of this effort. In spite of the fact that this policy could be enforced only with partial success, it increased the de jure as well as the de facto control of the empire over the chiefs. It also increased the imperial pressure on their economic resources and compelled many of them to seek imperial service as *mansabdars*. Administratively it tended to bring the land-revenue system of the chiefs in line with the Mughal pattern.

6. The Mughal emperors succeeded to a greater extent than their predecessors in compelling the autonomous chiefs to conform to imperial regulations, especially in regard to the maintenance of law and order and the freedom of transit. Not only were the emperors able to make the chiefs take vigorous action against rebels, criminals, and fugitives who happened to enter their territory, but they also claimed the right to dispense justice to those who appealed to the imperial government against their chiefs. For example, when Raj Suraj Singh of Bikaner arrested the retainers of his brother Dalpat, Jahangir ordered

[7]Detailed information on the assessment of *peshkash* from the *zamindar* of Trichnopoly from the years AH 1104–17 (1692–1706) may be seen in the Central Records Office, Hyderabad, Reg. no. 83 of Aurangzeb's reign.

that they be released.[8] Several *farmans* are in existence directing the chieftains not to harass traders passing through their territory or to levy taxes on them. Even though several instances are recorded of chiefs disobeying the imperial orders and levying unauthorized taxes on transit goods, there is no reason to doubt that such orders were generally respected.

The existence of a large number of independent principalities in the country and its political fragmentation could hardly have contributed to its progress. Internecine warfare, a logical corollary of such fragmentation, could not have been conducive to material progress. It is difficult to accept François Bernier's statement that the peasantry was better off under the autonomous rajas than in the rest of the empire,[9] not only because the French doctor's prejudice in favour of feudal rights apparently clouded his judgement, but also because the available original records indicate that the rate of assessment of land and other taxes paid by the peasants in the territories of the chiefs were no lower than those in the contiguous areas outside the chiefs' dominions.[10] Furthermore, if there had been no centralized empire subjecting the chiefs to the payment of tribute, which in the last resort was passed on to the peasants, some other powerful chieftain would have established his overlordship and extracted tribute of a similar type and magnitude.

A centralized empire, by establishing comparatively greater peace and security, by enabling trade and commerce to expand, and by increasing and diversifying the purchasing power of the consuming classes which led to the development of industries, brought about conditions favourable to the growth of a money economy. The emergence of a money economy began to affect agricultural production to a considerable extent, especially because revenue was being realized more and more in cash. It also led to the expansion of cash crops and the extension of the culivated area, partly as a result of the demand for greater

[8]*Farman* no. 29, dated 9 October 1614, in the *Descriptive List of Farmans, Manshurs and Nishans* (Bikaner, 1962), published by the Government of Rajasthan Directorate of Archives.

[9]François Bernier, *Travels in the Mughal Empire, 1656–1667*, trans. V.A. Smith (London, 1916), p. 205.

[10]Comparing the *arsattas* (monthly accounts of receipts and disbursements) of the *parganas* of Amber and Sawal Jaipur with those of the *parganas* of Chatsu and Hindaun reveals a general similarity in the rates of assessment (Rajasthan State Archives).

revenue.[11] To the extent that the Mughal empire succeeded in establishing its authority over the numerous chieftains and the considerable measure of success that it achieved in unifying the country politically and administratively, it played a progressive role in the development of Indian society.

There is no doubt that the Mughals were more successful than any of their predecessors in bringing the numerous chieftains within the pale of their empire. As a result of intensive military campaigning they compelled the chieftains in practically the whole country to accept their suzerainty. In accordance with the tenets of their policy enumerated above, they succeeded in securing loyalty and willing co-operation from the overwhelming majority of the chieftains and conformity with the broad aspects of their administrative policy. To this extent they were able to place curbs on the powers of the chiefs.

However, the policy of firmness coupled with friendship was able to resolve the contradiction between the chieftains and the imperial government only to a limited extent. Not all chiefs could have been granted high *mansabs* and lucrative *jagirs*. Furthermore, many of the nobles who were not *zamindars* envied the security enjoyed by the chiefs in imperial service and brought pressure on the emperor to restrict the grants of *mansabs* and *jagirs* to this class. As the pressure on *jagirs* increased, the emperor was no longer in a position to satisfy the aspirations of the chieftains. In such a situation many of the chiefs enjoying high positions in imperial service attempted to convert the *jagirs* assigned to them outside their ancestral territories into their hereditary dominions, as in the case of Sir Singh-deo Bundela during the reign of Jahangir and Jai Singh Sawai of Amber during the reign of Muhammad Shah. The imperial policy of demanding the payment of land revenue based on cultivated area could only have reduced the share of the chiefs. Rebellions were therefore inevitable. The chiefs hardly ever missed the opportunity of taking advantage of the difficulties facing the empire. For example, the chieftains of Orissa and Bengal supported Shahjahan when he rebelled against his father, but they quickly deserted the rebel prince when he was defeated by the imperial forces. On the other hand, whenever, because of various difficulties, the imperial government was unable to maintain its military pressure

[11]For an excellent discussion of the impact of money economy on agricultural production and for the nature of the agrarian relations existing in the Mughal empire, see Irfan Habib, *Agrarian System of Mughal India* (Bombay, 1963).

on the *zamindars,* the revolts became more frequent. Such was the case in the seventeenth century during the reign of Aurangzeb when the chieftains of Maharashtra, Bundelkhand, Mewat, and Rajputana, all took up arms against the Mughal empire and in their struggle drew upon the support of the lower classes of the *zamindars,* and also sometimes the peasants, especially when they belonged to the same clan or caste. The widespread dissatisfaction of the chiefs with the imperial government seriously weakened the military power of the Mughal empire. The empire depended too much on the support of the chiefs to have been successful in suppressing their power completely.

The frequent revolts of the chieftains, leading to long-drawn-out military campaigns and the inability of the imperial government to prevent the chiefs from expanding their dominions, placed a serious drain on the economy, adversely affected agricultural production in many cases, and weakened administrative unity. Consequently, by the close of the seventeenth century, the economic and administrative advantages of a unified empire had begun to disappear.

THE INTERMEDIARY *ZAMINDARS*

The category comprised the various types of *zamindars* who collected the revenue from the primary *zamindars* and paid it to the imperial treasury, or to the *jagirdars,* or to the chieftains—or in certain cases kept it themselves. Such intermediaries not only formed the backbone of land-revenue administration, but were also responsible for the maintenance of law and order. In return for their services they enjoyed various types of perquisites, such as commissions, deductions, revenue-free lands (*nankar* or *banth*), cesses, etc. Usually their share of the revenue ranged between 2.5 and 10 per cent. Most of the *zamindars* possessed hereditary rights, though in a few cases they held their position on short-term contracts.[12] Among the intermediaries may be included *chaudhuris, deshmukhs, desais, deshpandes,* certain types of *muqaddams, qanungos* and *ijaradars,* and the class of *zamindars* who contracted with the state to realize the revenue of a given territory and who began to be known during the second half of the seventeenth century by the generic designation of *talukdars.* Practically the entire country was under the jurisdiction of one or the other type of intermediary *zamindars.* The statement in the *Ain-i-Akbari* regarding the caste

[12]For a discussion of the various types of land rights, see B.R. Grover, 'Nature of Land Rights in Mughal India', *Indian Economic and Social History Review*, I, 1–23.

of *zamindars* in *parganas* other than those under the chieftains seems to refer to this class.[13] The fact that in the majority of the *parganas* the *zamindars* belonged to a single caste and also that persons of the same caste were the *zamindars* of many contiguous *parganas* suggests that certain families or clans held *zamindari* rights over large tracts.

While the rights of the intermediary *zamindars* were hereditary, the state reserved to itself the authority to interfere with succession and even to partition the jurisdiction among brothers or relations. In the case of imperial displeasure some of these intermediaries could be dismissed or transferred. An order of Akbar mentions the dismissal of a *chaudhuri* in Ilahabad on the grounds that he had been harassing the pilgrims going to the Triveni for holy baths.[14] A *nishan* (order) of Murad Bakhsh conferred the *desmukhi* of a *pargana* in *suba* Telingana on one Rama Reddy, rejecting the claim of half the deshmukhi of the *pargana* put forward by the adopted son of his elder deceased brother.[15] Aurangzeb issued an order that there could not be more than two *chaudhuris* in a *pargana*; if there were, they were to be dismissed.[16] In some cases the Mughal emperors conferred *zamindari* rights on persons appointed to maintain law and order or to facilitate the assessment and collection of land revenue.[17] Akbar's *farman* to Gopaldas conferring on him the rights of *chaudhuri* and *kanungo* in *sarkar* Tirhut formed the basis of the subsequent rise of the Darbhanga *raj*.[18] To satisfy the desire of the high *mansabdars* and nobles not belonging to the *zamindar*

[13] 'Account of the Twelve Subas', in H.S. Jarrett (trans.), Abul-Fazl-i'Allami's *Ain-i-Akbari* (2nd edn, Calcutta, 1949). II.

[14] Copies of a number of *farmans* issued in this connection by Akbar and Jahangir were made available to the writer by Dr. M.A. Ansari of Allahabad University.

[15] Andhra Pradesh State Archives, Hyderabad, Shahjahani Register, Vol. 40, no. 608, *nishan* dated 15 Ramazan, twenty-third regnal year of Shahjahan. The *suba* was a division of the empire, like a province.

[16] Habib, *Agrarian System*, p. 292.

[17] A *farman* of Shahjahan issued during the fifth regnal year promised *zamindari* rights to anyone who could bring the turbulent *zamindars* of the *parganas* of Kant and Gola under control. He was then to found a town named after the emperor in that region. A photostat of the *farman* is in the possession of the writer. See also Grover, 'Nature of Land Rights', p. 12.

[18] Qeyam Uddin Ahmed, 'Origin and Growth of Darbhanga Raj (1574–1666), Based on Some Contemporary and Unpublished Documents', *Proceedings of the Indian Historical Records Commission*, XXXVI, pp. 88–98. The *sarkar* was a government administrative district.

class to acquire hereditary territorial rights, the Mughal emperors instituted the practice of conferring *watan* and *altamgha jagirs*. In such cases the persons concerned were given permanent *jagirdari* rights. Usually the territories granted in such *jagirs* were small, comprising a single village or a small number of villages, though in some cases they were larger. The holders of these jagirs tried to acquire proprietary rights and in due course were often called upon to pay land revenue. For instance, the *watan jagirs* granted by Jahangir to Anirai Singh Dalan developed into large and powerful *zamindaris* of Anupshahr in Bulandshahr District. A similar case was that of the *watan jagir* granted during the reign of Jahangir to Miran Sadr Jahan at Pihani in Shahjahanpur District.

Most of the intermediaries were supposed to prepare the details of revenue assessment for the perusal of the state, help in the realization of the land revenue, encourage extension of cultivation, assist the imperial officers in the maintenance of law and order, and supply a fixed number of contingents. However, in actual practice, they were constantly struggling to enhance their rights and to appropriate to themselves a greater share of the revenue if not the whole of it. The extant records are full of references to the *zamindaran-i-zor-talab*, that is those who paid revenue only when it was demanded forcibly. Similarly, the intermediaries who contracted to collect revenue, either as *ijaradars* or as *talukdars* tried to avoid supplying detailed figures of assessment and only paid the stipulated amount. The Mughal custom of frequent transfers of *jagirs* encouraged the practice of revenue farming, or the letting of contracts to someone else to collect the revenue.

On the one hand, these intermediaries strove to consolidate their rights at the expense of the state; thus, for example, they often appropriated to themselves the state's right to dispose of the uncultivated wastelands. On the other hand, they intensified the exploitation of the rural population and attempted to depress the position of the primary *zamindars* under their jurisdiction. Since they had the responsibility to pay the land revenue, whether the primary *zamindars* paid it or not, they were led on occasion to collect the revenue directly from the peasants, in which case they were supposed to leave the primary *zamindars* the customary 'proprietary' share (*malikana*). But the temptation in such a situation to step into the place of the primary *zamindars* and become proprietors themselves must have been overwhelming.[19]

[19]For example, in 1703, Raja Ibadullah Kahn of Muhammadi contracted for

At they same time, they sought to build up hereditary territorial rights and, whenever the occasion arose, tried to become chieftains. As the Mughal empire became weak and the crisis of the *jagirdari* system was intensified, these intermediaries enhanced their power and frequently rose in rebellion along with the other intermediary *zamindars* of their own clan or joined hands with some of the chieftains who were in revolt against the imperial authority. Apart from the political and administrative disturbances which resulted from the tussle between such *zamindars* and the state, agricultural production and the position of the peasantry also suffered.

While the imperial authorities strove to subjugate the recalcitrant *zamindars* and attempted to force them to conform to the imperial land-revenue regulations, they could not afford to suppress this class as a whole. Under strong administrators the intermediaries generally performed their duties in accordance with imperial regulations and exercised their rights within specified limits. But under weak administrators the situation frequently got out of hand. The widespread revolt of these *zamindars* deprived the imperial officers of their income and consequently reduced their military strength. In turn, the officers started demanding transfers from the turbulent areas and even began to claim cash salaries instead of *jagirs*.[20]

The Primary *Zamindars*

The primary *zamindars* were for all practical purposes the holders of proprietary rights over agricultural as well as habitational lands. In this class may be included not only the peasant-proprietors who carried on cultivation themselves, or with the help of hired labour, but also the proprietors of one village or several villages. All agricultural lands in the empire belonged to one or the other type of the primary *zamindars*. The rights held by the primary *zamindars* were hereditary and alienable. Numerous sale deeds of such *zamindaris* dating back to the sixteenth

---

the whole of the *parganas* of Barwar-Anjana and Bhurwara in *sarkar* Khairabad, *suba* Awadh, and in course of time acquired proprietary rights over the whole estate.

[20]Numerous cases are cited in a number of contemporary documents included in the Durr-ul-Ulum, a collection of papers arranged by Sahib Rai Surdaj in 1688–9, now in the Bodleian Library, Oxford.

century are still available.[21] The Mughal state considered it its duty to protect the rights of these *zamindars* and encouraged the registration of transfer deeds at the court of the *qazi* so that a proper record of claims could be maintained.

In addition to those who had been enjoying these rights for generations or had acquired them by purchase, the Mughals conferred such *zamindari* rights on a large number of persons. In pursuance of their policy of extending the cultivated area, the emperors freely bestowed *zamindari* rights to those who would bring forest and waste under cultivation. It is also significant that the majority of the *madad maash* grants (revenue-free grants given for charitable purposes) related to uncultivated land. The *madad maash* grants required confirmation at the accession of each monarch, but the hereditary succession was not usually interfered with. In due course the *madad maash* grant also acquired the character of *zamindari*, as appears from the sale deeds of *madad maash* lands in the eighteenth century.

The *zamindars*, other than the peasant-proprietors, generally gave their lands in hereditary lease to their tenants, who enjoyed security of tenure in terms of the *patta* granted to them, on the condition that they paid their land revenue regularly. Even in cases of non-payment the tenant was not usually deprived of his landholding rights, but the arrears were realized by other means. Considering the fact that there was not much pressure on land, the rights of the landholding tenants were generally respected. At the same time, in view of the shortage of cultivators, the *zamindars* enjoyed the right to restrain the tenants from leaving their lands and to compel them to cultivate all arable land held by them.[22] From the evidence it seems that where the primary *zamindars* did not pay the land revenue, it was collected directly from the peasants, leaving about 10 per cent as the proprietary share (*malikana*) of the *zamindars*.[23] It may be inferred that this percentage represents the normal share of the *zamindars*. In addition to their share in land revenue, the *zamindars* were also entitled to a large variety of cesses, though a considerable portion of the income from such cesses had to be surrendered by the *zamindars* along with the land revenue.

[21]Numerous transfer deeds are preserved at the Central Records Office, Allahabad.

[22]See N.A. Siddiqi, 'Dasturul Amal-i-Bekas', *Proceedings of the Indian History Congress* (Aligarh, 1960).

[23]Grover 'Nature of Land Rights', p. 15.

The *zamindars* were deemed to be the *malguzars* or those on whom land revenue was assessed by the state. They were also expected to collect the revenue from the peasants and to deposit the share of the state with the higher authorities. It was their duty to assist the administration in the maintenance of law and order and in many cases to supply troops under the orders of their superiors.

Sandwiched as most of these *zamindars* were between the superior *zamindars* and the state on the one hand and the peasantry on the other, they were constantly struggling to improve their position and thus frequently came into conflict with both sides. Unless these *zamindars* were able to withstand pressure from above, they passed on the burden of revenue demands to the cultivators and so contributed to the intensification of the economic exploitation of the latter. On such occasions, they played an economically retrogressive role. But on many occasions they led the revolts of the peasantry against the growing exactions of the state, often utilizing the caste and clan appeal to rally support. Where revolts were not possible, many of these *zamindars* refused to pay the revenue until force was employed. As has been mentioned earlier, the intermediary *zamindars* often tried to depress the status of the primary *zamindars*, and where the attempt was successful a fresh category of subproprietary rights emerged. Sometimes the intermediary *zamindars* created a class of subproprietors, such as the *birtias*, in order to strengthen their position in the countryside.

Thus, there emerged not only a variety of land rights but also a kind of a pyramidal structure in agrarian relations wherein rights of various kinds were superimposed upon each other. The burden of the shares of the different categories of *zamindars* and also of the imperial revenue demand ultimately fell on the cultivator and placed such a strain on the agrarian economy that much progress was hardly possible. The imperial government tried its best to ensure that the peasant was not called upon to pay more than 50 per cent of the produce. But as imperial authority declined and as the pressure on *jagirs* increased, the agricultural economy had to face a crisis which began to deepen in the eighteenth century.

Politically and administratively, the *zamindar* class in general rendered loyal co-operation and assistance to the Mughal empire. Yet the conflict of interests between the *zamindars* and the state, and between the different classes of *zamindars*, could not be eliminated. The conflicts led to frequent clashes, disturbed law and order, and seriously weakened the administrative and military power of the state. The numerous measures adopted by the Mughal government to resolve these contradictions worked well, but only for a time. By the middle of the seventeenth century, strains began to appear, and after the death of Aurangzeb in 1707 the central government had become too weak to maintain the equilibrium between conflicting interests. In any case, the dependence of the Mughal empire on the various classes of the *zamindars* for its revenue resources as well as administration was far too deep for the conflict of interest between the empire and *zamindars* to be resolved. Only a class which was not dependent on the *zamindars* could have attempted to change the pattern of agrarian relations. Such a class had not emerged by the middle of the eighteenth century.

PART 3

Politics, Trade and Transformation

10
The Condition of the People in Aurangzīb's Reign*

Jadunath Sarkar

THE RAPID DECLINE OF THE MUGHAL EMPIRE

To all outer observers the Mughal empire seemed to have attained to its highest splendour and power when Aurangzib ascended the throne of Delhi. His tried ability and known character promised to the country undiminished prosperity if only he was spared to rule long enough over it; and he ruled over it for 50 years. The native genius of Akbar, the genial moderation of Jahangir, the sagacity, energy and refined taste of Shah Jahan, had left the Mughal empire without a rival throughout northern India and much of the Deccan too, and given peace, prosperity and culture to millions. 'The wealth of India' had become proverbial in far-off countries, and the magnificence of the Court of the Great Mughal had 'dazzled even eyes which were accustomed to the pomp of Versailles'. And when a trained administrator and experienced general, who was also a puritan in the simplicity and purity of his private life, succeeded to the guidance of this rich heritage in the fullness of his physical and mental powers, all people hoped that he would carry the empire to unimaginable heights of glory. And yet the result of Aurangzib's long and strenuous reign was utter dissolution and misery. The causes of this strange phenomenon it is the duty of the historian to investigate.

INTERNAL PEACE THE ROOT CAUSE OF INDIA'S PROSPERITY

In a warm, moist and fertile country like India—where the lavish bounty of nature speedily repairs the ravages of hostile man and beast, of

*From Jadunath Sarkar, *History of Aurangzib*, vol. 5 (Calcutta, 1924).

inclement sun and rain—order is the root of national life, in an even greater degree than in other lands. Given peace without and the spirit of progress within, the Indian people can advance in wealth, strength and civilization with a rapidity rivalled only by the marvellous growth of their vegetation after the monsoon showers.

A century of strong and wise government under Akbar and his son and grandson had given to the richer and more populous half of India such peace and impulse to improvement. A hundred victories since the second Panipat had taught the Indian world to believe that Mughal arms were invincible and Mughal territory inviolable. Shivaji broke this spell. And his destructive work was carried to undreamt-of lengths by his successors in the second half of Aurangzib's reign. Mughal peace—the sole justification of the Mughal empire—no longer existed in India at Aurangzib's death.

In a predominantly agricultural country like India, the tillers of the soil are the only source of national wealth. They produce the food and raw materials of clothing for the entire population. Directly or indirectly, the land alone adds to the 'annual national stock'. Even the craftsmen depend on the peasants and on the men enriched with the land revenue, for the sale of their goods, and if the latter have not enough foodstuff to spare, they cannot buy any handicraft. Hence, the ruin of the peasant means in India the ruin of the non-agricultural classes too. *Pauvres paysans, pauvre royaume,* is even truer of India than of France. Public peace and security of property are necessary not only for the peasant and the artisan, but also for the trader, who has to carry his goods over wide distances and give long credits before he can find a profitable market. Political unrest and insecure roads prevent the quick and cheap transport of grain from a district of bumper crops to one where the harvest has failed, and this circumstance makes famine relief slow and difficult.

Wealth, in the last resort, can accumulate only from savings out of the peasant's production. Whatever lowers the peasant's productive power or destroys his spirit of thrift by creating insecurity about his property, thereby prevents the growth of national capital and impairs the economic staying power of the country. Such are the universal and lasting effects of disorder and public insecurity in India. And the failure of Aurangzib affords the most striking illustration of this truth.

Economic Drain of Aurangzib's Ceaseless Warfare

The economic drain caused by Aurangzib's quarter century of warfare in the Deccan was appalling in its character and most far-reaching and durable in its effects. The operations of the imperial armies, especially their numerous sieges, led to a total destruction of forests and grass. The huge Mughal forces, totalling 170,000 troops according to the official records, with perhaps ten times that number of non-combatants, soon ate up everything green wherever they moved. In addition, the Maratha raiders destroyed whatever they could not carry off—feeding their horses on the standing crops, and burning the houses and property too heavy to be removed. At the siege of Satara, the Marathas had prepared for defence by burning the grass for 20 miles round the fort; while the Mughals in their turn, in building a raised battery opposite the fort tower 'had left not a single tree standing within a range of 60 or 80 miles from the place'.[1] The mischief was multiplied by the immense number of sieges in which the Mughals engaged in that land of the mountain and the flood. Hence, it is no wonder that when at last in 1705 Aurangzib retired after his last campaign, the country presented a scene of utter desolation. 'He left behind him the fields of these provinces devoid of trees and bare of crops, their places being taken by the bones of men of beasts.'[2]

This total and extensive deforestation had a most injurious effect on agriculture. At the same time, herds of cattle became extinct through robbery and lack of fodder. The pastoral tribes were ruined, and meat and milk supply ceased over much of Maharashtra.

The financial exhaustion of the empire in these endless wars left government and private owners alike too poor to repair buildings and roads worn out by the lapse of time. Indeed, in Aurangzib's last years, we read of urgent appeals from his officers for funds to make the most necessary repairs in important fortifications, which the emperor had to reject owing to lack of money! Civil buildings, water-works, *sarais* and roads could not expect any better treatment in such a state of things.

The labouring population suffered not only from violent capture, forced labour, and starvation, but also from epidemics which were very frequent during these campaigns. Even in the imperial camp, where

[1]Saqi Mustaid Khan, *Ma'asir-i Alamgiri*, Calcutta, 1871, English tr. by Jadunath Sarkar, Calcutta, 1947, p. 414.

[2]Niccolo Manucci, *Storia do Mogor*, tr. William Irvine, 4 vols, London, 1907–8, iv, p. 252.

greater comfort, security and civilization might have been expected, the annual wastage of the Deccan wars was one lakh of men, and three lakhs of horses, oxen, camels and elephants.[3] At the siege of Golkonda (1687)

> a famine broke out. In Haidarabad city the houses river and plain were filled with the dead. The same was the condition of the imperial camp . . . Kos after kos the eye fell only on mounds of corpses. The incessant rain melted away the flesh and skin . . . After some months when the rains ceased, the white ridges of bones looked from a distance like hills of snow.[4]

The same desolation overtook tracts which had hitherto enjoyed peace and prosperity. The acute observer Bhimsen writes about the eastern Karnatak: 'During the rule of the Bijapur Golkonda and Telinga [dynasties] the country was extensively cultivated. But now many places have been turned into wildernesses on account of the passage of the imperial armies, which has inflicted hardship and oppression on the people.'[5] The depopulation and impoverishment of the Madras coast in the closing decade of the seventeenth century is repeatedly noticed in the Madras Factory Diary and M. Martin's memoirs.

Pestilence and Natural Calamities

In 1688, Bijapur was visited by a desolating epidemic of bubonic plague, which is estimated to have carried off a 100,000 lives in three months.[6] So, too, we read of a plague in Prince Azam's camp in August 1694.[7] The English factors at Surat report similar devastating epidemics throughout western India in 1694 and 1696 (95,000 men perished).[8] To take one example only the drought and plague of 1702–4 killed two millions of men.[9] Thus, war and its constant attendant pestilence broke

[3]Ibid., iv, p. 96.

[4]*Ma'asir-i Alamgiri*, p. 292.

[5]Bhimsen, *Nuskha-i-Dilkusha*, British Museum, Ms. Or. 23; English tr. (incomplete) by V.G. Khobrekar, Bombay, 1972, f. ii, 114a also p. 136b about Berar.

[6]*Ma'asir-i Alamgiri*, p. 318.

[7]*Akhbarat-i-Darbar-i Mu'alla*, newsletters from the Imperial Court, Rajasthan State Archives, Bikaner, and Royal Asiatic Society Library, London, transcripts Sitamau, Malwa, and Sarkar Collection, National Library, Calcutta.

[8]Surat to Bom. 6 Oct. 1694; *Madras Diary*, 31 Dec. 1696: Karwar to Bom. 18 Nov.–28 Dec. 1696.

[9]*Storia*, iv. p. 96.

the placid repose of rural life in the Deccan and disturbed the old distribution of economic resources and activities.

The waste of army horses was terrible. In the newsletters, we constantly read of commanding officers begging for the grant of horses, as their troopers had lost their animals in the campaigns. Bhimsen describes how Nusrat Jang's cavalry had mostly to march on foot after a long chase of the Marathas.[10] This loss had to be made good by the government every year purchasing remounts in Afghanistan through its *subahdar*, and in Surat from Persian and Arab importers, as well as by sending an agent of its 'Purchase Officer' stationed at Surat to Persia for buying horses there and sending them to India.[11]

In addition to disease, great natural calamities like flood, drought and excessive and unseasonable rainfall were frequent in the Deccan at the beginning of the eighteenth century, which aggravated the sufferings of invaders and natives alike and still further reduced the population. The state of war, spread over nearly a generation of time, had left no savings, no power of resistance in the common people; everything they produced or had stored up was swept away by the hordes on both sides, so that when famine or drought came, the peasants and landless labourers perished helplessly like flies. Scarcity was chronic in the imperial camp and often deepened into famine. The former remarkable cheapness of grain in many parts of Khandesh, Berar and Konkan now became a forgotten myth; and even in the best years, in no place south of the Narmada did grain sell cheaper than six seers a rupee,[12] while in Multan and Bengal a bumper crop still brought prices down to two or even eight maunds a rupee. The Mughal army at last found life intolerable.

Injury to Trade and Industry by War, Disorder, and Official Exactions

There being no peace or safety for tillage, the starving and exasperated peasantry took to highway robbery as the only means of living. In many villages of the Deccan they gathered arms and horses and used to join the Marathas in their raids, and also sheltered enemy Maratha families in their houses while the menfolk were out roving. Raiding bands were

[10] *Nuskha-i Dilkusha*, ii, 135b.
[11] *Akhbarat.*
[12] *Nuskha-i Dilkusha*, ii, 146a.

also locally formed, which gave employment to many and chances of glory and wealth to the more spirited among the villagers.

Trade almost ceased in the Deccan during this unhappy quarter century. Caravans could travel south of the Narmada only under strong escort; hence they had to wait in the fortified towns, sometimes for four or five months, before they could get an opportunity of advancing further towards their destination in safety. We even read of the royal mail and baskets of fruits for the emperor's table being held up for five months at the Narmada by Maratha disturbances in the roads beyond it. A time came when even the emperor's letters could be carried to distant places only by spies who travelled in disguise—no escort being available for the regular couriers. Government stores and the personal effects of the nobles were all that could be transported under such conditions; the movement of tradesmen's goods was impossible.

Even where war was not raging (as in Bengal), the weakening of the central government emboldened provincial governors to defy imperial prohibitions, and to make money by forcing goods from traders at absurdly low prices and then selling them in the public marts, and also by exacting forbidden *abwabs* from craftsmen and merchants.[13]

In the absence of security at home and the impossibility of making purchases at distances, arts and crafts ceased to be practised except in the walled cities. Village industries and industrial classes together died out. The Madras coast, for instance, with its teeming weaving population, was so unsettled by the Mughal–Maratha struggle for the Karnatak (1690–8) that the English found it difficult to get enough clothes for loading their Europe-going ships.[14] As early as 1688, François Martin had foreseen the war between the Mughals and the Marathas and the consequent ruin of the textile industry of the Karnatak.[15] Thus ensued a great economic impoverishment of India—not only a decrease of the 'national stock', but also a rapid lowering of mechanical skill and standard of civilization, a disappearance of art and culture over wide tracts of the country.

[13]Jadunath Sarkar, *Mughal Administration*, reprint, Bombay, 1972, ch. 5.

[14]Ibid.

[15]P. Kaeppelin, *La Compagnie des Indes Orientales et François Martin: étude sur l'histoire du commerce et des établissements français dans l'Inde sous Louis XIV, 1664–1719*, reprint, New York, 1967, pp. 259, 293.

OTHER OPPRESSORS OF THE CULTIVATORS

In southern India, with many parts of it harried by more than a century of warfare, the peasantry had many enemies to dread besides the regular fighters on both sides. The Mughal soldiers on their march often trod down the crops, and though the emperor had a special body of officers for compensating the peasants for this loss (*paimali-i-zarait*), his financial difficulties led to the neglect of this humane rule. The worst oppressors of the peasants, however, were the tail of the army—the vast nondescript horde of servants, day labourers, *darvishes* and other vagrants who followed Aurangzib's 'moving city of tents' in the hope of picking up crumbs where such a crowd had gathered. Particularly the Baluchi camel-owners who hired out their animals to the army, and unattached Afghans searching for employment, plundered and beat the country people most mercilessly. The *banjaras* or wandering grain dealer tribe, who moved in bodies, sometimes of 5000 men, each with his couple of bullock loaded with grain, were so strong in their strength of numbers and contempt of the petty officers of government, that they sometimes looted the people on the wayside and fed their cattle on the crops in the fields, with impunity. Even the royal messengers (called *mewrahs* in Gujarat) who carried government letters, reports of spies, and baskets of fruits for presentation to the emperor, used to rob the people of the villages they passed by, sometimes under the pretext of making good the losses in the fruits they carried.[16] The emperor's repeated orders against this kind of iniquity were of no avail.[17]

In the trail of the Maratha soldiers appeared the *Berads* and even the *Pindaris*—who were brigands pure and simple, without even the pretence of belonging to any army or carrying out the orders of any government.

Then, there were the land-stewards of rival *jagirdars*—the incoming and the outgoing—of the same village. Under the plea of the never-to-be satisfied arrears of revenue, the late *jagirdar's* collector tried to squeeze everything out of the peasantry before he left, and even continued to stay in the village for some months after the arrival of his successor. And the newcomer, in order not to starve himself, passed the half-dead peasants through his fiscal grinding-mill.

[16]Sarkar, *Mughal Administration*, Ch. 5.

[17]Ali Mohammed Khan, *Mirat-i-Ahmadi*, ed. Nawab Ali, 2 vols and Supplement, Baroda, 1927–8 and 1930, p. 304.

Bankruptcy of Mughal Government

The English conquest of India was of a pulsatory character, it was achieved not by an uninterrupted succession of advances, but each aggressive governor-general was followed by a pacific, economical non-interventionist. A Warren Hastings filled the financial void created by the wars of Clive and Vansittart, and laid the basis for the military expansion of a Wellesley, while the bankruptcy caused by Wellesley's frenzy of conquest was repaired by the recuperation of a sober, plodding Barlow or Minto. The pacific Bentinck undid the ravages in the treasury made by the bellicose Marquis of Hastings and Earl of Amherst.

Not so Aurangzib. Ever since 1679, when he embarked on the spoliation of the kingdom of Marwar, his reign was one long warfare. He did not realize the necessity of intervals of peace and retrenchment, which would give breathing time to his subjects, recoup the losses of war, and lay by a reserve for future wars. He soon ran through his current revenue and the new tax (*jaziya*) imposed on the Hindus in 1679 and vigorously enforced by specially selected 'pious' collectors.[18] Then he ordered the accumulated treasures of his ancestors, from Akbar downwards, to be taken out of the vaults of Agra and Delhi forts and sent to him in the Deccan.[19]

Thus, the last reserve of the empire was exhausted, and public bankruptcy became inevitable. The salaries of the soldiers and civil officers alike fell into arrears for three years. The men starving from lack of pay and the exhaustion of their credit with the local grocers, sometimes created scenes in the emperor's court, sometimes abused and hustled their general's business manager, some, driven to desperation, beat to death the paymaster of their contingent.

The imperial government made reckless promises of money grant and high command to every enemy captain who was induced to desert and every enemy *qiladar* who was persuaded to surrender his fort. It was not humanly possible to keep all of these promises. The Mughal army, too, was immensely expanded in order to cope with the growing strength of the Marathas and their allies. The result was that the entire land in the empire proved insufficient for the total amount of *jagir* needed to satisfy the dues of all the officers included in the swollen army-list. As the imperial *diwan*, Inayatullah Khan, on being urged by

[18]Muhammad Hashim Khafi Khan, *Muntakhab-ul-Lubab*, eds. K.D. Ahmad and Wolseley Haig, 2 vols, Calcutta, 1869–74, ii, pp. 278, 378.

[19]Ibid., p. 411; *Storia*, p. 255.

Aurangzib to grant *jagirs* to every one and leave no claim unsatisfied, remarked in despair, 'The contingents of the officers who are daily passed in review before Your Majesty are unlimited in number, while the land available for granting as *jagir* is limited [in area]. How can a limited figure be made to equal an unlimited one?'[20]

Even when the grants of land in lieu of salary were drawn up by the Pay Office, they remained for years as mere orders on paper, the actual delivery of the villages to the grantees being impossible. At last the emperor used to cry out in bitterness of spirit to his paymasters. 'How often have I told you that I do not need any retainers? Why do you not dismiss them? You do not realise the badness of your action, but refuse to listen to your master's words!'[21] The interval between the order and the actual possession of the *jagir*, it was sarcastically said, was long enough to turn a boy into a greybeard.[22]

How impossible of realization were the promises of bribes made by the government to enemy captains and ministers and how ruinous was the price at which forts were bought by Aurangzib is strikingly illustrated by the case of Mutabar Ḵhan, the wise and able governor of Kalian. He had secured the capture of some forts in the Nasik and Thana districts by spending Rs 120,000 out of his own pocket in bribes to their commandants and his own army expenses; but the emperor in return granted him only Rs 30,000 or a quarter of his outlay, and even this small sum remained unpaid for years afterwards. If a minor Maratha hill-fort cost on an average Rs 45,000 in cash to take it peacefully, the emperor might well despair of taking all of them at this rate. And yet he obstinately went on capturing fort after fort by heavy bribery or by regular sieges which were ten times more costly. As Khafi Khan tells us,

> Most of Aurangzib's generals, whether posted in far-off provinces or conducting sieges under his eyes, after some fighting used in the end to secure the capitulation of the forts by bribing the *qiladars*. The Emperor was informed of it by his spies, and used to pay to the officer who had thus contrived the surrender the exact amount of the bribe (neither more, nor less), under the name of reward![23]

[20]Hamid-ud-Din, *Ahkam-i Alamgiri*, ed. and tr. as *Anecdotes of Aurangzeb's Reign*, Calcutta, 1912, section 57.

[21]*Muntakhab-ul-Lubab*, ii, pp. 411–12.

[22]Ibid., p. 379.

[23]Ibid., p. 503.

The spirit of the Mughal army in the Deccan was at least utterly broken. The soldiers grew sick of the endless and futile war,[24] but Aurangzib would listen to no protest or friendly advice. Even his grand *wazir*, Asad Khan, who had ventured to suggest that now that Bijapur and Golkonda had been conquered he had no more work to do and might as well return to Delhi, received a sharp reprimand, 'I wonder that a wise old servant like you has made such a request . . . So long as a single breath remains to this mortal life, there is no release from labour.'[25]

A generation of imperialists grew up in the Deccan who had never seen a city or house of brick or stone, but passed all their lives in tents, marching from one encampment to another.[26] The Rajput soldiers complained that their race would not be able to serve the empire in the next generation, as they had to pass their lifetime in the Deccan campaigns, without getting any respite for going home and rearing up children. One homesick noble offered the emperor a bribe of one lakh of rupees for transferring him to Delhi![27]

Administrative Decline and Public Disturbances in Northern India

The inflated expenditure and incessant warfare in the Deccan adversely reacted on the situation in northern India. The older, and more settled, peaceful and prosperous provinces of the empire were drained of their manhood, wealth, and talent. The best soldiers, the highest officers, and all the collected revenue were sent to the Deccan, while the *subahs* of Hindustan were henceforth left to minor officers with small contingents and incomes quite inadequate for maintaining viceregal authority. All classes of lawless men began to raise their heads in the north as well as the south, though later and more fitfully in Hindustan than in the Deccan. The new class of *subahdars* and *faujdars* were too low in rank and armed strength to repress them. The proud *zamindars*, whose grandfathers had been ruling princes before the coming of the Mughals, the Afghan families settled in various districts (especially Jaunpur, Malwa, Allahabad and north Orissa) and still dreaming of their lost

[24] 'Owing to my marching through deserts and forests, my officers long for my death.' Aurangzib to Muazzam in *Anecdotes*, section 11.

[25] *Ahkam-i Alamgiri*, section 46.

[26] *Nuskha-i Dilkusha*, ii, 141a.

[27] Samsam ud-Daula Shahnawaz Khan, *Ma'asir ul-Umara*, ed. Abd ur-Rahim and Ashraf Ali, 3 vols, Calcutta, 1891–95, English tr. by H. Beveridge with a volume of Index by Baini Prasad, Calcutta, 1964, i, p. 457.

empire in India, claimants to principalities dispossessed by order of Aurangzib, predatory tribes like the Jat peasantry west of Agra and the Mewatis south-west of Delhi, and turbulent Rajput peasantry like the Bais of Oudh and the Ujjainias of south Bihar, all rose in defiance of the government and began to lay hands on their weaker neighbours. The local viceroys could not cope with them with their normal contingents (*zabita*); they could hope to suppress the rebels only if they engaged troops in excess of the number for which their salary was fixed. And such extra retainers meant increased expenditure.[28]

Poverty and Powerlessness of Governors

But, at the same time, their income, inadequate even on paper for their heavy duties, was actually dwindling very fast. The general unrest naturally caused a falling off in the rent collection from the peasants. Then, the frequent changes of officers and transfers of their *jagirs* prevented them from gaining knowledge of the tenantry, establishing relations with them, and spreading the inevitable arrears of a lean year gently over a number of fat years. It is difficult to imagine a system more ruinous to the peasants and therefore in the long run more harmful to the state also, than the actual administration of Mughal *jagirs*. It ended in a mad looting of the peasants by rival *jagirdars*' agents or successive agents of the same *jagirdar*. The former I have described elsewhere. As for the latter, Bhimsen gives a lucid picture of it:

> There is no hope of a *jagir* being left with the same officer next year. When a *jagirdar* sends a collector to his *jagir*, he first takes an advance from the latter by way of loan. This collector, on arriving in the village, fearing lest a second man who had given a larger loan to the *jagirdar* was following (to supplant him), does not hesitate to collect the rent with every oppression . . . . The ryots have given up cultivation; the *jagirdars* do not get a penny.[29]

The same ruinous policy was followed in revenue collection in the crownlands, as we learn from the despatches of the *subahdar* of Orissa.[30]

The result of this policy was that the imperial officers, whether holding *jagirs* in the older or the newly conquered provinces, all alike starved on account of the rent collection of their fiefs always falling into arrears. Thus, a vicious circle was formed: political disorder (to

[28]*Nuskha-i Dilkusha*, ii, 139a–140a.
[29]Ibid.
[30]Jadunath Sarkar, *Studies in Mughal India*, Calcutta, 1919, p. 223.

which we must add, a wrong system of land administration) led to less and less money coming from the *jagirs;* this diminished income forced the governors to keep fewer and fewer men[31] in their pay; the decrease in their armed strength encouraged greater lawlessness among the people, from which followed a further impoverishment of the peasants and falling off in the land revenue. The evil was universal throughout the Deccan and also very noticeable in Bundelkhand, Malwa, and parts of Allahabad and Oudh.

War was the only occupation of the Rajputs and indeed of all the Hindus who claimed to belong to the Kshatriya caste. The Mughal peace established in northern India had left to them chances of employment only in the trans-frontier regions on the west or in the still-unsubdued parts of the Deccan. Rajputs had fought under the imperial banner in Central Asia and Qandahar. But in Aurangzib's reign Mughal military activity was contracted within the frontiers, though Kabul was still a part of his empire. His annexation of the remaining Deccan principalities caused unemployment among the Rajputs in two ways—first because he was under the necessity of giving employment to the masterless local troops of the subverted monarchies, and secondly because fewer territories were now left for him to conquer. In these circumstances aspiring scions of Rajput houses could only fight with their kinsfolk for their ancestral 'homes', take to robbery, or apostatize in order to get grants of estates from Aurangzib.

This situation was changed by the huge waste of life through pestilence and famine, even more than by actual slaughter, in the last years of the emperor's reign. The Hindu manhood of the north therefore continued to be drained for the Deccan war, but without any corresponding gain to Aurangzib; because the Rajputs with all their bravery were proverbially unfit for siege operations and hill-fighting, and at the same time his Deccani auxiliaries were untrustworthy.[32]

Decay of Indian Civilization under Aurangzib, its Causes and Signs

The retrogression of medieval Indian civilization under Aurangzib is noticeable not only in the fine arts—the decay of which was only the

[31] *Nuskha-i Dilkusha,* ii, 140b. 'Except these three men who have ancestral estates, viz., Rao Dalpat, Ram Singh Hada, and Jai Singh Kachhwaha, I have not seen a single noble who kept even a thousand troopers in his contingent.' The *Akhbarat* give reports of *hazaris* and 2-*hazaris* not keeping a single soldier under them.

[32] Ibid., ii, 146b.

outward manifestation of it—but still more in the low intellectual type of the new generation. As the seventeenth century wore on, the older nobility nourished on the manly traditions of Akbar and Shah Jahan, gifted with greater independence of spirit, and trained with greater resources and responsibility—gradually died out, and their places in camp and court were taken by smaller men, supplied with poorer resources by the suspicious Aurangzib, afraid to exercise responsibility and initiative, and seeking to advance themselves by sycophancy.[33] The exceptionally prolonged life of Aurangzib with its ever-increasing store of experience and information made him intellectually dwarf the younger generation. His self-sufficiency and obstinacy increased with age; till at last none dared to contradict him, none could give him honest advice or impart unpleasant truth. With the lack of leisure amidst the incessant warfare and rough camp-life in the far-off south, the culture of the aristocracy decayed, and, as the nobles set the tone of society, the whole of the intellectual classes of India slowly fell back to a lower level. A Jafar Jattali took the place of Faizi for their delectation.

Gloomy Outlook for India in the Eighteenth Century

The growing pessimism of the older men, which we find reflected in the letters and anecdotes of the time and even in the works of thoughtful historians, bears witness to the moral decay of the governing classes. It was too deep and too sincere to be passed off as an example of the familiar oriental habit of imagining a golden age in the past and looking down upon the present generation as the degenerate successors of their glorious ancestors. It finds utterance as early as the latter years of Shah Jahan, as we learn from the sayings of that monarch quoted in Aurangzib's letters.[34]

The historians Bhimsen and Khafi Khan were struck by the hopeless change for the worse that had seized the Indian world and looked wistfully back at the virtues and glories of the men of the times of Akbar and Shah Jahan.[35] We find the aged Aurangzib himself dolefully shaking his head over the prospect of the future and predicting a deluge after his death.[36] It is true, as Sadullah remarked in reply to a pessimist,

[33] Ibid, ii, 150b.
[34] Muhyi ud-Din Aurangzeb Alamgir, *Ruqaat-i Alamgiri*, Kanpur, 1267 AH.
[35] *Nuksha-i Dilkusha*, ii, 139a, 146a, esp. 157a; *Muntakhab-ul-Lubab*, ii, 550.
[36] *Anecdotes*, section ii.

'No age is without men of ability. What is needed is a wise master to find them out, cherish them, get his work done by them, and never lend his ears to the whispers of selfish men against such officers.'[37] But this wise principle was not followed in Aurangzib's latter years, and it was altogether discarded by his successors. Career was not freely opened to talent. The public service was not looked upon as a sacred trust, but as a means of gratifying the apostate, the sycophant, the well-groomed dandy, the great man's kinsmen, and sons of old official families. Bigotry and narrowness of outlook under Aurangzib and vice and sloth under the later Mughals, ruined the administration of the empire and dragged down the Indian people along with the falling empire.

Moral Degeneration of the Mughal Aristocracy

The moral decay was most noticeable among the nobility and it produced the greatest mischief. The character of the older nobility in the late seventeenth century was deplorable. In a mean spirit of jealousy they insulted and thwarted 'new men' drawn from the ranks[38] and ennobled for the most brilliant public services, and yet they themselves had grown utterly worthless. Aurangzib himself remarked in 1701: 'My nobles had opposed me in giving suitable rewards to Shaikh Nizam for the capture of Shambhu. So, too, they are now belittling the achievements of Md. Murad.'[39]

We have a significant example of the moral degeneration of the Mughal peerage. The prime minister's grandson, Mirza Tafakhkhur used to sally forth from his mansion in Delhi with his ruffians, plunder the shops in the bazar, kidnap Hindu women passing through the public streets in litters or going to the river, and dishonour them; and yet there was no judge to punish him, no police to prevent such crimes. 'Everytime such an occurrence was brought to the Emperor's notice by the news-letters or official reports, he referred it to the prime minister, and did nothing more.' At last after a Hindu artillery-man's wife had been forcibly abducted and his comrades threatened to mutiny, Aurangzib merely ordered the licentious youth to be prevented from coming out of his mansion.[40]

[37] *Ruqaat-i Alamgiri*, no. 46.

[38] Similarly the old effete French nobility of birth objected to the victor of Fontenoy being raised to the peerage by his grateful master.

[39] *Muntakhab-ul-Lubab*, ii, 489.

[40] *Ahkam-i Alamgiri*, section 48, author in *Ma'asir ul-Umara*, i, 320.

All the surplus produce of a fertile land under a most bounteous providence was swept into the coffers of the Mughal nobility and pampered them in a degree of luxury not dreamt of even by kings in Persia or Central Asia; as the court historian of Shah Jahan scornfully remarks, the revenue of the king of Balkh was less than the income of a third-grade peer of the Mughal empire.[41]

Evil Education of the Children of Nobles

Hence, in the houses of the Delhi nobility luxury was carried to an excess. The harems of many of them were filled with immense numbers[42] of women, of an infinite variety of races, intellect and character. Under Muslim law the sons of concubines are entitled to their patrimony equally with sons born in wedlock, and they occupy no inferior position in society. Even the sons of lawfully married wives became, at a precocious age, familiar with vice from what they saw and heard in the harem, while their mothers were insulted by the higher splendour and influence enjoyed in the same household by younger and fairer rivals of servile origin or easier virtue. The proud spirit and majestic dignity of a Cornelia is impossible in the crowded harem of a polygamist; and without Cornelias among the mothers there cannot be Gracchi among the sons.

There was no good education, no practical training, of the sons of the nobility. They were too much petted by eunuchs and maidservants and passed through a sheltered life from birth to manhood, every thorn being removed from their path by attendants. Early familiarized with vice, softened in their fibres by pleasure, they were yet taught to have an inordinately high opinion of their own wealth and importance in the scale of creation. Their domestic tutors were an unhappy class, powerless to do any good except by leave of their pupils, brow-beaten by the eunuchs (with the support of the ladies of the harem), disobeyed by the lads themselves, and forced to cultivate the arts of the courtier or the sneak, unless they were prepared to throw up their thankless office. The free give-and-take of life in a public school (which hardens character and at the same time removes its angularities), the salutary

[41] Abd ul-Hamid Lahori, *Padshahnama*, ed. Kabir-ud-Din Ahmad and Abd-ur Rahim, 2 vols, Calcutta, 1866–72, ii, 542.

[42] Hindu nobles and rich men were often as licentious, but they kept their mistresses in a separate establishment and not in their homes. Moreover, the children of such irregular unions among the Hindus formed a lower caste (*golak*), occupying a depressed rank in society.

discipline of training as subalterns in an orderly army, were unknown to the sons of the Mughal aristocracy. Hence, their moral decline was startlingly rapid and unchecked. Most of them, and even sons of Aurangzib like Shah Alam and Kam Bakhsh, were beyond correction. As Aurangzib, worn out with giving them unheeded counsels, cries out in despair, 'I have become garrulous by talking and talking; but none of you have taken heed from my words.'[43]

Vices of Society

In addition to unbridled sexual license and secret drinking, many members of the nobility and the middle class were tainted by pederasty. This vice was most prevalent among the Mongoloids of Central Asia, and there is reason to believe that even some of the so-called saints were not free from it. All Aurangzib's prohibitions and all the activity of his Censors of Public Morals failed to hold the Mughal aristocracy back from drink. Manucci notices it.[44] The newsletters of Aurangzib's court contain many reports of wine-selling and wine-drinking in the camp-bazars and houses of his nobles, and among the garrisons of forts. On 22 September 1698 the English governor of Madras presented 100 bottles of Canary to Nusrat Jang.[45] A similar present was made to his successor Daud Khan in November 1706. The drunken frolics of this Daud Khan are described in Wilks's *Mysoor.*[46] The freak pleasures and queer fancies of some of the nobles are noticed in the contemporary accounts.[47]

Popular Superstitions

All classes alike were sunk in the densest superstition. Astrology governed every act of life among rich and poor alike. Every king and nobleman maintained and always carried with himself a staff of star-gazers to point out the auspicious and evil days for his marches, entrance into cities or houses, receiving or making visits, besides domestic ceremonies. The planets hung like a lowering cloud over all men's lives. Relic worship was universal among Hindus and Muham-

[43] *Ruqa'at-i Alamgiri*, no. 2.

[44] *Storia*, ii, pp. 6, 1571, 393; iv, p. 131.

[45] Records of Fort St George, *Madras Diary and Consultation Book.*

[46] M. Wilks, *Historical Sketches of the South of India*, 3 vols, London, 1810–17, 2nd edn., i, pp. 133, 140n.

[47] e.g. *Storia*, iv, pp. 254–6, 262.

madans alike. Even the orthodox Aurangzib adored and walked devoutly round the pretended footprints and hair of the Prophet Muhammad (*asar-i-sharif*), as if these were representation of the Deity. It is difficult to distinguish between his attitude towards them and a Hindu's worship of Vishnu's footmarks on stone.[48] Trade in false relics was very brisk and highly profitable.

Man-worship of the grossest form degraded the character of the masses. Besides the adoration of *gurus* and *mahants* by Hindus and Sikhs, the Muslims, equally with the members of those two creeds, venerated saints and religious mendicants, and besought them to work miracles, and give them amulets, spells or marvellous medicines.[49] Pretended magicians did a roaring trade in these things, as well as in the philosopher's stone—being patronized by the nobles as well as the common people. Alchemy was believed to be a science and men of the highest status and education supported and encouraged the professors of this art, even undertaking to introduce them to the emperor.

The darker aspect of the subject was not wanting and we read of human sacrifice being performed to aid the quest for gold and the *elixir vitæ,* though it was criminal in law and punished whenever detected.[50] A lurid light is thrown on the medical art and beliefs of the age by Manucci's evidence that some Muhammadan doctors used human fat to cure their patients.[51]

Hindu superstition is further illustrated by the worship of long-armed men as incarnations of the monkey-god Hanuman. There was a Portuguese of St Thome whose hands reached below his knees, and whenever any Hindus met him they prostrated themselves, worshipping him like an idol. When another long-armed Portuguese visited Jagannath-Puri in Orissa,

> the Hindu priests and the people of the town conducted him to the temple with great veneration and made over to him the idols and all the wealth of the temple. He led a joyous life, regaling himself with delicate dishes and

[48]The universal and tumultuous exultation of the Muslim population of Srinagar when these bogus relics went to Kashmir is described in my *History of Aurangzib*, Calcutta, 1924, ch. 61, section 31.

[49]For example, the religious delusion of Sahibji's son-in-law, as described in Munshi Ghulam Husain Tabatabai, *Siyar-ul-Muta'khkhirin*, 3 vols, Lucknow (1840), English tr. Haji Mustafa, in 4 vols, Calcutta, 1902.

[50]*Muntakhab-ul-Lubub*, ii, p. 542.

[51]*Storia*, ii, p. 210.

requisitioning young girls whenever he pleased, they imagining he did them a great honour.

He afterwards departed secretly, with the wealth of the temple.[52]

As a natural consequence of their ignorance and pride, all classes felt contempt for foreigners. European gun-founders, artilleryists and doctors (a few) were no doubt patronized by the wealthy, because their superior efficiency had been demonstrated before their eyes; and European objects of luxury were eagerly bought. But no attempt was made by any Indian noble or scholar to learn European languages,[53] arts or military system. A modern Indian nationalist will best realize how blindly selfish and autocratic the Mughal emperors and the Indian aristocracy of the sixteenth and seventeenth centuries were, if he considers that while they spent lakhs every year in buying European objects of luxury or art, not a single printing press, not even a lithograph stone was imported, either for popular education or public business.

The moral and intellectual tone of Indian society was greatly lowered by the abundance of slaves. In addition to captives of war and vanquished families reduced to bondage, men and women were sold by their parents for money in famine times, or in discharge of debts. A defaulting debtor could himself be sold with his family at the demand of his creditor. This was an ancient legal practice of the Hindus and Muhammadans alike.[54] One way of punishing criminals of certain classes was to turn them into slaves and sell them to the public; the sale of female slaves of this class is noticed in the 'Peshwas' Diaries'. Slavery lingered down to the first quarter of the nineteenth century even in the British district of Purnia.[55] People often made eunuchs of children and sold them; Orissa and Sylhet were notorious for this offence, which was strongly condemned by Aurangzib.[56]

[52]Ibid., iii, p. 140.

[53]At the Mughal court interpretation was done for European visitors by Armenians or by Europeans who knew Persian. Only one Muhammadan (Mutamad Khan, *c.* 1703) is spoken of in Aurangzib's letters as knowing the English language. A few Shenvi Brahmans of Goa territory, who knew Portuguese, translated Marathi documents into the former language for the benefit of the English at Bombay. In Madras, the English and French factories employed Brahman interpreters who knew these languages besides 'Moor' (Persian).

[54]*Cf.* the story of Harishchandra.

[55]Martin's *Eastern India*.

[56]Ibid., ch. 38, section 4; esp. ref. in footnote.

Official Bribery, its Forms and Causes

The educated middle class was composed entirely of officials, if we except the handful of physicians and superior priestly families. Among the traders and lesser landowners there were many who ranked with the middle class in wealth, but not in education, nor did they ever cultivate literature. The Mughal administration, both civil and military, could be carried on only with the help of a vast army of clerks and accountants. Every department, every government store or factory, every *subah* and even *faujdari,* every field army, had a complete set of them. Their official pay was very low (like that of the East India Company's factory 'writers' in the early seventeenth century).[57]

But the exaction of official perquisites or gratuities from men who had to get business pushed through the public offices, was the universal and admitted practice, as in Tudor and Stuart England. In addition, many officials from the highest to the lowest took bribes for doing undeserved favours, or deflecting the course of justice. Official corruption was, however, admitted in society to be immoral, and was practised only in secrecy. There were many officers above corruption even in Aurangzib's reign.[58] But the receiving and even demanding of presents by men in power was the universal rule and publicly acknowledged.[59] Even the emperor was not exempt from it. Aurangzib asked an aspirant to a title, 'Your father gave to Shah Jahan one lakh of rupees for adding *alif* to his name and making him *Amir* Khan. How much will you pay me for the title I am giving you?'[60] Manohar Das (*qiladar* of Sholapur) gave him Rs 50,000 in return for the title of *Rajah.* Officers weary of the life in the Deccan, used to present him with large sums to induce him to transfer them to northern India, especially Delhi.

The ministers and influential courtiers round the emperor's person had the opportunity of reaping a golden harvest, by selling to suitors their good offices in speaking for them to the sovereign when in private

[57]For examples *Mirat-i-Ahmadi,* ii. p. 116.

[58]*Muntakhab-ul-Lubab,* ii, pp. 261, 374–82.

[59]Nur Jahan's father, when prime-minister under Jahangir was shameless in demanding presents. So also was Jafar Khan, one of the early *wazirs* of Aurangzib. Jai Singh offered a purse of Rs 30,000 to the *wazir* for inducing the emperor or retain him in the Deccan command [*Haft Anjuman,* Ben. Ms. 195b] Bhimsen's disgust at having to pay everybody at court in order to get or retain a common civil office may be found in *Dilkusha,* i, 194. On official bribery, see my *Mughal Administration* 2nd edn., p. 64.

[60]*Ma'asir-i 'Alamgiri,* p. 489.

attendance on him (*taqarrub*). Thus, Qabil in two and a half years of personal attendance on Aurangzib amassed 12 lakhs of rupees in cash, besides articles of value and a new house.[61] They were besought and bribed with presents and money to yield their protection to officers, to conceal the shortcomings (*ghaib-pushi*) of the latter, to intercede for them with the emperor (*wasila*), and in general to watch over their interests at court during their absence.

This pressure was passed from the emperor downwards to the peasant; each social grade trying to squeeze out of the class below itself what it had to pay the rank above it, the cultivator of the soil and the trader being the victim in the last resort.

Lower Official World, its Life and Character

The drink habit was widely prevalent among the clerks, both of the Kayastha[62] and Khatri castes—as well as among the Rajput soldiers. In spite of the prohibition of the Quran, the Muslim nobles and officers, both military and civil, were in many cases addicted to it. The Turks were specially notorious for their disobedience to this precept of their religion.

The lower official class, on account of their having to do their work far away from their homes, kept small harems of local concubines. This was the case with the Hindus no less than with the Muslims. The evil lingered on in British India till the middle of the nineteenth century. It was only the annihilation of distance by railways and moral reform effected by English education and theistic religious movements in the sixties of the last century, that put an end to this general immorality.

The clerks, both Hindus and Muhammadans, formed a brotherhood bound together by community of duties and interests, education and ideals, social life and even vices. We find in the memoirs of one of them, Bhimsen of Burhanpur, a pleasing picture of the clerkly world,

[61] Abdun Nabi, *faujdar* of Mathura, left a fortune of 13 lakhs of rupees, 93,000 *mohars* (worth Rs 14 each), and articles, jewels, etc. worth 4 1/2 lakhs more; Azam Khan Kokah (Fidai Kh.) governor of Bengal, 22 lakhs in rupees and 112,000 *mohars*; Hafiz Md. Amin Kh., *subahdar* of Gujarat, 70 lakhs in rupees, 135,000 *mohars*, 76 elephants, 432 horses, 117 camels, and 10 chests of china-ware; Abdul Wahhab, Chief Qazi for 16 years, 33 lakhs in rupees besides jewellery. *Ma'asir-i Alamgiri*, pp. 83, 169, 226. 169, 226. *Ma'asir-ul-Umara*, i, pp. 235–41.

[62] Several of Bhimsen's relatives, civil officers in their imperial army, died of drink.

with its mutual dancing parties, dinners, aid in trouble, consolation in sorrow, and union at sittings of Sufi devotional exuberance. The official world was marked by its hatred and contempt for intruders into its preserves. Offices were expected to be reserved for old families of clerks and accountants. Any official who was not a 'hereditary servant' (*khanahzad*) of state but had sprung from the ranks, was despised as a *novum homo* was in the official world of the dying republic of Rome. The speedy ruin of the state from the employment of such interlopers and upstarts was predicted.[63] This attitude was universal, from the higher nobility to the petty clerks.

The Purity and Delights of the Life of the Masses

The above picture of social life in Mughal India appears very dark, and must be declared incomplete and therefore untrue if we do not consider certain other aspects of it. When we turn our gaze from the crowded harems of the rich and the lax virtues of the Mongoloid and some other frontier tribes—we are bound to admit that among the teeming millions of the Indian people domestic life was pure and not without its simple colour and joy. This virtue alone saved the people from the doom of extinction which overtook the degenerate Romans of the later empire. We had many popular songs, ballads and stories, which assuaged the stricken human soul, taught heroic patience, and infused tenderness into the most unlettered hearts. The epic of Tulsidas, which is even now acted annually in every centre of population and recited in every Hindu home in the Hindi-speaking provinces, filled millions of people with love of duty, manliness, the spirit of self-sacrifice, and taught them wisdom in public and private life.

In Bengal, Tirhut, Orissa and Assam and certain other parts, the Vaishnavism taught by Shankardev and Chaitanya introduced an unknown gentleness and fervour, and tamed the rude if manly savagery of the Tantric worship and animism that used to prevail there before. The seventeenth century was the great period of the expansion of this new Vaishnavism—which was marked by enthusiastic personal devotion (as in the Christian revival movement), tenderness to children and the weak, the cultivation of literature (both Sanskrit and the current speech of the people), and the infusion of song and dance and a delicate romantic sentiment into the everyday life even of the poorest. It also bridged social gulfs and established a democracy of the spirit. Apart

[63] *Nuskha-i Dilkusha*, ii, 140b.

from this new popular religious literature, the masses[64] in different parts had their folk-songs, like the ballad of Ranjha and Hir (in the Panjab), which went to their very hearts and relieved for a time the dead weight of labour and political tyranny which pressed them down. The *kirtan* or chanting of religious narratives in verse (interspersed with songs and frequent improvisation) was the popular substitute for the sermon, the lecture, and literature throughout India—in the south as much as in the north—e.g. Shivaji doted on the *kirtan* and once risked his life and liberty in his passion to attend one. The common people were equally fond of these.[65]

The Muhammadans of that age (except the Hindi-speaking portion) had no vernacular religious poetry for the masses. But they had the annual celebrations of different saints (*urs*) at their tombs, which were attended by tens of thousands of pilgrims from distances, and where fairs were held which attracted men and women of all creeds. In addition, both sexes dwelling in cities, had their usual weekly outing to the garden-tombs of saints in the suburbs. The opportunity was utilized for pleasure rather than piety, and the spread of immorality that it caused led Aurangzib to issue an order for stopping the practice. But it was too popular to be put down.[66]

Visits to these periodical fairs and seats of pilgrimage were the sole joy of the Indian village population, and men and women were passionately eager to undertake them. Pilgrim centres like Ajmir, Kulbarga, Nizam-ud-din Auliya, and Burhanpur for the Muslims and Mathura, Allahabad, Benares, Nasik, Madura and Tanjore for the Hindus, served also to diffuse culture and to break down provincial isolation and narrowness of mental horizon.

[64] I have spoken of popular romance and religious poetry in the vernacular. But a vernacular literature for the *upper* classes was just missed by Aurangzib. It came into being under Wali of Aurangabad only ten years after his death.

[65] For a graphic description of such popular recitation among the Maratha villagers, see Acworth's *Ballads*, xxvii.

[66] *Storia*, iv, p. 205; Sarkar, *History of Aurangzib*, ch. 28, section 3.

11

Lower-class Uprisings in the Mughal Empire*

Wilfred Cantwell Smith

The history of India during the Muslim period has been presented until now chiefly by writers whose attention has been confined to the life of the upper class. Even within those narrow limits, their choice of subject-matter has been still further restricted in many cases to but two aspects of that life: war and government. The word 'history' instead of being used in its true meaning, as full as life itself, has been narrowed to describe that segment of specialized study which we ought to label merely 'political history'. And even more than today, before the rise of democracy, politics covered a very small area of life indeed. One of the chief tasks, therefore, facing the modern Indian historian is to broaden historiography so that it may include other aspects of the life of the upper class, becoming a true social and cultural history of the aristocracy instead of merely a court chronicle; and also, perhaps even more important, so to broaden it that it may include too something of the life of the other classes of society. At the same time, history must become analytical, rather than merely descriptive; and dynamic, rather than merely chronological. In other words, the historian must search for the way of life of all the people; and must search also for the slow transformations in that way of life, and for their causes.

Our present purpose is to investigate a little the life of the lower classes in the Mughal empire. The persons forming those classes constituted, of course, the overwhelming majority of the population. (It is doubtful whether the Mughal nobility comprised in all one-tenth of one

*From *Islamic Culture*, vol. 20, no. 1, 1946.

per cent of the people.)[1] No doubt, the individual lives of the peasantry and the town poor were very much less full, less varied, and less influential, than those of their rulers. Nonetheless, the humble folk were so immensely more numerous that, taken together, they are surely as important as the upper class. An unbiased historian would perhaps admit that the most important question to ask about a military campaign is not 'Who won it?' but 'How did it affect the common people?'; about an administrative system, not 'How efficient was it, or how much revenue did it bring to the state?' but 'How much income did it leave to the producer?'; about a reigning emperor, not 'What was his name?' or 'What sort of character did he have?' but 'How did the masses fare under his sway?'—and in general, the most important history of India is not the record of its kings but the story of its people.

Few historians would actually deny this principle explicitly. Those who have denied it in practice by writing history books or articles or doctorate theses in which the common man does not figure, have done so usually either by ignoring the issue, or on the plea that only for the upper class is source material available. With few exceptions,[2] they have not decided the issue in favour of the aristocratic minority after deliberation. Rather, their attention has simply not been called to the place of the lower classes in Oriental history; or, if it has been called, they answer that the extent sources deal only with the great ones of the earth.

This answer is on the whole true, and must be frankly faced even by those of us who deem the argument based on it invalid. The materials for constructing a history of Muslim India are primarily written

[1]Using W.H. Moreland's estimates, from his *India at the Death of Akbar*, one might put the total population of north India (including Bangāl and Gujarāt) in Mughal times at something like 70 million; of which 0.1 per cent is 70,000. The total numbers of Mughal *manṣabdārs* are given by Sri Ram Sharma, 'Organisation of Public Services in Mughal India, 1526–1707', *Journal of the Bihar and Orissa Research Society*, vol. XXII, Part II (1937), p. 16, as follows under

Akbar (1590)	1658
Jahāngīr	2069
Shāh Jahān (1637)	8000
Aurangzēb (1690)	11,456

These figures should be multiplied by, say, five in order to include families (though the standard histories devote very little space to the life of women and children in those days).

[2]Vincent A. Smith, *Akbar the Great Mogul*, p. 386.

materials; and the fact is that writing in those days was an undemocratic art. To it only a tiny minority, of nobles or of nobles' protégés, was initiate. With small exceptions (such as the wealthy foreign merchants' account books), the basis of modern historiography is literature produced by and/or for the upper class. Even the few non-written sources, such as architecture and coins, are monuments to the life of the rich.

This means that for us to learn about the poor in those days is difficult. It may be difficult; but it is also important. And perhaps even the difficulty will appear less formidable once one has boldly set oneself to deal with it. Perhaps the important explanation of modern Indian historiography's remoteness from the common people is not only that the medieval Persian chronicles were neither written nor read by the lower classes, but also that those lower classes still today are cut off from the academic historian. The modern writer, whether British imperialist or nationalist professor, has been in general not interested in the life of the villager or the town proletariat. (For this reason, our understanding even of medieval upper-class politics has been shallow.)

For material would not be entirely wanting for writers who undertook a social and cultural history of the Indian people. There is, for instance, the religious literature. Religion was life, and life was religion, for the ancient poor to a remarkable degree. A rich harvest awaits research workers who examine the poetry of, say, Tulsī Dās and the writings of the *Ṣūfīs* from this point of view; and the amount of social evolution that lies embedded in the rise of popular religious movements has still to be investigated, and is probably large. Moreover, stray references to the life of ordinary men and women are to be found here and there in almost all contemporary records, and could be assiduously culled and carefully studied. The comprehensive studies[3] of Moreland and Ashraf illustrate what can be done.

Without going so far afield, however, one can study one aspect of lower-class life in the writings of the upper class themselves; namely the conditions under which the two groups came in contact with each other. No doubt the aristocracy was much of the time unconcerned with the plebians; but they could not ignore them altogether, for, after all, they had to get their food from them. The most obvious and most continuous relation between the ruling class and the people was in revenue

[3]W.H. Moreland, *India at the Death of Akbar and From Akbar to Aurangzeb;* Kunwar Muhammad Ashraf, 'Life and Conditions of the People of Hindūstān (1200–1550 AD)', *Journal of the Asiatic Society of Bengal, Letters,* vol. I (1935), no.2.

collection. It involved the major part of the administrative system and a good deal of the army.

The upper class was enormously wealthy. But its wealth did not appear out of nothing, at the *fiat* of the emperor. It was taken from the lower class, by force or the threat of force, in the form of what is called 'taxes' or 'revenue'. Approximately one-third of the country's agricultural produce was taken for the nobility from the villagers who, by the sweat of their brow, produced it. Any notion that those villagers parted with their produce willingly is sheer romanticism. They paid their taxes only when they had to.

Bābur remarks of India in his *Mémoirs*: 'In many places the plain is covered by a thorny brushwood to such a degree that the people of the *parganas*, relying on these forests, take shelter in them, and trusting to their inaccessible situation, often continue in a state of revolt, refusing to pay their taxes.'[4] In other words, they seized any opportunity to evade payment; as is entirely natural. Such chance quotations could be multiplied many times. In fact, almost all modern historians have noted that the revenue was taken from the lower classes against their will. But they have failed to interpret this fact, or even much to consider it. We may choose almost any modern writer at random. Thus, Sir Jadū Nāth Sarkār, speaking of what he calls 'the Indian peasant's habitual reluctance to pay revenue',[5] remarks: 'A careful student of Indian history is very much struck by the chronic antagonism between the rent-payer and the rent-receiver from very ancient times. European travellers in India have noticed how the ryot was averse to paying even his legitimate rent and that force had to be employed to get from him the dues of the State.'[6] (The use of the word 'legitimate' betrays this writer's social bias.) Vincent Smith, in his life of Akbar, writes: 'The Faujdār was expected to reduce rebels, always numerous, and, whenever necessary, to use his troops against recalcitrant villagers in order to enforce payment of the government dues. . . . Akbar usually had a rebellion somewhere or other on his hands.'[7] Benī Pra<u>sh</u>ād, in his

[4]*Tūzuk-i-Bāburī*, in Elliot and Dowson, *The History of India as Told by Its Own Historians*, vol. IV, p. 222.

[5]Jadunath Sarkar, *Mughal Administration*, 1935 edn, p. 76; cf. Table of Contents, p. v.

[6]Jadunath Sarkar, *Mughal Administration*, p. 76, with reference to *Storia do Mogor*, ii, p. 450.

[7]Smith, *Akbar*, p. 381.

History of Jahangir, refers in passing to 'the village tendency to refuse payment of taxes'.[8] And Saksena, biographer of S͟hāh Jahān, says:

The mass of the people in medieval ages were more warlike and has a greater aversion to obedience and submission than now. Evidence of the existence of this spirit of defiance is to be found in the numerous expeditions undertaken to suppress local trouble in regions as near to the capital as the Doāb. Moreover troops were also stationed at important centres in a province to assist the *'Āmil* in revenue collection.[9]

And so on. The fact is that (in India as in the rest of the world) the relation of the upper class and the lower class was one primarily of conflict, and, in technical terms, of exploitation—that is the upper class expropriated from the lower a portion of the produce of their labour. Certainly there was at times sympathy from the nobles for the peasants, or alms, or redress of grievances. But the basic fact is that the villagers were having a portion of their little wealth regularly taken from them by their rulers, and they did not like it. Here then is the class struggle; permeating the whole of Mughal society, underlying all its aristocratic culture, colouring all its peasant life.

It is not our purpose here to investigate the Mughal revenue administration system as a class process. We shall confine ourselves to a few instances in which the class struggle broke out into overt violent form. One must bear in mind that the conflict between classes existing in all non-socialist societies is a continuous and inherent process, which perhaps only occasionally flares up in pitched battle, but at other times is suppressed, not absent. Perhaps it is also necessary to add that the socialist calls attention to class antagonism and to its causes not in order to stir up conflict, but on the contrary as a first step towards eliminating it. He believes that to solve the clash of interests between the rich and the poor, it is better to understand their struggle than, ostrich-like, to deny that it exists.

The struggles between classes in Mughal times are totally different from the conflicts within one class: between states, in which one ruling class fought another ruling class; or between individual nobles, fighting for position within the ruling hierarchy. Historians are slipshod who use the same word (for instance 'rebellion') for two quite different occurrences: on the one hand the rising of a provincial governor and his aristocratic entourage and army against the hegemony of the central

[8]Benī Pras͟hād, *History of Jahangir*, 1940 edn, p. 173.
[9]Banarsi Prasad Saksena, *History of Shahjahan of Dihli*, 1932, p. 283.

authority, and on the other hand the insurrection of peasants or workers against the local police. In the one case, members of the ruling class were trying, while preserving the system of rule intact, to replace others by themselves as chief custodians and beneficiaries of power. In the other case, members of the ruled class were trying to do away with the system altogether. Text books which fail to distinguish these are misleadingly gross. For one thing these class wars were always bitter, fierce, brutal; they usually ended in pillage, massacre, and a devastation that makes many upper-class wars of the time seem picnics. Secondly, the final result in their case was always the same: the upper class, with more or less atrocity, won, the lower class was beaten down. Thirdly, we may note that more frequently than with ruling class wars, tnese class struggles were fought with religious ideologies (this is also true of class struggles in Europe). Religion, often an opiate, is sometimes a powerful revolutionary force.

To illustrate the thesis of class conflict, some eight or ten active outbreaks of Mughal times may be considered.

We begin with three very minor instances from the reign of Jahāngīr. An uprising near Dihlī in 1610 is dismissed by the emperor in his *Mémoirs* in one solitary sentence: 'On Monday, the 24th, Mu'aẓẓam Khān was despatched to Delhi to punish the rebels and disaffected of that neighbourhood.'[10] Equally casual is his treatment of a peasant uprising two years later in Thatta: 'I sent 'Abdu-r-Razzāq, the *bakhshi* of the palace (*darkhāna*) to settle the country of Thatta (Sind) until a Sardar should be appointed who could conciliate the soldiery and the cultivators, and so bring the province into order.'[11] It is clear that the rulers expected to find, and probably did find, little trouble in suppressing such outbreaks. Between these two, however, a rising in the *dū'āb* was apparently serious enough to call forth extreme measures, and apparently annoyed Jahāngīr enough to make him vindictive—though he can still pass over the incident in a sentence: 'I ordered the Khankhanan to have a *jagir* in the *Subah* of Agra in the *Sarkars* of Qanauj and Kalpi, that he might inflict condign punishment on the rebels of that region and exterminate them (pull them out by the roots).'[12]

[10]*Tūzuk-i-Jahāngīrī, or Memoirs of Jahāngīr*, trans. A. Rogers, ed. H. Beveridge, London, 1909–14. vol. I, p. 171.

[11]Ibid., vol. I, p. 225.

[12]Ibid., vol. I, p. 199.

The royal wrath and contempt, however, were roused in earnest by our next instance, which was too formidable to be dismissed summarily or ignored: the seizure of Paṭnā by a proletarian mob which held the town for a week. This insurrection (1610) was led by a lower-class Muslim who impersonated the popular hero Khusraw, gathered about himself the discontented elements of the town and district poor, and, seizing an advantageous opportunity when the governor was absent from the capital, ousted the only upper-class representatives of authority, appropriated the treasury, and proceeded to dominate the city. After the success of his coup, numbers of the lower class aligned themselves with him. These proletarians even organized a minor army from amongst themselves, which they were foolish enough to send out against the upper-class army advancing under the irate governor. Of course, they quickly lost the ensuing encounter, some miles from the city. Within the fort, on the other hand, they were able to hold out for a considerable time; it was only with difficulty and after suffering several casualties, including 30 dead, that the imperial troops were able to overcome these commoners and restore upper-class 'order'.

Jahāngīr was furious. His reactions, both emotional and practical, were severe. He refers to the leader of this desperate venture, whose name was Quṭb, as 'an unknown man ... a mischievous and seditious fellow ... ' with 'the look of a dervish and the clothes of a beggar . ... that wretch',[13] and to his associates as 'men of those parts, who were always seditious ... those simpletons ... those rebels ... some of those wretched creatures who wait on events ... these scoundrels'.[14] Quṭb, though asking quarter, was summarily executed; and the *manṣabdārs* who had let the situation get out of hand in the first place were not treated as nobles would have been who had merely lost an encounter with equals, failing to suppress some ordinary upper-class conspiracy; but were publicly degraded and ridiculed at the imperial capital, being paraded through Āgrā on asses, heads all shaved and dressed as women.[15]

There is another, very minor, incident reported in Jahāngīr's autobiography, of a villagers' rising near Āgrā in 1618. 'In one of the villages of Agra,' he says,[16] 'which was not wanting in sedition'—

[13] *Tūzuk-i-Jahāngīrī*, vol. I, pp. 173, 175.

[14] Ibid., vol. I, pp. 73–5.

[15] For this whole incident, see *Tūzuk-i-Jahāngīrī*, vol. I, pp. 173–6; and Benī Prashād, *History of Jahangir*, pp. 143 f, with the other references given there.

[16] *Tūzuk-i-Jahāngīrī*, vol. II, p. 28.

notice how these lower-class people are hardly ever mentioned without some such epithet, about their rebelliousness—'the people rose to assist' a certain fugitive from the court, Subḥān Qulī, who had appeared among them and apparently incited their anti-imperialist feeling. When a detachment of the upper-class troops, however, arrived to take the matter in hand, those peasants, 'seeing their own ruin in the mirror of the case',[17] changed their minds, and gave the fugitive up. Nothing more is heard of this village; nor is it even clear whether the name ascribed to it (Jahanda) properly belongs to the village or to one of the characters in the story.[18] Referring to Subḥān—whose last name, Qulī, i.e. 'coolie', is perhaps significant for our purposes—Jahāngīr writes: 'This wretch ... this ungrateful fellow ... this scoundrel'.[19]

The final instance to be considered in Jahāngīr's reign is not so clear a case of class conflict. It is the disturbances in the Kishtwār district, between the Panjāb and Kashmīr. This area was taken from its Rājā (and some upper-class Chaks) by the Mughals in 1620; there were disturbances later, which were not effectively suppressed. The accounts do not make it quite clear who was involved in the insurrec tions. Then,

> An order was given to Irādat K . . . to inflict severe punishment on the rebels, and make such arrangements in the hill-country that the dust of dispersion and calamity might not settle on its frontiers. He, as ordered, hastened there and did approved service, and the people of sedition and disturbance, having turned their heads towards the desert of exile, escaped half dead. Thus once more was the thorn of calamity and mischief rooted out of that country.[20]

Later:

> As it was reported that the Zamindars of Kishtwār had again raised their heads in disobedience and sin, and engaged in sedition and disturbance, Irādat K. was ordered to proceed hot-foot, before they had time to establish themselves firmly, and having inflicted condign punishment on them to tear up the root of sedition. ... Irādat K., who had hastened to punish the rebels of Kishtwār, having killed many of them and regained the mastery and established himself firmly, returned to duty.[21]

[17]Ibid.

[18]See footnote 16 above.

[19]Ibid., vol. II, p. 27.

[20]Ibid., vol. II, p. 210. See also pp. 135–40, 170f.

[21]Ibid., vol. II, pp. 234f.

Still later: 'Thought Irādat K. had done his duty in Kishtwār well, yet as the ryots and inhabitants of Kashmir complained of his treatment of them, I promoted I'tiqād K. to the governorship of Kashmir'[22] and made the ex-Rājā of Kishtwār again Rājā.

From this rather confused account it would appear that the struggle was, in the beginning at least, between the Mughal ruling class and the Kishtwār ruling class (the princes and the landlords); but that the latter were able—probably partly because of the religious issue—to get extensive support from their own common people. Thus the affair took on also the characteristics of an inter-class conflict, and it seems evident that the lower classes—usually unconcerned in their rulers' quarrels—in this case both fought and suffered to a very considerable degree.

The reign of Aurangzēb presents instances of lower-class uprisings which were really formidable. The first two that we shall consider are those of the Jāṭs in Mathurā district (1669, and again in 1681, 1686) and of the Satnāmīs in Nārnawl. One of these outbreaks was occasioned by religious persecution, apparently; and the ideology under which both were fought was to some extent religious. (Actually, there seems to be less evidence than is usually assumed that communal differences were primary in the minds of the revolting Jāṭs). But, religious or not, these were lower-class uprisings in the straightforward sense that they were risings of lower-class people against their rulers. They desecrated some mosques, the symbol of their class enemies, perhaps much as a group of French workers in a German-occupied factory during the recent war might desecrate a swastika, the symbol of their exploiters. We are not suggesting that peasant or proletariat struggles fought in religious guise were in fact class conflicts rather than religious ones. We are not even contending that they were class conflicts in addition to being religious ones. Our thesis is that the two things are different but simultaneous aspects of the same fact. Religion expressed, motivated, and hallowed for these persons a struggle which the class situation engendered. It has been said that the French Revolution is the first major class struggle in history that was not religiously expressed.[23] It may also be pointed

[22]Ibid., vol. II, p. 238.

[23]This is doubtless not accurate. One apparent exception that comes to mind is Spartacus's revolt of the Roman slaves. Perhaps the French Revolution was the first *successful* class struggle with a secular ideology. All such generalizations, however, are much too sweeping to be put forward except as challenging ideas, or as hypotheses worth investigating.

out for India that, in Mughal times, no class revolt attained significant proportions that did not have a religious ideology to sustain it.

In the Jāṭ revolt, 1669,[24] thousands of peasants, under the leadership of one Goklā (a small landholder), rose; and overpowered the local military police, killing the commander and routing his forces. They then began to 'loot the neighbourhood'—which presumably means to loot the landlords and upper-class rich, not the peasants, since the latter sided with them more and more. The peasantry in neighbouring areas also rose in revolt against their exploiters; the villagers threw off the governmental yoke, and remained in control of the situation for almost a year (which is a very considerable while). Aurangzēb, of course, sent big forces against them; but they resisted long and bitterly. The final result is obvious: the upper class won; but only after a bloody struggle. These peasants had been able to muster a revolutionary army of 20,000, and their class spirit was so intense that the imperialist armies of the Mughal upper class, for all their artillery, training, and almost unlimited resources, could defeat them only with the utmost difficulty. And the havoc wrought on both sides was terrifying. The peasants lost 5000 dead and 7000 captured; the rulers, 4000 dead. These figures become more impressive when we compare this encounter with, for instance, the second battle of Pānīpat. There also the Hindū–Muslim issue was involved, but the fighting was between two sections of the upper class; one of the armies (Akbar's) was numerically of the same order as the Jāṭs' on this occasion; and the casualties on both sides in that instance were quite possibly no greater.

An interesting reflection on moral ideas, medieval and also modern, can be derived from a comparison of the penalties inflicted on the vanquished at these two battles. After Pānīpat, the captured Hēmū was brought before Bayram Khān and Akbar, and was executed. No attention is paid, by either ancient or modern historians, to the number of common soldiers or even subordinate officers who may have suffered or been killed in this battle; but much interest is taken in the question of whether Akbar did or did not kill this upper-class leader, presumably his equal. Those who believe that he did personally despatch Hēmū, seem to feel that this action requires apology; others, that it requires refuting. When it was a matter of suppressing the lower classes, on the other hand, not only was the punishment more severe, but also the need for condemnation or apology is less sensed, or is not sensed at all.

[24]For this revolt, see Jadunath Sarkar: *History of Aurangzib*, vol. III, pp. 334ff.

Goklā, taken to the imperial capital, had his limbs hacked off one by one in a public display; his family were forcibly made Muslims; and as late as the following spring those who had taken part in the insurrection were being killed or enslaved, their houses were being plundered, their families wiped out, by the upper-class troops. It is instructive to calculate that in half a dozen standard textbooks chosen at random,[25] more than two-thirds as much space has been devoted to the insignificant question of whether one Mughal emperor personally despatched an enemy ruler or merely watched it being done, as is given to the whole account of this Jāṭ uprising. (Two of these books,[26] which give a discussion of both sides of the former question, do not even mention Goklā's being hewn in pieces; one of them[27] does not even mention Goklā.)

The Jāṭ revolt was followed a couple of years later by a rising of some lower-class people in Nārnawl: the famous Satnāmī outbreak, 1672. This was a desperate class struggle, emotionally intensified by religious valuations. The persons involved were apparently small townsmen—petty traders and workers, either propertyless proletariat or men with a very small professional property—with perhaps some peasants as well. Musta'idd Khān describes them as 'goldsmiths, carpenters, sweepers, tanners, and other ignoble beings';[28] Khāfī Khān says that they were 'householders' who 'carry on agriculture and trade, though their trade is on a small scale'[29]—according to another translation, 'their trade is on a small capital'.[30] These men were held together in a small religious sect-community; this gave them, presumably, an intense community feeling and sense of solidarity, as such small sect-

[25]Ishwari Prasad, *Short History of Muslim Rule in India*, pp. 338, 654. Wolseley Haig, *Cambridge Shorter History of India*, pp. 339, 429. S.R. Sharma, *Mughal Empire in India*, 1940 edn, pp. 209, 530. S.C. Sarkar and K.K. Datta, *Text-Book of Modern Indian History*, 1937 edn., vol. I, pp. 51, 204. S.M. Edwardes and H.L.O. Garrett, *Mughal Rule in India*, pp. 24, 188. C.S. Srinivasachari and M.S. Ramaswami Aiyangar, *History of India*, Part II, pp. 213f, 237.

[26]Edwardes and Garrett, *Mughal Rule*; Srinivasachari and Aiyangar, *History of India*.

[27]Edwardes and Garrett, *Mughal Rule*.

[28]*Ma'āthir-i-Ālamgīrī*, p. 114, as translated in Elliot and Dowson *History of India*, vol. VII, p. 185.

[29]*Muntakhab al-Lubāb*, vol. VII, p. 252, as translated in Elliot and Dowson, *History of India*, vol. VII, p. 294.

[30]Jadunath Sarkar: *Short History of Aurangzib*, 1930, p. 162.

groupings habitually do. One contemporary historian charges them with immoral practices, but that kind of accusation is the common fate of isolated sects, and probably means no more in this case than that their social customs were different from those generally accepted; for instance, they ate pork and dog-meat.[31] Khāfī Khān pictures them as law-abiding citizens so long as they be not molested: 'They are not allowed to acquire wealth in any but a lawful calling. If anyone attempts to wrong or oppress them by force, or by exercise of authority, they will not endure it.'[32] It is interesting also to note, inasmuch as their revolt is usually dismissed as a Hindu–Muslim conflict, that 'they make no distinction between Hindus and Musalmans'.[33]

An instance of that molestation which they were said not to be able to endure occurred one day near Nārnawl: one member of this sect had his head broken by a minor government official (whether Hindū or Muslim is not mentioned) as a result of a quarrel. Other Satnāmīs came to his rescue and assaulted the official. What is more, they and their friends managed to overpower the police force subsequently sent to arrest them; and continued to defeat the larger and larger forces sent by higher and higher authorities. The regular troops of the city of Nārnawl proved equally ineffective; whereupon their commander appealed for help to nearby landlords (whether Hindū or Muslim is not mentioned), whose sympathy with the right rather than the left in a class struggle would be assured.[34] The Satnāmīs, however, defended themselves with a bravery and effectiveness which to their enemies and perhaps to themselves seemed miraculous and magical. All troops sent against them were defeated, until Nārnawl was left without an upper-class police force and without an upper-class commander. The Satnāmīs held the city.

What did they then do? Turn the city and district over to plunder and anarchy? Not according to the extant sources; rather, they at once organized an administration of their own, collecting revenue throughout the district and maintaining order. We can hardly believe that, even if they themselves did not turn to plunder, some rowdy element in the

[31] Ishwar Dās Nāgar, quoted in Sarkar, *History of Aurangzib*, vol. III, p. 337.

[32] Khāfī Khān, in Elliot and Dowson, *History of India*.

[33] Ishwar Dās Nāgar, quoted in Sarkar, *History of Aurangzib*.

[34] 'Matters grew worse, and the *faujdār* set about collecting more men, both horse and foot, and called to his assistance the *zamīndārs* of the neighbourhood'—Khāfī Khān, in Elliot and Dowson, *History of India*, vol. VII, p. 295.

area did not take advantage of the situation to commit excesses. Sir Jadū Nāth Sarkār accuses them of plundering and demolishing mosques in Nārnawl; this is perhaps based on the unpublished manuscript of Ishwar Dās Nāgar to which he refers.[35] No excesses are mentioned, however, by Khāfī Khān (who certainly had no reason to be partial to them); his account reads: 'The town of Nárnaul fell into the hands of the *Sat-námīs.* They proceeded to collect the taxes from the villages, and established posts of their own.'[36] The only disorders that he mentions were later, and not in Nārnawl itself but round about, and not from the common people but from the upper class attempting to establish their independence of Dihlī: 'The *zamindárs* of the neighbourhood, and some cowardly Rájpúts, seized the opportunity to throw off their obedience, and to withhold the government dues. They even broke into open violence, and the flames daily increased.'[37] Similarly, Musta'idd Khān says, 'Cities and towns were plundered',[38] but does not say by whom. In fact, in all the published source material, no charge of looting or disorder is laid against the Satnāmī brotherhood, or of violence except against the upper-class forces attacking them. Apparently they did not initiate any of the recorded fighting, and were not aggressive. Manucci, even, relates that they explicitly refused to take the offensive: 'Elated at having gained one battle, they would not consent to march any further, although urged on by the old woman'[39] who had been inciting them. Apparently they wanted to be left alone by the Mughal upper class and by the rest of the world, and to leave the rest of the world alone.

One wishes that there were some way of finding out more about the administration that they set up. How did they plan to spend the peasant revenue that they collected? Was the assessment for it less than or the same as that imposed by the Mughals? On the answer to such questions as these depends the status of this brotherhood in the annals of the people's movements of the world. It would seem that this group of lower-class townsfolk did not ally itself with the peasantry at large in its attempt to throw off upper-class control; if it also proceeded to exploit the villagers in the place of the Mughals, once it had seized

[35]Sarkar, *History of Aurangzib.*

[36]*Muntakhab al-Lubāb,* in Elliot and Dowson, *History of India.*

[37]Ibid.

[38]*Ma'āthir-i'Alamgīri,* in Elliot and Dowson, ibid., vol. VII, p. 186.

[39]Niccolao Manucci, *Storia do Mogor, or Mogul India 1653–1708,* trans. Irvine (1907), vol. II, p. 168.

power in the district , then it was sociologically confused. But it seems unlikely that this was the case; for the Satnāmīs had no power to enforce levies on the peasantry, and the defence outposts that they organized must have been manned by the villagers themselves. This is all presuming that the sentences in the sources are to be taken seriously. At least this much seems reliable: that the removal of upper-class rule was followed not by chaos but by some form of people's rule. Probably more than that we shall never be able to say definitely; it is a pity, for it would be interesting to know more of this early people's government in Hindūstān.

In any case, it was short-lived. Aurangzēb and his court were thoroughly alarmed. For one thing, we are told that the grain supply at Dihlī was becoming scanty;[40] which reminds us how dependent was the empire on its control and exploitation of the villages. The emperor fitted out a very formidable army, complete with important leaders, artillery, and magic spells; he being resolved 'to exterminate the insurgents'.[41] The battle was fierce and devastating, as class violence habitually is. Even Musta'idd Khān writes that it was just like any other class uprising: 'They fought with all the valour of former rebels whose deeds are recorded in history.'[42] In the end, of course, the upper class won; it is not so much that the Satnāmīs were suppressed as that they were wiped out. Khāfī Khān's version is: 'At length...several thousands of them were killed, and the rest were put to flight, so that the outbreak was quelled.'[43] Musta'idd Khān is even more vivid:

> The people of Hind have called this battle Mahábhárat, on account of the great slaughter of elephants on that trying day....These desperate men. The struggle was terrible. ...At length the enemy broke and fled, but were pursued with great slaughter. Few indeed escaped with their lives...and those regions were cleansed of the presence of the foul unbelievers.[44]...

He goes on to indicate the delight of Aurangzēb at the victory, and the honour with which he rewarded those who had effected it.

It seems entirely clear from a study of the sources that, in the minds of the Muslim ruling class, these people were their enemies and were to be crushed primarily because they were unsubmissive lower-class

[40] Sarkar, *Short History of Aurangzib*, p.163.
[41] Musta'idd *Khān*, Elliot Dowson, *History of India*, vol. VII, p. 186.
[42] Ibid.
[43] *Muntakhab al-Lubāb*, Elliot and Dowson, ibid., vol. VII, pp. 295f.
[44] *Ma'āthir-i-'Ālamgīrī.*

persons, not because they were Hindūs. In fact, the communal element is remarkably subordinated; what caused surprise, contempt, and horror was that such a challenge should be thrown to the empire by mere plebeians. It was always a surprise to the upper class when such uprisings were not at once suppressed. 'It is a cause for wonder...'[45] one of the most remarkable occurrencess ...[46] (cf. Jahāngîr on the lower-class successes at Paṭnā: 'a wonderful event').[47] Had a Hindū ruling class challenged the Mughals, they might have been perturbed or fanatical; but not surprised. Musta'idd Khān's attitude of class, rather than communal, antagonism is crystal-clear from his own words: he introduces his acount of the uprising as follows:

> It is a cause for wonder that a gang of bloody, miserable rebels, goldsmiths, carpenters, sweepers, tanners, and other ignoble beings, braggarts and fools of all descriptions, should become so puffed up with vain-glory as to cast themselves into the pit of self-destruction. This is how it came to pass. A malignant set of people, inhabitants of Mewát, collected suddenly as white ants spring from the ground, or locusts descend from the skies...

He continues the story, somewhat in this acrid vein, until after the fall of the city of Nārṇawl has been related and the matter has gone up to the emperor himself, who resolves to take action, fits out a well-equipped army, and finally sends it 'to effect the destruction of the *unbelievers*'[48] (emphasis mine). This last is his first reference in the whole account to the fact that the insurgents are not Muslims. It is true that later on he again refers to their being 'unbelievers', and calls the members of the finally victorious imperial army 'heroes of Islám'.[49] But this last is not strictly true; for Khāfī Khān mentions the 'great rájás' as well as the 'veteran amírs'[50] that were sent against them with powerful armies, and closes by stating that they were put down in the end 'by the exertions of Rájá Bishan Singh, Hamíd Khán, and others'.[51] Finally, we should note that of our three Indian authorities for the whole

[45]Ibid., p. 185

[46]*Muntakhab-al-Lubāb,* in Elliot and Dowson, *History of India*, vol. VII, p. 294.

[47]*Tūzuk-i-Jahāngīrī*, in Elliot and Dowson, ibid., vol. VI, p. 321.

[48]*Ma'āthir-i-Ālamgīrī*, Elliot and Dowson, ibid., vol. VII, pp. 185f.

[49]Ibid., p. 186.

[50]*Muntakhab al-Lubāb,* in Elliot and Dowson, *History of india*, vol. VII, p. 295.

[51]Ibid., pp. 295f.

affair, by far the most contemptuous and antagonistic[52] is Ishwar Dās Nāgar, an upper-class Hindū with a government job.

We do not mean to suggest that religion had nothing to do with this or similar outbreaks. On the contrary, it had much to do, colouring the affair vividly for many of the persons concerned. But essentially, the evidence suggests, it was a conflict of classes.

Lest it be said, moreover, that we have instanced as class struggles only those conflicts which might better be understood as communal riots, let us turn for our final illustrations to perhaps the most formidable people's movement by which the empire of the Mughals was challenged: the risings of the Paṭhāns. In this case, it was Muslim versus Muslim, as well as class versus class; and while the ideology of the insurrections was indeed religious to an important extent, yet it was not communal in the ordinary sense. Common people who were Hindū revolted against Mughal rule, as we have seen; but they did not revolt so successfully or so repeatedly as did at least one set of common people who were Muslim: those of the North-West Frontier.

The Paṭhāns rose against the Mughal upper class under two principal ideologies: the religious one of the Rawshanī movement (especially 1585, 1611–16, 1628ff), and the nationalist one expressed chiefly by the poetry of Khush-ḥāl Khān Khaṭak (1672–5). We have not the space here to investigate these uprisings in fine detail; the Rawshanī movement in itself, studied sociologically, could well form the subject of an entire assay. The results of research have already been published concerning, as usual, the leaders,[53] but little has been said about those many persons who followed them, or why they did so. Twenty-five thousand men are said to have participated in the Rawshanīs' unsuccessful fight against the Mughals in 1587; and five years later, according to Badā'ūnī, the number of prisoners taken by the imperial forces in an expedition against them reached 14,000. These figures,[54] without necessarily being accurate, are evidently significant; with them one may compare Niẓām ad-Dīn's contemptuous but impressive reference to 'this sect of Afghāns, who were as numerous as ants and locusts'.[55] Clearly, a very sizeable group of Paṭhāns saw some good reason for

[52]See quotations from his account in Sarkar, *History of Aurangzib*, vol. III, p. 337.

[53]See *The Encyclopaedia of Islam*, s. vv. 'Rawshaniya', D.S. Margoliouth, vol. III, pp. 1133f, and 'Bāyazīd Anṣārī Pīr Roshan Rawshaniya', H. Beveridge, vol. I, p. 686.

[54]Quoted by Margoliouth.

[55]*Ṭabaqāt-i-Akbarī*, in Elliot and Dowson, *History of India*, vol. V, p. 451.

joining in this movement. Something by no means negligible was stirring in their society.

Analysis will quickly reveal that probably this struggle of theirs, and certainly that under Khush-ḥāl, was not a clear class conflict in the strict sense which has been applicable to our previous examples. The reason is simple: that the Paṭhāns' society was not a class society in the same sense. These people live in a rather barren land where productivity is limited and therefore surplus wealth is small. Hence their society is not divided into two rigid economic classes, the rich and the poor, the one living off the labour of the other. Instead, it is strongly democratic; like other societies whose productivity is not abundant, such as Arabia where Islām arose, or the American frontier in the nineteenth century.

Paṭhān society, then, is not itself a class society, to a developed degree. Nonetheless, the attempt to impose on that society the rule of the Mughal state was in fact an attempt to impose on the common people there a ruling class, an attempt to make it a class society on the pattern of the rest of the Mughal empire. The idea was that a group of administrators appointed from Dihlī should collect tribute and issue orders, which the Paṭhāns were expected respectively to proffer and obey. The situation was complicated by the fact that the Mughals were astute enough to choose as members of their ruling class some of the Paṭhāns themselves; and we shall presently see the implications of this in at least one personality. In general it may be said without too great inaccuracy that the Frontier under the Mughals became a class community in which the common people, Paṭhāns, were the lower class and the rulers, Mughals (with some Paṭhān *khāns* in the Mughal imperial service), were the upper class. And when these two came into conflict with each other, it was a struggle between classes (the common people striving to throw off the rule of a group of people not of themselves), as well as between religious interpretations or between nationalities.

This analysis minimizes, then, the internal social structure of the Paṭhān community, according to which each tribe and subgroup had its leader, and these leaders taken together were distinct from the rest of the people. That structure, we feel, was not so rigid or so highly developed, and that distinction was not so sharp, but that we may feel fairly confident in almost ignoring them. Further research, however, might show that the class struggles which arose in this area were in fact significantly more complicated than here appears. With this word of caution, then, let us examine them.

The Raw<u>sh</u>anī movement was a socio-religious sect, comprising at different times very varying numbers of the Pa<u>th</u>ān masses who acknowledged as religious and political leader one Bāyazīd, whom they called Pīr Raw<u>sh</u>an (in Pa<u>sh</u>to: 'Ro<u>kh</u>ān,' 'Ro<u>sh</u>ān'), and later his descendants. He was influenced, through a Mullā Sulaymān,[56] by leftwing <u>Sh</u>ī'ah traditions—the depository in Islām for ideas of theological heresy and sociological revolution.[57] The doctrines of the sect included various metaphysical tenets, such as a form of theopanism; but the elements that chiefly interest a modern historian are the same as those which probably chiefly interested the Af<u>gh</u>ān commoner of that time such as freedom from observing the <u>sharī'at</u>, absolute obedience to the Pīr, lawfulness of seizing the property of non-Raw<u>sh</u>anīs, and the promise of 'in time, the dominion of the whole earth'.[58] It seems proven that had the movement confined itself to theology, it would hardly have attracted persecution; for the founder's son and subsequent successor, Jalāl ad-Dīn, was 'kindly received'[59] by Akbar (in 1580), and even the founder himself was acquitted in a heresy trial before the '*ulamā*' of Kābul.[60] The movement attracted repression for the same reason that it attracted followers: namely that it added to its theological principles practical exploits such as seizing caravans as they moved through the <u>Kh</u>aybar pass.

Akbar set out to 'repress this base sect'[61] not at the time of his meeting with Jalāl and presumably discussing metaphysics with him, but five years later when the latter and his men 'shut up the roads between Hindūstān and Kābul'.[62]

The first adherents of Bāyazīd were tribesmen of the <u>Kh</u>alīl and Maḥmūd-zā'ī, some of whom acted as missionaries and raiders for him. Later the Yūsuf- zā'ī joined the Raw<u>sh</u>anīyah; they presently abandoned

---

[56]In 'Kalindjār, S.W. of Allāhābād', according to Margoliouth; presumably Kālinjar is meant. H.G. Raverty, calls him 'Mullā Sulīmān Jālandharī,' *Selections from the Poetry of the Afghāns*, 1867, pp. 51–5: 'Notes on Mīrzā <u>Kh</u>ān, Anṣārī'.

[57]Students of Islamic history have recognized, but not adequately, the extent to which the <u>Sh</u>ī'ah movement, and especially the Ismā'īlī group and its later leftwing sects, have been connected with *social* discontent.

[58]Elphinstone, *History of India*, ed. Cowell, 9th edn, 1916, p. 505.

[59]*Ṭabaqāt-i-Akbarī*, in S.R. Sharma, *Mughal Empire in India, p. 277.*

[60]'For a consideration' Margoliouth, 'Raw<u>sh</u>aniya'.

[61]*Ṭabaqāt-i-Akbarī*, in S.R. Sharma, *Mughal Empire*, p. 278.

[62]Ibid., pp. 277f.

the cause and its leader and even fought against them, though continuing to fight against the Mughals also, under other ideologies. At one time enough of his fellow countrymen lent Bāyazīd their support for him to proclaim himself 'king' of Afghānistān and to dream of conquering the whole Mughal empire; and some, apparently, were willing to buy the drafts which he issued on Akbar's treasury. However, he was presently overcome by his enemies (Paṭhāns), and died. It was under his son Jalāl ad-Dīn's leadership (1585–1600) that the movement reached its most formidable proportions. The large figures that we have previously quoted belong to this period; tens of thousands of Paṭhāns became Rawshanīs and were prepared to sacrifice their lives for the cause which that represented. As such, they not only offered the Dihlī empire a serious challenge, but also in 1600 seized the city of Ghaznah. What they did with it is not clear, before they were shortly driven out.

Despite their very large numbers, they were not able to unite all the Paṭhāns. In fact, they continually attracted vituperation and persecution at the hands of one section of their own people. Their fight for freedom from outside control and for domination had to be waged as much against other Paṭhāns as against the Mughals.

In Jahāngīr's time, the numbers taking part in Rawshanī affairs seem very much smaller; though they again managed to give the Mughals much trouble. We first hear of them attacking Kābul in 1611, under the leadership of Jalāl ad-Dīn's son Aḥdād (Aḥad-dād). This was perhaps nothing more than a raid for booty, taking advantage of the governor's momentary absence; the accounts, written by their enemies, do not indicate whether the intention was to plunder or to rule.[63] In any case, the attack was beaten off, with the assistance of the local citizens.[64] Three years later we hear of 5000 followers of Aḥdād in another engagement. In two subsequent defeats the numbers of their losses to the imperialists are mentioned as 1500 and 400 respectively.[65] Apparently the Paṭhāns' interest in the movement was waning.

An interesting sidelight on the times is thrown by an incident a year or two later. The Paṭhāns of Bangash district, adopting perhaps not the theology or the name of the Rawshanīyah but at least its spirits, 'rebelled'—decided, presumably, not to pay tribute or to accept the domination of the alien rulers. In the encounter with the Mughal arms that ensued, they found as office-in-charge of a contingent facing them

[63]See Benī Prashād, *History of Jahangir*, pp. 186ff.

[64]Ibid., p. 186.

[65]Ibid., pp. 186f.

one other than a brother of Aḥdāno, called Allāh-dād, who had gone off to the imperial court and had been given by the Mughals a post in the government. His fellow Paṭhāns succeeded in making his conscience uncomfortable, it would seem; for he fought shamefully, and before long they had the joy of seeing him relinquish his imperial service and, instead of fighting against his own people, side with them in their fight for freedom.

The governor of Kābul was, of course, furious, and spent two years pursuing him. He was eventually caught, and was sent to the emperor for punishment. On condition that he totally renounce his nationalist activities, Jahāngīr magnanimously pardoned him and gave him back his official job. One does not know whether years later the Paṭhāns heard occasional reports and gossip trickling through to their home area of his very successful career in the distant government service: he showed no subsequent lapses from loyalty, and, earning his due reward, 'rose to high distinction under the title of Rashid Khan, during the reign of Shah Jahan'.[66]

These Bangashī continued to 'be troublesome' for the rest of Jahāngīr's reign, cutting to pieces at least one considerable army sent against them,[67] but seeing their lands devastated and their people slaughtered by the avenging Mughals.[68]

The last that one hears of Rawshanī exploits is under Shāh Jahān. Aḥdād was killed in 1625 or 1626 in an engagement with the imperial force (led by Ẓafar Khān); a year or two later a group of Paṭhāns accepting the leadership of his son, 'Abd al-Qādir, annihilated a Mughal army in the Khaybar (under the same Ẓafar Khān) and took much ootv. In 1628 Shāh Jahān, we are told,[69] took steps to crush the Rawsha ment. In the following year a number of Paṭhāns attacked Peshāwar, among whom was a group of Rawshanīs under 'Abd al-Qādir, as well as other Afghāns under another leader.[70] This attack was beaten off; also, the Rawshanīs lost their leader. For 'Abd al-

[66]Ibid., p.187. For instance, he was one of the chief officers under Prince Shujā in the Dakhin, 1633f. Saksena, History of Shahjahan of Dihli, p. 160. See further, ibid., pp. 82, 317.

[67]Under 'the impetuous Izzat Khan', Benī Prashād, *History of Jahangir*, p. 187.

[68]Ibid., p. 188: 'Rapine and slaughter filled Bangash.'

[69]Shāh Jahān Nāmah of Muḥammad Ṣāliḥ Kambū, cited in Margoliouth, 'Rawshaniya'.

[70]Kamāl ad-Dīn. Saksena, *History of Shahjahan*, p.124; Margoliouth, ibid.

Qādir was evidently persuaded of the futility of his career; he submitted to the Mughals, and four years later went off to join their imperial service. Shāh Jahān made him a manṣabdār of 1600, and later gave other honours to some of his relatives.

By this time, clearly, the movement was petering out. The loss of its leaders was probably not only a cause but also a result of that fact. There was a brother of Aḥdād and Allāh-dād, by the name of Karīm-dād; he had taken part in the assault on Peshāwar in 1629. The people of Bangash now asked him to come and lead them in their continued struggle. He did so, and in 1638 many of the tribes in that neighbourhood rose. Soon, however, they lost his leadership, and subsided; for the Mughals attacked vigorously, and succeeding in capturing him, put him to death.

From this time forward one reads of the Rawshanīyah only as a small group with certain religious predilections; they have undertaken, it appears, no further political or military enterprises. Some individuals are still perhaps to be found amongst the Paṭhāns who perpetuate till today traces of the theology of the sect,[71] and a few even have developed a separate heresy from it.[72] But after 1638 the movement drops out of political and military history, and has presumably negligible sociological significance.

Not, indeed, that it was long before the Paṭhāns were rising again against their Mughal would-be overlords. But by that time (under Aurangzēb's reign) they had a new ideology and new leaders. Before we observe their next uprisings, however, let us pause to ask what generalizations we can pass on the Rawshanīyah. From the above sketch it would seem fair to infer that the movement comprised different sets of persons at different times: in other words there was not really one movement but several. Of these, some are of sociological significance, others perhaps are not. Some those Paṭhāns who challenged the Mughal empire as Rawshanīs were fighting for freedom, some only for booty. There is no reason to doubt that there were individuals motivated towards both goals at once. A movement which promised its followers personal plunder and the liberation of their community and homeland, as well as religious salvation, would find that if one of these inducements was insufficient to attract many members, all three of them

[71] It is asserted that some relics of the community still exist in this (i.e. the Bangash) region, Margoliouth.

[72] The Isawī group. Ibid., citing T.C. Plowden, translation of the *Kālid-ī-Afghāni*, Lahore 1875 (sc. *Translation of the Kālidī-Afghāni*).

together would at times add up to do so. Finally, the sociologist notes that one finds almost to names of *khāns* attracted to the Rawshanīyah (also that the spokesman for its opponents amongst the Paṭhāns was an Akhūnd[73]): in all its different forms it remained a movement of the common people.

We need not detain ourselves over the Paṭhāns' later uprisings against Mughal imperialism; partly because they are already well known, being extensively treated in the standard histories, and partly because they were not people's movements unqualifiedly. For although the ordinary folk did take part, they were led by their own *khāns* and upper class. In 1667 the Yūsuf-zā'ī, with regal and religious trappings, set themselves up as an independent people, and attacked Mughal outposts.[74] The empire soon crushed them with great severity: thousands were killed, crops destroyed, villages burned. One is reminded of the accusation against the Roman empire: 'They made a desert, and they called it peace.'

The peace lasted in this case for five years. In 1672 the Afrīdī, whose grandsires had fought under Pīr Rawshan,[75] were enthusiastic when their *khān*, Akmal, set himself up as an independent ruler, with his own kingly crown and his own coins, and declared war on the Mughal empire. To his appeals that all tribes should join him to make this a united national movement, the other Paṭhāns listened with an interest which was heightened when they heard that the Afrīdī, annihilating a Mughal army in the Khaybar, had taken as booty, in cash and goods, more than 20 million rupees. (In appreciating this figure, one should recall the large purchasing power of the rupee in Mughal times.) The Khaṭak, whose *khān* was the inspiring anti-imperialist poet Khush-ḥal, were the first to join; it was not long before practically all the Paṭhāns were involved. It was a full nationalist movement. The people were ardent; the leaders well trained, many having served in the Mughal imperial service; and except for artillery, the Paṭhāns were as well armed as their would-be masters.

In fact, the empire was not able to down by military might this united Paṭhān resistance. Aurangzēb degraded his governor of Afghānistān, who proved helpless, and sent a new and formidable one.[76]

[73] 'Abd al-Karīm, Akhūnd Darwīzah, author of *Makhzan al-Islām*.

[74] For this and the following movement, see especially Sarkar: *History of Aurangzib*.

[75] Hell, article 'Afridis', in *The Encyclopaedia of Islām*, vol. I, p. 176b.

[76] Mahābat Khān. He had already proved his prowess at suppressing Afghāns.

He, too, was unsuccessful, and was degraded. Next, the suppressor of the Satnāmī uprising[77] was sent, and along with him one of the leading Rājpūt mahārājās.[78] The Pathāns defeated and slew the former; of the latter they frustrated every manœuvre. For four years, inspired and unified by the ideology and poetry of nationalism and by their own success, they held the empire at bay and would not be overcome. In the end, Aurangzēb's cunning won, where Mughal military strength had failed. He himself went north, and realizing that a united Pathān nation could not be conquered, managed to 'divide and rule'. By bribery; by gifts to the *khāns* of titles, of high-paid posts on the imperial service, and of jāgīrs; by the setting of one group against another in their traditional rivalries; and then by ruthless piecemeal terrorization of the remaining irreconcilables; imperialism was finally re-established.

At this point we end our study; though we have not, of course, exhausted the tale of folk warfare in Mughal times. Another nationalist movement against the empire under Aurangzēb could be called a people's movement, but only in a still more qualified sense: the rise of the Mahrattās. This was led by the Mahrattā feudal nobility; but the lower classes participated in it in its early stages, as V.V. Joshī has shown in his able work, *The Clash of Three Empires*. Their participation had also its religious aspect; for instance, in the democratic–nationalist ideology of Rām Dās's preaching. The rise of the Sikhs, similarly, awaits study from a class point of view. The writer has conceived the idea, too, that a sociologically minded investigator might find it worth his while to examine the repeated revolts[79] against Jahāngīr that were led by Khusrau, whose upper-class support was small, the suppression of whose uprisings was excruciating, and who undoubtedly caught the imagination of the masses, so that his name lived on among them as that of some legendary champion. One wonders how and why this prince succeeded in doing what most other aristocratic rulers of the time never even thought of trying to do, and would certainly have failed had they tried—namely to win the emotional and practical support of the common people in campaigns.

Before concluding, perhaps it is necessary to add, with a touch of emphasis, that the present essay is in no sense an attack on Mughal

[77] Shujā'at Khān.

[78] Jaswant Singh of Jodhpur.

[79] See Benī Prashād, *History of Jahangir* (pp. 120–34, and other references ibid. from the index). The leader of the Patnā outbreak, Qutb, pretended to be Khusrau.

civilization; which civilization was unquestionably one of the grand achievements of the human spirit in past history. The attainments of the Mughal rulers in many fields are the object of the most legitimate admiration. And not their least attainment was the very wide measure of peace and prosperity which they created for the common people under their sway. The peasants and the workers of north India enjoyed, while Mughal rule was at its height, a life of greater calm and comfort than their ancestors had known for centuries, and than their descendants were to know again for many a long day.

Our purpose is merely to point out that the Mughal empire, for all its virtues, and they are many, was none the less an empire. And all empires, and all class societies, whatever their virtues, involve along with rulers a group of ruled. The two tags which we quoted above with reference to the Mughals were first formulated to docket the Roman empire: it was Romans who made a desert and called it peace, and Romans who divided to rule. Yet anyone who in sympathy for the exploited of Roman days ignored the achievements of that empire would be dubbing himself a barbarian or crank rather than a liberal. Similarly for the Mughals: in examining the life of the poor, it would be unbalanced to forget the glories of the culture and contribution of the aristocracy—just as the more usual procedure, we have suggested, is unbalanced, whereby we note that aristocracy but overlook the poor. One does not choose between the two; for historical accuracy as well as human understanding one must realize that they went together.

Our particular thesis is simple, and we call attention to it only as one small but surely interesting aspect in the complex of Mughal culture. It is that throughout history, one group of men has lorded it over another; but that also, throughout history, from time to time the oppressed and exploited have risen in resistance and struggled that they might be free. This is true not only in Europe where it has been already studied, but throughout the world, including India. Until modern times it has not been possible that such movements should be successful; it is only recently that the objective conditions for social freedom and a classless society have been approximated. But we must appreciate, none the less, the attempts, however misguided, that man has made in the past; and must realize that the urge to freedom is universal, persistent, and in the end indomitable.

12
Review of the Crisis of the Jagirdari System*

Satish Chandra

The crisis of the *jagirdari* system in the Mughal empire was closely linked to economic and social relations in medieval India, specifically to the agrarian relations and the administrative superstructure reared upon these relations. As recent research has shown, rural society in medieval India was dominated by a large heterogeneous group of people called *zamindars* by the medieval writers. The *zamindars* were often closely linked with the cultivators organized on the basis of caste, clan or tribe. The caste, clan or tribe, it appears, often settled on land on a fairly compact territorial basis, so that groups of villages—12, 24, 48, etc.—'belonged' to certain castes. The necessity of collecting land revenue from the landholders who were often armed and organized on a caste/tribal basis, military-minded, and not prepared to part easily with any share of the agricultural surplus, created strong disintegrative tendencies. The *iqtadari* or the *jagirdari* systems which were specific features of the administrative system of the Sultanat and the Mughals should be viewed against this background. *Iqtadari* and *jagirdari* implied giving individual nobles a vested interest in collecting land revenue from the landholders in the tracts assigned to them in *iqta* or *jagir*. But for the presence of a class of powerful *zamindars* in the country, the *iqta* or *jagir* system could, perhaps, have been dispensed with, as was attempted by at least one ruler. It is true that control over land was also a matter of social prestige or status in an essentially feudal society. However, the dialectical relationship of the *zamindar*

*From Satish Chandra, *Medieval India: Society, the Jagirdari Crisis and the Village* (Delhi: Macmillan, 1982).

and the *jagirdari* system is cardinal in understanding the evolution of medieval Indian society. As is well known, the Sultanat and especially the Mughal rulers tried to limit the power and prerogatives of the *zamindars*, as well as utilized the *zamindars* in the task of revenue collection[1] Under the Mughals, a small proportion of the *zamindars* were offered *mansabs* and thus drawn closely into the central administrative system. However, the bulk of the *zamindars* were sought to be integrated into the working of the local land revenue system and the machinery for the maintenance of law and order. This was a complex process, with varying degrees of success in various areas, and depended upon a number of variables, such as the military strength of the *zamindar*, his association with the local community, the geographical location of the *zamindari*, etc.

Both caste and the structure of rural society played a significant role in the attempt of the Turkish and Mughal rulers to control and utilize the *zamindars* for their purposes. Recent evidence shows that though village society was segmented, a large proportion of cultivators who from ancient times had been considered owners of the land they cultivated, could not be dispossessed as long as they paid the land revenue. Moreover, bearing in mind the land–man ratio, cultivators were a major asset, and they could not be lightly dispensed with or forced to flee to neighbouring territories. These cultivators are called *khud-kasht* in seventeenth-and eighteenth-century Persian revenue documents. The khudkasht formed a privileged group in village society with well-recognized hereditary rights and duties.[2] Dominating a village or a group of villages in a region, a predominant section of the *khudkasht* was often drawn from one caste or clan. Thus, the Jats and Ahirs in north-western India, and Marathas in western India constituted the bulk of the privileged sections in many tracts of the regions. The local officials (*muqaddam, kulkarni, patel,* etc.) and even intermediary *zamindars* were often drawn from the *khudkasht*. The Sultans and later, in a more systematic manner, the Mughals tried to establish direct relations with the cultivators in order to determine the productivity, nature of crops, etc. thereby setting up a system of revenue administration on the basis of which they could fix and thereby limit the perquisites of the *zamindars*.

[1]S. Nurul Hasan, in this volume 'Zamindars under the Mughals'.

[2]See Satish Chandra, *Medieval India: Society, the Jagirdari Crisis and the Village*, Delhi, 1982, ch. IV, for a review of the position and role of the *khudkasht* and the *pahikasht*.

The growth of central authority and prestige under the Mughals, and the Mughal emphasis on justice, which broadly implied not permitting one group of people to encroach on the duties of another,[3] gradually created a situation in which various sections of society including the cultivators began to look to the central government, rather than to the local *zamindar* or chieftain, for protection and for the redress of their grievances if they went beyond a certain point. This led to the gradual development of a triangular or tripolar relationship between the central government, the *zamindars*, and the cultivators in which the *khudkasht* predominated. This apparently was the basis of the so-called 'Mughal stability'. This stability, which is a marked feature of the first half of the seventeenth century, lasted as long as the central government could convince the *zamindars* and the cultivators that it was more profitable for them to look to the central government for support and for the redress of their grievances than to join hands to resist and fight against it. The growth of the *pargana* administration and the *faujdari* system under the Mughals also aided this process. Unlike the *iqtadar* under the Sultanat, the Mughal *jagirdar* was largely divested of the administrative responsibility of the area assigned to him as *jagir*. The *faujdar* who was the lynchpin of the Mughal administrative system, had the dual responsibility of providing, where necessary, military support to the *jagirdar* in collecting his share of the land revenue, and also of providing a channel of redress against the exactions of the *jagirdar* and his agents, and the *zamindar*. The *waqianavis* was meant to watch over both the *jagirdar* and the *faujdar*. This system of checks and balances, rising up to the provincial and central levels, was an essential feature of the Mughal administrative system, and was designed as a safeguard against the abuse of power and authority at various levels.

By the very nature of medieval Indian society, the delicate social balance outlined above on which the Mughal administrative system rested was liable to be upset on a number of counts. The effects of a serious struggle for power at the centre, disaffection in the nobility, challenge to the empire by regional chiefs, etc., are some of the well-known factors. At the local and regional levels, augmentation of the power of the *zamindars*, directly or indirectly, or a serious weakening

[3]*Ain-i-Akbari*, Blochmann, p. 4. See also the views of the contemporary poet Tulsidas for whom this was the basis of social stability, in Savitri Chandra, 'Two Aspects of Hindu Social Life and Thought as Reflected in the Works of Tulsidasa', *Journal of the Economic and Social History of the Orient*, vol. XIX (1976), pp. 48–60.

of the position of the *khudkasht* could also have far-reaching consequences, though their effects were likely to be of a long-ranging nature and hence are less well documented. Tensions at the village or local level, sometimes on a caste basis, or large-scale local migrations also sometimes affected village society. Conflicts on a religious or ethnic basis could acquire an added historical significance, especially if it affected the villages.

Signs of a social and economic crisis appeared even during the first half of the seventeenth century, i.e. in the so-called period of stability. The crisis manifested itself in the shape of a financial and administrative crisis, namely as a growing gap between the revenue needed for assignment to the *mansabdars* and its availability. Without going into details, we may only note that the situation had become so serious that Shah Jahan, shortly after his accession, had to take official note of it. The introduction of the rule of one-third/one-fourth, and the month scales (*mahwar*) was aimed at reducing the emoluments and the obligations of the *mansabdars* in order to bridge the gap between the requirement and availability of revenue. Thus, in the twenty-seventh year of his reign, Shah Jahan ordered that a *mansabdar* on cash salary should not be more than eight monthly or less than four monthly.[4]

There has been considerable controversy regarding the factors which led to the introduction of the rule of one-third/one-fourth and the month scale, and their impact on the total emoluments of the nobles. Without entering into this controversy here, it may not be far wrong to draw the inference that the lowering of the effective share of the nobles in the agricultural surplus reflected in reality a social and economic crisis which the Mughal ruling class tried to resolve by administrative means. Since the land revenue demand had already been placed at the highest rate possible,[5] any augmentation of the resources available to the Mughal ruling class could be obtained only by (a) a further expansion of the empire; (b) expansion and improvement of cultivation; (c) improvement and expansion of non-agricultural production

[4]Ali Mohammad Khan, *Mirat-i-Ahmadi*, ed. Nawab Ali, Baroda, 1928, vol. I, pp. 227–8. In 1652, the *hasil* of the four *subahs* in the Deccan was less than one-third. Aurangzeb as Viceroy of the Deccan complained bitterly of being saddled with *jagirs* which were less productive than in the north. (*Adab*. 31a, 24b; J.N. Sarkar, *History of Aurangzib*, vol. I, Calcutta, 1912, pp. 99–100.) The situation did not improve materially under Aurangzeb. See *Selected Documents of Aurangzeb's Reign* (ed.), Y. Husain Khan (Hyderabad, 1958).

[5]Irfan Habib, *Agrarian System of Mughal India*, (Bombay 1963) p. 319.

and trade by application of science and technology; (d) efforts to squeeze the share of the various sections of agricultural classes to the point of diminishing returns. The Mughal ruling class or sections of it tried, in one way or another, all the methods outlined above. However, it was not able to solve the basic problem facing it, viz. the growing inadequacy of available revenue, largely because it was unable and unwilling to carry out any drastic changes in the existing social set-up, especially the agrarian relations which rested on the triad formed by the *jagirdars* (representing the central government, i.e. the Mughal ruling class), the *zamindars*, and the *khudkasht* landowners or the dominant section of the cultivators. There is evidence to show that the dominant or privileged body of peasants was generally reluctant to permit the landless peasants, or peasants with dwarf holdings, who often belonged to the low castes, to become landowners although there was no shortage of cultivable wasteland. A strong and confident central government could have taken the steps necessary to break the stranglehold of what modern sociologists might call 'the middle castes' on agricultural land, and provide to the underprivileged sections, viz. the low-caste preasants, the organization and financial means which would enable them to bring uncultivated wasteland under cultivation, and to acquire ownership rights over them. Although the Mughal government granted contracts on progressive rates (*istwah*) to those who brought virgin lands under cultivation, and inducements were held out to *pahis*, who were often drawn from the low castes, for rehabilitating ruined villages, setting up new villages, or for bringing surplus land under cultivation, a close reading of the sources suggests that the *pahis* entrusted with these tasks were generally those who had their own ploughs and oxen, i.e. those who were drawn from a comparatively privileged group in the village. Moreover, these activities were generally undertaken with the help of the local *zamindars* and *muqaddams* who, as we have noted above, generally belonged to the dominant landholding caste(s) in a village or region.[6] Thus, the Mughal government remained largely dependent on the backing and support of the *zamindars* and the dominant landowning castes at the village level.

As is well known, the working of the Mughal revenue system depended upon the ability of the Mughal government and its local representatives, the *faujdars, jagirdars*, etc. to overawe the *zamindars* and the cultivators with their superior military strength. However, the working of the rule of one-third/one-fourth and the month scale implied that

[6]See Chandra, *Medieval India*, ch. XIII.

the number of *sawars* employed by a *mansabdar* as well as the number and quality of the mounts were steadily lowered. Thus, a *mansabdar* of 4000/4000, if he had a *jagir* other than in the *subah* in which he was posted, and held a five-month *jagir*, employed 1000 *sawars* and 1000 horses. The number of *sawars* and the mounts was further reduced when the *jagir* was less than five monthly.[7] An adequate number of remounts was vital for the efficiency of the cavalry, and this had been ensured by the *dah-bisti* system under Akbar whereby a contingent of ten *sawars* had 20 to 22 horses. Under Shah Jahan, a five-month *jagir* became fairly normal, thus impairing the efficiency of the cavalry. The traditional reluctance of the *mansabdars* in engaging themselves in battles where they might endanger their horses, was further aggravated. The reduced number of *sawars* weakened the ability and willingness of the Mughal *faujdars* to give adequate support to the *jagirdars* in the task of collecting their share of land revenue. Writing with special reference to the Deccan after the Mughal conquest of Bijapur and Golconda, Bhimsen says that *faujdars* who had only small contingents (*jamiat*) compared to the earlier times, sat at home and took no action against the Maratha freebooters. The *wakil* of the Amber ruler wrote back that *mansabdars* of 7000 maintained contingents of only 700, and that due to the ineffectiveness of the *faujdars*, royal princes and their sons were roaming the countryside like *faujdars*.[8] The inability of the *mansabdars* to realize the income due from their *jagirs*, in turn, further eroded their military capabilities. This situation is pinpointed by Bhimsen who says that during the last part of Aurangzeb's rule, except Rama Singh Hada, Dalpat Bundela and Jai Singh Kachawa, *who had their own watans*, no *mansabdar* maintained more than 1000 *sawars*.[9]

We have argued above that the fundamental basis for the *jagirdari* crisis was the medieval social system which limited agricultural growth, and the administrative system was reared on this structure, the two acting and reacting on each other. A number of other factors can be considered contributory factors to the growth of the crisis. Of these, the one cited most frequently is the growth in the size of the ruling

[7] *Khulasat-us-Siyaq*, Ms. Aligarh Muslim University, ff. 54 a-b; Abd-ul Hamid Lahori, *Badshah Nama*, vol. II, eds., Maulvis Kabiruddin and Abdur Rahim, Calcutta, 1867–8, p. 507; Abdul Aziz, *Mansabdari System and the Mughal Army*, Lahore, 1945, p. 85.

[8] Bhimsen, *Nuskha-i-Dilkusha*, Br. Mus. Or. 23 f. 139a; *Akhbarat*, 27 *Ziqada* R.Y. 30/30 July 1693.

[9] Bhimsen, f. 140b, emphasis mine.

class, i.e. of the nobility and their dependents both of whom, directly or indirectly, subsisted on the revenue resources of the empire. The growing ostentatious lifestyle of the nobles limited the surplus available for expanding production, and this made for stagnation, i.e. a slow process of economic growth. However, this was common to all feudal societies, and hence hardly a new factor, ostentation itself depending on the size of the surplus. Aurangzeb was apparently concerned at the lifestyle of the nobles, and tried to establish an atmosphere of austerity by his personal example, e.g. banning the use of gold and silver vessels as being un-Islamic, giving up the weighing ceremony, etc. But it was of little avail. It is also true that not all the expenditure incurred by the nobles could be considered unproductive. Thus, they did provide employment to the artisans and craftsmen, and patronage to the artists, but within the framework of slow economic growth.

There is little doubt that there was a rapid increase during the seventeenth century of the number of those hankering for royal service. In addition to the influx of 'adventurers' from Central Asia, the number of *khanazads,* i.e. sons and relations of *mansabdars* grew rapidly, the *mansabdars* having many wives and mistresses and, in consequence, many sons and sons-in-law. For political reasons, it was necessary to include into the ruling class a number of *zamindars,* first the Rajputs and later the Marathas in the Deccan. In addition to these, *shaikhzadas* (i.e. sons of religious divines), and even petty officials, professional people such as *hakims,* etc. hankered for *mansabs* since a *mansab* had become a mark of social prestige. We are told that under Jahangir, even *hakims* and wrestlers were awarded *mansabs.* In consequence, there was the emergence of what we may call 'lobbyists', i.e. groups and individuals who canvassed with the ruler for *mansabs* for their relations, groups, etc. The so-called Irani, Turani factions, *khanazads,* etc. were a part of these 'lobbies'.

On balance, both Shah Jahan and, up to a point, Aurangzeb coped with this situation fairly well. Despite the 'lobbyists', the growth in the numbers of the nobility and their *mansabs* did not seriously outrun the available revenue resources of the empire. Aurangzeb put a severe check on the growth of *mansabs* and *mansabdars* after his accession to the throne.[10] Even after the conquest of Bijapur and Golconda, the growth in the numbers of the nobility was broadly matched by the

[10] Athar Ali, *The Mughal Nobility Under Aurangzeb,* Bombay, 1966, p. 10.

additional *jama* of the two *subahs.*[11] But in the process, some of the internal problems of the *jagirdari* system were aggravated. First, the induction of new elements into the nobility adversely affected the *khanazads*. Khafi Khan, who himself belonged to the category of *khanazads,* complains bitterly that on account of the inadequacy of *pai baqi*, and the appointment of innumerable *mansabdars,* especially large numbers of Marathas and Deccanis, the *khanazads* would sometimes not be able to get *jagirs* for four to five years.[12] The working of the central machinery of administration itself was such that there was great delay in granting *jagirs* to new entrants.[13] The new entrants, apparently the *khanazads,* had to sign a bond (*muchalka*) that they would not claim salary for the period between the preparation of their *yad-dasht* (claim) and the allotment of the *jagir*. Despite this, the *diwan-i-tan,* Musawi Khan, insisted that they must appoint their forces during the interval, but little attention was paid to their demand for the arrears. Khafi Khan says, 'Gradually, all regulations disappeared, and accounting was given up.'[14]

After the conquest of Bijapur and Golconda, Aurangzeb tried to put a limit on the further growth of the number of *mansabdars*. He repeatedly

[11]For *jama* and *hasil* figures of the empire, see Irfan Habib, *Agrarian System,* pp. 399–409. J.F. Richards in *Mughal Administration of Golconda,* Oxford, 1975, p. 272, has emphasized that while the nobility grew by 23.5 per cent, the *jama* grew by 23 per cent. Since neither total numbers, nor total *mansabs* give an adequate idea of the total salary (*talab*) payable to the nobles, on the basis of rule of one-third/one-fourth and the month scale, the above may be considered only a broad approximation.

[12]Muhammed Hashin Khafi Khan, *Muntakhab-ul Lubab,* vols I and II, eds K.S. Ahmad and Wolsley Haig, Calcutta, 1868–1974, vol. II, pp. 396–7. This is placed in R.Y. 35/1691–2.

[13]Mirza Yar Ali Khan, the *Darogha-i-Dak,* who was greatly favoured by Aurangzeb, remarked caustically, when the emperor objected that the man presented by him for grant of a *mansab* was too young in years, 'By the time he gets a *jagir* and is enrolled in the service, his hair would be grey.' Khafi Khan, *Muntakhab,* vol. II, pp. 378–9. This is placed in R.Y. 33/1689–90.

[14]Ibid., pp. 396–7. The author states that the *mansabdars* claimed the arrears of salary despite the *muchalka* so that substantial sums were owed to the *mansabdars* by the imperial government. However much the *mansabdars* wanted the account to be settled, the *mustaufi* paid no heed to it, and if a *mansabdar* as a result of his efforts, and with the support of protectors and his *wakil,* was able to establish his claim for a substantial amount, with great difficulty he would be able to get one-fourth of his demand.

declared that he did not need any new servants, and desired that no papers (*misl*) of new entrants be put up to him. But the *bakhshis*, under the pressure of the nobles, refused to co-operate. Ruhullah Khan, the *bakhshi*, continued to put fresh cases before the emperor on the plea that the empire consisted of seven Sultanats, i.e. it was vast, and that the emperor alone could say yes or no to the large number of needy *khanazads*. Later, after the death of Ruhullah Khan, Aurangzeb angrily turned down all the requests of the *bakhshi*, Mukhlis Khan. This led to great lamentation in the camp among those who had waited for an appointment for years. Imperial signature, i.e. grant of a *jagir*, became like giving one pomegranate to a hundred sick.[15] Inability on the part of *mansabdars* to secure suitable *mansabs* for their children and relations was bound to affect the future loyalty of these nobles to the empire. The problem posed by the *khanazads* continued to deteriorate, and became even more acute in the eighteenth century, under the successors of Aurangzeb.

Second, in order to cope with the military requirements of the empire, both Shah Jahan and Aurangzeb expanded the imperial *khalisa* or reserved lands. From one-ninth under Jahangir it grew to one-fifth under Aurangzeb.[16] While there is no evidence that the increase of the *khalisa* created a shortage of *paibaqi* lands, i.e. lands reserved for assignment in *jagirs* to the *mansabdars*, the manner of the demarcation of the *khalisa* lands created acute problems. The imperial *mutasaddis* usually chose for the *khalisa*, *jagirs*, which were *sair-hasil*, i.e. which were productive and easily manageable, leaving the *mansabdars* to deal with the less productive *jagirs*, especially those located in *zor-talab* areas, i.e. areas where realization was difficult due to the strength of the *zamindars* and the recalcitrance of the landowners. According to the *Hidayat-ul-Qawaid*,[17] the earlier rule was that *subahdars* should have

[15]Ibid., 411–12 (R.Y. 35/1691–2), 602. I have not agreed with the translation of the latter passage in Elliot and Dowson, *History of India as Told by Its Own Historians*, London, 1867–1877, vol. VII, p. 403. It is interesting to note that in another context, when Inayatullah Khan, the *diwan-i-tan-o-khalisa*, had complained to the emperor that the *paibaqi* was limited, while the number of applicants for a *jagir* was unlimited, Aurangzeb had observed that the world, i.e. the empire was vast, and that he should not lose heart (*Ahkam* 57).

[16]Irfan Habib, *Agrarian System*, pp. 272–3. A considerable part remained under *khalisa* in the conquered states of Bijapur and Golconda to provide for Mughal campaigns against the Marathas, and in the Karnataka.

[17]Hidayatullah Bihari, *Hidayat-ul-Qawaid*, Aligarh Muslim University Ms., f. 8a.

one-fourth *jagir* in *zor-talab* and rest in *ausat* (medium) areas; *diwans, bakhshis* and high grandees half in *ausat* and rest in *raiyati* areas; and the small *mansabdars* entirely in *raiyati* areas. It is difficult to say to what extent this was actually followed. However, it was thrown to the winds in large areas during the latter part of Aurangzeb's rule. Thus, we are told that Murshid Quli Khan brought large areas in Bengal under *khalisa,* assigning to *mansabdars jagirs* in the *zor-talab* areas in Orissa.[18] Aurangzeb followed a similar policy in the Deccan after the conquest of Bijapur and Golconda.[19]

Another practice mentioned by Khafi Khan, was that though many of the *jagirs* were lying waste (*viran*), and their realization amounted to almost nothing, the wretched *mutasaddis* continued to demand from the *jagirdars* payment for the feed of the animals (*khurak dawab*), and imprisoned the agents of the *jagirdars* for the purpose.[20] The struggle for *hasil jagirs* thus became a matter of life and death for *mansabdars,* and allowed the royal *mutasaddis* the opportunity to resort to all kinds of corrupt practices, including frequent transfers, of which Bhimsen complains bitterly.[21] Obviously, the smaller *mansabdars* were the worst hit.

The working of the *jagirdari* regulations also created problems. According to the branding regulations, when a noble failed to produce a contingent of requisite numbers and horses of the requisite quality, his *jagir* was to be resumed and brought under *paibaqi.* Due to the growing difficulties of realizing their share of the revenue from the *zamindars* and the landholders in the Deccan, many *mansabdars* failed to satisfy these conditions. As a result, large areas came under *paibaqi* and often remained unassigned for long periods.[22]

From the foregoing account it would appear that there was not so much an absolute shortage of lands available for distribution in *jagirs* as great delay in the grant of *jagirs* to the new entrants which affected the *khanazads* most, and the shortage of *sair-hasil* jagirs to the others,

[18]This is referred to in a letter of S. Abdullah Khan to Murshid Quli Khan in 1720. See Satish Chandra (ed.) *Balmukand Nama* Bombay, 1972, letter no. 20; Salimullah, *Tawarikh-i-Bangala,* I.O. Ms. 2995, ff. 36a–45b.

[19]Inayat Jung Collection, National Archives, New Delhi, 1/7/105; J.F. Richards, *Golconda,* pp. 158–9.

[20]Khafi Khan, *Muntakhab,* vol II, p. 602.

[21]Bhimsen, *Nuskha-i-Dilkusha,* f. 139a.

[22]J.F. Richards, *Golconda,* pp. 199–201. This is based on the papers in the Inayat Jung Collection. Whether this phenomenon was confined to some areas in the Deccan, or was a more general feature, needs to be studied further.

especially to the smaller *mansabdars.* That there was no real shortage of *paibaqi* lands has led some modern historians to deny the existence of a *jagirdari* crisis. However, the crisis of the *jagirdari* system should not be confused with *be-jagiri* which affected the new entrants rather than the existing incumbents. Central to the growth of the crisis of the *jagirdari* system was its increasing non-functionality, i.e. its inability to help in the maintenance of law and order and the collection of the central share of the land revenue over large parts of the empire. This, in turn, was bound to have repercussions on the rest of the empire in due course.

It has also been argued that a tendency to raise the revenue demand to a still higher magnitude, even beyond the level of subsistence, 'derived from the very nature of the *jagirdari* system', for a *jagirdar* who could not hope to hold his *jagir* for more than three to four years, could never follow a far-sighted policy of agricultural development.[23] While conceding that the interests of an individual *jagirdar* and the imperial administration did not necessarily coincide, the Mughal administrative machinery was designed to check abuse of power by individual *jagirdars,* and blatant abuse would have been checked *as long as the machinery of administration functioned normally.* Such a breakdown, it appears, did take place in some parts of the Deccan during the last years of Aurangzeb's reign, but it did not become a general feature till, in the eighteenth century, the central machinery of the administration was paralysed by factionalism and struggle between the *wazirs* and the monarch. Secondly, it should be remembered that the *jagirdars* supervised and generally collected the land revenue from a hereditary class holding superior rights in land, viz. the *zamindars.* There is little evidence to show that if the state had not centralized a large part of the revenue surplus through the *jagirdari* system, but left a larger part of it to the *zamindars,* the latter would have used it for the expansion and improvement of cultivation. The arguments of Bernier[24] and other European visitors of the time, that a hereditary landed aristocracy was a guarantor against oppression by the ruler, and that such a class would be an improving class is not borne out by the experience of the Rajputs and the Marathas, or the colonial period in India, nor any European country, excluding England.

[23]Irfan Habib, *Agrarian System,* p. 320.

[24]Bernier, *Travels in the Mughal Empire,* tr. A. Constable (Westminster 1891), p. 227. Bernier considered transferability of *jagirs* as the source of *all* evil in the Mughal empire, including oppression of peasants and artisans.

As a matter of fact, Bhimsen argued *not* against the practice of transfer of *jagirs* as such, but against too frequent transfers. Bhimsen says that uncertainty on the part of the *mansabdars* whether they would remain in possession of the *jagir* during the following year, exactions of the royal *mutasaddis* from the hapless *jagirdar*, and the latter's practice of taking a large advance payment (*qabz*) from the *amil* led to the neglect of the *jagir* and the ruination of the cultivators.[25] Hawkins, who had been awarded a *mansab* and *jagir* by Jahangir, complains bitterly of frequent transfers of *jagirs*.[26] Were transfers of *jagirs* more frequent under Aurangzeb than under earlier rulers? Did they affect the entire Mughal empire or only parts of it, especially those in the Deccan? Did they apply to high as well as to low grandees? Withough answering these questions it would be rash to make generalizations on the basis of Bhimsen's statement. Possibly, Bhimsen who was himself a small *mansabdar*, may have generalized the experience of small *mansabdars* who were at the mercy of the royal *mutasaddis*. As for the bigger *mansabdars*, they generally had to collect their share of the land revenue from big *zamindars*, some of whom possessed considerable military strength. As long as the *zamindars* as a class remained strong, frequent transfers of a *jagirdar* would not have affected the cultivators of the area to the extent made out by Bhimsen. As we have argued above, during Aurangzeb's reign, the *zamindars* of the Deccan and many other areas had become stronger *vis-à-vis* the *jagirdars* than in the earlier period, and the latter would hardly have been in a position to charge more than their sanctioned dues. Also, there are many examples of important Mughal *mansabdars* holding their *jagirs* for as long as ten years or more. According to a recent study,[27] large *mansabdars* accounted for over 80 per cent of the land assigned in *jagir*, and since transfer of *jagir* held by these *mansabdars* may not have been as frequent, the impact of frequent transfers of smaller *jagirdars* on the peasantry and on the agrarian system should not be overestimated. In fact, not frequent transfers but the decay of the practice of

[25]Bhimsen, *Nuskha-i-Dilkusha*, f. 139a.

[26]Hawkins, in *Early Travels in India 1583–1619*, ed. W. Foster, London 1921, p. 14: 'A man cannot continue half a yere in his living, but it is taken from him.'

[27]A. Jan Qaisar, 'Distribution of the Revenue Resources of the Mughal Empire Among the Nobility', *Proceedings, Indian History Congress*, 1967, pp. 239–40 (in this volume). This included *mansabdars* holding ranks of 500 *zat* and above in the twentieth year of Shah Jahan's reign.

periodic transfers of *jagirs* during the eighteenth century made the *jagirs* hereditary, and led to the further strengthening of the *zamindars* as a class. This accompanied and was followed by a gradual weakening of administrative checks which left the landowners and cultivators at the mercy of the new *jagirdars* and *zamindars*, thus paving the way for the disintegration of the empire.

Little detailed study has been done of the processes whereby the *zamindars* strengthened themselves as a class and squeezed the cultivators in various ways. It has been argued that the Mughal policy of integrating the *zamindars* with the machinery of administration for realizing land revenue from the cultivators, and also of giving them a guaranteed portion of the produce by including it in the *jama*, itself tended to strengthen the position of the *zamindars*. This, and the policy of extending and improving cultivation with the help and co-operation of the *zamindars* tended, in the long run, to identify the Mughal administration especially at the local level more closely with the *zamindars*, thus in turn alienating the cultivators including the *khudkasht* who had looked to the Mughal ruler for protection against local oppression. Reference has been made to the rise of opposition movements during the seventeenth century such as the Maratha and Jat movements. These are complex phenomena and cannot be regarded either as a simple manifestation of peasant discontent against the Mughal state due to over-exploitation, or a protest against the religious policies of the state. In both cases, the leadership was provided by smaller *zamindars*. There was clearly a divergence between the interests of the leaders who were claiming a better position for themselves in the prevailing socio-political set-up, and the sections of the peasantry who had rallied round them in the hope of justice—a term which could include such divergent things as a peasant utopia of egalitarianism, and an end to local oppression. In any case, these movements affected the moral position of the Mughal emperor, and tended to undermine the belief that he would act as the ultimate arbiter in case of oppression and injustice at any level.

Commenting on the situation brought about by the rise of the Marathas, the weakening of the position of the *jagirdars* in local administration and the growing strength and power of the *zamindars*, Bhimsen says: 'The province given to the *mansabdars* in *tankhwah* cannot be governed because of the smallness of their force (*jamiat*). The zamindars too have assumed strength, joined the Marathas, enlisted armies (*jamiat*) and laid the hands of oppression on the country.' Bhimsen goes on to say: 'Their [the *zamindars*'] oppression has no limit.

The *zamindars* pay not a *dam* or a *dirham* out of their pockets, but take it from the *riaya* and make the payment.'[28]

The strength and assertiveness of the *zamindars*, and the ineffectiveness of the *jagirdars* were opposite sides of the same coin. The net result was manifest inability to protect the landholders (*riaya*). The Mughals were thus unable to maintain, much less consolidate, the social balance which had enabled the Mughal central government to stand forth as the champion of the cultivators, and on that basis, to isolate the *zamindars*, reduce their perquisites, and centralize a large proportion of the revenue surplus. The growing crisis was not confined to the Deccan but extended to the north, as was shown by the Jat and other rebellions. The growing social imbalance was accompanied by an administrative and financial crisis, the two acting and reacting on each other.

Thus, the *jagirdari* system was a complex phenomenon closely linked to the structure and working of the village society, and the working of the Mughal system of administration both at the central and the local levels. The crisis of the *jagirdari* system leading to a breakdown in the eighteenth century was an outcome of a complex interplay between these social and administrative factors.

[28]Bhimsen, *Nuskha-i-Dilkusha*, ff. 139 a-b.

13
Trade and Politics in Eighteenth Century India*

Ashin Das Gupta

India's trade with other Asian countries underwent several important changes in the course of the eighteenth century. Traditional centres of trade like Surat, Calicut, Hughli and Masulipatam which had been in existence for a long time, gradually declined and gave place to new towns like Bombay, Madras and Calcutta. The orientation of export trade, which had previously been towards west Asia, going in the main to the Persian Gulf and the Red Sea, changed towards the east, directed more and more to China. In this process, the indigenous merchant class which had developed at the traditional centres of trade, suffered considerable losses, elements of it being virtually wiped out. Some managed to survive by migration to the new towns, where a trading structure developed through collaboration between the English and Indians. This new trade which developed in the second half of the century was dominated by the servants of the English East India Company trading as private merchants. A major element behind these shifts was the general crisis which overwhelmed the Indian empire of the Mughals during this time, and I shall contend that the decline of the older ports and the undermining of the mercantile classes were to a significant extent the results of the political breakdown understood in its broadest sense.

Before this discussion can be taken up in its details, it is essential to note the limitations imposed upon us by the nature of available source materials. The major source for an enquiry of this kind—the customs records of the Indian administrations—have totally disappeared. The

*From D.S. Richards (ed.), *Islam and the Trade of Asia* (Philadelphia, 1970).

second possible source—the papers of the Indian merchants—are, again, almost totally lost. The only surviving major document of this kind in our period is the diary kept by a Tamil merchant of Pondicherry, Ananda Ranga Pillai, which is available, with some gaps, for the years 1736 to1761.[1] Persian chronicles are available to students of political and administrative history, but they contain little on trade. The major source for us, therefore, has to be the papers of the various European companies and some private papers of their officials in India. It is necessary to realize that for the eighteenth century these papers are extremely voluminous and comprise a wide range of materials. Studies of the European companies trading in India have so far been based, by and large, upon the letters written to and from India and Europe. This is as it should be, but it should be noted that letters written from India to Europe tended to concentrate less upon local affairs and more upon things of general concern to the company in question. Apart from such letters an interesting range of documentation is available on day-to-day developments in various parts of India, which were naturally not summarized for the managers of the companies. Thus, Gujarati newsletters written by two Indian scribes, Dakhniram and Sampatram, in Dutch translation are available for the first two decades of the eighteenth century, giving in detail the developments in Delhi.[2] The Dutch company had an excellent regulation that, wherever its factors were settled, a *dag register* or a diary would be kept to note the events in the town as they happened. Unfortunately much of this series has been destroyed but extremely important material on towns like Surat and Hughli can

[1]J.F. Price and H.H. Dodwell (eds), *The Private Diary of Ananda Ranga Pillai,* 12 vols (Madras, 1904–28). Another interesting, though short, document of the same genre is the biography of the Parsi merchant of Surat, Rustamji Manakji, written by Mobed Jamshed Kaiqobad, private tutor to Rustamji's son Nowroji in the year 1711: 'Rustam Manock and the Persian Qisseh', full Persian text and extensive translations in English, by J.J. Modi, *Journal of the Royal Asiatic Society of Bombay* (1930), pp. 1–221. Attempts have been made by later scholars to reconstruct the history of some of the outstanding merchants and financiers of eighteenth-century India, the most important being J. H. Little, *The House of Jagat Seth,* originally published in *Bengal Past and Present* (1920–1), now available as a publication of the Calcutta Historical Society, ed. Professor N.K. Sinha.

[2]In 1720–1, in all 83 letters were received from Delhi and Agra of this kind: K(oloniaal) A(rchief) at The Hague, no. 1855, pp. 58–158. These decreased in volume later. In 1732 there is only one letter from Dakhniram desperately appealing for help, K.A. 2185, pp. 632–3.

still be found.[3] Account books and family histories of the Indian merchants are sometimes to be found in the legal records of the European settlements, which also provide a detailed source for commercial practices of the period.[4] Lastly, many details about Indian shipping can be pieced together from the various kinds of shipping lists available in the European papers.[5] When all this has been said, there are two difficulties about these sources, which have to be recognized. First, with all the local detail, these papers never penetrate far enough into the Indian society and a large number of Indian merchants remain only names. Second, the enormous volume of the documentation and the fact that the kind of enquiry we have set for ourselves in this essay is relatively

[3]For Surat the whole diary is available for the two years 1730 and 1731, but extracts are available for most other years, as is also the case with Hughli. These notes were made by the Secretary to the Dutch Council but there is no doubt that he obtained much of his information about what went on in town from the *bania* merchants who frequented the Dutch Lodge.

[4]Much information about the Konkani family of the Prabhus and the Jewish family of the Rahabis, both prominent in the trade at Cochin, are to be found in the documents dealing with a legal suit between them in 1772. I have dealt with it in *Malabar in Asian Trade, 1740–1800* (Cambridge, 1967), pp. 118–19. The quality of such documentation can be gauged from the series *Pleadings in the Mayor's Court* at Madras, which are available in print with some gaps for the years 1731 to 1745 (Record Office, Madras, 1936–43).

[5]This is a very important source of information for Indian shipping, especially the data available in the Dutch papers. These are of two kinds. On the one hand there are the lists of passes which the Dutch issued and which specify the name, the name of the owner and the tonnage of the ship, together with its destination, number of guns it carried and the name of its *nakhoda*. These lists, however, say nothing about the cargo carried, and it is entirely possible that the declared tonnage was short of its actual capacity. There are also available lists of incoming ships and an annual summary of their imports. These were obtained from the customs officials of the local administrations. The lists of imports are virtually unusable, because the units of measurement are innumerable and mostly totally obscure. For example the import of bullion at Surat are usually given in 'sacks' and 'chests', leaving it to conjecture how much these may have contained. The lists of the incoming vessels also varied in that some would only note ships above a certain size (e.g. at Surat) while in others (e.g. at Masulipatam) everything which sailed would be listed. The English never made proper lists but they usually noted arrival and departure of shipping. These provide useful checks on the Dutch data.

recent in Indian historiography, mean that there are wide gaps in our knowledge even so far as the European sources are concerned.[6]

It is also necessary to be clear about some of our concepts in this subject. Although we are concerned with 'Indian trade', it is not very easy to say what this meant in the eighteenth century. Towards the close of the seventeenth century the Mughal empire by its acquisition of the two southern kingdoms of Bijapur and Golconda became more or less coextensive with what came later to be known as British India, including the so-called native states. Thus for a time, and in a rather loose manner, India existed politically at the close of the seventeenth century, although the important trading area called the coast of Malabar, including the famous port of Calicut, was not in it. However, by the time the Mughal empire had reached its territorial limits, it had already been successfully challenged by the Marathas, based roughly around the city of Poona in western India. And within the first two decades of the eighteenth century Mughal central control had broken down over much of the empire. There was therefore no 'India', in the political sense, in the eighteenth century.[7] Economically and socially the position was even more intricate. There were areas in the subcontinent which were commercialized and where one would find clusters of trading cities and ports. Such areas were Gujarat, Malabar, Coromandel, Bengal and the two axes of the Mughal empire, the river Ganga (Ganges) laying down the broad artery of communication between the east and the heartland, and the roads connecting Surat in Gujarat and the region of Delhi and Agra. There were parts of the coastline where trade was less in evidence and the ports, naturally, smaller. Such was the area of the Indus basin with its old cluster of Thatta and Lahri Bandar, ports which had seen better days. Between Gujarat and Malabar, there was the area called Konkan, with its numerous roadsteads. And along the coast as it turned north and east after dipping its furthest at Cape Comorin, and before it became Coromandel, there

[6]As far as the eighteenth century is concerned there is no study of the Coromandel coast at all and none has so far made use of the Dutch documentation relating to Bengal. I have set out my findings about Malabar in the book cited above and I shall summarize some of the data on Gujarat in this essay.

[7]The standard account of these political developments are in Jadunath Sarkar, *History of Aurangzib*, 4 vols (Calcutta, 1912–19); William Irvine and Jadunath Sarkar, *The Later Mughals*, 2 vols (Calcutta, 1922), and Jadunath Sarkar, *The Fall of the Mughal Empire*, 4 vols (Calcutta, 1949–52, revised edn).

was Tinnevelly of sluggish but ancient trade. Beyond Coromandel and before Bengal, there was Orissa, only briefly alluded to in documents of trade and still something of a mystery.[8] This rough quadrilateral of trade—the two coasts and the two axes which connected the extremities of the coasts with the heartland of imperial cities like Delhi and Agra—was further connected with Central Asian trade via Lahore and Kabul. Major Indian cities crowded round these routes and the hinterland of each felt the pull of the market to a certain extent. But this pull naturally disappeared after a point, as the cost of transport over land was prohibitive. Thus interior India with its innumerable villages remained distinct from these other areas of trade and administration. The relationship between the two must have varied from region to region and has yet to be worked out in detail.

Granted the existence of these two different 'Indias'—in terms of society and economics—we are still to decide the extent to which the commercial areas formed one unit. Trade, of course, was itself a major link. Flow of trade was regular and continuous and these different areas had come to be interdependent to a significant measure. Thus the produce of the heartland of the empire, its indigo, and cloths of Lucknow, found their primary outlet through Surat, the port of Gujarat. And the cotton grown in Gujarat fed the weaving industry in Bengal.[9] The

[8]The most useful account of the Indian coastline is in William Milburn, *Oriental Commerce* (London, 1825), pp. 110 ff. Eighteenth-century topography as seen by Indian writers is discussed in Jadunath Sarkar, *The India of Aurangzeb* (Calcutta, 1901). One of the best discussions of the roads between Surat and Agra is by Dr J.P. Vogel in his introductory essay to the *Journal van. J.J. Ketelaar's Hofreis Naar den Groot Mogol te Lahore, 1711–1713* (The Hague, 1937).

[9]All relevant documents of the early eighteenth century, of course, speak of the export of Lucknow cloths and Agra indigo through Surat. A convenient assessment of the importance of this trade for Surat is in the memoir of J.J. Ketelaar written in January 1716 at Surat, K.A. 1777, pp. 99–102. The trade in cotton between Bengal and Surat, always of some importance, grew considerably in volume in the 1740s. In his letter to the Governor General at Batavia, Jan Schreuder noted in April 1742 that the price of cotton at Surat had risen by 23 per cent not merely because of a bad harvest but through a considerable export to Bengal by the English, French and Indian merchants, K.A. 2474, pp. 210–11. This complaint was repeated next year, K.A. 2502, p. 60. And the year after, the export to Bengal by the English alone was estimated as 16,000 bales, ibid., p. 114. Silk, on the other hand, was imported into Gujarat from Bengal and employed a large number of weavers. As early as the 1650s

structure of money and credit, without which such trade would be impossible, reinforced the links forged by the flow of goods. There are innumerable examples of how each major city was linked with the other, and I shall only cite one to show how sensitive the network was. In 1738, when news had come through of the fall of Peshawar to the advancing Persian army, the English were trying to remit a large sum of money from Surat to Bengal and they called on the leading shroff (*ṣarrāf*) in the former city who specialized in such remittances. This man, Tarwary Arjunji Nathji (Erjunjee Nautjee, in the document), informed the English Council

that the present rate of exchange was 104½ Surat rupees for one hundred sicca [coin current in Bengal], that if we had an inclination to remit a sum, he offered it as his advice that we should take bills in three or four days for that as Shaw Nadir advanced the exchange would rise or rather that it would be so precarious taking any bills that we might lose our money, that two considerable shroffs were already gone off from Muxadavad [Murshidabad, capital of the Mughal province of Bengal] and that as Judda Seit [Jagat Seth, leading financier in Bengal] was withdrawing all his money from the Europeans as well as natives, others might become Bankrupts [*sic*]. !10

Needless to say, cities in the same region were more closely linked through trade. Thus Madras and Pondicherry, although under hostile

---

this was an established commerce. In 1659 the landroutes were closed for a time by the wars of succession which brought Aurangzeb to the throne. Immediately after they were reopened, Gujarati merchants in Bengal sent a large quantity of silk overland to Ahmadabad via Agra, Pieter Van Dam, *Beschryvinge van de OostIndische Compagnie*, ed. F.W. Stapel (The Hague, 1932), book II, part ii, pp. 10–11. In the 1750s the Dutch made an unsuccessful attempt to take part in this trade. They were defeated by strong competition of the English and the Gujaratis as also their own inexperience. The story of this failure is in H(ooghe) R(egeering) te Batavia at the Algemeen Rijksarchief, no. 856, especially pp. 18–19.

[10] S(urat) F(actory) R(ecords), vol. XXIII, p. 83, at the India Office Library, London. Tarwary maintained a correspondent at Delhi who acted as a pivot in such transactions, ibid., p. 190. Such financial transactions between Gujarat and Bengal via Delhi were quite common and merchants in the course of their regular business took recourse to it, in addition to professional remitters like Tarwary. Thus Seth Laldas Vitaldas Parak undertook to transfer Rs 200,000 for the English in 1732 and did so through his trading connections at Delhi, S.F.R., vol. XVII, pp. 67, 80.

administrations were twin cities from the point of view of Indian merchants. Arunachala Chetti in a letter to Dupleix, governor of Pondicherry, said: 'As regards my mercantile dealings, I need hardly say more than that my food was there [Pondicherry] and water here [Madras].'[11] In addition, there was considerable social cohesion within each region, sometimes a trading community, dispersed in different areas, kept in social touch with each of its groups so scattered.[12] Thus it is possible to speak of some integration among these scattered towns along the sea coast and the major arteries of communication. There were, however, major differences, and trading between them was often far from easy. The growth of political diversity meant separate customs arrangements between the cities of different regions. By the fourth decade of the century trade had become difficult even between Bengal and Gujarat, two of the major Mughal *subahs*. The movement of money from one region to another was regulated by considerations similar to those governing transfers to 'foreign' parts, as, for example, transfers between Surat and Mocha.[13] So the conclusion one comes to is that it would be a mistake to regard the different towns as totally unconnected splinters, growing and dying in isolation, and it would be equally

[11]*The Private Diary of Ananda Ranga Pillai* (henceforth *Pillai*), vol. III, p. 172. Similarly the sons of Maliappa Chetti who had been in the employ of the French East India Company at Pondicherry moved to Cuddalore under English administration and set up in business, *Pillai*, vol. IV, p. 106.

[12]Considerable but scattered evidence of this can be found in the European archives as well as in the diaries of Pillai. A good example would be the correspondence between the Gujarati bania Jivandas Haridas at Delhi with his nephews at Surat, K.A. 2060, pp. 104–5, and K.A. 2094, p. 296.

[13]In 1744, for example, Sorabji and Ratanji, two Parsi merchants of Surat offered to buy a small ship from the Dutch and employ it in the trade to Bengal provided the vessel was given the necessary papers for it to pass as a Dutch vessel. The Parsis pointed out that although they were the subjects of the Mughal and Gujarat and Bengal were both Mughal *subahs*, nevertheless they were liable to pay taxes at both ends and were likely to be victimized, K.A. 2546, pp. 69–70. Transfers between Mocha and Surat figure prominently in the papers of both the English and the Dutch in the 1720s and 1730s, as every year the merchants of Surat transferred their profit in the Red Sea trade partly by bills through the Europeans. No doubt all major merchants in this trade would do the same. It is a sobering thought that Joseph Price, a free merchant in Bengal, could write in the 1770s that China had in the last few years robbed Bengal of its trade with Gujarat. J. Price, *Five Letters from a Free Merchant in Bengal* (London, 1778), p. 193.

unwarranted to make too much of the links which bound them together, and to speak of India or the Indian economy as an integral whole.

The only method that is left to us, therefore, if we are to form some idea of trade in India during the eighteenth century, is some kind of a *tour de horizon*, starting in Gujarat and covering the main trading areas of the country. It is, however, necessary to take a brief look at the nature of the political crisis which overwhelmed the Mughal empire and which affected trade in some form or other everywhere in the country. The classical accounts of the decline of the Mughal empire have accustomed us to the picture of a decrepit dynasty, overmighty subjects and the revolt of the Hindus against Muslim rule. All this still remains very true, but recent research has suggested that there may well have been something more to it than just that. This is a complex subject, still unresolved in several aspects. Here I must put it briefly, accepting all risks attendant on brevity. The mainstay of the empire was its system of nobility, the *mansabdārī* system. These noblemen of the Mughal empire, the *mansabdārs*, were assigned their respective personal ranks (*zat*) by the emperor, which carried with them an obligation to maintain a specified number of troops (*sawar*) and an assignment of revenues (*jāgīr*) to enable the officer to do so. Now, for various reasons the number of imperial *mansabdārs* increased spectacularly in the course of the seventeenth century, so that the total of *mansabdārs* of 1000 *zat* and above which had stood at 137 at the end of Akbar's reign (1605) climbed to 537 in the year of Aurangzeb's death (1707). It is true that the empire had also expanded in this time, so that there were more *jāgīrs* to take care of the fresh recruitment. But the rise in the number of *jāgīrs* had fallen greatly short of the expansion in the number of *mansabdārs*. So a time came towards the end of the seventeenth century when there were not enough *jāgīrs* to go round. Inayatullah Khān, the Imperial Pay Master General, is once said to have remonstrated with Emperor Aurangzeb, saying: 'The list of officers who are daily paraded before Your Majesty is unlimited, while the land for granting *jāgīrs* is limited. How can an unlimited quantity be equal to limited quantity?'[14] The emperor himself would say often about this problem: 'There is one pomegranet [sic] and a hundred sick men (*yak*

[14]In discussing the features of the crisis within the Mughal empire, I am following: Satish Chandra, *Parties and Politics at the Mughal Court, 1707–1740* (Asia Publications, 1959), Irfan Habib, *The Agrarian System of Mughal India* (Asia Publications, 1963) and M. Athar Ali, *The Mughal Nobility Under Aurangzeb* (Asia, 1966).

anār sad bīmār).' Added to this there was the problem of getting a good, that is a paying, *jāgīr*. From early in the seventeenth century it was officially acknowledged that the valuation of a *jāgīr* often fell short of its actual yield. In the reign of Aurangzeb it was decreed that the actual yield would be taken as no more than half the official calculation of its value. It had also to be considered whether the *jāgīr* was in a revenue-yielding tract or in a rebellious part of the empire. Thus there was a struggle not only for jāgīrs but for well-placed and remunerative ones. Socially and ethnically the Mughal nobility was an extremely heterogeneous group, comprising Iranis, Turanis, Afghans, Hindustani Muslims, and Rajput and other Hindu chieftains. In a situation of this sort internecine strife within such a body was inevitable and intense. Further, as the income of the noblemen fell steadily they put more and more pressure upon the *zamindārs*, that is the class of gentry who actually and permanently held much of the land in the empire. Naturally, much of this pressure was passed on to the peasant and in several cases the *zamindārs* led their peasants into rebellion against the imperial administration. Khafi Khān, a historian who wrote in the 1720s, summed up the situation in these words:

> It is clear to the wise and experienced that now, according to the ways of the time, thoughtfulness in managing the affairs of State (and the practice of) protecting the peasantry and encouraging the prosperity of the country and increase in produce, have all departed. Revenue collectors, who take the revenues on farm, having spent considerable amounts at the Court [to obtain it], proceed to the *mahals* and become a scourge for the revenue-paying peasantry. ... Since they have no confidence that they will be confirmed in their office the next year, nay even for the whole of the current year, they seize both parts of the produce (State's share as well as the peasant's) and sell them away. It is a God-fearing man, indeed, who limits himself to this and does not sell away the bullocks and carts (of the peasants), on which tillage depends, or, not contenting himself with extorting the amount of his expenses at the Court, of his troopers and of the deficit on his pledge, does not sell away whatever remains with the peasantry, down to the fruit-bearing trees and their proprietary and hereditary [rights in the] land. ... Many *parganas* and townships, which used to yield full revenue, have, owing to the oppression of the officials (*ḥukkām*) been so far ruined and devastated that they have become forests infested by tigers and lions; and the villages are so utterly ruined and desolate that there is no sign of habitation on the routes.[15]

[15]Quoted by Habib, *Agrarian System*, p. 325.

Another contemporary, Shāh Waliullāh (1703–62), the theological writer of Delhi, thought that the 'ruin of countries (or towns)' in his age was due, first, to the strain on the treasury from maintaining a large class of idlers. 'The second cause', he wrote, 'is the imposition of heavy taxes on the peasants, merchants and artisans, and then the oppression inflicted upon them, as a result of which the submissive ones flee and are destroyed and those who have got the power rise in rebellion.'[16] Thus the political collapse had produced strains which were engulfing all sections of the society. It is against this background that the details of the decline of Indian trade are to be seen.

The most important trading area in the Mughal empire was the subah of Gujarat with its chief port at Surat, from where the pilgrims for the Ḥajj sailed every year to the Red Sea. Although Surat was the main port, it was not in any important way a centre for production. The chief export of Gujarat, its various kinds of textiles, was in the main produced in villages in the neighbourhood of its capital city of Ahmadabad, 140 miles to the north, north-west of Surat and near Broach, Baroda and Cambay, other towns in between these two. Two varieties of indigo, Sarkhej and Jambusar, were also produced in, and exported from Gujarat, besides a host of other minor items. Surat was also the principal outlet for the whole axis connecting Gujarat with the heartland of the imperial cities. Thus particular varieties of cloth, manufactured in the neighbourhood of Lucknow, and the best kind of indigo, grown near Agra, were among the important items exported.[17] Naturally, merchants from all over northern, central and north-western India were to be found at Surat—Multanis, Kashmiris and northern Khatris, forming major groups among the local mercantile communities. The city itself was the home of wealthy Muslim merchants of the Bohra community. At the end of the seventeenth century the principal merchant among the Bohras, an old man called 'Abd al-Ghafūr, was the richest merchant at Surat, if not the whole of India. Beside this there were merchants simply

[16]Habib, ibid., p. 329.

[17]The best available discussion of Gujarati textiles in the seventeenth century is in John Irwin and P.R. Schwartz, *Studies in Indo-European Textile History* (Ahmadabad, 1966), pp. 15–27. Documentation in the eighteenth century usually omits the non-Gujarati places like Burhanpur and Sironj mentioned by Irwin and concentrates on Cambay and Broach. For the trade in indigo see W.H. Moreland, *From Akbar to Aurangzeb* (London, 1923), pp. 109 ff. Pieter Van Dam has a short discussion on the exports of Gujarat in *Beschryvinge*, Book II, pt. iii, p. 100.

called Muslims and others called Mughals. There was also an important clan of merchants called the Chellabies, always referred to as Turks. The Chellabies were the most important shipowners after the family of 'Abd al-Ghafūr. The most numerous among merchants were of course the *banias* of Gujarat and Rajasthan. In the main they conducted the business of trading in money as well, exchanging different currencies and remitting from one place to another. They also took charge of all kinds of marine insurance and were brokers for respondentia loans at sea. Apart from such 'Indian' merchants, there lived at Surat 'foreign' merchants who came from the Red Sea or the Persian Gulf areas, but it was not always easy to pick them out from the rest.[18]

At the turn of the eighteenth century, trade at Surat would appear to have been in a fairly favourable position. Indian shipping in particular seemed to be doing extremely well at the time. The English Council in their consultation on 19 April 1701, noted,

> The Inhabitants of this Citty having built such a number of shipping, that unless the Europeans interfear [*sic*], may in a little time make themselves by their frugallity [*sic*] the sole traders in India, they having of late sent two or three ships a year into the South Seas, the most profitable trade from this place w[hi]ch can't well be preserved, the Dutch employing double the stock as formerly to this place.[19]

[18]I have discussed some of these merchants in 'The Crisis at Surat, 1730–32', *Bengal Past and Present* (Calcutta, Diamond Jubilee Number, 1967), pp. 148–62. As to the Turkish family, it has to be noted that the European documents which were careful to distinguish between Mughals, Bohras, Arabs and even Arabs from Muscat, always spoke of this clan as Turks. These notes kept from day to day, year after year, by Europeans living at Surat are of course qualitatively different from occasional traveller's tales. It is interesting to note that Kaiqobād in his life of Rustamji Manakji calls the Chellabies 'Turki by caste (*jat*)', J.J. Modi, 'Rustam Manock and the Persian Qisseh', *Journal of the Royal Asiatic Society of Bombay* (1930), p. 38. 'Ali Muhammad Khān, the last of the Mughal *dīwāns* of Ahmadabad in his history, *Mirāt-i-Ahmadi* (English translation in Gaekwad Oriental Series, no. 146) (Baroda, 1965), spoke of the 'Rūmī' mercenaries in connection with this family, p. 522. As to the 'foreign merchants', they come up occasionally in the contemporary papers. Thus for example in 1706 when the Dutch were blocking the port of Surat 'the Turkish and Arab merchants' claimed full liberty of movement, as they were no 'subjects of Hindustan'. Among them of course none of the local Arabs or Turks were included: Letter from Risidas and Bhagwandas to Brindabandas, 29 December, 1706, K.A. 1611, p. 125.

[19]S.F.R., vol. VI, p. 92.

In the four months, February to May, in 1707, after the Dutch had lifted their two-year-old blockade of the port, as many as 57 Indian ships obtained their passport for the season, their declared total tonnage being 31,296 *khandies,* that is about 10,400 tons. Of these, 14 with a total declared tonnage of 10,875 *khandies,* that is about 3500 tons, belonged to 'Abd al-Ghafūr and 22 of the fifty-seven were destined to the Red Sea.[20] It is impossible to form an idea as to the total value of cargo these ships carried, but in the season 1698–9 the revenue from sea-customs is known to have yielded Rs 816,000, which calculated at 5 per cent, the maximum rate for customs, would give Rs 16,320,000 for the total turnover.[21] These years at the turn of the eighteenth century would thus appear to have been exceptionally good for trade at Surat, that is, for trade in Gujarat, and much of northern India.

But serious troubles began immediately after the death of Emperor Aurangzeb. In a letter from Surat, dated 4 February 1708, J. Grootenhuijs, the Dutch Directeur, noted that

> trade that had been hampered (*gestreemt*) after the death of Aurangzeb, was now [as the war of succession developed] at a standstill throughout the country, because the routes round about Agra are too unsafe in the lower lands [mainly to be understood as Gujarat] and about Ahmadabad things are somewhat more peaceful.[22]

The shroffs who remitted money to Agra had already suspended business and all merchants trading to that area were in trouble.[23] In 1710, however, it was again noted that trade was normal at Surat, Cambay, Broach and Ahmadabad.[24] All available evidence indicates that the first serious breakdown affected the heartland of the empire, and within the

[20] 'List of Passes', K.A. 1611, p. 125.

[21] This information is contained in an important daily diary kept by Joan Diodati, the Independent Fiscal of the Dutch Company at Surat, for the years 1698 to 1700. He noted it on 5 May 1699 and added 'it was what was said'. There is, therefore, the possibility of a considerable exaggeration. This figure was repeated in the Directeur Pieter Ketting's general letter to Batavia. We have to notice on the other hand that all the local merchants kept in close touch with the administration of customs and usually were remarkably well informed as to what went on, K.A. 1528, p. 221.

[22] Surat to Amsterdam, K.A. 1629, p. 28.

[23] Surat to Batavia, 12 May 1707, K.A. 1638, p. 250.

[24] Surat to Amsterdam, 19 March 1710, K.A. 1660, p. 1953. Slight difficulty was reported about customs at Cambay but this had nothing to do with the political collapse.

first two decades security of transport disappeared in the regions of Delhi and Agra. Simon Diodati, a young Dutch factor, who travelled from Agra to Surat towards the close of 1716, after closing down the Dutch factory at the former place, has left us an interesting and detailed account of his experiences on his way down this most important trade route. Although he travelled in the entourage of Qāsim Khān, the son of Haidar Quli Khān, the then governor of Surat, the journey proved perilous. The party decided to travel via Ujjain which, though longer, was deemed safer. But after a week of travelling, once they had crossed the river Chambal, they were repeatedly attacked by bands of 'armed peasants' (*gewapende boeren*) who were being led by their *zamindārs.* Diodati estimated that the largest group to attack them comprised about five thousand men of whom about two thousand carried small arms. As many as three attacks came in the course of one day on 2 January 1717, and on 16 January the party came to know of a Maratha advance immediately to the south. They then changed their route, cut across virtually trackless forests to Udaipur in the west, and then made their way to Gujarat. The impression that one gathers from this account is that tracts of the countryside, specially in the area inhabited by the Jats immediately to the south of the Mughal capitals, had gone over to brigandage.[25] The outcome of this, as far as trade was concerned, was twofold. On the one hand the export of the major products from the interior of India gradually died out, and on the other a glut developed at the port of Surat in those commodities which had a market in the upcountry towns. In 1720, the Dutch Council at Surat informed Amsterdam that the *Dariabadi chadar* (bedspreads from the neighbourhood of Lucknow) and the indigo *Biana* (best quality grown in the vicinity of Agra) were not to be procured till security of transport had been re-established. Those consignments which were now luckily coming through cost about 50 per cent of their purchase price more in transport, and to it was added a loss of 10–15 per cent on remittance from Surat to Agra.[26] At the same time it was found extremely difficult

[25]Diodati's travelogue is in K.A. 1805, pp. 86–129. The party set out on 26 December 1716 and reached Surat on 24 February 1717. It is of some interest to note that Diodati was regarded as an able young man by his superiors and had been commended for his knowledge of the local languages, K.A. 1694, p. 85.

[26]K.A. 1839, p. 209. The suspension of the procurement of *Dariabadi chadar* had been noted as early as 1708, K.A. 1645, p. 162. After this it was almost ritually repeated every year. This was also the case with *Biana* indigo which was stopped in 1710, K.A. 1689, pp. 224–5.

to sell any Indonesian spices at Surat. These depressed conditions in the market were repeatedly noted in the 1720s, and in 1726 Abraham Weijns recorded the specific case of the Kashmiri merchants, who were the largest exporters of spices to the interior, suspending business.[27]

The first consequences of the political breakdown were thus the cutting-off of Gujarat from the centres of production in north and central India as also the loss of these markets to the Gujarati traders. This was almost simultaneously followed by a breakdown within Gujarat itself. The first major Maratha inroad occurred in 1721, and the city of Surat was besieged for several weeks in November 1723. The Maratha army plundered up to the suburbs of the city, and Piloji Gaikwad, their general, arranged to have a fourth part of the revenues of the neighbouring villages collected for the Maratha treasury.[28] A

[27]In the season 1722–3, no bids at all were made for the imported spices for three months after the arrival of the ships and brokers reported that no merchant had the confidence to make purchases and that last year's imports were still in the city, K.A. 1891, pp. 44–5. On 26 April 1723 the Dutch Council at Surat wrote to the High Council of the Indies at Batavia: 'Surat at the moment is more than ever filled with imports and none of it can be sent out [to the north]', K.A. 1891, pp. 135–6. In 1725 the continuation of similar conditions was noted and it was said that the selling prices for imported commodities 'were now the lowest in many years', K.A. 1925, p. 33. The Kashmiri merchants of Surat were instructed by their principals, living in northern cities, to suspend their trade in Indonesian spices after a *qāfila* worth about Rs 200,000 had been plundered by the Marathas in spite of the fact that a safe-conduct for it had been obtained from them at a cost of Rs 1100, K.A. 1946, pp. 57, 82–3. A rupee at this time was worth between 2*s*. 3*d*. and 2*s*. 6*d*. The gross profit of the Dutch East India Company which in 1709–10 had stood at f.613,461 on an import valued at f.425,063 (K.A. 1704, p. 37) had fallen in 1722–3 to f.268,171 on an import of f.564,775 (K.A. 1946, p. 83).

[28]The first attack of the Marathas drove a large number of the villagers from the surrounding villages into Surat, but as the governor prepared for the defence of the town itself, the plunderers withdrew, K.A. 1855, p. 50 and K.A. 1875, p. 10. In the attack two year later, the Marathas trapped and destroyed some of the best officers and men of the governor Mu'min Khān, who was supposedly contemplating suicide. Many among the wealthy prepared for flight and Muḥammad 'Alī, the leading merchant in town, removed to one of his own vessels at the bar. However, after he had arranged for the collection of *chauth* (i.e. one-quarter of revenue) from the suburban villages, Piloji broke camp on 3 December, 1723, K.A. 1907, pp. 14–17. Evidence about these first raids, as available in English papers, can be seen in J.H. Gense and D.R. Banaji, *The Gaikwads of Baroda*, vol. I (Bombay, 1936).

struggle now developed between the Mughal forces and the light Maratha cavalry for the land revenue of Gujarat, and it gradually went against the Mughals, who, however, retained control over the main urban centres in the province. The position of the Mughal officers in Gujarat was therefore as follows: they had to spend a considerable amount of money at the imperial court in order to retain their various *mansabs* and ward off other competitors, they were forced to maintain much larger contingents of troops in order to fight off the Marathas or their brother nobles roving in search of *jāgīrs* and they lost much of the income which used to come from their revenue assignments. In this desperate situation their thoughts turned to the revenue to be extracted from trade and this process soon took on the aspect of a barely concealed plunder of the merchants of Gujarat. The story was the same in the different Gujarati trading centres like Ahmadabad, Cambay, Broach and Surat, but the documentation is much more complete in the case of the last-mentioned town. In the papers of the Dutch East India Company, however, have been preserved a remarkable series of letters from a Gujarati *bania* called Purushottamdas written from Ahmadabad in the years 1721–6 and then carried on after his death by his son Daaldas which chart the course of the crisis in the capital of Gujarat from 1728 to 1732. In 1721 Purushottamdas wrote of a 25 per cent rise in the prices of goods at Ahmadabad and noted that he was working without eating or sleeping, day and night, to get the *qāfila* for the Dutch ready in time while the merchants for the Red Sea were strenuously busy.[29] But this sense of an extremely busy trading metropolis disappears from his letters in four years time. In 1725 he spoke of a terror-stricken mercantile community, repeatedly forced to pay contributions to the governor Ḥamīd Khān, paying 100 per cent more in export duties, shut off from their sources of supply, meditating flight from the accursed city.[30] Ḥamīd Khān was succeeded by Sarbuland Khān, but the position only became worse. In his letters written in 1728, Purushottam's son Daaldas noted Sarbuland's misdeeds. In 1729 the Sunni Bohras of Ahmadabad defied the government and locked themselves in a *masjid*

[29]Letter received at Surat, 26 May 1721, K.A. 1875, pp. 98–9.

[30]Letter received at Surat, 9 September 1725, K.A. 1946, pp. 132–9. He described the development of the crisis in two more letters received respectively 28 October 1725 and 3 March, 1726, ibid., pp. 149–52, 172–3.

(mosque). A large number of merchants took to flight and government troops began to plunder their empty houses.[31] The approach of a new governor, Maharaja Abhay Singh, was hailed in 1730 as a great deliverance, and most of his initial measures were aimed at restoring confidence. But the fact was that what had broken down was a system and individual effort, however well meaning, was fruitless. Abhay Singh was recalled from Gujarat in 1731, and he was also guilty of similar oppressions immediately before he left.[32]

At Surat itself the old age and death of Emperor Aurangzeb had brought spells of anxiety but had produced no breakdown. Thanks to the firm action taken by the governor Amānat Khān, law and order had remained unaffected at the time, and three years after, in 1710, trade in the neighbourhood was reported as normal. It is useful to note that the conception of 'normal' would always make provision for local difficulties which never disappeared. Thus in the years immediately following we read in most letters from Surat of difficulties due to a scarcity of cash and increasing banditry. But the government continued to act against all threats to order, and in 1716 when Josua Ketelaar the outgoing Dutch Directeur, summed up the situation for his successor, he drew attention to the collapse at the imperial court and the slump

[31]Three letters from Daaldas were received by the Dutch Council at Surat and entered in their papers between July to December, 1729, K.A. 2060, pp. 134–6, 151–3, 162. Besides these, Daaldas wrote several letters to his brother Bhukendas at Surat which were also noted in the Dutch *dag register*, K.A. 2094, pp. 758–9, 767–8.

[32]The approach of Abhay Singh and the hopes it aroused at Ahmadabad were described by the Dutch diarist from time to time. For example on 14 August 1730 he noted that the leading citizens had fled and joined the vanguard of the Maharaja, K.A. 2094, p. 768. On 30 September 1730 he referred to the stories of Maharaja Abhay Singh's generosity to the people of the cities he was passing through and the punishment he was meting out to the oppressive officers of the previous administration, ibid., p. 799. On 8 November 1730 he noted the news that Abhay had reduced the duties on silk weaving to the customary 7 per cent from the extortionate 13 per cent under Sarbuland, ibid., pp. 834–5. However, on 7 November 1731 he noted that Abhay Singh had extorted Rs 800,000 from Seth Gosalji and a further Rs 200,000 from his nephew. The agent of Muḥammad 'Alī of Surat in the city was being molested for money, K.A. 2143, pp. 921–2.

in trade this had caused, but in his description of Gujarat he had nothing much out of the ordinary to chronicle. In fact he wrote optimistically about the prospects of trade for the Dutch and advised his successor to live in peace with the local government.[33] In the 1720s, however, the situation took a sharp turn for the worse. It is of importance to note that the dilemma of a conscientious Mughal official was made clear early on in the course of the collapse at Surat. Amānat Khān himself was known to rely heavily on his connections at the imperial court, but this had never been noted as a cause of distress at Surat. His able successor Haidar Quli Khān, however, became a topic for comment as his resolve not to rely on corruption in maintaining himself in power broke down and he stooped to familiar and unjust demands on the citizens. These two men, Haidar Quli at Surat in 1718–19 and Abhay Singh at Ahmadabad in 1730–1, were both known and admired as honest officials, but neither could maintain the posture of integrity they obviously valued. Honesty and integrity were the most prized of virtues, but clearly, by themselves, they were not enough.[34]

The first important attack by the Marathas, as distinct from occasional glancing forays, came, as we have seen, in November 1723. Within a short time of this the revenue of the 28 *parganas* (Mughal revenue units) which had been the mainstay of the administration at Surat virtually ceased to come in to the governor of the port any more. In the 1730s the city itself was obliged to agree to the payment of a fourth

[33]In his letter to Batavia of 2 April 1707, Grootenhuijs gave high praise to Amānat Khān for preserving law and order in town after the death of Aurangzeb, K.A. 1638, pp. 46–7. The relevant portions of Ketelaar's memoir are in K.A. 1777, pp. 87–109. This memoir contains a very helpful discussion on Gujarat's imports and exports at the time. It is interesting to note that in addition to the breakdown in the north, Ketelaar commented on the decline of the trade to Persia and the difficulties beginning to be felt in the trade to Mocha. He also noted that the English private traders sent only an occasional ship to Surat and these mostly laden with freight from Indian merchants.

[34]In January 1719 Haidar Quli asked for Rs 100,000 from the Dutch for his attempts on their behalf to obtain a piece of land for them at Surat. Daniel Hurgronje, the then Directeur, noted sadly how very changed the governor was through constant pressure upon him to furnish money to Delhi in order to maintain his office. When he first came he would hear nothing of illicit gratification (*corruptie penningen*) of this kind, K.A. 1820, p. 72.

part of its own revenues to the Marathas. Thus the Mughal officials of Surat were deprived of their means of subsistence.[35] To add to these difficulties, which were common to much of the empire, there were certain features of the administration of Surat which threw extra burdens on the meagre resources of the town. The administration of the city was divided between the port officer (*mutasaddī*), whom the Europeans always called the governor, and the officer in charge of the castle, who had nothing to do with the day-to-day running of the town. According to Mughal theory these two functionaries were to keep each other in check. But as the central control over the province weakened, conflicts between the two became frequent and on several occasions led to pitched battles in the streets of Surat.[36] Apart from the *mutasaddī* and the *qiladār* (the commander of the fort), the revenues of Surat had also to support a third functionary called the admiral of the Mughal fleet. This office was held successively by the chiefs of a clan of Africans settled at Danda Rajapuri to the south of Bombay. They were called the Sidis (probably a corruption of *Sayyidis*) and by virtue of a *farmān* issued by Emperor Aurangzeb they were to receive Rs 300,000 a year out of the sea-customs of the port. In exchange for this they were to protect the shipping of the port from piracy and maintain the security of the seas.[37] To these may be added the fact that for a long time before this, the Indian trading fleet of Surat had been regarded by anyone with a naval force as a suitable hostage for obtaining money

[35]An account of the revenues of Surat is in *Mīrāt-i-Aḥmadī, Khāṭima* (Gaekwad's Oriental Series), vol. LXIII (Baroda, 1928), pp. 188–9. 'Alī Muḥammad Khān gave the revenue of each *pargana* separately and the total was Rs 872,724. This was of course the official expectation in normal times. In 1730, the Raja of Mandavi, a neighbouring prince, took over the farm of these revenues from Sohrab 'Alī at Rs 400,000, although Piloji Gaikwad announced that he would see to it that the Raja derived no benefit from it, *Dag Register*, 15 September 1730 and 23 September 1730, K.A. 2094, pp. 787–8, 793–4. In the thirties as the Maratha control tightened over the countryside the administration at Surat had in fact to be content with what they allowed them to collect.

[36]A typical example was the street fighting in Surat in 1725 between Sohrab 'Ali Khān and Teg Bakht Khān in 1725, K.A. 2060, pp. 50–1.

[37]Indian historians usually call the 'Sidis' Ethiopians, but I believe it would be better to think of them as having come at some point of time from the 'Ḥabash' coast of the Red Sea without identifying them with present-day Ethiopians. For an account of the Sidis, see D.R. Banaji, *Bombay and the Sidis* (Bombay, 1932). The family tree of the Sidis is in Bowring's *Portfolio* at the India Office, London.

and other privileges from the governor of the port. The Europeans had made a habit of it, but others, such as the Arabs of Muscat, took recourse to it whenever necessary. In the 30 years from 1720 the merchants of Surat and the trade they carried thus came under tremendous pressure from all the local officials, who now had their backs to the wall, the Sidis, who for different reasons were fighting for their existence, and the English Company, which wished to share in the customs of the port and expand trade under threats of blockade. The most menacing for the merchants of the city among the three was, of course, the governor of the port. The impossible situation in which the governor was placed and the kinds of measures he would be likely to adopt in these years were seen fairly typically in the career of young Sohrab 'Alī who became the *mutasaddī* in 1725. His father had died shortly before this, fighting a curious combination of the Marathas and some of his fellow noblemen in the streets of Ahmadabad. Sohrab, who was seventeen years old at the time, was dismissed from his post in 1727 by the machinations of Teg Bakht Khān, a relation and a candidate of the governor of the castle. Teg Bakht was, however, unable to rule without unprecedentedly high taxation, and the unpopularity that he thus courted enabled the patrons of Sohrab to bring their young protégé back the next year. For the next four years Sohrab 'Alī hung on desperately, till he was forced out by a general rebellion of the merchants in the town. This was a unique kind of event in Indian history, when merchants recruited troops and fought pitched battles in the streets of the town. They were forced into this because they knew that Sohrab 'Alī had perfected plans for a general plunder of the wealthier among them, and that without it he could not possibly meet his financial obligations. But the tragedy of the situation was evident in the fact that when the merchants had won and it was for them to choose their own ruler, the man they selected was Teg Bakht Khān.[38] Thus the upshot was a temporary relaxation, and the character of the administration remained what it was. The oppression upon the merchants, the continuous quest for revenue, all remained as they were, and the leading mercantile families of Surat went under one by one.

The rebellion of the merchants at Surat was victorious in 1732, and within two years of it the port was blocked by the warships of the English East India Company. Henry Lowther, the chief of the English Factory, acted from complex motives. He was in the first place acting

[38]For this rebellion see my article 'The Crisis at Surat, 1730–2', *Bengal Past and Present* (Calcutta, 1967), pp. 148–62.

to protect the network of private trade that he and Robert Cowan, governor of Bombay, had built up over the last few years. He was also acting in order to protect all British private trade from being taxed by the Mughals. There were accounts outstanding between Teg Bakht Khān and Seth Jagannathdās Pārak, son and successor of Seth Lāldās Pārak, the principal business associate of Lowther. And finally there was the intent to make a gesture of suitable strength in order to cow the local administration at a time when the central power in the empire had crumbled.

The official excuse was that the action had been undertaken to preserve the English Company's 'privileges' which had been granted by the Mughals. Teg Bakht Khān was persuaded by the merchants to capitulate and it was agreed that English trade, public and private, was to be henceforth under no official scrutiny. In the process, however, almost the whole of the season 1733–4 was lost to the traders to the Red Sea, and Ahmad Chellaby, the leading merchant in town after the downfall of the family of Mulla 'Abd al-Ghafūr, calculated that his losses alone were about Rs 100,000. But more than that, the episode demonstrated the helplessness of the merchant caught between a totally unsympathetic and oppressive administration on the one hand, and a ruthlessly expanding trading structure on the other.[39]

The fact of this helplessness at a time when men who possessed some physical power were struggling desperately to keep alive, and the danger of it, were demonstrated yet again immediately after. The attack this time came from the African Sidis, who were in theory the naval guardians of the port. This peculiar clan of men were hopelessly divided among themselves by the 1730s and were engaged in a deadly encounter with the Marathas, who were steadily, and literally, driving them into the sea. The only source of income they were left with was the *t ınkha*, the assignment from the sea-customs of Surat. The fact was, of course, they did little to earn it, and the hard-pressed administration of Surat had long been defaulting in making this annual payment. In 1733 the Sidis had an acknowledged claim of Rs 600,000 due to them.[40] After various attempts, including naval demonstrations against the port, had failed to produce satisfactory results, the fleet of the Sidis swooped down on Surat Bar in March 1735 and arrested all the ships standing fully laden for the Red Sea. It was known at Surat that the English had

[39]The English blockade was begun in January 1734 and ended in early March, S.F.R., vol. XVIII, pp. 61–232.

[40]S.F.R., vol. XIX, pp. 75–7.

a close understanding with the Sidis and were assisting them against the Marathas. Henry Lowther was therefore called to the *darbār* and it was explained to him how 'their [i.e. of the administration] great poverty, the diminution of the revenues and the great expense they are at in maintaining their soldiers and complying with their engagement at Court' would not allow them to meet any 'high demand' from the Sidis.[41] Terrified merchants went into virtually non-stop sessions of consultations among themselves and all other interested groups, including the pilgrims waiting to set off for the Ḥajj. In a week's time when it seemed there was some slight chance of a settlement, the stupefied town learnt that the Sidi's fleet had made off in the night with six of their richly laden vessels.[42] In view of the close contact between the Sidis and the English, Henry Lowther considered it unwise to remain any further in town and retired on board a ship at the mouth of the river. He was, however, deeply disturbed at what had happened. On 15 March 1735 he wrote to his friends at the English Factory in town:

> None lament their [the merchants'] loss more than ourselves who have had nothing but plague and troubles for two months past on their account and had our advice taken place with Teg Beg Caun [Teg Bakht Khān] all might have been easy but instead of consulting this essential step, Interest has been the only motive that had any weight with him and it is such views as these that have brought on so many calamities upon the back of one another upon the back of the Inhabitants and the greatest of all is the impending storm, for without the ships are returned Surat can never recover itself again.[43]

After months of agonized waiting and ceaseless negotiations involving Surat, Bombay and Danda Rajapuri, the vessels were finally returned on 29 January 1736, but most probably much of their valued cargo had by this time disappeared. The merchants appear to have lost between Rs 100,000 and 300,000 in direct payment and the whole season in 1735 and much of it in 1736.[44] This episode of a struggle between the administration of the port and the admiral who was to look after its

[41]S.F.R., 9 March 1735, vol. XIX, p. 105.

[42]Ibid., pp. 105–8.

[43]Ibid., pp. 111–12.

[44]Again a day-to-day account of the stresses and strains in the town is available in S.F.R., vol. XIX, pp. 108ff. and S.F.R., vol. XX, pp. 1ff. Several payments were made in the course of the negotiations and the two figures I have cited appear to represent the minimum and maximum limits.

safety, showed how exclusively these two sets of men had come to rely on the revenue from trade and the inevitable plunder which followed.

These characteristics of the situation remained unchanged through the 1740s, and through many alarums and excursions the city of Surat went steadily to its own destruction. At the end of the decade the situation was described in a detailed memoir by the outgoing Dutch Directeur Jan Schreuder.[45] Delhi and Agra had by now virtually lost all their trade. The breakdown in security had not been mended and there was very little transport going up to the heartland of India. Ahmadabad, Schreuder noted, had been the capital and the largest city in Gujarat, with an impressive population. There was a very considerable trade there in textiles, especially in chintz and pieces worked with gold and silver threads. Now three-quarters of the city had been laid waste, and it was difficult to procure even a few pieces of cloth. The major reason for the decline, he thought, was the joint rule of the city by the Mughals and the Marathas and the plundering of its inhabitants by both. Both Cambay and Broach had also by now received Maratha officials to share in their administration. The results were more deadly for Cambay than for Broach, which retained some of its old network of procurement and, Schreuder thought, would retain these as long as there was some trade left at Surat. This last-mentioned town was the only one 'which had retained some traces of its previous prosperity'. But even then the losses had been grievous. The Muslim shipowners, for example, had by now lost much of what they once possessed. Now only about five ships sailed every year from the port where before these men had sent out at least 40. In an appendix to this memoir, Schreuder provided a list of the remaining 'capitalists' of Surat and their approximate fortunes. The usual figure ranged in the region of Rs 100,000 and no more than 30 people appeared on this list, with the predominance going to the *banias.* It is interesting to note that Mulla Fakhr al-dīn, the great-grandson of the famed millionaire Mulla 'Abd al-Ghafūr was credited with a fortune of exactly Rs 100,000. The total trade of the port had come down in 1740, the year Schreuder arrived at Surat, to Rs 5,000,000, of which the English carried about half and the Dutch about a tenth.

Thus, in course of the first 50 years of the eighteenth century India lost much of her trade in textiles and indigo which used to be channelled

[45] *Memoir of Jan Schreuder,* Hooghe Regeering, 838, pp. 17ff. In this as also in another memorandum which he wrote in 1746, Schreuder emphasized the growth of English private trade especially between Bengal and Surat and to China. H.R., 837, especially pp. 309–11.

through the ports of Gujarat, principally to the Red Sea. The commercial fleet, comprising about 60 sails in all, which had spanned the Arabian Sea every year, virtually disappeared. The strong links with Western Asia which had been maintained through the port of Surat were gravely weakened. The shipowners of Surat, who had been almost exclusively Muslim, were virtually wiped out. Although all figures must be regarded with some scepticism, the total trade of Surat appears to have dwindled to a third of its previous volume. The fact that one-third was retained has to be credited to a large extent to the expansion of English private trading.

Down the coast in Malabar, the other important trading area in western India, developments were in some respects quite different. This area of about 400 miles of green coastal belt, neatly sealed off from the interior at a distance of about 40 miles by the western Ghat, had never formed a part of the Mughal empire, or, for that matter, any other state of the interior. The most important port was Calicut, which was the oldest of the traditional centres of trade. In the sixteenth and again in the eighteenth century Cochin, to the south of Calicut, acquired considerable importance, although it never could measure up to its ancient rival. The Dutch East India Company had their Indian headquarters, as it were, at Cochin and the developments of this area as seen from Cochin are therefore well documented.[46] Unfortunately the port of Calicut itself is virtually without any documentation as, throughout much of the century, the European companies stayed away from it. Some documentation of less value is available from the archives of the English Company, which had two small establishments at Tellicherry and Anjengo in the north and south of Malabar. The main export of the coast was pepper, although there was a modest trade in textiles as well and some export of timber, sandalwood and coconut products. Because we do not have even a set of approximate figures relating to Calicut, it is impossible to estimate the total production of the coast at any time in the century. But to the south of Calicut available figures suggest that between 1760 and 1770 about 9000 *khandies* of

[46]In what I say about this coast I am briefly summarizing what I have said in *Malabar in Asian Trade, 1740–1800* and I shall not make any further specific reference to it. A very great deal of information about the coast in the eighteenth century is available in K.P. Padmanabha Menon, *A History of Kerala*, 4 vols (Ernakulam, 1924–37). An excellent discussion, especially of the imports and exports of the area, in A. Galletti, *The Dutch in Malabar* (Madras, 1911), in which two informative eighteenth-century memoirs have been edited with considerable care.

500 lb. each were exported every year. It seems possible that this was an increase over exports earlier in the century and it may have stayed at this level till the end of the century. All available evidence repeatedly refers to the dominating influence of the port of Calicut in Malabar, and if we posit a similar quantity exported from that port in the middle of the century we have a figure of about nine million pounds.[47] This must have been reduced from the 1760s onwards as the decline of Calicut began with the invasion of the coast from Mysore. Of these nine million pounds not more than a third was ever claimed by the European East India Companies, and in fact they never received as much as they wanted. The rest was sold, especially from the 1730s, to a heterogeneous group of Indian and Arab traders and private Europeans. The networks of supply were in the hands of Indian merchants of the coast, and their two important concentrations were, of course, at the two ports of Calicut and Cochin. We do not know very much about the business groups of Calicut, apart from the facts that they were the wealthiest in the area, owned ships and were predominantly Muslims. The two men about whom information is available were Isaac Surgun, a Jew, and Ḥājjī Yūsuf, a Mopla, that is a man of Arab descent. At Cochin the dominating groups were the Konkani Brahmans who had migrated down the coast in the sixteenth century from the environs of Goa and a strong community of Jewish traders led by the family of Ezechiel Rahabi. Although the Rahabis owned a few vessels, shipowning was by no means a major element in their business enterprise. Like other merchants of Cochin they concentrated on buying Indonesian spices from the Dutch and selling these, along with local produce, to the visiting Indian and Arab traders. Politically the coast had always been fragmented into little principalities, and this had been a blessing for the merchants of the coast, because the princes had tended their commerce for the transit revenues of customs.

There was no land revenue in Malabar till the 1760s, when it was introduced by the Mysorean conquerors. The princes lived in the main off their own lands and there was never any significant pressure on trade from the landed gentry. This somewhat idyllic picture changed sharply from about 1730. The first upsetting development was a boom

[47]For the estimate about southern pepper, see *Malabar*, pp. 58–9. In 1735 Ezechiel Rahabi estimated that 'in a period of complete peace and given a good harvest' the coast would produce 28,000 *khandies*, that is 14 million pounds of pepper, K.A. 2516, pp. 62–3. Thus the figure I have suggested is certainly a conservative estimate.

in the pepper market at Calicut, which occurred in the late 1720s. The price of pepper, which had remained between Rs 60 and Rs 62 for a *khandi* of 560 lb., shot up to between Rs 105 and Rs 125 in the 1750s. the reason for this sensational upsurge was the collapse of the Safavid dynasty in Persia and the ensuing dislocation of trade in the Persian Gulf. To this must be added the collapse of Surat and the closing of the main routes to the north. Businessmen who had previously found their pepper in the Gulf and at Surat were now presumably seeking their supply at Calicut. The dispersal from Surat may also have strengthened other centres in the area like Porbandar. At any rate it seems most probable that this new demand for Malabar pepper was at the expense of the Indonesian variety which the Dutch used to supply at Surat and then in the Gulf.[48] The second development, which followed almost immediately the first and was in some ways linked to it, was the transformation of a modest principality well to the south of the coast, by the name of Travancore, into an important kingdom which embraced all the coastline to the environs of Calicut. The emergence of this strong kingdom meant the end of the political fragmentation of Malabar, and it also meant the end of the coastal mercantile class in the area where the new kingdom stretched. The reason for the demise of the coastal merchants was that the kings of Travancore, Martanda Varma (1729–58) and Rama Varma (1758–98), built up their new kingdom with the help of a standing army and a bureaucracy which in the absence of land revenue could only be maintained out of the profits of the trade in pepper. A strict monopoly in this commerce was thus established which turned the merchants into officers of the state, and the commercial department of the kings of Travancore succeeded in establishing a control over both the production and distribution of this commodity in Malabar. Some of the merchants attempted to put up a

[48]In addition to the shipping lists of Cochin, we have copies of the passports which were issued to the Indian and Arab vessels by the Dutch for the years 1749–54, now preserved at the Madras Record Office. Our knowledge of these is therefore a little more complete than the ships of Surat or Hughli. More than half of them came from Porbandar, a small port a little to the west of Surat, and were owned by *bania* merchants there. They were small vessels, the usual declared tonnage being about 50 tons. The declared cargo never included pepper, but this was probably a little arrangement with the local Dutch officials, as pepper was on the Company's list of prohibited goods. In this connection we should note that from the papers relating to Surat it is clear that from the 1740s merchants at Surat were looking for other home-ports and the Dutch themselves were interested in developing their trade with Porbandar.

fight against this menace, but pressure from the bureaucracy, which soon changed into summary executions, prevailed over all opposition.

The distinction between what happened in Gujarat and the developments in southern Malabar was twofold. First, the merchants of Malabar were faced with a ruthless and efficient government, which saw its only salvation in the revenue it could have from trade and coolly proceeded to exploit this possibility. The struggle here was not against the crumbling administration of desperate, frightened men but against a new centralizing structure. Secondly, and following from it, the collapse of the mercantile classes did not therefore mean a decline in trade. It only stood for a new way of trading in which the profit went to the state. In the north of the coast—that is the area dominated by the famous port of Calicut—developments followed a more familiar line. The merchants of Calicut exploited the new boom in pepper to the full between 1730 and 1770, but then fell victim to the advancing armies of Mysore. Mysore, one of the several successor-states to the Mughal empire, was embattled with most of its neighbours and was desperately straitened for money. Haidar 'Alī, the Mysore ruler who first conquered Calicut in 1766, left the trade of the city unfettered in consideration of a large bribe which the merchants offered. But his son Tipu was unable to content himself with this arrangement and ruined much of this historic trade by following contradictory and capricious policies. In the first place he wished to establish a monopoly, probably on the model of Travancore, but was unable to obtain full advantage from it because the bureaucracy which had succeeded so brilliantly in the south was not available to him. Secondly, he followed the policy of concealed plunder as was done at Ahmadabad and Surat, and there is evidence of the wealthy merchants of Calicut undergoing similar tortures in the 1770s. In the third place, he attempted at times to destroy all trade by destroying the production of pepper and sandal, which he thought would inconvenience his deadly enemies, the Europeans. In the last decade of the eighteenth century there is thus enough evidence to show a considerable stagnation and decay in the major ports of Malabar, Calicut and Cochin. To some extent their place was taken by Alleppey, the new port of Travancore, which was managed by the commercial department of that kingdom. In the absence of relevant and adequate statistics it would be impossible to answer the question how far these developments denoted a total decline in the trade in pepper, but it seems clear that the direction of the trade was changed from northern India and Muscat to China. The number of vessels which called at Cochin from the north and west fell from 146 in 1774–5 to 22 in 1797–8 and it was noted at the end of the century that much of the pepper was being exported eastwards. Thus India's links with Western Asia through the trade in pepper would also appear to have been weakened in the eighteenth century.[49]

At the other end of the country, in eastern India, trading centres clustered along the two banks of a southern stretch of the river Ganga, and the dominating port was Hughli. This was the main port of the Mughal province of Bengal, and at the turn of the eighteenth century it had become the home of a large group of Indian and Asian traders, among whom the Shia Muslims, with Persian connections, were predominant. As Ghulām Husain Salīm writing in the 1780s noted of this earlier phase:

> The port of Hughli, in his time [that of the governor Murshid Quli Khān, 1701–26] became more populous than before. And merchants of all the ports of Arabia and *Ajam* [that is the non-Arab world] and English Christians who were shipowners and wealthy Mughals made their quarters there; but the credit of the Mughal merchants was greater than that belonging to other classes.[50]

Although Salīm knew of only the English as shipowners—and this certainly would appear to have been the case for about 50 years before Salīm wrote— in the early years of the century a fairly large number of Muslim ships operated from and called at Hughli. Dr Abdul Karim has counted 19 ships for the season 1705–6, relying on English data.[51] According to the Dutch list for departing vessels, 20 Muslim ships sailed in the season 1709–10. In the three months November 1719 to January 1720, the Dutch list comprised 18 such vessels.[52] In 1729–30 the number was 15 and in 1734 it was 11.[53] These falling numbers tell a tale

[49]The first figure is from the shipping list at Cochin and includes all kinds of vessels owned by non-Europeans, K.A. 3327, pp. 321–51. The second figure is from the *Report of Mr James Drummond on the Financial Position of the Dutch Possessions at Cochin, 1804*, at the Record Office, Madras, under Collectorate Records, no. 2557.

[50]*Riyazu-s-Salatin*, Ghulām Husain Salīm, tr. and ed. Mawlavi Abdus Salam (Calcutta, 1904), p. 30.

[51]A. Karīm, *Murshid Quli Khān and His Times* (Dacca, 1963), pp. 230–1. S. Chaudhuri cites the higher figures of 23 in 'The Rise and Decline of Hughli', *Bengal Past and Present*, vol. LXXXVI, especially note on p. 62.

[52]K.A. 1677, pp. 289–92 and K.A. 1854, pp. 36–9.

[53]K.A. 2057, pp. 296–301. The figure for 1734 is cited by Holden Furber in 'Glimpses of Life and Trade on the Hugli 1720–1770', *Bengal Past and Present*, vol. LXXXVI, pp. 14–23. He notes that the list for 1745 was 'shorter'.

which seems in its outlines acceptable. Muslim shipping which used to frequent the port dwindled, and there is some reason to believe that the port itself was damaged in the first half of the century. The details of the process are, however, unknown at present and all conclusions have to be strictly tentative. It is known for certain that the political collapse which affected Gujarat and other Mughal provinces in the early years of the century did not affect Bengal till the 1740s. On the contrary, a local process of consolidation under Murshid Quli and his son-in-law Shujā' al-dīn (Shuja Uddin) (1727–39) gave stability to this area.[54] It has been strongly urged that there was no economic decline in Bengal before Plassey,[55] but there is some evidence to the contrary. Salīm noticed that 'when oppression and extortion of the Faujdars increased, the port of Hughli declined, and Calcutta owing to the liberality and protection afforded by the English, and the lightness of duties levied there, became populous'.[56] This memory of past oppression was present in other writers as well, and there are two important contemporary documents which seem to bear this out. One is a memoir written at Hughli in 1732 by Jacob Sadelijn and the other, a similar document, drawn up in 1750 by Jan Huighens, both in the service of the Dutch East India Company. Sadelijn emphasized 'the decline of trade in this country', and as a major cause for it drew attention to the 'continuously increasing' oppressions of the local officials, 'which had so much impoverished the inhabitants that enterprising merchants of former years now scarcely earned their daily bread and leading families had been reduced to poverty'. In his opinion it was the 'brutal' and 'exhausting government' (*uijtputtende regeerings wijze*) of Shujā' Khān which had unleashed a spree of similar extortions among the lesser officials, that was the cause of it.[57] In the 1740s Bengal was attacked by the Marathas and the western part of it overrun. Hughli itself fell to the invaders and was under their control for a time. There was, however, no permanent annexation, and probably no lasting damage, as a result of it. However, when Huighens wrote in 1750, these events were very much present

[54]The standard book on political history is Jadunath Sarkar (ed.), *History of Bengal*, vol. II (Dacca, 1948).

[55]This is the view held by N.K. Sinha in his *Economic History of Bengal, 1757–1793*, 2 vols (Calcutta, 1956 and 1961), which provides the standard text for the second half of the century.

[56]Salīm, *Riyazu-s-Salatin*, p. 30. For further evidence, see the article by S. Chaudhuri, 'The Rise and Decline of Hughli'.

[57]K.A. 2088, pp. 421–3.

in his mind. He noticed the steady impoverishment of the Indian merchants and the problem this was creating for the procurement of merchandise for the Dutch. He also noticed that the pressure of the Maratha raid was to an extent being passed on to the merchants by the administration. Of the officials at Hughli he wrote

> the *naib fauzdar* Sheik Hedaytullah and his *dewan* Lahorimal are both reasonable men ... but the latter had recently been called to Murshidabad [the capital of the province] and compelled to supply Rs. 200,000/-. He will now certainly not scruple to export this amount from the local inhabitants and we must be careful that none of our men [Indians living under Dutch jurisdiction] fall into his hands.[58]

Apart from these strains developing within Bengal, the collapse in other parts of the country must have had repercussions on the trade of the area. This would seem to be borne out in the case of Gujarat, with which Bengal maintained a close trading connection. A major element in the Muslim shipping which used the port of Hughli every year was Gujarati, and much of the shipping was destined to the west of India. Thus in 1709–10 out of 20 vessels six were owned by merchants of Surat and nine were destined to that port.[59] Of the 18 ships recorded from November 1719 to January 1720, eight were for Surat, and it was noted that in the season 1720–1 eight ships belonging to Surat could not be ready in time and thus missed their passage.[60] Data collected from the list of passes issued by the Dutch at Surat bear out the importance of this link between Bengal and Surat in the early years of the century. Thus in 1707–8 the shipowners at Surat took out passes for nine of their vessels destined for Bengal and the total declared tonnage was 4425 *khandies* (about 1500 tons).[61] The collapse of Surat and the virtual disappearance of the Indian fleet based at that port would thus have been an event of major importance for Hughli, irrespective of local developments. It is interesting to note that in 1757 this was noticed in an account of Bengal compiled by a Dutchman called P. van

[58]This memoir dated 20 March 1750 is in K.A. 2655, which is unfortunately not paginated.

[59]K.A. 1677, pp. 289–92. Of the six ships two belonged to 'Abd al-Ghafūr.

[60]K.A. 1854, pp. 36–9, 187–90. Of the eight ships which missed their passage, four belonged to Muḥammad 'Alī, the grandson of Ghafūr. In the article cited above Professor Furber noted that of the eleven ships in 1734, five were from Surat.

[61]K.A. 1611, pp. 268–81.

den Velde at Batavia. 'The merchants of Gujarat', wrote Van den Velde, 'had for many years past [carried on their trade with Bengal] through a society they had set up under the name of Muḥammad 'Alī but it fell into misfortune when its directors were arrested on a charge of rebellion against lawfully constituted authority.'[62] In the last 'list of passes' to be found among the Dutch papers relating to Surat, 16 vessels are listed for the season 1735–6, of which five were destined for Bengal, and the total of their declared tonnage was 2600 *khandies* (about 850 tons). It is of great interest to note that all five of these were destined ultimately for China but were calling at Hughli on the way.[63]

This decline of Muslim shipping in general, and Gujarati shipping in particular, was made up to an extent by the remarkable development of English private shipping, and the decline of Hughli was matched by the growth of Calcutta. In the first decade of the eighteenth century Calcutta had been the home of about ten ships owned by resident Englishmen. This figure grew to 40 in 1722–3 and the figures for tonnage duty, which all such private shipping had to pay, show about 30 vessels operating in the early 1730s. There was a decline in the late 1730s and the number 25 in 1736–7 remained the highest till the 1750s, when it rose again to 30 and above. No figures are available for the 1760s and 1770s, but a great spurt in these years took the figures for English private ships using the port of Calcutta to 128 in 1783 and 591 in 1791.[64] Throughout the first half of the century much of this shipping was destined for the West, carrying Bengal's textiles, sugar and silk to Gujarat and Western Asia. With the decline of Muslim shipping Indian

[62]*Beschryvinge van Bengale* was one of many such collections which were done from time to time from the papers of the Dutch Company at Batavia, H.R. 244, p. 18. Muḥammad 'Alī was arrested at Surat after the rebellion of the merchants. The names of the other 'directors' of this 'society' can only be conjectured.

[63]K.A. 2282, pp. 1208–9. Two of these ships belonged to the great-grandsons of Ghafūr.

[64]For these figures and some of the references relating to Bengal I have used a paper called 'Private Enterprise and Company Monopoly: The British in Bengal in the Eighteenth Century' by P.J. Marshall of King's College, London, which he presented at the Conference on Modern South Asia at Cambridge in July 1968. I am grateful to him for his kind permission for this. The figures for private shipping at the end of the century are given by H.T. Colebrooke in *Remarks on the Present State of the Husbandry and Commerce of Bengal* (Calcutta, 1795), p. 154. It is necessary to note that Colebrooke added up the figures for arriving and departing shipping to obtain his totals.

merchants began to freight their goods on English bottoms. Marshall notes that in 1731 'the Guzzeratteers' complained to the Nawab that 'they should be very great sufferers' from any interruption in British shipping.[65] But political difficulties in Gujarat, the Persian Gulf and the Red Sea area, together with a surfeit of supplies to these markets, made the Western trade less attractive by the 1750s, and the great new shipping turned more and more towards the east. By the end of the eighteenth century only a few of the English ships were destined to the Western markets, while China, on the other hand, attracted most of them. In the years 1773–84, 94 private British ships arrived at Canton, while the figure for the following decade was 217.[66]

What is known about Bengal, and what can be reasonably conjectured, suggests three different phases of developments in the eighteenth century which should be distinguished one from another. In the first place we have the decline of the dominating traditional port and its replacement by the newly developing English trading centre. We do not yet know with any certainty the nature of this decline, but it would appear that the political pressures, so prominent elsewhere, played their role in this area as well. The kind of catastrophe which overtook Surat does not, however, seem to have taken place in Bengal. Secondly, the trading structure which developed in the second half of the century was dominated by the English private trader, and only those Indian merchants were allowed to operate who did not challenge this domination. The trade of Bengal was preserved in its old way, but the free play of demands which used to come from all quarters was resolutely turned back. During this phase the great turning of trade from the West to the East took place and the trade in textiles declined. Thirdly, the effects

[65]The source for this as for several other figures cited by Marshall is the Bengal Public Consultation series at the India Office Library, London.

[66]This great turning of trade in the Indian Ocean was first charted by Professor Holden Furber who, quite justifiably, hailed it as a 'commercial revolution', in *John Company at Work* (Harvard, 1948), p. 162. H.T. Colebrooke noted: 'To the gulphs of Arabia and Persia, Bengal sends grain, sugar, silk and cotton piece-goods, etc. This trade was formerly so considerable that the annual returns were estimated at thirty lakhs of rupees (Rs 3,000,000), but owing to anarchy which has prevailed in Persia since the death of Kherim Khan the successor of Nādir Shāh, and in Egypt since the overthrow of 'Alī Bey, with a variety of other causes, it has greatly declined of late', in *Remarks*, p. 165. Colebrooke's figures for shipping to the Persian Gulf and the Red Sea showed two ships from Bengal in that direction in 1783 and two in 1793. The corresponding figures for China were 13 and 33, ibid., pp. 150–1.

of the industrial revolution began to be felt from the 1780s onwards. It must be clearly realized that the industrial revolution did not break up a growing healthy structure of trade. It delivered the *coup de grâce* to a languishing commerce. In a large measure the switch from the manufacture and trade in textiles to one in agricultural products had already taken place. Now the industrial revolution took away the remaining trade with Europe and for the first time broke into India's home market.

It seems at present impossible even to suggest this kind of a conjectural pattern of development for the coast of Coromandel because of the paucity of our knowledge about it during the eighteenth century. In several important ways this coast appears to have differed from the other Indian trading areas. For one thing the political weakness which developed elsewhere at a certain time in the eighteenth century was present in Coromandel from about a hundred years before that. There was little in this area which could be called centralized political control either under the Muslim state of Golconda or the remnants of the once-powerful Hindu empire of Vijaynagar, which shared the coast during much of the seventeenth century. Farming of revenue, a feature which developed late in the Mughal empire, was the prevalent form in Coromandel at the beginning of the seventeenth century. W.H. Moreland in introducing a collection of travelogues wrote in an oft-quoted sentence: 'In essence, the administration was a scramble for immediate gain, without thought for the future, and this condition furnishes an adequate explanation of most of the difficulties experienced by Dutch and English merchants in establishing their trade in the seaports.'[67] An examination of the Dutch evidence relating to the seventeenth century has in general confirmed this verdict.[68] Thus the omnipresent political pressure was a reality the merchants of Coromandel had had to live with for a much longer period than their fellows elsewhere in the country. Possibly following from this, European settlements acquired an importance in this coast in the seventeenth century which they did not attain elsewhere before well on into the eighteenth. The best example of this would be the English settlement of Madras which, founded

[67]W.H. Moreland, *Relations of Golconda* (London, 1930), p. xvii. In this introductory essay Moreland gives one of the best available summaries of evidence about the coast in the seventeenth century.

[68]See T. Raychaudhuri, *Jan Company in Coromandel* (The Hague, 1962). Based on a detailed examination of the Dutch evidence this book is now the standard text for the seventeenth century.

in 1640, was a flourishing port by the end of the century.[69] This prosperity was steadily maintained, and in the 1740s Ananda Ranga Pillai, the diarist of Pondicherry, described it as the 'city of Kuvera', the god of wealth, and noted: 'It is not like other towns, where you may find ten rich men and all the rest beggars.'[70] In connection with this early emergence of European influence we should note the third peculiarity of the Coromandel coast, which consisted in some sort of a rough division between the northern and southern parts of the coastal belt. In the north, where the Muslim dynasty of Qutb Shāh ruled, there was the only major port of the area at Masulipatam, known for its shipping, the home of Mughal and Komati merchants. In the south, political power was fragmented among the local vassals of the Hindu kingdom ruling from the interior city of Vellore. It was in the south that the patterned textile goods were made which were the main exports of the coast, and they went, in the main, to South-east Asia. The north produced plain textiles which were in demand elsewhere in Asia. The south had no important trading centres when the English and the Dutch arrived early in the seventeenth century. This, presumably, was the reason for their flying start in spite of local vexations. An unexplored problem is the relationship between Masulipatam and the centres of production in the south, which presumably supplied its exports to Indonesia.

From the evidence which has so far been examined it would seem that there was an expansion in Indian trade in the second half of the seventeenth century. 'The mass of evidence provided by the factory records', writes Raychaudhuri,

> proves beyond doubt that in the latter half of the 17th century the trade of the Coromandel merchants had become one of the major facts in Asian commerce. They explored not only the regions directly or indirectly familiar to the Indian traders, but at least one new field—the Philippines. In the last quarter of the century this expansion of trading activities continued steadily in the face of

[69] The prosperity of Madras at the end of the seventeenth century is well brought out by the relevant volumes of *Diary and Consultation* of the English Council at that town, available in print. See especially *Diary and Consultation Book of 1701* (Madras, 1922), pp. 29, 88–96; *Diary and Consultation 1702*, p. 43; *Diary and Consultation 1704*, p. 29 (for a description of the large Indian mercantile community at Madras).

[70] This comment comes in a discussion of the sack of Madras in 1746 when an enormous booty was had by all, including most of Pillai's friends, *Pillai*, vol. IV, pp. 64–5.

immense problems thrown up by wars, famine and pestilence—a testimony to the resilience of the Indian commercial and production organization.[71]

The continued prosperity of Masulipatam and this resurgence of Indian trade suggest the important conclusion that, although administration upon the coast was geared to thoughtless and immediate gain, this placed no insuperable difficulty in the path of merchants, although it may well have set a limit to individual wealth.

The real problem is to account for the decline of this growing trade in the course of the eighteenth century. Raychaudhuri suggests tentatively that the competition from a resourceful and well-organized concern like the English East India Company may well have proved too much for the merchants of Coromandel.[72] If it did, then this is another respect in which Coromandel is unique in the history of Indian trade, because commercial competition from the English Company caused no concern to Indian merchants elsewhere. As we have seen, their competition was much more with the private trade of the Company's servants, and the enemy they dreaded was their own government. It is, however, possible to argue that the political weakness which had always been present in Coromandel broke down into total anarchy in the eighteenth century, and what should cause surprise is that some trade survived at the end. There were three major conflicts which simultaneously engulfed the coast from about 1730. At one level the Muslim power in the north of the coast reached down to the south and attempted an extirpation of the Hindu principalities. At another, the conflict between the Mughal empire and the Marathas, which had already touched the coast in the later years of the seventeenth century, broke out afresh in the 1740s. At a third level, the French and the English intervened decisively in the confused fighting which was going on and the whole of the coastline became an embattled area. Again, the contemporary evidence about the exact effects all this had on the trade of the coast has not yet been looked at. But evidence which is strongly suggestive of a general conclusion similar to that I have maintained in relation to other areas is available. Thus there is a series of memoirs written by the Dutch governors of Ceylon which illuminate the process of the collapse in Madura immediately to the south of Coromandel. The Dutch had a factory there at Tuticorin and they were interested in the trade

[71] T. Raychaudhuri, *Jan Company*, p. 128.

[72] Ibid. He also notes that the establishment of overall control by the British may have had something to do with it.

in textiles. As late as 1734, Jacob Christian Pielat noted: 'The trade in cotton goods on the coast of Madura is in a fairly flourishing condition, as is proved by the fact that 1510 bales of various descriptions of cotton were sent this year to the Fatherland; while the year before only 945 bales were sent.'[73] Six years later, when Madura had already experienced its first agonies, Baron Imhoff was more inclined to put down the decline in the profits of the Dutch Company to the dishonesty of its officials than to 'the troubles in the country', which, however, he was obliged to note.[74] Joan Gideon Loten in 1757 had to write extensively on the sustained political convulsions in the kingdom and the flight of the weavers due to official oppression, but he was still not sure that the Dutchmen at Tuticorin were not 'exaggerating' the difficulties.[75] All such doubts disappeared by the time Jan Schreuder came to write his appreciation of the situation in 1762. He was convinced that the country had been plunged into anarchy with the overthrow of its Hindu dynasty in 1736, and this anarchy was the central fact of the situation. 'The country', he wrote, 'is disturbed on all sides by (everyone, even its own) subjects ... and ravaged and plundered till it has gradually become (much smaller) and nothing but continual quarrels and dissensions exist among the lesser chieftains of which sometimes no true idea can be formed.'[76]

The comments noted almost daily by Ananda Ranga Pillai also bear out the fact of an overwhelming collapse in Coromandel. Every year his diary becomes more gloomy, and all of it cannot be explained away by the failure of the French or his personal frustrations. Typical laments in the year 1757 portray the physical breakdown at Pondicherry, where the French were forced to resort to large collective fines from the inhabitants in order to keep their wars going. It drove the peaceful men of Pondicherry nearly into rebellion and made Pillai often compare the 1730s most favourably with what was happening in the late 1750s. In typical style he summed up the situation on 1 May 1759: 'In times of decay order disappears giving place to disorder and justice to injustice.

[73]The Tinnevelly coast was Madura to the Dutch because political control came from that interior city, *Memoir of J.C. Pielat, 1734* (Colombo, 1905), p. 25.

[74]*Memoir of Gustaaf Willem Baron Van Imhoff, 1740* (Colombo, 1911), p. 41.

[75]*Memoir of Joan Gideon Loten, 1757* (Colombo, 1935), pp. 12–13, 32–3.

[76]*Memoir of Jan Schreuder, 1762* (Colombo, 1946), p. 33. This memoir contains the Dutch text along with the English translation and I have slightly amended the translation, in brackets, from the text.

Men no longer observe their caste rules but transgress their bounds, so that castes are confused and force governs.'[77] It is possible that Masulipatam had retained some of its famed prosperity till the 1740s. In the 1750s, however, it became one of the focal points in the Anglo-French struggle upon the coast. The French captured it in 1750 and the English took it over in 1759. Even before this the renters of revenue in the area had attempted to turn themselves into hereditary *zamindārs*, and had in effect become the actual rulers of the neighbourhood. It was noted that when the British took over the administration they found that

> the aims of government in the area immediately to the north-east of Masulipatam stopped short generally at the raising of revenue by heavy taxes on land and continuous and oppressive exactions on trade for the purpose of maintaining armed men. The agents of the Government were the *zamindars* who may be said to have combined military and executive functions.[78]

For a long time after the English took over the administration, the miseries of misrule continued. In 1783 the Masulipatam Council considered a report on the flight of weavers towards the interior.[79] In 1789 the Report of the Committee of Circuit drew attention to the bleeding of the countryside by the renters, and noted that they left only that much to the cultivator which would prevent large-scale desertion. The Report also characterized the rate of customs at Masulipatam as 'ruinous'.[80] Thus from the far south to the north of the coast, war and its attendant dislocation are the central facts of eighteenth-century Coromandel. It is but natural that Indian trade, which was totally unprotected, would not weather a crisis of this order.

It is equally natural that those elements of Indian trade which had found their footing at Madras, the principal centre of the ultimate victors, would, however, continue to flourish. Unlike Bombay and Calcutta, Madras had attained its prosperity early, and in an area where there was no pressure from a neighbouring indigenous port. It is therefore

[77] *Pillai*, vol. XI, p. 318. For comments on deterioration, see ibid., pp. 23–4, 95, 295–6. For the collective fine, see ibid., pp. 371ff, and Dodwell's editorial remark on p. xvii.

[78] *Guide to the Records of the Masulipatam District, 1682–1835*, vol. I (Madras, 1935), p. 3.

[79] Ibid., p. 67. Also see Gordon Mackenzie, *A Manual of Kistna District* (Madras, 1883), pp. 40 ff.

[80] *Guide to the Records of Masulipatam*, vol. I, pp. 153–4.

safe to suggest that the Indian merchants at Madras, who made good, represented a net addition to the world of Indian trade. In the case of Bombay, prosperity came only with the break-up of Surat, and was based on the stragglers from that city. Thus Bombay and Madras would seem to have represented two different ways in which the new structure of Indo-British trade came into existence. We have, however, to note that whether at Bombay, Madras or Calcutta, prosperity was possible only in co-operation with the Englishmen. It has been said that the relationship between the *dubash* and the Englishman was more of a kind of 'partnership between two young and ambitious merchants, each using one another for their mutual advantage', than one of master and servant.[81] But the exclusion of all independent trade, which competed with the trade of the English, was a fact, and so was the ultimate English control over the general directions of trade. Thus Indian merchants who had faced total extinction at the hands of Indian administration exchanged that dangerous position for a constricted existence. The English, in so far as they preserved islands of security, maintained an essential continuity in India's trade. But the trading structure which grew under English dispensation lacked the quality of freedom which, with all its wilfulness, the Mughal administration had preserved in the seventeenth century. The class which appears to have been wholly swept out in the process was that of the Muslim shipowners of Surat, Calicut, Masulipatam and Hughli. As the obviously wealthy element, they attracted the attention of the desperate, local officials, and as the obvious competitors they stood no chance of collaboration with the English. Thus much of Muslim trade disappeared along with Muslim administration in eighteenth-century India, and the close links they had stood for with Western Asia were loosened. It would be wrong to think, however, of a total breakdown in this Western trade, as some of it, of course, still continued. The strong emphasis on it, so marked earlier, was there no longer. One might say that for the mariner in Asian waters the Western shores gradually misted over while old landmarks in the East were picked out with a new brightness.

[81] John Gurney, 'The Debts of the Nawab of Arcot, 1763–1776', unpublished D.Phil. dissertation (University of Oxford, 1968), p. 44. In this work he has discussed the rise of a community of *dubashes* (literally 'interpreters' in fact 'agents') and their dominance in the trade of Madras. I am most grateful to him for letting me consult his work and to quote from it.

14

The 'Great Firm' Theory of the Decline of the Mughal Empire*

Karen Leonard

Most historians of the Mughal empire currently emphasize economic factors in their attempts to locate and measure the causes of imperial decline in seventeenth- and eighteenth-century India. Recent articles reiterate a standard set of tensions: those between monarch, military and service nobles (*mansabdars*), landholders (*zamindars*), and peasants.[1] Existing theories attribute the Mughal decline to the nature of the monarchy, the breakdown of the *mansabdari* administrative system, and the challenges from newly established regional rulers. One influential analysis points to the increasing burden of taxation and consequent *zamindar*–peasant rebellions throughout the empire as the

*A preliminary version of this article was presented at the Seminar on 'Decline of the Mughals' at the University of Pennsylvania, May 1974; criticism from the other participants, but even more from Dr John G. Leonard, has helped improve that version. First published in *Comparative Studies in Society and History*, vol. XXI, no. 2, 1979.

[1]Peter Hardy has referred to this standard 'diagram of tensions' in his commentary upon two of the most recent articles: P. Hardy, 'Commentary and Critique', *Journal of Asian Studies*, XXXV:2 (Feb. 1976), p. 257. The articles upon which he is commenting are M.N. Pearson, 'Shivaji and the Decline of the Mughal Empire', pp. 221–35, and J.F. Richards, 'The Imperial Crisis in the Deccan'. pp. 237–56, both in the same issue.

fundamental cause of decline.[2] The nobility and the *mansabdari* system have received most attention, however. Historians have emphasized the strains caused by numerical expansion, inflation of noble ranks, and the 'aristocratization' of the *mansabdars* through conspicuous consumption and hereditary control of positions.[3] Analyses of the availability and distribution of economic resources neglect one group whose relationship to the Mughal state and whose roles in the political system were crucial: the bankers—*sahukars, shroffs, mahajans*—particularly those in the 'great firms'. It will be argued here that the great banking firms of Mughal India played a key role in the decline of the empire.

The 'great firm' theory of Mughal decline, which relies on secondary sources for its comprehensive database, clarifies and extends existing economic theories of imperial decline. Indigenous banking firms were indispensable allies of the Mughal state, and the great firms' diversion of resources, both credit and trade, from the Mughals to other political powers in the Indian subcontinent contributed to the downfall of the empire. The period of imperial decline coincided with the increasing involvement of banking firms in revenue collection at regional and local levels, in preference to their continued provision of credit to the central Mughal government. This involvement increased from 1650 to 1750, and it brought bankers, more directly than before, into positions of political power all over India. This period of 'great firm' partnership with regional powers, among them the East India Company, was followed by political losses for the great banking firms. When in the 1750s the Company began to achieve political dominance throughout India, it turned against indigenous bankers and systematically displaced them, usurping their functions as bankers to the Company and to other political

[2]Irfan Habib, *The Agrarian System of Mughal India* (Bombay, 1963), argues for oppression and revolt. Two often-cited views focusing upon factions among the nobility are Satish Chandra, *Parties and Politics at the Mughal Court, 1707–1740* (Aligarh, 1959) and M. Athar Ali, *The Mughal Nobility Under Aurangzeb* (Aligarh, 1966). Two regional perspectives are given by Philip Calkins, 'The Formation of a Regionally Oriented Ruling Group in Bengal, 1700–1740', *Journal of Asian Studies,* XXIX:4 (Aug. 1970), and Karen Leonard, 'The Hyderabad Political System and Its Participants', *Journal of Asian Studies,* XX:3 (May 1971), pp. 569–82.

[3]See the two articles cited in footnote 1; Pearson argues that military efforts in the south and the defeats inflicted by Shivaji decisively affected the loyalty of the nobles, and Richards argues that policy miscalculations led to artificial *jagir* shortages and inattention to newly incorporated warrior élites in the south.

rulers and downgrading their roles in the collection of land revenue. One consequence was the relegation of indigenous bankers to less crucial roles in the political system. A second effect was the diminished historical awareness of the bankers' earlier importance in Mughal India.

The theoretical literature on historical bureaucratic empires points to the importance of the banking firms to the state. Imperial authority derived from a mixture of charismatic, legal–rational, and traditional religious and cultural factors.[4] A ruler's authority was strongest where the political order was closely interwoven with the cosmic, religious, and cultural order, that is where political legitimacy was based on the maintenance of that traditional order. In Mughal India, with a ruling class which was largely Muslim and initially drawn from outside, economic and political alliances were extremely important to maintenance of the state.[5]

The establishment of the Mughal empire required the conquerors to co-opt indigenous groups and institutions and to counter the opposition of various indigenous élites menaced by the imperial trend towards political centralization. Moreover, the Mughal emperors had to achieve some measure of legitimacy in traditional terms through political accommodation with traditional élites. And they had to form alliances with groups in the population which could benefit from the establishment of a more unified polity. Such allies theoretically could come from one of two categories: those (largely urban) economic, cultural, and professional groups who were by origin or interest opposed to the nobility and landholder, and the larger, lower-class groups (for example peasants) who could at least indirectly benefit from the weakening of aristocratic forces and the establishment of greater order. The Mughals had to find and utilize such new economic and political resources.[6]

The creation of the *mansabdari* system, a new organ of centralized administration directly supervised and staffed by new personnel was important in establishing the empire. But just as clearly, the Mughals depended upon urban merchants and bankers for the provision of goods

[4]Useful discussions are by S.N. Eisenstadt, *The Political Systems of Empires* (New York, 1963) and *The Decline of Empires* (New Jersey, 1967).

[5]The generalization has interesting implications for scholars of cultural and intellectual movements in medieval and early modern India, such as the *bhakti* movements, the development of vernacular poetry, the shifts of artistic patronage to regional courts, and those political movements led by Shivaji or the Sikh gurus.

[6]The analysis draws upon Eisenstadt, *Political Systems*, particularly ch. 12.

and commodities and cash, the latter for direct spending and payment for services. Given the geographic scope of the Mughal empire, the decentralized military forces and their employment in expansionist ventures, these financial resources had to be accessible and flexible. Since there was a monetized market economy and a highly developed system of credit in Mughal India, conditions of political stability encouraged the alliance of the Mughals and indigenous bankers and ensured a continuous flow of trade goods and notes of credit.

Yet the interests of the Mughal state and of the great banking firms sometimes came into conflict. The rulers had a constant need to mobilize extensive resources for military expansion. Such mobilization could either exhaust the available resources or strengthen the groups which produced and controlled those resources, making the bankers less dependent on the rulers and ultimately threatening the basis of the political system. For the banking firms, the conflict of interests was intensified by the practice of short-term loans, increasing the dependence of the rulers on them but possibly undermining the availability of resources in the long run.[7]

The ruler's relationships with diverse groups and institutions had to be carefully balanced, and any disruption could set off a chain of events weakening the empire. External pressures combined with internal tensions could intensify problems of imperial control. When other powers competed with the Mughals for the credit and other services offered by Indian bankers, the imperial bureaucracy was threatened. It became more dependent upon the banking firms and it had to develop better working methods or offer additional services to maintain the relationship.[8] The later Mughals, in policy and in practice, do not appear to have placed enough importance upon retaining the confidence of the great banking firms, and this was a critical error.

Most writers have treated bankers and other financial and merchant groups in India as 'segmental' rather than 'strategic' élites, viewing them as outside the governmental structure and not instrumental in decisions affecting society at large.[9] They have been analysed as 'hinge'

[7]Ibid., and his *Decline of Empires*, pp. 3–5; and A.L. Udovitch, 'Credit as a Means of Investment in Medieval Islamic Trade', *Journal of the American Oriental Society*, 87:3 (July–September 1967), pp. 60–4.

[8]S.N. Eisenstadt, *Essays on Comparative Institutions* (New York, 1965), p. 203, suggests this line of reasoning, which is clearly relevant to the Mughal empire.

groups, largely autonomous and apolitical,[10] or, even more negatively, as passive and parasitic beneficiaries of the conditions established by a strong imperial government.[11] Certainly they do not fit comfortably into the usual contemporary definitions of strategic élites, seldom being included in the ruling class of nobles and officials; yet they played a very large political role in Mughal India, as has been remarked in the cases of particular individuals. In fact, so little analysis of bankers and banking firms has been attempted that there is considerable confusion about the unit with which historians should be concerned. Should we be examining those famous individual bankers, or caste and merchant guilds in urban centres, or, rather more vaguely, 'banking castes', assumed to be following traditional occupations wherever they were?[12]

The 'great firms' has already been proposed here as the appropriate unit for historical analysis. This term has been used to describe a business firm engaged in a wide variety of enterprises, with several branches, often based on one 'household'.[13] For our purposes, a basic

[9]For an introductory discussion of 'Elites', see Suzanne Keller's article in the *International Encyclopedia of the Social Sciences,* Vol. 5 (New York, 1968), p. 28.

[10]This is Michael Pearson's view, particularly in his unpublished dissertation, 'Commerce and Compulsion: Gujarati Merchants and the Portuguese System in Western India, 1500–1600' (University of Michigan, 1971). He has modified his view of their role in politics to some extent in his article, 'Political Participation in Mughal India', *Indian Economic and Social History Review (IESHR),* IX:2 (April–June 1972), pp. 113–31.

[11]See Irfan Habib's three articles: 'Banking in Mughal India', *Contributions to Indian Economic History,* I (Calcutta, 1960), pp. 1–20; 'Potentialities of Capitalistic Development in the Economy of Mughal India', *Journal of Economic History,* XXIX (March 1969), pp. 32–78; and 'Usury in Medieval India', *Comparative Studies in Society and History,* VI:4 (July 1964), pp. 393–423. Also, W.C. Smith, 'The Mughal Empire and the Middle Class—A Hypothesis', *Islamic Culture,* XVIII:4 (Oct. 1942). pp. 349–63.

[12]For examples of such treatments, see Pearson, 'Political Participation', pp. 119–23; D.R. Gadgil, *Origins of the Modern Indian Business Class* (New York, 1959), especially pp. 23–8, and the same author's tentative conclusion that 'mahajans' in Poona were socio-religious organizations for immigrants, 'Immigrant Traders in Poona in the 18th Century', *Artha Vijnana* I (March 1959), 16; and K.L. Gillion, *Ahmedabad* (Berkeley, 1968), pp. 16–24.

[13]T.A. Timberg, 'A Study of a "Great" Marwari Firm: 1860–1914', *IESHR,* VIII:3 (July–Sept. 1971), pp. 267–8. Gadgil, in *Origins,* p. 34, speaks of firms based on kinship units. Neither defines the unit further.

functional distinction is essential: moneylenders were those individuals or firms habitually making loans, while bankers were those individuals or firms which not only made loans but received deposits and/or dealt in *hundis*, the written order for payment transmitted throughout India.[14] A further distinction in terms of customers proves useful: moneylenders dealt customarily with agriculturalists; bankers very seldom dealt with agriculturalists.[15] The last distinction directs us away from questions of the degree of monetization of the Mughal agrarian economy and brings us back to the extensive development of credit facilities, not those oriented towards the production of agricultural or other goods, but those oriented towards investment and profit through transactions with the Mughal government and its functionaries. A good working definition of the 'great firms' allied to the Mughal government should specify a certain magnitude of the firm's operations, both in volume of credit and in geographic range through the firms' branches: such specifications must await more empirical data.

'Great Firms' and the Mughal State: To 1750

Historians have found scattered evidence of the transactions between the great firms and the Mughal state. Irfan Habib's two articles on bankers and moneylenders in seventeenth-century India include many useful facts, although he places no emphasis on the political aspects of the transactions. Bankers performed important, but, in his view, limited services: they validated and minted money, maintained exchange ratios between different currencies, and issued *hundis*.[16] D.R. Gadgil has also discussed bankers at length, delineating their functions as money-changers and dealers in *hundis* and adding a major role in government finance. Here he mentions bankers serving as lenders of cash and credit, as receivers and remitters of land revenue, and as financiers of tax farmers.[17]

[14] L.C. Jain, *Indigenous Banking in India* (London, 1929), makes this distinction on p. 3. He also gives the best explanation of the *hundi* system which was extremely complex.

[15] V. Krishnan, *Indigenous Banking in South India* (Bombay, 1959), p. 9. In a twentieth-century survey, he found that 80 per cent of moneylenders dealt with agriculturalists, while only 3 per cent of the bankers did so.

[16] Habib, 'Banking', pp. 3–8.

[17] Gadgil, *Origins*, pp. 32–4. Hameeda Khatoon Naqvi, *Urban Centres and Industries in Upper India, 1556–1603* (New York, 1968), gives specific instances, pp. 62–3, 127–8, 286.

Particularly crucial were the bankers' roles as state treasurers. Specific banking firms were frequently appointed by a ruler to provide cash and credit for the payment of salaries and other expenses on a regular basis. Thus the delays and irregularities consequent upon sole dependence on the seasonally delivered land revenues to the capital could be avoided. There are many examples of such appointments.

The Jagat Seth firm gained fame in this treasurer role in mid-eighteenth-century Bengal. The Jain family firm had moved from Rajputana to Patna, and from there to Dacca and Murshidabad with the Mughal governors of Bengal. In the seventeenth century, the Mughal emperor Aurangzeb had personally honoured the firms's head, Manek Chand, for his large loans to the government. Manek Chand's nephew was appointed 'Imperial Treasurer' and awarded the title Jagat Seth by Emperor Farukhsiyar. Jagat Seth was accorded mint privileges by 1717, and after 1728 the imperial tribute from Bengal was sent to Delhi by draft on this banking house. The house of Jagat Seth had personal access to the Mughal emperor in the 1720s and 1730s, and it could allegedly obtain *farmans* of appointment for high officials.[18]

Other great firms served a treasurers to rulers throughout India. Kallidaikurichy Brahmin firms were bankers to the Rajas of Cochin and Travancore.[19] Branches of a single Marwari firm served as bankers to the Nawab of Fatehpur, the Pindari Nawabs, and Ranjit Singh.[20] Particular firms were named as bankers to the Nawab of Arcot and to the Nizam of Hyderabad.[21] Many other examples can be cited and the

[18]J.H. Little, 'The House of Jagatseth,' In *Bengal Past and Present,* XX (Jan.–June 1920), pp. 111–200, and XXII (Jan.–June 1921), pp. 1–119, is a fascinating history of this firm. The material used here comes from XX, pp. 112–32. Brijen K. Gupta, *Sirajuddaulah and the East India Company, 1756–1757* (Leiden, 1962), also documents this firm's closeness to the Mughals, especially pp. 30–1, 96–7.

[19]Krishnan, *Indigenous Banking,* p. 3.

[20]Timberg, 'A "Great" Marwari Firm', in the footnotes, pp. 272–4.

[21]For the Nawab of Arcot, Bavany Doss Nanasa Soucar and Dave Boocunji Cashee Dass Soukar were the largest creditors in 1805: Jain, *Indigenous Banking,* p. 21. For Hyderabad, there were the 'Panch Bhai' bankers, which in the early nineteenth century certainly included Seth Kishen Das (now a famous jewellery firm), Makhdum Seth, Mahanand Ram Puran Mal, probably Surat Ram Govind Ram, and perhaps Palmer and Company.

practice has been generally recognized; its significance, however, has been understated by historians.[22]

Other strong connections between great firms and the Mughal state came through the loans and credit extended to individual nobles and officials. Successive attempts by the state to regulate or prohibit these transactions testify to their persistence and to the state's perception of them as weakening imperial control. Nobles borrowed money frequently, using their *jagirs* ('land assignments') as security and giving claims upon the anticipated land revenues to bankers. High interest rates prevailed, but nobles allegedly preferred *jagirs* to payment of a cash salary, since *jagirs* were acceptable security for bankers.[23] Emperor Akbar tried to establish a royal treasury and avoid reliance on 'moneylenders', and he tried to advance loans from the treasury at an interest below that asked by bankers.[24] In the time of Aurangzeb, state officials served as intermediaries to recover debts for bankers from nobles: officials usually claimed one-fourth of the debt for this service, a practice Aurangzeb tried to stop.[25]

Both the central administration and its individual officials often had to transfer large amounts of money from one place to another, and this was done through banking firms. Habib's impression from the authorities he has seen is that the total amounts transferred on behalf of the Mughal government and individual officials 'rivalled if not exceeded' money remitted for purposes of trade.[26] In a similar attempt to estimate the volume and kind of various business transactions, Gadgil contradicts himself on whether the larger banking firms were more likely to be engaged in government financing or in trade.[27] These are questions of major historical importance, and while further empirical data

[22]Writers on later systems of finance and banking often referred to this prior function of indigenous banking firms, for example P. Datta, 'Rise of the Calcutta Money Market in Relation to Public Borrowing and Public Credit (1772–1833)', *Calcutta Review*, 46 (Feb. 1933), pp. 171–203, and N. Das, 'The Old Agency Houses of Calcutta', *Calcutta Review*, 46 (March 1933), pp. 317–26. But these and other authors completely fail to deal with the historical transition which the indigenous bankers have undergone, even at a descriptive level.

[23]Habib, 'Usury', pp. 408–9.

[24]Habib, 'Banking', p. 6, and 'Usury', p. 409.

[25]Habib, 'Usury', pp. 414–15.

[26]Habib, 'Banking', pp. 10–11.

[27]Gadgil, *Origins*, p. 34.

are obviously needed, the impressions of both of these scholars emphasize the political potential of the functions banking firms performed in Mughal India.

In addition to investment through the extension of credit to the central administration and its officials, three others types of profitable activities linked bankers to the Mughal state. These activities are often dismissed as examples of wasteful extravagance and dissipation of capital,[28] but that assessment must be reconsidered. First, there were the organized units of production and supply to the court, the *karkhanas*, which Gadgil suggests were the major banking firms' most direct connection with 'industry' at the time.[29] Second, contracting for the construction of public edifices in the sixteenth and seventeenth centuries—mosques, tombs, pleasure gardens and so forth—must have been extremely profitable. It was a major type of capital expenditure by the Mughal state.[30] Third, dealers in bullion and jewellery played major roles in economic life, and they were often involved in the great banking firms. Habib was surprised to find that *shroffs* rather than jewellers and goldsmiths were the chief buyers of foreign silver in Mughal India,[31] but in fact most banking firms were engaged in several enterprises and jewellery was a common sideline.[32] These court-related economic activities can no longer be viewed as superficial. Attempts must be made to measure them, ascertain who was engaged in them, and relate them to other areas of the Mughal economy.

Finally, there is the increasingly important role of banking firms in revenue collection. It is abundantly clear that by 1750 it was bankers who controlled access to the actual collection of land revenue, through

[28]Habib falls into this category most of the time. See his article 'Potentialities of Capitalistic Development', p. 69, where he sees the *karkhanas* as engaged in the 'production of luxury articles. . . This naturally set limits to their economic significance', and similar remarks on pp. 57–60.

[29]Significantly, Gadgil remarks that by 1750 such *karkhanas* had diminished in importance, *Origins*, pp. 34–35.

[30]Gadgil, *Origins*, p. 35.

[31]Ibid., p. 35; Habib, 'Banking', p. 4.

[32]In Hyderabad, a leading early banking firm is now noted as the leading jewellery firm, a business in which it had always engaged as well: Kishen Das, now Vithal Das. See also Qeyamuddin Ahmad, 'An Historical Account of the Banaras Mint in the Later Mughal Period, 1732–1776', in *Numismatic Society of India*, 23 (1961), pp. 198–215, where 'precious stones' pass through the mint, p. 209.

provision of credit or cash. They, rather than officials of the Mughal or any other ruler, were the people to deal with. The amount of interest set and the securities demanded by bankers were more critical economic conditions than the revenue demand fixed by a territorial ruler. Most of the evidence for this state of affairs is from the eighteenth century and seemingly linked to the practice of revenue farming. Bankers provided the funds which enabled *talukdars* ('contractors') to gain their positions as tax farmers, and bankers sent their own agents into the countryside to collect from the land given to them as security or mortgage.[33]

Historical instances of bankers involved in the land revenue system are numerous. In Bengal, the Jagat Seths presided over annual negotiations with leading *zamindars* at their Murshidabad residence, settling accounts and allocating fresh supplies of funds.[34] Other bankers in Bengal in the eighteenth century stood surety for landowners and paid the revenue on their behalf. They turned over to the East India Company sealed bags which were not opened, because the bankers were 'averse to the opening and inspection of them, declaring it contrary to established custom of the country and destructive of credit'.[35] Shah, discussing the revenue system of eighteenth-century Gujarat, terms moneylenders and bankers 'part of the entire system of state finance'. He notes that urban bankers made loans to rulers for military and other purposes and were in return authorized to collect the revenues.[36] Cohn shows many such instances in the Benares region in the eighteenth century, and he traces several bankers into official positions in the political system.[37] Lengthy descriptions of the Madras hinterland in the eighteenth

[33]Habib, 'Usury', p. 398.

[34]Little, 'House of Jagatseth', XX, p. 133, citing Hunter's *Statistical Account*, IX, p. 256.

[35]Jain, *Indigenous Banking*, pp. 18–19, citing Bengal District Records of the eighteenth century.

[36]A.M. Shah, 'Political Systems in 18th Century Gujarat', *Enquiry*, I:1 (Spring 1964), pp. 83–95, 92.

[37]See specific instances in the following articles by Bernard S. Cohn: 'The Initial British Impact on India, A Case Study of the Benares Region', *Journal of Asian Studies*, XIX:4 (August 1960) pp. 422–3; 'Recruitment of Elites in British India', in L. Plotnicov and A. Tuden (eds.), *Essays in Comparative Social Stratification* (Pittsburgh, 1970), pp. 128–9; 'Structural Change in Indian Rural Society, 1596–1885', in R. Frykenberg (ed.), *Land Control and Social Structure in Indian History* (Wisconsin, 1969), pp. 80–1; and 'Political Systems in Eighteenth Century India: The Benares Region', *Journal of the American Oriental Society*, 82:3 (July–Sept. 1962), p. 319.

century testify to the bankers' control of the land revenue; some of these bankers were based in Hyderabad and sent their agents out to collect revenue on lands ceded as security by *zamindars* in the circars.[38] It was in the Madras area also where 'customary arrangement' found a rural official collecting funds on the first of the month and then loaning the amount at interest to a banker, who used it as working capital until the official turned it over to the government on the twenty-eighth of the month.[39]

The banker's assumption of key positions in eighteenth-century systems of revenue collection has usually been attributed to the increasing weakness of the central government, leading to revenue contracting and emphasizing the need for capital to secure initial contracts. But so little is actually known about the operation of the Mughal land revenue system that it is hard to say where and when salaried officials were used, or whether there may have been an intermediate stage when collection was entrusted to private individuals working on commission.[40] Whether it is a symptom or a cause of imperial decline, the bankers' powerful role in regional and local land revenue system developed during the same period that bankers were redirecting their financial investments from the central Mughal administration to regional and local political powers.

From 1650 to 1750, several historical developments indicate why and how bankers were shifting their support and investment from the Mughals to other political rulers. First, the Mughals failed to protect bankers adequately in the second half of the seventeenth century. Shivaji's famous raids on Surat from 1664 on were far more significant for their impact upon the commercial interests there than upon the loyalties of the nobility.[41] This was the wealthiest port of Mughal India, and it has been shown that the sea trade here and in other Gujarati

[38]See L. Sundaram, 'Revenue Administration of the Northern Circars', *Journal of the Andhra Historical Research Society*, XIV (1943–4), pp. 22–58, and XV (1944–5), pp. 1–118, for details. The reference to Hyderabad firms: XV, p. 12.

[39]Krishnan, *Indigenous Banking*, pp. 19–20, notes that this was still done in the twentieth century; despite the failure to date its origin, it indicates the complex possibilities the revenue system offered for intermediary profits.

[40]Even for this commission method, an initial large *nazr* or payment seems to have been necessary.

[41]Pearson argues that the impact upon the nobility was crucial, 'Shivaji and the Decline'.

ports, and the customs revenue going to the Mughals, was far more considerable than has been generally recognized.[42] Leading officials and relatives of the Mughal emperor were involved in trading ventures.[43] Heads of the Gujarati great firms had access to the emperor in the seventeenth century, and successive emperors responded favourably to requests made by the Surat business community.[44] Yet Aurangzeb proved unable to protect Surat and other ports from raiders, and merchants and bankers left Surat for other cities.[45] Many eventually settled at Poona, capital of the Peshwas.[46]

Policies and actions of the later emperors Aurangzeb and Farukhsiyar indicate tensions between bankers and the Mughal state. By 1702, when Aurangzeb attempted to secure interest-free loans to pay troop arrears in the Deccan, he was turned down by banking firms.[47] Aurangzeb's expectation of financial support must have been perceived as contrary to the bankers' interests at this time, towards the end of the Deccan campaigns. Another indication of conflicting political and economic interests for the state and the banking firms was the emperor Farukhsiyar's need for money in 1712 and his plan to levy contributions on the rich merchants of Patna, including the Dutch and English merchants. His plan was thwarted by the governor of Bihar, who had his own dealings with the Europeans.[48] It has been suggested that Mughal officials at all levels were increasing their own commercial activities and actively competing with indigenous bankers and merchants at this

[42]Pearson, 'Shivaji and the Decline', pp. 227–8, and his 'Political Participation', pp. 118–19.

[43]Ibid., particularly the latter article, pp. 124, 129–30. See also Satish Chandra, 'Commercial Activities of the Mughal Emperors during the Seventeenth Century', *Bengal Past and Present*, 78:146 (July–Dec. 1959), 92–7, where he argues that the *jagir* crisis may have induced nobles to turn to commerce, and his 'Some Aspects of the Growth of a Money Economy in India during the Seventeenth Century', *IESHR*, III:4 (Dec. 1966), pp. 321–6.

[44]Pearson, 'Political Participation', pp. 122–7; Gillion, *Ahmedabad*, pp. 17–18, 21.

[45]Pearson, both articles cited above, and particularly 'Political Participation', p. 128, for emigration.

[46]Gadgil, 'Immigrant Traders in Poona', p. 16.

[47]Habib, 'Usury', pp. 408–9.

[48]Satish Chandra, 'Early Relations of Farrukh Siyar and the Saiyid Brothers', *Medieval India Quarterly*, 2:1&2 (1957) p. 142, for Husain Ali Khan's action (the governor of Bihar).

time,[49] though without a comparison with the past commercial networks and activities the evidence shows only commercial involvement.

Two other developments from 1650 to 1750 show the changing economic and political orientation of the great banking firms: the migration of bankers from Mughal urban centres to those of other powers, and the banker's extension of trade and credit transactions to newcomers, the Dutch and the English, in contrast to their earlier policies. Where the new commercial relationships have been noted, there has usually been no attempt to reconstruct the commercial networks of the banking firms prior to their connection with the European traders.[50]

Historical research on migration elsewhere has used empirical data to measure the opportunities available according to distance from the source of migration. Lack of systematic data on the movements of great firms in Mughal India prevents such an analysis here, but the information available supports the hypothesis that after 1650 banking firms moved to regional kingdoms and the commercial centres being established by European trading companies.[51] The emigrations from Surat have been mentioned; some of those bankers settled in Poona, where

[49]Satish Chandra, in his articles cited in footnote 43, suggests that Mughal commercial activities were increasing in the seventeenth century and persisted right through the eighteenth century; I suspect that their activities were characteristic earlier as well, and that his evidence supports the line of argument here for interdependence.

[50]For example S. Arasaratnam, 'Aspects of the Role and Activities of South Indian Merchants c. 1650–1750', *Proceedings of the First International Conference Seminar of Tamil Studies* (University of Malaya, 1968), vol. I, pp. 582–96. He prefaces his material on merchants dealing with Europeans after 1650 with these sentences (p. 582): 'After the decline of the great medieval collective enterprises, the mercantile tradition seems to have lived on among certain families with commercial roots in the past. When the European traders . . . came to southern India they . . . soon established firm relations with them.' See also, Susil Chaudhuri, *Trade and Commercial Organization in Bengal, 1650–1720: With Special Reference to the English East India Company* (Calcutta, 1975).

[51]B.G. Gokhale starts his 'Ahmadabad in the XVIIth Century' with the statement, 'The history of India in the seventeenth century is characterized by the emergence of various regions as distinct economic units', *Journal of Economic and Social History of the Orient*, XII: 2 (April 1969), p. 187; see also B. Ramachandra Rau, 'Some Specific Services of the Indigenous Bankers of Bombay', *Indian Historical Records Commission*, vol. 12 (1929), pp 54–9.

they gained mint privileges and became bankers to the Peshwa.[52] A Surat Brahmin firm moved to Calcutta through transactions with the East India Company in the eighteenth century, later on opening a Bombay branch.[53] The Jagat Seth firm's move to Dacca and Murshidabad was due to its tie to Murshid Quli Khan, governor of Bengal, in the early eighteenth century.[54] Firms based in the Nizam's capital city of Hyderabad moved into the northern circars, where they encountered the East India Company agents operating out of Madras. One Marwari firm gave up banking for Indian princes and moved to Calcutta, dealing in opium with the East India Company.[55]

These migrations have generally been attributed to negative factors, such as the Mughal inability to protect commerce or the raids of Marathas, Jats, and Afghans. No doubt the political instability and wars of the eighteenth century were destructive of some trade and commercial activities, but wars also offered positive inducements to many financiers and contractors.[56] The eighteenth century might be better viewed as a period of expansion and diversification for many banking firms and merchants.

The historical evidence for the process of realignment of leading banking firms with the East India Company during this century before 1750 is plentiful and unambiguous. Detailed evidence from Surat and from the Jagat Seth firm in Bengal documents an early and strong transition to doing business with the Company. While early seventeenth-century Dutch records from Surat show that the Mughals failed to protect Indian

[52]See footnote 46; also P.K. Gode, 'Keshavbhat Karve, a Poona Banker of the Peshwa Period and His Relations with the Peshwa and Damaji Gaikwad', *Journal of the University of Bombay*, vol. 6 (July 1937), pp. 87–91.

[53]B.A. Saletore, 'A Forgotten Gujarati Brahman Banker', *Indian Historical Records Commission*, XXX (1954), pp. 155–60.

[54]See Philip Calkins' article (cited in footnote 2) and his unpublished paper, 'The Role of Murshidabad as a Regional and Sub-regional Centre in Bengal', which suggests that the city's importance derived more from its commercial orientation towards European factories even in the seventeenth century than from its administrative orientation to the Mughals, pp. 8–14.

[55]For the Hyderabad firms, Sundaram, 'Revenue Administration', p. 12; for the Marwari firm, Timberg, 'A "Great" Marwari Firm', pp. 264–5, 283.

[56]This has been stated by Jain, *Indigenous Banking*, p. 17, and Gadgil, *Origins*, p. 32, where he notes that de Bussy in the Deccan and Karnatak obtained a loan from 'a great banker'. Instances of Kanara Saraswat merchants who allied themselves with the British are given in V.N. Kudra, *History of the Dakshinatya Saraswats* (Madras, 1972), pp. 117–18.

traders from Dutch and English competition from the sea trade then,[57] other records show at least eight leading Gujarati firms providing extensive credit to the English at Surat from 1634 to 1677.[58] Pearson shows that Gujarati merchants at Surat strongly opposed English traders in the 1620s, but by the 1660s they considered European traders to be among their best customers.[59] One Gujarati firm originally from Surat moved to Murshidabad, then to Calcutta and Benares, proudly claiming to be 'bankers to the Company' by the late eighteenth century. This firm showed a marked preference for the English throughout the second half of the eighteenth century. Its historian asks why that should have been the case and what the wealth of that firm and others like it actually was, when that firm alone lent one lakh of rupees a month to the English Company.[60]

The history of the Jagat Seth firm, already discussed in its Mughal context, is perhaps more fascinating in relation to the East India Company. Most accounts first link the firm to the English in mid-eighteenth-century Bengal, but in fact it had loaned funds to the English factory in Patna as early as 1652. An even stronger tie to the Company existed through the 'real' family of Jagat Seth—for Jagat Seth was the son of Manek Chand's sister, adopted by Manek Chand to continue his firm. Jagat Seth's natal family operated a great banking firm in Patna and Agra in the seventeenth century, the very firm which in 1714 extended credit to the English trade embassy from Calcutta when other leading Delhi bankers refused it credit. Mitra Sen of this firm, real brother to Jagat Seth, represented the East India Company in Delhi from 1712 to 1739, allegedly supervising its interests in all three presidencies.[61] The firm's prominent political role in the 1750s, when it helped the East India Company overthrow Nawab Sirajuddaula, is well known and

[57]Karl Fischer, 'The Beginning of Dutch Trade with Gujarat', unpublished paper, pp. 16–18.

[58]Saletore, 'A Forgotten Gujarati Brahman Banker', p. 155, citing early East India Company records which he lists in his footnote; see also Habib's charts in 'Usury', pp. 402–3. and H.Q. Naqvi, *Urban Centres and Industries*, pp. 63–4.

[59]Pearson, 'Political Participation', pp. 125–7. This is also clear in Ashin Das Gupta, 'The Merchants of Surat, *c.* 1700–50', in Edmund Leach and S.N. Mukherjee (eds), *Elites in South Asia* (Cambridge, 1970), pp. 201–22.

[60]Saletore, 'Forgotten Gujarati Brahman Banker', pp. 158–60.

[61]Little, 'The House of Jagatseth', vol. XX, pp. 115–16, for the 1652 loan, and pp. 126–9, 136–45 for the Mitra Sen firm.

caused Gadgil to term it 'exceptional'.[62] The argument here is that it was closer to the rule, as further research on banking firms' connections with political rulers will demonstrate.

'Great Firms' and the East India Company: After 1750

After 1750, the East India Company brought about major changes which were detrimental to the economic and political interests of the indigenous banking firms. The Company had relied upon Indian bankers as sources of credit, and often as agents for the collection of revenue, as it gained territory. Now the company displaced them, not only as the Company bankers but as bankers to Indian rulers as well. The Company also displaced bankers as the key intermediaries in the land revenue collection.

Thus, Clive's agreement with the Nawab of Bengal in 1765 specified that all revenues would go to the Company through a newly created board of ministers. This board consisted of the Nawab, the Diwan, and a Seth, the latter from the Jagat Seth firm. The Seth was still termed Company banker, but Clive insisted that all three men keep keys to the treasury, and that the Company be paid before repayment to back debts to the Seths. In 1770, Clive stopped the allowance which the Seths received as ministers of the Nawab. In 1772, the Company treasury was transferred from Murshidabad to Calcutta and the Seths ceased to be Company bankers. A later representative of the firm petitioned Hastings for reinstatement in the hereditary office of 'receiver and treasurer of government revenue', but he got robes of honour instead.[63] In the 1770s, an inquiry began into the whole system of revenue collection in Bengal, with the aim of 'placing the Company as nearly as can be in the stead of the Shroffs'. It was stated that revenue was being lost to the bankers, upon whom the Company was in any case too dependent.[64]

Similarly, the Company in Madras began to investigate *zamindar* indebtedness and the bankers' role in revenue collection in the 1770s.

[62]Gadgil, *Origins*, p. 32, Little's article, continued in vol. XXII, and Gupta, *Sirajuddaulah and the East India Company*, p. 132, all document the Hindu bankers' new alliance with the East India Company in Bengal by 1760. K.M. Panikkar, in *Asia and Western Dominance* (New York, 1953), carelessly generalizes that the powerful Indian merchant class worked with European traders because of its 'inherited hatred of Muslim rule', p. 99.

[63]Little, 'The House of Jagatseth', vol. XXII, pp. 97–103.

[64]Jain, *Indigenous Banking*, pp. 19–20, citing the Governor General's letter to the Collector of Rangpur, in vol. I.p. 33 of the Bengal District Records.

At first, the recommendation was to continue the 'agency of soucars' as 'innovations might be dangerous'.[65] In the 1780s, however, the Company tried to change the system, arguing that it 'gives the soucar very unreasonable advantage. ... '[66] But the reforms attempted encountered difficulties. The provision of security by *zamindars* themselves proved unworkable, and when the Company's inquiries appeared threatening, the principal bankers got together and refused to furnish security.[67] Noting that the prevalent system helped conceal information from the Company and kept the *zamindars* indebted to the bankers (who were always paid before the Company's current demand was met), a circuit committee in 1785 proposed drastic remedies. Reforms of the 'vicious system' succeeded in 'suppressing the private interests' and replaced 'commercial ideas by administrative ideas' in the collection of revenue in the circars.[68] At this time, of course, the Company itself was still a private and commercial concern.

Not only were indigenous banking firms displaced in Company territories, the Company acted against them in princely states. It did not enforce payment of debts to bankers when Company agents took over from or dealt with ruling princes. This happened in Benares in 1773, in Oudh in 1798, and in the case of the Nawab of Arcot in 1805.[69] The East India Company's view of bankers was much in evidence in the notorious case of Palmer and Company in Hyderabad State in the 1820s. Here, too, the ruler's debts to the banking firm were overlooked by the Company, and the Resident strongly disapproved of the political power exercised by the Palmers in Hyderabad. He said: '... it tends to draw them quite out of their sphere of merchants. ... I lament the power which they exercise ... in an authoritative manner not becoming their mercantile character . ...'[70]

By the nineteenth century, if one compares the functions of indigenous banking firms before and after the advent of foreign traders, a reversal, has occurred. Before, bankers had been state treasurers and were often directly involved in the collection of revenue. The financing of external trade before the seventeenth century had been chiefly in the hands of Indian trading firms; then it was taken over by European

[65]Sundaram, 'Revenue Administration', vol. XV, pp. 10–14.

[66]Ibid., p. 33, citing Macartney.

[67]Ibid., pp. 15, 34.

[68]Ibid., pp. 77–8.

[69]Jain, *Indigenous Banking*, pp. 20–2.

[70]This was Charles Metcalfe, in a letter to the Governor General, September, 1821: E.J. Thompson, *Life of Lord Metcalfe* (London, 1937), pp. 210–11.

firms; and, in the nineteenth century, by European banking institutions. With the 1835 imposition of uniform currency throughout British India, bankers lost much of their money-changing business as well as their mint privileges. In the nineteenth century, bankers and moneylenders were most noted for the financing of internal trade and the extension of agricultural credit; the British created government treasuries and a system of European banking institutions in India.[71] But we have come very far from Mughal India, and part of the reason for doing so is to demonstrate how historians have lost sight of the great Indian banking firms of those days.

Advantages of the 'Great Firm' Theory

The theory proposes that it was the redirection of economic and political support by the great banking firms of Mughal India from 1650 to 1750 which proved the decisive factor in the decline of the empire. The banking firms had been crucial to the functioning of the central government and to the functioning of many of its employees' households. It is not being argued that the great firms were directly incorporated into the governmental structure, or that a centrally directed economic policy was being implemented through them, for the Mughal state did not exercise tight control over these firms and their activities. Not only the state 'treasury', however, but individual *mansabdars*, *jagirdars*, *zamindars*, and *talukdars* were more than likely to be directly dependent upon these banking firms.

The situation of the bankers in Mughal India contrasts strongly with that of bankers in imperial China, and the contrast is an instructive one.[72]

[71] Jain, *Indigenous Banking*, pp. 23–5, makes this comparison. The best coverage of this transition period from the point of view of the Company is by B. Ramachandra Rau, 'Organized Banking in the Days of John Company', *Bengal Past and Present*, vol. 37 (Jan.–June 1929), pp. 145–57, and vol. 38 (July–Dec. 1929), pp. 60–80.

[72] Both Panikkar (*Asia and Western Dominance*, p. 99) and Gupta (*Sirajuddaulah and the East India Company*, p. 32) compare the Indian mercantile class to 'Shangahi compradors', but they do not investigate this comparison further. For China, see the following: E. Balazs, 'The Birth of Capitalism in China', in Eisenstadt (ed.), *Decline of Empires*, p. 109; Lien-sheng Yang, *Money and Credit in China, A Short History* (Cambridge, 1952); 'Economic Aspects of Public Works in Imperial China', in *Excursions in Sinology* (Cambridge, 1969); and 'Government Control of Urban Merchants in Traditional China', *Tsing Hua Journal of Chinese Studies*, new series (2nd) 8 (August 1970), pp. 186–206. See also Mark Elvin, *The Pattern of the Chinese Past* (London, 1973), particularly pp. 155, 161–2, 215–25, 285–97.

Most historians agree that the Chinese bureaucracy tightly regulated the merchant classes. For example when Chinese bankers invented 'flying money' (the equivalent of *hundis* in India). The government took over the system as a bureaucratic monopoly. The Chinese imperial bureaucracy was also able to establish control over promissory notes or paper currency, developed somewhat later. But in Mughal India, while there were attempts to regulate some aspects of banking activities, the regulation of *hundis* was never proposed, and other attempted regulations appear to have failed more often than not. The position of the bankers in India was that of an allied support group, one which provided essential resources to the state and had a good bargaining position with respect to it. Contrast their position with that of the *co-hong* merchants at the Chinese treaty ports, closely regulated and acting for their government as they carried out commercial transactions with foreigners.

Banking firms in Mughal India had greater power and autonomy than their Chinese counterparts. The tensions between short-term and long-term aims of the Mughal state and its creditors needed careful and constant attention. This was particularly true when military expansion or defence efforts impelled the state to call for more resources, or when banking firms were presented with alternative patrons or clients. From all indications, the later Mughal emperors did not give sufficient consideration to their relationships with the great banking firms, and many firms relocated and redirected their transaction after 1650.

While further research is admittedly necessary to test and fully substantiate this theory, it offers certain immediate advantages over other theories of Mughal decline and brings together the economic factors associated with the decline in a way that emphasizes their interrelationships. It also reorders the causative factors in significance, pointing to the economic decisions made by the great banking firms as the most important cause of irreversible decline, because so many of the other groups and institutions were dependent upon the banking firms. Virtually all government units of income and expenditure required the extension of credit or cash to continue operations. The refusal or diversion of resources by bankers contributed to the dissension among *mansabdars* and *jagirdars*, the impact of a real or artificially produced jagir shortage, the flagging zeal of the military, and so on.

Another advantage of the theory is its potential for measurement and testing. The systematic reconstruction of seventeenth- and eighteenth-century networks of great firms and their connections with Mughal institutions and functionaries, with each other, and with lower level firms and moneylenders should be possible. These were urban-based, well-organized and conspicuous institutions, limited in numbers at the level of operation in which we are interested. Changing patterns of trade and investment, relocation of firms and their branches, should provide yet other measures of loyalty, as well as the movements of individual nobles and themes in poetry and prose.[73] And there should be fewer units to analyse than in the cases of the *mansabdars, zamindars* and other categories of individuals.

A great advantage of this theory is that it relates the rise of the East India Company to the decline of the Mughal empire in a concrete and cumulative manner emphasizing processes rather than events or individuals. It lends continuity to revenue history, linking territorial conquest with the collection of land revenue through the agency of indigenous banking firms. It emphasizes the development by the Company of partnerships with the great firms, followed by Company displacement of them. The local and regional participants in that process of economic partnership and displacement can be discovered and compared throughout India.

Like any good theory, this one seems fairly obvious, and the puzzle is that it has gone unperceived and unresearched. There may have been a problem of sources,[74] but historians are now utilizing new sources and methods. Determined collection of data can result in the reconstruction of a grid of great firms and their relationships with the political powers of the time. New analytical perspectives will also be useful. Many who have theorized about merchants and bankers in Mughal India have done so from a Marxist perspective, forcing the data into a fairly rigid framework. Other researchers have seldom ventured beyond description, collecting detailed data on specific individuals, firms, or

[73]For example F. Lehmann, 'Shah Ayat Allah "Jauhri" and his Shahr Ashob', *Abdul Karim Sahitya-Visarad Commemoration Volume* (Dacca, 1972), and other writing on the eighteenth-century cultural laments.

[74]Timberg discusses the problem of sources in 'A "Great" Marwari Firm'. In an unpublished paper, 'Speculative Gains and Primitive Accumulation', which deals only with the nineteenth and twentieth centuries, Timberg's problem is the theoretical one of entrepreneurial values; he had no problems with sources. Morris D. Morris, in a recent unpublished paper, 'South Asian Entrepreneurship and the Rashomon Effect', also deals with the nineteenth and twentieth centuries and emphasizes the significance of indigenous banking and entrepreneurial activities and how little we still know about them (paper presented at a Conference on Colonial Port Cities in Berkeley in June 1976).

caste groups, following the traditional emphasis upon the diverse and specialized nature of financial communities in India. But now an attempt must be made to describe and analyse this heterogeneous category according to the organization and volume of their economic activities, focusing on the great indigenous banking firms of Mughal and early British India and their decisive participation in politics.

PART 4

Regions and Realms of Resistance

15

Conformity and Conflict: Tribes and the 'Agrarian System' of Mughal India*

Chetan Singh

I

Over the past twenty-five years or so, substantial contributions have been made by numerous scholars to our understanding of medieval Indian history. In keeping with the significance that has often been attached to socio-economic factors in historical processes, a considerable part of this relatively recent work has been directed towards examining the economic base of the medieval Indian state and society. It is, in turn, the predominantly agrarian aspect of the medieval Indian economy that has been subjected by scholars to the closest scrutiny.[1] What has emerged on account of this effort is an appreciably improved perception among historians about the rural society of that time.[2] More specifically,

*First published in the *Indian Economic and Social History Review*, vol. XXIII, no. 3, 1988.

[1]It is the earlier work of W.H. Moreland, *Agrarian System of Moslem India* (first published 1929), that seems to have acted as an example and many scholars have subsequently built upon it. For instance, Irfan Habib, *Agrarian System of Mughal India, 1556–1707* (Bombay, 1963); N.A. Siddiqi, *Land Revenue Administration under the Mughals, 1700–1750* (Bombay, 1970); Satish Chandra, *Medieval India; Society, the Jagirdari Crisis and the Village* (Delhi, 1982); S. Nurul Hasan, *Some Thoughts on Agrarian Relations* (Delhi, reprint, 1983); Harbans Mukhia, 'Was There Feudalism in Indian History?', *Proceedings of the Indian History Congress* (Waltair, 1979; separately printed text used).

[2]In this respect it is Irfan Habib's *Agrarian System* which seems to mark a sort of turning point. See Harbans Mukhia, 'Peasant Production and Medieval Indian Society', in Harbans Mukhia and T.J. Byres, eds, *Feudalism and Non-European Societies* (London, 1985), p. 239.

it is the image of agrarian society during the Mughal period that has apparently become sharper than ever before and which is also reflected in many related works on Indian history.[3]

To repeat what now appears a truism, the magnificent structure of the Mughal state and the continued dominance of its ruling élite rested upon the state's ability to appropriate a major part of the surplus generated by this agrarian society. The production of agricultural surplus, its systematic appropriation by the dominant *zamindars* and the Mughal state apparatus and subsequently its distribution amongst sections of the governing class (*jagirdars, madad-i-ma'ash* holders, and so on) together constituted much of what is now, quite acceptably, called the Mughal 'agrarian system'. Contributing to the emergence of this system and important to its functioning was the structure of the village community, its internal dynamics and response to forces and factors around it. One of the earlier expositions of the classical village community as a whole under Mughal rule has, probably, been made by Irfan Habib,[4] and some other researches have engaged in examining its details and variations.[5] Two features seem to have been almost

[3]M. Athar Ali, *The Mughal Nobility Under Aurangzeb* (Bombay, reprint, 1970); see also Ratnalekha Ray, *Change in Bengal Agrarian Society, c. 1760–1850* (Delhi, 1979), pp. 13–24. This image of the Mughal system is used as a beginning and a kind of reference point for explaining the manner in which agrarian society in Bengal differed. Another monograph that is influenced by this widely accepted picture of the 'agrarian system' of Mughal India is Indu Banga, *Agrarian System of the Sikhs* (Delhi, 1978); Tapan Raychaudhuri and Irfan Habib, eds, *Cambridge Economic History of India* (Delhi, 1984), vol. 1, pp. 48–75, 214–25, 235–48, has provided to this picture a more general acceptability.

[4]Irfan Habib, *Agrarian System*, pp. 111–35, Irfan Habib, 'Potentialities of Capitalistic Development in the Economy of Mughal India', *Enquiry*, vol. 3, no. 3 (1971), pp. 6–22.

[5]These researches are too numerous to all be mentioned here, but some of them are: B.R. Grover, 'Nature of Land-rights in Mughal India', *Indian Economic and Social History Review (IESHR)*, vol. 1, no. 1 (1963); B.R. Grover, 'Nature of Dehat-i-Ta'aluqa: Evolution of the Ta'alluqadari System During the Mughal Age', *IESHR*, vol. 2, no. 3 (1965); S. Nurul Hasan, 'The Position of the Zamindars in Mughal India', *IESHR*, vol. 1, no. 4 (1964); Satish Chandra, 'Some Aspects of the Village Society in Northern India During the 18th Century (Position of the Khud Kashta and Pahi Kashta)', *Indian Historical Review* (*IHR*), vol. 1, no. 1 (1974); Satish Chandra, 'Role of the Local Community, the Zamindars and the State in Providing Capital Inputs for the Growth and Expansion of Cultivation', in Satish Chandra, *Medieval India*, pp. 166–83.

essential to the village community; namely its considerably stratified nature and the pivotal role of the peasant in agricultural production.[6] The picture of the village community consisting of dominant *zamindars*, cultivating peasants, artisans and landless labourers, and so on, is only too familiar now to require repetition. Equally well acquainted are historians with the medieval Indian peasant, with his 'title to permanent and hereditary occupancy of the land he tilled', and the inviolability and saleability of these rights.[7] The strength of the peasant's rights was, however, matched by his inescapable obligation to cultivate the land over which he laid claim.[8] This in a nutshell is the framework within which the rural society of Mughal India is understood by scholars today.

Such a framework has, undoubtedly, gone a long way in eliminating, misconceived notions about the egalitarian structure of society. Yet it leaves out certain significant aspects of rural life in medieval India. One such aspect was the continued participation of tribal populations in the socio-economic processes that had been fundamental to the stabilization of agrarian society.[9] These tribal people were unlikely to have become completely irrelevant with the crystallization of the medieval village community and nor were their economic activities absolutely unrelated

[6]See Harbans Mukhia, 'Peasant Production and Medieval Indian Society', p. 239. Mukhia sees the emphasis on these two features as Habib's principal contribution towards altering the perception of medieval Indian rural society as 'an egalitarian structure by virtue of the absence of property in land'.

[7]Irfan Habib, *Agrarian System*, pp. 114–15. These rights would differ somewhat in *zamindari* areas, though they would be enjoyed to their fullest in the *raiyati* villages.

[8]Ibid., p. 115.

[9]Monographs on ancient Indian history repeatedly refer to the significant role of the tribes in this respect. See, for example D.D. Kosambi, *An Introduction to the Study of Indian History* (Bombay, 1975), pp. 115, 149, 241; R.S. Sharma, *Social Change in Early Medieval India, c. 500–1200* (Delhi, 1969); R.S. Sharma, *Sudras in Ancient India* (Delhi, 1980); R.S. Sharma, *Indian Feudalism* (Calcutta, 1965); A.N. Bose, *Social and Rural Economy of Northern India* (Calcutta, 1967, 2 vols). Irfan Habib, too, admits the importance of tribes in the formation of the 'menial proletariat' in rural society and suggests that the first millennium 'saw the completion of the great division between the peasantry and landless labour'. See Irfan Habib, 'Social Distribution of Landed Property in Pre-British India', in R.S. Sharma and Vivekanand Jha, eds, *Indian Society: Historical Probings* (Delhi, 1977), pp. 276–7; see also Irfan Habib, 'The Peasant in Indian History', *Proceedings of the Indian History Congress* (Kurukshetra, 1982, separately printed text used), pp. 21, 31. However, the significance of this process as a continuing phenomenon in medieval India is not very seriously considered.

to the interests of the Mughal 'agrarian system'. Tribal people do, nonetheless, appear incongruous with the image of rural society in medieval India that has so far been projected. This incongruity, however, was probably only an apparent one, and the Indian countryside under Mughal rule had not yet been disinfected from such socio-economic 'impurities' as tribal societies. On the contrary, the village communities of Mughal India probably lived in reasonable proximity to such societies.

There arises, at this point, a significant question. How much territory did the Mughal 'agrarian system' represent even within the Mughal empire? A very recent work of a statistical nature concludes that the gross cultivated area during the reign of Akbar was unlikely to have been more than 55 per cent of the gross cultivation in 1909–10.[10] This, in geographical terms, would represent an even smaller proportion when placed against the territorial extent of the Mughal empire. Large portions of the empire, though uncultivated, were however unlikely to have been totally devoid of human population. Many such areas were, in all probability, inhabited by societies for whom settled agriculture had not yet become a primary means of livelihood. Moreover, it is quite possible that even within the cultivated area there existed not only variations of the 'agrarian system',[11] but also socio-economic systems that were remarkably different from it.[12] Such seems to have been the

[10]Shireen Moosvi, *The Economy of the Mughal Empire, c. 1595: A Statistical Study* (Delhi, 1987), p. 65. In Punjab (which was one of the *zabti* [measured] areas of the empire) the gross cultivation in 1595 as compared with 1910 was 39.19 per cent.

[11]Harbans Mukhia, 'Peasant Production and Medieval Indian Society,' p. 245: 'even a grand state of imperial dimensions was able to establish its overarching system in the region only with considerable degree of variation'.

[12]The purpose here is to suggest that there existed other systems within the empire, which were capable of influencing considerably the Mughal 'agrarian system'. The latter's primacy, however, was obvious. It, probably, represents that 'one specific kind of production which predominates over the rest whose relations thus assign rank and influence to the others'. Karl Marx, *Grundrisse* (Martin Nicolaus tr., Harmondsworth, reprint, 1977), pp. 106–7. See also Chetan Singh, 'Interaction Between Divergent Social Formations: A Possible Explanation for Some Instances of Unrest in 17th Century Panjab', *Panjab History Conference* (Patiala, 1980), pp. 128–38; C.A. Bayly, *Rulers, Townsmen and Bazaars: North Indian Society in the Age of British Expansion 1770–1870* (Cambridge, 1983), p. 30.

case with the tribal Ghakkars and Janjuhas of the Salt Range in *suba* Lahore. In fact, the Mughal control over their territory was probably of a nominal nature, and the *arazi* figures provided for it in the *Ain-i-Akbari* were not calculated on the basis of any survey.[13] The need to provide these figures, in the first place, possibly arose from Abul Fazl's attempt to make social diversities appear in conformity with the 'system' that had evolved, particularly in areas that were largely under the close administrative control of the Mughals. Even tribal territories, which may have been only marginally agricultural were, therefore, represented as areas which were properly measured, regularly assessed and in no way different from those regions of the empire that were indeed agriculturally developed. This, in fact, is an impression that even modern historians have perpetuated.

A definite and comprehensive explanation of what constitutes a tribe, however, is not something upon which any substantial number of scholars can be easily united. Small points of disagreement, at the onset, tend to grow into major areas of confrontation as scholars proceed to elaborate their respective perceptions of what essentially characterizes tribal formations.[14] Even without entering into detailed definitional

---

It is rather difficult to arrive at any definite conclusion regarding the size of the population that might be classified as tribal. For more recent times, Denzil Ibbetson's, *Panjab Castes* (Patiala, reprint, 1970), based upon the *Census Report* of 1881, provides some information. By way of interest, it may be mentioned that in the British province of Punjab, 'Biloches, Pathans and allied races' constituted 56 per thousand of the total population, while 'minor dominant tribes' such as the Ghakkars, Awans, Khokhars, Kharrals, Dogars, Gujjars, and so on, numbered 67 per thousand of the total population. Even more difficult is the task of distinguishing, on the basis of available data, the tribal pastoral sections of the Jats from those that had for long been settled agriculturists. Certain Awan, Khokhar and Kharral groups returned themselves as Jats during the census. Moreover, tribes such as the Wattus, Bhattis and Janjuhas have been shown either as Jats or as Rajputs. The tribal and non-tribal elements of Punjab society, therefore, appear to have been inextricably intermeshed. To put it briefly, the tribal societies of medieval Punjab were, probably, quite considerable both in terms of population and socio-economic importance. See Denzil Ibbetson, *op.cit.*, pp. 38–9, 133–4, 140–1,144, 145–6, 151, 153–4, 166–7, 169, 172, 174.

[13]See Shireen Moosvi, *op. cit*, pp. 62, 64, 70.

[14]An interesting discussion in this context is Maurice Godelier, *Perspectives in Marxist Anthropology* (Cambridge, 1977), pp. 70–98.

complexities, however, it does appear from an examination of some of the medieval Indian sources that there existed during that period certain social formations, which although in many cases sedentarized, also relied considerably upon pastoralism.[15] This reliance upon pastoralism seems to have been integrated with a sense of social or communal cohesion that was characteristically distinct from the socio-economic hierarchy that normally marked the primarily agricultural village communities of Mughal India so graphically depicted by modern researchers.

Scholars of medieval Indian history have, however, generally been inclined either to ignore or to minimize the contribution of tribal societies to socio-economic processes.[16] Perhaps, the task of harmonizing the existence of tribal societies with a view of medieval India that is dominated by the stratified village community and the state proves to be an inconvenient one. To add to this difficulty is the problem of establishing a working relationship between the concepts of tribe, caste

[15]Quite interestingly, the Germanic tribes encountered by the Roman legions in the time of Caesar were of a similar nature. See Perry Anderson, *Passages from Antiquity to Feudalism* (Verso Edition, 1978), p. 107, who writes that these Germanic tribes 'were settled agriculturists, with a predominantly pastoral economy'.

[16]Among the exceptions are Amalendu Guha, 'Tribalism to Feudalism in Assam: 1600–1750', *IHR*, vol. 1, no. 1, pp. 65–76; K. Suresh Singh, 'A Study in State Formation Among Tribal Communities', in *Indian Society: Historical Probings*, pp. 317–36. Another exception is that of A.R. Khan, *Chieftains in the Mughal Empire During the Reign of Akbar* (Simla, 1977). In this case, the emphasis is more on the political aspects of tribal formations in their interaction with the Mughal state. See also A.R. Khan, 'Presidential Address' (medieval section), *Panjab History Conference* (1981), pp. 47–60; C.A. Bayly, however, comes closest to showing the true significance of tribal pastoralism to the larger socio-economic context, even though all too briefly (*Rulers, Townsmen and Bazaars*, pp. 20–1, 29, 91, 204, 363–4). Worth mentioning here is the view of D.D. Kosambi that 'The entire course of Indian history shows tribal elements being fused into a general society. This phenomenon, which lies at the very foundation of the most striking Indian social feature, caste, is also the great basic fact of ancient Indian history', D.D. Kosambi, *An Introduction to the Study of Indian History*, p. 27.

and peasant.[17] Modern scholars of medieval Indian history, however, have chosen to underplay the distinctiveness of tribes and attempted to accommodate them in social categories which are more easily explainable in the context of the commonly accepted notion of Mughal agrarian society. Terms such as '*zamindars*', 'chiefs', 'peasants', and 'caste' have been used for describing different tribal people, thereby giving the impression that the society being referred to was of the differentiated village community—'free peasantry' kind that constituted the classic Mughal 'agrarian system'.[18] Tribal societies, however, cannot be so easily wished away, and needless to say, such an approach

[17]It is hardly possible to examine here this intricate and awkward question. For a sociological analysis of all three concepts, see André Béteille, *Six Essays in Comparative Sociology* (Delhi, 1979), pp. 40–74. Regarding the comparison of tribe and caste, he emphasizes the 'relative isolation of tribes as compared with castes', and argues that 'a tribe is a world within itself having few external social ties, whereas a caste is by its nature a part of a larger whole'. Both are, however, to be viewed as a continuum. His definition of peasantry is a 'more or less homogeneous and undifferentiated community of families characterised by small holdings operated mainly by family labour'. These definitions, however, do not in any way simplify our task. See also E.R. Leach, 'What Should we Mean by Caste?', in E.R. Leach, ed., *Aspects of Caste in South India, Ceylon and North-West Pakistan* (Cambridge, 1969).

[18]Though scholars are not averse to using the term 'tribe', they do not give to it any distinct socio-economic significance. Irfan Habib, for instance, uses the term 'peasants' to describe the Mangecha tribals of Bhakkar. The original word used by Muhammad Masum is *mardum,* which is of a more general nature. See Muhammad Masum Bhakkari, *Tarikh-i-Sind,* U.M. Daudpota, ed. (Poona, 1938), p. 245. See also Irfan Habib, *Agrarian System,* pp. 161, 323, 332, 345, 346. While at one end of the picture certain tribes (Jud, Janjuha and Ghakkar) are classified as '*zamindars*', at the other the Dogars, Wattus and Gujjars are clubbed under the terms 'peasant' and 'caste'. The original word used by Sujan Rai to refer to these tribes is '*qaum*'. See Sujan Rai Bhandari, *Khulasat-ut-Tawarikh,* M. Zafar Hasan, ed. (Delhi, 1988), p. 63. This approach seems to dissolve these tribal societies into the two categories in which the Mughal emperors found it most convenient, for their own purposes, to view most of their subjects, namely *zamindars* and peasants. See also S. Nurul Hasan, *Thoughts on Agrarian Relations in Mughal India* (Delhi, 1983); idem. 'Zamindars Under the Mughals', in Robert E. Frykenberg, *Land Control and Social Structure in Indian History* (Delhi, 1979), pp. 17–32; Shireen Moosvi, *op. cit.*, pp. 62, 69–70.

oversimplifies an otherwise complex situation.[19] It ignores the possibility that the very existence of tribal formations in certain parts of the Mughal empire would result in the social distribution of power and property in a manner that corresponded with the tribal structure, and that this in turn would affect the nature of the Mughal state in those areas where strong tribal societies were to be found. The cursory treatment that tribal societies have received at the hands of historians appears to have been moulded and further fostered by the equally casual manner in which tribal formations are mentioned by medieval Indian sources. Even in these passing references, the significance of the tribal societies is indirectly represented as lying more in their ability to carry out quick and effective military mobilization rather than in any substantial contribution that they may have made to their larger social and economic environment. These very casual and indirect references to tribal societies in medieval Indian sources make it somewhat difficult to provide contemporary evidence on every single point.

II

Despite the limitation of scarce contemporary information on tribal formations, an attempt is made here to understand the structural dynamics underlying the changes which seem to have occurred in the tribal societies during the medieval period. The region of Punjab has been specifically chosen for this study. This effort is prompted by the existence of a reasonable possibility that tribal interaction with the 'agrarian system' of Mughal Punjab was fundamentally more significant for long-term developments in the region than it would appear from the manner in which tribal societies have been pushed towards the fringes of historical consciousness by medieval chroniclers and modern scholars alike.

Considering the close association that tribal societies normally have with pastoralism, it is quite possible that direct or indirect references to the latter phenomenon in contemporary sources are likely (not inevitable) pointers to the existence of tribal formations in the

[19]In one instance, however, Irfan Habib does lay emphasis on the distinctiveness of a tribe. But even here the reference is to ancient India. While referring to social change on account of changes in agriculture, he writes: 'In the Buddha's time, we begin to hear of *jatis,* "excellent as well as low"; but the tribe and *jati* were still only loosely differentiated; the Buddha could be said to belong to the Sakya *jati where it surely enough means the tribe*' (emphasis added). See Irfan Habib, 'The Peasant in Indian History,' p. 13.

region.[20] The existence, in the first instance, of pastoral populations is somewhat implicitly borne out by medieval historical sources.[21] Pastoralism was, probably, the primary source of sustenance for many of the tribes in Punjab during the Mughal period. Different tribes, nevertheless, responded divergently to their surroundings, and while their link with pastoralism remained strong, there were other variables in their economy which existed in dissimilar proportions in different tribes. These variables depended considerably upon the region which the tribe inhabited. It was, in fact, quite possible that the name by which a social group (or tribe) was known did not necessarily reflect its socio-economic similarity with other groups using the same tribal name, but located in different parts of Punjab.

In this respect, a long-term examination of the history of these tribes reveals an almost imperceptible process towards the sedentarization of those which were nomadic and to a great stratification amongst those which had already sedentarized.

The case of the Jats presents an interesting example. Their tribal origin has now, by and large, come to be accepted.[22] On the other hand, however, the divergent manner in which the Jats developed in different areas of Punjab up to the Mughal period, makes it difficult for us to study them as a single and integrated group. To begin with, their pastoral nature finds mention in some of the early accounts pertaining to Sind.[23] Subsequently, certain sections of the Jats appear to have moved into

[20]Tribal societies can also, however, be agricultural. André Béteille (*op. cit.*, p. 42), in fact, argues that 'while the non-tribal village is often too highly stratified to merit the name of peasant community, many of the so-called tribal villages in India are in fact communities of peasants'. Pastoral people, nevertheless, are more likely to have a tribal social organization. See also Chetan Singh, 'The Nature of Peasantry in Mughal Panjab', *Social Science Research Journal* (Panjab University, Chandigarh), Special Number, *Peasantry in India*, vol. 7, nos 1–2 (1982), pp. 75–6.

[21]This has been discussed in greater detail in Chetan Singh, 'Socio-Economic Conditions in Panjab During the Seventeenth Century' (unpublished Ph.D. thesis, Jawaharlal Nehru University, Delhi, 1984), pp. 227–39.

[22]A very convincing argument in this context is provided by Irfan Habib, 'The Jatts of the Panjab and Sind', in Harbans Singh and N.G. Barrier, eds, *Essays in Honour of Dr Ganda Singh* (Patiala, 1976), pp. 92–103. The period discussed is, by and large, pre-Mughal.

[23]Ibid., p. 94. In the time of Hiuen Tsang, the Jats appear to be living in the region of Sind. The *Chachnama* describes the same people and mentions their name as 'Jatt'.

Punjab, and wherever the geoclimatic situation permitted they, probably, abandoned (in part or as a whole) their predominantly pastoral habits in favour of settled agriculture. This socio-economic transition could hardly have been sudden, and even in areas where the change did occur it seems doubtful that it could have been a complete negation by the tribe of its pastoral heritage. The stray references that we find to the Jats in works pertaining to the period preceding Abul Fazl's *Ain-i-Akbari*, do give some passing hints to their pastoral habits. It was Babur who observed that 'if one goes into Hindustan, the Jats and Gujars always pour down in countless hordes from the hills and plains for loot in bullocks and buffaloes'.[24] These Jats and Gujjars, whom Babur referred to, resided in the mountains between Nil-ab and Bhira, and it appears that despite becoming settled agriculturists, they were inclined to retain animal husbandry as an important, though not fundamental, part of their economic and social system.[25] The description that Badaoni gives of his journey during the reign of Akbar, in the region of Multan, also seems to suggest that the Jats of the area represented a kind of transitory stage between pastoralism and settled agriculture, if not complete pastoralism itself.[26]

[24]Zahiruddin Muhammad Babur, *Baburnama*, A.S. Beveridge tr. (Delhi, 1970), p. 454.

[25]Ibid., pp. 379, 387. The fact that they did have permanent residences is gleaned from Babur's comments that the Jats, Gujjars and others were 'seated in villages everywhere on every rising ground . . . among the mountains of Nil-ab and Bhira'. That they were also engaged in agriculture is made clear by Babur's statement that the 'Ghakkars governed the Jats and Gujjars in the same manner as the Juds and Janjuhas ruled over the population subordinate to them'. About the Juds and Janjuhas we learn that they took from the cultivators 'one *shahrukhi* for each yoke of oxen and seven for headship'. The mention of 'yoke of oxen' makes the link with agriculture quite obvious.

[26]To begin with he tells us that the 'desert around Dipalpur' was 'the dwelling place of beasts of prey, wild animals and birds'. He further says that on his way to Shergarh to visit Shaikh Daud, he was passing through an uncultivated area ('perilous desert') and was stopped 'by Jats and highwaymen'. Upon being told that the purpose of his journey was to meet the Shaikh, the Jats abandoned their hostility and entertained him with 'milk, curds and such like refreshments'. Shergarh is mentioned as being half way between Multan and Pattan. All these comments of Badaoni, when juxtapositioned and seen in the context of the geography of the region, are pointers to a society in which agriculture was not the primary productive activity. Abdul Qadir Badaoni, *Muntakhab-ut-Tawarikh*, 3 vols; vol. 1, George S.A. Ranking, tr.; vol. 2, W.H. Lowe, tr.; vol. 3, Wolseley Haig, tr. (Patna, 1973). See vol. 3, pp. 50, 52, 80.

In addition to their pastoralist inclinations, the tribal nature of the Jats in some regions can be also surmised from a few of our sources. Badaoni, while relating some historical episodes of the Delhi sultanate period, refers to 'Malik Ikhtiyaruddin Altuniyah of Tabarhinda' (Bhatinda), who was supporting Sultan Razia and who 'having gained over certain of the Amirs and a body of Jats and Khukhars and all the landholders brought an army towards Delhi'.[27] From this statement, the impression gained is that neither the Jats nor the Khokhars are included by Badaoni among the *zamindars* or landholding group. On the other hand, if this 'body' of Jats and Khokhars were merely the retainers of these *zamindars*, there would hardly be the need to mention them separately; for the very act of military mobilization by a *zamindar* explicitly drew upon their retainers from all sources. Even if we assume that these Jats and Khokhars were in a politically subordinate position to the *zamindars*, their separate mention by Badaoni seems to imply a distinct social organization.[28] Manucci's depiction of the Jats as a 'race . . . four hundred leagues from Lahore, where there is much jungle', further strengthens this possibility.[29] It appears very likely, therefore, that under the tribal name of 'Jat', there were to be found in Punjab certain social entities which maintained a strong tribal identity and for whom the cultivation of land was, probably, not a primary economic activity.[30]

[27]Ibid., vol. 1, p. 121.

[28]Furthermore, from Jouher, writing about the time of Humayun, we learn that the Rana of Amarkot had Jat troops in his employ. It is not clear whether these Jats were agriculturists who lived within the Rana's territory or derived sustenance primarily from other sources, one of which was military service. What seems clearer, however, is the integrated nature of their society which causes this group to be referred to under the single name of 'Jat'. See Jouher, *The Tezkerah-al-Vakiat or Private Memoirs of the Mughal Emperor Humayun*, Major Charles Stewart, tr. (Delhi, 1972), p. 45.

[29]Niccolao Manucci, *Storia do Mogor*, William Irvine, tr. (Calcutta, 1965), vol. 2, p. 428. Even in this case, surmising from the nature of the area where Manucci says that the Jats (or Gett as he calls them) were located, agriculture was unlikely to have been of an extensive nature.

[30]For a much later date, we have the account of Alexander Burnes who says that there was a tribe of Jats in the region of Thatta, which lived in close proximity to the river Indus. He writes that 'they are industrious and very expert in reed or basket work, which they weave from the twigs of the tamarisk, and fit into all these vessels, thus rendering them dry and comfortable.' See Alexander Burnes, *Cabool* (London, 1842), p. 8. This description of the Jats, gving their association with boats, seems to re-create the centuries-old situation as described by chroniclers and travellers of the eleventh century. Refer Irfan Habib, 'Jatts of the Panjab and Sind', p. 95.

There was, however, another side to this picture, for it remains beyond doubt that by at least the sixteenth century, and probably even earlier, the Jats were also classified in Punjab as agriculturists.[31] It has been very convincingly argued by Irfan Habib that between the eleventh and sixteenth centuries, the Jats had converted from pastoralism to agriculture.[32] This is undoubtedly true of those areas of Punjab where climate and topography facilitated and even encouraged such a process of sedentarization. In the agriculturally prosperous areas of the region, therefore, the sedentarization of a large section of the Jats had probably occurred at a fairly early date.

The natural environment prevailing in the varying geographical areas which were inhabited by different sections of the Jats did, therefore, in all likelihood prompt structural changes in their society that

[31]The Jats are shown in the *Ain-i-Akbari* as *zamindars* in many of the *parganas* of the *subas* of Multan, Lahore and Delhi, besides Agra. Much of the peasantry in many of these *parganas* was likely to have been Jat, as there is little mention, even in later times, of any other castes being as predominant among the peasantry as them. See Abul Fazl, *Ain-i-Akbari*, H.S. Jarrett, tr. (Calcutta, 1948–9), vol. 2, pp. 321–5, 331–5. In the *Dabistan-i-Mazahib*, the Jatt (or Jat) is called a villager and a rustic. Refer Mohsin Fani, *Dabistan-i-Mazahib*, David Shea and Anthony Troyer, tr. and ed. (Paris, 1843), vol. 2, p. 252. Even here, however, the Jat villages may not have been of the highly differentiated kind. See also C.A. Bayly, *Rulers, Townsmen and Bazaars*, p. 22, where he suggests that 'a kind of tribal nationalism animated them [i.e. the Jats] rather than a nice calculation of caste difference'. See Eric Stokes, *The Peasant and the Raj: Studies in Agrarian Society and Peasant Rebellion in India* (Cambridge, 1978), pp. 82–3; Perry Anderson, *Passages from Antiquity to Feudalism*, pp. 130–1 regarding 'communal enclaves of the medieval village' being a 'Germanic inheritance'; Irfan Habib, *Agrarian System*, p. 332, however, chooses to call it 'the ties of caste'.

[32]Irfan Habib, 'Jatts of the Panjab and Sind', p. 96.. But, by taking into consideration only those Jats who had become settled agriculturists within the 'agrarian system', Irfan Habib is able to minimize the tribal significance of the Jats. Regarding the Persian-wheel as a factor contributing to the sedentarization of the Jats, see Irfan Habib, 'Technological Changes and Society: 13th and 14th Centuries', *Indian History Congress* (Varanasi, 1969). For a different view, see Chetan Singh, 'Well-Irrigation Methods in Medieval Panjab: The Persian-Wheel Reconsidered', *IESHR*, vol. 22, no. 1 (1985), pp. 73–88.

made many of these sections fundamentally and characteristically different from each other.[33] While the Jats had become settled peasants in the agricultural areas of Punjab, they continued to remain partially or wholly pastoral in the more inhospitable parts of the region. Quite interestingly, the pastoral habits of some Jat groups continued to survive in certain areas outside Punjab as late as the early twentieth century.[34] In the light of even the stray remarks of contemporary sources, it may be justifiable to suggest that even as late as the seventeenth century the process of transition among the tribal pastoralists of Punjab to a typically hierarchical agricultural society was by no means complete.

The Jats, however, were only one among the many such tribal societies of medieval Punjab. In fact, judging from the evidence available, one might even say with some confidence that the Jats were among those tribes, the greater part of which had already sedentarized and integrated with the agriculture based socio-economic system that Mughal Punjab was better known for. The other tribes, too, had over time been in the process of integrating in this manner. This is amply illustrated by the case of the Ghakkars, whose chieftains were incorporated into the Mughal imperial structure by the grant of

[33]The wide area in which people classified as Jats (Juts) were to be found in the early nineteenth century is shown by Elphinstone. It is noted by him that 'the provinces in the eastern bank of the Indus are generally peopled by a class of Hindkees called Juts, who also compose the Mussalman peasantry of the Panjaub, form the principal population of Sind, and are found mixed with Belouches throughout the south-west of Belochistan. . . . In Belochistan they are called Jugdalls as well as Juts and the tribe of them which inhabits Lus is called by the name of Jokha and Nomree. The great extent to which the Juts are scattered excites the same curiosity with the Taujiks, whose situation is very similar to that of the Juts.' See Mountstuart Elphinstone, *An Account of the Kingdom of Caubul* (Karachi, 1972, first published 1815), vol. 1, p. 413. This being the case, it is difficult to visualize the Jat tribe independent of the area where its different sections were to be found.

[34]According to the 1901 census, the Jats in Sind are mentioned as being a caste of cattle breeders, numbering 77,920 in all. See Irfan Habib, 'Jatts of the Panjab and Sind', p. 96.

mansabs.[35] The town of Gujrat was established by Akbar in order to enable the Gujjars to abandon their pastoral ways.[36] Even the case of the Khokhars was likely to have been similar.[37]

Another tribe whose different sections were, probably, at varying transitional stages even during the seventeenth century, was that of the Bhattis. The tribal and unsettled nature of Bhatti social organization in southern Punjab is borne out by some incidental references in our sources. The bardic tradition of Rajasthan recalls the expeditions of the rulers of Bikaner, conducted during the reign of Akbar, against the Bhatti 'raiders' who inhabited the northern borders of their territory.[38] The turbulent nature of the Bhattis and their lack of connection with agriculture seems to be a feature also of the reign of Jahangir.[39] Even

[35]The inclusion of the Ghakkars in the imperial structure took place during the reign of Akbar. See Abul Fazl, *Akbarnama*, H. Beveridge, tr. (Delhi, 1972), vol. 2, pp. 297–300. During the reign of Jahangir too, Akbar Quli Khan, the son of Jalal Khan, the chief of the Ghakkars was granted a *mansab* of 1000/1000. See Nuruddin Muhammad Jahangir, *Tuzuk-i-Jahangiri*, Alexander Rogers, tr. and Henry Beveridge, ed. (Delhi, 1968), vol. 2, p. 161. See also Perry Anderson, *Passages from Antiquity to Feudalism*, p. 110 for the inclusion of 'Germanic warriors', in the Roman armies and the 'client chiefs' who were kept in independence beyond the Roman borders.

[36]*Tuzuk-i-Jahangiri*, vol. 1, p. 91. The emergence of the town of Gujrat is, probably, only one of the numerous instances of the sedentarization process during the sixteenth century. This process, probably, continued throughout the later period for we know that the Gujjars survived as pastoralists right into the twentieth century. In many parts of Jammu and Kashmir and Himachal Pradesh they are still pastoralists.

[37]Abdul Qadir Badaoni, *op. cit.*, vol. 1, p. 121. As we have already seen, the Khokhars were classified by Badaoni in the same category as the Jats. Abul Fazl, however, has also mentioned them as *zamindars* in some *mahals* of both *subas* of Lahore and Multan. See Abul Fazl, *Ain-i Akbari*, vol. 2, pp. 320, 322, 325, 327, 334, 335. The fact that towards the end of the nineteenth century, the Khokhars were a 'tribe found among Jats, Rajputs, Arians and Chuhras', points significantly to the incorporation of the tribe into the hierarchical society at varying social levels. This was a development which was perhaps still in process during Mughal times. See H.A. Rose, *Glossary of Tribes and Castes of the Punjab and the North-West Frontier Province* (Patiala, reprint 1970), vol. 2, p. 539.

[38]L.P. Tessitori, 'Bardic and Historical Survey of Rajputana', *Journal and Proceedings of the Asiatic Society of Bengal*, vol. 13, no. 4 (1917), pp. 195–252. The particular song mentioned refers to the reign of Kalyan Mal of Bikaner.

the picture that Manucci paints of the Bhattis of this area is very much the same.[40] In fact, even until more recent times, the pastoral nature of the Bhattis in some parts of Punjab appears to have survived almost undisturbed.[41] As in the case of the Jats, however, there were other sections of this tribe which had already undergone the structural changes which enabled them to become very much part and parcel of a sedentarized and stratified agricultural society. Once again we can mention the *Ain-i-Akbari*'s listing of the Bhatti caste among the *zamindars* of Punjab.[42] Their appearance in this list of *zamindars* would not by itself prove conclusively that the Bhattis were part of the differentiated village community system, as it was always possible for non-agricultural but dominant tribal groups to appear in the *Ain-i-Akbari* as *zamindars.*[43] What asserts their participation in the 'Mughal system' is the fact that many Bhatti-dominated *mahals* (revenue districts) were located

[39]In an order to Sur Singh of Bikaner, Jahangir states that it is in his notice that 'Bhatti and other rebels of Lakhi Jangal etc., are committing lawlessness and brutality,' and the *raja* should 'punish those rebels in such a way as to leave no trace of them in those *parganas* and *mahals*'. This order is reproduced in *A Descriptive List of Farmans, Manshurs and Nishans Addressed by the Imperial Mughals to the Princes of Rajasthan* (Bikaner, 1962), p. 71. It is possible that the Bhatti rebels in this case were not cultivators, since the complete extermination or routing of cultivators would hardly be a punishment that the emperor would recommend to the raja.

[40]Niccolao Manucci, *op. cit.*, vol. 2, p. 430. This pertains to the reign of Aurangzeb.

[41]D. Ibbetson, *op. cit.*, p. 145. Regarding the sections of this tribe in the uplands of Gujranwala, Ibbetson says that historically they traced their pastoral life style to the area of Bhatner and, even at the time of writing, 'keep numerous herds of cattle which graze over the pasture lands of the *bar*, only plough just sufficient to grow food for their own necessities'. See also C.A. Bayly, *Rulers, Townsmen and Bazaars*, pp. 29, 52–3.

[42]Abul Fazl, *Ain-i-Akbari*, vol. 2, pp. 300–1, 320–3, 333–6. They appear in all three *subas* of Lahore, Multan and Delhi.

[43]Such a possibility would be in keeping with the loose manner in which the term *zamindar* was used during the Mughal period. This was apparently the case, for example, with the Ghakkars, Janjuhas and Khattars in the Sidhu–Sagar Doab of *suba* Lahore or the Junah, Bhim and Kharral in *suba* Multan. This argument has been elaborated in Chetan Singh, 'Socio-Economic Conditions in Panjab during the Seventeenth Century'.

in areas well known for intensive and commercialized agriculture.[44] It was observed by the author of *Ma'athir-ul-Umara* that the Bhatti tribe made its 'livelihood in the Punjab by *zamindari* and by robbery'.[45]

Arising out of the circumstances elaborated in the foregoing was a situation wherein different sections of a single tribe were to be found at varying levels of integration with the agrarian society that has traditionally been described by historians as one being typical of Mughal India. Those sections that had already merged successfully with this agricultural society would, probably, have exchanged their tribal identity for some kind of a caste status in a multicaste hierarchical society.[46] What concerns us here, however, is the position of that part of the population which retained its tribal character even at the height of Mughal power, but which was simultaneously affected by developments in its socio-economic environment; developments that, in turn, necessitated change in its social organization. This social change, when it did occur, was not haphazard and disorganized as might be imagined. Like all other societies, even the tribal-pastoral (or marginally agricultural) people had certain options according to which they could operate, and these options were in turn limited by the rationality that governed them.

More often than not, nomadism is found alongside pastoralism, and the two phenomena have almost invariably been examined together by scholars. Though it is somewhat difficult to say with any degree of certainty the extent of nomadism practised by the tribes in medieval Punjab, much of what Khazanov and Barth say about 'pastoral nomadism' seems to be of striking relevance to our present concern. 'Pastoral

[44]Ibid. For example, among the *mahals* of *suba* Lahore, Bhattis are noted as *zamindars* in Sultanpur in *sarkar* Bet Jalandhar Doab, Batala in *sarkar* Bari Doab. They also appear in Khizrabad in *sarkar* Sirhind of *suba* Delhi.

[45]Shahnawaz Khan, *The Ma'athir-ul-Umara*, H. Beveridge, tr. (Calcutta, 1911–41 and 1952), vol. 1, p. 467. This may also, however, be taken as a description of a tribe in transition.

[46]See D.D. Kosambi, *An Introduction to the Study of Indian History*, p. 27; R.S. Sharma, *Social Change in Early Medieval India*, pp. 12, 13, 15, 16, 19; Amalendu Guha, 'Tribalism to Feudalism in Assam', p. 75; Irfan Habib, 'Social Distribution of Landed Property in Pre-British India', p. 285. Irfan Habib refers to this process basically in connection with ancient India. See also Irfan Habib, 'The Peasant in Indian History', p. 13, where he suggests that the 'tribes [*janapadas*] disintegrated to be replaced by *jatis* [castes]'; Satish Chandra, *Medieval India*, p. 94; Harbans Mukhia, 'Peasant Production and Medieval Indian Society', pp. 243–4.

nomadism,' observes Khazanov, 'and in part even semi-nomadism are a result of passive adaptation of food-producing societies in ecological niches favouring their adaptation.'[47] The most marked feature of the pastoral-nomadic economy was its instability and consequently its inability to produce a regular surplus so as to fulfil the requirements of the whole society. There was a permanent need for additional agricultural products and handicrafts. Therefore, whatever the peculiarities, the nature of their links with the adjoining sedentary society, at least in our region of study, was likely to influence significantly their social values and economic calculations. Regarding the more recent condition of these people, it has been asserted that 'throughout the south-west Asian region . . . the nomads became tied in relations of dependence and reciprocity to sedentary communities in the area . . . their culture is such as to presuppose the presence of such communities and access to their products'.[48]

Many of the tribal-pastoralists of Punjab (irrespective of whether they were truly nomads or not) were, probably, placed in a similar situation, wherein social and economic differences with the agriculturists,

[47]A.M. Khazanov, 'The Early State among the Eurasian Nomads', mimeo, Tenth International Congress of Anthropological and Ethnological Sciences, Delhi (Post Conference: The Study of the State, December, 1978). In the term 'nomadism,' we can also venture to include transhumance. Transhumance, as has been observed by anthropologists, can either be wide-ranging or confined to small areas. It could range, as Fredrik Barth observes: 'from the movement of the whole population through a series of stable settlements in Indus Kohistan, to merely a month's residence in tent camps less than ten miles from the permanent villages in parts of Kurdistan,' See Fredrik Barth, 'Nomadism in the Mountain and Plateau Areas of South-West Asia', in *Arid Zone Research, XVII, Problems of the Arid Zone* (Proceedings of the Paris Symposium, UNESCO, 1962), p. 342. See also Akbar S. Ahmed, 'Nomadism as Ideological Expression: The Case of Gomal Nomads', *Economic and Political Weekly,* vol. 17. no. 27 (1982). pp. 1101–6, for the political factors for nomadism.

[48]Fredrik Barth, *op. cit.,* p. 345. Barth has further argued that: 'As far as the economic structure of an area is concerned, nomad and villager can, therefore, be regarded merely as specialised occupational groups within a single economic system.' In many parts of western Asia, too, we are told, 'pastoral lands were encircled by urban settlement, either partly or completely; the grazing lands visited by the nomads constituted enclaves partly or completely within the sedentary zone'. See M.B. Rowton, 'Autonomy and Nomadism in Western Asia', *Orientalia,* vol. 42 (1975).

though existent, were contained within a network of expanding economic relations.[49] If anthropological research is methodologically acceptable to historians, this interaction and exchange with sedentary society can be seen as taking some specific forms. The course likely to generate the least social friction was, probably, that of mediation by these tribes in trade between different sedentary societies or actual participation in exchange with neighbouring agricultural as well as urban areas.[50] There are some indications that interactions of this nature were to be found in medieval Punjab.

In so far as the question of mediation in trade is concerned, we have the example of the Lohanis, the best known of the 'tribal traders'. As early as the time of Babur, and probably even earlier, the Lohani Afghans carried merchandise from India to Kabul.[51] Abul Fazl, too, mentions in passing that 'the Lohani tribe practised buying and selling in Ghaznin'.[52] Though little is known about the trading activities of the Lohanis in the subsequent period, there is sufficient reason to believe that these continued into more modern times and that their field of operation included many parts of Punjab. Supporting such a possibility regarding this area in the early nineteenth century is the observation of Alexander Burnes that 'the Lohani Afghans are a pastoral and migratory people, and many of them proceed annually into India to purchase merchandise; and assembling here towards the end of April, and being joined by their families who have wintered on the banks of the Indus,

[49]This argument has been expanded in Chetan Singh, 'Socio-Economic Conditions in Panjab During the Seventeenth Century'. See also Fredrik Barth, *op. cit.*, p. 345. Barth observes here that not only are the nomads 'adapted to an environment containing villages and markets and specialised craftsmen—other occupational groups are adapted to an economic system which contains pastoral herders as one of its basic elements'.

[50]A.M. Khazanov, *op. cit.* See also Fredrik Barth, *op. cit.*, p. 346. Both of them observe the prevalence of these methods of interaction amongst nomadic tribes and sedentary populations.

[51]Around the region of Bannu in 1505, Babur's army plundered the goods of these Afghans. Babur writes: 'During the stay there, the foragers brought in from the villages in the Plain, masses of sheep and cattle and from Afghan traders met on the roads, white cloths, aromatic roots, sugar, tipuchaqs, and horses bred for trade. Hindi Mughal unhorsed Khwaja Khizr Lohani, a well-known and respected Afghan merchant, cutting off and bringing in his head', *Baburnama*, p. 235.

[52]Abul Fazl, *Akbarnama*, vol. 3, p. 1160.

they pass into Khorazan'.[53] This seasonal migration of the Lohanis was likely to have been not only very regular but also closely linked, either coincidentally or intentionally, to the trading pattern of the settled population.[54] Among the Afghan tribes, though we find mention only of the Lohanis in our sources, there were perhaps other lesser known ones which followed a similar method of interaction with sedentary society.[55] While movements of the Afghans encompassed a very large area outside Punjab, it is possible that some of the smaller tribes migrated within a smaller circle, and yet performed the same function as the Lohanis, albeit in a smaller way, with smaller stakes.[56] Mediation in trade to any great extent, nevertheless, required a fairly large field of operation coextensive with an equally wide-ranging migratory pattern.

[53]Alexander Burnes, *Cabool*, pp. 77–9. He further elaborates upon the branches of the tribe and the route which they followed in their migrations. Moreover, he notes that 'the extensive nature of the traffic is proved by the custom-house books, which show that 5,140 camels laden with merchandise passed up this year, exclusive of those carrying the tents and baggage of the people, which are rated at the enormous number of 24,000 camels'. This is also noted by Mohan Lal Kashmirian, *Travels in Panjab, Afghanistan and Turkistan* (Patiala, reprint, 1971), pp. 76–7. He writes: 'Trade has enriched the city of Kabul beyond any other capital in Afghanistan. The caravan of Lohanis, which consists of between six hundred and seven hundred camels, furnish it once a year with English and Indian goods. They come through Multan and Ghaznin.' Elsewhere he says that 'the trade of Bokhara to Multan is generally conducted by Lohanis and Shikarpuris' (p. 393).

[54]Alexander Burnes, *Cabool*, p. 78. Among others benefiting from this were, probably, the 'Hindoo merchants and travellers', who travelled with the Lohanis in their migrations.

[55]D. Ibbetson, *op. cit.*, p. 65. He says that the tribe of Pathan warrior-traders is included in the term Parwindah, and is engaged in the carrying trade between India and Afghanistan. Ibbetson elaborates upon their annual circle of migration, and adds that 'entering the Dera Ismail Khan district, they leave their families, stocks and some two-thirds of their fighting men in the great grazing grounds which lie on either side of the Indus and while some wander off in search of employment, others pass on with their laden camels and merchandise to Multan, Rajputana, Lahore, Amritsar, Delhi, Cawnpore and Benaras and even Patna'.

[56]B.R. Grover, 'An Integrated Pattern of Life in the Rural Society of North India During the 17th and 18th Centuries', *Proceedings of the Indian Historical Records Commission* (1966), p. 5. About the Gujjars, he has observed that some of them 'purchased and sold petty articles enroute their seasonal movements'.

The latter feature, however, never really characterized the pastoral tribes inhabiting Punjab proper.[57]

More convenient for these tribes, therefore, would have been to actually participate in the trade by exchanging their pastoral products with the neighbouring agriculturists for non-pastoral essentials. Quite possibly, the large quantities of pastoral products procured during Akbar's reign from *sarkar* Hisar-Firoza, for consumption in the imperial kitchen, were obtained in this manner.[58] The region of Sind, which adjoined this *sarkar*, was also rich in such products.[59] In this case too, one is tempted to argue that the surplus quantity of butter-oil purchased from the Sind region by merchants of the English East India Company was, in the ultimate analysis, a product of the pastoralists who probably entered into an exchange with the settled population of Sind.[60] So important to social stability was this kind of exchange between the

[57]We have already seen that the Punjab tribes were generally only semi-nomadic and their pastoral roaming was not very extensive in nature; for example, the Jats and Bhattis about whom Manucci informs us appear to have resided permanently in the Lakhi Jangal and to have held sway over this block of territory. See Niccolao Manucci, *op. cit.*, vol. 2, pp. 428, 430. These tribes were, probably, neither completely pastoral nor totally agricultural but had a mixed economy, with both aspects of the economy attempting to meet the balanced requirement for subsistence. The same might be equally true of those parts of *sarkar* Dipalpur where the Gujjars, Wattus and Dogars resided and where *jowar* and wheat were mentioned as the crops grown. See Sujan Rai Bhandari, *Khulasat-ut-Tawarikh*, p. 63. It has been noted that the Petlu community in the Shah Savan region of Azarbaijan in Iran, very recently, while still in the process of becoming sedentary, procured its essentials partly by agriculture and partly by pastoralism. See E. Sunderland, 'Pastoralism, Nomadism and Social Anthropology of Iran', in W.B. Fisher, ed., *Cambridge History of Iran* (Cambridge, 1968), p. 649. Sunderland, however, adds and 'it is difficult to assess the relative contribution of the two main types of occupations to the total income'. The need for exchange with completely sedentary agricultural society would, therefore, still exist.

[58]Abul Fazl, *Ain-i-Akbari*, vol. 1, p. 60. See also J.D. Cunningham, *History of the Sikhs* (Delhi, 1972), p. 14. The Juns and Kattias of Punjab provided butter to many of the towns.

[59]Due to certain obvious geographical similarities of Sind with southern Punjab, it is quite likely that the two regions had comparable socio-economic conditions. It is in that context that Sind is mentioned here.

[60]*English Factories in India* (*EFI*), W. Foster (ed.) (London); see vols. *1634–6*, pp. 119, 127.

societies concerned that it quite successfully continued to survive well into the twentieth century in some areas adjoining north Punjab.[61]

This pastoral–sedentary exchange could also, however, take a more political form in which the pastoralists either subordinated themselves to agricultural or urban societies, or, conversely, conquered and dominated them. There also existed, in addition, the possibility of the tribals carrying out periodic raids into the areas of sedentary societies.[62] Considering the contrasting geographical divisions of Punjab and the wide area over which the tribal groups were scattered, there is indeed a likelihood that some and perhaps even all of these alternatives were adopted at particular places or at particular points of time in this region.

While considering the possibility of tribal domination over an agricultural population, the Ghakkars come to mind as do the Juds and the Janjuhas. In its initial stages, the establishment of Ghakkar supremacy over Jat and Gujjar villages in north-west Punjab, probably, appeared in this form, even if the Ghakkars sedentarized with the passage of time.[63] The same may be said of the Juds and Janjuhas who were located

[61]See Fredrik Barth, *op. cit.*, p. 346. He says that though money had entered into the transactions in most areas, 'in some areas such as parts of North Pakistan, where money is still little known, standard exchange equivalents prevail (e.g., maize and milk are exchanged for each other in equal volume)'.

[62]Ibid., p. 346. Barth observes: 'Some of the subsidiary aspects of certain forms of nomad adaptation are at the bottom of far more of the conflicts between nomads and the settled world than are the primary aspects of nomadism. The most important of these subsidiary sources of non-pastoral wares have been, and are, warfare, robbery, landlord's rents, tenancy agriculture, migration, labour and trade.' See also A.M. Khazanov, *op. cit.*

[63]*Baburnama*, pp. 387, 391. Babur says that the villages of the Jats and Gujjars were governed by headmen of the Ghakkar tribe. Apart from the frequent raids by these subservient tribes for cattle, agriculture appears to be a feature of this region, as Babur mentions some sown fields while recounting his campaign against the Ghakkars who were led by Hati Ghakkar. It has been argued that even in those parts of the world where the nomads enjoyed a superior political position as conquerors, 'the early class relations attained by nomads in the course of conquest were beginning, although sometimes painfully and completely, to merge with more developed class relations of the conquered. The process of synthesis may have a negative impact on the development of sedentary societies, but accelerated the development of nomads', A.M. Khazanov, *op. cit.*

in the adjoining region.[64] Babur, in fact, specifically mentioned the supremacy established by these two tribes over the other people of the region and found in their methods of domination certain similarities.[65] By the late sixteenth century, however, it would have been extremely difficult for nomadic tribal groups to subordinate agriculturists. The most significant reason for this was that an expanding and vigorous Mughal state took upon itself the task of safeguarding the sedentary society on account of the land revenue that it obtained from the latter. Thus faced with the formidable Mughal state apparatus, the pastoralists would have had, by and large, to resort to some other means of fulfilling their non-pastoral requirements.

Though we have little recorded evidence to prove that pastoralists in medieval Punjab were subordinating themselves to the agriculturists it, nevertheless, does seem that this was a more likely possibility. Such subordination could entail the participation of the pastoralists as seasonal labour in agriculture or even require them to offer their services as a military body to the more powerful state apparatus.[66] Keeping in mind that during this period commercialized and intensive agriculture was becoming a common feature of the region, it was possible that the geographically peripheral areas, too, were being influenced by it. This commercialization of agriculture, which was by nature more labour intensive than subsistence farming, probably meant that a labour force larger than ever before would now be required. Such a requirement would become even greater with the expansion of the area under cultivation. It is not entirely improbable that this extra labour was forthcoming

[64]*Baburnama*, pp. 379–80. Babur writes that: 'These two from of old have been the rulers and lawful commanders of the peoples and hordes (*ulus*) of the country, between Bhira and Nil-ab.' The practice of pastoralism on the one hand is implied by his mention, on more than one occasion, of the 'various flocks and herds belonging to the country-people', on the other hand, the practice of agriculture in this area has been noted earlier. The levy of a tax by the Juds and Janjuhas based upon the number of ploughs has also been mentioned here.

[65]Ibid., pp. 379–80, 387.

[66]The references to the participation of tribal organizations in the military campaigns of the rulers and nobles of Delhi and Lahore are very frequent in the sources of medieval India, and of these a few examples have already been mentioned. However, the most explicit from our point of view is the comment of Manucci regarding the Bhattis of Lakhi Jangal that 'they enter the *faujdars*' service on small pay'. See Niccolao Manucci, *op. cit.*, vol. 2, p. 430. It shows quite clearly the poverty of the tribe and its need for an additional source of income.

from the neighbouring tribal area.[67] On the other hand, even the needs of the pastoralists (notwithstanding the commercialisation or otherwize of agriculture) could of their own volition draw them into the dominant agricultural society as seasonal cultivating tenants or as mere agricultural labourers.[68]

We might now also consider the final possibility of the Punjab tribes procuring their requirements by carrying out periodic raids into the agriculturally settled areas. Those appearing most frequently in our sources as a cause of turbulence are the Bhattis. Their marauding habits appear to have been a characteristic which survived through centuries. It has already been noted that as early as the time of Akbar, the Bhattis are known to have been raiders into the territory of the raja of Bikaner.[69] The reigns of all subsequent great Mughals witnessed these maraudings by the Bhattis into the neighbouring territories.[70] Most explicit, however, is Manucci's description of the Bhattis of Lakhi Jangal, when he informs us that they 'can place in the field six thousand cavalry and much infantry. ... These men are great thieves and plunderers of

[67]Considering the almost complete absence of information regarding the economic life of these tribals, it is difficult to provide definite contemporary evidence to prove their participation in Punjab as agricultural labourers on this account. That commercialized agriculture could, indeed, influence their activities is shown by the more recent examples of the Kattia and Jun tribes which inhabited the lower reaches of the Ravi in the early nineteenth century. Burnes observed that these pastoralists also cultivated tobacco with the help of irrigation. See Alexander Burnes, *Travels into Bokhara, with a Narrative of a Voyage on the Indus* (Oxford, 1973) vol. 2, p. 130. Tobacco, being a cash crop, probably linked these tribes to the market.

[68]Refer B.R. Grover, 'An Integrated Pattern of Commercial Life in the Rural Society of North India', p. 5. See also Fredrik Barth, *op. cit.*, p. 253; S.C. Misra, 'Social Mobility in Pre-Mughal India', *IHR*, vol. 1, no. 1, p. 42; C.A. Bayly, *Rulers, Townsmen and Bazaars*, pp. 219–22.

[69]L.P. Tessitori, 'Bardic and Historical Survey of Rajputana', p. 247. Though only one instance is given here, these raids of the Bhattis were, probably, a common feature.

[70]Mention is made of them in the reign of Jahangir. See *A Descriptive List of Farmans, Manshurs and Nishans Addressed by the Imperial Mughals to the Princes of Rajasthan*, p. 71. This seems to have continued even after the great Mughals. 'Robbery' is reported to be one of the means of 'livelihood' of the Bhattis. See Shahnawaz Khan, *op. cit.*, vol. 1, p. 467.

the roads and villages.[71] Later sources, too, suggest that the Bhattis continued to be known as thieves till more modern times and this was, probably, a method of meeting their non-pastoral requirements.[72] Another tribe of Punjab about which we find similar evidence is that of the Jats who, Manucci says 'were forever plundering the king's territories'.[73] Though contemporary evidence to this effect regarding the other tribes is lacking, the characteristics that they exhibited as recently as the end of the nineteenth century may provide reason enough to suggest that even in medieval times they obtained their essential non-pastoral goods through periodic raids into sedentary society.

About the Khattars residing near Attock in the north-west, we learn that Jahangir, while encamped at the village of Ahrohi (near Attock fort), was approached by its inhabitants who complained 'against the Khattars, who practised robberies and dacoities, etc.'[74] The other tribes which are mentioned as being inhabitants of Lakhi Jangal, apart from the Bhattis and Jats, were the Gujjars, Wattus and Dogars. It should

[71]Niccolao Manucci, *op. cit.*, vol. 2, pp. 428, 430. The nature of their raids seems to be mainly for essential commodities. The region which they inhabited does not appear to have been involved, to any great extent, in trade or manufacture, and it was unlikely that they were marauding for high quality goods.

[72]Shahnawaz Khan, *op. cit.*, vol. 2, p. 1029. In the biography of Zakariya Khan, he states that one of this noble's victories was over: 'Jang Panah of the Bhati caste, who was a sedition-monger and held sway from Hassan Abdal to the Banks of the Ravi.' See also D. Ibbetson, *op. cit.*, p. 145. Regarding the Bhattis of the Gujranwala uplands, he says they 'keep numerous herds of cattle which graze over the pasture lands of the *bar*, only plough just sufficient to grow food for their neccessities, and are famours cattle-lifters and notorious thieves'. See also C.A. Bayly, *Rulers, Townsmen and Bazaars*, p. 29, regarding Bhatti 'herdsmen-marauders' in the Haryana area.

[73]Niccolao Manucci, *op. cit.*, vol. 2, p. 428.

[74]Shahnawaz Khan, *op. cit.*, vol. 2 p. 1014. It is further noted that 'Zafar Khan was granted Attock as fief in place of Ahmed Beg Khan and he was ordered that the Khattars should by the time of the return of the Emperor, be removed to Lahore, and that their headmen should be imprisoned, and whatever they had taken from anyone restored'. See also H.A. Rose, *op. cit.*, vol. 1, pp. 532–4. Regarding the Khattars, the glossary quotes Col. Cracroft who says 'the Khattars enjoy an unenviable notoriety in regard to crime. Their tact has always been one in which heavy crime has flourished; they are bad agriculturists extravagant in their habits, keep hawks and horses, and are often backward in paying their revenue'.

come as no surprise to be told by a contemporary writer that these tribals were notorious for highway robbery, and that on account of the inhospitable nature of the terrain that they inhabited, they usually escaped unpunished.[75] Another tribe of marauding pastoralists may, possibly, have been the Kharrals. Though we do not have any contemporary evidence to support this, their social organization as recently as the late nineteenth century is a likely indicator of their earlier condition.[76] This last method of fulfilling non-pastoral requirements, though adopted by many of the tribes, often placed them in direct confrontation with the powerful Mughal state apparatus, the influence of which combined with expanding agriculture to encroach upon their traditional lifestyle.

Judging from the various alternatives that the pastoral-tribals in Punjab were likely to be faced with, it would appear that in the face of the economic and political developments occurring in the region under Mughal rule, the odds were weighed more in favour of the agricultural sedentarized society. In this context, the long-term movement towards the sedentarization of the pastoralists themselves seems to have been the most natural and logical course of change. Moreover, there is reason to argue that even in a situation where pastoral-nomadism thrives, there

[75]Sujan Rai Bhandari, *op. cit.*, p. 63. Supporting this description of the seventeenth century is the more recent observation of Ibbetson, that the Dogars 'like Gujars and Naipals are great thieves and prefer pasturing cattle to cultivating'. He further notes that: 'The Dogars of Lahore and Firozpur are essentially a riverside tribe; being found only on the river banks they bear the worst reputation, and appear . . . to have retained till quite lately some at least of the habits of a wild tribe.' About the Wattus, it is noted that 'the tribe was formerly almost purely pastoral and as turbulent and as great marauders as other pastoral tribes of the neighbourhood'. See D. Ibbetson, *op. cit.*, pp. 145–6, 177–8. Irfan Habib, *Agrarian System*, p. 323, however, refers to 'peasants' belonging to the 'refractory caste of Dogars' in Lakhi Jangal. Our suggestion here is that these Dogars were not completely sedentarized agriculturists and their status as 'peasants' is debatable. Their categorization as a 'caste' is equally questionable.

[76]See H.A. Rose, *op. cit.*, vol. 2, pp. 495–6. It is noted that 'the Kharrals are found in large numbers along the valley of the Ravi, from its junction with the Chenab to the boundary between Lahore and Montgomery. . . . The Kharrals have ever been notorious.' Further supporting the argument that their tribal and pastoral system of organization survived well into the nineteenth century is the observation that the Kharrals were being deprived of the refuge they sought after plunder, on account of the extension of cultivation into jungle areas.

continues simultaneously a movement in the direction of sedentarization.[77] In the Punjab context in particular, the growth of commercialized agriculture under the Mughals was likely to have encouraged and facilitated the absorption of previously pastoral people into the 'agrarian system'. It may be further argued that the monetization of the economy, along with the growth of internal trade, enabled a larger population to subsist on the same amount of cultivated land. On account of these developments, a larger area could be brought under cash crops while food requirements were obtained by import from areas producing surplus foodgrain. Even land that was not conducive to double-cropping could be devoted completely to commercial crops, and the monetary income obtained by their sale in the market subsequently utilized for the import of the foodgrain requirement of the much larger labour force now engaged in commercial agriculture.[78] The establishment of this cash nexus encouraged the emergence of a more complicated system of interaction between economically different sub-regions as well as organizationally different social sections.

If pastoral people were gradually moving into sedentary society in medieval Punjab, it must be assumed that the latter society was, indeed,

[77]See M.B. Rowton, 'Autonomy and Nomadism in Western Asia', *Orientalia*, vol. 42 (1975), p. 254. He argues that 'A process of continuous sedentarisation has to be recognised as a normal aspect of nomadism. The richest and the poorest among the nomads tend to sedentarise: the richest, when the size of their flocks exceed[s] the capacity of the grazing land available; the poorest, when the loss of livestock reduces their flocks below the minimum needed to support a family.' The argument of Barth can also be quoted here to further clarify this process. Barth observes that 'The diet of nomads is better balanced, containing a larger fraction of proteins than that of the villager; the sanitary and climatic conditions under which the nomads live are far better, and lower density makes the nomad population less susceptible to epidemics . . . there can be little doubt that other groups today, and most such groups in the past, are characterised by a strong positive balance between birth-and-death rates.' 'In any period of total population stability, this implies a continual population imbalance between nomads and sedentary society and a flow of migrants from nomadic to settled life-process, which has indeed been conspicuous throughout the history of the Middle East. Paradoxically, then, the net flow of population has been consistently from areas of low density to areas of high density and congestion.' See Fredrik Barth, *op. cit.*, p. 350.

[78]For the commercialization of agriculture and the growth of trade and handicraft in Punjab, see Chetan Singh, 'Socio-Economic Conditions in Panjab During the Seventeenth Century'.

in a position to accommodate and even absorb them. It is, in fact, quite likely that the Mughal 'agrarian system' actually required them in order to replenish its ever-growing agricultural labour force. However, the ability to support a natural population increase as well as to absorb new social sections, probably rests upon a continuous process of economic expansion in the society concerned. The more rapid the economic growth, the faster this process of amalgamation of the formerly pastoral population was likely to be. However, in the event of an agricultural/trade recession or economic crisis of a retrogressive nature, it is possible that the position of the newly incorporated sections of society (such as the recently sedentarized pastoralists) would be rather tenuous.[79] In such a situation, the newly settled areas and people on the fringes would be most precariously placed.[80] Under the circumstances there, indeed, existed the possibility of considerable social tension. It might even be suggested that at least part of the unrest which Punjab witnessed in the eighteenth century was in some manner linked to friction generated by processes that had been altering the structure of tribal societies in the region during the preceding period.[81]

[79]Though a return to pastoral-nomadism would be very difficult, it could not have been entirely impossible. It has been argued that in the event of harsh treatment by the central government or exploitation, the villagers could be 'induced to leave their villages and endeavour to resume a nomadic existence'. See E. Sunderland, 'Pastoralism, Nomadism and the Social Anthropology of Iran', p. 640.

[80]It has been observed with regard to village settlement that 'the older a class of places is, the lower the number of abandonments. From the oldest period of settlements there appear to be the fewest out settlements, more occur from the second wave of settlements and by far the most from subsequent periods. The reason for this is that in the first period settlers chose the best land; in the second period they have to choose less good land; the third far worse according to what is left. The number of abandonments for each settlement type, therefore, provides an indirect scale of assessing age'. See Robert C. Edit, 'Some Observations on the Role of Geography and History in the Development of Methodology for the Analysis of Settlements', *Proceedings of the I.G.U., Varanasi Symposium* (1975), R.L. Singh et al., eds, *Geographic Dimensions of Rural Settlements*, pp. 7–18.

[81]See Chetan Singh, 'Interaction between Divergent Social Formations: A Possible Explanation for some Instances of Unrest in 17th Century Panjab,' *Panjab History Conference* (1980), pp. 128–38; see C.A. Bayly, *Rulers, Townsmen and Bazaars*, pp. 20–1, for a somewhat similar argument.

Towards the end of Aurangzeb's reign the Wattus, Dogars and Gujjars are known to have rebelled in the *sarkar* of Dipalpur. Irfan Habib, *Agrarian System*, p. 346. In the Rachna Doab region of Punjab, the Bhattis, Kharrals and Gujjars

Structural change in the tribal societies, however, could not have been a matter of concern for tribals alone. So close a relationship did tribal pastoralism bear with the sedentary and commercialized agrarian society of Mughal Punjab, and so inextricably linked were its economic interests with those of the latter, that fundamental shifts in the structure of any one of these societies could hardly have left the other unaffected. To view these societies as constituting two separate worlds in themselves would, probably, be quite far from the truth. What remains important in the larger context is the significant part that tribal societies were likely to have played in the making of medieval Indian history. Though hardly in a position to withstand the growing pressure of the powerful Mughal state apparatus and the socio-economic system that it represented, these tribal societies, nevertheless, seem to have constituted an economically palpable and militarily influential element within the geographical boundaries of the Mughal empire. Moreover, if tribal-pastoral populations in other parts of the subcontinent, too, were as integral to the economy and society of adjacent agricultural societies (i.e. the Mughal 'agrarian system') as appears to have been the case in Punjab, it would hardly be possible to ignore them without jeopardizing, to a fair extent, our attempts to understand the structure of agrarian society in medieval India. Would it, therefore, be unfair to say that on account of the manner in which medieval Indian tribes have been disregarded by scholars, our knowledge today of the agrarian economy of medieval India might not only be more incomplete than we have so far imagined, but in certain ways, also more incorrect?

---

were very turbulent. *Asrar-i-Samadi,* M. Shujauddin, ed. (Lahore, 1965), p. 9; Muzaffar Alam, *The crisis of Empire in Mughal North India* (Delhi, 1986), p. 139. In 1700, Prince Muhammad Muizzuddin, who had been appointed Nazim of Multan, had to personally lead the imperial forces against the rebels. *Akhbarat* (Sitamau Transcripts), Aurangzeb 44th RY, 4th Zi-al-Hijja p. 235, 17th Zi-al-Hijja p. 245(a), 23rd Zi-al-Hijja p. 247, 3rd Rabi II p. 317(a), 21st Rabi II pp. 329–30. There was also the rebellion of Isa Khan Munj in *sarkar* Sirhind and Husain Khan Khweshgi in Qasur. See Shahnawaz Khan, *op. cit.*, vol. 1, pp. 641–3, 687–8. See also *Asrar-i-Samadi*, pp. 17, 19, 75.

16

Aspects of Agrarian Uprisings in North India in the Early Eighteenth Century*

Muzaffar Alam

Widespread agrarian uprisings causing and accelerating the decline of Mughal imperial authority took place in different regions of the empire in the early eighteenth century. In a number of modern works these uprisings have been examined in the context of the resistance launched by peasants, *zamīndārs* and other local social groups against the Mughals.[1] But as these studies are oriented towards explaining the decline of the Mughal empire, certain details of the history of the regions and the social classes involved in these uprisings have not received adequate attention. Similarly, it is difficult to identify the categories of the rural population which took part in and those which remained unconnected with these uprisings. The question of how urban groups, particularly merchants and artisans, reacted to them also needs careful examination. I have tried to examine some of these aspects in

*From S. Bhattacharya and R. Thapar (eds), *Situating Indian History* (Delhi, 1986).

[1] See Irfan Habib, *Agrarian System of Mughal India* (Bombay, 1963), pp. 330–51; Habib, 'Forms of Class Struggle in Mughal India', paper presented at the Bombay Session of the Indian History Congress, 1980; contributions by M.N. Pearson, J.F. Richards and P. Hardy to the symposium on the 'Decline of the Mughal Empire', *Journal of Asian Studies*, 35, no. 2 (February 1976); J.F. Richards and V.N. Rao, 'Banditry in Mughal India: Historical and Folk Perceptions', *The Indian Economic and Social History Review (IESHR)*, XVII, no. 1 (January–March 1980); Muzaffar Alam, '*Zamīndārs* and Mughal Power in the Deccan, 1686–1712', *IESHR*, XI, no. 1 (March 1973).

an earlier study of the Sikh movement in Punjab.[2] Here my study is extended to three other regions of north India and examines the nature and context of *zamīndārs*' clashes with the Mughal state. It also looks at the reasons for the participation or non-participation of other classes in such clashes. I have tried to see if the *zamīndārs*' fury was in all cases directed against Mughal authority and the extent to which social conditions made it possible for them to rise jointly against the Mughals. Turning to the limited evidence about the social and economic conditions of the regions where *zamīndārs* rose against the imperial power, the essay suggests that these uprisings could be explained in terms of their growing strength and prosperity in relation to the Mughal centre. It also asks if the initiative for these uprisings came from the *zamīndārs* themselves or whether they entered the fray after the 'peasants' had been up in arms and simply provided leadership for their war against the state. I shall also see if the *zamīndārs* on their own were capable of providing leadership to the process of a regional political formation in the wake of the decline of the imperial Mughal state.

My study is limited on two counts. In the first place, it is based on Persian sources. Apart from details of the political and military activities of *zamīndārs*, information about other classes is extremely limited in my sources. Even the *zamīndārs*' activities are generally mentioned briefly, in the context of the Mughal officials' military expeditions against them. Secondly, the study is restricted to only three regions of north India, namely the Morādābād–Bareilly region or the Mughal *sarkārs* (administrative divisions of a province) of Sambhal and Badāon; the Mughal province of Awadh and the Banāras region covering four eastern *sarkārs* of the Mughal province of Allāhābād, namely Jaunpūr, Ghazīpūr, Chūnār and Banāras. These regions have been chosen in the first place because they were contiguous with each other and together formed one large region, with Banāras as its eastern hinterland in the east and Morādābād with its north-western hinterland on the west, while Bahrāich and Gorakhpūr extending to modern Nepāl lay in the north and Baiswāṛa in the south. Secondly, the resources of

[2]M. Alam, 'Sikh Uprisings under Banda Bahādur', *Studies in History*, I, no. 2 (1979), pp. 197–213; see also R.P. Rana, 'Agrarian Revolts in Northern India During the Late 17th and Early 18th Century', *IESHR*, XVII, nos. 3&4 (July–December 1981), pp. 287–326. Rana has discussed in detail the participation/non-participation of the different categories of the *zamīndārs* and the peasants in Ajmēr–Ranthambor, Mewāt and Āgra–Kōl regions of upper India.

each of these regions sustained some kind of political stability even after the collapse of Mughal imperial authority in the eighteenth century.[3]

I

According to the *Ā'īn*, different castes and communities held *zamīndārī* rights in these three regions. In Morādābād–Bareilly, various clans of Rājpūts and Jāts shared the *zamīndārīs*. In a number of *maḥāls* (revenue districts) the Brahmans and certain other communities including the Muslims (Shaikhs and Saiyids) also held dominant positions. From the time of Shāhjahān the Afghāns also began to settle in the region and gradually acquired important *zamīndārī* holdings, especially in the new settlements. In Awadh the Rājpūts occupied the most prominent place as *zamīndārs*. However, the Muslims including the Afghāns and the Brahmans together with some other castes, also had a substantial share in the *zamīndārī* in the province. In the four *sarkārs* of the Banāras region, again, the Rājpūts on an average had the largest share in the *zamīndārī*, even though the Brahmans or Bhūmihārs had almost exclusive control over land in the core of the Banāras *sarkār*. In a number of *parganās* (divisions of a *sarkār*) in the other three *sarkārs* also the Bhūmihārs held *zamīndārīs*, while Muslims are mentioned as *zamīndārs* in some others. The Kāyasthas had *zamīndārīs* in two *maḥāls* of Ghazīpūr and Jaunpūr. In one *parganā* of Jaunpūr, significantly, the Kurmīs are also recorded as *zamīndārs*.[4]

[3]The Afghān states under the Rohilla Chiefs, 'Alī Muḥammad Khān and his sons and Ḥāfiẓ Raḥmat Khān in the Morādabād–Bareilly region, the *nawābī* founded and consolidated by Burhān ul-Mulk and Ṣafdar Jang, the Mughal governors in Awadh, and Banāras Rāj founded and consolidated by Mansā Rām and Balwant Singh in the Banāras region.

[4]*Ā'īn-i Akbarī*, II, Jarrett's English trans., ed., Jadunath Sarkar (Calcutta, 1949), pp. 293–5 for Badāon and Sambhal *sarkārs*, pp. 184–90 for Awadh; and pp. 173–6 for Jaunpūr, Ghāzīpūr, Chunār and Banāras *sarkārs*. For an analysis of the *Ā'īn*'s account of the *zamīndār* castes in Awadh, see S.Z.H. Jafri, 'The Land Controlling Classes in Awadh: A study of Changes in their Composition, 1600–1900', paper presented at the 43rd Session of the Indian History Congress, Kurukshetra, 1982. For Afghān settlements in the Morādābād–Bareilly region, see Iqbal Husain, 'Some Afghan Settlements in the Gangetic Doab, 1627–1707', *Proceedings of the Indian History Congress (PIHC)* (Varanasi, 1969); William Irvine, *Later Moghuls* (Delhi, reprint, 1971), pp. 117–18; Jadunath Sarkar, *Fall of the Mughal Empire* (Delhi, reprint, 1971), pp. 27–8.

Not all of these groups rose against the Mughals. But the *zamīndārs* who took to armed resistance posed a serious threat to imperial power in the region. Imperial campaigns against them were often led by *faujdārs* (area commandants) of the *sarkārs* and not infrequently by the *ṣūbadārs* (provincial governors), with heavy artillery to break their fortresses and armies sometimes exceeding 10,000 horsemen.[5] The governors were given additional powers, sometimes unprecedented, to deal effectively with the *zamīndār* revolts. In certain case additional offices were instituted with a view to absorbing leaders of the dominant local communities in the administration.[6] In 1708 the governor of Awadh resigned, protesting among other things against the inadequate authority he was given to encounter the threat from 'recalcitrant' *zamīndārs.*[7] It was probably to meet the threat from the *zamīndārs* that the *faujdārī* of Morādābād in the early eighteenth century was entrusted to such important nobles as Niẓām-u'l-Mulk, Muḥammad Amīn Khan and Qamar u'd-Dīn Khan, who all became *wazīrs* (principal revenue ministers) of the empire one after another in Muḥammad Shāh's reign (1719–48). In view of the magnitude of the problems, as also the vastness of the area, the *faujdār* of Morādābād was generally expected to have the calibre and stature of a *ṣūbadār.* Indeed, the office was considered at par with that of a govenor.[8] The enhancement of the *sarkār* to a full-fledged *ṣūba* (province), though for a brief period, under Farrukh Siyar (1712–18)[9] may also be seen against the background of the administrative difficulties caused by *zamīndār* uprisings.

[5]*Akhbārāt-i Darbār-i Mu'allā* (Akhbārāt), Farrukh Siyar (FS), 3rd Regnal Year (RY) Sitamau transcripts, pp. 22 and 143 for Mughal expeditions against the *zamīndārs* under the governor and the *faujdār* in Banāras region and Awadh. See also '*Ajā'ib u'l-Āfāq*, British Museum MS, Or. 1776, f. 35 for the governor of Awadh, Chhabēlē Rām's letter to the Emperor, Farrukh Siyar asking for additional arms and ammunitions from the centre to meet the threat from the *zamīndārs* to the provincial administration.

[6]See M. Alam, 'The Mughal Centre and the *Ṣūbas* of Awadh and the Punjab, 1707–1748', unpublished Ph.D. dissertation (Jawaharlal Nehru University, 1977), chs 2 and 3.

[7]Rustam 'Alī Shāhabādī, *Tārīkh-i Hindī*, Rieu iii 909a, Or. 1628, p. 217.

[8]Murtaẓa Ḥusain Bilgrāmī, for example, mentions Muḥammad Amīn, the *faujdār* of Morādābād in the reign of Bahādur Shāh, as the *ṣūbadār* of Morādābād Sambhal. cf. *Ḥadīqat u'l-Aqālīm* (Navalkishore Press, Lucknow), p. 127. See also Shāhnawāz Khān, *Ma'asir u'l-Umarā*, Bib. Indi., Calcutta, III, pp. 709 and 765 for the importance of Morādābād Sambhal region.

[9]Muḥammad Hādī Kāmwar Khān, *Tazkirat. u's-Salāṭīn Chaghtā*, ed. Muzaffar Alam (Bombay, 1980), pp. 251–2.

In a number of cases imperial campaigns were hardly able to force the rebels to submit. On 8 November 1709, for instance, a *zamīndār* of *ṭappa* (an administrative division) Faridnagar in *parganā* Mughalpūr of Morādābād refused to pay the revenue and rose in arms against the Mughal *'āmil* (revenue collector). Subsequently, Muḥammad Amīn Khān, the *faujdār,* led an expedition against the *zamīndār* and the campaign was carried out successfully. In August 1714 the same *zamīndār* was reported to have again created 'disturbances' in the *jāgīr* (revenue assignment) *maḥāls* of the *parganā.*[10] In another instance Madār Singh, a leading Rājpūt refractory *zamīndār* of the region, invaded and devastated the villages of different *jāgīr maḥāls* several times between 1710 and 1715.[11] The case of the Baiswāṛa *zamīndārs* in Awadh is yet another illustration of the magnitude of rural resistance against the Mughals in north India. A number of Baiswāṛa *parganās* had been disturbed by *zamīndār* revolts since the late seventeenth century. By the second decade of the eighteenth century the Bais had begun to offer more organized resistance against the imperial power. In 1714, although they had to submit to the Mughals under the command of the governor, Chhabēlē Rām, their submission was only temporary. Within a year and a half the Bais *zamīndārs* were again mobilized by their leaders, Mardān Singh of Dondia Kheṛā and Amar Singh of Jagatpūr, to show a much more effective strength against the Mughals.[12] In another case from Awadh repeated military expeditions under the command of the *ṣūbadārs* are reported to have been launched against the Rājpūts of *sarkār* Khairabād.[13] How the problem persisted until some arrangement was made with the rebels is further illustrated from the case of the *zamīndār* of Tiloi in *sarkār* Awadh. In March 1715 a military campaign against the *zamīndār* was commanded by no less a person than the nephew of the then governor, Girdhar Bahādur, who also became governor of the province in 1718. Again in 1716 the *zamīndār* refused to pay the revenue to the local agent of the *jagīrdār* (revenue assignee). The governor then sent another detachment to Tiloi.[14]

[10] *Akhbārāt*, Bahādur Shāh (BS), 3rd RY in the volume titled *Akhbārāt-i Aurangzēb*, I, p. 23; FS, 3rd RY, II, p. 41.

[11] Ibid., FS, 3rd RY, pp. 78, 170, 173; 4th RY, I, p. 152.

[12] Ibid., FS, 4th RY, I, p. 121; *'Ajā'ib u'l-Āfāq*, f. 18b. See also FS, 2nd RY, II, pp. 201, 238; 3rd RY, II, p. 98 for similar instances.

[13] *Ajā'ib u'l-Āfāq*; f. 36a; Saiyid Muḥammad Bilgrāmī, *Tabṣirat un-Nāẓirīn*, Aligarh MS, *Fārsiya Akhbār*, 204, f. 55a.

The successes against the *zamīndārs* were, thus, only temporary and showed at best the marginal military and strategic superiority of the Mughals in certain cases. In the Banāras region, the *zamīndārs* seem to have consistently scored over imperial power. In 1708 the *faujdār* of Ghāzīpūr invaded the habitats of the rebel *zamīndārs* in Zamānia and reportedly killed scores of them. But within a few days the *zamīndārs*, reinforced by about 11,000 Ujjainiyas from across the borders in Bihār, overpowered the imperial force. The *faujdār*, wounded and humbled, then fled and took shelter in a *ra'iyatī* village in *sarkār* Jaunpūr in the neighbourhood.[15] In another instance, in 1709, one Dhruban Singh with his clansmen invaded Ghāzīpūr and held up the town and suburbs when the *faujdār* had apparently gone on an expedition to the countryside. In the battle which followed the arrival of the *faujdār* with his army to the rescue of the townsfolk, the *zamīndār* defeated the Mughals. The *faujdār* was injured. The rebels then set the town on fire, plundered properties, pulled down trees in the orchards and demolished mosques.[16]

The strength of armed bands under the command of the *zamīndārs* and also the fortresses they had under their control are to be particularly noted for an assessment of the magnitude of the threat their risings may have posed to the Mughals. In 1714, a *zamīndār* of Parganā Aihar, in Baiswāṛa district of Awadh, led an army of 2000 horsemen, in addition to scores of foot soldiers, against Mughal forces under the command of the governor. No less than 25 fortresses were under the control of the Gaur Rājpūt rebels of *sarkār* Khairabād. In 1715, according to a report, only four out of a number of fortresses belonging to the Afghān rebel zamīndārs of *sarkār* Lucknow could be subjugated by the Mughals.[17] The strength of the Ujjainiyas who reinforced the *zamīndārs* of Zamānia in 1708 has been given as 11,000, and the strength of the *faujdār's* army which invaded the habitats of the rebels as 15,000.[18] In Morādābād at least 12 fortresses are reported to have been in control of the *zamīndār* of *tappā* Farīdnagar. No less than 4000 Afghan

[14] *Akhbārāt* FS, 4th RY, I, p. 7; and 5th RY, II, p. 122. Still, the *zamīndār* of Tiloi continued to be a major source of disturbance until about 1742 when Ṣafdar Jang finally reconciled him by conceding him some military and administrative authority over his *zamīndārī*.

[15] Ibid., BS, 2nd RY, p. 77.

[16] Ibid., RY, p. 213.

[17] *'Ajā'ib u'l-Āfāq*, f. 36; *Akhbārat*, FS, 2nd RY. II, pp. 99, 130, 154; 3rd RY, II, p. 78; 4th RY, I, p. 149; 4th RY, I, p. 4.

[18] *Akhbārāt*, BS, 2nd RY, p. 77.

mercenaries fought with Madār Singh. The Afghāns also constituted a substantial part of the armed forces of the Rājpūt *zamīndār* of Mainpūr. In another case, a Muslim *zamīndār* of *parganā* Sahwān employed a large number of Afghāns.[19]

My sources are not clear about the strength of local peasants other than the *zamīndārs*' own *jama'iyat* in the retinue of these rebels. It is known that *zamīndārs* customarily had their own armed contingents.[20] In the context of the cases examined it is interesting to note that the terms used in the *Akhbārāt* (newsletters) for the armed bands of the *zamīndārs* are in general, *jama'iyat*, occasionally *ulūs*, literally 'group' and 'kinsfolk', and *sipāh*—a common word for soldiers and mercenaries. Sometimes the plurals of *mufsid* (disturber and mischief-monger) and *zamīndār*, namely *mufsidān* and *zamīndārān* are interchanged with, for instance, *Rajpūtān* or *Afghānān*, the plurals of the words Rājpūt and Afghān, or with the other caste and clan names of the rebels.[21]

II

However, the strength that the *zamīndārs* achieved through their links with peasants was often impaired by internal social conditions. The *zamīndārs* were divided among themselves on caste, clan and territorial lines, and were perpetually at war with each other. Each group feared the other and thus each had to demonstrate its strength to safeguard itself against the actual or threatened encroachment of the other. The need of a power from outside to enable each of them to protect and promote its interests was, in a large measure, the consequence of its social structure. In the absence of an effective paramount power, as was the case in the early eighteenth century, the stronger among them tended to extend their power and subjugate the others in the neighbourhood. Thus the rural populations also became victims of these raids. In Morādābād, for instance, the *zamīndārs* of Lonī, a village in *parganā* Āonla, suffered heavily at the hands of the armed bands of Madār

[19]Ibid., 3rd RY, in the volume titled *Akhbarāt-i Aurangzēb*, I. p. 23; FS, 3rd RY, II, p. 78; and 4th RY, II, pp. 156, 187.

[20]Compare Irfan Habib, *Agrarian System of Mughal India*, pp. 163–5.

[21]*Jama'iyat* (group or clan and kinsfolk), *sipāh* (soldiers) and *qila'cha* or *qila'* (fortress or fort) are almost invariably mentioned in the context of a *zamīndārī* disturbance. Similarly in a number of cases, e.g. the case of the Rājpūts of Khairabād and Afghāns of Lucknow, the rebel *zamīndārs* have been mentioned by their clan names.

Singh.[22] In 1711, an Afghān *zamīndār* of Ḥasanpūr attacked and ravaged the villages in the suburbs of Badāon with an army of over 2000.[23] In another instance, the villages around Bareilly and Morādābād are reported to have been devastated by a Rājpūt *zamīndār* of *parganā* Rājpūr.[24] Sometimes those *chaudhurīs* (village headmen) and *qānūngos* (revenue officials) who were still with the Mughāls were the targets of the rebels, and when they could not collect money and valuables from them they would capture some of the *zamīndārs* along with the animals and run off. Some cases from Awadh show the peasants and cultivators having suffered at the hands of rebels.[25] According to one tradition, a major advantage that the Bais *zamīndārs* took of their increasing strength in Baiswāṛa was the extortion of a higher share from the peasants.[26] In October 1715 three such *zamīndārī* disturbances were reported from the Banāras region in which local people, and not Mughal officials, were victims of the rebels' fury. On 10 October 1715 one Rājā Rām, the *zamīndār* of Samīnpūr, together with the *zamīndār* of *parganā* Bhagwant, invaded and killed the *zamīndār* and the *ri'āyā* (peasants) of Bahrāmganj, about four miles from Chūnār. The *qila'dār* (fort commandant) of Chūnār was reportedly too scared to come out and protect the victims. On 24 October the villages around Ghāzīpūr were plundered by the armed bands of a *zamīndār*. On 30 October Gaharwār Rājpūt *zamīndārs* of Sekar, in Banāras *sarkār*, were reported to have invaded, besieged and devastated the villages of *parganā* Mawai in *sarkār* Chūnār.[27]

A study of the relevant records from some other regions of northern India also shows that the fury of the *zamīndārs* was not always directed against the Mughals. Out of the four cases of *zamīndār* rising in *chaklā* Etawah taken randomly from the *Akhbārāt*, two represented rather the conflict among the various *zamīndār* groups themselves than their resistance as a class against the Mughal state. In both these cases the victims expected and appealed to the Mughal officials to come to their help.[28] Again, in Punjāb, the agrarian revolts in the early

[22] *Akhbārāt*, FS, 3rd RY, II, p. 78.

[23] Ibid., BS, 5th RY, p. 421.

[24] Ibid., FS, 4th RY, I, p. 24.

[25] Shivdās Lakhnawī, *Shāhnāma-i Munawwar Kalām* (Shivdās), Rieu i 274a, Or. 26, ff. 72b–73a.

[26] Compare Charles Alfred Elliot, *Chronicles of Oonao* (Allāhabād, 1862), p. 73.

[27] *Akhbārāt*, FS, 4th RY, II, pp. 87, 131, 143.

[28] Ibid., 3rd RY, II, pp. 213, 275.

eighteenth century sometimes caused serious damage to peasants and villages.[29]

These revolts were thus sometimes a menace to some local *zamīndārs* and peasants and posed a threat to Mughal power as well. According to my sources, the *zamīndārs* supported the Mughals in a number of cases in their bid to chastise rebels. In Awadh in some cases even the *ri'āyā* seem to have actively taken part in campaigns against rebels, while there is clear evidence for the presence of the parganā-level *zamīndārs* and intermediaries in the imperial armies in all these three regions.[30] In some cases, as is illustrated from the encounters between the *zamīndārs* of *parganā* Majhauli of Gorakhpur *sarkār* and the Ujjainiyas of Bihār, the *zamīndār* fought the rebels independently to defend and protect Mughal interests.[31] It was with the help of local *zamīndārs* that stability in Banāras could be restored following the subjugation of the Rājpūts by a Brahman *zamīndār* of the region.[32]

One can ascribe the internal conflict among *zamīndār* to caste, clan and community differences, an ascription that appears to be supported by some instances of mutual clash or assistance on grounds of caste or community identities. The Rājputs of Ghāzīpur, as we have seen above, appear to have often been supported by their clansmen from Bihar. In Morādābād, in one case, the village of a Mughal *zamīndār* was devastated by an Afghān *zamīndār* in 1715.[33] In Awadh in a number of cases the hostility of the Rājpūt *zamīndārs* was directed against the Muslim

[29]M. Alam, 'Sikh Uprisings under Banda Bahādur'.

[30]See Shivdās, f. 73f, for instance for the presence of the *zamīndārs* and the *ri'āyā* in the army of Girdhar Bahādur, the governor of Awadh, against the Gaurs of Khairabād; Ghulām Ḥusain Kamboh, *Tārīkh-i Banāras* (Kamboh), Bānkipore, Patna MS, ff. 5a, 7a, 12a, 15, 16b–17a, 21b–24b, 28, 29a, 37b–38a and 57, for the presence of Mansā Rām, Balwant Singh and the *zamīndār* of Kāntit (*sarkār* Allāhabād) in the Mughal military expeditions against the Rājpūts *zamīndārs* of Banāras region; see also Khair u'd-Din Muḥammad Khān, *Tuḥfa-i Tāza* or *Balwantnāma (Tuḥfa)*, Bānkipore MS, ff. 4a, 8, 9a.

[31]*Akhbārāt*, FS, 6th–8th RY, p. 169. See also R.P. Rana, p. 307 for the *chaudhurīs*' and the *qānūngos*' support to the Mughals in the regions under his review.

[32]Compare Kamboh and *Tuḥfa* for the details of how Mansā Rām, a Brahman *zamīndār* of Gangāpūr in Banāras, and his son got access to Mīr Rustam 'Ali Khān, the Mughal official of the region, obtained *mustā'jirī*, and mobilized their kinsmen in support of the Mughals against the rebel *zamīndārs*.

[33]*Akhbārāt*, FS, 4th RY, p. 156.

madad-i-ma'āsh (revenue grant) holders who had begun to behave like *zamīndārs* by the beginning of the eighteenth century.[34]

The Mughals also seem to have been aware of the importance of playing on caste differences among *zamīndārs* to meet and overcome the danger from them. In Awadh they appointed *zamīndārs* and encouraged *zamīndārīs* by purchase in the caste bastions of the Rājpūts. In *parganā* Unāo, where Bais enjoyed dominance, efforts were made to promote the Saiyid *zamīndārīs*. The choice of the Saiyids was determined by the fact that they had once enjoyed eminence and had strong *ulūs* in the *parganā*.[35] In another case Burhān u'l-Mulk, the governor of Awadh (1722–39), promoted one Muṭahhir 'Alī Khān in Rasūlabād. By 1740 Rasūlabād was made the headquarters of a *parganā* wherein all the important offices were held by Muṭahhir 'Alī's family.[36] Again, in the early eighteenth century the Muslim *chaudhurīs* of *parganā* Sandīlā appear to have strengthened their position by purchasing a number of *zamīndārīs* in the *parganā*.[37] In 1714 one Saroman Das, son of 'Ālam Chand, apparently a Kāyastha *qānūngo*, obtained an *in'ām* (gift, revenue-free land) of 30,000 *dāms* (copper coins) in *parganā* Sānḍī, *sarkār* Khairabād for the plantation of some orchards around the town of Sānḍī. In 1716 in the same *parganā* the village of Kankhat was granted to him as *in'ām* for raising a *sarāi* (walled lodging and storehouse) and a fortress. The village was subsequently known as the *qasbā* (small town) of Saroman Nagar *alias* Kankhat.[38] In some cases difficulties were created by the Mughals and the local *chaudhurī* to force Rājpūt *zamīndārs* to sell their *zamīndārīs* to the non-Rājpūts in their caste strongholds.[39] In Banāras region the Brahmans or Bhūmihārs who as a zamīndārs caste held a strong position in Banāras district proper, seem to have been specially encouraged and united against Rājpūt rebels of the region. Indeed the policy of the local agent of the Mughal

[34] M. Alam, 'Some Aspects of the Changes in the Position of the *Madad-i Ma'āsh* holders in Awadh, 1676–1722', *PIHC* (Jādavpur, 1974), pp. 198–207.

[35] Bhūpat Rāi, *Inshā-i Roshan Kalām*, Nizāmi Press, Kānpur, n.d., pp. 7, 36.

[36] *Chronicles of Oonao*, p. 56

[37] Allāhābād Documents (Persian Records preserved at the Uttar Pradesh State Archives, Allāhābād), nos. 516, 522, 611.

[38] Ibid., nos. 2, 7, 11.

[39] Ibid., no. 536.

jāgīrdār to promote the Bhūmihārs contributed to the conditions leading to the rise of the Banārs Rāj in the eighteenth century.[40]

However, the caste factor explains only in part the inter-*zamīndārī* clashes. The internal conflict among *zamīndārs* cannot be ascribed solely to their caste and community positions. On the contrary the evidence shows a number of cases of intracaste conflict to which fellow caste men invited outside intervention to their obvious detriment. By promoting one or the other family line, the Mughals and their agents in the region thus also used, to their advantage, the difference within a caste group. Evidence illustrating a similar case comes from the Banāras region and relates to the insubordination of the Rājpūts of *parganā* (*ta'alluqā*) Thaṭra. They had refused to submit the full sum and insisted on paying according to their own assessment. In 1735 when Mansā Rām, the *mustā'jir* (revenue farmer) and *'āmil* of the region, realizing the difficulty of direct confrontation with them, engaged one Lāl Sāhī, a Rājpūt *zamīndār* of the neighbouring *parganā* of Majhwā, to maintain a virtually autonomous status in revenue matters of their district, they naturally resented this arrangement and reportedly agreed to pay the stipulated amount. But when Mansā Rām intended to remove Lāil Sahī, his son, Balwant Singh, who was to become the future Rājā of Banāras, advised him to retain Lāl Sāhī so that 'the Rājpūts fight among themselves. For whosoever is killed, it would be to our benefit'. The subsequent killings between Lāl Sāhī of Majhwā and the *zamīndārs* of Thaṭra weakened the positions of the Rājpūts of both the *maḥāls* which eventually enabled a close relative of Mansā Rām to take charge of the area.[41] Thus if on the one hand Balwant Singh's aim to weaken the Rājpūts and place a Bhūmihār in power in Thaṭra and Majhwā shows the importance of caste, the caste ties on the other hand could not prevent the Rājpūts of these two *parganās* from fighting among themselves and hastening their own destruction. Again, in Morādābād, Madār Singh, a Rājpūt, fought against Debī Chand, the Rājpūts chief of Kumāon. Similarly, the Rājpūt *zamīndār* of Rājpūr made encroachments into the territory of the Kumāon chief. There was no love lost between Kalyān Chand, the Rājpūt *zamīndār* of Kāshīpūr and

[40]Compare Kamboh, f. 5a; see also Ghūlām Ḥusain Khān, *Zikr u's-Siyar*, British Museum MS, Or. 6652, ff. 5b–7a.

[41]Kamboh, ff. 54b–55a; see also Saiyid Maẓhar Ḥusain Korwī, *Tārīkh-i Banāras* (Urdū), vol. II (Banāras, 1916), pp. 111–14.

Khemkaran, another Rājpūt rebel of the region.[42] In Awadh after the Bais Rājpūts had reconciled with Burhān u'l-Mulk, they readily fought with the governor against some of their own clansmen.[43] These are some of the complexities which militate against any unqualified and simple generalizations.

III

These uprisings cannot be generalized to embrace the entire rural community, but they certainly highlighted in very large measure the reaction of certain regional groups to the imperial power. They perhaps expressed the anger of local members of the ruling class, who did not lack in resources and were strong and rich enough to raise and maintain an army to meet the military strength of the local Mughal official. Notable in this connection is the evidence of the availability of considerable money with *zamīndārs* and in villages. In 1714, Madār Singh paid over Rs 52,000 to his Afghān soldiers out of the cash and valuables he had plundered from the villages in *parganā* Āonla in Morādābād.[44] In 1712, when Farrukh Siyar needed money on his way from Patnā to Āgrā to avenge the death of his father and contest the throne against Jahāndār Shāh, he was able to appropriate Rs 100,000 from a Banāras *zamīndār* in addition to what he obtained from the *sāhūkārs* (bankers) in the city.[45]

One indication of the prosperity of agriculture in these regions is their brisk trade. A very large number of *banjāras* (roving bands of grain and cattle merchants) carried items of trade between Bihār and Awadh in the 1730s.[46] Valuables and merchandise of the *banjārās* worth Rs 400,000 were reported to have been among the goods plundered by the *zamīndār* of *parganā* Rājpūr in Morādabād in 1715.[47] A number of new towns signifying the expanding network of local trade are also mentioned in my sources. The *zamīndārs* around these towns took as plunder, among other things, the animals

[42]*Akhbārāt*,, FS, 4th RY, I, p. 224; Lālā Awadhī Lāl, *Manṣūr u'l-Maktūbāt*, Lucknow University MS, p. 179; Qudratu'llāh 'Shauq', *Jām-i Jahan Numā*, II, p. 33.

[43]cf. *Chronicles of Oonao*, p. 75.

[44]*Akhbārāt*, FS, 3rd RY, II, p. 78.

[45]Saiyid Maẓhar Ḥusain Korwī, *Tārīkh-i Banāras*, p. 56.

[46]Karam 'Ali, *Muzaffarnāma*, BānKipore, Patna MS, ff. 11b, 25b–26a.

[47]*Akhbārāt*, FS, 4th RY, I, p. 24.

which, together with the plough, were the basic prerequisites of investment in, and extension of, agriculture.[48] At this time such animals were also the most effective means of transport on land in the countryside.[49]

Developments in the Banāras region in the late seventeenth and early eighteenth centuries are to be particularly noted in this connection. At least three large market centres for local products, namely Ā'ẓamgaṛh, Bhadohī and Mirzāpūr, came into existence and occupied an important place in the region during this period.[50]

The area under the modern district of Ā'ẓamgaṛh which formed part of the Mughal *parganā* of Niẓāmābād seems to have witnessed a considerable increase in cultivation since the time of Jahāṅgīr (1605–26). Jahāṅgīr is reported to have awarded *zamīndārīs* to the Gautam

[48]Compare Tapan Raychaudhuri and Irfan Habib (eds), *Cambridge Economic History of India,* vol. I: *c.* 1200–1750 (Cambridge, 1982), p. 84.

[49]For the importance and extensive use of animals as means of transport in trade in agricultural produce, see Irfan Habib, *Agrarian System of Mughal India,* pp. 61–3. See also *Cambridge Economic History of India*, vol. I, p. 339.

[50]Information about Ā'ẓamgaṛh in the following four paragraphs is based on the manuscript copies of a local history of the family of the Rājās of Ā'ẓamgaṛh. This history was originally written by one Gridhārī, a member of the local Kāyastha *qānūngo* family, in 1801. Gridhārī claims to have drawn for his work on the *qānūngo* papers of his ancestors. The title of his work is *Intiẓām-u'l-Rāj,* or *Intiẓam-i- Raj Ā'ẓamgarh* as the cataloguer puts it. But there is little on *intiẓām* (administration) in the book. It is a straight political and genealogical history in very involved and highly ornate Persian. The prose is interrupted by poetic compositions, sometimes from the classical Persian poets but often from Gridhārī's own compositions. A manuscript copy of the work (no. 238) is preserved in the University Library, Edinburgh.

Later, in the second half of the nineteenth century, two other histories of Ā'ẓamgaṛh (actually based on Gridhārī's work) were compiled. These are in simple, direct Persian prose style. A copy of one of these titled *Sarguẓasht-i Rājahāi Ā'ẓamgaṛh* by Saiyid Amīr 'Alī Riẓwī is preserved in the Edinburgh University Library (no. 237) while the other, titled *Tārīkh-i A'ẓamgaṛh*, is in the India Office Library (IOL), London (IO, 4038). The author of the IOL manuscript is not known. Individual references in this paper are from the IOL manuscript, as the other two manuscripts of Edinburgh are not foliated. Some information contained in these manuscripts is available in the District Gazetteers of Ā'ẓamgaṛh. Mr Najmul Raza Rizwī of Allāhābād University has also based his brief narrative of the Ā'ẓamgaṛh Rāj family on these manuscripts. Compare *PIHC,* 41st Session (Bombay, 1980), pp. 239–44.

Rājpūts of the region. He encouraged them to settle in the area and build habitats and villages for the cultivators. Subsequently a number of Gautam Rājpūts villages and *zamīndārī* settlements came up. By the beginning of Aurangzēb's reign (1658–1707) the Gautams of *parganā* Niẓāmābād were strong enough to command armed contingents, artillery and a large number of elephants and horses. They made inroads into the *zamīndārīs* of *sarkār* Gorakhpūr in the neighbourhood and levied *na'lbandī* from the peasants of *zamīndārīs.*[51] This meant that they made a bid to extend their zamīndārīs or intermediary position to parts of Gorakhpūr as well. In this they were apparently supported by the Mughals who had encountered difficulties against the erstwhile *zamīndārs* of Gorakhpūr.

Sometime during the last years of the seventeenth century, the chief of the Gautams, one Bikramājīt Singh, had to convert to Islam to avoid execution at Aurangzēb's order for a conspiracy the chief had hatched to kill his brother, Rudra Singh. Aurangzēb's order followed an appeal from the widow of the deceased. On conversion to Islam, Bikramājīt Singh married, as the tradition goes, a Mughal woman in Delhi who bore him two sons, Muḥammad A'ẓam Khān and Muḥammad 'Aẓmat Khān. Subsequently, after the death of Bikramājīt, when A'ẓam Khān succeeded him as the chief of the Gautams, he founded the town of Ā'ẓamgaṛh after his own name while his brother, 'Aẓmat Khān founded another town, 'Aẓmatgaṛh.[52] By 1720 Ā'ẓamgaṛh had grown into an important administrative centre (*chaklā* headquarters), next only to Jaunpūr in the area. A'ẓam Khān is also reported to have cut out a canal connecting the river Tons with the Kol.[53]

In the early decades of the eighteenth century, a number of bazaars and *ganjs* (grain markets) were founded by the successors of A'ẓam Khān and 'Aẓmat Khān. At almost the same time, when Mahābat Khān,

[51] *Tārīkh-i'Āẓamgaṛh*, IO, 4038, f. 15a. *Na'lbandī:* a contribution exacted by the medieval Indian ruler from petty princes or the peasantry, on the plea of keeping up the cavalry of the state or as the price of preventing the horsemen from devastating the country, from H.H. Wilson, *A Glossary of Judicial and Revenue Terms* (Delhi, reprint, 1968) p. 365.

[52] Ibid., ff. 14b–17a.

[53] Ibid., ff. 15 and 26b. *Chaklā* was a territorial division and was often identical with a *sarkār*, but in general a *chaklā* was considered a smaller unit than a *sarkār*. In Bengal, however, a *chaklā* consisted of a group of *sarkārs* in the eighteenth century. cf. Irfan Habib, *Agrarian System of Mughal India*, p. 277n.

a son of 'Aẓmat K͟hān, revolted against the Mughals, 'Aẓmat K͟hān's other son, Babū Irādat K͟hān, built a bazaar in Kopāganj. In addition, 'in a number öf places Irādat Khān founded a *ganj* after his own name'. All of these *ganjs* survived till the middle of the nineteenth century.[54] Subsequently, at least five more *ganjs* and a *zamīndārī* centre with a fortress were built by the members of these neo-Muslim Rājpūt *zamīndārs*. Irādat K͟hān's son, Jahān K͟hān, built Mahrājganj, Jahānganj and Shāhgaṛh, while his cousins, Babū Ṣūfī Bahādur, Babū Husain K͟hān and Babū Jahāngīr K͟hān, founded Sūfīganj, Husaingaj and Jahāngīr-ganj, named after themselves.[55]

The growth of A'ẓamgaṛh into a *chaklā* headquarters together with the founding of these *ganjs* or grain markets must have followed a substantial increase in commercialized agriculture and the prosperity of *zamīndārs*. In the same period of development, however, Mughal imperial authority in the Banāras region was seriously jeopardized by the revolts of Mahābat K͟hān and the other *zamīndārs* of Ā'ẓamgaṛh.[56] The rebels could finally be subdued only when they totally failed against the artillery of Sa'ādat Khān, Burhān u'l-Mulk, the founder of the Awadh *nawābī*.[57] The strength of the region can also be conjectured from the nineteenth-century legend of Mahābat K͟hān's brave and ar-rogant reply to the emperor's *shuqqa* (letter) admonishing him to refrain from 'recalcitrance'.[58]

Bhadohī was another important town in the Banāras region which came into prominence in the early eighteenth century. Around Bhadohī too, successive village settlements began to grow from the time of Jahāngīr. I have found references to no less than 12 villages having come up in the immediate vicinity of the town from a quick survey of an early nineteenth-century local history. This history, it may be noted,

---

[54]Ibid., f. 26b.

[55]Ibid., ff. 27.

[56]*Akhbārāt*, FS, 3rd RY, II, pp. 23 and 268 for *zamīndār* uprising in *parganā* Niẓāmābād and Ā'ẓamgaṛh.

[57]*Tārikh-i-Ā'ẓamgaṛh*, ff. 24. It was the cannons of the governor of Awadh which forced Mahābat and other *zamīndārs* to submit to him. The title of Burhan-u'l-Mulk in the perception of these 'rustic' Gautams was 'Bharbhunja'.

[58]Ibid., f. 24a. According to this, Mahābat's reply to the emperor's *shuqqa* was very brief and ran as follows:

If his Majesty has suddenly decided to fight [let us fight] in the name of God, and if your Excellency likes peace, God bless you.

The brave ones do not turn their faces from fighting anyone.

Here is the battlefield, there is the playground and here is the ball.

was purportedly written to highlight, and establish the claims to, the powers and properties of just one family of the town.[59] A number of *maḥallās* are mentioned as having been settled and inhabited by immigrants during the seventeenth century. Some members of a *qānūngo* of Kaṛā, for example, who had earlier migrated to Jaunpūr, came and settled in Bhadoḥī in Shāhjahān's time. The same years saw the rise of a *maḥallā* inhabited by the Fārūqī Shaikhs of Manḍiān. Towards the end of Aurangzēb's reign the Malik family of Rāmpūr came in and founded *maḥallā* Malikāna.[60] At least four important bazaars of the town, namely Bazaar Ṣalābat Khān, Bazaar Rustam Khān, Bazaar Aḥmadganj and Kaṭrā (marketplace) Rusukhiat Khān, were founded during the 25 years between 1712 and 1737.[61]

The growth of Mirzāpūr in the late seventeenth century with its central position, second only to Banāras in the economy of the region during the eighteenth and early nineteenth centuries, further shows that the explanation of *zamīndār* revolts also lay in their wealth and increased strength. We know very little of the antecedents of the founding of the town. But the little available information does suggest that the hinterlands of Mirzāpūr responded to the demands of regional and perhaps also long-distance trade. According to the *Tārīkh-i-Bhadohīn*, one Mirzā 'Abd u'l-Bāqi Bēg was sent to the area sometime in the last years of Aurangzēb (when the emperor was in the Deccan) to deal with the rebel *zamīndārs* of *parganā* Kāntit. The Mirzā was welcomed by the Omars, a local merchant community, and they also appear to have assisted him in his campaigns against the *zamīndārs*. Subsequently, following the emperor's order, the chief of the Omar community, Nand Lāl Omar, founded a town on the bank of the Ganges and named it after the Mirzā. Soon after, Mirzāpur was linked to the trade between the region and beyond *mandvī* (market) Phūlpūr and Banāras. By the time of Muḥammad Shāh, Mirzāpūr had grown into a major town with a large *kaṭrā* in its centre and at least three *ganjs*, Muzaffarganj, Lālganj and Munnūganj, in its vicinity to connect it with its rural hinterlands. The town like the other big towns of the Mughal empire, had a full-fledged *shahṇā/kotwāl* (superintendent of markets/chief police official)

[59]Qāẓī Muḥammad Sharīf of Bhadohīn, *Tārīkh-i Bhadohīn*, U37, India Office Library, compiled in 1847.

[60]Ibid., ff. 9, 11, 14b, 15a, 16b, 17b, 19a.

[61]Ibid., ff. 21b, 26, 30b.

in Muḥammad Shāh's time.[62] It is very likely that the trade of Mirzāpūr provided a major incentive for the subsequent clearance of jungles and extension of agriculture around Latīfpūr and Ahraurā under Balwant Singh and Chait Singh, the Rājās of Banāras.[63]

Some general references, even though scattered and irritatingly brief, to the prosperity of the city of Banāras are notable, In 1740 the city, according to an eyewitness account, had large numbers of the community of *mahājans* (money-changers). Two of them, Gopāldās and Gowāldās, controlled the bulk of the monetary transactions of the city. Gowāldās was very rich but, since he had financed Mīr Rustam 'Alī Khān whom Mansā Rām, the founder of the Banāras Rāj, had replaced as the chief *mustā'jir* of the region, he lost his position under Balwant Singh to Gopāldās. Subsequently, he allegedly involved himself in a plot to assassinate the Rājā, was captured, and released only when he agreed to pay the Rājā a sum of Rs 5,00,000. Initially, Balwant Singh demanded Rs 10,00,000 and it was on Gopāldās's intercession that the amount was reduced to Rs 5,00,000, which Gowāldās paid within a week's time. Gopāldās is mentioned as the sole financier of the Banāras Rāj. At his accession to the Rāj, Balwant paid at least Rs 24,00,000 annually to the Nawāb of Awadh while towards the end of his time the revenues of Banāras had certainly gone up to over Rs 50,00,000. By the middle of the eighteenth century (1752–3), Banāras city was noted in particular for its wealth and money (*anqusht numā ba farāwānī-e-zar*).[64]

[62]Ibid., ff. 37b–38. For Lālganj and Munnūganj, see Ghulām 'Ali Khān, *Shāh 'Ālam Nāma*, ed. Al-Māmūn Suhruwardī and Āqā Muḥammad Kāẓim Shīrāzī, Bib. Ind. (Calcutta, 1874), p. 87.

[63]Ghulām Ḥusain Khān, *Zikr u's-Siyar*, ff. 22a, 26b–27a, 31–7. For a comprehensive study of the growth of the towns, grain markets and their links to agricultural production in the Banāras region in the later half of the eighteenth century, see C.A. Bayly, *Rulers, Townsmen and Bazaars: North Indian Society in the Age of British Expansion, 1770–1870* (Cambridge University Press, 1983), chs 2–5. See also K.P. Mishra, *Banaras in Transition, 1738–1795*, (Delhi, 1975), pp. 93–167.

[64]*Zikr u's-Siyar*, ff. 65b, 70b, 71a. The descendants of Gopāldās and Gowāldās survived to continue as leading *mahājans* of Banāras in the late eighteenth century. C.A Bayly, 'Indian Merchants in Traditional Setting: 1780–1830', in Clive Dewey and A.G. Hopkins, *The Imperial Impact: Studies in the Economic History of Africa and India* (London, 1978), pp. 171–93; K.P. Mishra, *Banaras in Transition*, pp. 172–4.

The prosperity of the city of Banāras certainly owed a great deal to its leading position as an entrepôt for the medium-level and long-distance trade. The geographical location of Banāras in the intra- and inter-region trade also encouraged local industries, which in turn further enriched the city. The extent of the percolation of the city's wealth to the countryside in our period is a matter for conjecture, but there is ample evidence of this for the later period.[65] It is, however, interesting to recognize that in a period of ten years in the middle of Muḥammad Shāh's reign, 1731–41, the revenues from the *khāliṣa* from *parganā ḥavelī* Banāras rose from Rs 42, 248–7½ in 1731 and Rs 49,246–7½ in 1737 to Rs 77,000 in 1741. What is significant is the fact that in nine out of these ten years the actual collections were 100 per cent of the *jama'* (assessed revenues), and that reasons for shortfall in 1740 were purely administrative.[66] The rise in state demand had a bearing on the prosperity of intermediaries, specially when there is evidence to show that the amount paid to the treasury during this period was sometimes much less than what they actually collected from the assesses. According to Ghulām Husain Kamboh, in the late 1720s and early 1730s, Mansā Rām, as a *mustā'jir* of the *parganās* which later formed the core of the Banāras Rāj, paid only Rs 5,00,000 while his actual collection was no less than Rs 20,00,000.[67] This gap probably explains how within a decade Mansā Rām so easily built up enough power to displace his Mughal patron. When the region came under the control of Burhān u'l-Mulk he demanded and obtained Rs 13,00,000 for the same *parganās*, while his successor, Ṣafdar Jang, insisted on a still higher sum from Mansā Rām's son, Rājā Balwant Singh.[68] Far from being an index of the actual state of production, the rise and fall in the revenues in a number of cases probably simply showed the strength or weakness of the collector. With the change of the collector or the terms dictating his position, there was sometimes a very substantial rise in the revenues.[69]

[65]C.A. Bayly, *Rulers, Townsmen and Bazaars*, ch. 2.

[66]*Kaifiyat-i Jama '-Maḥālāt-i Khāliṣa*, I.O., 4491.

[67]Kamboh, f. 45a.

[68]*Tuḥfa*, ff. 10a–11b; Kamboh, f. 65b.

[69]IO, 4491 for increase from Rs 49,246–7 1/2 in 1146 *faṣlī* to Rs 75,000 in 1147 with a change from the *'āmilī* of one 'Abd u'r-Raḥīm to the *ta'ahhud* of one Mīr 'Abdu'llāh. It may be noted that 'Abd u'r-Raḥīm collected (or submitted from his collections) only Rs 17,000 in 1146 *faṣlī*.

Region	*Jama'* in *dāms* in the *Ā'īn*	Jama' in *dāms* in the early and mid-18th century	
Awadh	20,17,58,172	37,46,74,559 (rose by 17,29,16,387)	*c.* 1755
Banāras	8,45,05,384	17,51,27,980 (rose by 9,06,22,596)	*c.* 1720
Morādābād–Bareilly	10,17,58,494	35,35,07,068 (rose by 25,17,48,574)	*c.* 1750

That agriculture in the regions under study registered a marked development in the course of the seventeenth and early eighteenth centuries is illustrated from a comparison of the available revenue figures of the early and mid-eighteenth century with those of the late sixteenth century as recorded by Abu'l Fazl in the *Ā'īn-i-Akbarī*. The rise in *jama'* since the time of the Ā'īn (1595) was spectacular. In Awadh the *jama'* rose by over 85 per cent, in the Banāras region by over 107 per cent, while in the Morādābād–Bareilly region the rise, according to my figures, was almost incredibly over 247 per cent.[70] The spectacular rise in the *jama'* figures could possibly be easily explained in terms of the influx of the precious white metal and the consequent rise in prices, if only one had the prices of foodgrains and other commodities for these regions in the seventeenth and early eighteenth centuries. But since the figures for such contiguous areas as Awadh and the Morādābād–Bareilly region varied so radically, we can presume that the rise in *jama'* had

[70]For *Ā'īn*'s figures, see ibid., vol. II (Jarrett's trans.), pp. 173–6, 184, 293–6. For the eighteenth-century figures, compare IO, 4485, 4487 and 4489. The break-up of the figures for the Morādābād–Bareilly and Banāras regions in my sources is as follow:

Region		*Jama'* in *dāms* in the *Ā'in*	*Jama'* in *dāms* in the early and mid-18th century	
1		2	3	
Sarkār	Sambhal	6,69,41,431	21,16,82,068	*c.* 1750
-	Badāon	3,48,17,063	14,18,25,000	
-	Jaunpūr	5,63,94,107	9,27,02,303	*c.* 1720
-	Ghāzīpūr	1,34,31,308	3,42,30,204	
-	Chūnār	58,10,654	2,88,36,578	
-	Banāras	88,69,315	1,93,38,895	

a bearing on the increase in agricultural production too. We can not, also, overlook the evidence of new settlements in some parts of the regions under review.[71]

The *ḥāṣil* (collection) figures, whether taken as representing the actual yields or as the revenues collected by state officials, also show that the *jama'* figures bore a relationship to the actual production and the paying capacity of the assessees. The *ḥāṣil* in Awadh was 63 per cent of the *jama'* while in Banāras and Morādābād–Bareilly the *ḥāṣil* figures ranged between 84 per cent and 86 per cent of the assessed revenues. Over a number of years in Aurangzēb's reign, even in Awadh, in most of the *maḥāls*, the *ḥāṣil* approximated the *jama'* figures, while in some *parganās* the former also exceeded the latter.[72]

The *ḥāṣil* figures probably showed more clearly the ability of the Mughals to collect from intermediaries. In this context it is interesting to note that in most of the revenue papers of north India which the indigenous officials prepared for the East India Company, they mentioned the *jama'dāmi,* together with the maximum of the collections (*ḥāṣil shud*) and the minimum of what was estimated to be collected in a year (*jama'-i sāl tamām*) since about the middle of the seventeenth century. As the East India Company officials experienced special problems with the *zamīndārs* in Bengāl, they might have insisted on getting all these figures and also the reasons—such as war, drought or flood (*āfāt-i arẓī-o-samāwī*)—if any, for the shortfall. In other words, the difference between the minimum of *sāl-i tamām* and the maximum of the *ḥāṣil shud* if not explained in terms of reductions due to war, famine, drought and flood, etc. indicated the range of the revenues appropriated by the *zamīndār* in addition to his customary perquisites and *mālikāna.* Significantly, the resistance of *zamīndārs* to the Mughals expressed itself initially in their bid to 'misappropriate' revenues collected from the peasants (*zar-i maḥsūl rā mutaṣarrif mī shawand*).

Against this background it is interesting to note the *qānūngos*' reported answer to Burhān u'l-Mulk's enquiry about the state of agriculture in Baiswāṛa. According to one tradition, early in Muḥammad Shāh's reign when Nawāb Burhān u'l-Mulk took over charge of Awadh

[71]For some such evidence, see M. Alam, 'The Mughal Centre and the *Sūbas* of Awadh and the Punjab, 1707–1748', ch. 3.

[72]IO, 4489 and 4485. However, the fact that the *ḥāṣil* figures in most of the cases included not only the collections of the current year but also the arrears of the past and the repayment of the *taqāvī* should not be overlooked while considering the relationship these figures bore to the assessed revenues.

as its governor, he made a tour of Baiswāṛa in a bid to deal with the turbulent *zamīndārs* and set right the revenue administration. When he summoned the local *qānūngos* and asked for the revenue roll, the latter enquired as to which revenue roll the nawāb wanted, 'the man's' or 'the coward's'. On being asked the meaning of their answer, they explained that there were two figures which a *qānūngo* could give. In a 'coward's roll', against every landowner's name was written only the sum which had been fixed for him at the last assessment, but in the 'man's roll' everyone's rent was indicated on the basis of what it should have been, taking into account the improvement that had taken place in land. Burhān u'l-Mulk asked for the 'man's roll' and, on that basis, doubled the assessment.[73]

In this connection some early European observations on the soil conditions of these regions are worth noting. Northern Rohilkhand, the central districts of Awadh around Lucknow and Faiẓābād and the alluvial tracts along the river Ganges between Chunār and Banāras down towards Buxar, were noted by Europeans in the eighteenth century as some of the most fertile and populated parts of the whole subcontinent. The Banāras region was exceptionally rich and had much in common with contemporary Bengāl. Cultivation in central and southern Awadh could be resumed without much capital as the soil was moderately light and fertile, and the water table was not so low as to make the cost of irrigation prohibitive. In the Banāras region good natural irrigation was also available for watering the *rabī'* crops while parts of the Morādābād–Bareilly region profited splendidly from spring torrents 'which rushed down into the plains from the foothills of the

[73] *Chronicles of Oonao*, p. 73. The story, besides showing the *qānūngos'* loyalty to Mughal authority, throws considerable light on the nature of the relations between the big and powerful *zamīndārs* and the peasants. The Ujjainiya intermediaries of Bihār are also reported to have enjoyed over a fairly long period the benefits of the gap between the *tahṣīl*, which went on increasing and the *jama'-i dami*, which remained constant. Compare S̤. Nurul Hasan, *Thoughts of Agrarian Relations in Mughal India*, (Delhi, 1973), p. 35. The same situation seems to have prevailed in Bengāl. According to the *Risāla-i Zarā'at*, no assessment was made since the days of Akbar and the *jama'- i tashkhīsh* in most of the districts registered many fold increase over the *jama'-i ṭūmār* by the beginning of the eighteenth century. cf. *Rīsāla-i Zarā'at*, Edinburgh University Library MS no. 144, ff. 8b–9a. But the evidence of the *Risāla-i Zarā'at* regarding the absence of assessment is to be accepted with reservations. Some figures available in, for instance, British Museum, Add. 6586 and 6599 for the seventeenth century suggest substantial increase in the *jama'* of the province.

Himalayas'.[74] It is also significant that European merchants rushed to these regions following the East India Company's victory over the Nawāb of Awadh in 1764 at Buxar. The growth of exports from these regions to Bengāl was 'spectacular' in response to 'the great expansion' of Calcutta's seaborne trade in the late eighteenth century.[75]

In the regions under study, the initiative for the rural resistance against imperial power appears to have come from *zamīndārs*. Rich and strong as they were, they endeavoured to control the region with the objective of having some kind of autonomy, or at least a greater share in the revenue. But their success depended on their assuming the leadership of the region by binding together different local communities in their bid to take over power from the Mughals. This they were unable to achieve. Their social distinctions seldom allowed them to rise jointly as a local challenge to imperial power. Again, if they struck the Mughals, they also let loose terror among the traders, the townsfolk

[74]Compare C.A. Bayly, *Rulers, Townsmen and Bazaars*, ch. 2.

[75]Compare P.J. Marshall, 'Economic and Political Expansion: The Case of Oudh', *Modern Asian Studies*, 9, 4 (1975), pp. 465–82; Tom G. Kessinger in his article on the northern Indian economy (1757–1857) also notes expansion of production and trade in the region in response to the stimulus which came from the demand for export goods. cf. Dharma Kumar and Meghnad Desai (eds), *The Cambridge Economic History of India*, vol. II: *c*. 1957–*c*. 1770. (Cambridge University Press, 1983), pp. 242–70. Almost the entire northern Indian region east of Delhi seems to have responded positively to this stimulus. For some evidence about Aligarh and Etah regions, see S. Nurul Hasan's comments on 'Du Jardin Papers', *The Indian Historical Review*, V, 1–2 (July 1978–January 1979). See also T. Raychaudhuri and Irfan Habib (eds), *Cambridge Economic History of India*, I, pp. 177–8 and Dharma Kumar and Meghnad Desai, *Cambridge Economic History*, II, Introduction, for T. Raychaudhuri's remarks about the mid-eighteenth century social and economic conditions. But these qualifications do not substantially alter the general framework of the history of the Mughal Indian agrarian economy in *Cambridge Economic History of India*, I. cf. Harbans Mukhia's review of vol. I in *IESHR*, 21, no. 1, 1984. But just as Awadh, Banāras and parts of Rohilkhand were developing in our period, large areas of the Mughal heartland were declining or were, at least, developing less fast. I have discussed the economic decline of Punjab and the consequent political instability in the province in 'The Mughal Centre and the Ṣūbas of Awadh and the Punjab', ch. 5. C.A. Bayly mentions the relative decline of sales of Bayāna indigo, the decline of the Persian market for Punjab cloth and the gullying and the decline of the water table in the Jamuna. He also notes the silting of the canals north of Delhi and the consequences of early Jāt disturbances at the emperor's back-door in *Rulers, Townsmen and Bazaars*, pp. 84–92 and 156–7.

and even the *zamīndārs* and peasants of other castes. The peasants of the other castes not only became victims of the *zamīndārs*' raids, but sometimes also sought protection from and fought with the Mughals against them. In Morādābād, *banjārās* became victims of their raids while in the Banāras region, in a bid to blockade the passage of the Bengāl treasury from Paṭna through Banāras and Allāhābād to Delhi, they also plundered and killed traders and wayfarers.

Numerous cases of this are illustrated from the *Akhbārāt* relating to Awadh. The *zamīndārs* attacked the offices of *qazis* (justices) as well as *madrasas* (colleges) and mosques, and created panic among the town dwellers. Their raids could in part be explained in terms of their fury against the *madad-i ma'āsh* holders, who they regarded as the local representatives and symbols of imperial power. But when they pulled down orchards and set towns on fire, they also terrorized traders and artisans and thus destroyed some of the major ingredients of the region's strength. Perhaps they also saw the traders—some of whom certainly linked the regions of the empire and thus created and fostered the necessity of imperial unity—as serving the interests of imperial power. All the more so because members of certain trading communities were closely associated with Mughal administraion.[76]

I have no evidence to show the reaction of urban sections to the uprisings in these regions. But it is interesting that in another region of north India, traders and artisans stood on the Mughal side. The traders perhaps saw their interests tied up with the Mughal system. The Mughals had provided some uniformity in different regions, and their revenue system had also created markets for different goods—to the extent that Irfan Habib suggests the possibility of the commercial structure and urban growth of the seventeenth century parasitical, or 'depending upon a system of direct agrarian exploitation by a small ruling class'.[77]

[76]See. M. Alam, 'The Mughal Centre and the *Ṣūbas* of Awadh and the Punjab, 1707–1748', ch. 4, for some such evidence about the Punjābī Khatrīs and a few northern Indian Baniyās.

[77]Irfan Habib, 'Potentialities of Capitalistic Development in the Economy of Mughal India', *Enquiry*, New Series, III, 3 (Winter 1971), p. 55:.see also M. Athar Ali, 'The Passing of Empire: The Mughal Case', *Modern Asian Studies*, 9, 3 (1975), pp. 389–90. But *Zikr u's-Siyar's* evidence about the relationship between the Rājās of Banāras and Gopāldās shows a different trend. Compare ff. 65b, 70b and 71a. C.A. Bayly also mentions a growing relationship between smaller local merchant communities and the emerging ruling *zamīndārs* in the late eighteenth century. cf. *Rulers, Townsmen and Bazaars*, ch. 2.

The *zamīndār* revolts, in a number of cases in the regions under review, had no bearing on the decline in the agricultural produce and its markets. It appears that it was in the wake of their prosperity and enrichment following the region's integration into the wider area in the seventeenth century that these *zamīndārs* found themselves strong enough to rise against the Mughals, asking for greater share in political power and produce in the area under their control. Their enrichment disturbed the existing rural relations and also emboldened them to give express and violent form to their conflict with imperial Delhi. This aspect of the history of the regions and the communities in revolt tends to be overlooked when we examine the problem with an objective of explaining only the decline of the Mughal empire. The Mughal decline perspective has prevented us from going out of the confines of the Mughal empire into the regions to look for the causes of the turmoil or stability in different parts of the empire. We have tended to remain imprisoned within the precincts of the empire to locate the causes of the developments in the region in terms of either the decisions and policies of the emperors or the structural flaws in the Mughal system.

In the cases where their enrichment enabled the *zamīndārs* to be up in arms, they not only led the poor peasants' resistance, capitalizing only on the latter's grievances against the Mughal ruling class, but also took the initiative in mobilizing the peasants for their own political ends. Their success depended on the strength of their kinsfolk in the region. But as they relied on support from their caste, their position as 'local despots' and leaders of the region was crippled. The strength of these rebel *zamīndārs* was impaired by divisions within the *zamīndār* class. Since their goal was limited, narrow and parochial, they were unable to appreciate that it was the region's economic strength which enabled them to rise against the Mughals effectively and that only by incorporating the interests of the different regional groups in their programmes could they fight for themselves successfully. Thus, not only the peasants of the other castes, but also the townsmen and traders became victims of their raids, even if their actions emanated from the aspirations of the region to become independent of imperial control. These *zamīndārs* remained leaders of only their own communities. Often they could not think beyond their goal of limited political power and a share in the revenues and therefore were unable to destroy the Mughal system and establish a viable regions power on their own. The political formations in these regions in the eighteenth century were thus not only within the Mughal institutional framework but also under the aegis of the Mughal nobles or their protégés.[78]

[78]Professors Satish Chandra and S. Nurul Hasan were generous with their time to discuss the sources and questions relating to this paper. Dr C.A. Bayly, N. Bhattacharya, Professors S. Bhattacharya and Romila Thapar commented on an earlier draft of this paper. I am grateful to all of them.

Persian words, names and place names drawn from Persian sources have been transliterated in this paper according to the system followed by F. Steingass in his *Comprehensive Persian–English Dictionary.* I have used ṛ and ṭ to represent the harder sounds in Hindi.

17
Two Frontier Uprisings in Mughal India*[1]

Gautam Bhadra

INTRODUCTION

The existence of a long tradition of peasant and tribal uprisings in India is now a well-recognized fact.[2] These uprisings are no longer ignored by historians as a subject not worthy of study. Perhaps the political role played by peasants in the nationalist and communist movements in the Third World during this century as well as the programme of agrarian revolution initiated by their radical leaders, have forced historians of all political persuasions to revalue a hitherto submerged and neglected tradition. Some historians, however, are attempting to appropriate this tradition of peasant resistance on behalf of the ruling élites of Third World countries. The polemics have already begun.[3]

*First published in Ranajit Guha (ed.), *Subaltern Studies*, vol. II (Delhi, 1984).

[1]I am grateful to Mrs Mandira Sen and Maulavi M.A. Quddus for their help and suggestions. The sketch map of the Mughal north-eastern frontier where the rebellions occurred, is based on Rennell's *Bengal Atlas* (1779) and the district map of Kamrup with additional information from *Kamrupār Buranji* and *Baharistan*. I am indebted to Mrs Keya Dasgupta for drawing the map.

[2]One of the earliest works is W.C. Smith, 'Lower Class Uprisings in the Mughal Empire', *Islamic Culture* (1946). For the best available general introduction to the subject, see Irfan Habib, *Agrarian System of Mughal India* (Bombay, 1963), ch. IX. My article in Bengali, 'Mughal Juge Krishok Vidroha' ('Peasant Uprisings in Mughal India') *Ekshan*, Autumn Number (1385 BS).

[3]Eric Stokes, 'The Return of the Peasant of South History', in *The Peasant and the Raj* (Delhi, 1978). For a review of this book, see Gyanendra Pandey, 'A View of the Observable etc.', *Journal of Peasant Studies*, 7:3 (1980). Also see Joy Mukhopadhyay, 'Bharate Krishok Bidroher Itihas Lekhar Samasya' ('Problems of Writing the History of Peasant Uprisings in India': in Bengali), *Deshapremik*, Autumn Number (1387 BS).

Before we can understand the dynamics of such resistance movements throughout the Third World, I suggest that we begin with an analysis of what took place in our own countries and with this in mind I propose to discuss two frontier uprisings in Mughal India.

In order to avoid certain misconceptions, let me point out that I do not pretend to have discovered any new material. The source materials used in this study are well known to the scholars of Mughal India. Again, so far as the scope of the study is concerned, my treatment is not comprehensive but selective. I have chosen to examine one region—Kamrup–Goalpara in north-eastern India. This is partly because of the availability of sources and partly because important political developments in this region have once again brought it to our attention at the present. In this essay, after analysing the two revolts separately, I will consider their overall importance to the evolving Mughal polity in the context of the problems of integration and domination and of subjection and defiance.

The Revolt of Sanatan Sardar

The revolt of Sanatan Sardar occurred during Jahangir's reign.[4] During this time the Mughals were expanding their empire in eastern India, and there were numerous revolts throughout Kuch Bihar and on the borders of Assam.[5] This revolt originally started at Khuntaghat, situated on the south bank of the Brahmaputra and within the present district

[4]The principal source is *Baharistan-i-Ghaybi* by Mirza Nathan, a contemporary Mughal general, who participated in all the major campaigns in the north-eastern region during the reign of Jahangir. I have consulted the transcribed copy of the only existing manuscript in the Bibliothèque Nationale, Paris, preserved in the Jadunath Sarkar Collection, National Library, Calcutta. All subsequent references for pagination given in this article are to this copy of the Sarkar Collection (nos. 61–3) cited henceforth as *Baharistan (Sarkar)*. M.I. Borah has made a reliable translation of the same text in Borah, *Baharistan-i-Ghaybi*, 2 vols (Gauhati, 1936). Notes appended to this translation have been extremely helpful. References to this work are cited below as Borah, I–II.

[5]For a general description of Mughal expansion in this region during the period, see Jadunath Sarkar (ed.) *The History of Bengal*, vol. II (reprint, Patna, 1973), *passim;* Sudhindra Nath Bhattacharya, *Mughal North-East Frontier Policy* (Calcutta, 1929). An account of the rebellion of Sanatan Paik has been given in E.W. Gait, *A History of Assam* (Calcutta, 1926). It is inaccurate and confused in the sequence of events.

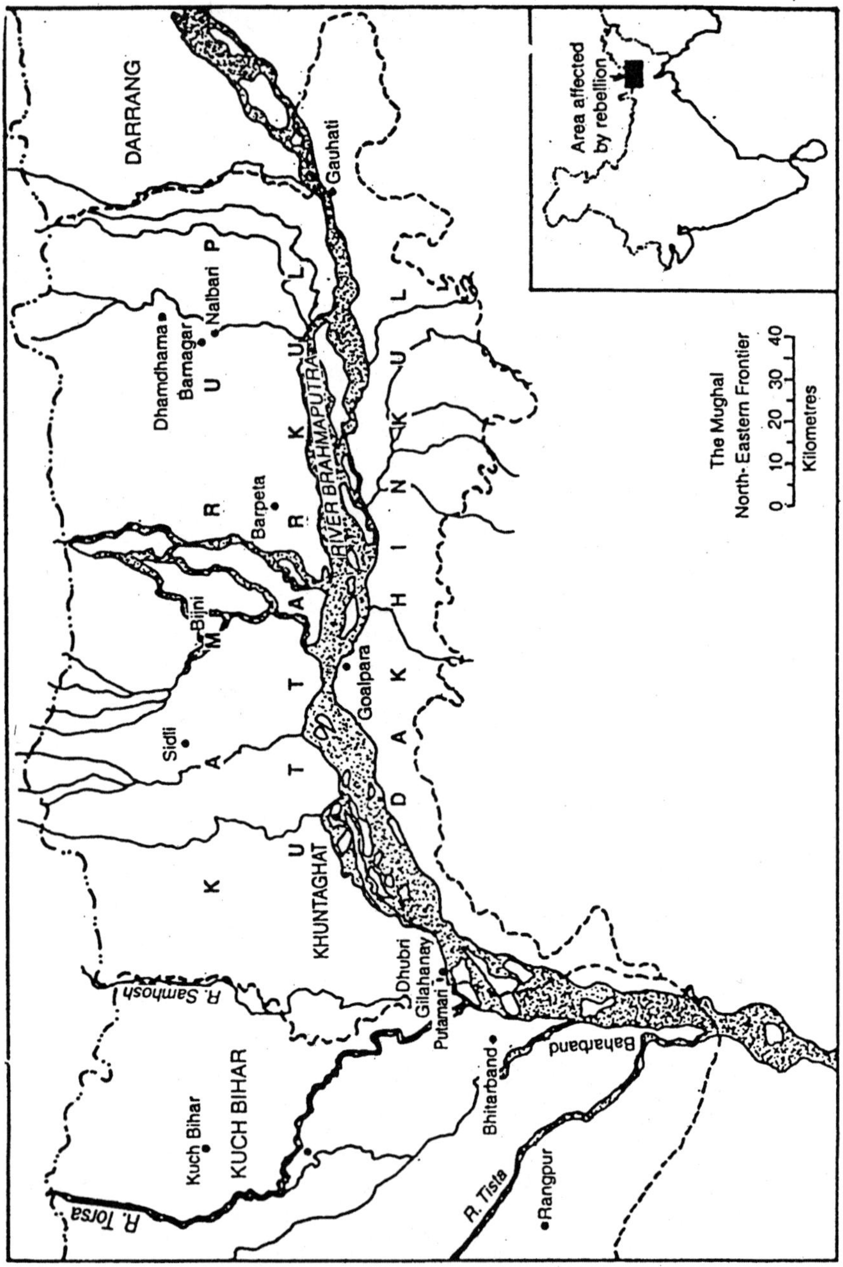

The Mughal North-Eastern Frontier

of Goalpara (AD 1614). It spread later to Kamrup, where Sanatan, a headman of the *paiks*, emerged as its leader (AD 1615).[6]

The immediate context of the revolt was the Mughal annexation of Kuch Bihar and Kamrup. The death of the governor, Islam Khan, shortly thereafter led to the appointment of Qasim Khan in his place. Qasim Khan inaugurated a new administrative system in the conquered territories. Under his direction, Mirza Hasan divided the *parganas* of Kuch Bihar into 20 clearly defined circles. Muhammad Zaman Tabrizi was appointed the *karori* (revenue collector) of the *pargana* of Khuntaghat. *Karoris* were revenue officers who collected revenue from the conquered area. Apart from the *karoris*, Mirza Hasan also appointed *mustajirs* or revenue farmers and received the bond *(qubuliat)* from them for the *parganas* given to them.

As the *karori* of Khuntaghat *pargana*, Muhammad Zaman Tabrizi began to tyrannize the peasants *(raiyat)* and abducted their beautiful daughters and sons for his harem. The peasants killed him by poisoning,[7] took action against other *karoris* and *mustajirs* who continued to misappropriate vast sums. Shaykh Ibrahim, the *karori* at Kamrup, for instance, increased his wealth by nearly seven lakh rupees. The extent

[6]In the text, these *paiks* are called archers *(paikan yani tirandazan): Baharistan (Sarkar)*, vol. II, f. 152a. In another place, it is said that Raja Parikshit of Kamrup fought the Mughals with the *kandi paiks* or the archers: *Baharistan (Sarkar)*, vol. I, f. 115a. *Kandi* may be derived from the term *kari*, i.e. archers. In local dialect '*kar*' means arrow: see glossary appended to *Thangkhungiya Buranji*, edited and translated by S. K. Bhuyan (Calcutta, 1933), p. 237. Also see *Baharistan (Sarkar)*, vol. II, ff. 146b.

[7]*Baharistan (Sarkar)*, vol. II, no. 62, 146a–146b; Borah, I, pp. 272–3. In the course of a description of black magic and sorcery as practised by the inhabitants of this region, Mirza Nathan mentions some details to show how the petty exactions and oppressions of local officials such as *dihidars* and *pattadars* (tenure holders or revenue farmers) created an atmosphere of antagonism there. The demand for fish at midnight when fish was not available and the use of violence and torture in order to force the subjects to satisfy the whims of the bailiffs had, according to Nathan, compelled the peasants to use 'black magic' against them. That the Mughal officials came to attribute magical faculties to the local population is itself an index of the mistrust which developed between them and their new rulers. The latter were, as a result, always haunted by a sense of uncertainty and fear. After Muhammad Zaman's death Salim Beg Khaksar, Mirza Babu and a Brahmin (*zunnar-dar*, i.e. holder of the sacred thread) named Raja Ram were sent there as *mustajirs*. None had a very creditable record with the people.

and nature of these revenue abuses perpetrated on the newly annexed areas can be gauged from contemporary records. In *Baharistan*, there is a description of the changes introduced by the Mughals, which also enables us to gain some idea of the pre-Mughal system of administration. Hence it deserves to be quoted in full:

> After Rajah Lakshminarayan's departure Mir Safi . . . introduced a number of changes in the revenue assessment of all the parganas of Jahangirabad and the allowances made in the form of salaries for the *paiks*, that is, archers *(mujrai' ulf-e paikan yani tirandazan)* of this area were also charged to revenue assessment *(bar jama' i' afzuda)*.
>
> Owing to his lack of intelligence, he did not pay any heed to the discord in the region and the sedition of the cultivators and considered himself to be loyal . . . . One portion of the parganas was handed over to the *karoris* and another portion to the *mustajirs*. Then he left them after making necessary A arrangements for each of them. When the *mustajirs* after a slight increase in assessment *(juzw-e bar jama' afzuda)* brought the *parganas* under their own possession and thought of increasing it more for their own benefit and expenses *(bar nafa' wa ikhrajat)*, it augmented the causes of discontent among the *ri'aya*.[8]

Mir Safi was, however, removed from the office of *Diwan* and *Bakshi* in Kamrup owing to several complaints against him; but despite this the situation did not improve much.

After the annexation of the north-eastern kingdoms the Mughals had not taken any direct action against the princes of this region. Islam Khan and Qasim Khan had promised to maintain the dignity of Lakshminarayan, king of Kuch Bihar, and Parikshitnarayan, king of Kamrup. But in blatant violation of his promise, Qasim Khan placed Lakshminarayan and Parikshitnarayan under surveillance *(nazr band)* and deported them to the distant court of the Mughal emperor. This action roused the nobles and exacerbated tension leading to the outbreak of the revolt at Khuntaghat. During 1615–16 the peasants killed the *karoris* and *mustajirs*. The Kuch nobles joined their rebellion and proclaimed one of themselves as the *raja*. The Mughal commander Allama Beg was killed along with many of his soldiers. The rebels occupied the land up to Rangamati and besieged Jahangirabad, formerly Gilahanay (about ten miles north of Dhubri),the principal administrative centre, and the fortified residence of King Parikshit. Mughal authority almost disappeared from this region.[9] Mirza Yusuf Barlas, *thanadar*

[8] *Baharistan (Sarkar)*, vol. II. no. 62, 152a; cf. Borah, I, pp. 288–9. This description has been corroborated by the Assamese sources, S.K. Bhuyan (ed.) *Kamrupār Buranji* (Calcutta, 1930), p. 27.

from Dakhinkul, south Kamrup, described the helplessness of the Mughal army pleading for immediate help and pointing out that without aid he and his forces would suffer the same fate as Allama Beg's army had:

This is a serious uprising of the enemies and they are driving us from place to place. They have not stopped chasing us and we have been driven back to the bank of the Brahmaputra. For the third day, we are encamped on the sandy plains and we are besieged by the enemy in such a way that even a straw was not available for horses, not to speak of grains.[10]

The rebels were finally defeated by their own vacillation and the strategy of Mirza Nathan. But it was not a lasting defeat. Despite the imprisonment of the rebel leader and the destruction of their forts at Putamari and Takunia, the peasants of Khuntaghat were not effectively subdued. They continued to offer resistance, especially during the rainy season when Mughal communication links were weakened and Mirza Nathan was absent.

It was at this moment that Sanatan, the Kuch chief of the *paiks*, began to harass the *karori*, Shaykh Ibrahim, and declared his revolt in Kamrup.

Sanatan, one of the Kuchs in the area of Kamrup assumed kingship *(Sanatan ke yek-i az kuchan dar mulk-e Kamrup ba rajgi bardashta)* and put Shaykh Ibrahim to great straits.[11]

The *paiks* alleged that 'Shaykh Ibrahim not only put us to distress but also takes away the beautiful girls and handsome boys of our families and he is persisting in doing this'.[12]

The Mughal army, under the leadership of Mirza Nathan, was ineffective against Sanatan due to his alliance with the local peasants. The Mughals failed to occupy the *paik*'s fort, Dhamdhama, which was situated in the Nalbari *pargana* of Kamrup. Mirza Nathan sent proposals for peace, with the assurance that Shaykh Ibrahim would be dismissed. Sanatan's reply has been preserved in the writing of Mirza Nathan. As the voice of a rebel leader, it is a very important document:

The oppression perpetuated in this region you have been informed of. Now the cultivators (*ri'aya*) have no strength or capacity *(qudrat wa taqat)* to pay attention to sending revenue (*malguzari*). So how can your coming here satisfy

[9]The paragraph is based on the events described in *Baharistan (Sarkar)*, vol. II, ff. 153, 153a–b, ff. 169a; cf. Borah, I, chs. II and IV, pp. 290–352.

[10]*Baharistan (Sarkar)*, vol, II, f. 158a; Borah, I, p. 302.

[11]*Baharistan (Sarkar)*, vol. II, f. 179a.

[12]Ibid., ff. 180b; Borah, I, p. 360.

me? Two of our great princes have surrendered to the emperor and paid lakhs and crores of rupees. What benefits have they reaped which I may consider as advantages? However, I agree to the following terms. I shall hand over one of my brothers for Your Excellency's service (*ba khidmat-e huzur*) on the condition that first, stern punishment should be meted out to Shaykh Ibrahim; secondly, the revenue should be remitted for full one year; thirdly, the Mughal soldiers will have to return to Gilahanay; fourthly, the allowance of the *paiks* should be paid direct to them and should not be made as an addition to the revenue due to the government (*mujarai'paikan ra dakhil jama'na karda*).[13]

Mirza Nathan accepted Sanatan's first proposal but not the others. As a result Sanatan continued the resistance. Direct assaults on his fort were repelled again and again. Sanatan's success permitted him to declare himself raja. In retaliation Mirza Nathan razed the neighbouring villages to the ground so that the rebels' sources of supply were destroyed.

It took Mirza Nathan two days to destroy those villages; nearly 2000 food suppliers were killed or taken prisoner by him. These details are an indication of the support and loyalty enjoyed by the Kuch rebel leader in the neighbouring villages.[14] The rebel fortress fell to the Mughals after a siege lasting about three months. Sanatan was forced to flee to the hill tracts, from where he continued his resistance against Mughal authority. When Raja Parikshit's brother Baladev also known as Balinarayan, rose in rebellion, Sanatan joined him and attacked Mirza Yusuf. Later when Shaykh Ibrahim himself defied imperial orders and took up arms, Sanatan joined him, helping his erstwhile enemy.[15]

The *Hathikheda* Uprising

Hathi kheda (capture of elephants) sparked off the second uprising in 1621. Khuntaghat was once again the centre. Elephants were indispensable for the army: they carried war materials into the jungles of Assam and were used to seize forts in the hill tracts. It was one of the duties of the *ryots* to help the Mughal army to capture elephants. The services of the *palis* were necessary in order to keep the elephants confined within the enclosure *(qamargah)* while those of the *gharduwari paiks* (auxiliary footmen) were required to drive the elephants into the enclosure. Government officers were sent with special instruments to

[13] *Baharistan (Sarkar)*, vol. II, ff. 180b–181a; cf. Borah, I. p. 370.
[14] *Baharistan (Sarkar)*, ff. 183b–184b; Borah, I, pp. 378–81.
[15] *Baharistan (Sarkar)*, ff. 207a–b.

draft the *gharduwari paiks* from their lands.[16] This practice disrupted the ryots' work on their own lands and was naturally resented by them.

Baqir Khan, a Mughal officer, carried out *a hathi kheda.* Some of the elephants escaped while being put in chains. In consequence, the leading elephant drivers among the *pali* and *gharduwari paiks* were sentenced to death and the others were whipped. Baqir Khan ordered: 'Either bring the escaped elephants here or pay rupees one thousand for each elephant.' This was the immediate cause of the revolt. In the words of Mirza Nathan,

> These discontented people instigated the people of the region (*ahl-e mulk ra*) against him, and they attacked at night. Baqir Khan was caught alive and was cut in two pieces. The soldiers of the army who fought were all killed and the others were held prisoners, and all the elephants of the government were confiscated. They proclaimed a headman of the elephant-drivers as their king, rose in open revolt and created an amazing situation.[17]

The rebellion spread to other classes. Bhaba Singh, the Kuch noble and brother of Raja Parikshit, became involved in it. The tyranny of Balabhadra, the Hindu *diwan* of Mirza Nathan, had roused the peasants who joined the insurrection. The rebels imprisoned the family of Qulij Khan, the Mughal commander of Kuch Bihar. Jahangirabad was raided and stockades were built at Bangaoan and Madhupur on either side of the river at Goalpara. Mirza Nathan suppressed this uprising after much effort. The words of his rivals suggest that this revolt was conducted by the ordinary people belonging to a particular lower caste. 'Have you subdued any rebel', they taunted, 'other than a group of fishermen *(machwagiri)* who built a fort at Goalpara?'[18]

THE *PAIK* SYSTEM

An analysis of these two rebellions makes a few things clear. First, these took place in the same area, though they sprang from different causes. In the first place, it was the coercion of the cultivators by the Mughal revenue collectors and the revenue farmers which was the main cause of the conflict. In order to understand the nature of the uprising, however, it is necessary to look at the complaints of the *paiks.* These were peasants who also worked as the nobles' soldiers or armed

[16] *Baharistan (Sarkar),* vol. III, no. 63, ff. 287b–288a; Borah, II, p. 676.

[17] *Baharistan (Sarkar),* vol. III, ff. 274a; Borah, II, pp. 638–9.

[18] *Baharistan (Sarkar),* vol. III, f. 287b; Borah, II, p. 651. It is to be noted that *machwas* meant *jaliya keota* in this region in the mid-nineteenth century. See W.W. Hunter, *A Statistical Account of Assam* (London, 1879), vol. II, p. 44.

retainers. In return for serving their masters in war or manning the border regions they were given arable land free of revenue charges. Such land was known as *paikan* or *chakran*. In reality, in Kuch Bihar and Assam peasants customarily paid revenue in terms of labour and not in cash, receiving land in return. In fact the evidence of *Fathiya-i-ibriya* by Shihabuddin Talish, *waqai navis* (a news reporter) of Mir Jumla and the Mughal *sanads* for the *zamindari* of Gauripur in 1676 indicates the existence of rights over land granted in exchange for this kind of service.[19]

The genealogy of the princely family of Kuch Bihar and the stone inscriptions on temples built by Chila Roy shows that the grantees of *paikan* land fell into different categories according to the services for which such grants were made. For instance, land was given to 140 families of votaries of the temples, among whom were blacksmiths, weavers, messengers, panegyrists and so on.[20] The official history of Shah Jahan's reign states that such people 'were given *jagirs* by order of the king. Those soldiers are known as *paiks* . . . for their livelihood they are employed in the work of cultivation *(ba zira'at)* and also in capturing and driving elephants.'[21] A similar account has been given in the *Fathiya-i-ibriya*. 'To collect revenue from the peasant of these areas is not the rule. From every house one person in every three was brought for the services to the king *(az har khana fi seh nafar yak nafar ba khidmat-e raja qaim numayad)*.[22]

[19]Ranajit Guha, 'A Report on Gauripur Archives', in *Annual Report, Regional Record Survey Committee, West Bengal, 1955–56.*

[20]K.L. Barua, *Early History of Kamrup* (Shillong, 1933), pp. 298–300.

[21]Abdul Hamid Lahori, *Padshah Namah*, edited by Maulavi Kabiruddin and Maulavi Abdur Rahim, Bibliotheca Indica, vol. II (Calcutta, 1867–8), p. 71.

[22]*Fathiya-i-ibriya*, Mss. Sarkar Collection (a copy of Asiatic Society of Bengal Ms.) no. 77, ff. 57a. For a detailed discussion, see Amalendu Guha, 'Medieval North East India: Polity, Society & Economy, 1200–1500 AD', *Occasional Papers, No. 19*, Centre for Studies in Social Sciences, Calcutta (mimeo). There is a suggestion in some of the sources that thanks to the elaborate revenue arrangements made by the imperial officials the pressure on the peasants was to be less acute in the territory of the chiefs than in that directly administered by the Mughals (Habib, *op. cit.*, p. 336). Under the administrative system of the Ahoms, the *paiks* were allowed to hold two *pauras* of the best rice-lands. To an extent too they had also a voice in the election of their leaders, *saikias, boras* or *hazarikas*. Most of the land owned by the chiefs was, however, cultivated by the slaves. See Gait, *op. cit.*, pp. 239–40, 241–2; Bhuyan, *Kamrupār Buranji*, p. 112; Francis Buchanan-Hamilton, *An Account of Assam*, ed., S.K. Bhuyan (Gauhati, 1963), pp. 22–4.

It is clear that the *paikan* system played an important role in the agricultural economy of Assam and Kuch Bihar. All active males other than the higher officials, slaves and priests were brought within the purview of the *paikan* system through *gote* ('service'). Each *gote* generally consisted of four peasants. A peasant became a *paik* by rotation. He would render his services to the king for one year while other members of his *gote* looked after his land. Some difficulties regarding the analysis of the *paikan* system should however be considered. The evidence from contemporary Persian sources points to a system of land tenure based on labour service in this region on the eve of the Mughal administration. But the indigenous sources are of later origin and refer to the nature of Ahom administration in Kamrup in the late seventeenth and early eighteenth centuries rather than to the Kuch administrative system in the late fifteenth and early sixteenth centuries. However, it seems that the features are broadly similar, though in a subsequent period social differentiation developed more fully. In Darrang, there is an account of the *paikan* system established by Naranarayan in pre-Mughal days. 'The king afterwards made a census and created the *paiks*. . . . He made four people *(chari pawa)* equivalent to a *gote* of *paiks*.'[23] There is, of course, confirmation on the working of the system from other *vamshavalis* written in almost the same period. It was said that the soldiers of the Kuch king were given about 12 *bighas* of land as an allowance in lieu of a cash payment.[24] It can therefore be concluded that on the whole the general information, if not the detail, supplied by these local sources of the later period confirms the working of the system as depicted in the Persian chronicles.

The Assamese sources written during Ahom rule in Kamrup in the late seventeenth and eighteenth centuries indicate two other important features of the *paikan* system. According to the *Buranjis*, *karis* or archers were associated with the lower castes. In general, under the Ahom administration, the *karis* were treated as people of inferior status and enjoyed fewer privileges than the *chamuas* who were skilled artisans and not bound to go to war. A *kari* was allowed to enter an upper-caste

[23]Baldev Surya-Khari Daibagya, *Darrang Raj Vamshavali*, ed., Navinchandra Sharma (Gauhati, 1963), p. 64. The text however is a history of the Kuch kings written in the late eighteenth century.

[24]Khan Chaudhury Amanatullah Ahmed, *Koch-Beharer Itihas* (in Bengali; Calcutta, 1936), p. 125. Ripunjay Das, *Maharaj-Vamshabali*, ed., Nripendra Nath Pal (Kuchbihar, 1383 BS), p. 4. Amanatullah Ahmed's book is probably one of the best local histories written in Bengali on the basis of the information provided by *vamshavalis* in this region.

group, but his position was still marked by a social stigma.[25] The Kuch, too, who constituted the bulk of the *paiks*, were treated by the eighteenth-century Ahoms as being of rather low status. Thus among the *paiks* there were many who came from lower-caste professions and were treated as social inferiors by the Ahom élite.

Secondly, the Assamese evidence suggests a kind of growing differentiation within this region. Haliram Dhekyal Phukan mentioned *paiks* who did not pay labour service (*gamati*). They were called *chamua*, as mentioned earlier. He also referred to a privileged land tenure called *bhala manuhiya zamin* or the lands enjoyed by the *bhadralok*. He compared this with a situation when the entire land had been held revenue-free. In *Kamrupār Buranji* it was suggested that Shaykh Ibrahim introduced the *pargana* land administration in this area. After 1684 the Ahoms made a hierarchical structure of revenue administration, following the Mughal tradition, and introduced a variety of tenures with different terms and obligations.[26] Some of the inscriptions of this period also suggest the existence of various kinds of land tenure in this area.[27] We may infer from these Assamese sources that the impact of the Mughal and the Ahom administrations in the seventeenth and eighteenth centuries led to a growing differentiation within the peasantry. Moreover, in the late fifteenth and early sixteenth centuries the community bondage among the *paiks*, soldiers as well as cultivators, was perhaps stronger within a less differentiated agrarian society, especially where the bulk of the cultivators belonged to the same caste group. The *paikan* system was perhaps sufficiently well integrated with the community to make any disruption in the distributive machinery affect both *sardars* and cultivators. This would explain why their reactions were so violent and quick. Land assessment and the rigid *jama* or collection were seen as evils by the ordinary peasant because these left him less room for manoeuvre. The Mughal land revenue administration aimed at and achieved greater control through the *karoris* and *mustajirs* who became, consequently, the target of the peasants' anger.

[25]For a detailed discussion, see S.K. Bhuyan, *Ahomer Din* (in Assamese, Jorhat, 1918), pp. 52–3, 55, 72. Haliram Dhekyal Phukan, *Assam Buranji* (1829), ed., J.M. Bhattacharya (Gauhati, 1369 BS), p. 54. It is an informative account of the Ahom administrative system in Kamrup during the eighteenth century by a person long connected with the administrative system in this region. He himself belonged to the family of a local customs official of Kamrup.

[26]Phukan, *op. cit.*, pp. 51–4; Bhuyan, *Kamrupār Buranji*, p. 112–13.

[27]Maheswar Neogi (ed.), *Prachya Sasanavali* (Gauhati, 1974), pp. 118–19.

The Mughal System Versus the *Paik* System

As the Mughals had the *mansabdari* system for procuring soldiers and since they emphasized the importance of the collection of revenue directly in cash, they were not interested in maintaining the *paikan* system. Consequently, this new system acted against the interest of the *paiks* and their chiefs, that is those who were their leaders in times of war. Moreover, the Mughals brought the hitherto untaxed *paikan* land under assessment. Taxes had now to be paid in crops or in cash. Besides, the farmers increased the rate of revenue. Conflicts arose between the fiscal system of cash or crop payment based on a rent-roll and the centralized military system on the one hand, and the extraction of revenue in terms of labour-service based on decentralized local powers on the other. As pointed out earlier, Sanatan, in his letter, spoke directly in favour of the latter system which had been seriously disrupted by the Mughals. He asked, therefore, for a remission of revenue and for an exemption of the land of the *paiks* from assessment. His proposals did not agree, of course, with the Mughal practice of extracting the maximum possible social surplus. Common subjects and *paiks*, or those who were both cultivators and soldiers, revolted. It was in the context of a general atmosphere of agrarian discontent that the rebellion led by the Kuch nobles became formidable.

Three currents of discontent can be perceived in the first of these rebellions as having arisen from the grievances of (a) the ordinary *ryots*, (b) the *paiks* or a special class of *ryots* and soldiers, and (c) the Kuch nobility. The existence and leadership of armed *ryots* in Kamrup transformed this revolt into a resistance which commanded wide support from the people for a long time. At one stage the Mughal state power even came out with the proposal for a cease-fire and was prepared to compromise.

In the second uprising at Khuntaghat the immediate cause for the disturbance was the state's demand of service for catching elephants. Here the *ryots* who trapped and tamed elephants as a profession, were the first to rise in revolt, and were then joined by other oppressed cultivators. They probably belonged to a low caste, and their leadership fell into the hands of one of their own headmen. The second rebellion was, therefore, the work of a comparatively lower and poorer section of the peasants. Here too we find the name of a Kuch noble, but the part he played is rather obscure. It appears that the leadership lay in the hands of *ryots* of the lower strata and not in those of any upper-caste group. This was perhaps because specialization in chasing elephants had to be acquired by a particular class of *ryots*, giving rise to solidarity. Since they were a cohesive group, it might have been comparatively easy for them to provide the requisite leadership. It is clearly indicated in the writings of Nathan that the *ryots* engaged in chasing elephants were skilled in a particular profession and that it was they who took the initiative to mobilize the common people. This uprising arose from two currents connected with (a) the grievances of *gharduwari paiks* and *pali paiks*, and (b) those of the ordinary cultivators.

In terms of participation and mobilization one point is to be particularly emphasized. Some of the rebellions had an obviously aristocratic linkage. The humiliation suffered by the traditional rulers was certainly a factor behind the uprising. For instance, Sanatan, the rebel leader, possessed a fort and was once described by Mirza as a *raja.*[28] In his petition, he also referred to the injustice meted out to his kings. Hence the vertical linkages within a landed society, operating between lords, vassals and ordinary subjects, might have been invoked to mobilize the people. These vertical linkages had a special importance in the context of the specific historical development of the frontier region. The period immediately preceding Mughal penetration here had witnessed the rise of the Kuch principality under Naranarayan. It has been suggested that they belonged to the Mech, or Bodo tribal groups.[29] It was during this period that they were transforming themselves into a dominant caste. With the establishment of a strong principality in the course of the fifteenth century, Naranarayan renovated the temples of

[28]Nathan says, 'This Rajah and his fort are not of that nature from which you can expect any income after the conquest': *Baharistan (Sarkar)*, vol. II, f. 180a. The sentence is suggestive of the fact that Sanatan was not a prosperous chief. However, Sanatan did belong to the category of a *zamindar* or a feudal chief, and was probably a hereditary leader of a number of *paiks*. Under the Ahom king chief officials like Burha Gohain, Bar Gohain and Bar Patra Gohain commanded the services of 10,000 *paiks* each. Such posts were ordinarily confined to particular clans and were hereditary in nature: Borah, II, p. 846.

[29]B.R. Hodgson, 'Koch, Bodo and Dhimal Tribes', *Journal of the Asiatic Society of Bengal*, vol. XVIII, part II (1849), pp. 704–5. In the genealogy of this dynasty, the fugitive Kshatriya princes were said to have married Mech women and 12 powerful Mech houses descended from those unions. The wife of Haria Mundal, the chief of the Mech, gave birth to a son named Vishnu who was the real founder of the royal house of Kuch Bihar (Daibagya, *op. cit.*, pp. 8–10). The legend is suggestive of that well-known social process by which a tribe aspiring for access to economic power and political domination used the puranic tradition to bolster its prestige within the caste hierarchy.

the goddess Kamakhya, patronized Sanskrit scholars and established a claim to his family's connection with the mythical exploits of Parashuram against the Kshatriyas.[30] Later on the Kuchs were also to assume the appellation Rajbanshi in this area.[31] Hence, in the early sixteenth century the Kuch nobility and population may have felt a strong attachment to their royal house, which became a focal point and visible symbol of their social mobility and of the social power in this region. This bond was strong, as suggested by Nathan's account about the reaction of the Kuch nobles to the arrest of their kings.

Due to the circulation in the territory of Kuch of the news of the arrest of the two *rajas,* some of the Kuch chiefs *(raiyan-e kuchan)* in order to wipe off their bad reputation *(badnami)* raised an insurrection.[32]

The suggestion of disgrace felt by the Kuch nobility because of the dishonour to their rulers at the hands of the Mughal authorities is unmistakable here. The attitude of Sanatan Sardar merely underlined the same sense of disgrace. The frequent insurrections by Parashuram in Dakhinkul and Jadu Nayak, another *sardar* of *the paiks,* in this area also suggested the general antipathy felt by the *sardars* against Mughal conquest.[33] Again, in the early nineteenth century, Francis Buchanan hinted at the caste composition of the agrarian population in this area saying, 'Thus in the territory of the Khuntaghat on the Bisne river, belonging to one of their powerful chiefs, almost every cultivator is called a Rajbanshi.'[34] Hence, in this type of agrarian society, where most of the cultivators as well as their chiefs belonged to the same caste group, mobilization often followed the lines of social linkages binding *rajas, sardars* and cultivators in a common struggle. Dishonourable treatment meted out to a royal house, or a breach of trust with respect to the latter, could easily have been construed as an affront to the prestige of the community, particularly to that of the chiefs.

But in the *Hathikheda* rebellion, the opposite seems to have been the case. It was a spontaneous insurrection of the elephant-catchers and the language used by Mirza Nathan indicates that they themselves

[30]Ahmed, *op cit.*, pp. 126–9. Daibagya, *op. cit.*, pp. 67–8. 102–12, 123–5.

[31]E. Dalton, *Descriptive Ethnology of Bengal* (Calcutta, 1872), p. 89; W.W. Hunter, A *Statistical Account of Bengal,* vol. X (Calcutta, 1876), p. 353.

[32]*Baharistan (Sarkar),* vol. II, f. 153b.

[33]Borah, II, pp. 505–23, 532–3, 662–4.

[34]Buchanan-Hamilton, *Report on Rungpur,* Mss. Eur. D. 74, book II, ff. 140–1.

elected a leader from their midst. The *ryots* oppressed by Balabhadra quickly joined their ranks. The Kuch nobles came later. It seems that here the initiative lay with the lower strata of the peasantry and their action was an incentive to others to follow them. These two contrasting types of mobilization suggest that the uprisings of the peasants under the leadership and initiative of the *zamindars* was not the only type of peasant revolt witnessed in this area. There might have been other types too characterized by a different kind of mobilization.

In spite of differences two common tendencies may be observed in these two revolts. First, there was a tradition of frequent resistance on the part of the peasants and their chiefs against the Mughal imperial power. Whatever might be the cause of conflict, whether over collection of additional revenue or over the right to capture elephants, the peasants of this region time and again rose in rebellion. Secondly, it appears that those who were already engaged in strictly specialized professions or were moving towards some degree of specialization, were in the vanguard of rebellion, as were the militiamen and archers in the revolt headed by Sanatan and the *gharduwari* and *pali paiks* in that of the elephant-catchers.

The regional characteristics of these two revolts should also be noted. Both revolts erupted in the border areas of Bengal and Assam. The Mughals had recently conquered these regions. Further, the social system and fiscal organization were quite different in these parts from those in India. The existence of tribes over a wide area made the polity of this region more complicated. Hence, it was comparatively easy for the *ryots* to rise in revolt ever so often against the relatively weak Mughal forces in these outposts of the empire.

In fact, the discontent among the peasantry of this region was never anything but acute, and it reared its head as soon as an opportunity arose. Thus the *ryots* of Putamari deferred payments to the Mughals when Balabhadra, the Hindu officer of Mirza Nathan, went there. The *ryots* of Khatribag, the *jagir* of Nathan himself, refused to pay revenue, taking advantage of the floods. Afterwards, they were subdued with the help of the local *zamindars*. When some merchants went to collect rations for the Mughal soldiers, the peasants from the villages of Kendugiri and Badhantara attacked and plundered them.[35] Mirza Nathan, after he was awarded the title 'Khan', became dissatisfied with the work of the elephant-chasers and whipped the headman of the *paiks*. In conse-

[35] *Baharistan (Sarkar)*, vol. II, ff. 169a.

quence, the latter became sorely aggrieved, and the danger of another violent insurrection loomed large. The crisis passed when another Mughal officer, Khwaja Sadat Khan, found himself in a tight corner and was forced to release the *sardars* and conciliate Baki Laskar, the headman of elephant-catcher *paiks.*[36] Again, during the reign of Aurangzeb, the people of Kuch Bihar revolted in support of their chief against the revenue arrangement of Mir Jumla.[37] Thus the defiance of Mughal authority by various groups of people was a constant feature in this region from Jahangir's reign to Aurangzeb's and the elaborate system of dominance evolved by the Mughal authority was frequently challenged both by the people and their chiefs.

Violence and counter-violence embedded in this type of rebellion deserve our attention. Both Baqir Khan and Mirza Nathan demonstrably punished the *pali* and *gharduwari paiks* for their failure in duty. The rebels also reacted with violence in no uncertain terms against Baqir Khan. One of the attributes of any authority lies in a right to punish. This appears to have been understood both by the Mughal power and the lowly peasants. Hence a counter-assertion of power by the rebels always took the form of violent punishment meted out to the officials such as Allama Beg or Baqir Khan. This was invariably a signal of the temporary suspension of Mughal authority in this region and created an atmosphere of general insurrection.

Conclusion

These revolts were not very large in scale and were ultimately suppressed. But their frequent recurrence in this frontier area was an index of the relative failure on the part of the Mughals to integrate peripheral zones within the state structure. In this area the cultivators, under the leadership of some specialized groups, participated in the insurrection. These were more popular in character because caste solidarity as well as community bonds were stronger in these parts for various reasons. Horizontal and vertical linkages of mobilization were both operative in this region. Here, however, a relatively organized system based on service-tenure was replaced by a more centralized and hierarchical system. The Mughal state power appeared to be an intrusion to the chiefs as well as the members of the society. The fact of its existence as well

[36]Ibid., vol. III, ff. 288b.

[37]*Fathiya*, ff. 80a–b.

as the mode of its operation were disruptive to all who constituted the agrarian society. The prestige of one of the autonomous chiefs regarded as powerful even by the Mughal chronicler was at stake. The status of the *sardars* was threatened. The oppression on the family as well as the property of the ordinary cultivators was perpetuated. Rural life was in fact greatly disturbed. Hence, the exercise of Mughal authority led inevitably to turmoil and disintegration within this society. In this situation defiance and rebellion was the only recourse people had. In this sense, frontier uprisings with all their variations were a part of the general tradition of rebellion and agrarian resistance that rocked the Mughal state time and again. In this area these uprisings also marked the beginning of a tradition of peasant resistance that was invoked again and again in various forms against Mir Jumla, against the Ahoms during the Moamaria revolt and against British rule in the late nineteenth century.

18

Banditry in Mughal India: Historical and Folk Perceptions*

J.F. Richards and V. Narayana Rao

INTRODUCTION

In the course of a century or more of administrative and political consolidation, by the last quarter of the seventeenth century, the Muslim rulers of Golconda had succeeded in creating and sustaining a remarkably stable and wealthy kingdom in the eastern Deccan.[1] By this time, in interior Telengana, and coastal Andhra, the two major Telugu-speaking[2] regions to the north of the Krishna river, a prosperous, relatively peaceful society could be found. At the apex of the society was a small political–military élite of Muslim soldiers, administrators and political figures, a nobility composed of aristocratic Persian and Deccani or native-born Indian Muslims. Below this numerically small, but immensely powerful group, an influential and sizeable Muslim gentry consisting of lesser officials, merchants, and *'ulama* (the Muslim religious élite) dominated the vigorous life of Hyderabad, Warangal, and the other towns of the kingdom. In the countryside, an equally influential Telugu warrior aristocracy, although initially defeated,

*First published in the *Indian Economic and Social History Review*, vol. XVII, no. 1, 1980.

[1]See J.F. Richards, 'The Seventeenth Century Concentration of Power in Hyderabad', *Journal of the Pakistan Historical Society*, XXIII, (1975), pp. 1–35.

[2]Telugu is a major language of south India spoken by millions of persons in the linguistic state of Andhra Pradesh. Telugu has a vigorous cultural and literary tradition. The term is also used to refer to those peoples speaking the language and sharing in the culture, e.g. the Telugu peoples.

continued to control the rural population (i.e., the clean Sudra caste Telugu peasants and a wide range of other Telugu clean and unclean artisan and other service groups).

After coming to a flexible series of political accommodations and arrangements with its Muslim conquerors, the Telugu warrior aristocracy was left armed, with retainers, kinsmen, and troops under its local command, and with undisturbed local social status and hereditary local offices. These warriors, also left with much of the responsibility for collection of the land tax, disposed of most of the surplus agricultural production of the area. In addition, some of the more prominent and powerful Telugu aristocrats served their Muslim overlords as military commanders, as fortress commanders or even as courtiers who appear noticeably in the descriptions of court assemblages for great state occasions at Golconda's magnificent court.

Literate Telugu Brahmins, from the secular secretarial groups of that large caste grouping, also found lucrative and less obviously powerful careers as agents for all great men (whether Telugu warrior-aristocrats [*nayaks*] or Muslim grandees), entrepreneurial farmers of taxes or as technicians and lesser officials in the formal machinery of the state. During the early 1670s two such Telugu Brahmins, the brothers Madanna and Akkanna, rose by means of administrative skill and political acumen to become the chief minister and chief army commander respectively for Abul Hasan Qutb Shah (1670–86), the last independent Muslim king of Golconda. Within a short time the two Brahmin officials, given full powers of administration and appointment by the king, were able to exercise virtually complete control over the state apparatus. For a decade they pursued two linked goals: increased consolidation of state power and enhanced Brahmin, Hindu control of the state. Resistance to this threat from the Muslim noble élite, although bitter, was ineffectual until intervention by the Mughal emperor Aurangzeb (1658–1707), the titular suzerain of Abul Hasan.

Spurred by Muslim complaints and worried by an alliance negotiated by Madanna between Abul Hasan Qutb Shah and Shambhaji, the rebel Maratha king, who ruled a compact aggressive state in the western Deccan, the emperor Aurangzeb put increasing pressure on Golconda in the 1680s. Eventually this military and political pressure culminated in a Muslim coup and the assassination of the two Brahmin officials. However, this measure did not prevent invasion, a siege and the final conquest and annexation of the kingdom of Golconda by the Mughal emperor in 1686–7.

The Mughal conquest did not immediately radically change the existing political and social configuration of society in the eastern Deccan.[3] To be sure, the Muslim élite of Golconda dispersed within the imperial service to be replaced by cadre of experienced Mughal officials. The king of Golconda, deposed, was replaced by a Mughal governor, a servant of the Mughal emperor. The great Telugu warrior-aristocrats, no longer employed as military commanders, returned to their purely local domains. The terminology and operation of administration changed. But apart from this, after recovery from the effects of the extended siege, drought, and famine (in the years 1686–90), the basic structure of local society seemed little altered in the decade 1690 to 1700.

By 1700, however, this picture had begun to change.[4] For the next 13 years, steadily weakening imperial power during Aurangzeb's last years and the reign of Bahadur Shah (1708–12), his son and immediate successor, put continued pressure on the society of Hyderabad. Imperial credibility was irreparably damaged by a series of punishing raids in force, carried out in Hyderabad province in the years 1702 and 1704 by rebel Maratha commanders. The demoralized Mughal governor and other imperial officers unsupported by the emperor, failed to drive off or even to seriously oppose the intruders. As the power, efficacy, and credibility of the empire declined in a descending spiral, local men, both Muslim officials and Telugu aristocrats, faced an unpredictable future. A devastating drought and famine in these same years lowered productivity, and forced many peasants and artisans into flight from their homes. The governor, and other imperial commanders, manoeuvred, ignored orders, built up their personal forces, and illegally extorted funds from the populace.

In 1707–8 political insecurity culminated in the long-awaited war of succession, which broke out among three princes upon the death of the aged Aurangzeb. During this struggle, the youngest of the contenders, Prince Muhammad Kam Bakhsh, formally governor of the eastern Deccan in his father's lifetime, retreated to Hyderabad city to make a stand against his victorious brother, soon to be Emperor Bahadur Shah. In the desperate weeks which prince Kam Bakhsh spent in Hyderabad, he clashed with the incumbent Mughal governor, who had ostensibly acted in previous years as the Prince's deputy in his

[3]For an extended examination of Mughal policy, See J.F. Richards, *Mughal Administration in Golconda* (Oxford, 1975).

[4]See ibid., pp. 213 ff, for a full discussion of these events.

administration of the province. The Mughal deputy governor, Rustam Dil Khan, his powers swollen by an illegally and harshly extracted fortune, and by a newly enlarged personal army, was reluctant to defer in more than a symbolic fashion to the prince. Moreover, after nearly 20 years of continuous high office in Hyderabad province, the over-mighty governor had carefully built up a series of alliances with the most powerful Telugu aristocrats, and with at least one prominent bandit leader in the region. The nearly inevitable clash between prince and governor ended with the execution of the governor by the prince's forces. Shortly thereafter prince Muhammad Kam Bakhsh died in battle with his brother, victim to the rigorous rule of Mughal succession disputes.

Between 1708 and 1713, after the war of succession, two successive imperial governors, lacking even minimal support from the centre, failed to restore order and stability in Hyderabad. Despite one notably successful campaign against a powerful bandit chief (see below) the first governor, Yusuf Khan, was unable to pay his troops, who finally mutinied for their long-due back pay. By 1711, several examples had been recorded of Mughal military commanders in Hyderabad plundering the countryside, trying desperately to seize goods, food and money in order to fend off the insistent demands of their violently mutinous followers. This descent to directionless plundering by imperial troops represented a near-terminal stage for imperial authority in the Telugu lands of the eastern Deccan. Simultaneously, members of the Telugu regional warrior aristocracy, who in various capacities, acted to collect and, after suitable allowances, to transmit the state's share of the land tax to imperial officials, suffered a crisis of confidence. They no longer thought it prudent to make payments to a regime which seemed to be so obviously failing. Thus, the combined effect of weak or non-existent central direction, control and support from the imperial throne at Delhi, and inability of local imperial administrators to collect revenues, virtually paralysed the state.

The Impact of Political Disorder

Against this background of weakening central authority and deteriorating public order, the power, wealth and security of many, if not the majority, of the members of the major élite groups in the province was seriously threatened. In the years after 1700, those Brahmins associated with state service were obviously hard hit. Members of the Telugu warrior aristocracy, especially those who had held semi-hereditary, state-appointed posts as village or subdistrict headmen *(deshmukhs)* in the countryside, felt the loss of state authority and power. Most of the higher ranking Mughal officials, their pay and emoluments eroding, became increasingly demoralized. Members of the urban Islamic élite, their revenues and positions directly dependent on the vitality and strength of the state, also suffered. At the same time, however, exceptionally shrewd and forceful individuals, such as the Mughal governor, or some Telugu raja moved quickly and aggressively to secure and retain new and, in the context of the imperial system, illegitimate powers. As the state declined, able men, whether Muslim official or Telugu warrior chief, could use their official positions or their local position to prosper. Often such aggrandizement was at the expense of less adaptable or ruthless men. As in any situation of rapid political change, some persons gained and some lost power.

However, other individuals who possessed neither legitimate official status nor hereditary dominance in Telugu society also rose during this period. These were the bandit leaders whose activities constituted a grave threat to both Muslim and Telugu élites. The breakdown of state power and public order, and economic distress, touched off by a series of droughts, pushed 'troops of impoverished men', from their normal occupations as peasants or artisans, into various forms of beggary, vagabondage and brigandage. Unpaid, disbanded soldiers also turned to banditry. These men coalesced in bands around a number of leaders, whose names have not survived. But the two most prominent bandit chiefs of this period, each of whom attracted and commanded enormous numbers of followers, were known and feared by their contemporaries. Thus, we have considerable information about Riza Khan (d. 1712), an ex-Mughal military governor *(faujdar)* turned bandit leader, and Papadu[5] (d. 1710), a low-caste Telugu bandit chief, from descriptions and comments found in official news reports, chronicles, and reports from European merchants trading in the region. They became 'historically visible' in other words. Both men were active for approximately the same period of time, in northern Golconda north of the Krishna river. Apparently hostile rivals rather than allies, they were each equally successful in their violent careers, as they and their followers burnt and desolated villages and towns. Each, after evading capture for more than a decade, was eventually suppressed and killed by imperial authorities.

[5]Papadu is the name given in the Telugu versions. Khafi Khan corrupts this to Papra in the Persian chronicle.

Nevertheless, despite the similarities between the careers of the two men, at least one important difference exists. Notorious as he was in his own time, Riza Khan has left no discernible trace in the folk memory of either Muslims or Telugu Hindus. Papadu, on the other hand, has survived two and a half centuries after his death in the folk tradition of the Telugu country. His exploits are still sung today in great detail by wandering singers. The dramatic story of his life has even formed the subject of recent Telugu film and drama. It is this difference between the two bandits and differences and similarities between the folk view and the contemporary official and/or alien view of Papra which we wish to explore. The questions surrounding bandits as folk heroes and bandits as folk predators, complex and subtle as they are, have not been satisfactorily resolved. To look carefully at both the folk image and the contemporary official view account in one particular case, is a beginning which may suggest further lines of inquiry for the future.

Riza Khan

In either AD 1700 or 1701, the Mughal emperor Aurangzeb sent Riza Khan, a Muslim Afghan officer *(mansabdar)*, to take over as military governor of Ramgir, a town in the Deccan province of Bidar. Ramgir is located just north of Hyderabad province's northern boundary, near the district town of Elgandel. When Riza Khan arrived at his new post, however, the incumbent governor, refusing to leave, defied the emperor's order. In response Riza Khan recruited additional soldiers, seized the governor and forcibly took control of Ramgir district. But such was the state of imperial authority in the Deccan, at this time, that Riza Khan, with scarcely any delay, himself rebelled. Assembling a large irregular force, he began to seize the imperial revenues, and to plunder caravan traffic moving along the roads.[6]

Riza Khan wasted little time in moving south to the richer targets offered in and around Hyderabad city, the central market and focus for long-distance trading in the Deccan. Within a year, the new bandit chief had assembled a following of 9000 to 10,000 men, described by Dutch

[6]The scattered references to Riza Khan and his activities, which have been drawn upon for the following account, are from the memoirs of Niccolao Manucci, *Storia do Mogor, 1653–1708*, trs. and ed. by W. Irvine, Indian Texts Series (4 vols, London, 1907–8), III, 501; IV, 248–9, and also from references in the Dutch Trading Company records. The Mughal news report of Riza Khan's death is from the reign of Jahandar Shah, *Akhbārāt-i Darbār-i Mu'allā*, vol. I (12 Ramazan), p. 278.

merchants as 'rogues and cow-thieves'. During 1702, he had made it unsafe for caravans operating between metropolitan Hyderabad and its principal sea port on the coast, 300 miles to the east. He, and other bandits operating in the region, had also begun to cut off caravan traffic coming into Hyderabad along the trade routes of the interior, from Gujarat on the west coast, and from north India (Hindustan).

In addition to attacks on highway traffic, Riza Khan's massed forces sacked towns and villages coming into their path. In 1703, the Dutch merchants wrote, from their trading establishment at Machilipatnam, that Riza Khan had desolated most of the villages lying to the north-east of that town, and had left them in ashes. But despite the size of his following, Riza Khan does not seem to have attacked Warangal, Machilipatnam or the larger towns of the region. In the smaller towns and villages the residents caught in his path lost their goods and cattle, if not their lives.

Three Dutch estimates, made in 1703 and 1704, put the size of Riza Khan's forces at 10,000 to 12,000 men.[7] The exact composition of the band is unknown, or the details of its organization. Some men, especially the large number, perhaps as many as 5000 with horses, might have been deserters or unpaid soldiers from the Mughal armies. Others must have been recruits from the bands of impoverished men which the Dutch reported infesting the roads at this time. Undoubtedly, the ravages of the band itself must have contributed to the general social and economic disorder which generated recruits for banditry. The one reasonably certain fact is that Riza Khan's personal and military qualities were such that he could attract, organize and hold an extremely large following over a period of years. Nor do we find any trace of direct opposition to the bandit leader. Neither the demoralized Mughal officers nor the great Telugu rural aristocrats (*zamindars*) wished to engage in open battle with Riza Khan's horde, as long as they were not attacked. Thus, Riza Khan continued to hold up caravan traffic and to move freely through Hyderabad, from as early as 1702, until his death in 1711. At least one source suggested the bandit chief had begun to regularize his pillaging, exacting 'from one district after another the tributes that they pay the king'.[8] However, the scattered references remaining give no indication as to the location of a permanent base or camp for Riza Khan. Possibly Ramgir town, from which he began his

[7]Manucci (cf. Irvine) estimated 15,000 horse and 30,000 foot.

[8]Manucci (cf. Irvine), IV, p. 249.

operations, served such a purpose during the hot season when campaigning slowed.

As the years passed, and Riza Khan's reputation and his resources grew, the bandit chief gained increasing recognition as a power to be reckoned with in the turbulent politics of early eighteenth-century Hyderabad. In AD 1706, the Mughal deputy governor of Hyderabad, Rustam Dil Khan, came under intense pressure from the emperor Aurangzeb to seize and punish the other notorious bandit leader operating in Hyderabad at that time. Papra, a low-caste Telugu bandit chief, had carried out a series of abductions of well-born women, wives and daughters of both Hindu and Muslim notables. These activities had spurred a protest from Hyderabad, which travelled directly to the emperor's court, and resulted in a direct order for the suppression of Papra. Thus, Dutch observers noted in May 1706 that Rustam Dil Khan had made overtures to Riza Khan and had asked for the bandit chief's assistance in pursuing Papra. Just over a year later, at the outset of the war of succession after the death of the emperor Aurangzeb, Rustam Dil Khan, trying to strengthen his position in the province, sent some of his men to Riza Khan once again to ask for help in putting down the 'malefactor'. On this occasion, Riza Khan is reported to have responded by sending a very large sum of money back to the Mughal governor, in reply to this request. The following year, in 1708, Riza Khan sent troops to assist Rustam Dil Khan in an armed confrontation brewing between the governor and Prince Kam Bakhsh, one of the contenders in the succession war, who had just arrived in Hyderabad. Throughout this period, Riza Khan also seems to have occasionally negotiated, and at times plundered with Maratha raiders, entering Hyderabad province from the western Deccan.

But in January 1709, when the new emperor, Bahadur Shah, victor in the succession war, held audiences in Hyderabad, Riza Khan, rather than attend and possibly put himself in jeopardy, prudently stayed away from the imperial audience tent (unlike Papra, who seems to have appeared before the new emperor bearing an extremely large payment in goods and money [see below]).

Nonetheless, when Riza Khan later saw an advantage to be gained in supporting the steadily weakening provincial administration in Hyderabad, he did not hesitate to do so. In 1711, following the death of the incumbent Mughal governor, when a general revolt of the leading Telugu aristocrats of the region had begun, the chief Mughal fiscal officer of Hyderabad was reported to be planning to send a punitive force of 2000 to 3000 cavalry against one of the leading rebels. To command that force he had asked one of his own officers, and also Riza Khan, the rover 'who had excoriated the coastal districts of Golconda i.e., Hyderabad these last many long years'. Whether or not Riza Khan actually participated in this expedition is uncertain. The fact that he was considered for such a role suggests the ambivalence of his position, and the intimacy which his relations with the imperial Mughal officers of Hyderabad could sometimes attain. One might suggest that this occasional intimacy reflected a commonality of attitudes and interests retained, despite Riza Khan's rebellion and bandit career, from common experiences as imperial officers and by the attitudes and values shared by that status group. Certainly, the other major bandit leader, Papra, remained completely aloof from any similar involvement with the provincial cadre of Hyderabad.

Eventually, in 1712, Riza Khan's political skills failed him. According to an official Mughal report, when the newly arrived Mughal governor of Hyderabad marched from the capital, in an attempt to restore order in the province, Riza Khan, the malefactor *(mufisid)*, in alliance with the rebellious Telugu aristocrats tried to seize the governor. However, the Mughal governor, 'having skilfully called him [Riza Khan] before him' seized the bandit leader, and killed him and most of his followers.

Papadu: The Historical Account

The early eighteenth-century chronicler, Khafi Khan, includes in his work an extended description of the career of Papadu, the Telugu bandit chief. This lengthy description, from which our discussion is drawn, illustrates the notoriety which Papadu's exploits gained him in the wider world of the empire.[9] Khafi Khan begins his account by mentioning that the Muslim judge *(qazi)*, and other notable inhabitants of the district of Warangal in Hyderabad province, complained in a body directly to Bahadur Shah, the Mughal emperor. Since the time of Bahadur Shah's father, Aurangzeb, in the governorship of Rustam Dil Khan, Papadu had been active in the province. With this introduction, Khafi Khan proceeds to give the known facts about the bandit leader. Papadu was of base lineage, from a disreputable caste of toddy (palm wine) sellers. However, his sister was well-to-do, the widow of a wealthy man. While living with her, he discovered her valuables and cash, gathered some

[9] Muhammad Hashim Khafi Khan, *Muntakhab-ul Lubab*, Bibliotheca Indica, Calcutta, no. 60, vol. II, pp. 630–43.

companions, and tortured her (by burning her body) for her possessions. With this brutally acquired capital, he set out on a life of villainy, probably about AD 1700.

Enlisting many followers, he found a hill top refuge and strong point nearby (apparently near the minor chiefdom [*pargana*] of Kilpak, his birthplace). From this lair, Papadu began robbing travellers on the highway (presumably that running to Hyderabad city), and peasants in the vicinity. He was successful to the point that he gathered many more adherents and acquired more arms, and 'the materials for exercising rebellion'. But, very soon, the imperial military officers and the Telugu rural warrior aristocracy of the region reacted and planned to capture him. Papadu, learning of this, fled and took service as an officer in the military establishment of Venkat Rao, the *zamindar of* Kaulas (a minor chiefdom located some distance from his former habitat). There, Papadu quickly found a congenial associate, another officer named Chinahanuvant *(sic),* who joined him in using their position to plunder travellers. Their employer, Venkat Rao, learning of these activities, seized both men, and threw them into his prison under rigorous confinement. This might have been the end of Papadu's story, but he and his companion were suddenly released when the Kaulas *zamindar* freed all his prisoners as a means of religious propitiation, in the hope of curing his son of a serious illness.

Once free, Papadu travelled to Bhongir district, adjacent to Hyderabad, to the village of Shahpur where one Sarva, one of the 'foremost notorious malefactors' also newly arrived in Bhongir, had begun operations. Together, the two began to plunder and rob in all directions. Their headquarters at Shahpur was a newly constructed crude fort, done in the local style. From this strong point, Papadu led a series of raids in all directions. He quickly developed, as a speciality, the practice of abducting beautiful and wealthy upper-class women, whether Hindu or Muslim. Finally, a deputation of local notables from Hyderabad complained directly to the Mughal emperor about Papadu and Sarva. Acting upon direct orders from the emperor, the deputy governor of Hyderabad, Rustam Dil Khan, placed one of his most trusted officers as military governor at Kilpak, a town located about 20 miles from Shahpur, Papadu's stronghold. As soon as he arrived at Kilpak (which had not been the seat of a military governor earlier), Qasim Khan Afghan led a large contingent of cavalry in pursuit of the bandits. Finally, when a pitched battle did occur, a fortuitous shot killed the Mughal commander, and saved the bandits from near-certain defeat and capture. Thereafter, when another of his officers also failed to take Papadu and

Sarva, Rustam Dil Khan led an army in person against Shahpur. At the conclusion of a two-month siege, the governor took and destroyed the bandit fort, but Papadu and Sarva eluded him.

As soon as the governor's army returned to Hyderabad, Papadu and Sarva rebuilt their fortress at Shahpur with stone and mortar. They also began to acquire a stock of artillery. Returning to their marauding, the bandits' activities increased to the point that for a distance of 40 to 50 miles from Shahpur 'no person could sleep comfortably at night'. In this interval, Sarva, in a duel with one of his officers carried out 'as the rule of the Deccan' in single combat, died, as did his opponent. Papadu, now in sole command, vigorously built his army. He began to assault a number of the small forts (presumably of the Telugu *zamindars)* in the neighbourhood.

So threatening had Papadu become that Rustam Dil Khan led the imperial cavalry against Shahpur once more, in either AD 1706 or possibly 1707. But, a two- or three-month siege produced no effect on the rebuilt fortress and its garrison. In the end, Rustam Dil Khan, accepting a large sum of money from the bandit leader, quietly returned to Hyderabad. Although Khafi Khan does not state this, the political uncertainties surrounding the expected death of the emperor must have contributed to the Mughal officer's lack of resolution. Thus, it is clear that, in the course of perhaps six to seven years, Papadu had built up the essentials for survival. A fort, an army, a treasury, a reputation, all acquired in a time of political disorder, might well have ensured that he could have made the transition to a petty chief, who, with possibly a new, fictive genealogy might well have become a Telugu *zamindar* or *raja*.

Instead, Papadu chose a riskier path. During the political confusion surrounding the war of succession, he posed a direct challenge to the dominance and security of both the Muslim urban nobility and the Telugu aristocracy of the region. This challenge to the most powerful groups in the regional social order ultimately brought about a deputation of local notables to the emperor Bahadur Shah, and the capture and execution of the bandit chief. According to the Mughal chronicler's narrative, on the night of 22 March 1708, Papadu, at the head of 2000 to 3000 infantry and 400 to 500 cavalry, rode to the foot of the walls of Warangal fort. The former capital of the last great independent Telugu dynasty, Warangal town was a major commercial centre in inland Telengana, famous for its carpet manufactures. Blocking the road, one segment of the bandit army carried out a silent escalade of the fort walls using the traditional Deccan technique of throwing, from their saddles, nooses over projections in the fortifications to anchor the rope scaling ladders. The other portion of the army moved to assault the town. Both Muslim and Hindu inhabitants of Warangal were busy during the night, constructing replicas of the tomb of the martyred Husain for the Muharram festival procession to come the next day. But in the early dawn instead of a festival 12,000 to 15,000 inhabitants of Warangal fell captive to Papadu's forces. For two or three days, the bandits plundered both fort and town, seizing large sums of money and any movable property. Eventually, after obtaining what they could in loot, the bandits left Warangal in desolation. Few of the noble persons of the town retained their wealth or honour. After abducting the wife and eight-year-old daughter of the judge of Warangal, the most prominent member of the Muslim community, Papadu enrolled the mother in his harem, and placed the daughter in a troupe of dancers to be trained for that profession.

Within a short time, Papadu tried to repeat his success at Bhongir, another sizeable hill fort and market town located near Hyderabad city. But on this occasion, the night assault on the fort failed; the alarm was given. The bandits had to be content with looting Bhongir town for several hours, before retreating with 2000 to 3000 captives. As they left, Papadu ordered the stacks of unhusked rice in his route to be burnt so that the smoke would blind the fire of the Mughal musketeers and cannoneers from the fort overlooking the town.

In the aftermath of his notorious plundering of two of the most sizeable towns of Hyderabad province, Papadu began to extend his territorial base and to acquire more and more elements of a royal style.[10] The son of a low-caste toddy tapper now employed a bodyguard of

[10]A Dutch letter sent from Negapatam to Batavia in May 1709 includes a report from Hyderabad city to the effect that the emperor Bahadur Shah had admitted to an imperial audience *'den rover serwapaper'* who had been marauding in the region for some years. The *'rover'* who seems to have been Papra, offered the emperor as tribute one million four hundred thousand rupees, as well as large amounts of foodstuffs and other provisions for his army. In return the emperor presented a ceremonial robe of honour to the bandit. The incident, as yet unconfirmed by other sources, took place in the course of Bahadur Shah's brief stay in Hyderabad after the defeat and killing of his brother Prince Muhammad Kam Bakhsh. If the Dutch account is accurate and this was indeed Papra, we could better understand the indignation of the local Muslim notables, and the moral pressure which they were subsequently able to exert upon the Emperor. KA 1670 (7.5.1709) fol. 41.

700 horsemen, each armed with large double-chambered muskets which (according to Khafi Khan) could fire a second round without reloading. These unusually armed troopers surrounded their leader's litter *(palki)* and/or riding horse when he travelled. The former mode of conveyance was usually reserved to kings or to men of extremely high rank. About ten miles from Shahpur, on another hilltop near the village of Tarikonda, Papadu erected another stronghold. Beneath it he established a small market town. Here in Tarikonda were imprisoned the rapidly growing body of captives which the bandit leader had seized.

As was the practice for kings and generals in the Deccan, he summoned a band of itinerant grain merchants and bulk carriers *(banjaras)* who, driving herds of thousands of pack bullocks, supplied the armies and urban markets of the region with bulk foodgrains, salt, and raw cotton. But instead of paying their price, Papadu simply imprisoned the merchants and plundered the cash and foodstuffs carried by their bullocks. He put the 10,000 or more pack animals to work, ploughing in the area around his forts.

During this period Papadu was also reputed to have offered five silver rupees reward to those soldiers in his army who brought in Muslim women as captives. Whenever noblewomen from well-known *(mashaikh)* families were brought in, he reportedly paid five gold *hun* (i.e. fifteen silver rupees). Lavish marriage ceremonies, the mark of all well-born families, which attracted Papadu's attention, resulted in the abduction of the bride by the bandit leader. As a result, 'the sighs and cries of woe of the oppressed continually reached the sky'. Certainly, the threatened members of the Muslim gentry wasted little time in complaining directly to Bahadur Shah. Shah Inayat, well-known pious *shaikh,* whose daughter and granddaughter were seized by the bandit at Warangal (they were the wife and the daughter of the town judge) led the deputation to the emperor. Seeing only inaction on the part of the latter, Shah Inayat retired to his home, arranged his affairs, freed his servants, and, after 40 days, died of sorrow and disgrace. The emperor, responding to growing pressure, commissioned a new governor for the province, Yusuf Khan, and emphasized to him the importance of capturing Papadu.

When he arrived in Hyderabad in 1709, Yusuf Khan found that the Muslim gentry were not alone in their fears. Papadu was then busily engaged in a siege of the town of Kilpak. The Telugu *zamindar* of that town, whom the bandit wanted to kill, repeatedly sent requests to Hyderabad for assistance. The new governor ordered a relief force to Kilpak, consisting of a body of imperial Afghan troops under the command of Dilawar Khan, an experienced officer. Upon arrival, the Mughal troops defeated and dispersed Pāpadu's forces, in a battle outside the Kilpak walls. The bandit withdrew with his battered forces to Shahpur fort, taking along the great cannon 'Lal Laxman' which he had used in the siege. The Mughal forces did not immediately exploit this victory (which may not have been as decisive as Khafi Khan implies). Instead, Dilawar Khan established a fortified camp (*thana*) near Kilpak, and waited for an opportunity to capture the bandit chief.

Such an opportunity came with the rebellion of a group of prisoners held captive by Papadu in Shahpur fort. Among the captives in the fort was Papadu's wife's brother (imprisoned for a reason not explained by Khafi Khan). With files secretly brought by his wife along with his food, this man cut his chains. Along with a group of his fellow prisoners, he overcame the guards at a time when the fort garrison was depleted, and Papadu was absent. Mughal pressure had apparently slackened somewhat at this time, for Papadu had just sent, as a grisly warning to the *zamindar* of Kilpak, the severed tongue of the latter's wife, together with the message 'to keep his eye on the road and his ear for the sound of cannon'. When news of the rebellion reached Papadu, his first reaction was one of disbelief. He ordered the tongue of the unfortunate messenger cut out. But, when he arrived to find the cannon of Shahpur firing at him, he quickly reacted by igniting the main gate of the fort, in preparation for an assault. The bandit and a few followers, putting on blood-soaked hides of freshly slaughtered cattle and sheep, tried unsuccessfully to pass through the flames and enter the fort. Concomitantly, the Mughal army led by Dilawar Khan, followed by the *zamindar* of Kilpak's forces, reached Shahpur. These joint forces drove off Papadu's confused army, and rescued the captives in Shahpur fort. Papadu led his men to Tarikonda fort, his second and newest refuge.

Four days later, the chief fiscal officer of Hyderabad province, Mirza Ali, arrived at Shahpur with 5000 to 6000 cavalry, and orders from Yusuf Khan, the governor, to attack Tarikonda. Despite these fresh forces, Mirza Ali's assault failed to gain him entrance to Tarikonda fort. When the siege had gone on for three to four months, Yusuf Khan came to take command in person, at the head of an additional 5000 to 6000 cavalry. At this point in the siege, the imperial forces were also augmented by 10,000 to 12,000 horsemen and 20,000 infantry brought by the local fort commanders, and by the *zamindars* in the vicinity of Shahpur. The bandit garrison resisted for another nine months, according to the chronicler, until Yusuf Khan made direct overtures to the bandit rank and file. He offered employment at double the pay and rations for any deserters, while continuing to attack the fort daily. Ultimately, with his followers deserting and his gunpowder depleted, Papadu, seeing the 'time of the perverseness of his fate', decided to escape. Alone, at night, he fled the fort by an underground tunnel, leaving his sons to face the imperial assault.

The *dénouement*, as depicted by Khafi Khan, shows Papadu in disguise reaching Hasanabad town (located two days march from Tarikonda) and, tired and thirsty, ordering toddy to drink. The toddy seller, a member of his caste, recognized the fugitive. Keeping his customer waiting for a superior brand of toddy, the seller went to the deputy military governor of the town (the former captive, Papadu's wife's brother) who brought 200 to 300 men to capture the bandit. They carried the bandit leader, wounded in the leg, to Yusuf Khan, who tried for several days to locate Papadu's treasure, but only met with defiance from his 'obscene and abusive tongue'. Finally he was cut into pieces, the head to be sent to the emperor in Delhi, and the remainder of the corpse to be displayed on the walls of Hyderabad city. However, the Mughal news report of this event, not exploiting the dramatic ironies of Papadu's end, merely records the taking of Tarikonda fort, the casualties suffered on each side, and the capture of the notorious brigand.[11]

PAPADU: THE FOLK NARRATION[12]

According to the most recently recorded oral version of the Telugu song, Sarvayi Papadu was born into a caste of toddy (liquor) sellers

[11] *Akhbarat*, Bahadur Shah IV (23 Muharram), p. 32; (11 Rabi II), p. 96; (1 Jumada II), p. 158; (20 Rajab), p. 263.

[12] The story of Sarvayi Papadu is available in two versions, one long oral version, and a shorter written version based on the oral song. The oral version we used was recorded on 29 October 1974 by Gene Roghair at Gadevaripalle, Guntur district. It was sung by Pudota Kotilingam, Pudota Balayya, and Pudota Mallayya of the Jangam caste. The singers say that they belong to Gogulapadu, Gurajala Taluk, Guntur district. However, their accent indicates that they originate from Telengana. The earliest known reference to the sung version was by J.A. Boyle, in 'Telugu Ballad Poetry', *Indian Antiquary*, vol. III, 1874, pp. 1–6. Boyle states that he heard the story of Papadu from a person of the Boya caste from Bellary district. The text of the song given by Boyle, as indicated by the excerpts he quotes, considerably differs from the song as it is sung today. But the theme does not seem different. This is precisely the way oral tradition operates: it has a fixed theme, a fixed metre, but not necessarily a fixed text.

The earliest known printed version was published by Westward and Co., Madras in 1931. There are several reprints and republications by other publishers, but all of them use the same text. Printed versions of oral songs usually result from someone writing down the song while the singer speaks his text at a slower speed to facilitate writing. When a singer, who is accustomed to create his song as he sings during a public performance, is asked to say his text slowly, it distorts his text and also makes his song considerably shorter, as is confirmed by disconnected sentences and disjointed areas appearing in the printed version. It is not possible to state that differences between the present sung version and the printed version which is based on a past sung version are wholly due to distortions resulting from slow singing. Some of them, at least, are results of the creativity of the individual singers and the passage of time. What is however interesting is that there are large areas of similarity between the printed text which dates at least from 1931 and the sung version of 1974.

The following are the aspects of the printed version that differ from the sung version. The family name of Papadu is Nasana, and his mother's name is Sarvamma. Other details of Papadu's family do not occur in the printed version. The band of the associates of Papadu consists of 12 persons whose names are: Asen, Usen, Turka Himan, Dudekula Pur, Jakkula Perumallu, Nelluri Hanumanthu, Cakali Sarvanna, Mangali Masappa, Kummari Govindu, Karyala Miryalu, Medara Yenganna, and Kotwal Miri Saheb. The printed version has no reference to the killing of the cobra. The prediction of the Brahmins is also considerably different. They say that Papadu is destined to rule Golconda for seven hours. A girl of the fortune-telling (and criminal) *yerikala* caste, who comes later in the story, makes the other predictions, which, according to the sung version, are made by Brahmins themselves. There is no reference to the cause of Papadu's death in the printed version. The palm tree of the king, the plot to poison Papadu, and the story of the donkey and the festival which Papadu attends do not appear in the printed version. The printed text measures the money that Papadu's mother saved as seven *kopperas* full. (A *koppera* is a large metal cauldron.) There is no mention of the *golla* village and related incidents, and neither Vajranabhudu nor Venkat Rao appear in the printed version.

According to the printed text, the king had the horoscope of Papadu read at the time of the battle, and having, found that Papadu was destined to sit on the throne of Golconda for seven hours, he let him fulfil his destiny. At the end of the seven hours, the king defeated Papadu in the battle.

The story of the boy killing Papadu and the following incident about Papadu's head being received on a golden plate, do not appear in the printed version. However, Papadu in this text also kills himself when he finds his fortunes in the battle reversed.

(gavandla).[13] He was born in Pulagam, grew up in Tarikonda, and his family name was known as Mogili. His father was a village officer *(patel)*, his mother was Sarvamma. He had a sister named Jaggayi, and a brother who was a petty army commander *(sardar)*. When he was twelve, Papadu went to his mother dressed like a soldier, with a sword and spear. He asked her to direct him to do things suitable to his ability. She said he was too young to achieve anything, and asked him instead to take the cows out to graze. He called his friends and associates (the story-teller says he had 12 friends and five associates, but lists the names of eight of them: Asen, Usen, Dudekula Peer, Yerikala Cittel, Yenadi Pasel, Kummari Govindu, Mangali Masappa, Jakkula Perumallu), and they followed him.

Instead of guarding the cattle, Papadu simply commanded the cows to behave themselves, and not to trespass into the fields of farmers. The obedient cattle stayed within limits, and grazed only on the permitted areas. At noon, he directed his followers to go to their homes and eat their meals. He himself rested under a mango tree and went to sleep. A twelve-hooded cobra saw Papadu, and recognized his noble features, which indicated that he would become a king. The cobra decided to provide shade for him against the sun for seven hours. Some

---

The story of Papadu has also received the attention of several scholars in Telugu. Mallampalli Somasekhara Sarma is the first historian to take notice of this song in 'Sarvayi Papadu', *Amaravati Stupamu*, Madras, 1932. Hari Adiseshuvu, *Janapadageya Vangmaya Paricayamu*, Guntur: Navya Vignana Pracunanabu, 1967, pp. 73–9, praises the artistic qualities of the song. B. Ramaraju, *Telugu Janapadageya Sahitayamu*, Hyderabad: Andhra Racayitala Sangham 1958, pp. 220–8, discusses the song as a folk ballad in relation to its historical references in Khafi Khan. All the scholars mention the oral version of the song but base their study on the printed version alone, Moreover, they tend to pay tribute to Papadu as a Telugu warrior and show little interest in analysing either the song or the historical version. In a way, these scholars appear to be participating in the continuing myths of Sarvayi Papadu.

The authors wish to thank Gene Roghair for making available to them his tape of the oral song.

[13]Gavandla is an alternative term for the Gamalla, a caste of 'toddy drawers, and distillers and vendors of arrack in the Telugu country'. More prosperous members of the caste sell toddy and the less prosperous extract toddy from toddy palms. In the nineteenth century some Gamallas were also employed as cooks and domestic servants. cf. E. Thurston, *Castes and Tribes of Southern India*, Madras, 9 vols, 1909, II, pp. 253–7.

Brahmins who were passing that way to Banaras saw the boy and the cobra, and cried out to warn him of the snake. The boy woke up, saw the reptile curled on his chest, and spreading its hood. He attempted to kill it. But the Brahmins prevented him from doing so. They said it was a twelve-hooded cobra, was not an ordinary one, but was a symbol of royalty. It would be a sin to kill it. The Brahmins then asking for his given name and family name, read his horoscope. They predicted that Papadu was destined to be king of Golconda. He would invade Bandar (i.e. the port) city, and Kandanur fort. He would ride on a palanquin, a vehicle that only kings and nobles would have, with a *golla* (cowherding caste) girl for his bride. He would also have a mistress, named Nancharu, of the fortune-telling *yerikala* caste. He would have 12 concubines, who would bring him great good fortune. He would grow to be so powerful that the ruler of Golconda, fearing him, would leave his kingdom and run away to Delhi. However, Papadu would die at the hands of a 12-year-old boy, the son of Jinkala Venkanna of the Muttarasu family in Golconda.

Papadu was pleased with the predictions. The one about his death did not bother him; he thought that a great life, though short, was better than a long and poor life. He decided not to graze cattle again. He went to his mother, and bowed to her. He requested her to direct him to do things suitable to his ability. She again said that he was too young to achieve great things. In addition, there was nothing better in the world that a person could carry out than his caste profession *(kula vidya)*. So, she asked him to sell toddy. Papadu did not want to perform low-caste work. He called his friends, and told them what his mother had asked him to do. They decided there was fun in toddy; they could get drunk. The toddy they drank sometime ago was not strong enough: it was Golconda toddy. This time they wanted to go to Jidigallu, where the king of Golconda had his private palm from which he got his supply of toddy. The ruler had ordered 12 soldiers to watch the palm tree, and had placed silver and gold rings on it indicating that it was a royal palm. No one else was permitted to drink from that tree. Now, Papadu and his friends decided to get toddy from that tree.

Arriving at Jidigallu they commanded Jidanna, the chief of the grove, who was also a *gavandla* caste person, to give them the best toddy available. Jidanna did not want to give Papadu the toddy from the royal palm, but neither did he want to be beaten by Papadu. Therefore he lied to Papadu: it was summertime and all the trees were dry. If only Papadu came in the right season, Jidanna would have as much toddy as Papadu and his associates could drink. But Papadu was not satisfied with such a feeble reply. He asked Jidanna to go into his grove and command the trees to yield toddy, in the name of Papadu. Even now Jidanna did not want to drain toddy from the royal palm. Instead he preferred to cut the *katamayya* palm. This was the tree he reserved in the name of his family diety, Katamayya, and never slashed for toddy. Now he cut this palm in 12 places and attached pots to it. But the tree was too proud and did not yield any toddy. Papadu, growing angry, went into the grove and commanded the palm to yield toddy immediately. The tree not only gave toddy, but bent down to the earth to deliver the toddy to Papadu.

Jidanna saw that Papadu was too strong for an ordinary man to resist. But he did not want to be abused and ill-treated either. Therefore, he plotted to kill Papadu by putting poison in his toddy. However, Papadu was too strong for any poison; he would not die—such a plan was futile. Papadu and his friends, having drunk as much as they liked, gave the leftover toddy to their donkey to drink. Still much toddy remained. Papadu then commanded the donkey to carry the toddy to his mother's home. When the donkey was unable to do so, because it was completely intoxicated, Papadu cut its nose and ears. The donkey, running for its life, went to Golconda to seek refuge. Three thousand donkeys at the outskirts of Golconda, having seen the fate of this donkey, and all fearing the same kind of treatment at the hands of Papadu, fled to Delhi.

Papadu and his friends now decided to go to the festival of Ramasvami, at Jidigallu. But they had no money. Papadu therefore went to his mother and asked for a little money. When she replied that she had none, Papadu became angry and frustrated. He ordered his friends to get some oil and boil it hot. He then approached his mother affectionately and pretending to request her help, poured the hot oil on her body. He continued to torture her until she revealed all the secret places where she had hidden her money. It turned out that she had quite a large sum hoarded in secret places. One such hiding spot was the temple of Yellamma, their family deity, where his mother kept the money buried underground. Papadu went to the temple and commanded Yellamma to dig out all the money from that ground. He then ordered Yellamma out of the temple; Papadu said that he himself was god; there was no place for two deities in the family.

Papadu collected the money consecrated to the goddess, which amounted to several hundred thousand rupees. He had a golden palanquin made for himself, and set out to Jidigallu with his followers. On his way, Papadu reached a village of cowherders. The daughter of the headman had been married that day. The bride and bridegroom were sleeping in the house. Papadu invaded it, and raped the bride, while the bridegroom fled for his life. A warrior named Venkat Rao came to punish Papadu, but was defeated in single combat by the hero. Thereafter, Papadu plundered the village, and acquired much gold and silver.

Papadu, continuing his exploits, attacked the city of Bandar (Machilipatnam), and Kandanur. In the course of these adventures he met a gypsy girl, Yerikala Nancharu, who was going to tell the fortune of the sultan of Delhi. Papadu stopped her, and said that he was greater than the sultan. He took her to be his mistress, put her in one of his forts, and continued his plundering raids. A celebrated Telugu warrior, Vajranabhudu, fought him unsuccessfully. Vajranabhudu then sought the help of the king of Golconda in controlling Papadu. But even he could not stand the power of Papadu, who fought a fierce battle with the Muslim ruler, and emerged victorious. The king left his city, and fled to Delhi. Papadu ordered Golconda to be plundered. He and his followers carried all the riches on carts to his home. But on the way back, Papadu encountered death.

The 12-year-old son of Jinkala Venkanna had set a snare to catch deer. When Papadu approached in the darkness, the boy thought it was a deer, and shot him with his gun. Papadu realized it was his destiny. But, he did not want to die by someone else's hands. He therefore beheaded himself with his sword. The severed head shot up into the sky. Just at that time, the king of Golconda was returning form Delhi to see if Papadu's army had left his city. He saw the head hanging in the sky, and placed it upon a golden plate. The ruler declared the greatness of Papadu as a hero, and had his body buried with royal honours. He proclaimed the Kartika Pournami, the full moon day in October-November as the annual ritual day in honour of Papadu. With this dramatic finale ends the legend of a bandit turned into a mythical hero.

Convergences between Chronicle and Ballad

At first glance, the folk legend, sung in Telugu verse, some two and a half centuries after its subject lived, seems in its mythical and fantastic episodes to be far removed from the historical account of Khafi Khan. Nevertheless, enough details are common to both ballad and chronicle to make an identification possible. Among the more important of these are the name, origins and caste of the bandit leader. Papadu, in the Persian text, is described as of 'base lineage, from a caste *(qaum)* of toddy sellers; without respectability'. In the Telugu ballad (in both versions), Sarvayi Papadu is described more precisely as a member of the *gavandla* caste of toddy sellers.

In the ensuing narrative, other major points of agreement can be seen. The ballad, like the chronicle, portrays the bandit as a cruel, ruthless, ambitious figure who begins his career by defying his caste role, and deliberately choosing to become a desperado. Both sources show that Papadu acquires his first working capital by assaulting and torturing a female relative (his mother in the ballad, and his widowed sister in the chronicle). In each account, the erstwhile bandit assembles a large army, and adopts elements of the kingly style. In the Persian narrative, he employs a formidable personal bodyguard, rides on a palanquin (reserved for great men), and controls a miniature state around his forts. In the Telugu ballad, the Brahmins predict that he is destined to become king of Golconda, to have an army of 12,000 men, 12 mistresses, and to ride on a palanquin. In both accounts, Papadu successfully assaults several major towns: Warangal and Bhongir in the chronicle, Golconda, Bandar and Kandanur in the ballad, he fights the chief Muslim political figure in the region: Rustam Dil Khan and Yusuf Khan, the Mughal governors of Hyderabad, and the 'Navab [king] of Golconda'. All the sources agree that the bandit leader met a violent end; that he was decapitated; and that the actions of one of his fellow caste members caused his death.

In addition to these main structural features, other smaller points increase our confidence in this identification. The constant references to Papadu's cruelty and lustfulness in Khafi Khan's version are matched in the Telugu songs. References to mutilation by cutting out the tongues of his victims, in the Persian account, find an echo in the longer Telugu version, in which the protagonist cuts the nose and ears of a donkey. The bandit's continuing abduction of women, and his assaults on marriage parties are paralleled by the Telugu description of his attack on a *golla* wedding, and the ravishing of the bride. Papadu's plundering activities, and especially his incessant hunt for hoarded and buried treasure, in the chronicle, also appear in the ballads. The account of Khafi Khan describes Papadu's conflicts with Venkat Rao, the *zamindar* of Kaulas, while the ballad describes a duel with a warrior of the same name.

On some matters, the Telugu ballads supply information not known to or not included by Khafi Khan. Thus, we find Tarikonda mentioned as the place in which Papadu was reared as well as mention of his birthplace. Papadu's first name, Sarvayi, as given in the sung ballad, is not used by the Mughal chronicler. This helps to alleviate some of the confusion surrounding the identity of Sarva, Papadu's associate who is a separate person, and the Sarvapapra named in the Dutch account of the bandit leader's audience with Bahadur Shah, the Mughal emperor. We also can see, from the identification given at the beginning of the ballad, that Papadu was of a caste ranking very low in the ritual hierarchy of Hindu society, having a lowly traditional occupation (i.e. tapping toddy palms, making and selling toddy); but, in the chronicle, Papadu's family actually belonged to the upper strata of the peasantry. His father was a village headman, his brother a military commander. Thus, there was some form of previous political, military and administrative experience in his family background. This also explains the existence of considerable hoarded family funds.

Perhaps most important is the list of Papadu's immediate followers given in both ballads. These include members of both Hindu and Muslim low or untouchable castes, and some low tribal castes: Muslim quilt makers and cotton cleaners, Hindu potters and barbers both unclean, and tribal animal breeders, itinerant fortune-tellers and thieves, singers and performers make up the list.[14] If this list accurately reflects the low or unclean caste composition of Papadu's immediate followers, it is probable that Papadu was leading a revolt against political, economic and ritual domination by the locally powerful classes of Hyderabad, both Muslim and Hindu. What seems to be a disjuncture between the attained secular status of Papadu's family, and the ritual and occupational status of his caste, helps to explain his flat rejection of his caste role.

[14]Most of the names of Papadu's followers, according to either version, show that they come from lower castes of both Muslim and Hindu communities. Dudekula is a Muslim caste of cotton cleaners and quilt makers. *Yerikala, jakkula,* and *yenadi* are tribal groups of itinerant fortune-tellers, thieves, animal breeders, singers, and performers. *Cakali* (washerman), *mangali* (barber), *kummari* (potter), and *medari* (basket weaver) are marginal Hindu castes. Among the group, Nelluri Hanumanthu is probably a clean-caste Hindu. The use of the family name Nelluri, rather than a low-caste name, indicates a possible higher social status. The status of the others, Asen, Usen and Turka Himan, is also uncertain. Kotwal Miri Saheb is probably a person of higher status among Muslims. But the company of low-caste persons makes even a clean-caste person unclean.

Conclusion: The Historical Bandit and Folk Hero

The sudden collapse of imperial power in the eastern Deccan severed the lines of simultaneous support and control from the centre of imperial authority to Hyderabad province. The connections between the emperor and the provincial corps of imperial officers in Hyderabad (the *mansabdars);* between the emperor and the local Muslim élite of the towns and cities; and between the emperor and the partially assimilated Telugu regional rural aristocracy (the *zamindars)* had snapped. This development was coupled with Maratha plundering raids, the social and economic dislocation attendant upon them, and upon widespread dearth from drought in the countryside. The breakdown of imperial guarantees and public order, as well as the confused movement of large numbers of impoverished peasants, artisans and former soldiers, explains the success of both Riza Khan and Papadu.

Under these circumstances, a Mughal district military commander could ignore the emperor's orders, build up a following, harry the roads and survive. So also could an able, ambitious, low-caste Telugu brigand build up an army large enough to assault two of the largest towns in the region.

But if the rise of each of these men can be attributed to the same social and political context, some important distinctions can be made as well. First, Riza Khan did not seem to threaten the Muslim-dominated imperial, social, and political order in the same way as did Papadu. In his account of Papadu's life and in his general treatment of the period, Khafi Khan ignores Riza Khan. The fragmentary account which we have compiled of the latter's activities comes from official news reports, from references to him made by Dutch merchants in their correspondence, and from a Venetian adventurer long in Mughal service. Unlike his Telugu counterpart, the former Mughal officer seems to have established no fortified territorial base. His targets were apparently restricted to road traffic and villages. Nor did he make any spectacular attacks on major towns. Nor did he assault and kidnap members of the Muslim nobility or Telugu *zamindars.* Although technically in revolt, Riza Khan sustained very close connections with the governor, and other Mughal administrators in Hyderabad. On occasion, he could even be approached by the latter for fiscal and military assistance against Papadu.

By contrast, Khafi Khan portrays Papadu as a cruel, lustful infidel who was an open threat to the personal and collective honour of Muslims and the Muslim empire. But Khafi Khan also reveals that he was as dangerous for the Telugu *zamindars* whom he was displacing in the countryside. The key point here is that Papadu was engaged in dual rebellion: against the Muslim-controlled, urban-focused state structure and against the local domination of the Telugu *zamindars*. The latter were the political and military arm of the Brahmin-controlled Sanskritic high culture of the Telugu-speaking areas. The *zamindars*, acting as attenuated, much reduced versions of Hindu monarchs of the pre-Muslim period, enforced and regulated the rigidly stratified caste system. Prompted and supported by their Brahmin advisers and priests, the Telugu aristocracy buttressed the local caste system with its stress on differential ritual status, on proper caste behaviour and occupation, and on proper deference for lower castes. In his revolt against this caste occupation and in his attack upon the Telugu *zamindars*, Papadu struck at the most basic ordering of society—an ordering long accepted and supported by the Muslim overlords of the eastern Deccan.

Here we approach a plausible explanation for the notoriety which Papadu attained among the Muslim élite, and for his origin as a hero of folk legend. Riza Khan, alien in origins, Muslim, aristocratic, a former imperial officer, offered no substantial menace to the imperial or local social order. Papadu rebelled against both. His radical social threat may be seen as the origin of his appeal to the Telugu folk culture—which was distinct from the high Brahminical Sanskritic tradition. However, this original appeal becomes overshadowed by a mythical, a legendary quality which overtakes the circumstances surrounding the human, historical figure of Papadu.

A person who defies his low social role and reaches high positions of power, exhibiting great courage in the process, has always enjoyed a certain degree of admiration. If such a person has the added dimension of fighting for social justice, however vaguely perceived the concept might be, the daring hero becomes a demigod. Papadu was one such hero and thus, he became eligible to be elevated into a legend.

Folk-songs about historically identifiable heroes in Telugu have not yet been systematically studied as a genre in literature; nor has their structure been examined in relation to myths. An attempt is being made here to suggest that the transformation from history to legend in this folk-song conforms to identifiable structures of Telugu folk mythology.

In folk mythology, destiny plays the supreme role in the development of a hero. His birth, or the beginning of his heroic activities, is related to a higher power manifesting itself in the course of the activities of the hero. (Papadu is destined to be king of Golconda.) In the same way his death also becomes an act of destiny. A hero does not die because he is killed or for such other normal reasons. He dies because his role has come to an end. (Papadu kills himself. The incident of Jinkala Venkanna's son only serves as a reminder to Papadu that his role ended.) Anything that the hero does between these two points—between his emergence as destined hero and his exit from the active world—is therefore removed from the realm of human standards. The acts of the hero are not subject to normal judgement of the mundane world. The hero is superhuman, and therefore is above human understanding. The fantastic element in the folk narratives confirms the superiority of the hero, and often establishes his communication with powers that normal human beings do not control. The presence of magic numbers such as 12 or 7 in the fantastic events connected with the hero apparently strengthens this function.

Papadu's story, subject to the established structure of a folk legend, begins with a snake providing shade to him, thus indicating his royal destiny. A prediction by Brahmins, basing their forecast on the Vedas, serves as a confirmation as well as a Sanskritization[15] of the legend, of which we will have more to say later. Destiny which has to be fulfilled has been revealed by the sacred snake, and is confirmed by the infallible Vedas as interpreted by the Brahmins. Given this destiny, the cruel, ambitious, and ruthless acts of the historical account take a different complexion; they are the superhuman acts of a superhuman hero. The heroe's personality is built layer by layer, until his superiority is established in the minds of the listeners. Papadu orders the cows to graze within their limits; they obey him. Papadu demands of the Brahmins to read his horoscope; they obey him. Cows and Brahmins, two sacred institutions of the society, submit to him. The trees in the toddy grove, including the royal palm and the palm of the deity Katamayya, obey him. Papadu always commands, and commands everyone—people, animals, trees, or gods; either they obey him or he punishes them. Cruel acts of intimidation mentioned in the historical account become acts of punishment, deserved for not obeying a superhuman hero. Even the type of punishment is changed to suit a folk legend. It is not cutting the tongue as the historical account indicates; it is cutting the nose and ears. This is a typical punishment that repeatedly occurs

[15]Sanskritization in this context refers to imitation of the forms of classical Sanskrit literature. More broadly, it also refers to admission of the superiority of Brahminical high culture as opposed to the less sophisticated culture of the lower castes.

in a number of legends. It acquires a stylized mention by the rhyming of the words meaning nose and ears, '*mukku cevulu*' and the word meaning three, '*mudu*'.

After a structured narration establishing Papadu's control of, and communication with, all the universe around him—humans, animals and vegetation—now the story-teller is ready to relate the specific act of his torturing his mother, and later his ravishing a married woman. These are heinous crimes, destructive of the very values of stability, of family organization which is so very central to society. But insulated by the preceding events, which established a superhuman and the all-pervading personality of the hero, the acts do not shock the listeners. On the other hand (to continue the analogy), they galvanize the hero. In the context of the fulfilment of the mission of a hero who is god, anyone who does not collaborate and co-operate with him is punishable, and whatever treatment he receives at the hands of the hero, however cruel it is, is deserved punishment. The mother, had she only given him the money when he had asked, would have had the respectable status of a co-operating agent in the acts of the hero. But she did not, and so follows the punishment. The story-teller does not indicate any sense of disapproval of the act of Papadu, nor does he make the mother's character that of a helpless innocent sufferer.

Papadu's death also gets transformed into the legend, following the established pattern. He does not die at anyone's hand. No poison kills him. No warrior kills him. The accident caused by the 12-year-old son of Jinkala Venkanna, which was predicted by the Brahmins, alone leads to his death. Even that mishap only serves as an indication that his preordained task in this world has come to an end. Papadu kills himself, dramatizing the fact that there is no one equal to him on this earth.

According to the historical account, Papadu was beheaded, his head was sent to Delhi, and his body was cut into pieces. A mystification of this incident is now in order, to make a fitting end to the legend. Fact gets transformed into fantasy; the nawab holds the head falling from the sky on a golden plate. He orders a royal funeral for Papadu, and declares Papadu's greatness to all the world.

Central to the structure of a folk legend is often its supernatural mistresses symbolism. Papadu's story has a repeated occurrence of the number 12 and the number seven. Papadu is 12 years old, the snake has 12 hoods; Papadu has 12 friends; the number of his mistresses is 12; the royal palm in the toddy grove has 12 rings and 12 watchmen.

Papadu's army is 12,000 strong, and his death is caused by a 12-year-old boy.[16] Similarly, there is a recurrence of the number seven. The snake provides shade for Papadu for seven hours; Papadu has seven wives; he is destined to rule Golconda for seven hours. The number of pots of toddy the palm gives is seven. While the precise meaning of this numerical symbolism is not clear, it is obvious that it has no relationship to actual fact. Numbers 12, seven, five, and three occur repeatedly in many folk legends in Telugu.

Subsequent to the transformation of history into a folk legend, a layer of Sanskritization is added to it. The folk-singer, trying to imitate the external form of a Purana story, begins the song with an invocation to the god Siva, and ends it with *mangalam*, an auspicious song to god. All through the narration, the singer uses a language full of hyperforms, imitating the Brahmin dialect of Sanskritized Telugu. The structure of the legend and its internal incidents are folk, while the element of Sanskritization is clearly a latch adjunct to it.

The story of Sarvayi Papadu is a continuing legend. Compared to the myths of India, it is a very young myth; hardly two and a half centuries old. But the transformations it has undergone, and is still undergoing, give a fascinating possibility to speculate into the process of myth-making, and relates the process to greater Indian myths.

In a recent play entitled *Sardaru Papadu,* a noted Telugu author, P.V. Rajamannar, has transformed the story of the singers very significantly.[17] Papadu in this play is a very highly principled man, who has decided to become a warrior to redress the grievances of the suffering common people in the hands of rich and cruel lords. He commands his followers never to intimidate women, nor to oppress helpless

[16]John W. Spellman, 'The Number Twelve in Ancient India', *Journal of Asian Studies,* XXII-I, November 1962, draws the attention of scholars to the symbolic significance of the number 12. He suggests that 'it implies the restoration of *dharma* or expiation of guilt'. Spellman has used only Sanskrit sources in his study. If we take folk sources into consideration, the significance of the number of symbols would need a different interpretation. It is clear that the numbers 12 and seven in this story are associated with royalty and destiny in some way. But we cannot say with certainty that the concept of *dharma* is accepted in this-folk song or in Telugu folk literature in general.

[17]P.V. Rajamannar, *Sardaru Papadu,* Machilipatnam: M. Seshachelam & Co., 1972.

people. He marries his beloved Nancharu of the 'criminal' *yerikala* caste, who predicts that he will become king of Golconda. This is a marriage by consent and even mutual love. Nancharu, Papadu's gypsy wife, according to this story, turns out to be a girl of the *gavandla* caste kidnapped, when she was an infant, by *yerikalas*. Thus, the story keeps the caste honour of *gavandlas* and at the same time confirms the thieving quality of the *yerikalas* in one stroke.

He asks his mother for money to pay for an army and threatens to burn her body if she does not give the money. But his wife Nancharu, who, by now has become a very affectionate daughter-in-law, interprets the threat as a remark made under the influence of liquor. The mother, trying to help her son, reveals a small source of money. Papadu, however, wants more money and to get it from her, threatens to kill himself with the sword he has in his belt. In this version no torturing of the mother occurs. Instead we find the Gandhian ethic of self-mortification as a means of convincing others of the nobility of one's actions.

Papadu, in this story, is an ideal son, an ideal husband, an ideal friend, and also an ideal hero. Nancharu is an ideal wife, and Papadu's friends are ideal friends who die along with Papadu. Even Jidanna, who, in the legned, tries to poison him, becomes his ideal brother-in-law as Nancharu's own brother. Jidanna is also a willing host to Papadu when the latter goes to drink at his grove with his band of followers. The element of fantasy is completely eliminated except for the snake incident and fortune-telling by the gypsy girl. These incidents serve merely as a confirmation of the heroic stature of Papadu. Comparing the folk-singer's version to the modern play, it is obvious that while Papadu undergoes a deification in the folk legend, he is idealized in the written play. By deification, the folk legend elevates Papadu to a higher plane, above human judgement. Through idealization, Papadu is depicted as a great human hero in the written play.

One is tempted to make a comparison with the story of Krishna, or Rama. They are made gods. Their births and deaths are presented as manifestations and withdrawals of the Supreme God, and thus, questionable acts, like illicit association with others' wives in the case of Krishna or killing Vali by deception in the case of Rama, are placed above human judgement. To the extent they are made gods, their actions are removed from human criticism. Rama of Tulsi Das is the Supreme God. Even his victims are his devotees who chose to reach him through enmity, a special form of devotion named *vairabhakti.* Similarly, Krishna of *Bhagavata Purana* is only blessing the women with liberation when he was involved with them in what might look like a sexual orgy to the irreverent reader. In other stories, Rama and Krishna undergo a process of idealization. In those versions, they are depicted less as gods, and more as ideal human beings, with a minimum mention of their godly origins. The best example of a Rama story, where Rama is depicted more as an ideal king rather than god, is Valmiki's *Ramayana.* Similarly, Krishna of the *Mahabharata* appears more as a highly idealized diplomat, friend, charioteer and leader rather than as the God in Supreme which he is the *Bhagavata Purana.*

Idealization and deification seem to be two processes which myths in India undergo in the course of being retold in time. It appears that the myth of Sarvayi Papadu is participating in the same process as that of larger and older myths.

A further aspect that is important is that the folk legend shows a thin layer of Sanskritization on it. As a story of a person that was originally opposed to Sanskritized upper-caste groups and one that was sung by lower-caste groups, the basic narrative is not very sympathetic to Brahmins. Papadu's irreverent attitude to the Brahmins who read his horoscope is clear evidence of the point. As such, the presence of Sanskritization suggests a process through which myths of lower castes become assimilated into a 'great tradition'.

Bibliography

The bibliography on Mughal India in the form of research papers and monographs is vast; this listing is thus far from comprehensive. To our knowledge, no recent bibliography exists either, that by S.R. Sharma being considerably out of date. Its compilation should hence be accorded high priority by bibliographers and librarians. In the interim, useful bibliographies and references to both primary and secondary literature exist in Irfan Habib, *The Agrarian System of Mughal India* (1963), more recently in the *Cambridge Economic History of India*, vol. I (1982) and in Muzaffar Alam, *The Crisis of Empire in Mughal North India* (1986). The recent synthetic work by J.F. Richards, *The Mughal Empire* (1993), contains a brief bibliographic essay.

The annual *Proceedings of the Indian History Congress* normally sees Mughal studies well represented, and is a point of reference for articles that are however usually limited in size, and usually aimed at bringing to light documentation. In recent years, the papers have however been of declining quality, and dominated by scholars of the 'Aligarh School' to the exclusion of other viewpoints. Amongst periodicals, now defunct journals such as the *Medieval India Quarterly*, *Medieval India—A Miscellany*, and *Enquiry*, published a number of important papers on the Mughals over the years. From the 1940s to the 1960s, the Hyderabad-based *Islamic Culture* also published extensively on the Mughals, though since then, its focus has shifted elsewhere. A very large number of substantive papers on aspects of Mughal society and economy have been published in the *Indian Economic and Social History Review*, and to a lesser extent the *Indian Historical Review*, and *Studies in History*. Amongst journals published outside of India, mention should be made of the *Journal of the Historical Society of Pakistan,* and the *Journal of the Asiatic Society of Pakistan* (later Bangladesh). In the West, occasional papers on the Mughals have appeared in the *Journal of the Economic and Social History of the Orient,* and *Modern Asian Studies,* besides a few other journals.

1. Research Aids

The following listing provides a sample of aids on literature, prosopography of notables, guides to manuscripts, and periodical and monographic literature.

'Abdu'l Ghani, Muhammad, *A History of Persian Language and Literature at the Mughal Court, with a Brief Survey of the Growth of Urdu Language,* 2 vols, Allahabad: The Indian Press Ltd, 1930; Rpt, Westmead: Gregg International Publishers Ltd, 1972.

Athar Ali, M., *The Apparatus of Empire: Awards of Ranks, Offices and Titles to the Mughal Nobility 1573–1658*, Delhi: Oxford University Press, 1985.

Encyclopaedia of Islam (eds B. Lewis, V. L. Ménage, Ch. Pellat and J. Schacht), 2nd edn, Leiden–London: E.J. Brill-Luzac & Co., vols I, 1962.

Habib, Irfan *An Atlas of the Mughal Empire: Political and Economic Maps with Detailed Notes, Bibliography and Index,* Aligarh, Centre of Advanced Study in History, Aligarh Muslim University, Delhi: Oxford University Press, 1982 (2nd revised edn 1986).

Index Islamicus 1906–1955, A Catalogue of Articles on Islamic Subjects in Periodicals and Other Collective Publications, compiled by J.D. Pearson, with the assistance of J.F. Ashton, Cambridge, W. Heffer, 1958; *Supplement 1956–1960,* comp. J.D. Pearson, Cambridge, 1962; *Second Supplement 1961–1965, idem,* 1967; *Third Supplement, 1966–1970,* comp. J.D. Pearson and Ann Walsh, London: Mansell, 1972; *Fourth Supplement,* Part I, 1971–1972, *idem,* 1973; Part II, 1972–1973, *idem* 1973; Part, III, 1973–1974, *idem,* 1975; Part IV 1974–1975, *idem,* 1976.

Index Islamicus, 1976–1980, part 1, Articles, comp. J.D. Pearson, London: Mansell, 1983; rpt, 1986; Part 2, Monographs, comp. J.D. Pearson and Wolfgang Behn, *idem,* 1983; rpt, 1986.

Index Islamicus, 1981–1985, A Bibliography of Books and Articles of the Muslim World, compiled and edited by G.J. Roper, 2 vols, London: Mansell, 1991.

Khalidi, Omar, *Dakan under the Sultans, 1296–1724: A Bibliography of Monographic and Periodical Literature,* Wichita (Kansas): Haydarabad Historical Society, 1987.

Marshall, D.N., *Mughals in India. A Bibliographical Survey of Manuscripts* (1967), London–New York: Mansell, 1985.

Momin, Mohiuddin, *The Chancellery and Persian Epistolography under the Mughals (Babur to Shahjahan),* Calcutta: Iran Society, 1971.

Schwartzberg, Joseph E., ed., *A Historical Atlas of South Asia* (1978); second impression with additional material, New York–Oxford: Oxford University Press, 1992. (Association for Asian Studies Reference Studies, No. 2).

Sharma, Sri Ram, A *Bibliography of Mughal India (1526–1707* A.D.), Bombay, *c.* 1939; rpt, Bombay: Karnatak Publishing House, n.d.

Storey, Charles Ambrose, *Persian Literature. A Bio-Bibliographical Survey,* London: Royal Asiatic Society, 1937–9; rpt, Leiden: E.J. Brill, 1977.

Taraporevala, V.D.D. and D.N. Marshall, *Mughal Bibliography. Select Persian Sources for the Study of Mughals in India,* Bombay: New Book Co., 1962.

2. Art History

As an important additional source of material on Mughal court culture, some major reference works on Mughal art history are listed below.

Beach, Milo Cleveland, *Early Mughal Painting,* Cambridge, (Mass.): Harvard University Press, 1987.

——, *Mughal and Rajput Painting* (The New Cambridge History of India, vol. I.3), Cambridge: Cambridge University Press, 1992.

Binyon, Laurence, *The Court Painters of the Grand Moguls,* with historical introduction and notes by T.W. Arnold, London–Bombay: Humphrey Milford, Oxford University Press, 1921.

Brand, Michael and Glenn D. Lowry, *Akbar*'s *India. Art from the Mughal City of Victory,* New York: Asia Society Galleries, 1985.

Goswami, B.N. and Eberhard Fischer, *Wonders of a Golden Age. Painting at the Court of the Great Mughals. Indian Art of the 16th and 17th Centuries from Collections in Switzerland,* Munich: Museum Rietberg, 1987.

Verma, Som Prakash, 'Elements of Historicity in the Portraits of the Mughal School', *The Indian Historical Review,* vol. IX (1/2), 1982–3, pp. 63–73.

——, *Mughal Painters and Their Work: A Biographical Survey and Comprehensive Catalogue*, Delhi: Oxford University Press, 1994.

Welch, Stuart Cary, Annemarie Schimmel, Marie L. Swietochowski, and Wheeler M. Thackson, *The Emperor's Album. Images of Mughal India*, New York: Metropolitan Museum of Art, 1987.

3. General Studies

There is a surprising lack of good general histories of the Mughal state. Amongst popular, illustrated treatments by amateurs, that of Gascoigne is relatively acceptable. The recent volume by Richards in the *New Cambridge History of India* bravely attempts to bridge the gap between orthodox viewpoints and recent research. Aziz Ahmad's work is still a valuable point of reference. For the rest, the essay by I.H. Qureshi represents his 'orthodox' viewpoint well enough, and must be read with caution, like the works of Srivastava and Sharma.

Ahmad, Aziz, *Studies in Islamic Cultures in the Indian Environment*, Oxford: Clarendon Press, 1964.

Athar Ali, M., 'Towards an Interpretation of the Mughal Empire', *Journal of the Asiatic Society of Great Britain and Ireland*, 1978, no. 1, pp. 38–49.

Gascoigne, Bamber, *The Great Moghuls*, London, Jonathan Cape, 1971; rpt, 1974, 1976, 1979, 1985; paperback edn, Delhi: Time Books International, 1987.

Habib, Irfan, *Essays in Indian History: Towards a Marxist Perception*, Delhi: Tulika, 1995.

Qureshi, I.H., 'India under the Mughals', in P.M. Holt, Ann K.S. Lambton and Bernard Lewis, eds, *The Cambridge History of Islam*, Cambridge: Cambridge University Press, 1970, vol. II, pp. 35–63.

——, *The Muslim Community in the Indo-Pakistani Subcontinent*, The Hague: Mouton, 1963.

Richards, J.F., *The Mughal Empire* (The New Cambridge History of India, vol. I.5). Cambridge: Cambridge University Press, 1993.

Sharma, Sri Ram, *Mughal Empire in India. A Systematic Study Including Source Material*, 3rd ed., Bombay: Karnatak Publishing House, 1947; revised edn, Agra: Lakshmi Narain Agarwal, *c*. 1966.

Srivastava, A.L., *The Mughal Empire 1526–1803* AD, Agra: S.L. Agarwala, 1977.

Tripathi, R.P., *Rise and Fall of the Mughal Empire*, Allahabad, 1956.

4. Comparative Studies

The Mughal empire has usually been seen comparatively in terms of the Asiatic Mode of Production (as in Athar Ali's essay), or in terms of one of a number of 'despotic' states seeking vainly to escape the inevitable onslaught of Western capitalism. But there have also been a number of independent attempts at comparison.

Anderson, Perry, *Lineages of the Absolutist State,* London: New Left Books, 1974.

Athar Ali, M., 'Political Structures of the Islamic Orient in the Sixteenth and Seventeenth Centuries', in Irfan Habib ed., *Medieval India 1: Researches in the History of India, 1200–1750,* Delhi: Oxford University Press, 1992, pp. 129–40.

Bayly, C.A., *Imperial Meridian: The British Empire and the World 1780–1830,* London: Longman, 1989.

Blake, Stephen P., 'The Patrimonial-Bureaucratic Empire of the Mughals', *Journal of Asian Studies,* vol. xxix (1), 1979, pp. 77–94.

Hodgson, Marshall G.S., *The Venture of Islam Vol. III: The Gunpowder Empires and Modern Times,* Chicago: The University of Chicago Press, 1974.

Kunt, I. Metin, 'The Later Muslim Empires: Ottomans, Safavids, Mughals', in Marjorie Kelly, ed., *Islam: The Religious and Political Life of a World Community,* New York: Praeger, 1984, pp. 112–36.

Richards, J.F., 'Mughal State Finance and the Premodern World Economy', *Comparative Studies in Society and History,* vol. xxiii (2), 1981, pp. 285–308.

——, 'The Seventeenth-century Crisis in South Asia', *Modern Asian Studies,* vol. xxiv (4), 1990, pp. 625–38.

Streusand, Douglas E., *The Formation of the Mughal Empire,* Delhi: Oxford University Press, 1989.

Subrahmanyam, Sanjay, 'Iranians Abroad: Intra-Asian Elite Migration and Early Modern State Formation', *Journal of Asian Studies,* vol. li (2), 1992, pp. 340–63.

——, 'The Mughal State—Structure or Process? Reflections on Recent Western Historiography', *Indian Economic and Social History Review,* vol. xxix (3) 1992, pp. 291–321.

Washbrook, David A., 'South Asia, the World System and World Capitalism', *The Journal of Asian Studies,* vol. xlix (3), 1990, pp. 479–508.

5. Biographies and Personality-centred Works

Traditional histories remain personality-oriented, as do the great bulk of courses on the Mughals. Over the years, a large number of imperial and sub-imperial biographies have flourished, though rarely with an explicitly psychological orientation.

Avasthy, Rama Shanker, *The Mughal Emperor Humayun*, Allahabad, History Department, University of Allahabad, 1967.

Banerji S.K., *Humāyūn Bādshāh*, 2 vols, vol. I, London: Oxford University Press, 1938; vol. II, Lucknow: Maxwell Co., 1941.

Dale, Stephen Frederic, 'Steppe Humanism: The Autobiographical Writings of Zahir al-Din Muhammad Babur, 1483–1530', *International Journal of Middle Eastern Studies*, vol. XXII, 1990, pp. 37–58.

Datta, K.K., *Alivardi and His Times*, Calcutta, 1939.

Hasan, Mohibbul, *Babur: Founder of the Mughal Empire in India*, Delhi: Manohar, 1985.

Husain, Yusuf, *The First Nizām: Life and Times of Nizam-ul-mulk, Asaf Jah I*, 2nd edn, Bombay, 1963.

Karim, Abdul, *Murshid Quli and His Times*, Dacca: Asiatic Society of Pakistan, 1963.

Khan, Iqtidar Alam, *The Political Biography of a Mughal Noble, Mun'im Khan Khan-i Khanan 1497–1575*, Delhi: Orient Longman, 1973.

——, *Mirza Kamran, A Biographical Study*, Bombay: Asia Publishing House, 1964.

——, 'Akbar's Personality Traits and World Outlook: A Critical Reappraisal', *Social Scientist*, vol.xx, nos. 9–10 (no. 232–3), 1992, pp. 16–30.

Malik, Zahir Uddin, *A Mughal Statesman of the Eighteenth Century: Khan-i Dauran, Mir Bakhshi of Muhammad Shah, 1719–1739*, Bombay: Asia Publishing House, 1973.

Naik, Chhotubhai Ranchhodji, *'Abdu'r-Rahīm Khān-i-Khānān and His Literary Circle*, Ahmedabad: Gujarat University, 1966. (Theses Publication Series, No. 2).

Prasad, Beni, *History of Jahangir*, Allahabad, 1930.

Prasad, Ishwari, *The Life and Times of Humayun*, Calcutta, 1955; Bombay: Orient Longman, 1955; rpt, Allahabad: Central Book Depot, 1976.

Qanungo, Kalika Ranjan, *Sher Shah and His Times: An Old Story Retold by the Author After Decades from a Fresh Standpoint*, Bombay: Orient Longman, 1965.

Rahim, A., 'Islām Shāh Sūr', *Journal of the Pakistan Historical Society*, vol. IV (4), Oct. 1956, pp. 245–77.

Ray, Sukumar, *Bairam Khan*, ed., M.H.A. Beg, Karachi: Institute of Central and West Asian Studies, University of Karachi, 1992.

Rushbrook Williams, L.F., *An Empire-Builder of the Sixteenth Century: Babur*, London, 1918.

Saksena, Banarsi Prasad, *History of Shahjahan of Dihli*, Allahabad, 1932.

Sarkar, Jadunath. *History of Aurangzib*, 5 vols, rpt, Calcutta, 1973.

Sarkar, Jagadish Narayan, *The Life of Mir Jumla, the General of Aurangzeb*, 2nd edn, Delhi: Janaki Prakashan, 1979.

Siddiqui, Iqtidar Husain, *History of Sher Shah Sur*, Aligarh: P.C. Dwadash Shreni, 1971.

Smith, Vincent A., *Akbar the Great Mogul*, Oxford: Clarendon Press, 1917.

Srivastava, A.L., *Akbar the Great*, 3 vols, Agra: S.L. Agarwala, 1973.

6: Religious, Ideological and Cultural Issues

Under this head, we have grouped an admittedly diverse set of materials, ranging from Buckler's controversial essays on Mughal sovereignty, to the Mughal link with Sufis and Sufi orders, to writings on Mughal architecture as a symbol of sovereignty, and an expression of shifting imperial ideology. A particularly outstanding and neglected piece, is Simon Digby's analysis of Dattu Sarvani's memoirs, an engaging early example of the 'history of mentalities' as applied to the first years of Mughal history.

Abdul Aziz, S., *The Imperial Library of the Mughals*, ed., A. Shakoor Ahsan, Lahore: Panjab University Press, 1967; rpt, Delhi: Idarah-i Adabiyat-i Delli, 1974.

Agravāl, Sarayū Prasād, *Akbarī darbār ke hindī kavī*, Lucknow: Lakhnau Visvavidyalaya, 1950.

Ahmad, Nazir, 'Some Cultural and Literary Remains of Emperor Humayun's Visit to Iran and Back to India', *Indo-Iranica*, vol. XXVIII, nos. I–IV, 1975, pp. 1–33.

Ali, Mubarak, 'The Mughal Court Ceremonies', *Journal of the Pakistan Historical Society*, vol. XXVIII (1), 1980, pp. 42–62.

Alvi, Sajida Sultana, *Advice on the Art of Governance: Mau'izah-i Jahāngīrī, of Muhammad Bāqir Najm-i Sānī, An Indo-Islamic Mirror for Princes*, Albany: State University of New York Press, 1989.

Asher, Catherine B., *Architecture of Mughal India,* vol. I, 4, The New Cambridge History of India, Cambridge: Cambridge University Press, 1992.

Begley, Wayne E., 'The Myth of the Taj Mahal and a New Theory of Its Symbolic Meaning', *The Art Bulletin,* no. 61, 1979, pp. 7–37.

Buckler, F.W., *Legitimacy and Symbols: The South Asian Writings of F.W. Buckler,* ed., M.N. Pearson, Ann Arbor: University of Michigan, 1985.

Chandra, Satish, *Mughal Religious Policies, the Rajputs and the Deccan,* Delhi: Vikas, 1993.

Digby, Simon, 'Dreams and Reminiscences of Dattu Sarvani, A Sixteenth Century Indo-Afghan Soldier' (in 2 parts), *The Indian Economic and Social History Review,* vol. II (1), 1965, pp. 52–80; vol. II (2), 1965 pp. 178–94.

Digby, Simon, 'Abd al-Quddus Gangohi (1456–1537 AD): The Personality and Attitudes of a Medieval Indian Sufi', in *Medieval India—A Miscellany,* vol. III, Bombay: Asia Publishing House, 1975, pp. 1–66.

Friedmann, Yohannan, *Shaykh Ahmad Sirhindi: An Outline of His Thought and a Study of His Image in the Eyes of Posterity,* Montreal: McGill University, 1971.

Gaborieau, Marc, 'Les oulémas/soufis dans l'Inde moghole: Anthropologie historique des religieux musulmans', *Annales E.S.C.,* 1989, no. 5, pp. 1185–1204.

Habib, Irfan, 'Political Role of Shaikh Ahmad Sirhindi and Shah Waliullah', *Proceedings of the Indian History Congress,* 1960, pp. 209–23.

Koch, Ebba, *Mughal Architecture: An Outline of Its History and Development (1528–1858),* Munich: Prestel, 1991.

Mukhia, Harbans, *Historians and Historiography during the Reign of Akbar,* Delhi: Vikas Publishing House, 1976.

Nizami, Khaliq Ahmad, 'Naqshbandi Influence on Mughal Rulers and Politics', *Islamic Culture,* vol. XXXIX, 1965, pp. 41–52.

——, *Akbar and Religion,* Delhi, 1989.

Qaisar, Ahsan Jan, *The Indian Response to European Technology and Culture, 1498–1707* AD, Delhi: Oxford University Press, 1982.

Rizvi, S.A.A., *Religious and Intellectual History of the Muslims in Akbar's Reign, with Special Reference to Abu'l Fazl, 1556–1605,* Delhi: Munshiram Manoharlal, 1975.

Rizvi, Saiyid Athar Abbas, *Muslim Revivalist Movements in Northern India in the Sixteenth and Seventeenth Centuries*, Agra: Agra University, 1965.

——, *A History of Sufism in India*, 2 vols, Delhi: Munshiram Manoharlal, vol. I, Early Sufism and Its History in India to 1600 AD, 1978; vol. II, From Sixteenth Century to Modern Century, 1983.

Russell, Ralph and Khurshidul Islam, *Three Mughal Poets: Mir, Sauda, Mir Hasan*, Cambridge (Mass.): Harvard University Press, 1968.

Sharma, Sri Ram, *The Religious Policy of the Mughal Emperors*, 3rd edn, Agra: S.L. Agarwala, 1972.

7. State and Economy

The methodological bases for an understanding of the Mughal state and its relations with the economy that exist today (e.g. in the *Cambridge Economic History of India*, vol. I), were in fact laid by W.H. Moreland in three monographs in the 1920s. Since then, scholars from the 'Aligarh school' and elsewhere have modified it in minor ways, enriched its details and corrected factual errors, but produced no fundamental shift in the paradigm (cf. works of Habib, Moosvi, etc.). More recent scholarship, however, has begun to call into question the Moreland–Habib model of a centralized fiscal despotism.

Alam, Muzaffar, 'Trade, State Policy and Regional Change: Aspects of Mughal–Uzbek Commercial Relations, *c.* 1550–1750', *Journal of the Economic and Social History of the Orient*, vol. XXXVII (2), 1994, pp. 202–27.

Bagchi, A.K. 'The Mughal Economy: A Quantitative Study', *Indian Historical Review*, vol. XIII (1–2), 1986–7, pp. 174–80.

Bhattacharya, S., 'Towards an Interpretation of the Pre-Colonial Economy', *Economic and Political Weekly*, 1 October, 1983, pp. 1707–11.

Brennig, Joseph J., 'The Textile Trade of Seventeenth-century Northern Coromandel: A Study of a Pre-modern Asian Export Industry', Ph.D. thesis, University of Wisconsin, Madison, 1975.

Chandra, Satish, 'Some Aspects of the Growth of a Money Economy during the Seventeenth Century', *The Indian Economic and Social History Review*, vol. III (4), 1966.

Chaudhuri, K.N., *The Trading World of Asia and the English East India Company, 1660–1760*, Cambridge: Cambridge University Press, 1978.

Chaudhuri, Sushil, *Trade and Commercial Organisation in Bengal, 1650–1720,* Calcutta: K.P. Bagchi, 1975.

Dale, Stephen Frederic, *Indian Merchants and Eurasian Trade, 1600–1750,* Cambridge: Cambridge University Press, 1994.

Das Gupta, Ashin, *Indian Merchants and the Decline of Surat, c. 1700–1750,* Wiesbaden: Franz Steiner Verlag, 1979.

Desai, Ashok V., 'Population and Standards of Living in Akbar's Time', *The Indian Economic and Social History Review,* vol. IX, 1972.

——, 'Population and Standards of Living in Akbar's Time—A Second Look', *The Indian Economic and Social History Review,* vol. XV (1), 1978, pp. 53–79.

Gopal, Surendra, *Commerce and Crafts in Gujarat, 16th–17th Centuries,* Delhi: People's Publishing House, 1975.

Grover, B.R., 'Nature of Land Rights in Mughal India', *Indian Economic and Social History Review,* vol. I (1), 1963.

——, 'Nature of Dehat-i-Taluqa and the Evolution of the Taaluqdari System during the Mughal Age', *The Indian Economic and Social History Review,* vol. II (3), 1965.

Habib, Irfan, 'The Technology and Economy of Mughal India', *The Indian Economic and Social History Review,* vol. XVII (1), 1980, pp. 1–34.

——, 'Potentialities of Capitalistic Development in the Economy of Mughal India', *The Journal of Economic History,* vol. XXIX (1), 1969, pp. 32–78.

——, *The Agrarian System of Mughal India (1556–1707),* London and Bombay: Asia Publishing House, 1963.

Hasan, S. Nurul, *Thoughts on Agrarian Relations in Mughal India,* Delhi, 1973 (rpt, 1984).

Moosvi, Shireen, 'The Gross National Product of the Mughal Empire, c. 1600', *The Indian Historical Review,* vol. XIII (1/2), 1986–7, pp. 75–87.

——, *The Economy of the Mughal Empire c. 1595: A Statistical Study,* Delhi: Oxford University Press, 1987.

Moreland, W.H., *India at the Death of Akbar: An Economic Study* (lst edn., London, 1920), Delhi: Low Price Publications, 1990.

——, *From Akbar to Aurangzeb: A Study in Indian Economic History,* London, 1923.

——, *The Agrarian System of Moslem India: A Historical Essay with Appendices,* Cambridge: Cambridge University Press, 1929.

Perlin, Frank, 'Proto-industrialisation and Pre-colonial South Asia', *Past and Present,* no. 98, 1983, pp. 30–95.

Prakash, Om, *The Dutch East India Company and the Economy of Bengal, 1630–1720,* Princeton: Princeton University Press, 1985.

Raychaudhuri, Tapan and Irfan Habib, eds., *The Cambridge Economic History of India,* vol. I (*c.* 1200–1757), Cambridge: Cambridge University Press, 1982.

Richards, J.F., ed., *The Imperial Monetary System of Mughal India,* Delhi: Oxford University Press, 1987.

Siddiqi, Noman Ahmad, *Land Revenue Administration under the Mughals, 1700–1750,* Bombay: Asia Publishing House, 1970.

Subrahmanyam, Sanjay, *The Political Economy of Commerce: Southern India, 1500–1650,* Cambridge: Cambridge University Press, 1990.

——, 'Rural Industry and Commercial Agriculture in Late Seventeenth-century South-eastern India', *Past and Present,* no. 126, 1990, pp. 95–126.

——, 'The Portuguese, Thatta, and the External Trade of Sind, 1515–1635', *Revista de Cultura,* (Macau), nos. 13/14, 1991, pp. 48–58.

Van Santen, H.W., 'De Verenigde Oost-Indische Compagnie in Gujarat en Hindustan, 1620–1660', Ph.D. dissertation, Leiden University, 1982.

8. Mughal Administrative Institutions

Many aspects of Mughal administration are already touched on in the writings cited in the two preceding sections. These are some additional writings, from a primarily institutional viewpoint.

Aziz, Abdul, *The Mansabdari System and the Mughal Army,* London, 1945.

Habib, Irfan. 'The *Mansab* System, 1595–1637', in *Proceedings of the Indian History Congress,* 29th Session, Patiala, 1967, pp. 221–42.

Hasan, Ibn, *The Central Structure of the Mughal Empire,* rpt, New Delhi: Munshiram Manoharlal, 1980 (lst edn, 1936).

Irvine, William, *The Army of the Indian Moghuls: Its Organization and Administration* (1903), rpt, Delhi: Eurasia, 1962.

Khan, Ahsan Raza. *Chieftains in the Mughal Empire during the Reign of Akbar,* Simla: Indian Institute of Advanced Study, 1977.

Khan, Iqtidar Alam, 'The Mughal Assignment System during Akbar's Early Years, 1556–1575', in Irfan Habib, ed., *Medieval India I: Researches in the History of India, 1200–1750,* Delhi: Oxford University Press, 1992, pp. 62–128.

Moosvi, Shireen, 'Evolution of the *Mansab* System under Akbar until 1596–97', *Journal of the Royal Asiatic Society of Great Britain and Ireland,* 1981, no. 2, pp. 178–85.

Qureshi, I.H., *The Administration of the Mughal Empire,* Karachi, 1966.

Richards, J.F., 'Norms of Comportment among Imperial Mughal Officers', in Barbara Daly Metcalf, ed., *Moral Conduct and Authority: The Place of Adab in South Asian Islam,* Berkeley: University of California Press, 1984, pp. 255–89.

Saran, Paramatma, *The Provincial Government of the Mughals,* 2nd edn, Bombay: Asia Publishing House, 1973.

Sarkar, Jadunath, *Mughal Administration,* 3rd edn, (1935), rpt, Bombay: Orient Longman, 1972.

Tripathi, R.P., *Some Aspects of Muslim Administration,* 2nd edn, Allahabad, 1959.

Trivedi, K.K., 'The Share of *Mansabdars* in State Revenue-Resources: A Study of the Maintenance of Animals', *The Indian Economic and Social History Review;* vol. XXIV (4), 1987.

Zaidi, Sunita, 'Problems of Mughal Administration in Sind during the First Half of the Seventeenth Century', *Islamic Culture,* April 1983, pp. 153–62.

9. Aspects of Social and Urban History

Some of the more significant writings on the interface of the Mughal state and the society over which it ruled, including its 'tribal' components, are presented here, as are some models of both urban and general societal formation, as applied to the Mughals.

Blake, Stephen P., *Shahjahanabad: The Sovereign City in Mughal India, 1639–1739,* Cambridge: Cambridge University Press, 1991.

Fox, Richard G., *Kin, Clan, Raja and Rule: State–Hinterland Relations in Pre-industrial India,* Berkeley: University of California Press, 1971.

Gokhale, B.G., *Surat in the Seventeenth Century: A Study in the Urban History of Pre-Modern India,* Copenhagen: Institute of Asian Studies, 1979.

Gupta, I.P., *Urban Glimpses of Mughal India: Agra, the Imperial Capital (16th and 17th Centuries),* Delhi: Discovery, 1986.

Khan, Iqtidar Alam, 'The Middle Classes in the Mughal Empire', Presidential Address to the Medieval Section, *Proceedings of the Indian History Congress,* 36th Session, Aligarh, 1975, pp. 113–41.

Kolff, Dirk H.A., *Naukar, Rajput and Sepoy: The Ethnohistory of the Military Labour Market in Hindustan, 1450–1850*, Cambridge: Cambridge University Press, 1990.

Leonard, Karen Isaksen, *Social History of an Indian Caste: The Kayasths of Hyderabad*, Berkeley: University of California Press, 1978.

Naqvi, Hamida Khatoon, *Urban Centres and Industries in Upper India, 1556–1803*, Bombay, 1968.

——, *Urbanization and Urban Centres under the Great Mughals, 1556–1707*, Simla: Institute of Advanced Studies, 1971.

Pearson, M.N., 'Political Participation in Mughal India', *Indian Economic and Social History Review*, vol. IX (2), 1972, pp. 113–31.

——, *Merchants and Rulers in Gujarat: The Response to the Portuguese in the Sixteenth Century*, Berkeley: University of California Press, 1976.

Sanyal, Hitesranjan, 'Mallabhum', in Surajit Sinha, ed., *Tribal Politics and State Systems in Precolonial Eastern and Northeastern India*, Calcutta, 1987, pp. 74–142.

Siddiqui, Iqtidar Husain, *Mughal Relations with the Indian Ruling Elite*, Delhi: Munshiram Manoharlal, 1983.

Singh, Chetan, 'Forests, Pastoralists and Agrarian Society in Mughal India', in David Arnold and Ramachandra Guha, eds, *Nature, Culture, Imperialism: Essays on the Environmental History of South Asia*, Delhi: Oxford University Press, 1995, pp. 21–48.

Trivedi, K.K., 'Changes in Caste-Composition of the *Zamindar* Class in Western Uttar Pradesh, 1595–ca.1900', *The Indian Historical Review*, vol. II (1), 1975.

10. Diplomatic Contacts

A large number of studies of individual embassies (and texts of the writings of European ambassadors) exist. Here, we have grouped together some of the more important writings on intra-Asian diplomatic contacts, as well as rivalries, together with a small sample on European embassies.

Askari, Syed Hasan, 'The Mughal–Magh Relations Down to the Time of Islam Khan Mashhadi', *Proceedings of the Indian History Congress, 29th Session, Gauhati (1959)*, Bombay, 1960, pp. 201–13.

Donzel, E. van, *Foreign Relations of Ethiopia, 1642–1700: Documents Relating to the Journeys of Khodja Murad*, Leiden: E.J. Brill, 1979.

Farooqi, Naimur Rehman, *Mughal–Ottoman Relations: A Study of Political and Diplomatic Relations Between Mughal India and the Ottoman Empire, 1556–1748*, Delhi: Idarah-i Adabiyat-i Delli, 1989.

Foster, William, ed., *Early Travels in India, 1583–1619*, London: Humphrey Milford, 1921.

Haider, Mansura, 'Relations of Abdullah Khan Uzbeg with Akbar', *Cahiers du Monde Russe et Soviétique*, vol. XXIII (3–4), 1982, pp. 313–31.

Pearson, M.N., 'The Mughals and the Hajj', *Journal of the Oriental Society of Australia*, vols XVIII–XIX, 1986–7, pp. 164–79.

Renick, M.S., 'Akbar's First Embassy to Goa: Its Diplomatic and Religious Aspects', *Indica*, vol. VII, 1970, pp. 32–47.

Riazul Islam, *Indo-Persian Relations: A Study of the Political and Diplomatic Relations Between the Mughal Empire and Iran*, Teheran: Iranian Culture Foundation, 1970.

——, A *Calendar of Documents on Indo-Persian Relations (1500–1700)*, 2 vols, Teheran: Iranian Culture Foundation/Karachi: Institute of Central and West Asian Studies, University of Karachi, 1979–82.

11. Regional Studies

The studies under this head could potentially be vast, reflecting the work of generations of local historians. Some selectivity has hence had to be exercised, but at the same time, a flavour of the variety of regional studies has been sought to be maintained. Amongst these studies, two may be singled out for mention: Richards's classic work on Golconda, published in the mid-1970s, and from a considerably different perspective, the recent work of Eaton on the long-term developments in Bengal. Besides these, Kulke's meticulous essays on Orissa before and during the Mughal period are useful for a regional approach.

Akhtar, Shirin, *The Role of Zamindars in Bengal, 1707–1772*, Dacca: Asiatic Society of Bangladesh, 1982.

Alam, Muzaffar, 'The Zamindars and Mughal Power in the Deccan, 1686–1712', *The Indian Economic and Social History Review*, vol. XI (1), 1974, pp. 74–91.

Banga, Indu, *Agrarian System of the Sikhs*, Delhi: Manohar, 1978.

Barnett, Richard B., *North India Between Empires: Awadh, the Mughals and the British, 1720–1801*, Berkeley: University of California Press, 1980.

Bayly, Susan, *Saints, Goddesses and Kings: Muslims and Christians in South Indian Society, 1700–1900*, Cambridge: Cambridge University Press, 1989.

Calkins, Philip B., 'The Formation of a Regionally-oriented Ruling Group in Bengal, 1700–1740', *The Journal of Asian Studies*, vol. XXIX (4), 1970, pp. 799–806.

Chatterjee, Anjali, *Bengal in the Reign of Aurangzeb 1658–1707*, Calcutta: Progressive Publishers, 1967.

Chaube, Jharkhande, *History of the Gujarat Kingdom, 1458–1537*, Delhi: Munshiram Manoharlal, 1975.

Cohn, Bernard S., 'Political Systems in Eighteenth-Century India: The Benares Region', *Journal of the American Oriental Society*, vol. LXXXII (3), 1962, pp. 312–19.

Dutta, S.C., *The Northeast and the Mughals, 1661–1714*, Delhi, 1984.

Eaton, Richard M., 'Islam in Bengal', in George Michell, ed., *The Islamic Heritage of Bengal*, Paris: UNESCO, 1984, pp. 23–36.

——, *The Rise of Islam and the Bengal Frontier, 1204–1760*, Delhi: Oxford University Press, 1994.

Fukazawa, Hiroshi, *The Medieval Deccan: Peasants, Social Systems, and States, Sixteenth to Eighteenth Centuries*, Delhi: Oxford University Press, 1991.

Gupta, S.P., *The Agrarian System of Eastern Rajasthan, c. 1650–c. 1750*, Delhi: Manohar, 1986.

Khuhro, Hamida, ed., *Sind Through the Centuries*, Karachi: Oxford University Press, 1981.

Kulke, Hermann, *Kings and Cults: State Formation and Legitimation in India and Southeast Asia*, Delhi: Manohar, 1993.

Leonard, Karen, 'The Hyderabad Political System and its Participants, *The Journal of Asian Studies*, vol. XXX (3), 1971, pp. 569–82.

Malik, Zahir Uddin, 'Documents Relating to Pargana Administration in the Deccan under Asaf Jah I', in *Medieval India: A Miscellany*, vol. III, Bombay: Asia Publishing House, 1975, pp. 152–83.

McLane, John R., *Land and Local Kingship in Eighteenth-century Bengal*, Cambridge: Cambridge University Press, 1993.

Ramaswami, N.S., *Political History of the Carnatic under the Nawabs* Delhi, 1984.

Ray, B.C., *Orissa under the Mughals*, Calcutta, 1981.

Raychaudhuri, Tapan, *Bengal under Akbar and Jahangir: An Introductory Study in Social History*, 2nd edn, Delhi: Munshiram Manoharlal, 1966.

Richards, J.F., *Mughal Administration in Golconda*, Oxford: Oxford University Press, 1975.

Sharma, G.D., *Rajput Polity: A Study of Politics and Administration of the State of Marwar, 1638–1749*, Delhi: Manohar, 1977.

Singh, Chetan, *Region and Empire: Panjab in the Seventeenth Century*, Delhi: Oxford University Press, 1991.

Singh, Dilbagh, *The Peasant and the State: Eastern Rajasthan in the Eighteenth Century*, Delhi: Manohar, 1990.

Sinha, S.N., *Subah of Allahabad under the Great Mughals*, Delhi, 1974.

Wink, André, *Land and Sovereignty in India: Agrarian Society and Politics under the Eighteenth-century Maratha Svarajya*, Cambridge: Cambridge University Press, 1986.

12. The 'Crisis' of the Mughal Empire

The issue of the 'crisis' of the Mughal state, whether from the late seventeenth or the early eighteenth century onward, has generated much debate in the past decade and a half. An earlier consensus, which was partaken of broadly by writers as diverse as Spear, Sarkar, Athar Ali, and Irfan Habib, has now been replaced by a fierce debate on the nature and character of the 'crisis', its central and regional dimensions, and its political and economic ramifications.

Some of the major contributions to the debate have been reproduced in the volume; listed below are some other works that have played a role in establishing one or the other position in the debate, as well as some newer voices and perspectives. Some recent papers of orthodox historians that effectively do no more than repeat older arguments, without advancing the debate, have been excluded.

Alam, Muzaffar, *The Crisis of Empire in Mughal North India: Awadh and the Punjab, 1707–1748*, Delhi: Oxford University Press, 1986.

——, 'Eastern India in the Early Eighteenth-century 'Crisis': Some Evidence from Bihar', *The Indian Economic and Social History Review*, vol. XXVIII (1), 1991, pp. 43–71.

Athar Ali, M., *The Mughal Nobility under Aurangzeb*, revised edn, Oxford University Press, Delhi: 1997.

——, 'The Passing of Empire: The Mughal Case', *Modern Asian Studies*, vol. IX (3), 1975, pp. 385–96.

——, 'The Eighteenth Century: An Interpretation', *The Indian Historical Review*, vol. V (1–2), 1978–9, pp. 175–86.

Bayly, C.A., *Rulers, Townsmen and Bazaars: North Indian Society in the Age of British Expansion*, Cambridge: Cambridge University Press, 1983.

——, *Indian Society and the Making of the British Empire* (The New Cambridge History of India, vol. II 2), Cambridge: Cambridge University Press, 1988.

Chandra, Satish, *Medieval India: Society, the Jagirdari Crisis and the Village*, Delhi, 1982.

——, *Parties and Politics at the Mughal Court, 1707–1740*, 3rd edn, Delhi: People's Publishing House, 1979.

——, *The Eighteenth Century in India: Its Economy and the Role of the Marathas, the Jats, the Sikhs and the Afghans*, Delhi, 1986.

Goetz, Hermann, *The Crisis of Indian Civilization in the Eighteenth and Early Nineteenth Centuries*, Calcutta: University of Calcutta, 1938.

Gommans, Jos J.L., *The Rise of the Indo-Afghan Empire, c. 1710–1780*, Leiden: E.J. Brill, 1995.

Husain, Iqbal, *The Rise and Decline of the Ruhela Chieftaincies in 18th Century India*, Delhi: Oxford University Press, 1994.

Irvine, William, *Later Mughuls*, rev. Jadunath Sarkar, rpt, Delhi, 1971.

Malik, Zahir Uddin, *The Reign of Muhammad Shah: 1719–1748*, Bombay: Asia Publishing House, 1977.

Pearson, M.N., 'Shivaji and the Decline of the Mughal empire', *The Journal of Asian Studies*, vol. XXXV (2), 1976, pp. 221–35.

Sarkar, Jadunath, *Fall of the Mughal Empire*, 4 vols, Calcutta, 1912–30, rpt, Bombay: Orient Longman, 1971–5.

Spear, Percival, *Twilight of the Moghuls*, Cambridge: Cambridge University Press, 1951.